LAND AND LABOR IN EUROPE 1900—1950

STUDIES
IN SOCIAL LIFE
IV

EDITORS:
GUNTHER BEYER
JULIUS ISAAC

LAND AND LABOR
IN EUROPE
1900 – 1950

A COMPARATIVE SURVEY OF RECENT AGRARIAN HISTORY

by

FOLKE DOVRING

WITH A CHAPTER ON
LAND REFORM AS A PROPAGANDA THEME

by

KARIN DOVRING

MARTINUS NIJHOFF / THE HAGUE
1956

PRINTED IN THE NETHERLANDS

CONTENTS

PREFACE

This book is the outcome of research which was initiated in the fall of 1951. My research in agrarian history of past centuries in Continental Western Europe and Scandinavia had focussed my attention on the entanglement of things old and new in the rural world. It also made me feel the lack of a comprehensive survey of modern agrarian problems. An attempt to synthesize the most recent experiences in the field of the land question in the light of a half century's history could not have been started until the main lines of the political behavior in post-war Europe had become somewhat stabilized. It is only recently that statistical material referring to the situation around 1950 has become available from most countries in Europe. The lacunas remaining in this respect might to some extent have been filled if the publication of the volume were to have been postponed. This, on the other hand, would have made the bulk of the results less up to date than they are now.

In the initial stage the enquiry was supported by a travel grant from the Swedish State Council for Social Research. During seven months' travel over large parts of Southern and Continental Europe many governmental offices, institutions, politicians, and scholars, gave precious help in finding facts and information about agrarian situations and policies in their countries. They also largely helped in establishing invaluable contacts with local technicians and with different strata of the farming population. The generous hospitality I met everywhere was both helpful and charming.

For this book my work in the service of the United Nations' Economic Commission for Europe in Geneva and the Food and Agriculture Organization of the United Nations in Rome has been a source of great inspiration. The interest shown by my chiefs and colleagues at these institutions and ample exchanges of

views with them have helped me forward with my work. I am
specially thankful to Mr D. K. Britton of FAO/ECE, Geneva.

A one-year fellowship from the Rockefeller Foundation of
New York made possible a period of concentrated activity on
this book. A special grant allowed the employment of a computing
assistant for three months who carried out part of the computations underlying the tables in Chapter 3. Apart from this
assistance all the research for chapters 1 through 6 has been
done entirely by myself.

The research for the seventh chapter has been done by its
author, Dr Karin Dovring under discussions with Professor
Harold D. Lasswell of Yale University who attentively followed
her work and read it in manuscript and proofs.

Mr R. A. Bishop and Mr L. Lind of FAO, Rome, have kindly
advised me on my English and helped checking the proofs.

I am grateful to them all.

Rome, October 1955

Folke Dovring

INTRODUCTION

THE LAND QUESTION

(1) Ever since the eighteenth century brought human social conditions under serious discussion, the land question has been one of the basic issues of any program for social and economic reforms. It has been looked at under almost all conceivable aspects, but in practically all socio-economic systems it retains its fundamental importance and originality. It has proved difficult to fit into general theoretical conceptions and always seems to call for special treatment. Some schools of thought, for example the Physiocrats and Georgeists, regard land as the basic source of human wealth; others look upon agriculture as the most important among the factors which retard progress. Individual ownership of land is one of the most important principles of Roman law and Liberal economic thought; other systems regard it as a theft from the community. Whichever the underlying general views were, most land policies have failed, more or less, to reach the goals set for them. Under the changing conditions of modern times, the land question shows itself in a new light, a continually changing riddle provoking new controversies.

(2) As well as focussing interest upon social agrarian structure, we must keep in mind some of the basic economic issues. Social structure is here understood mainly as the stratification and organization of economic wealth and economic power. The traditional main factors were land and labor. On a stage of higher economic development, invested capital contributes to complicating the relationship between the two. Even so, a conjunction of land and labor is always fundamental for agricultural wealth. The organization of land in relation to labor and vice versa forms the core of social agrarian structure, and its development is the essential content of social agrarian history.

(3) The land question is not only a matter of distribution of economic wealth. It is as much one of economic power, which is basic in relation to economic wealth. The question of organization and decision-making in agrarian society is part of the general socio-economic problems of our days and is involved in the ideological debate around these. Large and small enterprise, individualism and common action, rights, duties and responsibilities of the individual, all this is debated as hotly as ever. A growing conviction that the choice is one of degree rather than of principle does not make the choice any easier or less loaded with sentiment. Socialism and Communism, as well as various Neo-Liberal and Neo-Conservative trends of thought, all tend to put different stress on economic, social and human values.

In the ideological debate there is a tendency to concentrate upon the urban-rural contrast, often conceived as representing the contrast between handicraft and urban-industrial ways of production. Socialism took the urban-industrial process of production as a point of departure, passing judgment on both agriculture and economic life as a whole on the assumption that the same mechanical requirement of organization into large units applied to both. Some of its modern opponents in thought and policy, on the other hand, tend to start from the rural way of living with its extremely familistic pattern of life. While Communist land policy strives to make farming industry operate in large enterprises, there are, in opposition, those who would like to maintain as much as possible of urban handicraft and even decentralize manufacturing industries into something akin to a family farm structure. As far as urban industries are concerned, this sort of organization is rarely achieved. It is in the realm of agriculture that the debate really influences practice. Thus, the rural milieu becomes a battleground for contrasting social and human ideals. The family enterprise is a general social program but derives its validity mainly from agrarian realities. The big industrial enterprise, with its vast hierarchy of decision-making among directors and employees, on the other hand, is mainly an urban reality, resulting from modern development of manufacturing industries. Thus, two distinct historical strata of human life stand one against the other and claim that between them lies the decision for the future of mankind. This is one of

the reasons why agrarian problems are basic to any discussion
of social problems even in modern Europe. Another reason lies
in the still considerable size of the agrarian sector in most
countries, even in many of those in Europe.

(4) It is difficult to say how far a scientific analysis can modify
basic political conceptions of what human life should be. Political
decisions will always in the last instance be taken from considerations of values, in themselves profoundly irrational. The
task of the scientist is not to advise or convert but to contribute to showing more clearly than before what the consequence will be of the alternatives discussed. Our scope here is
not to advocate a definite program of action. We hope instead
to contribute to making adherents of different programs see more
clearly than before the real nature of their assumptions. Perhaps
even, for some readers, the choice between old controversial
solutions may become obsolete and give way to a re-formulation
of the problem. However striking the contrast may seem to be
between two historical strata of society, it may not always have
the significance the ideologies tend to ascribe to it. A survey of
Europe, on an historical and comparative basis, may throw some
new light on the land question. The conclusions are likely to be
of interest even outside our continent.

AN HISTORICAL APPROACH

(5) Sometimes, the most important thing about a problem is
not so much its status as its trend of development. A situation
may be full of difficulties and nevertheless be left alone, if it
shows distinct signs of improving by itself. Another situation,
though for the moment no worse, may call for urgent measures
if it tends to deteriorate gravely. This is only one of the general
reasons for a short-term historical approach to problems of social
and economic policy. A reason for a long-term historical outlook
lies, and in Europe no less than elsewhere, in the presence of
different historical strata side by side in the actual situation of
today. Not only does rural society develop slower than urban
society, but perhaps even more striking are the disparities within
rural development. European rural areas show many lingering
relics of past centuries, more or less interwoven with quite modern

features. This is a powerful factor in rural psychology, making the reaction to modern development not only often retarded but sometimes also paradoxical. Even in highly developed areas, it is well established that it takes at least a generation for a change to penetrate the countryside. In this book, the attempt will be made to describe agrarian structure in Europe since around 1900. The more general and remote historical background will be kept in mind, when useful and possible.

(6) Another reason for an historical approach to modern land questions is the importance of history as a social science. The frequent use and misuse of historical arguments in discussions on such themes makes it especially appropriate to furnish correct arguments. The tendency to interpret the present by the aid of the past, though generally sound, may also be overdone. The use of common terms to cover realities from different epochs, often conceals the real differences. "Feudalism" is only one of the most striking examples of an historical terminology causing confusion through over-simplification. The dilemma facing the historian as a social scientist is between specialized knowledge and synthesis.

Strangely enough, History is supposed to embrace fairly vast areas of knowledge when dealing with long epochs in a remote past. The very same knowledge in a short space of modern time, on the contrary, belongs to a number of specialized disciplines— economics, political science, sociology etc., or even such of a purely technical character as agronomy or industrial technology. It sounds, sometimes, as if only the dizzy perspective of remote centuries could lead to an historical approach. Views of this kind underlie the low reliability characterizing much current historical information.

Synthesis, of course, is not a scientific method, but rather a way of handling scientific results. As recently stated, History — — as, for instance, Geography — is not a distinct scientific discipline along with others, but rather "a branch of study, carried out according to scientific principles"[a]. Critical analysis of sources is not the specific sign of the historian, it is only an application of the general critical principle inherent in all science.

When handling various methods of research belonging to our theme, we are therefore conscious of owing the reader the same effort as the specialists of each branch would try to offer. An historical approach in this book does not mean adoption of a "synthetic" method of work that would diminish the reliability of the results. On the contrary, we aim at using historical arguments only when they are well founded. The rules of probability are everywhere the same, and a conclusion or a generalization that does not hold good on the basis of modern material does not do so any more on the basis of Mediaeval material.

On the other hand, experience in handling modern material and the pitfalls of probability it engenders, is likely to produce valuable contributions to the methodology of social history. It is our hope that the critical reflections on various modern sources made here will explain some of our scepticism towards much current information on social history in remote epochs.

(7) If it is generally true that most of the knowledge that belongs to the history of our time is brought forth by others than historians, then this is probably even more true about modern rural history. It is commonplace to say that agrarian history as such is neglected — the fact is too obvious to be denied, except by people almost entirely ignorant of the subject. It has been pointed out recently that a profound ignorance of agrarian matters has been at least partly responsible for some of the most spectacular political failures of our time[a]. One of the great shortcomings of agrarian policy seems in fact to be that these matters have been treated mainly from different technical points of view. The approach of the historian is required, along with that of the technician, for the formation of both expert and public opinion.

WHY EUROPE?

(8) The choice of region for this enquiry may need a short explanation. Why Europe, why not only a somewhat homogeneous group of countries, and why limit our scope to our own continent? The question may seem superfluous to many readers, but not to answer it might cause some misunderstanding.

First of all: when making a "choice" out of a given material, there is always the risk of being arbitrary. Choosing a continent as traditionally defined does away with objections of this kind.

From this geographical scope, our main exclusion is European Turkey, as part of an essentially Asiatic state.

At the beginning of the period here considered, Europe had a kind of inner unity. An essentially common ideological framework and many resemblances in past social history formed the background for the pros and cons of public debate. Despite great differences, conditions seemed basically comparable from one country to another. Manifold contacts all over the continent created a consciousness of unity and common ways of expression. In many respects, the contrasts were smaller than they are now, and the idea of comparative surveys of Europe might perhaps have seemed more natural then from a static point of view.

How this unit came to fall apart is a story one side of which it is our intention to tell in this book. Other sides have to be told by those analyzing other parts of recent social and economic history. Wars and revolutions are mainly symptoms, even if sometimes bringing to fruition the development that generated them. One of the most fascinating problems is why the social and economic disparities in Europe should have become ever greater. This is the explanation for a comparative enquiry of our continent, while the presence of widely varying yet comparable social patterns as well as contrasting trends of development, make it a model subject for a comparative analysis, from which conclusions which are generally valid might emerge.

The possibility of reintegration of Europe — or some large part of it — in the future that is, of re-creating the lost unity, cannot be treated here. It is only our hope that this book may contribute to a better understanding of the agrarian problems involved in the integration issue.

A COMPARATIVE APPROACH

(9) Comparative research in agrarian social science is especially necessary in connection with definitions of concepts and for a better understanding of current trends of development.

Even basic concepts are often used in a way which implies a varying sense in the same word. Everybody talks about villages and dispersed settlement, large and small property, large and small farms, private versus collective property, only to mention some important examples. When considering the opinions of various writers on "villages", for instance, one observes that many of them give a special sense to the term, influenced by conditions in the writer's own country. Intuitive views influenced by tacit assumptions within each one country are not only less comparable, but as a whole less reliable than concepts defined in the light of the experience of many countries. Even such a factor as the social role of property may remain partly unexplored as long as it is treated within the framework of one legal system only. From a fundamentally positivistic viewpoint of legal phenomena, which is necessary for a social scientist, legal terms like property could not possibly have any other sense than that derived from a close description of their real function in each society.

Since the countries of Europe today, as well as half a century ago, represent different stages of socio-economic development, a comparison between them and their trends of development is likely to furnish precious information as to the probable sequence of evolution in certain respects. If such factors as overpopulation, extensive monoculture, latifundia and microfundia, only to mention some of the most notorious elements of Mediterranean misery, are to be attacked with some success, it is of course of interest to see what became of similar conditions in countries with a different recent development. Especially when exploring the critical margins, the proportions that distinguish a sound society from a suffering one, comparative research may have something useful to say.

AGRARIAN STRUCTURE — NATURAL AND POLITICAL

(10) "Agrarian structure" is a somewhat vague but generally used term for the whole institutional framework within which agriculture does its work. All the complex structural questions in Europe cannot be dealt with in one book. We will here focus interest on a number of main topics with direct bearings on the land-labor relationships.

Agricultural settlement will thus be treated here from the viewpoint of the allocation of manpower in relation to the land.

At the same time, current policies and discussion will be viewed, as ascribing a specific social value to one or the other settlement form. Layout and fragmentation of land will be treated as a question of allocation of land in relation to manpower, and the consolidation and country-planning issues as attempts at solving problems which are both economic and political. Resources in land and manpower will be discussed, both in order to determine the trend of development in the direct quantitative relations between land and labor and, by weighting the productive resources, to map out the real importance of land hunger. On the same lines, the size of holdings will be compared and weighted, so that farm structure problems may be judged on a solid quantitative basis. Systems of land tenure will be scrutinized, in order to settle how far the differences in legal structure have real socio-economic bearings. It is also necessary to understand agricultural co-operation, as limiting and modifying the owner-ship-tenancy situation and as bringing about important modifi-cations in the system of decision-making.

(11) The research items mentioned would not, however, alone fulfill the goal of our analysis. Every structure in a somewhat developed society is more or less the result of a compromise between artificial and spontaneous tendencies in social life. We call the latter "natural", the former "political" factors. We are conscious that the real difference between these sets of factors is more one of degree than of kind. Also "spontaneous", "popular" reactions, insofar as they result from superstition or class antagonism, for instance, may be inadequate and may be regarded as a sort of policy at a smaller scale and at a lower level. And of course the inner compulsion of economic and social circumstances may leave no alternative to the policy which is actually pursued. However, the contrast between "spontaneous" and "artificial" factors is distinguishable more or less throughout social life, though the borderline may not always be clear. Summing up the main trends in land policy and their consequences will contribute towards showing some of the inherent necessities of each situation.

As already hinted, a policy is not merely a systematic action for realizing a scheme that was thought useful or rational. Any coherent action is inspired by a system of thought which, more often than not, is founded on some sort of ideological conception of human life. The critical point is not that the politician is driven by his wishes. No one amongst us can even drive a nail in the wall without being driven by some sort of a wish. But the difference between the technical experts and the ideological politicians does not lie here. The former may disagree as to the ways to reach the same goal, because their knowledge is different and they estimate unknown factors differently. The ideological politicians, on the contrary, work towards different goals, inspired by different attitudes towards irrational values. The underlying basis of a policy can only in a very imperfect way be concluded from overt actions. Therefore, the last chapter of this book analyses some of the most important ideological conceptions underlying recent land policies in Europe. This study will illustrate also the possibilities of modern quantitative semantics in conjunction with social research on the same subject matter as the propaganda analysed.

CHAPTER 1

AGRICULTURAL SETTLEMENT
THE ALLOCATION OF LABOR

(12) The importance of the form of rural settlement for social life in the agricultural community is often stressed, both in theoretical research and in practical planning. Discussion on the topic is however often unclear, because different issues are kept together and the difference in their bearing on the subject is overlooked.

The basic contrast which it has been attempted to characterize and to explain is that between concentration and dispersion. These terms may be taken either in an absolute or in a relative sense. Absolute concentration means the size (in population numbers) of nucleated villages or other centers. Relative concentration should be an expression of the degree to which a rural population is allocated as between such centers, and in settlement of a decentralized character, respectively. Obviously, these two concepts do not relate to the same sort of problem. The bearing which relative concentration could have upon both land-labor relationships and other sides of rural social life is closely connected with the density of population. A loose cluster of houses, with rather long distances between them, may be regarded as a sort of village if surrounded by vast unsettled areas. The same or even smaller distances between the houses in vast stretches of very densely settled open countryside does not evoke the idea of a village either for the residents or for outside observers[a].

Questions of relative concentration are of importance mainly for human geography, especially in connection with the sociology of cohabitation. Size and scope of rural communities, the way in which a nucleated village is related to its surroundings, and social relations within it, etc., are questions which will be the subject of our enquiry mainly in connection with agricultural co-operation. For our main topic, land-labor relationships, absolute concentration becomes the most interesting aspect of rural settlement. The absolute size of a village has important bearings upon the distance factor and the layout of the land. These will be discussed later in this chapter, after the presentation of a comprehensive map of the size factor in European agricultural villages.

MEASURING VILLAGE SIZE

(13) Historical and geographical research on villages started with attempts at establishing qualitative criteria, especially such as were supposed to reveal different ethnic characters of the peoples that founded the settlement[a]. Later research, which was more historical in its approach though less so in its ambitions, revealed the strongly relative character of the type classifications and the difficulty of tracing ethnographic peculiarities through the settlement systems[b]. Close research on individual villages over a long period also tends to show that villages may change their "type" when growing in size[c]. Though the qualitative description of the "type" may retain some interest as a form of layout of the settled area, this recent discussion has weakened interest in village typologies. Recent geographic discussion especially has been focussed on quantitative aspects.

(14) One approach to the concentration issue is to study the interdependency of bigger and smaller nuclei, as attempted especially by W. CHRISTALLER and research following him[a]. The question, which are the settled nuclei that are dependent upon others and which are the ones that exercise "central" functions, is likely to be different depending upon what relations we are asking for, and the answer will vary with the question. If asking for a "geographical primary region", we must remember that such a thing does not exist in itself, but can only be understood as an abstraction that is likely to be useful for the generalization of some types of information.

From more general and less purposive points of departure, French settlement research, under DEMANGEON and his followers,

attempted to establish universally valid criteria by which to
characterize settlement as concentrated or dispersed[b]. The
application of Demangeon's general formula, which will soon be
discussed, was dubious even for the country for which it was
conceived[c], and called for modifications when applied to other
countries[d]. One of the main difficulties was in distinguishing the
"centers" from their "periphery", and the delimitation of the
territory dominated by each center. Because there was no
generally accepted criterion as to what should be regarded as a
"village", many geographers contented themselves with vaguely
qualitative criteria. In doing so, they could profit from their
intimate knowledge of their own countries[e], but on such a basis
an international comparison would be impossible. Finally,
attempts have also been made to reduce the spatial extension of
buildings to a map, so that concentration and dispersion might
be at least visually perceptible[f]. The latter method illustrates
the location and size of houses but has no direct bearing upon
the importance of manpower or its functional relationship to the
land.

For obvious reasons, the area covered by houses would not be
very instructive as to concentration of population. Nor would
the number of houses be an expression of the degree of co-
habitation, because even the number of living-houses does not
always correspond directly with the number of families. As an
extreme example of co-habitation under one roof, it may be
mentioned that there are manorial constructions in the Iberian
countries where all the permanent employees on the estate live
under the same roof.

(15) The point of departure for the formula proposed by
DEMANGEON was the wide-spread, though somewhat unclear,
distinction between villages and hamlets, which has equivalents
in most European languages[a]. Considering forms of transition,
as well as regions where dispersed and concentrated settlement
forms compete within the same area, Demangeon established the
following formula, intended to demonstrate the relative importance of "central" villages, as opposed to "peripheral" hamlets
and isolated farmsteads:

$$\frac{E \cdot N}{T} = K$$

where E represents the population of all "écarts" (i.e., settled points other than the center of the community), N the number of these écarts, T the total population of the community, and K the wanted coefficient. If the community has no écarts at all, only one village, then both E and N will be = 0, and K too, consequently. Thus, 0 would mean full concentration, while high degrees of dispersion would be represented by high K-values. Even before publishing the final results in the Atlas de France, the formula had been criticized because it did not take into account the different size of the communities. Demangeon therefore attempted to formulate a modified version of the formula, including the area factor in it. Its application on one French department gave a representation profoundly different from that produced under the first formula. Any factors could be put into such a formula, which is a compound index of non-comparable data.

While the formula, in order to express real points of interest, would require communities of essentially the same size everywhere, there is even in France too great a variation in this respect. Some communities are so small that their center is only a hamlet and cannot be considered as the center of any geographical region. Turning to southern Europe, we find rural communities so large that many of them contain two or more large villages. A formula could not be applied to them on the community basis. Here, we would need another definition of the "village" as well as of its "territory". This could only result from very time-consuming field research, which so far has barely started.

In countries where the community could not serve as even an approximate basis, a suggestion might be to start with distinctions between villages and hamlets that are accepted within each region. We have attempted this, on the basis of the population census material from Croatia and the settlement classification contained therein [b]. The conclusion was mainly that such a classification, founded on "inside" regional information, is too variable from one small region to another. Abandoning any attempt to classify relative concentration, we will try to establish a kind of universally applicable expression for absolute concentration.

(16) The bearing of village size upon land-labor relationships calls for an expression of village size, as measured in manpower

and in land. Directly, neither can be found on the basis of existing statistics[a]. Both can with some reservations be derived from a measure based on total population dependent on agriculture.

The size of villages as expressed in agricultural population can but seldom be found directly in census material, but can with relatively little uncertainty be calculated on the basis of data on total, rural, and agricultural population by districts. Details of such calculations are presented in Appendix 1. The question remains in which form such population figures should be presented to best advantage[b].

Arithmetical averages would not be very instructive, because a number of small hamlets and isolated farms could dominate the picture through their number rather than through their importance. Even regions heavily dominated by big villages might appear as more or less "dispersed", and to a degree that might vary independently of the importance of the central village. A simple index which serves the purpose of our enquiry is the median. It represents the average situation as regards the distance factor and related circumstances. If the median is 500, it means that half the agricultural population of the district lives in villages with more than 500 inhabitants (of agricultural population), the other half in villages or other settlements with less than 500 agricultural inhabitants. Of course, the median values express the situation in a somewhat imperfect way. Fractiles (deciles, for instance) would have given a fuller picture of the details of the situation, by showing the contrasts between distinct strata of the settlement situation. For the purpose of a map, however, one single index had to be adopted.

(17) As will be described in detail in Appendix 1, we have established median values, by provinces or districts, for most European countries on the basis of population censuses. The material ranges from 1926 (Russia) to 1951 (Ireland, the Netherlands). In countries where such values could not be calculated directly, different estimates had to be made.

For the representation on the map, the figures had to be grouped according to a limited number of size-classes. The following seven categories were adopted[a]:

under 100 inhabitants (dispersed settlements —
hamlets and open country)

100–200	,,	(small villages)
200–400	,,	(medium-sized villages)
400–1000	,,	(big villages)
1000–2000	,,	(very big villages)
2000–5000	,,	(small agro-towns)
over 5000	,,	(big agro-towns)

The map shows that hamlets and open country prevail in the
Scandinavian-Baltic area, most of the British Isles and France,
in an important part of northern and central Italy, and in the
north western corner of the Iberian peninsula. Small villages
dominate in eastern England, north eastern France and large
parts of western and northern Germany, the Alpine region,
Poland, northern Russia, and parts of central Portugal and
northern Spain. Medium-sized villages are the dominating feature
in large parts of Germany and Poland, in Czechoslovakia, north
eastern and central Russia, on the Dinaric mountain range along
the eastern border of the Adriatic sea, some departments in
southern France, and parts of the Iberian countries. Big villages
are represented mainly in northern Spain and in a vast zone
running from Greece over the central Balkans and western
Hungary, Slovakia and central Russia to the Ural mountains.
South of the agro-town zone, they again dominate the picture
on the Volga steppe and in the Caucasian mountains. Very big
villages are important in southern Spain, on Sardinia and in
central and southern Italy, the eastern parts of the Balkans and
the Danube basin, the whole of Ukraina, and parts of south
eastern Russia. Small agro-towns characterize great parts of
southern Spain, some districts in southern Italy, part of the great
Hungarian plain (the Alföld) and its continuation into Yugoslav
Vojvodina and some other districts along the Danube, and some
regions in Northern Caucasia. Big agro-towns, finally, though
individually represented in large areas of southern and eastern
Europe, entirely dominate the settlement situation in one Spanish
province (Ciudad Real), most of Sicily and Apulia, and a great
central zone in Northern Caucasus. The map and Appendix 1
fill out the detail of these broad outlines.

(18) As a very rough generalisation, it is easy to observe that

great concentration and big villages are mainly a southern feature, whereas dispersed settlement is at its maximum in the north-western parts of Europe. If the map were our only source of information, it would be easy to misinterpret this trend as an expression of the dominating influence of physical geography. It is true that the zoning found on the map may to some extent be due to the impact of climate, as is likely on the Iberian peninsula and in Russia. But it is also true that the sudden change of pattern in central Italy has nothing to do with climate or other factors of physical geography. The sharp borderline along the Danube is much more due to historical conditions, caused by centuries of military frontier, than to geographical contrasts.

The most important geographical factor which is held to account for concentration of rural settlement is lack of water. In arid regions people would be forced to settle near the few wells. Also the physical character of the rock is sometimes invoked as an explanation: granitic ground with plenty of wells should facilitate dispersion of settlement, while impermeable minerals would tend in the same direction as an arid climate. However, this kind of explanation would not hold good for the appearance of agro-towns with many thousands of agricultural inhabitants each, and it would leave many other regional features unexplained too. A short survey of the recent history of settlement, under the main aspect of concentration versus dispersion, will show that the contrast is much more an expression of factors in social and economic history than of geographical necessities.

TRENDS OF DEVELOPMENT

(19) Since it proved impossible to produce one map for the state of settlement as around 1900 and another representing the stage reached in each country around 1950, something should first be said to account for our opinion that the picture offered by the map by and large refers to conditions in 1950.

As regards western and northern Europe, the data used are quite recent. The figures from the Iberian countries are from 1940, those from Italy from 1936. In the two former countries very little can have happened up to 1950 to change the settlement pattern, and in Italy not very much more. The artificially dispersed settlement on the Agro Pontino was already recorded, and the dispersed settlements created in the recent land reform areas came into being mainly after 1950. The census material used from Austria and Yugoslavia is also quite recent. The Greek data are as old as 1929, but samples taken in the first available results from the 1950 population census showed essentially unchanged settlement conditions, as far the concentration-dispersion conditions and the size of villages are concerned. As in southern Europe, the Bulgarian settlement conditions are not likely to have changed much since 1934, nor the Rumanian since 1941 nor the Hungarian since 1930. As regards Czechoslovakia and present-day Poland, it is of course merely a supposition that the settlement patterns of the pre-war period have by and large been maintained.

The greatest problem of continuity however concerns Russia. The pattern of settlement which was reflected by the census of 1926 represented a transitional stage in more than one respect. As late as the beginning of this century, most agricultural settlement in Russia was in nucleated villages. The main exceptions were in very thinly settled regions in the north and in the Ural mountains. Following the Stolypin reform, isolated farmsteads had been created on a large scale during the first two decades of this century, mainly up to World War I. Part of these isolated farms were again abolished during the period of war communism, when village communities were restored to their former positions and many owners of isolated settlements were forced to return to the village they had left some years or decades earlier. Presumably, some isolated farmsteads survived, and others may have been re-established or founded during the NEP-period in the twenties. Whichever was most frequent, there did exist a considerable number of dispersed farmsteads in Russia according to the 1926 census. It is noteworthy that part of this dispersed settlement must even have survived collectivisation for quite a number of years. It was not until the end of the thirties that abolition of the isolated farmsteads was ordered by decree[a]. This was at the eve of World War II. It is not possible at present to know how far the decree was carried out before the German invasion. At any rate, full application of the decree seems to have been achieved after the war, around 1950. Thus, concentration ought to have increased. On the other hand, agricultural population has decreased considerably, which should have balanced the loss of the isolated farmsteads, from the viewpoint of village size as expressed in population numbers. For these reasons, the medians may have remained at essentially the same levels as before. After World War II, still further concentration of settlements was attempted, in connection with the amalgamation of the kolkhozy. As will be commented upon later, these attempts are likely to have had little effect upon the settlement system. The pattern reflected by the 1926 census is likely to be still tolerably similar to actual conditions in most of the USSR.

A special problem is connected with the Baltic States. Obviously, it is the policy of the USSR to abolish the system of isolated farmsteads that became prevalent in these countries in the twenties. As late as in 1948, at least, not very much seems to have been achieved in this direction [b].

(20) In a farther perspective, the history of agricultural settlement cannot be said to represent any clear line of development. On the contrary, there have been many changes of direction. The clearest theoretical pattern so far outlined is that presented by DEMANGEON [a], trying to find one continuous line from primary dispersion followed by concentration in ages of uncertainty and oppression; followed anew by dispersion in modern time, when military and civil development made villages out of date. As will be seen later in this chapter, modern technical developments have again changed the frame of reference for a discussion on the subject. At the same time, patterns of settlement have become involved in the general ideological debate between collectivism and individualism in agriculture. Some main features of recent settlement history will serve as background to understanding this debate and its bearing upon realities.

(21) In the Scandinavian-Baltic area, the current prevailing pattern of dispersed settlement is only in part original. Isolated farmsteads have always characterized Norway and Iceland. Recent colonization in the woodlands of central and northern Sweden and in Finland generally started as isolated farmsteads eventually developing in the course of centuries into small

hamlets, in some regions of northern Sweden even into real villages. In most parts of central Sweden, even prehistoric settlement was mainly in large isolated farmsteads or in small hamlets. Southernmost Sweden, and the whole of Denmark, in ancient times had villages of very much the same size and shape as in northern Germany. Their dissolution into mainly isolated farmsteads, leaving but small village nuclei, is an artificial feature. It was brought about through the enclosure movement in the late 18th and the early 19th century, led by a highly rationalistic trend of thought among the governing classes, often resisted by the peasants and often deplored later on[a]. The same sort of movement a little later, in the course of the 19th century, dissolved may small villages and hamlets in both Sweden and Finland, but left essentially untouched those of northern Sweden. In the latter, crop production was on the whole secondary to animal husbandry, forestry, and handicraft, and high population pressure on the land made enclosures little practical.

On the same lines as in Denmark and southern Sweden, villages were dissolved in the Baltic States, partly already in the 19th century, partly in connection with the land reforms in the twenties[b]. In this region, however, nucleated villages were not a very old feature. It seems to be proved that as late as in the 16th century, the dominating settlement form was in small, loose hamlets, organized in groupings of a rather indefinitely regional character. The nucleated villages seem to have been brought about by the so-called German colonization — introduction of "Gutsherrschaft" in the Prussian sense — in connection with demographic increase. Dissolution of the villages in modern time was not likely therefore to have met with resistance from the peasants but was felt rather as a liberation from the domination of the landlords.

(22) Also in the British Isles, the dispersed character of agricultural settlement in most districts is only partially original. Irish settlement seems always to have been of a prevailingly dispersed character, mainly as small hamlets without nucleation[a]. The thoroughgoing dissolution of even these small centers, in connection with land reform measures during the last sixty or seventy years, does not therefore mean a profound change, viewed from the standpoint of our enquiry. Also in the Welsh counties, dispersed settlement appears to have been the original

pattern [b]. In England, on the contrary, many villages have declined, both in connection with enclosures and through decrease in numbers of the farming population [c].

Even more than in the British Isles, villages and larger hamlets have declined in parts of France in relatively recent times. The movement has been a double one. On the one hand, there are many instances where existing villages declined. Above all, the smaller ones among them have failed to fulfill any important social mission and therefore have tended to succumb under the pressure of the technical necessity of living close to the farm land. The greater villages, on the contrary, have resisted better because they had social advantages to offer in exchange [d]. Parallel with this, there has been a strong tendency, at least since the 18th century, for new settlements to be established as isolated farmsteads [e]. Finally, the rural exodus is likely to have contributed towards making French villages less important than before in comparison with the dispersed settlement. The exceptions only contribute to underlining the general trend [f].

(23) Very much on the same lines, agricultural villages began to decline at a rather early epoch in northern and central Italy. The present predominance of isolated farmsteads in large areas is caused by a long-term change in farming patterns which has produced a result similar to that provoked by the enclosures in England and Scandinavia, though in a less spectacular way and without attracting general interest to the same degree [a]. The movement is emphasized by the existence of parallel movements, though not so radical, in almost all other parts of the country, even those where the large villages have remained the dominating feature. Dispersion has resulted not only from deliberate policies, as on the Agro Pontino and elsewhere, but has also come about spontaneously as in Sardinia [b].

The limited area of mainly dispersed settlement in the north-western corner of the Iberian peninsula is partly dominated by hamlets rather than isolated farms, and also has a certain number of agro-towns in contrast to the general pattern. The mainly dispersed settlement here seems to descend from antiquity, being long linked with the land tenure system of the region [c]. Other historical features are even more illustrative of the strength of the spontaneous trend towards dispersed settlement as a means to live close to the land. A trend in this direction in other parts of northern Spain, even of a semi-arid character, was prohibited by royal decrees in the 16th century[d]. Had such measures not intervened, there would no doubt have been more dispersed settlement than there actually is on the Spanish plateau. The dispersed settlement that actually exists there is not negligible in importance, though largely inferior to the nucleated villages. It is of rather recent origin and, if anything, still expanding. In Portugal too, it is well documented that the recent spontaneous trend is for ever greater dispersion[e].

More or less the same movement could be shown to be going on in most areas of Western Europe, even in regions where villages continue to predominate, partly because of lack of flexibility in the agricultural community[f].

(24) No less instructive are the corresponding developments in Eastern Europe. We have already mentioned that in the Baltic countries, settlement was mainly of a dispersed character before the German colonization in the 16th century, showing that the recent deconcentration was by no means contrary to geographical conditions for farming. The same evidence emerges from the partial dissolution of Russian villages which had already occurred to some extent late in the 19th century but became of great importance after the Stolypin reform decrees from 1905 onwards. The movement was especially important in the north west but also, for instance, in Ukraina. The semi-arid climate was thus no absolute bar, and the age-old settlement system is likely to have been an expression of former social systems rather than of geographical necessity.

Policies in the inter-war period also caused some rural settlement to become dispersed in Poland, apparently without any great resistance from the peasants, who seem rather to have seen their advantage in the movement[a]. Likewise, the recent creation of a great many isolated farmsteads on the Hungarian plains must have corresponded to real needs of farming activities[b]. Though controversial in its implementation, this movement forms an interesting counterweight to the increase in size of the Hungarian villages that was a consequence of demographic increase. This ambivalent movement contrasts with the fairly consistent concentration that was going on in the Balkan countries.

(25) The comparatively strong recent growth of population in the Balkan countries allows us to see stages of development that many other countries passed much earlier. In Turkish times population was rather scanty. Beginning at different periods during the 19th century, a very quick demographic increase changed the pattern of settlement. In many regions, there were villages, though scarcely any larger than those of contemporary France or Denmark. In others, there were only small hamlets, and new ones were founded throughout the colonization movements that followed the liberation of each area. Small groups of farmsteads, maybe only a few farms located at some distance from each other, increased through subdivisions and were gradually tightened into large nucleated villages *a*. At the same time, there was a certain shift from mountain to plain settlement; the former even diminished in absolute importance in many areas when conditions for living on the better land improved *b*. Thus, there has not only been a recent trend towards increasing concentration of settlement, but there has even been a tendency to diminishing absolute importance of dispersed settlement.

This movement is likely to have shown many similarities with what went on in Western Europe in the High Middle Ages. Population increase on the spot made the villages grow; newly acquired defensive needs together with lingering·cohesion of the enlarged family group kept them together. The contrast with Hungary is only partial. It is true that in the latter country, a great many isolated farms were created in recent decades. This has only partly counterbalanced the strong increase in size of many villages. Some agro-towns on the Alföld had only a few hundreds of inhabitants in the 18th century *c*.

(26) It can thus be said that the most general spontaneous tendency in modern times has been for increased importance of dispersed settlement. This tendency has been most important in those countries where liberal ideas have exercised most influence. These are also by and large the same countries where economic progress was strongest. Enclosures and consolidation of fragmented land, mobilization of private land ownership, commercialization of land affairs and abandoning of age-old group collectivism have attacked existing village structures, despite different age and varying character. In pre-liberal

Europe, dispersed settlement predominated mainly in mountainous or recently settled areas. If hamlets are also reckoned as dispersed settlement, then the latter has played a fairly important historical role in land settlement, especially in epochs before the impact of landlord rule. There is no doubt that both local rulers and local defense necessities once played an important part in concentration of the settlements that could not always be easily abandoned after the original incentives had ceased to operate. The agro-town of Mediterranean Europe probably has its roots in the city of antiquity, which was a farming community with much stress upon stockraising and the urgent necessity of local self-defense. For many centuries, feudal oppression kept them together, and recent overpopulation gave little incentive to leave them. The huge concentrations in northern Caucasus were also mainly pastoral communities, until some decades ago also living under the pressure of military incertainty. There is no evidence to show that the huge concentrations were harmless to crop production. The scope of the trend towards dispersed settlement should be judged not only in view of the specific forces that promoted it, but equally in view of the hindrances it must have met in lingering tradition, lack of incentives and lack of means to bring about a change.

The contrast in south eastern Europe results from a stage in historical development which has long been passed in the rest of Europe. This movement therefore reflects the conditions of living at such a stage, rather than any conditions valid for all stages of development. The same, of course, may be true about the modern trend of dispersal.

How the size-of-village factor is related to the technical conditions of farming cannot be judged on the basis of data on village population only. It is also necessary to take into account village size in terms of land area.

TERRITORIAL EXTENSION

(27) The size of village territories is important also from other viewpoints than that of distance and other technical preconditions for work, which is the main issue for our enquiry. It is, for instance, often argued that dispersed agricultural settlement tends to sharpen the traditional antagonism between town and

countryside[a], and that concentration of agricultural population into big centers ("agro-towns") would contribute towards diminishing this antagonism. In a positive sense, it is sometimes argued that dispersed settlement, on the contrary, may contribute to making the individuals somewhat less linked up with the place where they were born than is often the case with big villages. The latter may too often mean "the world" for their inhabitants; when the village is big enough to confine most of both marital and commercial relationships to its own orbit, it may show a tendency to remain closed to the outside world.

One of the most interesting possible consequences of such village isolation concerns the structure of agricultural co-operation, as will be discussed in Chapter 5. Another consequence is the hampering influence on national integration. Above all in south-eastern Europe, centuries of self-reliance within the big villages contributed powerfully to preserving the hopeless mixture of nationalities living side by side at short distances, without any tendency for the minorities to be assimilated into the linguistic and cultural pattern of the majority population. It is only recently that forced migrations have simplified the situation somewhat. Apart from this, a village with thousands of inhabitants of a certain nationality could live almost all its economic and social life without entering into any close contact with neighbouring villages of other nationalities. The Danube basin is the most famous demonstration of this principle: German villages were scattered all over the old Hungarian monarchy, deep into present Yugoslavia and Rumania; Hungarian, Serbian and Rumanian villages lay side by side in broad zones of transition without any distinct borderlines between the nationalities; even the different Slavonic nationalities might live unmixed at slight distance from each other, as when the "boundary colonization" of the 18th century placed Serbian and Slovakian villages close to each other in Vojvodina where they still exist side by side without relaxing their original linguistic and cultural differences. Albanian and Greek settlements in southern Italy and German villages in Ukraina furnish other examples, and even a single Swedish village in Ukraina survived two centuries of national isolation until it was dissolved through repatriation and emigration a short time ago.

A similar persistence of different nationalities would be much more difficult in regions of dispersed settlement or even of small nuclei. Finnish settlers in Sweden became relatively quickly assimilated when dispersed in Swedish parishes. Islets of French and Rhaeto-romanic language in south-western Germany also disappeared rather quietly, in a region where the dominating settlement feature was villages of moderate size.

(28) Our main concern with the settlement system in this enquiry is, as already mentioned, its bearings upon the land-labor relations, especially through the development of the distance factor as a consequence of the extension of village territories. These consequences, however, are likely to vary according to population density and the intensity of cultivation. The denser the population and, consequently, the bigger settled nucleus within the same village territory, the greater will be the need for intensive land use. Thus, in a village territory of a given size, the distance factor is likely to mean more waste of time the bigger the village is, as measured in agricultural population. This observation tends to be true up to a certain limit; thereafter, when the village becomes really overcrowded, there will be such a huge labor surplus that it does not matter very much any more whether available manpower is used rationally or not. Even despite this, experience seems to show that peripheral lands may be entirely abandoned and left uncultivated because of large distances.

Because village territories as such are almost never taken into account in census material[a], the only way of getting an idea of the size of village territories in general is by means of population figures. The medians for agricultural population, as briefly presented above, can be multiplied by an index expressing the number of hectares of land per person of the agricultural population in the country or district concerned. The index may be based on figures for cultivated land or for total area. The choice between these alternatives largely depends on the geographical character of the region. If all the intensively used land is grouped in the proximity of the village, and only extensively used land is located at large distances, then it seems that the figure for cultivated land would be best. But if, as is the case for instance in the Balkan mountains, cultivated land is spread all over the village territory, with streaks of pasture and mountain slopes between them, then the figures for total area must be preferred. In areas where most land is subject to relatively intensive use, the choice would be of little importance.

(29) Details of land medians, calculated along the lines just discussed, can be seen in Appendix 1. Of course, these land medians are even more theoretical and should be taken with much more reserve than the population medians from which they are derived. They are however indicative of the order of magnitude of the distance problems that may derive from the settlement system. In a broad generalization, the following outline can be drawn of the occurrence of typical village territory sizes in Europe.

A village territory size safely below 100 hectares predominates in most of the Scandinavian-Baltic area and the British Isles, in a number of Western departments in France, Belgian Flanders and Dutch Overijssel and Gelderland, some provinces in the north-west of the Iberian peninsula, part of northern and central Italy and in Slovenia and Montenegro (the latter with reservations for the effect of mountainous topography).

Between 100 and 200 hectares is most important in eastern England and most of France, and part of the northern districts in Portugal, Spain, and Italy.

Between 200 and 400 hectares has a high frequency in great parts of the Netherlands and northern France, in north-western Germany as a whole, some Alpine provinces in Italy, Niederösterreich, most of Switzerland, western Croatia, Bosnia, Hercegovina, and the Kosmet district in Yugoslavia.

Between 400 and 1,000 hectares dominate some northern and some very southern departments in France, Belgium except Flanders, south-western and parts of eastern Germany, Bohemia, northern and central Poland, great parts of northern and central Russia, central Portugal, some northern provinces in Spain, some scattered provinces in Italy, most of Greece, Albania, Yugoslavian Macedonia, Old Serbia, central Croatia and the Carpathian districts of Rumania.

Between 1,000 and 2,000 hectares is most common in two southern French departments and some southern German districts, great parts of Austria and most of Moravia-Silesia and

Slovakia, a number of central Russian districts, southern Portugal, some central Spanish provinces, some provinces in southern Italy and Greece, and important parts of Bulgaria and Rumania.

Between 2,000 and 5,000 hectares is more or less dominant in great parts of the Iberian peninsula, a number of Italian provinces, Yugoslavian Vojvodina, western and northern Hungary, most of Bulgaria, the Danube and Tisza valleys in Rumania, most of Ukraina and important parts of southern Russia.

Between 5,000 and 10,000 hectares have been calculated to be frequent in 9 Spanish and 9 Italian provinces and some districts in south-eastern Hungary (on the Great Plains, or Alföld), and are also likely to be of importance in Ukraina and Caucasus.

Over 10,000 hectares appear to be normal in some provinces of southern Spain and at least two on the Italian mainland, at least half of Sicily, parts of the Hungarian Alföld, and must also be important in some southern areas of the Soviet Union, especially Northern Caucasus.

(30) These figures mainly refer to total area. Especially for dairying, but also for other forms of relatively intensive land use for animal husbandry, large distances are perhaps as great an inconvenience as for the cultivation of arable land. It is true that primitive stockraising, especially in southern Europe, has shown a capacity for adapting itself to the vast distances between village centers and peripheral pasture lands. Many shepherds sleep under the open sky with their flocks rather than go home in the evening. Even the last Greek agricultural census reckons with the case that a stockman may not have any fixed domicile. But these are extensive forms of land use and seem to exclude, for instance, regular delivery of fresh milk. The settlement system is not a consequence of such practices, and to some extent it is responsible for land use systems lingering on which for other reasons should now be obsolete.

(31) When discussing the technical aspects of the size of village territories it should be observed that the occurrence of nucleated villages in Europe to a considerable extent is due to dense population on the countryside. For any comparison, for instance with the U.S.A., the difference in population density must be kept present. American farms are for the most part located on

the land they run, as isolated farmsteads, whereas villages are relatively few and mainly service centers with but a few, if any, farmers living in the village. This pattern of settlement is not only related to another style of living and farming than that of European agricultural villages, but is also conditioned by the distance factor, as determined by the different ratio between labor and land. The number of hectares of agricultural land per head of the population that lives from agriculture, in most European areas ranges from 2 down to less than 1; in the U.S.A. it is something like 10. A village of 1,000 hectares, which is rather exceptional in Northern and Central Europe and predominant mainly in depressed areas of Southern and Eastern Europe, would mean an agglomeration of 500–1,000 persons according to European population density standards, and perhaps a hundred farm units, if no more. In the U.S.A., the same territory, even if farmed out from one settled spot, would support a farming population of scarcely a hundred persons, and perhaps 10–15 farms. This, obviously, would not constitute a village in the sense of a social center. It would just be a hamlet with very few community functions to justify its existence. In most respects, it would remain as dependent on services rendered by non-agricultural centers as are the isolated farmsteads. As will be seen in the following, a territory of 1,000 hectares already implies undesirable technical consequences. It is therefore vital for all discussion of the future of agricultural villages to keep in mind the possibilities of change in size of farms. The development of other industries in rural villages also constitutes an issue and is likely to require different solutions as regards the location of stables and other farmbuildings. But, as far as the settlement of the agricultural population is concerned, the relation between the desirable maximum distances and the desirable maximum density of population may prove a dilemma which rules out the nucleated village.

Of course, the prospects for agricultural settlement in villages are different according to the type of farming that prevails. In districts with very intensive land use, like the Spanish *huerta* around Valencia and Murcia, or the flower district in the Netherlands, the conditions for village living in the long run are clearly more favorable than elsewhere. The more the labor really needed for farming a given area, the more manpower can live in the same place without inconvenience because of distance away from the land. In the ordinary types of arable and livestock farming, the viability of villages will in the long run depend upon how the land-labor relationships in general are solved.

(32) The theory of the distance factor may be worked out by extension from an ideal case. Suppose that the whole countryside is a normally fertile plain, with almost exclusively arable land and good grassland. On such a plain, village territories may be laid out as squares, as envisaged in planning the new Dutch polders[a]. The distance from one village to another would then be equal to the side of the square. The shortest distance from the village center to peripheral land would then vary between half the side of the square (that is, to the mid-point of the side of the square), up to 1.415 times as much:

$$\sqrt{2 \cdot (\tfrac{1}{2}S)^2} = \sqrt{2} \cdot \frac{S}{2} = 1.415 \cdot \frac{S}{2}$$

S being the side of the square.

Thus, if the square is 4 km², or 400 hectares, the side is 2 kms, which is then also the distance to the next village, and the shortest distance to peripheral land will be 1 and 1.42 km respectively, and average distance within the village territory would range from 700 to 1,000 metres. This ideal case seems to correspond with the tolerable distance maxima of 1 to 1.5 kms, as calculated in recent Swedish and German labor research[b].

According to this result, the distance factor caused by village settlement would be of negligible importance in the British Isles and most of France, in the Scandinavian-Baltic area, in northern and central Poland, Bohemia, the Atlantic corner of the Iberian peninsula, the Po valley and in northern and parts of central Italy. In most other European regions, the distance factor, as a direct consequence of the village system, appears to be a more than negligible hindrance to farming, though to a varying degree.

(33) The ideal case described is, however, theoretical only. It is likely to occur relatively seldom, except in recently planned areas like the new Dutch polders. The ideal case requires that roads go straight from the center to the periphery and are laid out with mathematical precision. In practice, this is seldom

so, for both topographic and historical reasons. The way the roads go may increase the effective distance considerably, as also does the occurrence of rocky or other waste land. To a certain extent, these kinds of increase in the distance factor may be outbalanced if the village is not too closely nucleated. Especially so-called "road villages" may present even smaller distances than those theoretically calculated on the basis of the area of the village territory. This effect, however, depends upon the degree to which each farm has its land, or most of it, located in parts of the village territory that lie in the same direction as the farm center. As a whole, the average distance from the farm center to its land is likely to be longer rather than shorter than in the ideal case. 400 hectares (1,000 acres) is then a maximum that could barely be exceeded when planning nucleated agricultural villages. Even this may be too much if the farm land is inter-mingled with large tracts of waste land.

In most regions, the distance factor is much increased for topographical reasons. This is so not only in mountain regions but also in forest areas, as in most of Scandinavia. Also in regions of low mountains and little forest, as in some densely cultivated regions of central Europe, there are certainly many villages with less than 400 hectares of agricultural land where distances are burdensome because of the layout of the village territory and its roads.

(34) As already stressed, distances resulting from the village system are as a rule much longer in southern and eastern Europe than in the west. An area of 1,000 hectares, which is rather small in many southern and eastern regions, makes the side of a square territory 3.16 kms, with consequent minimum distances to peripheral lands of 1.6–2.2 kms. Moreover, in these areas it is rather exceptional that the village territories have a regular form and layout. Supposing the village lies at the foot of a mountain, with its agricultural territory in front of itself, in the form of a semi-circle. The calculation would then start from the radius of a circular area twice as large as the actual agricultural territory of the village. For 1,000 hectares of agricultural land, the radius would then be 2.5 kms. If the form of the village territory is not regularly shaped, the distance will be even wider. For exceptionally vast village territories of 15,000 hectares, the

minimum radius would be 6.8 kms. The irregularities of the road system will increase the effective distances further, and any theoretical calculation remains an understatement. From the Peloponnesos, where our median values point to villages of about 1,000 hectares of agricultural land, special enquiries tell us that 5–6 kms distance to peripheral land is looked upon as quite normal, while instances are found of 15 and even up to 25 kms[a]. This is already comparable to some of the most "agro-town" dominated areas of New Castilla, Sicily, and the Hungarian Alföld. In the latter, normal village territories of some 10,000 to 20,000 hectares (100 to 200 square kms) should cause distances of 5 to 15 kms. In a country like Bosnia-Hercegovina, where our medians show villages barely exceeding the tolerable limits in the ideal case, the mountainous topography sometimes causes a village *zadruga* (co-operative farm) to have 300 hectares of agricultural land spread over an area of 80 square kms[b].

It is evident that village size and layout in the South often causes serious waste of labor, which sometimes even impedes a somewhat rational use of the land[c]. This is the case not only in the areas where the villages are biggest. Some aspects of this problem will be set forth in connection with the analysis of settlement policy. In this connection it must be stressed, to avoid confusion, that any calculation of the waste of labor starts from the assumption that labor has a value and could better be used in some other way. Against calculations of maximum distance, like that set forth above, it is sometimes objected that experience shows villages with much larger distances to have existed for centuries without preventing farming operations. It is then frequently overlooked that in a locally autarcic farming of a primitive type, surplus labor may have very little value, if any at all. If the surplus labor cannot be employed elsewhere, it represents a fixed capital and its maintenance a fixed expenditure. The time lost through the distances may then not mean any loss in economic values to the villagers. Once the autarcic circle is broken through increasing exchange of goods and services with other industries, labor must acquire a market value. It is on this assumption that we will examine the disadvantages of the distance factor.

Even apart from this, there are types of farming where

distance is a drawback in itself, regardless of the cost of labor. Irrigation agriculture to a great extent requires the immediate presence of the farmer several times a day ("pyjama farming"). Many forms of intensive land use equally make it necessary to be able to look over the land frequently. Unreliable weather conditions in the harvest season may also create a case for living close to the land.

MODERN TRENDS OF POLICY

(35) In thought and action regarding agricultural settlement, technical and economic considerations are weighed against social values. The former tend to be more or less the same, when measured according to the same methodology and in regions with somewhat similar conditions. The social values, on the contrary, depend largely upon different appreciation of non-measurable assets.

As already mentioned, the consolidation movement, from the 18th century onwards, caused large-scale dispersal of settlement, dissolving or reducing nucleated villages in large parts of western Europe. Similar movements, though less comprehensive in their scope, tended to transform the countryside in Russia, Poland and Hungary. At present, different ideological conceptions of social life make for different solutions. An illustration of some of the main lines in recent discussion and policy may show the implications of one and the other standpoint.

Continued spreading of settlement through creation of new isolated farmsteads still goes on in Italy in connection with the current measures of land reform and land improvement. The main policy is that the farmers should live close to the land they run, and that their situation should be made less difficult through the construction of new service centers[a]. The most important reason lies in the technical implications of intensive cultivation, which call for as small distances as possible between the farm-stead and the land. Actual experience in Italy also favors this line. The isolated farms in northern and central Italy compare favorably to the regions of agro-towns in the deep south, where large distances often impede women from participating in agricultural work and sometimes cause land use to be less intensive than it otherwise could be. A social viewpoint, favoring an individualistic way of living rather than collectivistic tendencies, is not expressly stated in official documents on the subject, but seems nevertheless to underlie the line of action. An intermediate solution is sometimes sought in a sort of "village" where the homesteads are scattered over an inner area of intensively cultivated land, with zones of less intensively used land at some distance from the settled area. Similar experiments, with the view to maintain the advantages of both village living and living close to the land, are being made in Portugal, also a country with considerable experience of dispersed settlement [b].

(36) The idea that farmers should live close to the land they run is also followed in the recent Dutch colonization schemes on the new polders. Practically all farmsteads are scattered, and it is contemplated that both the farmers and their full-time employees should live there. Only temporary farmhands are to live in nucleated community centers, together with non-agricultural rural service personnel [a]. The trend reflects experiences in a country with highly intensive cultivation of the land as well as important animal husbandry.

Also in recent Swiss and German discussion, the tendency has been to prefer dispersed settlement [b]. Here, technical considerations have been prevalent. The contrary desire to have nucleated centers as a basis for rural social life sometimes inspires attempts at model solutions to maintain as much as possible of both ways [c]. Even so, it has been clearly stated that a village could not exceed 10–12 farms of about 25 hectares each, which would already make the village embrace 300–400 hectares. This would give maximum distances of 800–1000 metres and average distances of 500–600 metres [d]. If the farms grow even bigger, the cluster would not be a village any more, only a hamlet.

Both in England and Scandinavia, there has been much talking about re-constructing the agricultural village as an agreeable unit for social life on the countryside. In practice, little has been done, except the preservation of some existing villages from dissolution. This discussion often seems to neglect the technical difficulties of creating really important agricultural centers which do not involve burdensome distances to the land. The problem must be viewed under modern conditions of farming, with the size of farms nowadays held to be suitable, and the possibilities for future development that are envisaged. As late as in 1949, the authorities handling the creation of new smallholdings in England recommended to avoid the village type of settlement in all cases where it does not meet with the needs of farming [e].

(37) Thus, in Western Europe, the prevailing tendency is still to prefer dispersed agricultural settlement. The main reason for objecting to this seems to lie in the cost of electrifying the isolated farmsteads. Other social needs, such as schools, church, shops, etc., will be met, it is generally considered, by parish or community centers, which may also break the monotony of the open country. Sometimes, the extra costs involved in creating new dispersed farmsteads are quoted as arguments in favor of the old villages. When new farm buildings are needed, the costs would at any rate be a fixed investment, and for buildings other than the living house it would in any case be difficult to find other use even in a nucleated village. The problem of planning building investments is therefore one which touches the farm structure policy more than settlement policy.

Another type of objection is that a farm population that has for generations lived in big villages could not easily get accustomed to the isolation of the open countryside. Some concessions to this viewpoint can be found in countryplanning schemes in southern Italy. A more direct consequence of this view is to be found in Spain with the foundation of entire new communities on recently irrigated land. The new settlements are founded as nucleated villages, generally without any isolated farms at all in the periphery. This does not depend exclusively upon the deep-rooted instincts of village living among the peasants in many Spanish regions, but also arises from the difficulties of finding wells and suitable village sites. Even here, the distance factor causes the new villages to be considerably smaller than the old ones; they may reach some 1000–2000 inhabitants, and thus no attempt is made to copy the old agro-towns. The inconveniencies of large distances are moreover diminished by locating the village in the proximity of the intensively cultivated irrigated land, while the extensively used dry lands are farther off.

(38) Even in Western Europe, voices are heard ni favor of

village settlement as an ideal external framework for far-reaching agricultural co-operation [a]. In eastern Europe, this viewpoint is obviously important in the attempt to concentrate the farming population. The Bulgarian statute on collective farms directly presupposes that each village forms one co-operative, and the peasants are supposed to belong to a village [b]. Even if the term "village" should here embrace the dispersed settlements at the outskirts of a community as well, the choice of term remains significant. Recent Hungarian plans for changing the settlement pattern of the country seem to be more concerned with abolishing the isolated farmsteads than with dispersing the very big villages. In fact, villages of 6,000 to 8,000 inhabitants have been advocated as a model solution, though it is contemplated that the inhabitants should live not only from agriculture, but that there should also be a considerable growth of local industries [c].

The Soviet Russian thesis, that dispersed settlement is to the detriment of both the farming population and the farming industry, may here be illustrated by one of the attempts based on it to change the situation in the Baltic countries. It is argued that settlement policy is one of the basic socio-economic problems; dispersed settlements were to be an important hindrance against the liquidation of the traditional antagonism between farmers and townsmen. It is held that isolated farmsteads serve the individualism of the peasant, at the same time as causing unnecessary expenditure, especially when modern technical services become more and more important [d].

However, even the best laid plans to concentrate agricultural population on few and large centers cannot avoid all the difficulties caused by large distances. In the re-planning of Yugoslav Vojvodina (which is the most village-dominated part of that country), it has been found necessary to maintain some of the existing isolated farmsteads as livestock farms. The heavy transport requirements for manure, hay and straw are considered to debar distances much above 1 km, if good labor economy is to be maintained. A similar exception has also been allowed in the Soviet Union, although the maximum permissible distance was longer. Beyond 8 kms from the center of the kolkhoz, peripheral livestock farms should be established, with buildings for permanent personnel [e].

More important than these exceptions is the fact which seems to emerge from available recent information on Soviet settlement, that the planned large-scale merger of villages into "agro-towns" has not been successful. Probably this was already so when the propaganda drive on the settlement concentration was discontinued. It is now being confirmed by the appearance of research on the layout of agricultural land, where it is recognized as inevitable in many cases to maintain more than one settled center within the same kolkhoz[1]. It is here stated that, after the merger of the kolkhozy, 58 per cent of all kolkhozy in the Odessa district had more than one (up to seven) settled points. This is in Ukraina, a country where big villages prevail. Although the view is consequently held that settled points within a kolkhoz should be as few as possible, much attention is focussed upon the problem of giving a good layout even in the case where more settled points must be maintained. The internal relations of the concentration that has been brought about are only stressed through the recommendation to keep each brigade settled in the nucleus immediately surrounded by the land run by the same brigade. This passage reveals how difficult it is for agricultural organization to free itself from the influence of the settlement pattern. On this point, the comparison with the kolkhozy themselves will be instructive.

CHAPTER 2

LAYOUT OF LAND

(39) The distance factor would be no more complicated than analyzed in Chapter I, if every settled point were the seat of one single agricultural enterprise with all its land allocated in a solid bloc around the farm center. This would be true whether the enterprise were a family farm, a large estate, or a kolkhoz. As already mentioned, even a kolkhoz may have more than one settled point some distance apart, which is often also the case on large private estates. This is indeed a partial response to the problems arising as farms grow extremely large. In Europe outside the Soviet Union, agricultural settlement in villages means as a rule the occurrence of many farms with their centers close to each other, and correspondingly less close to their land than under a system of dispersed settlement. Variation in the layout of the land may affect the organization of work and the time wasted on moving large distances, whatever the farm structure. Such things as road systems, drainage systems, irrigation systems and the relief of the land, its modification through levelling, contour plowing and terracing, create problems common to the large farm and the peasant village. More specific for the latter are the problems created by fragmentation and the need for consolidation of fragmented holdings; in addition these problems become more complicated depending on the impact of the layout of the land in general.

This chapter will deal with fragmentation, consolidation, and country planning, in their bearings upon the social problems of land-labor relationships. An attempt will be made to assess their importance, outline their recent history and the present trends of research and policy. As a background, the source material and its basic definitions must be presented.

LAND REGISTRATION DOCUMENTS

(40) To the student of agrarian affairs, cadastral and other land registration documents are interesting not only for the direct information they give on the disposition and the layout of the land at the time the documents were established. The way in which these documents are organized also reflects an important aspect of agrarian history. The occurrence of regular cadastres mainly in countries that have applied land taxation, and also the different ways in which the documents are drawn up, witness the impact of different social systems in the past. According to the varying character of the tax system, the object of registration (the cadastral unit) may be different. Consequently the possibility of getting a large-scale view of the layout of the farms (the operational holdings) at the present moment will vary. The differing age of the documents, and the various systems for bringing them up to date, only make matters more complicated.

(41) Not all countries in Europe have cadastral records. They are entirely lacking in the United Kingdom and Norway, and very incomplete in the Iberian and Balkan countries. In the rest of the continent, cadastres are at best inconsistent if not incomplete. As will be further discussed in Chapter 4, the most important distinction is between registration of individual parcels of land, and registration of entire land holdings. The latter was regular in Europe of the High Middle Ages, when the *mansus* and similar units were registered as units without mentioning their composition of various plots of land. The breakup of these units, at various periods mainly in the Late Middle Ages, caused more and more landlords to register each plot of land as a separate object of lease. These detailed parcel registers are the origin of modern parcel cadastres. Late mediaeval rules on farm indivisibility, which will also be dealt with in Chapter 4, caused the *mansus*-principle to survive in limited areas of Scandinavia, Germany and some other countries. These came to form the basis for a concept of the cadastral unit different from that of the parcel cadastre.

(42) In the countries under Roman Law, in principle, every parcel of land was a separate object for all sorts of legal transactions. This was so until recently, and to some extent still is.

The cadastral system for these countries, as developed mainly in France and Italy, had its main scope in assessing land tax separately on each plot. If kept well up to date, such a cadastre gives a good idea of the degree of fragmentation of the units of property. Only vague inferences can be drawn from them, however, concerning fragmentation of operational holdings (farm units).

The French cadastre was created by a statute of 1807 after preparatory work during the revolution, absorbing the experience of former land registers. It was completed towards the middle of the 19th century and is a classical example of both the advantages and the drawbacks of such a system[a]. At the time that a cadastre sheet is finished, it presents a good picture of the local land situation; but because the documents were drawn up to serve as the basis for an unchangeable land tax, they were in principle unchangeable too, and hence after some time become materially obsolete. This rigid cadastre has more than once called for revision, both during the latter half of the 19th century, in 1907, and in 1918. It was not until 1930 that the revision was placed on a firm legal basis. By 1946, about half the country had a revised cadastre. Some districts still only have land registers from the epoch before the revolution in 1789.

For our purpose, it is of special importance that available statistics on cadastral plots dates back to the years around 1900. The number of cadastral plots does not give all the information on fragmentation of property. Parallel data on "ilots de propriété" are also given. These may consist of two or more cadastral plots together forming one solid bloc of land. Where there is extensive fragmentation, "ilots" may be rented as units, without further subdivision, but the opposite may also be frequent.

(43) On more or less the same lines as in France, the Italian cadastre is based on the individual land plot as the unit. Originally, fiscal interests were more important. In modern time, however, the Italian parcel cadastre is being developed into a first-class instrument for country planning. Historically, the Italian cadastre developed from various systems applied in the different States, among which the most important was the Austrian cadastre in Milano[a]. At present, most regions have cadastres from the 1920's or 1930's or even later.

In the Iberian countries, not even the system of land taxes was able to foster the establishment of a cadastre in the proper sense of the word. Recently, such work has been taken up with considerable energy, on the basis of the Italian system. In both Spain and Portugal, the start was made in the South of the country. The large estates prevailing in these parts of the countries made the task easiest there. In the northern regions, where most farms are small and land fragmentation very advanced, the work must necessarily cost more and they are still waiting for their cadastre. The Spanish cadastre has by now come to embrace the major part of the country [b]. The new Portuguese cadastre so far covers mainly the southern part of the country. In the central and northern parts, merely some pilot surveys only have been carried out [c]. Annual taxation statistics give information on the number of separately registered tax units, which ought to correspond to some concept of land parcel. The 1952 census of agriculture indicates, however, that the concept of separate land plots within the operational holdings is considerably different from that of the tax registers.

(44) Based on traditions more favorable to the unity of the farm, the German cadastres and land registers took into account the property units (which might be more than one per owner) and the various plots of land which compose them [a]. This comes close to operational holdings, provided that there is little leased land and few mixed holdings. Essentially on the basis of the German cadastre, the modern Greek cadastre was drawn up in the twenties [b]. It had the immediate objective of registering the state of affairs resulting from the land reform, and so far it does not cover much more than the areas where this reform was carried out. In these regions, the registration was relatively simple; leasehold plays a small part and registered units are close to operational holdings. In regions where small farms have been prevalent for a century, land fragmentation is more advanced, while mixed tenures are more frequent and more important.

Similar principles also applied to the famous Austro-Hungarian cadastre, also kept up to date by means of annual revisions [c]. The Austrian cadastre has had a decisive influence upon the systems in most of the succession States. For instance, the still incomplete

Yugoslav cadastre derives most of its merits from the Austrian tradition[d].

Other countries in eastern Europe have so far lacked a regular land registration system. This does mean that there may not locally have been fairly good order in land affairs. In Bulgaria, for instance, there were no written land registers, but the system of oral recording seems to have functioned satisfactorily[e]. For our purpose, figures based on such local recording may be more reliable than those derived from a cadastre of the French type, because the concept of land parcel is likely to have been kept closer to realities.

From post-war Bulgaria, land registers are incidentally mentioned in connection with the collective farms[f]. It may be that this is due to the adoption of model statutes for the collective farms which rely to a great extent upon Russian patterns. For each Russian kolkhoz, a local land register (*shnurovaia kniga*) is supposed to exist[g]. This, however, is a gestion document within the farm. Public land registration need only concern itself with the large farm units and is likely therefore to be rather a simple affair as far as the countryside is concerned.

(45) The land registers in Denmark, Sweden, and Finland are based on the operational holding[a]. For the study of land layout, however, this approach is useful mainly where the register was drawn up recently, or where the farm pattern has not changed since. In general, the original farm units have become crystallised as register units. Further subdivisions are duly registered, but the amalgamation of two or more old units into one operational holding is not necessarily so. A statistical basis for the study of fragmentation would therefore require special enquiries.

The absence of a cadastre in Great Britain makes information on land layout equally dependent on special enquiries, as for instance the National Farm Survey in 1943. For civil purposes, the ordnance survey sheets and the Land Registers (which are obligatory in Scotland and in practice rather comprehensive in England) serve many of the purposes otherwise fulfilled by the cadastres[b].

(46) According to the land systems that have put their stamp upon the registration documents, the registration unit may be an individual parcel of land, or an agglomeration of parcels

forming together some kind of unit, or an ideal unit of prorata shares in common land. For the study of land layout, only the first of these units would serve, and even this depends on the concept of land parcel. As already mentioned, the French cadastre has two kinds of parcels: the *ilot de propriété*, which is a coherent piece of land belonging to the same owner and on all sides surrounded by the property of others, and the *parcelle*, which may be only a part of the former, and subject to one only among the main types of land use current in the region [a].

The same kind of distinction also plays some part in the Spanish cadastre, which reckons with *parcelas* and *subparcelas* [b]. Dutch research has also taken the distinction between *kavel* and *perceel* in the same sense [c].

This distinction is specially significant because the most important material we have to fill out the results of defective cadastre statistics are agricultural censuses which register the number of separate plots of land. There, regularly, the concept of parcel is that of the *ilot de propriété* (the Bulgarian census of 1934 is an exception). Within such a plot, there may be distinct patches of land which are temporarily or permanently destined to different kinds of land use. They may even be separated by hedges, broad ditches, or other obstacles of a permanent character. The latter is regularly the case within consolidated en-bloc holdings of some considerable extension.

For our present purpose, it is of course interesting to know how far the fragmentation of the land coincides with or differs from the land use divisions. The same number of land plots may vary in significance, depending upon their distribution over different categories of permanent land utilization.

LAND FRAGMENTATION

(47) The division of land in a great number of distinct parcels has often been deplored as a major cause of backwardness in agriculture. It is a complicated issue with various aspects that must be kept apart.

First, the division into many plots of the land area dependent upon a point of settlement means a multiplication of the distance factor as analysed in the preceding chapter. This can be directly studied by means of statistics on the number and size of plots, as available in a number of countries, on the basis of either cadastres or farm censuses.

Secondly, the difference it would make if all the plots belonging to the same operational holding were consolidated into one bloc of land, depends largely on the farm size structure. The smaller the farms are, the more the increase in total distance factor is due to this structure and the less to the number and average size of the plots, because there will then be fewer plots per farm, *ceteris paribus*. In other words, more would be gained through consolidation of large than of small farms.

Further, the division of the land in many distinct plots may be only the most striking feature of bad layout of the land. A bad layout of roads, ditches etc. often makes the access to some plots difficult. This is not a necessary result of fragmentation as such, only a commonly concurrent evil.

TABLE 1. *Land fragmentation and need for consolidation*

	Average size of plot (hectares)	Plots per hectare	Plots per farm	Area in need of consolidation	
				(ooo ha)	As per cent of agri- cultural area
United Kingdom . . .	..	..	..	..	..
Ireland	..	..	..	..	..
Norway	..	..	..	..	..
Denmark	..	..	..	150	5
Sweden	..	..	..	250	5
Finland (1938)	4.5	0,2	2,6	300	10
Netherlands (1950) . .	2.3	0.4	3.2	1,000	43
Belgium (1950)	1.1	0.9	6.8	500	28
France (1901)	0.9	1.1	18	9,000	30
Switzerland (1939) . . .	0.5	2.0	9.7	450	38
W. Germany (1949) . .	0.7	1.4	10.0	6,000	50
E. Germany.	..	..	..	..	..
Poland	..	..	..	4,000	20
Czechoslovakia (1938) .	0.3	3.3	30	3,500	50
Austria.	..	..	..	1,000	40
Hungary (1935)	1.4	0.7	3.4	3,500	50
Rumania (1948)	0.9	1.1	6.6	7,000	50
Bulgaria (1934)	0.4	2.5	13.4	1,900	40
Yugoslavia	..	..	..	5,000	50
Greece (1929)	0.7	1.4	5.5	850	25
,, (1950)	0.5	2.1	5.6		
Italy (1935)	0.6	1.6	10.6	6,500	40
Spain (1945)	1.6	0.6	7.0	12,000	50
Portugal (1940)	0.6	1.6	26	2,800	60
USSR	..	..	..	..	..

In order to grasp some of the facts about land fragmentation in Europe, the above table has been compiled from available statistics[a]. Sources and some further details are given in Appendix 2.

The year indicated within brackets is that to which the basic statistics relate, and also the averages given in the three first columns. The over-all estimates in the two last columns are adjusted so as to refer to 1950. Thus, in the countries of Eastern Europe, the effect of collectivization has been taken into account in this respect.

As a conclusion to be drawn from the table, it may be said that at least one-third of Europe's agricultural land is in need of consolidation.

(48) The information contained in this table and in Appendix 2 can be carried further by calculating the average effect of the degree of fragmentation in different countries and regions.

Theoretically, the fragmentation of a village territory would be a function of the size of the territory multiplied by the average number of plots per hectare. Combining our fragmentation data with figures for typical village size given in Chapter 1, the situation may be illustrated for some countries.

TABLE 2. *The impact of fragmentation on the distance factor*
Selected countries

Countries	Plots per hectare	Village size, hectares	Plots per village	Theoretical distance factor:	
				Average per plot, km	Total per village, km
Belgium	0.9	100–400	100–400	0.3–1	30–400
Netherlands. . .	0.4	100–400	50–2,000	0.3–1	15–2,000
Switzerland . .	2.0	100–500	200–1,000	0.3–1	60–1,000
France	1.1	100–2,000	100–2,000	0.3–2	30–4,000
W. Germany . .	1.4	100–2,000	150–3,000	0.3–2	50–6,000
Bulgaria	2.5	2,000	5,000	2	10,000
Rumania	1.1	900–3,000	1,000–3,000	0.7–2.5	700–8,000
Spain	0.6	100–32,000	60–20,000	0.3–6	20–120,000

The figures can also be broken down by regions. In northwestern Spain, with small hamlets, plots averaging 0.7 per ha would lie at an average distance from the center of about ⅓ km and a total distance factor of only 12 km. The maximum figures shown for Spain refer to the province of Ciudad Real, in New Castilla; but also on the northern part of the plateau, where villages are of modest size and fragmentation relatively advanced, there may be thousands of plots in a village, at average distances exceeding 1 km. In Rumania, some regions of Transylvania have 2.5 plots per hectare, combined with village territories averaging 1,000–2,000 hectares, which would add up to a total distance factor of 5,000–6,000 km; but also Dobrogea, with only 0.4 plots per hectare, combined with village territories of 3,000 hectares, seems to have typical average total distances of 3,000 km.

(49) The average of the total distance factor, thus calculated, is of course both an overstatement and an understatement, in extreme cases.

Even for an isolated en-bloc farm, or a small hamlet with well consolidated farms, the total distance factor could scarcely approach zero. It would do so only where all the land-use divisions reached right up to the farm center. This is seldom likely to be so. Generally, at least some of the land-use divisions lie at some distance. The total distance factor would further depend upon how often each plot was visited.

At the other end of the scale, that is the case when the plots are very numerous, the calculated total distance factor is over-stated. If each plot is large enough to absorb entire labor days in each of the major operations, then it is the average distance in the village territory that is of importance and not the number of plots. If, on the other hand, the plots are very small, so that more than one has to be visited and worked on during the same day, then it is not very likely that the farmer or worker always goes home in between. It is more probable that he works successively on plots that are not very far from one another. The distance he has to walk during the day or half-day is then not equal to the sum of the distances of the plots to the village center. It is rather the total of the distances of the first and the last plot (taken once each), plus the distances between the plots.

The result is that the total average distance to be walked or driven each day or half-day is likely to exceed the total average distance factor of the village, as soon as the number of plots per farm seriously exceeds the number of different crops grown at the same time but with different timing or different technique of operation. The total average distance to be walked or driven is never inferior to the total average distance of the village, except when the plots are so large as to allow some considerable part of the distance to be covered during the work operations. The latter will seldom be of importance in large villages divided into small farms but rather on large-scale farms (an argument sometimes advanced in Soviet literature).

It is thus safe to say that purely theoretical calculations will not show too much about the real impact of the fragmentation upon the distance factor. On the other hand, the distance factor may increase through the impact of other features in the layout of the land. Empirical measurements indicate that, when the distance grows to 6 km, this may double the total cost of labor for the plot concerned [a].

(50) Another way to illustrate the importance of the average size of plot and the number of plots is to ask what parts of the land and farms are subject to excessive fragmentation. This can to some extent be studied in agricultural censuses, when the number of plots by size of holding is shown, so that separate averages can be calculated by size-class.

Generally, the average size of plot has some correlation with the size of holding, i.e. the smallest holdings have also the smallest plots, on the average, and inversely. The average size of plot for the whole country is also characteristic for a distinct part of the size-class structure: that is in the size-classes (or size-class) occupying approximately the same percentage in holding area and number of plots. The occurrence of en-bloc holdings among both the smallest and the largest farms may modify the distribution. Even so, the point of balance we are discussing appears to have considerable importance for the interpretation of data on fragmentation.

Many factors in the farm size structure are likely to affect the distribution of fragmentation. Therefore, it is scarcely possible to establish any *a priori* rule for calculating in which size-class the average situation should occur. Empirically, however, a sort of rule can be established. For some countries, we have laid out distribution curves of the factors in question: the distribution of the land and the distribution of the number of plots. The curves intersect in the proximity of the median for the size of holding.

In Bulgaria (1934) the curves coincided from about the 42nd to about the 49th percentile, in W. Germany (1949) from the 40th to the 44th percentile, in the Netherlands (1950) from the 40th to the 48th percentile. In Belgium (1950), the corresponding intersection started as early as the 30th percentile, but this was evidently due to the exceptionally great role of dwarf holdings in that country. This category is largely made up of one-plot family gardens. When it was taken out of the picture and the curves laid out anew on the basis of the rest of the farm structure, then the intersection occurred slightly above the median.

The Belgian example is instructive as to the factors that may disturb our main rule. In a normal farm structure, with no important discrepancies between the size-classes, the median is likely to represent the size-class for which the average data on fragmentation are applicable.

(51) The identification of the median farm as the size-class where the average size of plot predominates is a main key to appreciating the consequences of fragmentation for the distance factor in agricultural holdings. The number of plots in the median farm is of course in general greater than the average number of plots per farm. The significance of this is that while the farms which are smaller than the median have smaller plots, they also have fewer. Inversely, the farms over the median size, while they have often even more plots than the median farm, have larger plots, which may counterbalance part of the inconvenience of their number. The very large farms are often consolidated and fall out of the picture.

The four countries mentioned in the preceding paragraph may illustrate the conclusions. In Belgium, in 1950, the area median was about 10 hectares of agricultural land. With an average size of plot of 0.9 ha, this makes 11 plots on a median farm, which is already on the margin of the excessive number. The 10–20 hectare farms will have many plots, yet they are too small to take advantage of the increasing size of the plots. Fragmentation then becomes a serious problem. The same is true of Western Germany. With a median over 13 ha (agricultural land), and an average size of plot of 0.7 ha, the median farm will have about

20 plots. Here, already, the main problem may be with the farms close to the median. Among those above 20 hectares, the increasing size of plots may already be of some advantage. In the Netherlands, the plots are both fewer and larger. The farm median is close to 15 hectares (still agricultural land), and with an average plot size of 2.3, the median farm should have only 6–7 plots. To some extent, this may be due to the regional differences; there are regions in the Netherlands where fragmentation plays a very small role, so that the picture would have been more typical of the Netherlands, if the fragmented regions had been taken out and considered separately. But even so, it appears as if the official estimate of the need for consolidation had taken into account more of other factors in a bad land layout than is usual in other countries. A higher technical level of agriculture brings about different standards of judgement and makes comparisons as to the "need" for consolidation difficult.

Our figures from Bulgaria are from the thirties. At that time, the median farm had about 7 hectares of agricultural land, and with an average size of plot of scarcely 0.4 ha, the median farm should have had about 20 plots, which indicates a very advanced fragmentation. In the still remaining "private" sector of Bulgarian agriculture, the median farm is only about 4 hectares. With the same average size of plot as before, this farm would have about 12 plots. The importance of fragmentation was thus reduced as the farms grew smaller, but it has not disappeared.

For some more countries a similar computation is more difficult to work out because the criteria are not consistent. In France and Czechoslovakia the farm structure is measured in total area; since our figures for average size of plot etc. are modelled upon agricultural area, a direct application of the plot size and number factors to the figures for farm structure would lead to an over-estimation of the impact of fragmentation. Despite this, it is obvious that in both these countries, the impact of fragmentation is greater than in any of the four countries discussed above, because the plots are smaller or more numerous than in Belgium, Germany or the Netherlands, while the farms are larger than in Bulgaria. In a country like Italy, the importance of fragmentation is even more difficult to assess, because of the contrasts within the farm structure: the large estates, which are seldom bothered by fragmentation, tend to increase the average and median size of farm. Insofar as fragmentation is mainly a matter for the small holdings, it may be of limited importance because of the smallness of the holdings. The same is more or less true about the Iberian countries. The recent Portuguese farm census, however, shows that the number of plots may sometimes be very high even among farms of a middle size, according to the conditions of the country.

(52) The impact of fragmentation upon the distance factor — the amount of time consumed in moving between the plots — thus results from a combination of size and number of the plots. The above observations tend to show that the inconvenience of strip farming is likely to be felt most by the farms around or above the median. The very large holdings are in general well enough consolidated to be little interested in the issue. The very small holdings, on the other hand, have too little land and too much manpower to feel the loss of time as a very important circumstance, as compared with the costs and the risks of a consolidation operation. Legal rules which require the adherence of the majority of the farmers of the village to a consolidation project are therefore likely to meet with very great difficulties. The majority of the farmers have, by definition, farms below the median size. As soon as the median holdings are in serious need of consolidation, this means a need for reallocating the whole village. At any rate, the holdings around the median represent a considerable proportion of the farming industry of the region. If their well-felt need for consolidation is not shared by a numerical majority of small farmers, then the structure may appear to be responsible for the continuation of fragmentation.

(53) Most treatises on land fragmentation try to illustrate the phenomenon by publishing some "horrifying examples" of extremely fragmented villages. By doing so, and by stressing the exceedingly great number of plots existing in these extreme cases, they risk overstating the problem and thereby indirectly weaken interest in its bearing upon the broad mass of cases. Experience shows that the latter are not nearly so startling either by the number or by the size of plots. Examination of maps of fragmented villages is on the other hand likely to bring to

attention another factor which may often be of equal or even greater importance than fragmentation. The occurrence of a bad layout, a complicated road system and extensive intermingling of different holdings, may both increase the distance factor very much and make it difficult or impossible to apply rational drainage, irrigation, and planning of work as a whole. This is a reason why the need for reallocation of land is judged differently at different stages of technical development. We have already mentioned that, as far as number and size of plots are concerned, the Netherlands would appear to be far better off than France, and yet the need for consolidation is officially estimated to be higher. A special enquiry in Belgium, where fragmentation is at any rate less stressed than in France, showed that as an average 16 per cent of all plots were enclaved, so that they could be reached only by walking over the land of other farmers. This makes at least one enclaved plot per farm [a].

It was for a long period largely overlooked that already a good system of roads might by itself substantially improve working conditions in the villages, even though the plots continued to be numerous [b]. Nowadays, the prospects are more encouraging for a layout where there might still be a number of different plots belonging to the same farm; especially the use of light machinery, and of joint machinery use, offer interesting possibilities [c]. On the other hand, it is more and more evident that there may exist grave cases of bad layout of the land, even if the number of plots is not very great. The war-time farm survey in England revealed bad layout on 13 per cent of all farms (with 12 per cent of the farm land). Only "fair" layout was found on 33 per cent of the farms (with 33 per cent of the farm land). Really good layout was thus found on 54 per cent of the farms (with 55 per cent of the farm land). 75 per cent of the farms were found to be in one single bloc of land, while 25 per cent of the farms were "severed", i.e. constituted of more than one plot of land [d]. These proportions indicate that the cases with rather many plots per farm must have been fewer than those where the layout was really bad. It is also obvious that many farms with only a "fair" layout were en-bloc farms. Most cases of fragmentation were found in eastern England and were ascribed to the lingering impact of the Saxon villages. Even so, this factor can only be responsible for part of the need for country planning and improved layout in England.

Also in Scandinavia, where consolidations are reputed to have been carried out radically at an early stage, any inside observer is aware of the fact that there is great need of country planning with a view to make the layout of the land correspond better to the needs of agricultural work.

These views justify the conclusion that far more than half the agricultural land of Europe is in need of country planning measures.

HISTORY OF FRAGMENTATION AND CONSOLIDATION

(54) Land fragmentation is often regarded as an inheritance from the European Middle Ages. It should then have been brought to an end first in those countries where Mediaeval traditions were earliest to disappear, along with the general development of these countries. It should also be lingering longest where social life of the Mediaeval type maintained its influence longest.

This kind of view illustrates a tendency to overstate the lack of mobility in rural society and is rather contrary to the results of modern research in the field. Pilot enquiries in Mediaeval village structure show that the original fragmentation was quite modest. Even in Western Europe, most of the now existing fragmentation is the result of partitions of inheritance over a few generations. To some extent, this happened already in the late Middle Ages, but to a great extent during various periods of recent centuries[a]. This experience, that fragmentation often develops quickly over a relatively short period of time, is amply confirmed by recent material from eastern Europe. In many areas both in the Balkans and in other eastern countries, settlement itself is so relatively recent that the fragmentation existing nowadays could not possibly be older than about a century. Many Serbian, Bosnian, and Bulgarian villages, for instance, show a degree of fragmentation which is much more due to rapid population increase since the villages were founded about a century ago than to any impact of Mediaeval institutions.

Another reason why the degree of fragmentation does not measure the age of the phenomenon lies in a tendency to self-checking when fragmentation goes too far even for a crowded primitive farming community. From Sardinia, there is evidence that fragmentation, especially on peripheral land, may practically extinguish land value. Spontaneous local consolidation is then the natural sequel [b].

The speed with which fragmentation may develop, if it is not checked, may also be illustrated by examples of modern consolidations being undone. In the eastern parts of Austria, it has been held that villages consolidated about sixty years ago were already fragmented once more and should be consolidated again [c].

(55) The history of land fragmentation and consolidation does to some extent reflect the double fact that fragmentation advanced earliest in countries of old settlement and old population density. Among these were also found some of the countries where a higher degree of efficiency in farming was first felt necessary. The early consolidation movement was thus an expression of the need for coercive improvement felt by the State or by the leading classes of these countries.

The famous English enclosures, begun in the late Middle Ages and for the most part brought to completion during the 18th century, were less a consolidation of peasant villages than of large estates. The en-bloc layout of small farms that followed was mainly an indirect consequence thereof.

In Scandinavia, the consolidation movement started in the middle of the 18th century and achieved its greatest successes during the first half of the 19th [a]. To some extent, this development was due to the influence of English technique and to incentives from the English market. It is however interesting to note that, at least in Sweden, interest in consolidations stirred just at a period of strongly increasing land fragmentation. A drive toward fresh land clearance at the border of the old villages was accompanied by a wave of subdivisions of farm units that had remained stable for generations.

(56) Next to the British Isles and Scandinavia, land consolidation made its greatest progress, before World War I, in northern Germany. Prussian legislation especially had good results, though mainly in the eastern parts of the country; a big factor were the low requirements for majority in the village. The Rhine province, on the contrary, saw few consolidations and remained badly fragmented. In southern Germany, almost nothing was done and

the area has remained up till now among the worst fragmented
in Europe[a]. The drive towards consolidation in the inter-war
years[b], and in these last years, has not yet had results of the
same magnitude as those of the early Prussian consolidations.

In Switzerland, land consolidation was to some extent carried
out around 1900. Before World War II, however, the results were
rather modest, and it seems as if fragmentation had increased
somewhat over the period 1905–1939[c]. During the last war,
important results were brought about in some cantons, but the
bulk of the work still remains to be done. Also in Austria,
consolidations started decades ago but have as yet touched only
the smaller parts of the areas in need of reallocation. The recent
Dutch initiatives also mark a relatively new drive towards
greater energy in such operations, after bringing about only
modest results during decades past[d].

Despite repeated legislative attempts, French consolidations
remained unimportant, apart from the necessary reallocations
of devastated frontier districts, during the whole inter-war
period. After the last war, the increased drive towards mechanization has increased interest in the issue and provoked consolidation
activity at a much larger scale than ever before[e]. It remains
essentially confined to the northern parts of the country, where
the farms are largest and the perspectives for mechanization
most promising. In Belgium, the initiative for consolidation is
only quite recent and has only just begun to be effective[f].

(57) In southern Europe, other rural problems have been more
urgent and very little has so far been done about the consolidation
problem. Among other things, the land tenure conditions have
been little favorable for a positive solution. The unit to consolidate
would be the operational holding, but this is in much of southern
Europe a quickly changing compound of plots held under
different and, till recently at least, precarious contracts. The
population pressure has probably been an even stronger disincentive. The most important initiative so far is the recent
Spanish consolidation statute, marking a serious attempt to
cope with the problem along lines similar to those applied in
France. The stress is, however, more on property than on operational holdings[a]. In Portugal, the problem is only as yet being
studied. The issue is there complicated through its gravity: in

many instances, trees belong to other owners than the land, and co-ownership in both plots and trees make any conceivable reallocation an extremely complicated operation. In Greece, where the land of the Old Kingdom has already become badly fragmented since 1830, the land reform in the twenties and thirties had to yield to the farmers' habits in so far that the new holdings were laid out in a small number of plots each. As regards the old small holdings, legislation has so far been confined to deciding a minimum size of plots at land divisions [b].

(58) In eastern Europe before the Communist régimes, land consolidation was applied on a modest scale only. As far as it occurred, it relied upon patterns borrowed from Austria and Scandinavia. The former influence inspired the consolidation movement in Czechoslovakia. Especially in industrialized Silesia there had been a not negligible amount of land consolidation since the nineties [a]. In Bohemia and Moravia the movement was still of small importance, and in Slovakia almost non-existant. In Tsarist Russia, the villages had become badly fragmented through the land régime established after the liberation of the serfs in 1861. At the beginning of the century, when Stolypin attempted to transform the Russian peasantry into individualistic farmers, Scandinavian expertise was employed for designing consolidation measures; the same attempt was made in Rumania in the inter-war period [b]. In other eastern countries, little was done in the field in the inter-war period, and fragmentation increased [c].

Early Communist policy, before the collectivization drives, tried to bring about some consolidation in the Soviet Union in the twenties and still tries to do so here and there in eastern Europe. Of much greater practical importance is the consolidation that occurs in connection with collectivization. In theory, it was carried through in almost all the Soviet Union in the thirties, even though there were limitations in practice to the fulfilment of the goal [d]. Since the amalgamation drive around 1950, the remainder of fragmentation ought to have disappeared, even if no comprehensive material is available to show the degree of application. In other eastern European countries, the collectivization which has been going on since the late forties is supposed to bring about large-scale consolidation.

THE CHANGING ARGUMENTS

(59) Consolidation of land is a field where arguments, old and new, tend to cross each other and no clear-cut lines separate the adherents to different ideologies. The way in which different ideological issues are here moved by technical considerations towards similar practical solutions is especially instructive.

The liberal standpoint, which dominated 19th century land policy and still inspired, for instance, the Stolypin attempt at land reform, was to deliver landed property from any bonds linking it to others and their property. Consolidation, to a large extent, meant the dissolution of common rights in undivided land and the abolition of passage rights and other servitudes. At the same time, it also meant the liberation from collective constraint as regards the timing of field work and grazing. While consolidation did all this to make property more individualistic than before, it was also taken to include constraint on the individual to cede the plots of land he held and accept other plots in exchange. From this viewpoint, the operation meant a violent assault on the sanctity of individual property rights.

This dilemma of legal ideology was capable of, and did crystallize into strongly contrasting results, according to the conditions. In countries where a class of leading farmers or landowners had much to gain through consolidation, they brought it about one way or another, in the alleged interest of their individual property. In cases where not so much seemed to gain for the leading class, the resistance of the broad mass of small peasants weighed heavier, and consolidation was hindered, in favor of the individual property of the latter. In both cases, the economic needs of society as a whole was formally disregarded, since it was supposed to be best served by the same measures as those promoting individual interests.

Since the first world war, there has been a gradual and lately almost universal switch-over towards regarding the interests of society as a whole as decisive for what to do with the land. Productivist policies try to support the urge of progressive farmers towards consolidation, at the same time as technical progress itself tends in the same direction. The dilemma is no longer between the individual's right to do what he wants and his right not to be prevented from progress by his neighbors. The new dilemma is in the choice between different ways of carrying out the consolidations, so as to lower the costs without missing the essential benefits of the operation.

(60) Technically, the size and shape of the plots change in importance as farming technique changes. The long and narrow strips in the classical three-field system were technically well adjusted to ploughing with large teams of oxen, difficult to turn. The enclosures in England and Scandinavia seem to have had something to do with the introduction of a new type of plough, drawn by two horses and much easier to turn. By contrast, heavy tractors and combine harvesters require plots to be not only larger but above all longer. For a period of time, mechanized harvesting required plots as close to a square form as possible, because of manual harvesting of the borders of the plot. Self-propelled combines and hay-harvesters pushed in front of a tractor again tend to make this requirement obsolete. For heavy combine harvesters, it is held that plots should not be smaller than 10 hectares, and for such a special device as electrical tractor ploughing in dryfarming areas, even 100 hectares are mentioned as a minimum size of plot for economic management. Under conditions of small-scale mechanization, several writers have pointed out 2 hectares as the probable minimum size for economic operations. The most recent developments in special machinery for small farms tend to adjust the machinery to the existing plots rather than the other way around, as a cheaper solution than consolidation. The requirements for minimum size of plots then tend to be even lower.

Along with the question of the size of plots, also the views on their number and distance have varied considerably in recent research. Radical consolidation, creating en-bloc holdings around isolated farmsteads, was a great technical and economic success in Scandinavia and the Baltic countries. It took place at a time when farm buildings were simple, cheap, and easy to remove. Reallocation of settlement largely was carried out through local mutual aid among the interested farmers. Also, there were few invested values to take into consideration. At present, the value of solid farm buildings, roads of a permanent character, the drainage system, and other investments tend to outgrow the value of the land. At the same time, electrification and other modern amenities make the isolated farm less advantageous as a form of settlement than it used to be. In modern research, the tendency is therefore to try and tolerate such fragmentation as does not directly hamper the farm operations. Even up to a dozen plots per farm is sometimes regarded as quite acceptable.

(61) Economically, it has always been observed that fragmentation meant waste of time and draught power. It is of special interest that this side of the issue tends to prevent the introduction of modern machinery. The work done on making the machines ready for work and on bringing them out on the fields are relatively fixed costs, increasing only with the distance. They do not decrease because the plots are small. The smaller the plots are, the greater will be the part of total labor costs taken by these parts of the operation. Thus, small and distant plots tend to attract primitive methods of farming. Together, it is estimated that up to half the working time may be unproductive[a]. Total costs of production should then be lowered through consolidation; a cost reduction of some 20 per cent is a figure which is not regarded as an overstatement[b]. The fact that a not negligible amount of land is being wasted along the borders of too many plots, and may be won back through consolidation, also tends to increase the economic gain of the operation. The counter-charge is the cost of consolidation, i.e. the investment needed to bring about this increase in land value[c].

As already mentioned, the early enclosures and consolidations in England, Scandinavia, and the Baltic countries worked with relatively low costs. The technical requirements on the accuracy of the measurements were not quite so high as now, and country planning was not yet thought of. The layout then introduced therefore does not always meet with modern requirements. The opposite of these conditions nowadays threatens to make consolidation an extremely costly affair. The search is towards finding cheaper practical solutions. One of the main preoccupations is that the detailed consideration tends to make the operation last over several years[d]. Simplified methods now make it possible to finish the whole consolidation within a year, at the same time as costs are lowered[e].

Thus far, the new layout which issues from the consolidation is in most cases the result of intuitive pondering rather than of systematical calculation. Formulas of mathematically tested layout which will be adaptable to conceivable changes in the farm structure are only just beginning to be considered [f].

ACTUAL LEGISLATION AND PRACTICE

(62) As mentioned above, the success of consolidation has always depended on what majority of farmers is necessary to get it approved. Generally, the numerical majority was in such a situation that it was little interested, materially. Nowadays, one would expect that the question as to the majority would be less important than before. High costs have forced most legislators to make the State assume the burden of most if not all the costs. The whole operation, as being to the benefit of the whole community, enters into the framework of a social land policy. On this point, the recent German consolidation statute has gone farther than any. The participants may not be asked their opinion at all, the decision is taken entirely by competent authorities [a]. The same statute has a clause about distributing losses of land through expropriation between all the landowners of the neighborhood (§ 87 : 1), through a special kind of consolidation. In striking contrast to this, the current French consolidation statute still tries to maintain a democratic decision as the basis for really efficient consolidation legislation [b]. Persuasion alone should be able to bring about free adherence to this radical change in the life of a village. The changed tenancy situation is likely to be in favor of this line of action. The majority required for approval is that of the holders rather than of the owners. The regions where consolidation is most badly needed in the interest of mechanization are also those where there are most tenants, by and large. Also the Austrian, Dutch and Belgian statutes tend to rely upon voluntary persuasion, even though the public interest in consolidation is clearly recognized [c].

Among the countries in southern Europe, Greece and Spain have recently enacted statutes on land consolidation [d]. Both are so written as to make it probable that only limited activity will take place during the next few years. The southern countries have so many other and more urgent problems to solve on the countryside that large-scale public investment of this kind has low priority. It is along these lines that the absence of efficient legislation in this field in Italy and Portugal can most easily be understood.

(63) In none of the countries where consolidation plays an important role can it be said that the problem is likely to be done away with over some short period of time. It may be recalled also that in those countries where the problem was mostly solved long ago, the work lasted several decades.

It will appear from the above discussion that the technical arguments for consolidation, and for rational country planning as a whole, are changing in character. More important is, or has been, the fact that these considerations are not always practical. The inconvenience of fragmentation for introduction of modern machinery is not a factor until it becomes possible, for other reasons, to introduce such machinery. This is why the issue has not been fully appreciated in central Europe until recently, and this is why it still remains in the shadow in southern Europe. The same answer refers to the problem which is in the center of our discussion, namely to the labor waste caused by fragmentation. The inconvenience of it only really begins to be felt at the moment when manpower begins to be scarce. As long as the countryside is very over-equipped with manpower, there is no very great sense in saving labor. This is especially true of small under-sized family holdings. This observation also applies both to the recent interest in the problem in central Europe and to its being still dormant in southern Europe. Both the spread of fragmentation and its remaining more prevalent in some regions than in others thus becomes an aspect of the ratio between manpower and productive resources which is the main theme of this book.

In this connection it is of interest how actual policies look at the task of consolidation. Most of the consolidation action in western Europe looks to redesigning into better shape the operational holdings actually existing[a]. No doubt some slight adjustment is envisaged, in so far as some of the weakest holdings are amalgamated in connection with the consolidation. Sometimes, it is explicitly stated that consolidation should wait until the farm structure has been improved by elimination of some of the under-sized holdings.

On this point, Communist land policy claims to be superior, because the amalgamation of the small holdings into large collective ones does not foresee any future adjustments of the farm structure at all. The large-scale enterprise should be able to undertake all the necessary adjustments within its own boundaries. Despite this, the amalgamation of small kolkhozy in the Soviet Union into larger ones around 1950 meant a kind of consolidation as well [b]. The result will then depend upon the viability of these new units. If they were to be reexamined, this might also upset the land layout in the future.

In contrast to this, the argument can be advanced that, if the fields are laid out according to a scheme for production rather than for dependance on distinct production units, it should be possible to shape them so as to function independently of any changes in the structure of operational holdings. Like the blocks of a town, which are successively occupied by buildings of different size and purpose, it should be possible to create land blocks within the agricultural land, making them to function as multi-purpose elements, useable for a great variety of agricultural purposes. If this kind of planning can be realized, the whole issue will be made independent of the social questions of land ownership and holding structure.

CHAPTER 3

LAND SUPPLY AND FARM STRUCTURE

(64) A factor basic to all questions of social organization in agriculture is the land supply per man. The average land area available per unit of manpower, and the way it changes, exercise an important influence upon the kind of farming, as regards both intensity and type of production. This in turn cannot but affect the holding structure and the attempts to change it.

The impact of demographic development may seem simple enough at first sight. Increasing population on the land would immediately call for more intensive cultivation, by methods of production which produce more by employing more manpower. Decrease of manpower may act in the opposite way, towards more extensive and less labor-consuming kinds of land use, though it need not necessarily do so, because as a rule it forms an incentive to technical progress. The degree to which it does this depends upon market conditions outside the agricultural sector of the society.

The impact of technical progress upon employment is more complicated. Under conditions of stable or increasing agricultural population, technical progress may be difficult, because manpower is abundant and cheap. If nevertheless it occurs, it will have the same effect as population increase, making for more intensive and labor-consuming ways of production. Under such conditions, technical progress is likely to be halting and slow, unless economic incentives are very strong. Under conditions of decreasing manpower, as a consequence of rural exodus, technical progress is likely to respond to the challenge, both by rationalizing the most labor-consuming operations in the peak seasons, and by adopting production combinations which distribute the work more evenly over the year. If the latter is chosen to any great extent, it will mean fuller employment for the manpower remaining in agriculture. The example of the USA during the first half of this century is instructive on this point. Through the expansion of vegetables, fruit, and other labor-consuming branches of production, total consumption of labor in US agriculture has gone down much less than one might expect when considering only the dramatic reductions in labor expenditure in some branches of production, as wheat. Above all, total labor consumption has gone down much less than total manpower, so that the level of employment must have improved considerably[a].

Under these general aspects, this chapter will deal with the man-land ratio, the levels of employment, the farm structure, and the inter-relationship between these factors.

DEFINITIONS

(65) There are many different definitions as to what land should be reckoned as agricultural. In particular there are many different ways of treating pastures, the best of which are generally included in "agricultural land", while the less valuable may or may not be excluded. In order to make an analysis of the holding structure according to farm censuses, it is unavoidable to accept the definitions of each census, for reasons of statistical overlap which will be discussed in due course. For a direct comparison of the importance of the man-land ratio and the changes in it during the period covered by our enquiry, some kind of uniform definition has to be found. Later it will be shown that relatively little can be gained by taking the formal definitions of various categories of land. For the moment, we must try to find a criterion that can be applied somewhat uniformly in each country at the beginning and the end of the period under review. The alternatives to choose from are

– the cultivated area only (arable and horticultural land = "cropland");

– the cultivated area in a broader sense, including either harvested meadows or, in addition, pastures that are cultivated in one way or another (by fertilizing, for instance);

– the agricultural area in the broad sense, that is including all rough grazings, but excluding forest land;

– the total useful area of agricultural holdings, that is including farm forests; and

– the total area strictly speaking, that is the total area of the agricultural holdings of the whole country, excluding only urban areas and other non-farm land.

Among these alternatives, the first can be rejected practically at once, because it would give a very wrong idea about the volume of agricultural resources in countries where unploughed grassland plays an important part in production, as in Great Britain and the Netherlands. The second alternative would be difficult to apply, because the distinction between rough grazings and meadows is not given in the statistics of all countries. The third alternative, total agricultural area, is rather more attractive, among other things because it is closer to a natural measure. Over the period considered in this book, most changes in land use have taken place within this definition of agricultural land, either by ploughing of natural grassland or by returning plough-land to grazing. Forest clearing and draining of swamps has played a far less important role. On such a basis, therefore, it is easier to make tolerable estimates for the period around 1900. The alternative of including forest and waste land, obviously, risks using figures devoid of any significance and cannot therefore be considered. In the following paragraphs, we therefore choose the definition of "agricultural land" in the broad sense, despite the shortcomings in even this definition.

(66) The manpower in agriculture is composed of men and women and persons of different ages. For an exact analysis of the manpower situation in a country it is therefore necessary to consider the total working population, weighted according to capacity, skill, and time effectively devoted to agriculture. For this broad survey, and especially because it covers half a century, a very rough generalization is unavoidable.

First, it will be necessary to count men only. This does not mean that we regard female labor as of secondary importance. In a number of countries it is of primary importance, in some countries perhaps even more important than male labor. But the participation of women in agricultural work is not only unevenly distributed from country to country and within countries. It is also very unevenly recorded in the statistics, in both time and space. In some instances, the increasing tendency to record female labor has caused the erroneous impression that the agricultural population is increasing [a]. In other instances, as in Spain, female workers are so unevenly distributed over the country that it is difficult to say how far these regional differences are real or are due to regional differences of attitude in answering the census. The importance of female labor in agriculture cannot therefore be dealt with here except in very broad terms. The limitation of manpower figures to male workers only is thus a necessity imposed by the statistical sources. On the other hand, whatever the actual participation of women in agricultural work, they represent potentially about the same additional working resource, other things being equal. The figures for active males in agriculture therefore represent the most useful index that can be provided to illustrate the trends of change in manpower. Only, these figures must not be taken as indicating the actual labor force.

(67) The working capacity of men is not the same at all ages, and in national enquiries different systems have been tried for weighting workers of different age (and sex), in order to express the total available manpower in "man-equivalents". The weights used vary from one country to another and sometimes from one enquiry to another. For our comparative purpose, these weights are not sufficiently well founded to serve. No attempt will therefore be made here to weight the different age-strata of males working in agriculture.

It must moreover be accepted that different censuses use different age-limits for drawing the lower (and, sometimes, the upper) limit of the working population. Among other things, the age at and above which people are regularly gainfully employed is not the same in all countries, to some extent depending on the age at which children leave school. When no age-limit is given, we have therefore accepted the figures for "active males in agriculture" given by national statistics. When the lower age-limit is unusually low, it would have been desirable to eliminate the strata below the generally accepted limit of 15 or 16 years, but this was impossible in practice. It would be impossible to state the extent to which other persons in the same age strata are recorded not as working but as schoolchildren, etc. In cases where the age-stratification of active males in agriculture was available, we have tried to standardize the data so as to refer to persons between 15 and 65 years of age. The same applies to cases where estimates had to be made on the basis of typical age-distribution in the country.

The Russian census of 1897 and the Serbian of 1900 come in a special category. Both start at a lower age-limit of 20, which evidently under-estimates the available manpower. In these cases we have therefore added allowances for people between 15 and 20 years of age, based on figures for the age-distribution of rural population. In those countries and at that epoch, very few rural youngsters over 15 could have been at school, and there can be no doubt that they participated in agricultural work. The high birthrate and the low average expectation of life in these cases also make these age strata unusually important.

(68) The way in which the type of occupation is defined is also important for the comparability of the data. In many cases, available statistics do not separate people engaged in forestry, fishing and hunting from those engaged in agriculture and live-stock husbandry. Especially when looking at statistics of about 1900, such a distinction is in quite a number of cases impossible. The association of these activities with agriculture is often so close that separate figures would be difficult to produce. Region-ally, the distinction may be important but, for entire countries, it is mainly in Norway and Scotland that the fishing population really distorts the man-land ratio. The difference will be particu-larly pronounced when we come to an analysis by size of holding of the distribution of manpower in the farm structure. Apart from that analysis, for comparability we take agricultural manpower as including those engaged in the above-mentioned associated occupations.

As regards the dividing line with urban occupations, on the whole, the classification of the censuses has been accepted. The figures are thus assumed to include those for which agriculture etc. was the main occupation and not those for which it was an accessory occupation. The latter are thus taken to be counter-balanced, by and large, by the occurrence of non-agricultural accessory occupations among the agricultural workers.

THE MAN-LAND RATIO

(69) On the basis of these principles, the following table has been drawn up to show the amount of agricultural land in each country in Europe, within their present boundaries, around 1900 and around 1950, and the number of male workers active in agriculture and related occupations around 1900, 1930, and 1950. Sources and methods applied are given in some detail in Appendix 3.

TABLE 3. *Land and man-power 1900–1950*

Countries	Agricultural land, 000 hectares		Active males in agriculture in 000's			Hectares per man	
	1900	1950	1900	1930	1950	1900	1950
England & Wales	12,400	12,082	1,221	} 1,181	970	10.2	12.5
Scotland	6,400	6,208	197		164	32.5	37.9
N. Ireland	1,200*	1,203	166	135	120*	7.2	10.0
Eire	5,070	4,689	624	542	470	8.1	10.0
BRITISH ISLES	25,070	24,182	2,208	1,858	1,724	11.4	14.0
Norway	1,112	1,046	292	373	325	3.8	3.2
Finland	2,600*	2,949	420*	570*	543	6.2	5.4
Sweden	4,966	4,437	720	799	585	6.9	7.6
Denmark	3,170	3,162	358	438	376	8.9	8.4
SCANDINAVIA	11,848	11,594	1,790	2,180	1,829	6.6	6.3
Netherlands	2,116	2,413	513	546	601	4.1	4.0
Belgium.	1,917	1,792	575	497	362	3.3	5.0
Luxemburg	154	143	27	24	21	5.7	6.7
Switzerland	2,127	2,197	376	362	326	5.7	6.7
France	35,554	33,542	5,867	4,510	4,022	6.1	8.3
Saar	150	136	47	21	21	3.2	6.5
W. Germany.	13,691	13,768	2,729	2,323	2,344	5.0	5.9
WEST-CENTRAL EUROPE	55,709	53,991	10,134	8,283	7,697	5.5	7.0
E. Germany	6,845	6,378	861	829	880	8.0	7.2
Poland	20,763	20,864	3,550	4,200	3,450	5.9	6.0
Czechoslovakia	8,325*	7,536	1,837	1,554	1,100	4.5	6.9
Austria	4,513	4,080	854	655	513	5.3	8.0
EAST-CENTRAL EUROPE.	40,446	38,858	7,102	7,238	5,943	5.7	6.5
Hungary	7,500*	7,362	1,400*	1,560	1,611	5.4	4.6
Rumania	13,000*	13,000*	2,540*	3,260	3,325	5.1	3.9
Bulgaria	5,500*	5,500*	800*	1,350*	1,600	6.9	3.4
Yugoslavia	13,800*	13,882	2,700*	3,234	3,104	5.1	4.5
Albania	1,200*	1,200*	175*	250*	300	6.9	4.0
Greece	8,000*	8,660	750*	1,008	1,193	10.1	7.3
DANUBE-BALKAN REGION	49,000	49,604	8,365	10,662	11,133	5.9	4.5

TABLE 3. *Land and man-power 1900–1950 (continued)*

Countries	Agricultural land, 000 hectares		Active males in agriculture, in 000's			Hectares per man	
	1900	1950	1900	1930	1950	1900	1950
Italy	22,260	21,775	6,390	6,621	6,096	3.5	3.6
Spain	30,000*	30,000*	4,300*	3,775	4,830	7.0	6.2
Portugal	4,860*	4,864	1,147	1,122	1,330	4.2	3.7
SOUTH-WESTERN EUROPE	57,120	56,639	11,837	11,518	12,256	4.8	4.6
SUB-TOTAL: EUROPE OUTSIDE the USSR	239,193	234,868	41,436	41,739	40,582	5.8	5.8
Estonia	2,500*	2,750*	200*	218	200*	12.5	14
Latvia	3,600*	3,600*	300*	387	350*	12	10
Lithuania	4,000*	4,200*	500*	600*	600*	8	7
Belorussia	10,000*	10,800*	1,700*	1,900*	1,500*	6	7
Ukraina and Moldova	47,500*	47,500*	7,300*	9,700*	7,000*	6½	7
European RSFSR and Carelia	153,400*	153,400*	13,800*	17,000*	12,700*	11	12
Transcaucasia	9,000*	9,000*	1,200*	1,200*	1,200*	7½	7½
SUB-TOTAL: USSR IN EUROPE . . .	230,000*	231,000*	25,000*	31,000*	23,500*	9	10
GRAND TOTAL: EUROPE	469,000	466,000	66,500	73,000	64,000	7	7

(70) The main importance of the table consists in the trends of demographic development it displays, and the resulting changes in the ratio between land and manpower. Although the grand totals for Europe turn out rather similar for 1900 and 1950, this global figure tends to conceal extremely important national and regional developments. In very broad terms, these developments can be said to mean an increasing difference in land supply in different parts of our continent. Especially in central Europe and the Danube-Balkan region, it appears that a sharp contrast has emerged from what was originally rather uniform. Since this movement has been in the same direction as the trends of general economic development of different parts of the continent, it reemphasises the relative disintegration that has taken place in Europe over the period here studied. The fact that the most vital climatic condition for agriculture — rainfall — is by and large distributed in much the same way as industrial development up to now, only makes the disintegration the more striking. Discussion of some regional features will underline this observation even more.

(71) In Great Britain, the figures from 1900 to 1930 represent a late stage in a slow downward trend in agricultural population [a]. The downward movement continued till late in the thirties and was violently reversed during the war. The new peak in agricultural manpower was reached in 1948, with a level not very far from that around 1900. Thereafter, the trend was downwards again and had by 1950 reached a level close to that of 1930; later it again reached the low level of the late thirties. The war-time discontinuity is thus now over. It did not affect the picture of Great Britain as the country in Europe where land supply per man is richest.

In contrast to Great Britain, Ireland was till lately a pronounced agricultural country. The strong downward trend in the agricultural population of Eire seems to be almost parallelled in Northern Ireland, although it has had to be estimated over the last quarter of a century. The process is only partly due to industrialization but depends also to a large extent on emigration continuing still in this century. The figures from the last fifty years only represent the last phase of what is perhaps the most striking example of solving a problem of rural overpopulation through large-scale emigration.

(72) West-Central Europe, taken together, also displays a distinct downward trend in its agricultural population. The most striking individual features are the even quicker decline in Belgium and parts of France, and the contrasting upward movement in the Netherlands. Western Germany stands at an intermediate position close to the average in this part of the continent.

The strong downward trend in agricultural manpower in France becomes the more striking when the regional differences within the country are viewed. The distribution over the period may be seen from Table 4.

Thus, the movement which over half a century reduced agricultural manpower by about a third, was very unevenly distributed. The reduction was to almost one-half in the north-eastern departments and the Alps, but only to $4/5$ in Bretagne, the northwest, and the Mediterranean departments. The latter feature is remarkable since French rural depopulation has been especially much deplored in the southernmost departments. The inflow of Italians and Spaniards to fill some of the lacunas was, in con-

TABLE 4. *Land and manpower in France, by regions*

Region	Agricultural land, 000 hectares		Active males in agriculture, in 000's		Hectares per man	
	1892	1929	1896	1946	1896	1946
East	4,317	3,831	466	253	9.3	15.1
North	5,935	5,614	842	596	7,1	9.4
Alsace-Lorraine	765[a]	900	193[a]	112	4.0	8.0
North-Center.	6,798	6,543	954	635	7.1	10.3
Bretagne	2,380	2,516	575	428	4.1	5.9
Center-SW	8,588	8,051	1,400	1,016	6.1	7.9
Center-SE	3,428	3,173	738	469	4.6	6.8
South-West	636	647	185	127	3.4	5.1
Alps	393	344	51	29	7.7	11.9
Corsica	462	322	55	32	8.4	10.1
Mediterranean region . .	1,852	1,601	408	325	4.5	4.9
FRANCE	35,554	33,542	5,867	4,022	6.1	8.3

[a] Refers to 1907 (derived from the German farm census)

sequence, overestimated in importance[a]. As will be seen later, the regions where manpower declined least include both some of the poorest and some of the richest areas of France.

The upward trend in the Netherlands is part of the unusually strong population increase as a whole in that country, exceptional for Western Europe in this century. The increase in numbers has been compensated by winning of new land. As will be seen later, it has been more than compensated by the high degree of intensity in farming.

The trend in Western Germany has been complicated through the influx of a great number of refugees from eastern Europe. Manpower in German agriculture was already declining at the beginning of the century. The number of active males in German agriculture was 5.54 million in 1895 (in the whole of Imperial Germany), as against 5.28 million in 1907, a fact often overlooked because of the increasing numbers of female workers recorded by the statistics[b]. During World War I, there was a certain increase, followed by a renewed decrease. During the second war, there was again a certain increase, which may however have been at least partially apparent only. In 1950, the number of 2.32 million included 0.29 million refugees. The regional distribution of these features may be seen from Table 5.

TABLE 5. *Land and manpower in Western Germany, by regions*

Lands	Agricultural land, 000 hectares		Active males in agri-culture, in 000's				Hectares per man		
	1907	1949	1907	1939	1950a	1950b	1907	1950a	1950
Schleswig-Holstein	1,150	1,160	121	117	151	108	9.5	7.7	10.7
Niedersachsen with Hamburg and Bremen . . .	2,498	2,843	416	404	462	364	6.0	6.2	7.8
Nordrhein-Westfalen . . .	1,960	1,960	418	340	330	292	4.7	5.9	6.7
Hessen	1,135	1,018	244	198	189	170	4.6	5.4	6.0
Rheinland-Pfalz	880	916	259	218	220	211	3.4	4.2	4.3
Baden-Württemberg . . .	1,939	1,970	523	394	358	338	3.7	5.5	5.8
Bayern	4,030	3,901	749	652	634	572	5.4	6.2	6.8
W. GERMANY	13,592	13,768	2,729	2,323	2,344	2,055	5.0	5.9	6.7

1950a = total number; 1950b = total number less the refugees

It thus appears that the downward trend was rather general and steady; even though not entirely uniform, it may be said to have been more so than the corresponding movement in France. The presence of the refugees may to some extent have acted as an incentive for local residents to leave agriculture for other occupations. Even so, the trend 1907–39 indicates that rural exodus was important everywhere. It appears however from the figures for Schleswig-Holstein and Niedersachsen as if the unusual influx of refugees had speeded up the rural exodus among the original inhabitants. As a conclusion it may be said that, had there been no refugees, the manpower figure would not have turned out quite as low as our figures for 1950b (without the refugees). Perhaps the total might have been 2.1 million by 1950.

(73) The apparently parallel movement in the group of countries here called East-Central Europe has to a great extent been influenced by events connected with the last war. Of these four countries only Austria shows by and large the same sort of development as would have taken place without the influence of these events. In that country, a strong downward trend in agricultural manpower witnesses the impact of a rapid urbanization. The same refers partly also to Czechoslovakia. In the latter country, however, the movement is largely confined to the western provinces, where it was accentuated by the expulsion of the German elements. In Slovakia, it almost appears as if

agricultural population were rising slowly as late as around 1930[a]. This impression is also supported by the official figures for total population dependent on agriculture[b].

TABLE 6. *Population living by agriculture in Czechoslovakia (thousands)*

	1900	1910	1921	1930	1947
Bohemia	2,255	2,185	1,980	1,714	1,100
Moravia-Silesia	1,364	1,303	1,176	1,019	685
Slovakia	1,823	1,807	1,819	1,901	1,615
TOTAL	5,442	5,295	4,975	4,634	3,400

Since it is normal that active males in agriculture are not very far from being one-third of total agricultural population, these figures express roughly the same trend as those for active males, in the following table.

TABLE 7. *Land and manpower in Czechoslovakia, by regions*

	Agricultural land 000 hectares		Active males in agriculture (thousands)			Hectares per man	
	1900	1947	1900	1930	1947	1900	1947
Bohemia	3,512	3,138	816	642	350*	4.3	9.0
Moravia-Silesia .	1,813	1,621	440	345	225*	4.1	7.2
Slovakia	3,000*	2,777	581	567	525*	5.2	5.3
TOTAL	8,325*	7,536	1,837	1,554	1,100	4.5	6.9

Until recently, the Czechoslovak territory thus displayed a widening difference between the parts once belonging to the Austrian and those once belonging to the Hungarian monarchy. Within its boundaries, Czechoslovakia experienced the same disintegration between central and south-eastern Europe as we have stressed above to be one of the fundamental features of the development of the man-land ratio. Up to 1947, this trend had barely been reversed. Since then, changes have probably taken place, but no figures are available. It can be supposed that the difference between the regions has diminished, but this conclusion is not altogether certain.

Also in Eastern Germany, the man-land ratio has been influenced by war events. Statistics published as relating to 1946 indicate a strong increase in agricultural population, as compared both with 1939 and with 1907 [c], not only in Eastern Germany as a whole but also in each of the five Länder then distinguished. Later available data, shown in Table 3, indicate much the same level of manpower as at the beginning of the century. In 1939, the figure was 829,000, thus somewhat lower than in 1907. Around 1950, the number would scarcely have exceeded 800,000 if there had been no refugees. By and large, the situation is comparable to Schleswig-Holstein and Niedersachsen.

Poland, finally, is a country where great regional contrasts are covered by the national averages, and where war events have played a decisive role in the actual picture. The western and northern parts of the country had a demographic history, before the last war, similar to that of northern and eastern Germany. The eastern and central parts of Poland, on the other hand, were typically Eastern European regions with a fast demographic increase, continuing the extremely rapid rise which the Polish population showed throughout the 19th century [d]. Grouping the districts distinguishable in 1949 in three main regions, roughly corresponding to historical distinctions, we get the following main picture.

TABLE 8. *Land and manpower in Poland, by regions*

	Agricultural land 000 hectares		Active males in agri- culture (thousands)			Hectares per man	
	1900	1950	1900	1930	1949	1900	1949
West	10,628	10,309	1,510	1,500*	1,420	7.0	7.3
East	7,773	8,244	1,335	1,900*	1,440	5.8	5.7
South	2,362	2,311	705	800*	590	3.3	3.9
TOTAL . . .	20,763	20,864	3,550	4,200*	3,450	5.9	6.0

The rapid increase between 1900 and 1930 was thus mainly concentrated in the purely Polish regions. The western parts behaved very much like other eastern regions in the old German empire. The disintegration we see here was, however, mostly along the State border rather than within the same State, as in Czechoslovakia. On the other hand, the pressure of increasing Polish population made itself strongly felt in mixed districts on both sides of the boundaries. The violent changes since the war,

including the expulsion of the German population and re-settlement with Polish elements, has sharpened rather than lessened
the difference between regions, so far as our figures go. Changes
that may have occurred since 1949 remain unknown. The net
diminution in population would have turned out even greater
if there had not at the same time been a population exchange
over the new eastern boundary of Poland, which seems to have
resulted in a net gain in numbers to Poland.

From the viewpoint of general demographic history, the present
agricultural inhabitants of Poland are the offspring of a part
only of the old inhabitants of the country. The 1949 level of
3.45 million should, from this point of view, be compared with
about 2.6 million around 1900, rather than with the 3.6 million
then existing in the present territory of the country.

(74) The development of the man-land ratio in the Scandinavian
countries has followed a kind of common line which lies somewhere between the patterns of Central and Eastern Europe. The
inheritance from the 19th century was a strong demographic
increase on the countryside, despite large-scale overseas emigration. The upward trend is seen to have continued over the first
quarter of this century. Thereafter, a reversal occurred which,
by 1950, has brought numbers back to the level of 1900, for the
region taken as a whole. This downward movement started first
in Sweden and has so far been strongest there. The other countries
still have more manpower in agriculture than they had around
1900. The downward trend showed up last in Finland, though
partly concealed through the concentration of almost the whole
of the population on about $^9/_{10}$ of the old agricultural territory.
The table shows the population living on the present State
territory, so that the Carelians are included in the 1950 figure
but not in those from 1900 or 1930. But for this change, the downward movement in Finland would have been more marked.

(75) The Danube-Balkan region is dominated by the East
European pattern of rapidly rising numbers in agriculture. This
increase is however very different according to countries and
regions, and for partly different reasons.

The increase has been strongest in Bulgaria, where agricultural
manpower was doubled over half a century. It was weakest in
Hungary, with only about 10 per cent increase over the same

period. Between these limits Yugoslavia displays each of the extreme trends in various regions. The southernmost regions, taken over from the Turkish empire as late as 1912, have had the same rapid increase as Bulgaria. In addition, Old Serbia, Bosnia-Hercegovina, and Montenegro had a rapidly increasing agricultural population. Vojvodina, once part of Hungary, showed only a slight increase, if anything even slower than Hungary. Croatia and Slovenia, also former parts of the Austro-Hungarian monarchy, show diminishing numbers in agriculture in the latest decades. Yugoslavia, like Czechoslovakia, has thus also been the scene of an inner disintegration, due to the same kind of difference in the historical background. Only, the contrasts were even sharper.

In Rumania, it seems as if there were also a difference between the formerly Hungarian regions (Transilvania and the Tisza valley), with a slower increase than the national average, and the Old Kingdom, Dobrogea, and Bucovina, where the East European pattern was more dominant. This contrast has however not been so striking as in Yugoslavia or even in Czechoslovakia.

The figures on Albania are estimated and do not allow for any precise conclusions.

Greece had in reality a far less marked increase in numbers on the countryside than appears from the figures of the table. The strong increase over the period is to a great extent due to the exchange of population between Greece and Turkey, which is known to have meant a great net increase to the Greek population, both total and agricultural.

In all these countries, a strong drive for industrialization since the last war is likely to have modified the inherited structure. The results cannot however be properly distinguished on the basis of material so far available.

(76) The three countries in south-western Europe exemplify a late phase in a slow secular increase of population on the land. On the one hand, these countries have had relatively good emigration possibilities, which partially accounts for the slowness of the increase. On the other hand, birthrates are slowly declining and not nearly so high as in most countries of Eastern Europe. Northern Italy has already practically reached a standstill in

population growth, with slowly falling numbers in agriculture. This trend is however overbalanced by a continued slow increase in the southern and central parts of the country. The all-over decrease shown by the latest census figure for Italy is probably apparent only, due to statistical differences. The regional figures for agricultural manpower were not fully available for this enquiry, so that the distribution of different trends cannot be described.

Also in Spain interesting regional trends appear from the details of the last census (See Appendix 3). The figures we have for around 1900 are partly estimated. It seems, however, certain that the considerable decrease which took place over the twenties was much stronger than the average in Galicia, the traditional recruitment area for emigrants to Brazil. On the other hand, there was even in the twenties a net increase in agricultural population in Andalucia, known as an area where agrarian unrest was specially strong in the early thirties.

Available material from Portugal is sufficient to show the interaction between natural increase among the agricultural population and overseas emigration.

TABLE 9. *Active males in Portuguese agriculture, by regions (thousands)*

	1900	1930	1950
North	660	587	679
South	332	380	470
Algarve	60	62	74
Islands	95	93	107
TOTAL	1,147	1,122	1,330

Available figures on agricultural area are estimates to such an extent as to make worthless the calculation of separate quotients for hectares per man. Even without such data, the figures show clearly that in the northern part of the country numbers in agriculture diminished for a certain period but have since offset the decrease. The southern parts did not correspondingly profit by emigration possibilities and went on increasing over the whole period.

The probable conclusion is that there has been a slow process of inner disintegration within the Mediterranean countries, owing to inadequate mobility of manpower within the countries. This, in its turn, depends upon many factors, but one of importance must have been the great density of agricultural population everywhere in these countries.

The characteristic difference between the south-western countries and the Balkans lies in the duration of the overpopulation problem. In the former countries, a situation already of long standing simply did not change much over the period under review. In the Balkans, a similar critically high pressure of people on the land came into being during this period.

(77) The figures from the European part of the Soviet Union demonstrate how an imminent crisis of agricultural overpopulation came to be at least relatively eased by the rapid absorption of manpower into other activities. The process is the same as that now going on in the Danube-Balkan region, though the break in the demographic trend occurred earlier and more violently. The rising tide of agrarian overpopulation was already checked by about 1930, associated with the collectivization drive. Wholesale destruction and expatriation of elements resisting collectivization was probably responsible for most of the actual decrease in numbers. Industrialization was, at best, no more than able to absorb the still great annual natural increase.

Apart from direct loss of life during the collectivization drive and during World War II, migration also played a part. On the one hand, there has been a continuation of the traditional colonization in Siberia. On the other hand, considerable numbers of Poles, Germans and Finns have left the territories recently annexed to the USSR. Even so, the present level of agricultural manpower is only slightly lower than the level around 1900. The difference may be due to war losses and, if female labor were better documented, it would probably be shown to be at least as numerous as around 1900.

So far as our estimates go, it appears that there were considerable regional differences within the union. The Baltic countries, relatively sparsely populated during the Tsarist epoch, cannot be said to have been faced by any overpopulation crisis. The changes seem to be smaller than the average in Belorussia and

Transcaucasia, while the changes in Ukraina were certainly more radical than the average for the USSR. For the European part of the Russian republic (including Carelia), it may be interesting to look at a tentative regional distribution of the figures and their trend.

TABLE 10. *Land and manpower in European RSFSR (and Carelia), by regions (all figures estimated)*

	Agricultural land, 000 hectares	Active males in agriculture (thousands)			Hectares per man		
	1900–1950	1900	1926	1950	1900	1926	1950
North and Lake regions with Carelia and Kaliningrad district	12,000	1,400	1,800	1,400	8½	7	8½
Central and Middle Volga regions	34,000	4,000	5,000	3,500	8½	7	10
Volga and Volga-Don regions with Astrakhan district . .	59,000	4,000	5,000	3,800	15	12	16
Central Black Soil region . .	17,400	2,500	3,000	2,000	7	6	9
Northern Caucasus with Rostov District and Daghestan	31,000	1,900	2,200	2,000	16	14	15½
TOTAL	153,400	13,800	17,000	12,700	11	9	12

The figures in this table show something about the regional distribution of the man-land ratio. That it is as high as 11–12 ha is thus seen to be due to the impact of the vast steppe regions in the south east. In the western regions, as in Belorussia and Ukraina, it is rather close to what is normal in Europe. If the differences in climate are kept in mind, it becomes clear that Russia in the twenties was no longer a country with an ample supply of land.

(78) As already stressed, the demographic development on the land, as represented by the figures of our tables, has meant progressive disintegration within Europe. There can be no doubt that the differences in land supply (hectares per man) between countries and regions are now greater than they were half a century ago. This fact forms an important background to the economical and political disparities appearing in our continent and to the attempts towards easing them.

Until relatively lately, rural exodus and declining agricultural population have in general been judged as a sign of weakness in the community. For reasons of general policy which will be discussed at greater length in a later chapter, diminution of the agricultural population, both absolute and relative, has often been deplored [a]. The opposite view based more on economic than on sociological or political motives, is however now being heard more and more frequently [b]. It is also stressed more and more that the diminution of the population directly engaged in agriculture fits into a process of specialization which is one of the main conditions for economic progress [c].

In this connection it is only appropriate to point out, too, that increasing land supply per man does not automatically mean increasing productivity. Partly, the movement merely reflects increasing specialization. When part of the labor force working in agriculture is set free for other industries, it will to some extent produce investment goods and other commodities which are basic for agricultural production. At an early stage of the process, the diminution of manpower on the land might mean that those leaving agriculture went into manufacturing industries making clothes, shoes, tools etc., which the farmers used to make themselves. Eventually, part-time handicraft cannot meet the competition, and the employment of those remaining in agriculture is more strictly than before confined to production of crops and livestock products. A mere increase in the space available for cultivation per unit of manpower may then be an apparent advantage rather than a real one. As regards the productivity and well-being of agriculture, it is probably more important to be able to measure the intensity of land-use rather than the direct ratio between man-power and land-area, in geometrical terms. In all circumstances, the increase in net labor productivity, which is a real change, will be smaller than the increase in gross labor productivity, which is mainly a formal one since the inputs into agriculture are also increasing.

(79) The interesting variations shown in Table 3 and the following tables are those in agricultural manpower and population. Variations in agricultural land in each country are not very great, in many countries not even known. Europe has not been the scene of very large reclamation schemes during this century. The continent has, by and large, been occupied for centuries. Some of the countries where there was no dense

population before the 19th century had nevertheless done most of their land clearance by about 1900. The definition of agricultural land used in this chapter does not permit of much expansion of agricultural land. In south eastern Europe, including Ukraina and southern Russia, expansion of the sown area has largely taken place at the expense of natural grassland. Among greater reclamation projects one may mention the new polders in the Netherlands, extensive forest clearing in Finland, and the draining of the Pontine marshes in Italy. The two former have affected the picture of land supply in the two small countries, though not overwhelmingly. In Italy, the fluctuations in definition between rough grazing and waste land have dwarfed the impact of land clearance upon the picture.

The abandonment of agricultural land, in France for instance, may also to some extent be only apparent. Part of the abandoned lands are probably still used as pastures. Differences in definitions over a long period thus make it unwise to build on the relatively small changes that can be observed in some countries.

The main conclusions of this section therefore belong to the history of population and manpower. The figures for hectares per man do not in themselves tell very much about absolute land hunger, only about the trend. It is true that area per man is high in England and France, and low in southern Europe and on the Balkans. The quotient is however low also in the Netherlands and high in the Soviet Union, as well as on the Spanish plateau. It must be admitted that the bare number of hectares per man does not give the reason for wealth or poverty in a country's agriculture. Italian and Spanish cadastral valuations report differences in land value, per hectare of different kinds of land, ranging from 1 to 1,000. Even if this is extreme, differences in land quality are nevertheless almost everywhere so considerable as to make necessary another measure than the unweighted area of agricultural land.

WEIGHTING LAND AND LIVESTOCK

(80) Because unweighted areas say too little, some kind of weighting has to be devised. The need for this has been felt by many scientists, and various systems have been tried. We may

here quote the system proposed by W. E. MOORE in his survey
of the economic demography of southern and eastern Europe[a].
Arable land was taken as 1, horticultural land as 4, meadows as
0.4, and pastures as 0.2. The weighted unit thus produced was
christened "arable equivalent land". The main fault with this
scale is that it is uniform everywhere and therefore fails to take
account of some of the most interesting differences in land value
from region to region. In fact, even within the traditional
category of arable land, there are such differences in fertility and
value, especially for climatic reasons, that figures for "arable-
equivalent" land are little better than unweighted areas. At the
other end of the scale, the value of rough grazings is in many
instances infinitesimal, far less than one-fifth of normal arable
land. But, in some countries, pasture land may have the same
value per hectare as arable land. The method adopted by Moore
leads at the same time to a pronounced underestimate of agricultural resources in a country like the Netherlands, and a strong
overestimate of resources in a country like Spain. A good scale
of weights cannot be based on such simple and stereotyped
categories but must take into account geographical and other
differences between countries and regions.

From some countries, detailed valuation scales are available,
which make possible some kind of weighting of the economic
value of farm land within the country. The scale proposed by
J. KLATZMANN for France is based on the rental value of the
land in each individual case which is, or can be made, known for
all French land[b]. By adopting it, one would undoubtedly go far
in assessing the land situation in different parts of France. The
Italian cadastre valuations, which are, at least in principle,
applied over the whole country, could also be used to illustrate
the differences in land supply within that country[c]. Similar
systems will probably issue from the Spanish and Portuguese
cadastres, when they approach completion.

For Spain one might, for the time being, use the land value
scales furnished by current agricultural statistics, on the basis
of output. A similar method has been attempted here and there
with varying success.

It is a matter of question whether one or other of these
weighting systems would satisfy the purpose of this enquiry,

which is to illustrate the social distribution of economic resources. In this case, rental values, like those mentioned from France and Italy, would tend to illustrate the values which become available for the owners of the land or of capital invested in the land, rather than those available for the people working on the land. The rental values would tend to represent marginal surpluses rather than the comprehensive asset which the land means in the hands of those who work on it.

Output values, however interesting in themselves, would cause difficulties from two viewpoints. One is that the value of gross output is to a very great extent dependent upon the intensity of input and thus only represents the value of the land mainly on the assumption that the intensity of input is always and everywhere in the same proportion to the natural fertility of the land. More important, however, is another point. All valuation scales based on output will necessarily depend on commodity prices in money; but money is not only an artificial, man-made unit, it is also a unit the relations of which to various natural units vary, both according to any rule of demand and supply (the results of which might be entirely disproportionate to the effort needed to produce the commodity units), and at least as much according to the economic policy of each country. The price relation between, say, wheat and milk, is nowadays largely not a result of the demand and supply of the two commodities, but much more a result of the economic policy conducted in order to protect either consumers from exorbitant prices or producers from destructive competition. Any value ascribed to the land is, therefore, in a sense a value that corresponds to political issues. For the purpose of our enquiry, we must look for a natural measure, one that can be said to be basically comparable from country to country.

(81) On the output side, a scale can scarcely be constructed without using prices in some way or other. Comparing calorie values would understate too much high-priced items like grapes and, besides, many industrial crops do not have any calorie value at all. Only within the same specific kind of land use would it be possible to use a natural weight if the output side were taken into account. Measurement of the value of grassland through the dairy cow furnishes a good example of this limited approach[a].

Looking towards the input side, consumption of human labor appears as the most widely applicable measure available. Human labor not only represents the largest single item of input in almost all countries but has at the same time the advantage of being measurable in units which are essentially the same from country to country. The problem of whether farmers, grown-up members of their families, and agricultural workmen have or have not full employment, is much the same in many countries, and certainly in most of the countries of Europe. We will therefore use as a measure the volume of employment available to the farming population in existing crop and livestock enterprises. The latter will for our purposes also represent those parts of the agricultural area which are not directly cultivated, insofar as no separate labor norms are available for them. Each important crop on arable, horticultural and orchard land will be given a separate weight in accordance with the amount of labor taken to cultivate it, and each kind of livestock a separate weight in accordance with the amount of labor required to tend a unit of stock.

(82) This weighting should, in the first place, be done separately for each country on the basis of labor norms applicable in that country and representing a reasonable level of technology under the circumstances prevailing in the country. It would at this stage be impossible to apply one and the same set of labor norms everywhere. The amount of labor needed would depend both on the climate and on the methods of cultivation imposed by it. It would also depend on the amount of machinery and other invested capital existing in the country, which may modify the conditions of work. It would finally also depend on the general level of technology and education in the country concerned.

By weighting land and livestock in each country separately according to national labor standards we can form an idea of the volume of employment available for the agricultural population. The resulting figures are comparable from country to country for the purposes of social science. The level of employment and hidden or open unemployment means essentially the same thing in relation to agricultural population in each country. They are not, however, directly comparable from the purely economic point of view, because the level of employment found in each country depends on different technical and economic levels. The method of making these levels roughly comparable is to apply, in addition, a single set of labor norms to all countries. We talk expressly about this as a second step in the weighting enquiry, because it will necessarily be more hypothetical and less realistic than weighting by national standards. For this purpose, we have chosen American labor standards of 1945/48, as representing a technical level essentially higher than that found in any European country and at the same time derived from fairly mature and well-founded research on agricultural labor. They have also the advantage of representing a weighted average from a country where agriculture is a very big industry, and with about the same climatic zones as Europe.

(83) The idea of measuring labor operations in order to make them quicker and more economical was formulated in the USA late in the 19th century. Taylorism, first devised for manufacturing industries, soon spread to the early industrialized agriculture of its country of origin. USA has been able to provide over-all surveys of the amount and efficiency of agricultural labor from as early a date as 1910 and onwards[a]. In Europe, a similar start was made in Germany immediately after World War I, and a number of other countries followed the same road during the twenties and thirties[b]. The issue was of special concern to the Soviet Union in connection with the collectivization of its agriculture, and especially around 1930 a number of studies of general interest were produced there[c]. Since about the same time, some countries have kept regular accounting services which have also tended to increase interest in and the extent and reliability of research on agricultural labor. After the last war, the tendency has been to intensify such research. It is nowadays possible to assess the labor consumption in various countries' agriculture with a margin of certainty that makes it of real interest for our purpose. The relatively recent character of this research makes it, on the other hand, advisable not to apply it, as yet at least, to earlier periods except where the persistence till lately of primitive farming methods indicates that no great changes have occurred.

Details of the norms used for weighting in different countries, and methodological considerations in connection with them, are collected in Appendix 4.

THE LEVELS OF EMPLOYMENT

(84) The materials thus produced give us, in the first place, the volume of employment available to the agricultural population. The data refer to the land and livestock existing at a given moment and thus reflect the pattern of intensity at that very moment. This makes it possible to calculate the level of employment per man working in agriculture.

Some distinctions must be kept in mind. There is a difference between open and hidden underemployment. The former is an evil that mainly hits salaried workers, because the landlords or peasants employing them may not be able or willing to offer constant employment. The latter is something that touches all workers in agriculture as soon as they have too little land to find it practical and economical to conform to the standards of efficiency which are possible and somewhat generally applied in their country or region. The question of hidden underemployment will be discussed later on. We note here that our term "levels of employment" refers to the relatively efficient employment that is possible in each region and that the degree of underemployment refers to lower efficiency more often than to physical lack of work.

The labor year cannot be discussed without some consideration of the distribution of different kinds of work during the year. The climate may for instance create a dead season when there is insufficient or no employment. This factor must not, however, be overemphasized. In north-western Europe, agricultural work is dominated by livestock which is, if anything, more labor-consuming in the winter than in the summer. In the far north, where the winter is very long, there is, in return, much forestry work with which to fill out the year. In southern Europe, where there is little forest nor much livestock there is, on the other hand, in general a rather short dead season or none at all. The continuity of cultivation there makes seasonal unemployment a matter of agricultural practice — avoiding monoculture — rather than of physical possibilities. The regions where winter unemployment may still be an important deficit item in the labor year are on the vast woodless plains along the Danube, in Ukraina, and parts of southern Russia.

In most instances, seasonal variations in the availability of labor are self-compensatory in that shorter or fewer labor days in the off seasons are off-set by longer labor days in the rush periods. The same applies also to the breaks caused by bad weather (which, moreover, affect a minor part only of all work in modern agriculture).

It is therefore not too inexact to reckon on the same length of the labor year in all parts of Europe. We have taken a year of 2,500 hours (or 250 days, reckoning 10 hours a day) as standard full employment. This is also rather close to a full labor year in urban occupations. A different year is applied in this study only where the underlying labor norms are based on a different assumption; the Belgian norms thus presuppose 3,120 hours as a full labor year.

The degree of employment should, for reasons discussed above, be calculated on the basis of figures for male manpower only. These figures ought, however, to be raised in order to allow for a certain amount of female labor, which actually takes place in all countries. American labor standards, which play an important part in this analysis, imply a level of employment in US agriculture close to 120 per cent of the male workers. The actual participation of female workers in the countries of north-western Europe also seems to be of the order of magnitude of 20 per cent of the male workers. We therefore calculate the level of employment on the basis of 120 per cent of the male labor force. In some countries, this may lead to an over-estimate of the actual level of efficient employment, because the actual participation of female labor is higher.

Apart from the level of employment, the weighting also gives a measure of agricultural land resources which is more instructive than the figures for unweighted land area. In order to make the weighted figures comparable with the unweighted, a unit should be found which equates the weighted with the unweighted land area, under normal agricultural conditions. No unit of crop area seems to be appropriate for this purpose. Weighted average labor consumption per hectare of arable land would not serve, since it would vary with the crop pattern. Taking one single crop, wheat for instance, as an indication, there would be reflected the very great variations in labor consumption in that crop. Livestock, on the other hand, shows much lesser variations in labor consumption per head, so far as available material on European labor norms goes to show. For dairy cows especially, the variations within Europe are modest. In addition to the figures on levels of employment, the following table therefore also contains figures for "cow-units" of labor. This unit represents the number of days or hours required to tend a milk cow per year. The approximative equality between this figure and the

TABLE 11. *Labor potential and levels of employment in selected countries, calculated according to national labor standards. Data refer to a year close to 1950 except when otherwise stated*

Countries	Agri-cultural land 000 ha	Labor available:			Manpower:		Per cent employ-ment
		Million hours	Cow-units, 000	Man-years, 000	Active males, 000	Active males plus 20 %	
United Kingdom	19,493	2,924	17,200	1,170	1,254	1,505	78
Eire	4,689	708	4,166	283	470	564	50
Norway	1,046	500	2,900	190	263 [a]	316	60
Finland	2,949	900	5,600	360	543	652	55
Sweden (1932)	4,500	1,700	10,600	680	800	960	71
Denmark	3,162	873	5,453	349	376	451	77
Netherlands	2,413	1,300	6,255	417	601	721	58
Belgium	1,792	900	4,328	289	362	434	67
France	33,542	10,600	51,620	4,239	4,022	4,826	88
W. Germany	13,768	5,075	29,861	2,030	2,344	2,813	72
Poland	20,864	9,900	32,443	3,958	3,450	4,140	96
Czechoslovakia (1946) . .	7,536	2,700	13,494	1,089	1,100	1,320	83
Austria	4,080	1,075	6,313	429	513	616	70
Hungary	7,362	3,000	11,550	1,150	1,611	1,943	64
Bulgaria (1940)	5,500	3,975	12,822	1,590	1,600	1,920	83
Greece	8,660	3,100	10,039	1,245	1,193	1,432	87
Italy	21,775	12,200	70,500	4,884	6,096	7,315	67
Spain	30,000	9,060	57,487	3,625	4,830	5,796	62
Portugal	4,864	2,500	12,600	1,000	1,330	1,596	63
Estonia	2,750	440	1,900	175	200	240	73
Lithuania	4,200	1,100	4,715	434	600	720	60
Belorussia	10,800	2,800	12,100	1,110	1,500	1,800	62
Ukraina and Moldova . .	47,500	11,650	50,600	4,655	7,000	8,400	55
USSR (incl. Asiatic parts)	..	60,000	285,000	24,000	29,000	34,800	69

[a] Excluding those engaged mainly in fishing

areas of agricultural land depends especially on the fact that in a year a cow eats something like the amount of grass that comes off 0.8–1 hectare of normal grassland.

The ratio between unweighted areas and cow-units thus illustrates the degree of labor intensity in the use of the land. The ratio between man-years needed and manpower available illustrates, schematically, the level of employment.

(85) The application of the weighting scale implies in each case an hypothesis as to the technical level that would be attainable in each country without significant new investment, under the condition of no structural defects creating unproductive work and no labor surplus to act as a deterrent against reaching this efficiency level. The resulting level of employment is of course dependent on the correctness of this hypothesis and the figures should be read in conjunction with the following remarks.

This assumption is likely to be approximately correct in most of the western European countries, as will be shown, among other things, in the structural analysis presented later in this chapter. It is not correct as regards Eire, where British norms were applied for the sake of direct comparison with the United Kingdom. In practice, the level of employment in Irish agriculture is likely to be higher than shown on the table, while technical efficiency is lower than in the U.K.

The assumption is also likely to be approximately true in the countries of southern Europe, and in Bulgaria, Hungary, and Czechoslovakia. It is not correct for Poland and the Soviet Union (and those countries within the latter represented in the table). This case is the opposite to that of Eire; because tolerably correct information on the actual level of efficiency and employment was not available, the level of employment has here been calculated hypothetically on the assumption of primitive techniques, thus disregarding mechanization and other modern farming practices recently introduced. In reality, efficiency in these countries is higher and the level of employment correspondingly lower. The consequences of these observations will become clearer when the comparison is made with the measurement based on American labor standards.

For both southern and eastern Europe, the level of employment is overestimated because the input of female labor has been

calculated at the same low level as in north-western Europe. If
the actual degree of female employment were used in the calculation, efficient employment would show up even lower in
comparison with labor forces available and put into productive
use.

Although several different sets of national labor norms have
been used, as further demonstrated in Appendix 4, it is nevertheless possible to distinguish in the table four general strata of
efficiency. The norms applied in the United Kingdom, Eire,
Denmark, Norway, and Sweden belong to a stage of development
where there is far-reaching mechanization of farming operations.
The norms in Belgium, the Netherlands, Western Germany, and
Austria belong to a stage that can be labelled half-way mechanization. Those in Finland, France, and Czechoslovakia (the latter
because of striking a balance between the higher level in the
Czech provinces and the lower one in Slovakia) correspond to a
level of agricultural technique where horse-drawn implements
only are still in use but, among these, several advanced machines
like the self-binder. The levels in southern and eastern Europe,
finally, represent essentially primitive farming, where besides
the plough there are few horse- or ox- drawn implements and
most operations (notably harvesting and threshing) are essentially manual.

(86) Against the background of these general observations,
the table already makes it possible to correct some of the misleading impressions derived from the figures for unweighted areas,
as given in Table 3 and some following tables. The very large
supply of land per man in Great Britain is obviously largely due
to the extent of low-yielding rough grazings. Even so, the United
Kingdom remains the best employed of the countries on the table,
considering the fact that this employment is calculated on the
basis of advanced mechanization. However, the gap in relation to
the continental countries has narrowed. The countries of continental Western Europe, on the other hand, appear relatively
speaking better off in this table than according to unweighted
hectarages. Especially, it becomes clear that the Netherlands
are hardly less employed than other continental countries. The
higher degree of intensity in land use, in connection with the
higher natural fertility of the land itself, has to a great extent

compensated the narrow geometrical space. The situation is of course also affected by the use of imported fodder for part of the livestock that also enters in the resources offering employment.

In both southern and eastern Europe, the noteworthy point is that the employment level turns out as low as it does, despite the fact that the low level of efficiency and the low participation of female labor that were assumed ought to have made employment appear higher than it really is. Only Poland has apparently approached full employment as a result of both these assumptions. In southern Europe, the large land supply in Spain is clearly outweighted because of extensive farming on most of the land, while the much higher intensity of Italian farming results in somewhat better employment on a much narrower area. It is also noteworthy that Greece appears to be better employed than the other Mediterranean countries, on the basis of norms on essentially the same level. The apparent advantage of Bulgaria, as compared to Hungary is, on the contrary, essentially due to higher norms in grain production.

The computation for the Soviet Union is based, as far as crops are concerned, on the plan target figures for 1950; for livestock, the figures published in 1953 were used. Since the plan targets were not fully reached, the level of employment is, if anything, overestimated correspondingly, in addition to what has been said above. For those countries within the USSR represented in the table, plan figures only were available for livestock as well, and overestimation of the employment level may therefore be even greater. The contrast between the north-western countries and Ukraina depends essentially upon the fact that lower norms for grain production are indicated for the latter country.

A full evaluation of these results can better be made by means of measurement on a single scale: the American labor standard of 1945–48. This measurement will also serve as basis for an attempt to trace some main lines of historical development.

(87) Concerning the choice of scale by which to make the labor situation comparable in many countries of Europe, even a purely fictitious scale would have done, if it had been so constructed as to reflect the situation in the countries concerned in a somewhat homogeneous way. If a scale actually experienced in one of the countries involved in the comparison had been chosen there

TABLE 12. *Labor potential and levels of employment in selcted countries, calculated on the basis of American labor standards from 1945–48. Data refer to a year close to 1950 except when otherwise stated*

Countries	Agricultural land, 000	Labor available:			Manpower: Active males plus 20 %	Employment level	
		Million hours	Cowunits, 000	Manyears, 000		Per cent	As per cent of national standard
United Kingdom	19,493	1,872	13,869	749	1,505	50	64
Eire	4,689	508	3,765	203	564	36	72
Denmark	3,162	491	3,637	196	451	44	56
Finland	2,949	550	4,070	220	652	34	61
Norway	1,046	345	2,650	139	316[a]	44	73
Sweden 1932	4,500	1,200	8,327	450	960	47	66
Netherlands	2,413	543	4,026	217	721	30	52
Belgium	1,792	390	2,891	156	434	36	54
France	33,542	4,088	30,281	1,635	4,826	34	39
W. Germany	13,768	2,344	17,366	938	2,813	33	46
Poland	20,864	2,160	16,000	865	4,140	21	22
Czechoslovakia	7,537	1,060	7,860	424	1,320	32	39
Austria	4,080	467	3,456	187	616	30	44
Hungary	7,362	700	5,200	280	1,943	14	23
Bulgaria	5,500	700	5,200	280	1,920	15	18
Greece	8,660	870	6,435	347	1,432	24	28
Italy	21,775	3,828	28,350	1,530	7,315	21	31
Spain	30,000	2,320	17,175	930	5,796	16	26
Portugal	4,864	545	4,000	220	1,596	14	22
Estonia	2,750	157	1,165	54	240	23	31
Lithuania	4,200	320	2,376	128	720	18	29
Belorussia	10,800	930	6,890	370	1,800	21	33
Ukraina and Moldova . .	47,500	4,675	34,650	1,870	8,400	22	40
USSR (incl. Asiatic parts) .	. .	17,000	126,000	6,800	34,800	20	28

[a] Excluding those engaged mainly in fishing.

would have been a risk of favoring that country and thus biassing the verdict on other countries. The only country in Europe which has a varied enough agriculture to provide a generally applicable scale is France. From that country, however, only very incomplete data are available on agricultural labor, and the lacunas would have had to be filled in with material from other countries. In comparison with a fictitious scale, the American set of labor norms has the advantage to be based on experience and to relate to a great agricultural country within about the same climatic zones as is Europe.

However, we must stress the theoretical nature of the computation on the basis of American labor standards. Measurement on the basis of national labor norms always refers to a situation which exists — or has existed — in the country. It therefore makes clear what might be gained in labor productivity, and in prosperity for those remaining in agriculture, by releasing part of the existing manpower for other industries. Measurement by the American scale does not in the same way refer to existing or foreseeable possibilities. It is a theoretical computation only to substitute, say, Italian agricultural technique by that of another country. In practice, the question would arise whether Italian agricultural resources are susceptible to the foreign technique. In many instances, a higher level of efficiency would call for another system of land utilization, with another combination of crops and livestock, which in the end might cause a diminution in the volume of production. This does not mean that higher efficiency could not be achieved at any cost. It only means that the road to higher technical efficiency may be different from that taken by the more advanced countries. It has been rightly stated that Italian cultivated land is essentially an artifact, a man-made thing. It is the result of a continuing patient effort, transforming soil which was not from the outset capable of producing what it produces now. The same is true of agricultural land in many other countries, and not only in the Mediterranean region. Highly productive land is only to be understood in its context. This is the reason why in the first place we attempted weighting agricultural resources, and the resulting employment level, on the basis of national labor standards.

(88) All this admitted, it nevertheless remains true that measurement on the basis of American labor standards has the advantage of being strictly comparable from country to country. It makes it possible to distinguish clearly the different strata of national efficiency we briefly mentioned in a preceding paragraph, on the basis of Table 11. The English and Scandinavian mechanized standard thus corresponds to 55–70 per cent of the American standard. The half-way mechanized and the horse-drawn standards represented in continental Western Europe and in Finland vary between 40–45 per cent of the American standard. Most countries in southern and eastern Europe appear to reach only 20–30 per

cent of the American standard, if the low efficiency level used in the computation on the national basis is accepted. If it is not accepted, then the ratio to American standard will improve, but the level of employment will drop correspondingly. The case of Ukraina is instructive on this point.

The levels of employment thus theoretically computed and presented in Table 12 give an idea as to the comparable volume of agricultural resources in each country. It emerges that the available productive resources are two to three times greater, per man, in Great Britain and Scandinavia than in southern and eastern Europe. They are 1½ to 2 times greater in continental Western Europe than in southern and eastern Europe.

Among the more remarkable features is the difference between Italy and the Iberian countries, which now appears considerably greater than before. This means that employment in Italian agriculture is more than in the Iberian countries based on branches of production which require a high input of manual labor. These branches are more likely than the easily mechanized branches to furnish lasting employment for a long time ahead. In the Iberian countries a major share of the two thirds level of employment according to the calculation based on national norms is derived from extensive grain growing. This is especially sensitive to reduction of labor through mechanization and thus is less likely to support lasting employment for many hands in agriculture than, say, horticultural production and dairy farming.

It also emerges that Greece shows much the same advantage compared with Italy as on the basis of national standards. The difference between Bulgaria and Hungary has disappeared, and Poland is reduced to being one of the poor countries. Czecho-slovakia still maintains a position on the central European level.

(89) Another salient feature is the low level of employment that would result in the Soviet Union, if American efficiency standards were generally applied there. The situation can scarcely be overstated, since the basic data are plan target figures, which were not fully reached (they may have been reached later, however). According to our calculations, Soviet agriculture would employ only about 7 million men if it were managed at the American level of efficiency. This result is not very astonishing since population figures indicate that Soviet and US agriculture

should be industries of roughly the same magnitude, and US agriculture actually employs some 6–7 million men. The estimate for active males in Soviet agriculture, or 29 million, may be a weak one. In any case, since about half the population of the USSR is known to derive its livelihood from agriculture, there can be no doubt that working males in Soviet agriculture are many times those working in US agriculture. The conclusion is that either Soviet agriculture does not work at the high technical level the authorities of the USSR often claim, or there must be a lot of hidden or open unemployment in Soviet agriculture.

The latter may very well be true, if a high degree of mechanization in certain labor operations is combined with the survival of purely manual work in other functions. The official livestock norms do not indicate that a high level of technical efficiency is normal. If, for instance, grain is harvested by combine but weeds are picked manually in the wheat fields — there seems to be some evidence of that — then the over-all efficiency level may be low at any case. Shortcomings in labor organization, often stressed in official reports on Soviet agriculture, may also undo part of the results of machine use. The disparity between the man-power situation and the volume of productive resources is, in any case, such as to provoke strong doubts whether large-scale mechanization has after all been of any great use in Soviet agriculture, so far.

(90) A comparison of the levels of employment of countries within Europe, and between European countries, and other parts of the world, does not of course tell the whole story about the distribution of agricultural wealth. Other parts of that story are the natural fertility of the land and the capacity of the country's farmers to achieve high yields per unit of land and livestock. The higher the yield, the more it is economically justifiable to make a high input of labor per productive unit. This topic cannot be further investigated in this book but is likely to be the theme of many future enquiries.

Tentatively, it can be supposed that labor productivity in the strict sense — output per man-hour—in some western European countries is much closer to American standards than is the level of efficiency measured only in number of hours per productive unit. A country like the Netherlands, for instance, would come close to American labor productivity if there were no labor surplus and the efficiency standard characteristic of the larger and middle-sized holdings in the country were to be found throughout the country's agriculture. The higher input per unit is to a very great extent justified by the higher output per unit. The combination of a fertile soil and a good climate with systematic efforts to make the technically best possible out of the natural factors can thus create a type of farming which, while it is profoundly different from American farming, yet has the same degree of economic justification as any other.

In Western Europe, it is quite possible that the existing labor surpluses may be absorbed in other industries within a foreseeable period of time. In southern and eastern Europe, on the other hand, the task of absorbing agricultural surplus labor appears to be much heavier. Urban industries are as yet only of the same magnitude as agriculture, when measured in manpower, and absorption of the bulk of agricultural manpower therefore presupposes a very large expansion relatively speaking in other industries. This observation still seems to be true also of the Soviet Union, even if the latter has accomplished a swifter change in the pattern of its economy than any other of the countries just now discussed. Any drive for modernization and mechanization of agriculture in these countries constantly threatens to release more manpower than it creates new employment openings through more intensive farming methods. For a considerable period of time to come, the manpower surplus in these countries will continue to act as the traditional disincentive against mechanized and labor-saving farming methods.

(91) An enquiry into the recent history of the development of productive resources would have been instructive concerning the forces which promote or retard agricultural advancement. To study the successive expansion of intensive cultivation and intensive livestock husbandry in Western Europe cannot however yet be undertaken, because no adequate method of research is developed. The only way would be to apply the same set of labor norms to agricultural statistics from various epochs and observe the changes in the volume of labor potential and resulting employment. On the other hand, such a method would run the risk of producing illusory results, because the effect of a

changing technique is not the same in all branches of production, and a constant unchanging scale applied to a changing crop and livestock pattern would distort some important features.

So far, we can only state that agricultural resources in terms of labor potential have obviously expanded continuously in western Europe, at least during the period under review here. An important exception is Eire; possibly another may be France. In both cases, this is likely to be the cause behind the slowness of mechanization. In Scandinavia, the first expansion of productive resources followed the challenge of population increase, which stimulated land clearance and increase of livestock production. Thereafter, when manpower began to decline, mechanization started to meet the challenge of manpower shortage and competition with other industries for manpower. A similar double process has been going on in continental Western Europe. As a whole, it may be supposed that productive resources in agriculture as measured by an identical measure, have never been as great as they are now. At the same time, the level of efficient employment is likely to have declined, because rural exodus has not kept pace with the labor-saving devices of the new technique. The west European labor surplus is practically all due to technical advances. How it happens that the surplus does not disappear will be reviewed in a later section.

(92) In countries where agricultural technique has remained essentially unchanged it is, on the contrary, perfectly feasible to calculate the development of productive resources over a period. In doing so, one must of course appreciate the weakness and the limited comparability of agricultural statistics. The following table illustrates this development in some countries where the computation proved possible.

Here the development of labor potentials should be studied only on the basis of national labor standards. The parallel calculation on the basis of American labor standards has been made with the view to obtaining a test on the usefulness of the method. The two sets of figures run tolerably parallel in Portugal, Bulgaria, Hungary, and Ukraina. The relatively higher increase in labor potentialities as measured in American instead of in national standards in Spain and Greece results from a certain shift in production patterns towards branches where high labor input is

TABLE 13. *Development of labor potentialities in selected countries. Owing to the method of calculation, no conclusion should be drawn on the basis of small changes or differences*

Country, year	Man-years available, national standard (000)	Approximate change, per cent	Man-years available, American standard (000)	Approximate change, per cent
Italy				
1930	4,656		..	..
1950	4,884	+ 5 % in 20 years	1,530	..
Spain				
1920	3,585		818	
1930	3,840	+ 5 % in 10 years	913	+ 15 % in 10 years
1950	3,625	— 5 % in 20 years	927	—
Portugal				
1900	750		175	
1920	730	—	163	—
1936	890	+ 20 % in 16 years	200	+ 20 % in 16 years
1950	1,000	+ 10 % in 14 years	220	+ 10 % in 14 years
Greece				
1922	725		155	
1929	870	+ 20 % in 7 years	210	+ 35 % in 7 years
1934/38	1,221	+ 40 % in 7–8 years	347	+ 60 % in 7–8 years
1951	1,245	—	305	— 20 % in 15 years
Bulgaria				
1900	1,113		191	
1926	1,386	+ 25 % in 26 years	238	+ 25 % in 26 years
1940	1,590	+ 15 % in 14 years	282	+ 15 % in 14 years
Hungary				
1911/15	1,226		307	
1931/35	1,194	—	289	—
1947	1,150	—	277	—
Ukraina				
1928	3,837		1,400	
1950 (Plan) . . .	4,655	(see p. 98)	1,870	(see p. 98)

likely to prevail even under technically advanced conditions. The disadvantage of Spain in this respect, as compared with Italy, has thus been somewhat diminished, at least over the twenties and the early thirties. The corresponding advantage in Greece seems to a considerable extent to be the fruit of recent expansion.

Apart from these observations of a methodological and relative nature, it is interesting to note how far the expansion of resources that is, of more intensive land utilization patterns, or higher numbers of livestock, or both in conjunction, has run parallel to the development of population pressure on the land. Italy, with more or less constant farm population over the last decades, has developed its resources, though not in any revolutionary way, and covering a fraction only of the labor surplus. In Spain, the moderate expansion in the twenties was due to higher livestock numbers. The subsequent decline was due above all to events connected with the civil war and has been made good in years after 1950. Portugal, with more virgin resources than Italy and with no war by contrast with Spain has developed its productive resources, though not very much faster than population increase. The level of employment has improved only slightly, if at all.

The lately liberated countries of southern Balkan have shown a more dynamic pattern. Radical land reform in Greece, for the purpose of accomodating a million refugees in a small and poor country, was accompanied by very significant improvements of agriculture. Even if it is legitimate to differ as to the reliability of early Greek agricultural statistics, it remains undeniable that Greece's agricultural resources in the twenties and thirties developed faster than its agricultural population, despite the large influx of refugees. War and civil war again damaged the country's economy, and the recovery was by 1951 not complete.

At the beginning of the period here under review, the larger part of present-day Bulgaria had been free from the Turks for a couple of decades, and much of the initial land clearance was over. The subsequent improvements up to 1940 are nevertheless very remarkable. Territorial changes were not then acting to make the figures look better than they really were. Bulgaria had lost fertile Dobrudsha and won some rather meagre tracts of mountain land in the south. An accumulated increase of 45 per cent of the original labor potential was a great performance. Over about the same period, agricultural manpower almost doubled. Population pressure on the land must have increased, and is the main explanation of the constant drive to quantitative expansion. Lack of statistical sources makes it impossible to pursue the inquiry over the last decade.

In contrast to Bulgaria, Hungary has not shown any significant change. If anything, the volume of agricultural labor potential has declined somewhat. The 1947 figure may, however, be influenced by war events. At any rate, this stability in a country where agricultural manpower increased by only 10 per cent over the period, forms an interesting contrast to the case of Bulgaria.

Ukrainian development is partly obscured by the fact that the country is now much larger than it was in 1929 (incorporation of south-western Poland, easternmost Czechoslovakia, northern Bucovina and part of Bessarabia, and Crimea). Further, we have included Moldova in the figures for Ukraina in 1950. Finally, the basic 1950 figures are plan target figures. If all this is kept in mind, it appears that no very significant expansion of agricultural resources can have taken place in Ukraina over the period. Even if there has been an increase, it can not be more significant than the corresponding movement in Italy.

(93) Regional distribution of labor surpluses is of interest in the larger countries where regional differences may be of the same magnitude as the differences between countries. In Eastern Europe, studies of this aspect are hampered by the lack of available regional statistics. The same is partly true also about Italy, where regional manpower data from the latest population census are slow of publication.

In Western Germany, there is a noteworthy difference in the magnitude of the labor surplus as between Schleswig-Holstein and Niedersachsen on the one hand, where it is below the average for the Federal Republic and no greater than in Denmark, and the southern and western Länder on the other, where the surplus is at or above the federal average[a]. In France, considerable regional differences can also be shown to exist. Some of the richest regions in northern France have virtually full employment in agriculture, even with a technical level considerably higher than the average for the country. At the other end of the scale, Corsica and the departments along the Mediterranean have an employment level not very much above that of the Mediterranean countries. This result is, however, due to the fact that a higher standard of efficiency is supposed to be achieved in all parts of France than in any of the Mediterranean countries. When measured according to American efficiency standards, the Mediterranean departments turn out to have among the highest enduring employment levels in France, because of the great importance of the vineyards [b].

In Italy, comparison of regional data for labor consumption with population figures from earlier censuses shows a considerable superiority of northern Italy over both central and southern Italy. The latter are thus under the Italian average, with only about 60 per cent employment. In Spain a superiority of the Mediterranean region (Cataluña and the Levante) above the national average was partly dispelled by a sharper decline there than the national average over the last fifteen years of our period. Regional population figures from 1920 and 1930, read in conjunction with figures for the development of labor potentials, indicate that the Mediterranean region profited most from the general improvement over the twenties, while Andalucia deteriorated in weighted as well as in unweighted values (See Appendix 3).

THE FARM STRUCTURE

(94) The disposition of productive resources on units of management — the farms — is commonly regarded as one of the most important features of the agrarian structure, both socially and economically. The contrast between farms of different size is also one of the most controversial issues of agrarian policy, no matter what the ideological background may be. Socialist doctrine condemns the exploitation of agricultural workmen on medium-sized and large farms. Productivistic thinking is anxious to develop general efficiency, and worries about the high level of farm household consumption in a farm structure where small subsistence holdings are dominant.

Unfortunately, the definitions of farm size are not very clear nor very consistent. The family farm especially is obscure in definition. The varying principles of classification used in statistics from different countries contribute to the difficulty of making comparative judgments about farm structures.

In order to distinguish the pure family farm from such types of enterprise as rely to some considerable extent upon hired labor it would be interesting to analyze available figures on the distribution of manpower by size-classes [a]. It cannot however be taken for granted that labor is always or even mainly occupied on the same holdings as returned and, besides, such a breakdown of man-power data on the size-class structure of farms is often incomplete.

In order to determine the importance of different size-classes of farms, we will therefore first look at their distribution in the size-classes used in the different farm censuses. Thereafter, it will be shown how these size-classes refer to land supply (hectares per man working in agriculture). As a second step in the enquiry, we will then try to apply the system of weighting land and livestock to the size-classified statistics and compare the outcome with the distribution of manpower by size-classes.

(95) Farm censuses generally furnish figures regarding the number of holdings (which may or may not be identical with the farms) in each of the size-classes used by the census. Often, but not always, there are also data on the distribution of area by size-classes. If this is not so, approximate calculations can be made to show the distribution of the area that is the criterion for size-classification. Only when the size-classes are very few are such calculations likely to be very uncertain as to reliability. Even then, a distribution curve can help settle the true averages per size-class. If the size-class at the top of the structure is very important, however, extrapolations for a subdivision of it may be very uncertain.

It has been often attempted to describe a given farm structure by presenting the proportions between farm number and farm area in each size-class, so as to show the degree of disparity or inequality in the structure. Often this is done simply by presenting a table taken from a farm census. The comments put forward different criteria as being important, according to circumstances or the bias of the author. For a comparative enquiry, such a presentation would not do at all, because the criteria for classi-fication are not the same in all censuses. Even if the same criterion were used, it may not have the same significance everywhere.

It has therefore been attempted to make data on farm structures comparable by means of curves and indices of con-centration. The most consistent attempt was made by the Mexican statistician G. Loyo, on the basis of disparity indices developed by the Italian mathematician C. Gini [a]. The procedure can easiest be described by referring to the device known as Lorentz' curve. The percentage of farm numbers found in each size-class is represented in one dimension and the share of each size-class in farm area in the other. The greater the disparity the deeper the resulting curve. In the case of a completely equal distribution — a theoretical one — the curve would turn out to be a straight line, the diagonal of the chart. In that case, the concentration index would be zero. The deeper the curve is, the higher the concentration index, which cannot, however, in practice ever reach 100. Mathematically, all the drawbacks due to different kinds of size classification would have been remedied.

For our enquiry this procedure is however of little value because there is not, and could scarcely be, a completely uniform and universally valid definition of what a farm is. The units of the farm censuses are seldom defined rigorously according to the same principles. The lower limit especially towards allotments and home gardens, is in many instances decisive for the whole concentration index. To take a simple example, the West German farm census of 1949 counts 2.1 million units larger than half a hectare of total land area and 1.9 million units over half a hectare of agricultural land. The subsequent census of holdings below the former limit enumerates 4.5 million such units. The farm census of 1907 counts 3.3 million units over 500 square metres (0,05 hectare); over a half hectare, there were then 2.0 million units. If there had not been a common size limit of half a hectare, any comparison would have been void of sense. Even so, the classification criterion was not exactly the same, because the two censuses used somewhat different definitions of "agricultural land". Thus, even the common size-class limit at a half hectare is not identical; some precisely similar units are counted below that limit in 1907 and above in 1949.

The same difficulty can be shown to distort most comparisons, except in some instances when comparison is possible between censuses from the same country. Even when there is one size-limit which is formally the same everywhere — 1 hectare, for instance — this limit may refer to different things as between countries to such an extent that the comparison would loose much of its meaning.

(96) Because it is so difficult to define the lower limit for what

should be reckoned as a farm in an internationally comparable way, we will, for this enquiry, abandon the number-of-farms factor and try to analyze the structure merely on the basis of the distribution of farm areas by size-classes. This can easily be done by means of distribution curves and can be read off as fractile values. In this connection, the median is not the only interesting value. Experience seems to show that something less than deciles will be unsatisfactory. If, for instance, only quartiles are presented, a considerable amount of large farms might remain hidden.

It is true that even so, it is of some importance how farms are separated from non-farms. As far as the small units are concerned, this is of very limited significance. Though very numerous, family gardens seldom include more than an extremely small fraction of the land included in the census. Of greater importance is the treatment of the large public and private forestry holdings and the publicly-held tracts of waste land. At least the public holdings of forest and waste land should if possible be kept outside the material under review. This is the case in many censuses, and occurs automatically when the classification criterion is not total area but agricultural or arable land.

Accordingly, Table 14 has been drawn up to show the farm structure in most European countries. In general, at least a year at the beginning and a year at the end of the period under review are represented, to show the main changes. Some of the most important differences in the definitions in the statistics underlying our figures are discussed immediately after the table. Sources and methods are set forth in Appendix 5.

(97) The table gives witness to the importance of the classification criterion for the picture of the farm structure. All instances where the higher fractiles contain farm-sizes of thousands of hectares refer to a classification according to total area. The case of England and Wales and Scotland is especially instructive as to the effects of the choice of criterion for classifying farm size.

It would, however, be misleading to divide the material into two groups only, i.e. censuses where total area, or where agricultural area is the criterion of classification. "Total area" may mean different things, according to what is included. The occurrence of vast and meagre rough grazings in a country like Scotland is one factor which makes total area a poor indicator of the social distribution of landed wealth. The inclusion of large tracts of land in public possession in Austria and Czechoslovakia contributes largely to an impression of the great importance of large farms in these countries. In the Italian figures — on the basis of property statistics rather than statistics on farms — the alternative figures on private property only reveal the importance of public property (generally vast tracts of land with low unit value) for the farm structure picture. The censuses of Ireland, France, and some of the Eastern countries do not include any large public holdings, and at once their structure looks more akin to those classified according to agricultural area.

Also the classification criterion "agricultural land" may have a sense that varies considerably. For instance, in Germany in 1907, it excluded "Geringere Weiden und Hutungen", corresponding to rough grazings in other classification systems. In 1949, the same category is included. This category happens to be a small one in Germany. The effect of a change in the criterion thus depends on the geographical character of the country.

For all these reasons, a direct comparison between the farm structures of the countries under review, on the basis of these fractile values only, would have very limited value. Further calculations will be needed to show the real differences in the distribution of the land of the countries by different size-classes of farms.

(98) On the other hand, this table already allows certain conclusions regarding the development of the farm structure in most of the countries, and the following interpretation may be given of the changes in fractile values.

The movement in the upper fractiles directly reflects the change in the importance of the larger farms. Decreasing values of the higher fractiles indicate decreasing importance for large farms, and inversely. On the contrary, the movement in the low fractiles is opposite to the changes in the importance of small holdings. Decrease in the low fractiles means increase in the relative importance of small holdings, while rising values of the low fractiles indicate decreasing importance of small farms.

It is easy to see that, during the first half of the period, large holdings were decreasing everywhere in Europe. As far as our

TABLE 14. *Fractile values of farm structure: unweighted. Farm size (under the definitions of each census) found at each of the following deciles*

Country	Year	1	2	3	4	M	6	7	8	9	Land category used as classification criterion
England & Wales	1875	14	27	39	52	70	90	115	145	210	Crops and grass
,,	1924	13	24	36	49	63	80	105	125	200	id.
,,	1949	13	26	37	50	65	80	100	130	200	id.
,,	1950	18	34	45	59	76	95	125	175	300	id. + rough grazings
Scotland	1949	13	26	37	47	59	70	90*	120*	180*	Crops and grass
,,	1950	43	93	175	340	620	1,100*	2,000*	4,000*	7,000*	id. + rough grazings
N. Ireland	1900	5	8	11	15	19	25	35	52	110	Total area
,,	1950	5*	10*	16*	21*	25*	30*	35*	45*	65*	id.
Eire	1900	7	12	20	28	40	62	110	175	250*	Total area
,,	1949	7,5	12	17	21	27	36	48	67	125	id.
Norway	1907	1,3	2,8	4,5	6,5	9	11	15	22	35	Crops and cult. gr.
,,	1949	1,9	3,2	4,3	5,5	7	9	12	17	27	Agricultural area
Finland	1896	4*	6*	9*	11*	16*	25*	140*	200*	300*	Arable land
,,	1950	3,2	5,5	7	9	11	14	18	24	35	id.
Sweden	1900	3	6	10	14	18	25	36	55	100	Arable land
,,	1932	4	6	9	12	16	22	31	50	105	id.
,,	1951	4	6,5	10	13	17	23	35	55	105	id.
Denmark	1901	9	17	24	31	40	50	65	110	300*	Agricultural area
,,	1951	7	11	16	20	24	30	38	48	67	id.
Netherlands	1949	8	11	14	18	23	32	42	59	105	Total area
,,	1910	4	7	10	15	20	25	33	42	55	Agricultural area
,,	1950	4	7	9	12	15	19	25	34	46	id.
Belgium	1895	2	3,5	5,5	8	11	15	20	25	36	Agricultural area
,,	1950	2	3,8	5,6	8	10	14	18	26	45	id.
France	1892	5	9	15	21	30	43	80	190	500*	Total area
,,	1929	5,5	9	13	19	26	36	49	75	180	id.
,,	1942	7,5	12	17	22	28	37	49	74	160	id. restricted application
W. Germany	1907	2,7	4,5	6,5	10	13	17	23	33	61	Agricultural area

Region	Year										Area
Poland: East[a]	1951	3,5	6	7	8	10	13	20	35	70*	id.
„ : South	1892/1909	4,5	7	8	10	13	19	140	1,000*	2,000*	Total area
„ : West	1902	2	3	4	5	7	10	22	150*	200*	id.
Poland: Total	1907	6	10	16	28	50	90	175*	330*	600*	Agricultural area
Czechoslovakia	1949	3	4	6	7	9	10	12	18	80	Total area
„	1930	3,5	6,5	10	16	25	54	95	145	400*	Total area
„	1949	3,5	6,5	9	13	19	55	100*	400*	500*	id.
Austria	1902	7	14	24	40	65	200*	600*	2,000*	10,000*	Total area
„	1951	7	14	21	33	64	180	750	2,400	10,000	id.
Hungary	1900[a]	4	9	20	55	180*	600*	1,900*	5,000*	15,000*	Total area
„	1935	3	6	11	18	35	125	425	850	1,600*	id.
„	1949	3	4	6	9	16	50*	130*	450*	1,300*	id.
Rumania: Old	1913	2	3	4	6	8	14	60*	450*	1,300*	Agricultural area
„ : West	1900	3	4	5	6	7	8	11	15	25	id.
„	1948	2,5	3,5	4	5	6	8	11	16	26	Total area
Bulgaria	1908	3	4,5	6	8	10	13	16	23	43	Total area
„	1934	3	4	5	6	7	9	11	13	18	id.
„	1946	1,5	2	2,5	3	4	6	9	16	30	id.
Yugoslavia: Old Serbia	1897	3	5	6	8	10	13	18	20	30	Arable area
„ : Vojvodina[a]	1900	4	6	9	11	14	17	20	25	35	Total area
„ : Croatia[a]	1900	2	4	5	7	9	11	14	18	25	id.
„ : Slovenia	1902	4	6	8	10	14	20	28	36	45	Total area
„ : Total	1950	2,4	3,5	4,4	5,5	7	8	11	14	20	Arable area
Greece	1929	1,2	1,5	2,9	5,0	9	16	50	100*	200*	Agricultural area
Italy	1930	2,5	5	8	14	26	58	170	640	2,400	Total area
„ a	1946	1,4	3.6	8	18	42	96	225	600	1,700	id.
„ a,b	1946	1,1	2.6	4.7	10	17	36	75	180	430	id.
Portugal: Algarve	1952	2,4	4	6	9	12	15	20	30	60	Arable area
„ : Alenteje	1952	21	60	150	320	590	900	1,250	1,800	3,200*	id.
„ : Estremadura etc.	1952	1	2	4	8	18	45	130	350	700*	id.
„ : Center	1952	1	1	2	2	2.5	5	7	10	16	id.
European Russia[a c]	1905	7	10	14	20	37	100	550	1,900	10 000*	Total area

a Units of property rather than farms
b Private properties only
c Except the Northern Region

figures go, they have decreased over the whole period in all the countries except England and Sweden, where the opposite has been true over the last decades, and Belgium, where the criterion is not identical.

The decline of large holdings has, however, varying significance. In the land reform countries in Eastern Europe, and in Denmark, Finland, and the Netherlands, the decline of the large holdings has been accompanied by a general decrease in all the decile values. This is the sign of a relatively radical social land policy, which is also reflected by the fact that the decline of large holdings has been very considerable, in some cases almost total. The main exception to the latter rule is the Netherlands, where the whole change is rather modest and depends more on the farm pattern created on land of recent reclamation than on any radical remodelling of the structure of the old land resources. The various reform measures leading to these results will be discussed further in Chapter 6.

In most of the countries of Western Europe, where there was no radical policy of changing the farm structure, the large holdings have none the less declined, although not in so spectacular a way as in the land reform countries. The most radical change is in France. However, the computation underlying our figures involves several uncertain factors, the most important of which is the reliability of the census data from 1892. Even if the decline of large holdings which we believe to have been able to outline is a fairly general phenomenon in France, there are nevertheless interesting regional differences which indicate that most of the movement is real and only a minor part of it may derive from statistical errors [a].

Also in Ireland the decline of large farms has been considerable. This is, as is well known, only the last phase of a land reform, although here, the smallest farms too have declined in importance a result of the different character of the Irish land reform as compared with those in eastern Europe.

In Germany, Belgium, Sweden and Norway, and in England up to the thirties, the decline of large farms was less radical. Both in these countries and in France, the movement was accompanied by an opposite movement in the lower part of the structure. The lowest fractile values have increased, that is, the importance of the very small farms has been decreasing. The movement was thus towards the center, increasing the importance of middle-sized farms. Along with the considerable stability of the west European farm structure, this centripetal movement is the most interesting feature of development. On the basis of regional figures, it can be shown also to have taken place in most major regions of England, France, and Germany. The most striking exception is the Mediterranean region in France, where the movement has been in the opposite direction: maintenance of most of the importance of large holdings, decline of the middle-sized farms, and increased importance of small holdings[a]. In chapter 6 some considerations will be given to show that this centripetal movement of the farm structure, however modest, at any rate by far exceeded the changes that have been brought about through deliberate land policy in Western Europe.

Recently, the trend has shifted in England and Sweden. In the former country, it can be shown that the renewed increase of large holdings is really important in eastern England, where large farms have always been important. In some of the eastern counties, the area of large farms is now larger, even in absolute figures, than it was in 1912. On the other hand, parts of western England, and especially Wales, show very few signs, if any, of increase among the large holdings. The interpretation of this difference is closely connected with the mechanization of arable farming. Wales and western England, where livestock husbandry is dominant, may not react in the same way to mechanization[b].

The revolutionary destruction of large farms in eastern Europe has to a very considerable extent gone on spontaneously, independently of land reform measures. It will be seen from our figures that both Yugoslavia and Bulgaria had very few large farms at the beginning of the century, and the same is true of western Rumania. Also in Russia and Poland, many of the large estates were crumbling by themselves, under the pressure of land hunger of increasing peasant masses, in combination with the increasing economic difficulties of the estate owners. The land reforms have contributed more by improving the conditions of tenants than by dividing large farms into smaller ones.

The pattern prevailing in the three countries of south-western Europe contrasts both with the radical changes in eastern Europe and the persisting consolidation of family-sized farms in western Europe. The striking contrast between latifundia and a mass of very small farms in Italy has an interesting parallel in the Mediterranean zone of France. The development of Italian farm structure cannot be described on the basis of statistics. Expert opinion indicates that there must have been a slow, long-term trend towards increased importance of small farms, along with the general trend of intensification of agriculture.

No corresponding statements can be made with respect to the Iberian countries. The Spanish farm structure is not very well known, since no farm census has taken place so far. The first Portuguese farm census, taken in successive rounds in 1952–54, shows enormous contrasts between the extensively farmed plateau land, where most of the land is in big estates, and the intensively cultivated, garden-like agriculture of the central and northern parts of the country. This contrast, it is known in various ways, has persisted throughout many centuries. Something similar must, broadly speaking, be true of the plateau and of the zones of intensive cultivation in Spain.

In Italy and Spain, measures of land reform and domestic colonization are under way and already contribute to modifying the farm structure. No figures are however available to show the scope of this movement in the framework of the farm structure of the countries as a whole.

(99) However, the significance of the changes that have taken place can be measured in other ways too. The meaning of increasing or decreasing farm size is essentially different under different demographic situations. In order to illustrate some of these differences, we will again show the fractiles of farm structures, converted now into "man-land units". This means that, in the framework of each farm census, the total of the land which is distributed by size-classes according to the fractile values, is divided by the number of active males in agriculture at the-same epoch. The resulting "man-land unit" may differ from the corresponding units shown on Table 3, depending upon the criterion used for classifying the farms by size groups. Dividing each fractile value by the relevant "man-land unit", we obtain the farm structure expressed in equal population shares, under the theoretical condition that all land is equal.

TABLE 15. *Fractile values of farm structure in man-land units: unweighted. Farm size (under the same definitions as on Table 14), found at each of the following fractiles, as expressed in man-land units*

Country	Year	1	2	3	4	M	6	7	8	9
England & Wales.	1900	1.6	3	4	6	8	10	13	16	24
,, ,, ...	1924	1.0	1.8	3	4	5	6	8	10	15
,, ,, . . . ; . .	1949	1.3	2.5	4	5	7	8	10	13	20
,, ,, ...	1950	1.4	2.7	4	5	6	8	10	14	24
Scotland	1949	0.8	1.6	2	3	4	5	6	7	11
,, ...	1950	1.1	2.4	5	9	16	29	55	103	184
N. Ireland	1900	0.7	1.1	1.5	2	2.5	3	5	7	15
,, ...	1950	0.5	1.0	1.6	2	2.5	3	4	5	7
Eire	1900	0.6	1.1	1.9	2.5	3.5	6	10	16	23
,, ...	1949	0.5	0.8	1.1	1.5	2	2,5	3	5	9
Norway	1907	0.5	1.1	1.9	3	4	5	6	9	14
,, ...	1949	0.6	1.0	1.3	1.7	2	3	4	5	8
Finland	1896	1.7	2.6	4	5	7	11	61	87	140
,, ...	1950	0.7	1.2	1.6	2	2.5	3	4	5	8
Sweden	1900	0.6	1.1	1.9	2.6	4	5	7	11	19
,, ...	1951	0.6	1.0	1.5	2	3	4	6	9	17
Denmark	1901	1.0	2	2.5	3.5	4.5	5.5	7	12	30
,, ...	1951	0.9	1.4	1.9	2.3	3	4	4.5	6	8
Netherlands	1910	1.1	2	3	4	5	7	9	11	15
,, ...	1950	1.0	1.7	2.4	3	4	5	6	9	12
Belgium	1895	0.6	1.1	1.7	2.3	3	4.5	6	8	11
,, ...	1950	0.4	0.8	1.1	1.5	2	3	4	5	9
France	1892	0.6	1.2	2	3	4	6	10	25	65
,, ...	1929	0.5	0.9	1.3	2	2.5	3.5	5	7	18
,, ...	1942	0.9	1.4	2	2.5	3.5	4.5	6	9	19
W. Germany	1907	0.6	0.9	1.4	2	3	3.5	5	7	13
,, ...	1939	0.6	0.9	1.3	1.8	2.3	3	4	6	10
,, ...	1949	0.6	0.9	1.3	1.7	2.2	3	4	5	9
E. Germany	1907	0.5	1.1	1.8	3	4.5	7	16	24	39
,, ...	1939	0.6	1.0	1.5	2.3	3.5	5	11	22	38
,, ...	1951	0.5	0.8	0.9	1.1	1.4	1.8	2.5	5	9
Poland: East.	1892–1909	0.6	0.9	1.1	1.4	1.8	2.5	19	135	255
,, : South	1902	0.7	1.1	1.4	1.7	2	3	7	47	130
,, : West	1907	0.8	1.4	2.2	4	7	13	19	46	84
,, : Total	1949	0.5	0.8	1.0	1.2	1.5	1.7	2	3	14
Czechoslovakia	1930	0.4	0.8	1.3	2	3	7	12	17	50
,, ...	1949	0.3	0.6	0.8	1.2	1.8	5	9	18	47

TABLE 15. *(continued)*

Country	Year	1	2	3	4	M	6	7	8	9
Austria	1902	0.8	1.6	2.7	4	7	12	19	25	35
,, ...	1951	0.5	1.0	1.5	2.5	5	9	13	17	22
Hungary	1900	0.5	1.2	2.7	8	25	84	265	700	2,000
,, ...	1935	0.5	1.0	1.7	3	6	20	65	135	250
,, ...	1949	0.5	0.7	1.0	1.4	2.5	8	20	70	200
Rumania: Old	1913	0.5	0.7	0.9	1.3	1.8	3	14	100	600
,, : West	1900	0.5	0.8	0.9	1.3	1.5	2	3	4	5
,, : Total	1948	0.5	0.7	0.8	0.9	1.2	1.5	2	3	5
Bulgaria	1908	0.5	0.8	1.1	1.4	1.7	2	3	4	7
,, ...	1934	0.9	1.2	1.5	1.9	2.2	2.5	3	4	6
,, ...	1946	0.5	0.7	0.8	1.0	1.4	2	3	5	10
Yugoslavia: Old Serbia . .	1897	1.1	1.6	2	2.5	3	4	6	7	10
,, : Vojvodina . .	1900	0.7	1.1	1.5	2	2.5	3	3.5	4	6
,, : Croatia . . .	1900	0.4	0.9	1.3	1.7	2.2	2.7	3.3	5	6
,, : Slovenia . . .	1902	1.1	1.5	1.9	2.5	3.5	5	7	9	12
,, : Total	1951	0.6	0.8	1.0	1.3	1.6	2	2.5	3	5
Greece	1929	0.3	0.4	0.8	1.3	2.5	4	13	25	50
Italy	1930	0.6	1.3	2	3.5	6.5	15	45	160	600
,, (private)	1946	0.3	0.7	1.2	2.4	4	9	20	45	110
Portugal: Algarve	1952	0.8	1.4	2	3	4	5	7	10	20
,, : Alentejo	1952	3	5	20	43	80	120	165	240	425

(100) Methodologically, this table throws interesting light upon the consequences of different size-classification systems. The choice between agricultural and total area as the classification criterion appears now to be of small importance in a country like England, where rough grazings and waste land are not dominant and are relatively evenly spread over the different farm sizes. In a country like Scotland, where the opposite is true, the choice of criterion turns out to be decisive for the picture. It is easy to imagine that the inclusion of vast tracts of very meagre land has stretched the scale far too much, and that the figures referring to 1950 do not tell any important part of the story.

The same difference as between England and Scotland is

certainly also observable between various other countries where the criterion for classification is total area. For the direct comparison between different countries, figures based on unweighted hectarages are still too little instructive.

For describing the development that took place over the period under review, on the other hand, this treatment of the material adds some new features. To a certain extent, it makes visible how the development of farm size refers to demographic development. The interplay between land hunger and changes in land distribution will, among other things, work out as changed proportions between full-sized family farms, under-sized or subsistence farms, and large farms using hired labor to a considerable extent. These proportions will not appear directly from the figures of Table 15, because the areas are still unweighted. Even so, these figures will give indications as to the trend.

In the land reform countries in eastern Europe, the dominating feature is still the strong increase of farms which are too small to hire any labor, and also of those that must be too small for employment of a family. In Rumania, Yugoslavia and Greece, there must at the date of the latest census have been very little scope for hired labor on farms, and in eastern Germany, such scope must have been small, if any at all outside State farms. In Poland, Czechoslovakia and Hungary (especially the latter), the classification criterion does not allow for seeing how far hired labor may still be playing a part (we know from other sources that it was almost wiped out).

The effect of the demographic trends is however different even in the countries of Eastern Europe. In Czechoslovakia, the change in farm structure as measured in hectares was modest, yet the change as measured in man-land units is considerable. The background is the heavy decrease of agricultural manpower, which made the man-land unit larger and the size of each farm smaller, as measured in the number of hands employed. In Bulgaria, for instance, the decrease in farm size since the beginning of the century — partly through division of inheritance, partly through land reform measures — was greater when measured in hectares than when measured in man-land units. In contrast to Czechoslovakia, Bulgarian agricultural manpower doubled over the period. The man-land unit went on shrinking, and each farm size becomes the sphere of employment for more and more hands.

Under constant farm structure, the trend would thus have been towards more family enterprises (without hired hands) when manpower is decreasing, and towards more hired labor when manpower is increasing. This accounts for the radical nature of the reforms in the Balkans, and also for their moderate or late character in Czechoslovakia and Hungary.

In Western Europe, the trend of diminishing size of farms is universal over the period, again with the sole exceptions of England and Sweden in the very last decades. By contrast with Table 14, there is no longer any impression of a "concentration towards the center". All the fractiles appear to be declining (the French data from 1942 are not fully comparable to those of 1929 and do not allow any positive conclusion). The background is again, as in Czechoslovakia, the diminution of agricultural manpower. In the Netherlands and Finland, the decrease in farm size has at any rate gone faster than the increase in agricultural manpower. In the latter countries, therefore, the decrease in farm size, as measured in hectares, has been speeded by population pressure on the land, as in the Balkans though less rapidly. In the rest of Western Europe, the decrease in manpower has speeded development of more and more pure family enterprises. Both in France and in Germany, rural exodus is likely to have operated a partial, not clearly visible "land reform", in the sense of making the occurrence of farms with considerable scope for hired labor less frequent.

In both eastern and western Europe, therefore, most of the development of farm size and agricultural manpower over the period has tended to increase the part played by the family farm. It has also tended to increase the part played by the under-sized farm. On the basis of unweighted figures, only the trend can be described but not the absolute proportions of each category. The same refers to the contrasting recent trend in England and Sweden. The trend is now towards larger farms in both these countries. How far this affects the part played by family farms, under-sized farms, and farms hiring labor, can only be described on the basis of data where the farm size has been weighted according to the intensity of land use.

CHART

*The correlation between
village median and average size of kolkhoz
in the thirties*

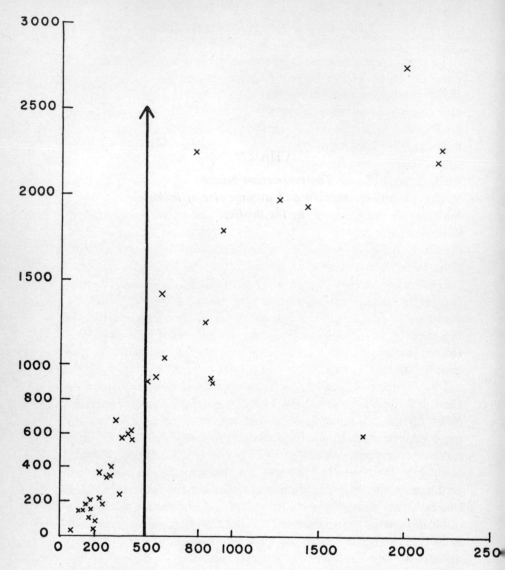

The correlation between village median and average size of kolkhoz in the thirties (both expressed in area of arable land): The vertical scale represents the area of median villages, the horizontal one the area of the kolkhoz, in each district. The arrow, at 500 hectares, represents the ideal size of kolkhoz at that time, and the points should have clustered around this line if the ideal size had been followed. There is a slight tendency to such clustering, although the correlation with village size is more marked.

In southern Europe, no clear statement can be made as regards even the trend in the respect here discussed. Expert opinion in Italy claims that the family farm has been slowly gaining ground, and this may very well be so, even if also some of the large farms have intensified their activities and therefore may be able to hire more hands than before. The trend of unweighted farm sizes in southern France would be indicative of a contrasting movement in Mediterranean Europe, if Mediterranean agriculture were not so diversified as it is. Even if it can be shown that small farms are growing even smaller and large farms even larger, as vaguely indicated also by the fragmentation data from Portugal, this does not tell the true story since small and large farms have entirely different farming practices and levels of intensity.

(101) The successive breakdown of all large private farms, completed in eastern Europe in the later forties, was already complete in Russia at the revolution of 1917. Amalgamation of the many small subsistence holdings issuing from such a radical reform is going on in eastern Europe and will be described in the chapter on land policy.

In a countryside which is over-populated in the sense that there is not, under existing technical conditions, enough employment for all hands, radical re-distribution of the land means a more equal distribution of the burden of underemployment. The creation of large co-operative or collective farms, already completed in Russia in the early thirties, creates new structural problems if the over-population is not radically dealt with. This can be done either by withdrawal of the manpower surplus to other industries or by intensification of the agricultural activities so as to absorb more labor, or by a combination of both kinds of measures. Our inquiry on employment levels showed that, although both measures have been applied, the goal of removing underemployment is far from having been reached.

The first Soviet collectivization drive in the early thirties aimed at creating units for which the model size was 500 hectares of sown area. Figures from the thirties show that practice did not come very close to this ideal. In fact, there was a clear correlation between the average size of the kolkhoz in each district and the median size of village in the same district (see Chart).

The small size of the kolkhozy in many districts is a striking feature. Thus, the settlement pattern, for some time, hampered the realization of the large-scale collective farm.

Around 1950, steps were taken to overcome the situation. The number of kolkhozy was reduced from some 240,000 to about 94,000, thus to barely 40 per cent of the number originally created. The average size, which had been about 650 hectares of arable land, rose to about 1700 hectares, as an average for the whole Union. It was underlined that this action was especially important in the north where the kolkhozy, it was now overtly stated, had not been sufficiently large from the outset. If the action had been confined to these regions, then its effect might be interpreted as raising the size of kolkhozy there to a level similar to that long existing in southern, large-village districts. Actually, there appear to have been many instances of kolkhoz amalgamation in Ukraina and other southern areas too. This must have increased the average kolkhoz size there. Since part of the total effect of the action was thus located in areas where the kolkhozy were already very large, the inescapable conclusion is that much of the difference in kolkhoz size between north and south has survived, although at a higher level. The northern kolkhozy may now have reached the original target of averageing 500 hectares, but those in the southern regions have gone very far beyond the original plans. Details are not known except for very scanty local data.

(102) A similar connection between size of collective farm and size of village is to some extent, though very vaguely, distinguishable in other countries of eastern Europe. The following figures for size of collective farm in the early fifties [a] may be compared with the characteristic size of village territory according to our calculations in Chapter 1.

The percentage of collectivization is of interest because the connection between farm size and village size is clearest in Bulgaria, where collectivization had reached farthest at that time. In Hungary, on the other hand, no connection was visible at all. The existing collectives must, at that time and as an average, have embraced only fractions of villages each. The relatively high percentage of collectivization therefore indicates that most of the large villages had at least one co-operative farm operating

TABLE 16. *Village size and size of collective farm in eastern Europe*

Country	Year	Size of co-operative farm, agricultural area	Per cent collectivization	Size of villages, agricultural area
Bulgaria.	1952	914	51	950– 2,200
Czechoslovakia . . .	1952	332	34	500– 800
Eastern Germany. .	1953	154	11	300– 600
Hungary	1952	282	21	1,000–10,000
Poland	1953	170	7	300– 1,500
Rumania	1953	246	7	900– 3,000
Yugoslavia.	1952	476	21	50– 4,000

a minor part only of the land of the village.

In Yugoslavia, most of the then existing co-operative farms were in Serbia and the Vojvodina. The former country has villages, which do not very much exceed the size of the average co-operative farm in the country as a whole, while settlement in the Vojvodina is close to the Hungarian pattern.

In Poland, it is known that most of the then existing co-operative farms were in the western parts of the country and largely coincide with former German villages where a few large farms dominated the picture. This only underlines the connnection with the settlement pattern, as these are some of the regions where Polish villages are smallest.

WEIGHTING THE FARM STRUCTURE

(103) The reasons for weighting land and livestock, as discussed in an earlier section, are of course, if anything, even more important for weighting the farm structure as for weighting the resources of a whole country. Large farms often tend to have more of the poorest qualities of land, subject to extensive use, while the small farms often have the most fertile land under extremely intensive use. We have also underlined in the comments to Tables 14 and 15 that the figures do not allow for any but very rough comparisons between countries, and that even the trend of development they display is merely indicative and does not show the absolute magnitude of the problems inherent

in the structural discrepancies between small and large farms.
The idea of measuring the degrees of intensity in farming by
the different rate of labor input is not entirely the same idea as

TABLE 17.   *Farm structure — weighted and unweighted. Size of farm, under the
definition of each census, found at each of the following fractiles, when
weighted according to labor norms of the national standard. Unweighted
data taken from Table 14 are included for the sake of comparison*

Country	Year	1	2	3	4	M	6	7	8	9
England and Wales										
Unweighted . .	1924	13	24	36	49	63	80	105	125	200
Weighted . . .	1924	9.5	20	31	43	59	75	97	130	195
Weighted . . .	1942	10.5	20	30	42	55	70	90	124	190
Eire										
Unweighted . .	1949	7.5	12	17	21	27	36	48	67	125
Weighted . . .	1949	4.8	8.5	12	16	20	25	31	44	71
Norway										
Unweighted . .	1949	1.9	3.2	4.3	5.5	7	9	12	17	27
Weighted . . .	1949	1.4	2.4	3.6	4.7	6	7	10	14	23
Finland										
Unweighted . .	1950	3.2	5.5	7	9	11	14	18	24	35
Weighted . . .	1950	3.6	5.1	6.5	8	10	13	15	21	33
Denmark										
Unweighted . .	1951	7	11	16	20	24	30	38	48	67
Weighted . . .	1951	6	9	13	16	20	25	32	44	59
Netherlands										
Unweighted . .	1950	4	7	9	12	15	19	25	34	46
Weighted . . .	1950	2.8	5	7.5	10	14	17	20	26	37
Belgium										
Unweighted . .	1950	2	3.8	5.6	8	10	14	18	26	45
Weighted . . .	1950	1.7	3.4	4.8	6.5	9	11	14	20	34
France										
Unweighted . .	1942	7.5	12	17	22	28	37	49	74	160
Weighted . . .	1942	6.2	10	13	17	22	28	36	50	85
W. Germany										
Unweighted . .	1949	3.3	5.2	7.5	10	13	17	23	32	53
Weighted . . .	1949	2.6	4.4	6.7	9	12	15	20	28	45
Austria										
Unweighted . .	1951	7	14	21	33	64	180	750	2,400	10,000
Weighted . . .	1951	3.7	6.5	10	14	18	21	28	40	100
Bulgaria										
Unweighted . .	1934	3	4	5	6	7	9	11	13	18
Weighted . . .	1934	2.1	3.3	4	5	6	8	10	12	16

that of measuring labor efficiency, as advanced by Taylorism.
In fact, the former idea was to some extent set forth earlier than
the latter[a]. So far, the principle has been applied mainly on

TABLE 18. *Farm structure, weighted and unweighted, in man-land units. Farm
size (under the same definitions as on Table 14) found at each one of
the following fractiles, converted into units of full man-years of work
(not man-quotients of weighted land and livestock). Corresponding
data from Table 15 are brought in for the sake of comparison*

Country	Year	1	2	3	4	M	6	7	8	9
England and Wales										
Unweighted . .	1924	1.0	1.8	3	4	5	6	8	10	15
Weighted . . .	1924	0.9	1.4	2	3	4	4.5	6	8	13
Weighted . . .	1942	1.1	1.7	2	3	4	4.5	6	8	15
Eire										
Unweighted . .	1949	0.5	0.8	1.1	1.5	2	2.5	3	5	9
Weighted . . .	1949	0.5	0.7	0.9	1.1	1.3	1.5	1.7	2	3
Norway										
Unweighted . .	1949	0.6	1.0	1.3	1.7	2	3	4	5	8
Weighted . . .	1949	0.3	0.5	0.7	0.8	1.0	1.3	1.6	2	3
Finland										
Unweighted . .	1950	0.7	1.2	1.6	2	2.5	3	4	5	8
Weighted . . .	1950	0.8	1.1	1.4	1.8	2.2	2.7	3.4	4	7
Denmark										
Unweighted . .	1951	0.9	1.4	1.9	2.3	3	4	4.5	6	8
Weighted . . .	1951	0.8	1.2	1.5	1.7	1.9	2.1	2.4	3	5
Netherlands . . .										
Unweighted . .	1950	1.0	1.7	2.4	3	4	5	6	9	12
Weighted . . .	1950	0.7	1.1	1.3	1.5	1.8	2.2	2.7	4	5
Belgium										
Unweighted . .	1950	0.4	0.8	1.1	1.5	2	3	4	5	9
Weighted . . .	1950	0.3	0.6	0.8	1.0	1.2	1.4	1.8	3	5
France										
Unweighted . .	1942	0.9	1.4	2	2.5	3.5	4.5	6	9	19
Weighted . . .	1942	0.8	1.1	1.4	1.7	2.0	2.5	3.4	5	7.5
W. Germany										
Unweighted . .	1949	0.6	0.9	1.3	1.7	2.2	3	4	5	9
Weighted . . .	1949	0.5	0.8	1.1	1.3	1.6	2.1	2.8	4	7
Austria										
Unweighted . .	1951	0.5	1.0	1.5	2.5	5	9	13	17	22
Weighted . . .	1951	0.4	0.6	1.0	1.3	1.5	1.7	1.9	2.2	5
Bulgaria										
Unweighted . .	1934	0.9	1.2	1.5	1.9	2.2	2.5	3	4	6
Weighted . . .	1934	1.0	1.3	1.6	1.9	2.1	2.6	3.2	3.4	5

chosen cases or, at best, on a sample basis[b]. For this enquiry, the weighting has had to be undertaken with the same national labor weights as in the above section on weighting productive resources. Some preliminary results have been published separately[c].

(104) The man-years given in Table 18 are not fully analogous to those shown in Table 15. The latter represent the share of the land that would come to each man if the land were equally divided among all males active in agriculture. The full man-years, on the other hand, show the amount of labor that could be fully employed on farms of the size shown under each fractile.

The first table shows that, from the methodological point of view, an analysis founded on size classification according to agricultural area might give a tolerably good result under the conditions prevailing in western Europe. This observation of course takes into account that the calculation is made on the basis of global figures from entire countries. Especially in the larger countries, regional extremes may outbalance each other in the national figures. It is therefore possible that larger discrepancies between unweighted and weighted figures might show up if the farm structure is weighted within small and geographically homogeneous areas which do not represent the average of the geographical conditions for the whole country.

Further, the two tables tell us that the west European farm pattern, besides being so rigid over a long period, is also astonishingly similar from country to country, when weighted according to the normal labor consumption in each branch of production within each size-class separately. The median farm size ranges from only 1 man-year in Norway to 2 man-years in France, the extremes on the Continent. In none of the continental countries does the ninth decile reach 10 man-years. Family-sized farms appear to be dominant, while farms with regular hired labor occupy a minor share of the Continent's land. It is clear that "agrarian industry" only plays a small part on the Continent. In England, the traditional home of large farms, the median is 4 man-years, just double that of France, and only the 15–20 per cent at the top represent really large-scale enterprise.

The weights are the same as for land and livestock in a previous section of this chapter. Hence the weights are not the same everywhere. In France, the norms applied are lower than in the surrounding Continental countries, while they are higher in England, Eire, Norway and Denmark. This gives a further reminder of the real uniformity of the farm structure. For instance, the real structural differences between France and Germany must be very small.

The norms used in Bulgaria are even lower and represent rather primitive and very labor consuming practices. The resulting figures are therefore not at all comparable to those from the western countries.

For the interpretation of all these data it should be kept in mind that the weighting of land and livestock within each size-class separately involves a certain amount of statistical over-lapping. The result of the weighting calculation is a sum of labor that should be necessary within each size-class separately, and thus results in an average labor consumption per size class, which is then the basis for computation of fractiles. But the size-classes are homogeneous only when not weighted, even though their homogeneity is then fictitious. Economically, and also as regards labor consumption, some farms are larger and some others smaller than indicated by the size-class limits. If the weighting had been done individually, farm by farm, and the size-classification thereafter had been undertaken in size-classes of labor-consumption, then the scale would have been spelled out sharper than now. The median would have remained about the same, but the low fractiles would have turned out lower and the high fractiles higher than now. The difference would have been greater the more considerable the difference is between weighted and unweighted hectarages. Thus the effect of over-lapping must be greatest in Austria among the countries in Tables 17 and 18. It is also likely to be somewhat greater in France than in Germany, for instance.

(105) A separate weighting by size-class according to American labor standards does not seem to have any great value, since it would merely show a theoretical result. European farms as they exist now are not at all adapted to American methods of production. That a drastic reduction of labor consumption must have serious effects upon the viability of the existing farms is clear without much comments.

For the same kind of reasons as discussed above, it is not feasible at present to undertake the weighting of the farm structures in western Europe for earlier epochs. The progressive intensification of farming has been accompanied by technical advancement reducing the amount of human labor necessary. At the same time, as the above analysis should have shown, farms have dropped in size, even when measured in hectares. Their size, in units of labor, has been further reduced through rural exodus. Both the family-sized farm and the under-sized farm should have increased in importance in western Europe over the period. The rigidity of the farm pattern seems to have contributed to this development. Even though the development cannot be followed in detail, it may nevertheless be possible to see where the labor surplus lies within the existing farm structure. This can be done in so far as census returns give also the distribution of manpower by size-classes. Even though the principles followed in registration of manpower are not by far the same everywhere, the data on distribution of manpower on the size-classes can be made to illustrate both the reliability of our weighting calculations and the localization of the labor surplus.

TABLE 19. *Labor available and needed in England and Wales, by size of holding, in 1924 and 1942*

Size-class, acres	Thousands				Id. as average per holding in the size-class	
	Manpower available		Manpower needed			
	1924	1942	1924	1942	1924	1942
1– 5	73	82	16	14	0.2	0.2
5– 20	151	126	58	48	0.5	0.6
20– 50	159	138	94	97	1.2	1.4
50–100	173	171	140	156	2.3	2.5
100–150	128	125	117	126	3.7	3.9
150–300	217	200	218	212	6	6
300–500	98	94	108	97	11	11
500 and over	62	72	78	71	24	25
TOTAL.	1,061	1,008	830	821		
Sub-total, – 50 acres .	383	346	168	159		
Sub-total, 50 acres and over	678	662	661	662		

(106.) For the presentation of the weighted farm structure in England and Wales, manpower data, though of different

character, are available for 1924 and for 1942. In the former
year, complete data on various categories of workers have here
been weighted according to the scale indicated by T. WILLIAMS,
though with some simplification[a]. For 1942, only the number of
workers, casual and regular, was available. To this, the number
of holdings was added, on the assumption that each holding has
a holder working on it. This procedure is likely to lead to some
overstatement of the real manpower. However, the two resulting
figures are of the same magnitude, and the difference between
them is considerably smaller than the labor surplus.

(107) In Scandinavia and the Benelux countries, calculations
have been made to show the amount of real labor input, by size
of farm. The procedures behind these calculations can be discovered from the farm censuses taken in these countries in
1949–51. Here, it should only be mentioned that the Norwegian
calculation includes housework. In order to reduce these figures
to a significance closer to that of our calculation, we have therefore subtracted one labor-year per holding.

TABLE 20. *Labor input and needed in the Netherlands and Belgium, in 1950,
by size of farm*

Size-class, hectares	Thousands				Id. as average per farm	
	Labor input		Manpower needed			
	Nether-lands	Belgium	Nether-lands	Belgium	Nether-lands	Belgium
1– 5	194	248	79	88	0.6	0.5
5– 10	133	139	92	71	1.4	1.2
10– 20	134	96	118	68	2.4	2.1
20– 30	57	28	59	26	3.7	3.3
30– 50	47	16	46	17	5.3	4.7
50–100	17	11	15	14	7.6	7.8
100 and over	5	3,5	5	4	30	13
TOTAL.	587	542	414	288		
Sub-total, – 20 ha . .	461	483	289	227		
Sub-total, 20 ha and over	126	59	125	61		

Corresponding figures for Denmark have already been
published[a]. The difference in size-classification system makes it
difficult to render them directly comparable to those of the other
Scandinavian countries.

(108) On the Continent, there is a special interest in trying to render comparable the figures from France, Germany, and Austria. The differences in size-classification are likely to produce characteristic differences in the picture of the structure.

TABLE 21. *Labor input and need in Norway and Finland, 1949–50, by size of farm*

Size-class, hectares	Thousands				Id. as average per farm	
	Labor input		Manpower needed			
	Norway	Finland	Norway	Finland	Norway	Finland
– 5	121	121	72	68	0.6	0.7
5–10	63	158	53	101	1.3	1.2
10–20	32	132	34	98	2.2	1.8
20–50	17	67	18	62	3.7	3.6
50 and over	3.5	14	4	15	13	18
Total.	236.5	492	181	344		
Sub-total, – 10 ha . .	184	279	125	169		
Sub-total, 10 ha and over	52,5	213	56	176		

Manpower data are not available in such a perfect form as from the Benelux and Scandinavian countries. German data per size-class refer to male manpower in 1949, when agricultural manpower was still overstated [a]. Since no better compensation device can be produced, these data are taken as indicative of the distribution of manpower among size-classes. The French figures on agricultural labor force in 1946 have recently been worked out by size of farm according to the 1942 census [b], but the seasonal workers were left out, as belonging to no special farms. Here, we have tentatively ascribed them to the farms over 50 hectares. From the Austrian census, data on permanent workers have been completed by the number of holders whose main occupation is farming. This gives a total somewhat lower than the total for agricultural manpower according to Tables 11 and 12 (because female labor is represented by less than 20 per cent of the males), but higher than in Table 3 (because some female holders are included).

(109) The Bulgarian farm structure in 1934 represents a stage through which all the Eastern European countries have passed at some time, though of different duration. Because the actual labor conditions were very different from those in Western Europe

alternative calculations should be presented also for the real input
of female labor, which was about equal to the input of male labor.

TABLE 22. *Manpower available and needed in W. Germany, France, and Austria (1949, 1942/46, and 1951, respectively), by size of farm*

| Size-class, hectares | Thousands | | | | | | Id. as average per farm | | |
| | Manpower available | | | Manpower needed | | | | | |
	W. Germany	France	Austria	W. Germany	France	Austria	W.G.	F.	A.
− 5	822	768	143	449	260	64	0.5	0.5	0.3
5– 10	646	882	113	445	500	67	1.1	1.0	0.8
10– 20	557	1,165	136	517	942	112	2.1	1.7	1.5
20– 50	378	1,046	117	444	993	118	4.0	3.4	2.3
50–100	94	650*	23	107	719	24	8.5	6.0	3.0
100–200	41	190*	11	38	201	13	17	10	3.9
200 and over . . .	34	100*	31	30	105	31	38	16	17
Total	2,572	4,800	574	2,030	3,720	429			
Sub-total, − 20 ha.	2,025	2,815	392	1,411	1,702	243			
Sub-total, 20 ha and over . . .	547	1,985	182	619	2,018	186			

TABLE 23. *Manpower available and needed in Bulgaria, in 1934, by size of farm*

| Size-class, hectares | Manpower available (thousands) | | | Man-years needed | |
	Males only	Males plus 20 per cent	Males and females	Total	As average per farm in the size-class
− 1	105	126	216	45	0.4
1– 2	142	170	306	92	0.8
2– 3	157	188	338	131	1.1
3– 4	158	190	341	153	1.4
4– 5	150	180	322	161	1.7
5– 6	123	148	264	146	2.0
6– 7	103	124	219	126	2.2
7– 8	82	98	175	107	2.5
8– 9	67	80	142	92	2.7
9–10	53	64	111	75	3.0
10–15	141	169	292	223	3.6
15–20	48	58	97	89	4.7
20–30	28	34	55	59	6.1
30–40	6	7	12	15	7.8
40–50	2	2	3	5	9.3
50 and over . .	3	3	4	8	14.3
TOTAL . . .	1,368	1,642	2,897	1,527	
Sub-total, − 5 ha . .	712	854	1,523	582	
Sub-total, 5–15 ha. .	569	683	1,203	769	
Sub-total, 15 ha and over . .	87	104	171	176	

It should be noted that this table does not refer either to the same year or to the same territory as the global calculations set forth above.

(110) All the calculations from Western Europe give evidence of the tolerable reliability of the method chosen. In all of them, the calculated need of manpower is fairly coincident with the manpower actually available in all the higher size-classes. The tolerable similarity of the two calculations for England and Wales also indicates that the result is in touch with reality, since somewhat different procedures, applied on material somewhat differently presented in the statistical sources, have given essentially the same picture. The Bulgarian table will be commented upon later. Its apparent labor shortage in the highest size-classes is small in absolute figures. The compensation, in the form of additional seasonal employment, which it may have offered the small farmers cannot therefore have eased their situation much.

The material used for the calculations is not always identical with that underlying the over-all calculations. Among other things, the breakdown of land use and livestock is often less detailed in the tabulations by size of holding than in non-size-classified tabulations. Further, the farm censuses with breakdown of land use and livestock by size of holding do not always refer to the same year as was chosen for the over-all calculations. Despite these differences, it is obvious that the labor surpluses shown through the size-classified calculations are of more or less the same magnitude, country by country, as in the global calculations set forth above.

The remarkable coincidence between labor force available and needed, not only on the large but also on the middle-sized holdings, is a good argument for our opinion that the labor need on these holdings has been calculated with a degree of accuracy allowing some general conclusions.

(111) In all the western countries under review, the point upwards from which there is fairly good coincidence between labor available and needed according to our calculations, lies close to the point in the farm structure where the labor need averages two man-years. There are deviations from this rule, but it is difficult to calculate the deviations exactly because we have generally speaking too few size-classes for an exact interpolation

of this kind. This result is in accordance with the results derived by a similar method, on a small scale, by Dutch and American scholars[a]. In the hectare scale, the critical point seems to lie, in most countries, somewhere around 15 or between 15 and 20 hectares. In Norway, exceptionally, it lies below 10 hectares; the explanation seems to be in the unusually great importance of grazings which are not included in the land area on which the size-classification was based.

It seems thus established that the West European labor surplus is essentially localized in the small holdings[b]. In them, it is above all localized in the very smallest ones, and the relative importance of the labor surplus diminishes upwards, until it disappears at a point close to a farm size that absorbs two full man-years. This is not astonishing. Two full man-years is about the amount of labor that a normal farm family produces. When the holding is large enough to absorb the work of the family, working by rational methods, the family becomes of course fully employed. When the holding is too large to be worked by the family alone, outside labor is hired, though seldom to an extent that seriously exceeds the need. Thus, almost a priori, employment should continue to be full in all the upper strata of the farm structure, from the fully employed family farm upwards.

The result of our weighting of the farm structure is, first, to give a measure to the phenomenon. The relative importance of labor surplus can be grasped, size-class by size-class, as far as the data on manpower available are reliable. Next, the enquiry also shows that the medium-sized farms are technically about as efficient as the large farms. At least they absorb their manpower about as well. It is even possible — although the evidence is scanty and difficult to interpret so far — that the very largest holdings have a certain labor surplus. This appears at least to be so in the Netherlands, Germany, and Austria. At any rate, one would have expected the opposite, since the large farms have more possibility to really profit from labor-saving devices. The fact that they do even so consume as much labor as the family holdings, in comparison with the intensity pattern of the farms, indicates that the family holdings have a peculiar advantage in the elasticity of their labor organization. It may be too great a risk for the large farms to rely entirely on the labor market for hands when they are really needed. They may be obliged to hire more permanent hands than are necessary all the year round, just not to run the risk of being without them — or too many of them — at rush seasons. The family farm, with its limited scope, can rely much more on the willingness of the family members to work many over-time hours when the interest of the family economy requires it, and take the compensation of under-employment in off seasons.

(112) The different degrees to which available manpower is absorbed also have bearings on the degree of utilisation of fixed capital equipment and on the differences in the level of output per productive unit.

As far as capital equipment is concerned, a measurement could be made mainly on the basis of accounting holdings but these are, at least in most countries so far, not proper statistical samples capable of being raised. It may only be said here that this is probably the very point where the large holdings hold advantages over the medium-sized holdings, which may outbalance a slight advantage of the latter in the labor organization. It may also outbalance the advantage enjoyed by family holdings of some-what higher unit yields, if this is really the case. All this tends to show that the large and the family-sized holdings have advantages of different kinds that may counterbalance each other and eventually lead to the conclusion that both are about equally viable and that slight changes in economic policy may cause a shift in favor of one or the other.

As regards small holdings, it is more difficult to see how the specific advantages of small-scale enterprise could counterbalance the double disadvantage of both a heavy over-equipment with labor and the tendency to over-equipment with fixed capital. Especially the buildings will often imply fixed investments which cannot be amortized to the same degree on all sizes of farms.

We set apart the cases when the very small holdings have reached such a degree of specialization as to really absorb the work of the holder and his family. In this case it is not a very small holding any more but a family-sized farm. We have already stressed that, if these apparently small but really middle-sized farms could be taken out of the picture, then the over-equipment of the other small holdings with manpower would appear even more striking. The main chance these holdings have of improving the situation is in the possibility of reaching higher yields, in each branch of production, to justify the higher input of labor. Not very much material is available on differential yields by size of holding. Recent Danish calculations, which we have already quoted in the discussion on the advantages of different farm sizes, indicate an over-all advantage of the magnitude of ten per cent, when small holdings are compared with medium-sized farms, and of the magnitude of 25 per cent when they are compared with large farms[a]. This obviously cannot counterbalance the disadvantage of putting in some 50 per cent more labor. On the other hand, the differences in yields may lead to the conclusion that the farms are economically viable at a somewhat (though not very much) smaller size than would appear from our calculations. In a country like Denmark, the disadvantage may not be very great on farms around 10 hectares. How the principle works out in other countries can only be settled on the basis of information from each country.

The conclusion is then that in most western countries, about half or even more of the agricultural resources are disposed of on farms which are too small to be fully viable under modern conditions. In quite a number of countries, a very considerable amount of the resources are in farms considerably too small for viability under modern conditions. Also a large proportion of those working in West European agriculture are to be found on such farms. This seems to be the main obstacle against a considerable rise in the productivity of farm labor in western Europe.

To what extent workers on small holdings find supplementary income in other occupations, is a topic largely unexplored. In the Scandinavian and Benelux countries, work on other farms for pay is already taken into account in the material underlying our tables. The exercise of two professions is one of the main sources of error for any calculation of labor productivity. It may be a matter for doubt whether it represents a good and durable solution for an industry like farming.

(113) The East European situation, as represented on Table 23 on Bulgaria, is characterized by two main differences as compared with the West European situation just analyzed. One is the much lower technical level and the much lower efficiency of labor. The

other is the high degree of actual labor performance by female workers[a]. The sub-totals of Table 23 show that, if only 120 per cent of the males were counted as labor force, there would be over 90 per cent employment. This employment would have been distributed as a surplus on the holdings under 5 hectares, thereafter tolerable balance for a few size-classes representing a farm size of 2–3 man-years, and finally a considerable shortage of labor in the higher size-classes. When the actual input of female labor is considered, there appears to have been only about 53 per cent employment. This is distributed as a considerable labor surplus in almost all the size-classes up to about 15 hectares, thereafter a tolerably good balance on the holdings between 15–30 hectares (representing 5–6 full labor years each), and a shortage of permanent workers on the very few large holdings. When this situation is compared with that of Western Europe, it must be remembered that Bulgarian farm families were large at that epoch.

The larger family working at a lower efficiency level reached full employment on farms of about the same size as the fully employed farms in Western Europe. There may of course have been serious difficulties in finding enough hands in rush seasons. Despite a remarkable trend of intensification, Bulgarian agriculture was still essentially grain production. This, too, is characteristic of the East European countries over most of the period here reviewed.

For one thing, this tremendous pressure of underemployed people on the land must have precipitated the subdivision of large estates and the expansion of small-scale production in agriculture. The advantages of the labor organization of the family farm must have been decisive when labor was so abundant and yet could not be had for nothing, as in an economy based on slavery or bondage. The question is whether the abundance of manpower even contributed to the abolition of bondage, since the family farmer may produce even more efficiently than the bondsman.

On the other hand, there cannot have been much incentive for mechanization in such a farm structure. The motive for saving labor cannot have been great, and the opportunity to pay for the machinery must have remained with the few large farms only.

It is on this point that Communist land policy had to make its choice. One way was to favor competition among farmers, ruining some and allowing others to expand to fully employed family farmers, eventually hiring some extra hands. The other way was collectivization of the many small farms. The latter way was more in line with the ideological claim for equality. But, did it also bring about the advance in agriculture that was envisaged?

It will have appeared from the above analyses that collectivization in Soviet agriculture has not solved the problem of population pressure on the land and under-employment among those who work the land. If anything, it may have tended to intensify under-employment by mechanizing a few key operations. Those carrying out these operations — the tractorists, among others — will then have had the chance of doing efficient work. Those left over for the non-mechanized operations are likely to produce less than ever per unit of time put into the work. It is fairly possible that employment opportunities are far from evenly distributed among the members of a kolkhoz. Even more, the relations between the kolkhoz and the machine-and-tractor station may be to the benefit of the latter and to the detriment of the former. If this is so, then the old inequality between holders of farms of different size has been followed by an inequality between holders of differently remunerated jobs.

The key problem for East European agriculture, which is apparent to the eye of a reader of Table 23, is the small possibility of higher labor productivity. The response is partly in expansion and intensification of farming, partly in a rapid rural exodus. The collective farm does not specifically promote any of these solutions. It might do so on a level where efficiency and productivity were already high enough to pay for the new investments needed. On a population level which calls for a maximum of human labor and a minimum of money expenditure, the collective farm has not furnished any decisive solutions.

(114) The situations of Southern Europe, though not very well known in detail, furnish some sharp contrasts which are interesting to analyze in broad outline.

The basic contrast in all three countries is that between large extensive farms on the dry areas which so far have been most adapted for grain growing, and a mass of largely under-sized family farms in the restricted zones of intensive farming on irrigated land. Important parts of Italy, however, occupy an intermediary position. Despite a low level of efficiency per working hour, there is an astonishingly high degree of efficiency in the sense of producing much on lands that would not look very productive in their natural state. The intensively cultivated rice fields of the Po valley are thus mostly in large farms, because small-scale enterprisers would not have managed the heavy job of draining the vast plain. Much of the grain growing in northern and central Italy, on the other hand, is in family farms of a mixed character, which have come into existence over a drawn-out period of expansion for small-scale production in agriculture.

For one thing, the holders of the vast latifundia have not been very willing to sell parts of their land, because the social framework of these countries has, until recently at least, retained the archaic view of landed property as a sign of nobility, as something valuable apart from its economic value. On the other hand, there seems to be evidence from the Iberian countries that, even though latifundia owners to some extent have sold off some of their lands, the new small-holders who bought the land — and bought it expensively — were not capable of surviving a series of dry years and collapsed economically. The landlords then had the chance to buy back the land cheaper than they sold it. Without some kind of collective or public support, small farmers are not capable of carrying through the irrigation and other land improvement enterprises necessary for the establishment of intensive farming on the dry plateaus of the south.

On the other hand, there are obvious limits to the viability of the large farms in Southern Europe too. Even apart from the small tenancies and mortgaged freeholds in the zones of very intensive cultivation, the principle of abundant family labor as the cheapest source of working power shows its strength in the vast zones of Mediterranean sharecropping. The systems range from that of enterprising landlords supervising sharecroppers that are little but workmen paid in kind, to sharecroppers who are independent entrepreneurs, only paying a share rent to a passive landlord. In either case, the landlord's willingness to farm out some of the risk of the enterprise, even though he may be losing some of the profit too, reveals the weakness of the large-scale enterprise in farming. Its dilemma is between having too many people on the permanent payroll or risking not to have enough hands in the rush season. This dilemma becomes especially embarrassing under conditions of primitive farming with little machinery and other outside investments. When the land and the labor are the sole or main production factors, the family farmer's willingness to work overtime in his own interest will be a powerful factor in land reforms. The spontaneous shift towards small-scale farming in the hands of sharecroppers and short-term lessees, however, has other drawbacks that will be discussed in the next chapter.

FARM STRUCTURE AND DEMOGRAPHIC STRUCTURE

(115) The disposition of the productive resources on productive units — the farms — has some interesting bearings upon the composition of the farming population, although the real meaning of these relationships is not easy to describe.

One ratio which it would have been highly desirable to describe is that between farmers and hired hands. This would give a supplementary indication as to the social significance of the farm structure. However, a table describing this ratio in various countries at different points of the period under review would turn out both incomplete and deceptive as to trends. The limit between the small farmer who also does some work for pay on other farms, and the hired hand who has some land of his own is a tricky one to define. Eventually, a deterioration in the situation of the farmhands may produce a statistical illusion that independent farmers were increasing and farmhands decreasing: this will be the impression if some of the part-time farmers who are also part-time farmhands do not find any employment outside their own small holdings any more. Further, figures of the ratio between farmers (and their family members) on the one hand, and the hired hands on the other, will not be entirely comparable for one more reason. In some countries, it is fairly customary for the grown-up son of a farmer to leave the farm and accept paid jobs on other farms, in order to broaden his experience and increase his independency. Meantime, the father may hire a farm worker — who may be a son of another farmer —

to fill the gap. This practice will create the impression of a relatively high ratio of hired hands. In other countries, where this practice is not so frequent, the resultant impression of this ratio will therefore not be comparable to that of the former countries.

The ratio between family and non-family workers can therefore be given only a very rough outline. The trend of development will be observable only in cases of extremely rapid change.

With these reservations, it seems established that hired hands constitute about two-thirds of the agricultural manpower in England and Portugal. In Spain, hired hands — under the definitions of Spanish statistics — are about 40–45 per cent of the population working in agriculture. The proportion was similar in Hungary and Eastern Germany before the war but has since dropped heavily; in the former country, at least, there seems to have remained a stratum of farmhands of the magnitude of 15 per cent in service of State farms and "kulaks". In most of Western Europe, the ratio is on the level of 15 to 30 per cent. It is not clear how far this is influenced by the inclusion of many farmers' sons among the paid farm workers. Even in Poland and Czechoslovakia, landless farm workers seem still to play a role which is far from negligible. In the Balkans, landless farm workers were of the order of less than 10 per cent before the war and should since then have dropped further.

In very over-populated countries, like the Balkans, the radical land reforms will automatically do away with the system of paid farm workers. When almost all farms are too small to absorb more labor than the farm family can provide, there will be almost no employment to be had for others than the farm families. Those who used to be part-time farmers and part-time farm workmen will then become full-time farmers because of lack of outside employment. Of course, the radical land reform distributes the burden of under-employment more evenly. It even does away with some of it through the intensification it makes feasible. But much of the underemployment is likely to stay whatever the changes in the farm structure.

(116) The ratio between the social strata on the countryside is not only a consequence of the farm structure. It is also likely to produce different trends in the demographic development of the farming population.

It is fairly generally recognized that the attitude towards marriage and family size is not the same in all strata of society, even if the differences cannot be said to be very well explored so far. The same observation appears to be true, at least in certain instances, about the different strata of the farming community, although here, the differences are even less explored. Some features can however be quoted.

It is not infrequent that statistics seem to show that farmers have larger families than landless farm workmen. This may to a great extent be a statistical illusion. The cohesion of the family may be greater among the farmers than among the workmen. Further, the age composition of both groups is important. Those individuals who begin their career as landless workmen and later on advance to farmers, will contribute to the impression that farmers had larger families than the workmen.

The deceptiveness of such statistics was shown from Hungary in the thirties. If crude values were used, farmers had more children, but when the age of persons and marriages were also considered, the opposite turned out to be true [a].

French data on numbers of children under 14 years of age indicate considerable social differences, though with different bearing in different regions. In most departments, it appears as if agricultural workmen and employees have fewer children than independent farmers. The same reasons as quoted from Hungary may play a part here, even if the difference varies considerably from one department to another. On the other hand, in some 30 departments, agricultural workmen and employees appear to have larger families than the farmers. This is, broadly speaking, in the richest agricultural regions of France [b]. In this case, the general economic level of the countryside may have provoked contrasting social reactions to marriage and family size.

Since the limit between farmers and workmen is fluid among the smallholders, the question may arise whether the demographic behavior is different according to size of farm. The Hungarian farm census of 1935 seemed to give an indication to that effect, though a very weak one, and it remains doubtful whether the difference was real [c]. In some parts of Germany, it has been shown that there used to be a positive correlation between farm size and birthrates, but this tendency has disappeared [d]. In other areas of the same country, it was found that there was no correlation of the kind [e].

The issue is complicated through the possibility of differential fertility in relation to land tenure. In a number of countries, there appears to be a tendency for leaseholders to have larger families than owner-operators. Again, the age composition is of importance for the interpretation. On the other hand, farms held under lease are often larger, as an average, than owner-operated farms. Only differential figures would therefore prove anything.

No general rule can therefore be formulated in this respect. The differences in birthrates in various strata of the agricultural society are not likely to be the same everywhere or at all epochs in the same country.

The field is one where future research may harvest interesting results. In Europe, most differences of this kind are likely to lie in the past. They may be of more direct concern to social policy in regions of the world where "the population explosion" is still far from slowing down.

CHAPTER 4

LAND TENURE

(117) Wherever there is land in use, somebody may be said to hold the land. In most cases, he is an individual, but it could equally well be a group, either of individuals, or a society, or a community. The most generally used distinction, between owner-operated and rented land, represents a simplification, founded on certain traditional concepts of legal doctrine. It may really be asked, under modern conditions, what the fundamental difference is between ownership and tenancy. The psychological difference, however important it may be in many instances, ultimately derives from the concepts of legal ideology and is likely to change with the changes of the legal situation.

In an introductory section of this chapter, we will try to draw up the broad lines of discussion on the principles. Ownership and tenancy will be regarded under the viewpoint of the basic relativity of their social and economic implications, to some extent also in their legal structure. In the following sections of the chapter, we will try to outline the occurrence of different types of land tenure in Europe and their implications for the land-labor relationships.

FEUDAL AND QUASI-FEUDAL TENURE

(118) A short historical outline of certain older forms of land tenure in Europe is likely to contribute towards understanding the immediate background existing at the beginning of the period here under review. It may also yield some contribution to the formulation of a general theory of land tenure.

From the Roman Empire, Mediaeval Europe had inherited mainly two types of tenure situations under owners of large landed estates. One was the protected bondage (the colonate), the other was the system of large estates farmed by slave labor. Free smallholders also existed and must have increased in connection with the migrations of Germanic tribes. The dominant features were however the two main tenure situations under large landowners. In those parts of Eastern and Northern Europe which had never been under Roman domination, primitive tribal communities survived, eventually developing into large landholdings of tribal chiefs, these also making extensive use of slave labor.

The colonate was a form of tenancy, protected from unjustified eviction of the tenant by the landlord. At the same time, the colon was forbidden to leave unless somebody else was put in his place. According to an often quoted formula, he was *servus glebae, non hominis* (serf of the land but not of any man). This kind of glebe-fixed, protected tenancy had been introduced by the late Roman State in order to make safe the payment of taxes and to prevent the desertion of the land.

On the large estates, slaves worked under the supervision of other slaves. The supervisors, as slaves, were formally deprived of all civil rights, as well as those whom they supervised. As a matter of fact, they enjoyed quite a different social position. Because it was materially necessary to conclude contracts with slaves in responsible positions, this was also done already in the High Antiquity. Reluctantly, Roman law began to recognize these acts as "quasi-contracts". At the beginning of the Middle Ages, slaves in responsible positions were a quite normal feature in estate management.

With the downfall of public power, the position of the colons deteriorated. During the Black Centuries (800–1000), they became very little better than slaves of the landlords. At the same time, slavery as an institution declined, and the two categories became amalgamated into one: the bondsmen. Only some unimportant formal features in the composition of land rents sometimes make it possible to distinguish later which holdings were originally held by slaves from those of the free colons. At this stage, feudalism came in as a stabilizing element.

As long as the threat of invasion and devastation was constant and State protection not very efficient, landowners could treat their tenants very much as they liked. The distinction between slave-tenant and colon-tenant was not therefore of any great practical importance. At the same time, social and political relationships within the ruling class were reorganized through classical feudalism, regulating the personal bond of fidelity, established through certain ceremonies. It was complemented through counteracting rules of social and legal relations, even those of kinship. The system was apparently disintegrated, but answered in a sense to the needs of the chaotic epoch. It created a framework for elementary defense and a relative inner peace. The renewed rise of European economy in the High Middle Ages may very well have been promoted by the feudal social order, but in its turn it prepared the downfall of classical feudalism.

(119) When landlords became the vassals of counts or kings, they renounced the property rights to their estates and received them back as feuda. At the same time, most small freeholders became vassals of landlords, and likewise gave up their freeholds and received them back as feudal tenures. Sooner or later, the same régime was applied also to the other tenants — the "serf"-tenants, as the bondsmen were called, irrespective of the position they or their ancestors had originally held. Thus, the peasants regularly became the vassals of the landlords. Their title to the glebe they tilled then came to be of very much the same nature as the landlord's title to his estates. They did not own their land, but the landlord did not own it either. He in his turn held it from his suzerain, who also might depend upon a higher suzerain, eventually the Emperor or another distant monarch. The hierachy of feudal tenure was often more complicated than that, because more than one seigneur could derive special rights from the same glebe. The vassal-tenant could then be brought, if not to serve more than one master, at least to pay rents and rights to more than one. It is characteristic of European Mediaeval land law, before Roman Law was again brought into force along with the decay of classical feudalism, that the ownership of land was seldom talked about. The object sold and bought, or rented, or contested, was seldom a glebe or a territory. More generally, it was a specified right derived from a certain glebe or territory, or even from a specified tenant without indication of the territorial extension of the tenure. In this relativity of rights, only

one person had a concrete and materially well defined position in relation to the land: he who tilled it. When feudal social order crumbled, there could be a strong case for the tenant to become owner.

When sometimes a freehold occurred in Mediaeval feudal Western Europe, it was characterized as "feud of the sun" (*Sonnenlehn*, in German). More frequently, its freedom was denied: no land could be without a seigneur. This is an over-simplification of the situation which showed many variations all over Europe. It reached its classical shape above all in northern France and certain surrounding regions. It maintained its character of a customary legal order, smoothly following the variations of the practical situations, as long as legal order depended mainly upon oral tradition. When legal order again came to be a question of written evidence, the development of feudal tenure gave different results according to the situation of the region.

(120) Generally, the trend was for cultivation to expand during the High Middle Ages of Western Europe. Different landlords, temporal and spiritual, competed for available manpower and were led to improve the conditions of their tenants. Under the pressure of this leading incentive, bondage conditions became successively mitigated or even abolished. The relation between the seigneur and the vassal-tenant tended to become more and more contractual. Because already classical feudalism had very soon reabsorbed the right of inheritance as regards the feudal estates of the landlords, the same rule was largely applied to the tenants, so much the more when tenants became scarce.

The liberation of the tenants from formal bondage, which took place in most regions of Western Europe successively during the Late Middle Ages, therefore eventually might mean a deprivation of the right of inheritance, or even of the right to lifetime possession, and make the position of the tenant less safe than before. This was largely the case in Italy, where such "liberation" was brought about at an early stage and landlords were often urban merchants who managed their estates in accordance with the principles of early capitalism. In England, the early rise of wool industry and trade may be held responsible for a similar development, but also some peculiar features in English feudalism contributed to the result. In both cases, the land went back to the big landlords. In France and the western parts of the German empire, the titles of the peasants to lifetime and inheritable tenancy, in general, did not become abolished when bondage was abolished. At least in France, this was due to the King's protection of the lower classes. A general situation where the seigneurs became more and more dependent upon the rents from their land may also have contributed to the result. When Roman Law made its comeback, and it was necessary to explain the legal nature of a situation where both landlord and tenant had inheritable rights to the same land, it made use of the theory of *dominium divisum* or divided ownership. In many cases, when the value of rents fixed in money was destroyed through currency depreciation, the ownership of the seigneur remained only nominal. Instances of the same process occurred also in England and elsewhere though not so frequently as in France and surrounding regions.

(121) It is therefore a big historical mistake to state that the French Revolution abolished feudalism. This mistake is due to the makers of the revolution, who belonged to an age when the distinction between sounds and things had only just begun, and confusion was frequent between legal terminology and legal and social reality. The revolution abolished the land rent derived from Mediaeval feudal tenures. It did not change very profoundly the agrarian structure of the countries it touched at first hand, and scarcely needed do so either, since the farm structure was already essentially the family farm structure we know. The "inferior" ownership of French and neighbouring peasants was converted into full ownership. Generally, this implied the same kind of change as the abolition of hypothecs. The abolition of feudalism had gone on silently during the Late Middle Ages. The subsequent centuries had built up the farm structure of a "bourgeois" type still prevailing in Continental Western Europe.

The mistake as to the true nature of feudalism as a framework for land tenure maintained itself largely during the 19th century. Especially through the influence of Marxist theory, the term "feudalism" is nowadays used almost more often for phenomena different from classical feudalism. Because it seems now to be impossible to get rid of this use of the term, we will here adopt the slightly different term "quasi-feudalism" as a collective name for a number of tenure situations often described as feudal without being so in the legal sense.

It is only too characteristic of the confusion in the use of the terms that it is sometimes stated that feudalism should have survived especially long in Spain. As a matter of fact, true feudalism never prevailed in Spain. It existed mainly in some Northern regions of the country, which are nowadays considered to be the most progressive parts of Spain. It scarcely developed at all in the regions which are nowadays dominated by latifundia.

(122) Tenure situations which may be described as quasi-feudal are derived from two main background situations: land-lord-patriarchalism and tribal communities. Both historically and socially, the difference is important, even though there are forms of transition.

When some estates in the Iberian countries, and even in Italy, are sometimes described as feudal, this does not mean that the landlords have any civil rights over the persons of the tenants or their families. Juridically, there does not exist any feudalism at all in Europe to-day, nor has there existed any during the last half century. What we have in mind when talking about feudalism on large estates is the fact that a big landlord may have such a dominating position in the community that he can exercise a personal influence in matters where he has no legal right. This is of course only one of the many instances — occurring more or less in all societies — when legal and actual power do not coincide. The often crucial distinction between crime and policy is likely to depend on the political climate and the legal civilization of the country concerned. The individual situations where landlords act as local rulers vary too widely to be described as a comprehensive system, comparable to classical feudalism.

Another side of South European quasi-feudalism is the kind of title the landlord may have to the land. Nowadays, it is always full property according to Roman Law. The accession has in many instances taken place during the 19th century on the basis of feudal claims to common lands of the villages. These claims may not always have been juridically well founded, even in the framework of the rules under which they were advanced. In

other instances, much of the land came in the possession of the
landlords through 19th century secularization of common lands.
This operation was supposed to serve Liberal ideals when it
was carried through but materially led to a strengthening of the
positions of the class of big landlords.

(123) Of greater importance for the social history of modern
Europe is the dominance of landlords long existing in large parts
of Eastern Europe.

The so-called German colonization created a system of large
estates, cultivated by serfs with almost no civil rights, not only
in the eastern parts of the German empire but also in the Baltic
countries, Poland (with present Belorussia), and the Austrian
empire, including its non-German parts[a].

The Hungarian crown also expanded the rule of big landlords,
along with its military and political dominance of the Danube
Basin. Thus, the liberation of that region from the Turks
contributed to creating mighty social problems for the future.

As in these countries, and even more, landlords were the
dominant social class in 18th century Russia. There was scarcely
any compensation for the peasants, in the form of legal protection.
The claims for land reform could scarcely try to modify existing
institutions and therefore turned out so much the more radical.

However destructive the domination of the Turks over the
Balkans may have been from many points of view, it seems
nevertheless that it did not mean as much oppression of the
peasants as occurred in other parts of Eastern Europe. The
landlord, generally, claimed only a rent in money, without any
personal service[b]. Under the rule of the Turkish landlords, therefore, Balkan tribal society could to some extent survive, even
apart from its survival in free mountain communities. After
liberation, this allowed the constitution of the famous *zadruga*-
community, as a stage of transition towards the society of
individual peasants.

THE FORMATION OF HOLDINGS

(124) The way in which a feudal or quasi-feudal order was
broken up, be it long ago or recently, in many ways proved decisive
for the main features of both the farm structure and the systems
of tenure. These changes developed in constant interaction with

the changes in the organization of the peasant families, due to
the rate of transition from primitive self-sufficiency to integration
into a market economy. This process has also been of basic
importance for the size structure of holdings, as a background to
the methods by which social control is nowadays established over
the division and use of land. These regulations, to a large extent,
mean an intensification of State functions that in remote centuries
were the affair of groups and corporations responsible for what are
nowadays considered as public affairs.

In the Early Middle Ages, most of Western Europe's land was
organized as large domaines, managed on the basis of local self-
sufficiency. The division of farm land and the formation of
productive units (the operational holdings) lay in the hands of
the big landlords, and there was perhaps little risk of excessive
fragmentation. The famous Mediaeval *manse* is likely to have
been more of a cell in the domanial organization than an expression of familistic peasant independence, even if it be true
that it was the home of an enlarged family group. In the large
landed domains created by the German colonization, by the
Hungarian political expansion, or by the rise of power of the
Russian boyar's, equally, the landlords must have had rather a
free hand to create such tenant holdings as they found suitable.
The same may be true of the remaining zones of large landed
domains in Southern Europe, to-day.

(125) The progressive decline of domanial authority in Western
Europe, mostly during the Late Middle Ages, was accompanied
by the breaking up of the enlarged family group and the manse,
and the strengthening of the conjugal tenant family in its
possession of the land it cultivated. On large parts of the Continent
north of the Alps, the feudal concept of possession tended to
crystallize into a deliberate theory of divided ownership. These
forms of protected tenancy might go as far as to allow the tenant
to divide the land among his heirs, or even to sell his rights to
another tenant. Thus, the landlord's power to create such holdings
as he thought suitable slipped out of his hands in the same
moment as he ceased to be the leader of a great agricultural
enterprise and confined himself to merely receiving perpetual
rents. This process, for all that it was undeniably beneficial to
the farming class and the farming industry, at the same time let

loose anarchy of land division, promoting excessive subdivision of holdings and extreme fragmentation of plots. To some extent, landlords may have enforced rules of indivisibility of the peasant inheritance. However, most customs of restricted inheritance that were introduced from the Late Middle Ages and onwards seem to be due to the peasants themselves and their familistic sentiment.

(126) In Scandinavia, primitive freehold yeomanry succeeded in partially holding its own. Rules of indivisibility of farms were introduced in the Late Middle Ages, partly in the fiscal interest of the Crown, but also due to the peasants' interest in equal tax distribution. This development laid the foundation for the modern concept of the farm as a unit and prepared the ground for the reappearance of the indivisible freehold as the dominating agrarian feature. In particular, the resurgence of yeomanry in Denmark, during the 19th century, gives a strong impression of the importance of this Scandinavian tradition.

In the British Isles and in Southern Europe, the peasants largely failed to be incorporated in the feudal tenure system and therefore were not established as "sub-owners" in the way that was usual on the Continent. The dominance of British landlords and the weakness of other holders of rights in land made possible the big enclosures, from the Late Middle Ages to the early 19th century. The absentee character of the landlords in Ireland was an important hindrance to the formation and maintenance of large-scale enterprises in agriculture in that country. The dominance of small-scale tenancy made possible the 19th century appeal to full security of tenancy and even free sale of tenanted land. These claims recall to mind the Continental concept of divided ownership. Some decades of agitation and political struggle brought to victory not only these claims but also the full emancipation of most farm land in the hands of small-scale owner-operators. The process, thus rapidly brought about was, in substance, the same as had gone on slowly for centuries on the western parts of the Continent. The presence of the landlords in Great Britain, and the fact that they were often interested in the farming industry itself and not only in the income it might provide, accounts at least partly for the special development of that country.

In the Mediterranean countries, no clear features of development in these respects can be outlined. The secularization of ecclesiastical and communal land in the 19th century ought to have increased the landed property of big landlords, but the variations in their creation of holdings cannot be followed. As indicated in connection with the farm structure, in Chapter 3, there have been successive expansions and contractions of small-scale farming, following the variations in the economic possibility of small-scale production. The geographical diversity of these countries has probably caused the pressure towards formation of small holdings to be confined to zones where this was relatively the best under existing conditions.

(127) Divided ownership was done away with and protected tenants were made full owners, in part of Switzerland as early as the Late Middle Ages, in the Netherlands somewhat later through the effect of bourgeois capital penetration on the land, but on the bulk of the western Continent only through the French Revolution. At the same time, the land held by unprotected tenants became recognized as full property of the landlord. For the future, tenancy law became separated from inheritance rules. The only exception is in the lingering remnants of the institution called *emphyteusis* in the Mediterranean countries. Formation of owner-operated holdings could no more be influenced by the landlords, and society at large had not yet recognized its possible responsibilities in this respect.

One consequence of the Revolution was the increased importance of Roman Law. Especially through the French Code Civil and other legal codifications based upon it, many customs of restricted inheritance were done away with. This was the case not only in parts of Western Germany but also in many regions of France, Spain, and Portugal. The fact that such customs have mainly survived in Germanic countries, or countries under direct and strong Germanic influence such as Bohemia, has created the illusion, that such customs were specifically Germanic in origin [a]. It would be more appropriate to characterize them as offsprings of Late Mediaeval legal civilization.

(128) A parallel development of liberating peasant tenant holdings, making them freeholds, took place in Eastern Europe at a much later epoch. General development was later, and the

rule of landlords was still the dominating agrarian feature in the
19th century and remained so in eastern Germany, Hungary and
part of Poland until quite recently. There was progressive
dissolution of the large estates into small-scale tenancy farms
during the liberal era and therefore the idea of divided ownership
did not occur. The choice was a radical one: between precarious
contract terms and full independence.

In early stages of peasant liberation, the tendency was to
create loose associations for common landowning, more or less
founded upon tribal organization, like the Balkan *zadruga* and
the Russian *mir*. Both of them could to some extent counterbalance the common drawbacks of peasant proprietorship, such
as unrestricted land division and uncontrolled fragmentation.
This kind of organization, however, never lasted very long and
had for the most part lost its importance at the beginning of this
century, or shortly after.

Increased commercial contacts made self-supporting local
nuclei out of date. The enlarged family group was progressively
dissolved, as it had been in Western Europe in the expansion
period of the High Middle Ages. Lingering remnants are to be
seen in some remote parts of the Balkans but no longer have any
sizeable importance. At the dissolution of the ownership associations and the enlarged family group in Eastern Europe, generally
in the later half of the 19th century, there were no institutions
to form a link with operational holdings, by restricted inheritance
or by other measures. In the Balkans, on the contrary, the influence of Roman Law in its Byzantine form only served to
strengthen the liberalizing influence of the legal system of the
Code Civil[a]. In some of the most Western parts of the area,
however, in Bohemia and some other regions under Austrian rule,
this development started so much earlier that the whole pattern
came to be more similar to that of Western Europe. Strong
demographic increase was the driving force behind the land reform
in Eastern Europe. In time, more and more land was split up
into often very fragmented small holdings, and in the area there
are many extreme instances of the inconveniencies of free land
division.

(129) Despite the dominance of Liberal thought in economic
and legal matters, there were quite a few instances of an active

land policy even in the 19th century and at the beginning of the 20th. The land reforms only represented some of the most dramatic instances of departure from Liberal ideas. Homestead policy in many Western countries also underline the impression that it was already felt that the farming industry could not be left quite as alone as urban industries. In some countries, there was also at an early stage some elements of legislation on forestry which forecast the modern idea that society as a whole should have a say in the use of the nation's fixed capital.

In overt opposition to Liberal ideas was the Socialist line of thought, which throughout the 19th century recognized the basic importance of the land question. It was complemented, after the nineties, by the Catholic social program for expanding small-scale ownership of land. Since the first World War, the problems of self-sufficiency in food have produced more and more public regulation of the farming industry, and the second war only brought to maturation tendencies that were already in existence before it. The increasing demand for an active social policy has also contributed to bring about profound changes in the legal structure of agricultural enterprises. At present, it may well be said that the very foundation for land law in Europe is profoundly different from what it was before World War I, or even during the inter-war period. Distinguishing some main lines in recent developments in this field will help to make clear the importance of the change and to characterize the present legal structure.

Before entering upon these questions of recent legal and social development, something must be said on the statistical distribution of landed property and tenancy.

LAND OWNERSHIP
(STATISTICAL)

(130) Throughout the span of modern agrarian history with which we are here concerned, there are two main statistical observations concerning landed property. One is that interest shifts from units of property to those of management (the operational holdings). The other lies in the scarcity and the limited reliability of statistics on landed property.

On the former point, it seems appropriate to state that the

shift from interest in property distribution to interest in the distribution of operational holdings or farms is symptomatic of modern developments. The holder has gradually become more important than the owner. Inversely, it can be stated that the degree to which the stress lies upon one and the other aspect is significant of the degree to which this modern development has been realized.

Statistics on landed property were available in most countries in Europe around the beginning of the period here under review, or slightly before. In England, figures were compiled in 1875, in France in 1882, in Germany, Austria, Hungary, and Russia, around 1900. Since then, very few statistics of this kind have been compiled in Europe. They are nowadays available mainly from Italy, Spain, and Portugal.

Of course, in countries where most land is operated by the owners themselves, the distribution of landed property comes rather close to the farm structure. It is not in these cases that the distribution of landed property is really crucial, but in the countries where much land is let. It then becomes interesting to know whether those owning the rented land are a vast stratum of small-scale capitalists who have placed their personal savings in land, or a small group of large-scale capitalists, capable of managing and dominating the land market to their advantage. The issue is interesting mainly where landholders are unprotected. If, as the case is in most countries of Europe to-day, leaseholders are efficiently protected, the power of the owners becomes less important and the structure of the owner group less interesting to observe.

(131) Part of the social phenomenon of the distribution of landed property can be made comprehensible through figures on modes of tenure and on mixed tenures. Such figures will illustrate mainly the negative side of the issue so to speak, that is the relative lack of ownership among those who cultivate the land. The positive side of ownership concentration, or the degree to which landed property is concentrated in a few hands (or the contrary, as the case may be), could be fully known only through statistics on ownership where all land belonging to the same owner is shown together as a statistical unit. Such material is only very seldom available.

The difficulties on this point are illustrated by an enquiry on the figures derived from the so-called New Domesday Book in England, which was compiled in 1875. Double returns for landlords owning land in different regions made the 525 members of the peerage to be counted as over 1500 "owners" [a]. The same factor makes it in most other instances extremely difficult to assess the real importance of the concentration of landed property, except through investigations similar to the English enquiry we just quoted. All available statements on the concentration of landed property in Spain and Portugal are, for instance, grossly inaccurate because they are founded on figures based on registration of property rights separately within each administrative district. Such figures often illustrate more clearly the general degree of subdivision and fragmentation of the land than the distribution of landed property. The latter may thus be much more concentrated than indicated by such figures [b].

A remarkable exception is in the Hungarian statistics on landed property which were attached to the population census of 1900 [c]. It is stressed here that the results are not a farm census. They indicate the distribution of landed wealth among persons in different parts of the country. A holding was registered where the holder resided, not where the holding was located. Thus, the great concentration of landed property was illustrated.

As a consequence of these considerations, it must be stated that a general table showing the concentration or dispersion of *landed property*, as opposed to land holdings, cannot be drawn up with any degree of accuracy. Only in some few instances can the elements be produced. For comparative purposes, property distribution can be approached mainly through the indirect information given by the figures on distribution of the modes of tenure.

OWNERSHIP VERSUS TENANCY
(STATISTICAL)

(132) The coincidence of the farm structure with the property structure thus depends upon the dominance of owner-operators. Conversely, the existence of tenancy implies differences between farm structure and property structure, the more important the

larger the share of the land that is held by tenants. The main interest of the tenure structure is in the distribution of decision-making, that is in the degree of independency that characterizes the holder of the land, with all the implications it has upon the economic results of his farming and upon his social status. In this respect, the statistical information only gives a one-sided, basic information, which must thereafter be interpreted in the light of the legal rules and social customs that give the tenure structure its content.

For a judgement on the impact of the different modes of tenure in different countries, it is therefore of first interest to show the quantitative importance of existing modes of tenure. In accordance with our general approach, to assess the volume of the productive resources and their distribution, we will first view the distribution of the farm land on the categories of land tenure. Unfortunately, weighting is impossible at this stage, on the basis of published materials. Even so, it will to some extent be possible to evaluate the significance of the unweighted figures in the light of what has been shown above on the basis of the weighting thus far attempted. Also the regional distribution of the modes of tenure can contribute to characterize them. The following table can be drawn up to show the distribution of farm land, under the definitions of each census.

(133) As a comment on this table, it may first be underlined that owner-operated land predominates in most of Europe. This is especially the case in several countries not included on the table (Finland, and Eastern Europe outside the USSR). Soviet land tenure does not fit into the pattern here discussed and will be commented upon later.

Rented land is more common, however, in Great Britain, the Benelux countries, and Italy. In France, there is strong regional differentiation, with rented land dominant in the north western parts of the country, by and large the richest from the agricultural point of view. Also in Sweden, there are regions where rented land occupies not very much less than half of the cultivated land, and these regions are also among the most fertile of the country. Even in Western Germany, where leaseholds play a much smaller part, they are more important in Niedersachsen than in the agriculturally less fortunate southern Länder.

TABLE 24. *Tenure structure in selected countries*: *per cent distribution of farm area, under the definition of each census*

Country	Year	Owner-operated	Rented	Share-cropped	Under other modes of tenure
England and Wales . .	1950	38.0	62.0	—	—
Scotland	1950	42,5	57.5	—	—
N. Ireland	1950	100*	—*	—	—
Eire	1949	95.7	4.3	—	—
Norway	1949	90*	10*	—	—
Sweden	1951	74.2	25.8	—	—
Denmark	1946	93.7	6.3	—	—
Netherlands	1950	44.1	55.9	—	—
Belgium	1950	32.3	67.7	—	—
France	1892	52.9	36.3	10.8	—
,, ...	1929	60	30	10	—
,, ...	1946	53.9	33.5	10.5	2.1
Germany	1907	86.1	12.8	—	1.1
W. Germany	1939	87.5	11.5	—	1*
,, ...	1949	87.5	12.2	—	0.3
Austria	1951	95.3	4.7	—	—
Czechoslovakia	1930	90.1	9.9	—	—
Hungary	1949	82	18	—	—
Rumania	1913[a]	60	40	..	—
,, ...	1948	94.4	1.5	2.8	1.3
Bulgaria	1934	90.0	10.0	—	—
Greece	1950	91.7	5.4	2.1	0.8
Italy	1930[b]	66.9	14.7	18.4	—
,, ...	1947[b]	48.1	18.6	33.3	—
Spain	1952	63.6	22.3	14.1	—

[a] Old Kingdom only. The same territory, in 1948, shows the same structure as the rest of Rumania in 1948.

[b] The 1930 and the 1947 figures are not comparable because they are founded upon a different approach to certain tenure forms causing a different limitation of what should be reckoned as operated by the big landowners themselves. The 1947 figures are best adapted for a comparison with the rest of the table, while the 1930 figures also allow comparisons with the number of farms and the occurrence of mixed tenures.

Apparently, leaseholds appear to be associated with a high level of agricultural development. The French material especially seems to support this conclusion. The same trend is seen also in Norway[a].

On the other hand, the part played by "owner-operators" in the Mediterranean countries is overstated in the figures. The high percentages of owner-operators include many large estates which are only formally run by the owners themselves but in reality by managers who carry out operations of an often rather simple and backward, extensive type of farming with very little supervision, if any at all, from the owners. It would have been more instructive if this type of situation would have been set apart as a special category. It would then have become obvious that only a minor share of the land in these countries is farmed by the owners themselves. This, of course, upsets all the conclusions on the role of peasant ownership and different forms of land renting and enforces a re-formulation of the problem.

For one thing, sharecropping is not comparable to leaseholds with fixed rent, whether in cash or in kind. It is well known that sharecropping is a symptom of lack of capital among the farming class. In France and the Iberian countries it is also known that it is associated with poor soils and backward methods of farming, and with regions where such conditions are frequent [b]. In Italy, the situation is more complicated because of the various types of sharecropping in that country.

Historically, the trend has been towards increased importance of peasant ownership. The Rumanian figures are an example of the tendency of the late 19th and early 20th land reform movements. A similar trend, though slower and less radical, has also operated in the Scandinavian countries [c]. Russian statistics on landed property from 1882 and 1897 show that, even between the waves of land reform policy, more and more land was slipping out of the hands of the big landlords, partly to be converted into peasant property [d].

On the continent of Western Europe, however, the development has been almost nil. The stability revealed by the German figures is rather striking, and the change in the French figures is mainly illusory. In fact, the definitions of the censuses were so different that they may alone explain the whole difference in the figures, and there is scarcely any evidence of real changes in the tenure structure [e]. The coincidence of the percentage distribution in 1892 and 1946 seems, on the contrary, to indicate that very little has changed. Of course, many things have happened locally or even regionally, even though it is seldom that the change can be grasped statistically [f]. The national picture has barely undergone any great change.

(134) Despite what has been said in the preceding chapter on the difficulties of comparing the number of farms in one country with those of another, it will in this connection be interesting to

compare the distribution of farm numbers in various types of tenure. In countries where a greater proportion of the number than of the area of the farms is operated by the owners, this will indicate that the owner-operated farms are smaller than the rented ones; and conversely. This, of course, has some importance for a judgement on the socio-economic bearings of tenancy. The following table has been drawn up to show the importance of this factor.

TABLE 25. *Tenure structure in selected countries: per cent distribution of the number of farms, under the definition of each census*

Country	Year	Owner-operated	Rented	Share-cropped	Under other modes of tenure
England and Wales . .	1950	42.7	57.3	—	—
Scotland	1950	26.7	73.3	—	—
Norway	1949	91.3	8.7	—	—
Finland.	1950	97.6	2.4	—	—
Sweden.	1951	82.6	17.4	—	—
Denmark	1946	96.5	3.5	—	—
Belgium	1950	36.4	63.6	—	—
France	1892	71.8	21.4	6.8	—
,, ...	1929	74.6	20.0	5.4	—
,, ...	1946	65.2	26.2	6.6	—
W. Germany	1949	80.5	19.5	—	—
Austria.	1900	90*	10*	—	—
,, ...	1951	89.8	10.2	—	—
Czechoslovakia	1930	79.6	20.4	—	—
Hungary	1949	94.5	3.5	—	—
Bulgaria	1934	92.4	7.6	—	—
Greece	1929	80.7	5.9	3.3	10.1
,, ...	1950	97.2	1.9	0.5	0.4
Italy.	1930	69.4	15.8	14.8	—
Spain	1952	56.3	31.4	12.3	—
Portugal	1950 [a]	76	24	—	—
Portugal South	1950 [a]	80.3	19.7	—	—
,, ,,	1952 [b]	78.8	14.2	7.0	—

[a] These data refer to the status of holders, rather than to holdings, and are derived from population census data. They serve to illustrate the general distribution, since the consistency with farm census data is good, judging from appearances in the South.
[b] Farm census data for the southernmost parts of the country. The figures derived from the population census and referring to the South cover the same area as these farm census data.

(135) When comparing the two tables, it is interesting to note that rented farms take a larger share of the area than of the number of farms — that is, they are larger — than the owner-

operated ones, in England and France. The result, as regards the latter country, is quite obvious and appears in all three censuses despite the differences in definitions. It is also true of both lease-hold and sharecropping, taken separately. The opposite is apparently true in Spain, where the extensively cultivated latifundia are at least partly returned as owner-operated. It is also the case in countries like Germany and Czechoslovakia, that is in agriculturally well developed countries where owner-operators predominate. In Italy, apparently, the position is uncertain. In that country, it is possible that regional contrasts counterbalance each other in the national picture. Some regions have features similar to those of Spain, others are reminiscent of the English farm system, others are more like Continental peasant farming.

It would therefore barely be appropriate to ascribe to tenancy a distinct role on the ladder of agricultural development, regardless of the general conditions of the country. It appears as if owner-operated land predominates in cases where the land is too poor to pay any rent at all, as in French Massif Central and the mountain regions of Southern Europe. It seems to be predominant also where farming has been intensified to such a level that scarcely anyone except the family farmer could achieve the high labor input required and make it economic. Sharecropping would represent a variation of the former situation, under conditions in which the farming class has either never got hold of the land, for historical reasons, or again and again looses its grip on it, because of great variations in weather and harvests. Capitalist enterprise, operating with a considerable amount of hired labor, on the other hand represents an intermediate situation, when the land is fertile enough to create considerable profit, and yet not sufficiently fertile —or not fortunately enough situated in relation to markets — to pay for the over-input of labor which is usual on small family farms. The association between the capitalist principle and fixed rent contracts then seems obvious. This analysis explains many features of the distribution of tenure forms in Europe. Of course it cannot explain them all. Historical incidents have created too many of the actual features to allow them to express clearly any kind of general law.

MIXED TENURES

(136) The picture of the distribution of the modes of tenure is substantially modified because of the occurrence of mixed forms of tenure. This factor partly underlies the smallness of rented holdings in Germany and their large size in France. Statistically, the impact of mixed tenures is difficult to grasp. There seems to be a general tendency to underestimate the phenomenon.

In Tables 24 and 25, the mixed tenures have been spread over the "pure" types. Some of the quoted farm censuses have themselves assessed the real amounts of land rented and owned, on the basis of separate returns, while others have made more or less justifiable assumptions as to the impact of mixed tenures. These observations serve to underline the importance of the following figures.

TABLE 26. *Mixed tenures, in selected countries, as per cent of the number of holdings and of the farm area, according to the definitions of each census*

Country	Year	Per cent of	
		Farm number	Farm area
Belgium	1950	53	52
France	1892	15*	..
,, ...	1929	19.6	..
W. Germany	1907	32	40
,, ...	1939	48.1	29.8
,, ...	1949	53.5	32.5
Austria	1951	25.2	14.0
Czechoslovakia	1930	36.6	..
Hungary.	1949	5	..
Bulgaria	1934	29	34.5
Greece.	1929	0.5	..
,, ...	1950	11.1	16.6
Italy	1930	14.8	14.0
Portugal South	1952	13.9	..

(137) The lack of data from many countries does not by any means imply that mixed tenures were of negligible importance in these countries. On the contrary it seems to mean, in most cases, that the phenomenon is overlooked, hidden, so that we cannot see the differences in the picture of the tenure situation

they would indicate. The point can be illustrated by quoting some
contrasting information from Spain. Despite the fact that this
information derives from different periods, the contrast is too
striking to be due to any sudden real changes. The recent
tenancy enquiry thus states that owner-operated farms are
dominant, not only in Spain as a whole but also in most provinces,
and especially in those on the plateau — in Castilla and Leonesa [a].
By contrast, it is stated in a German enquiry from the thirties
on agrarian conditions on the northern part of the plateau
(Leonesa and Old Castilla) [b] that mixed tenures are in a large
majority, as far as the numbers of farms were concerned. On the
plateau, at least 80 per cent of the farms had some rented land,
in some provinces as León, Palencia, Burgos and Valladolid even
90 per cent. In the provinces of Valladolid and Zamora, less than
5 per cent of all farmers relied entirely upon land they owned
themselves. On the other hand, pure leaseholds embrace less than
10 per cent of the farms on the plateau. These figures indicate
that rented land is of a very great importance.

It may of course be a matter of judgement how the mixed
tenures should be allocated as between mainly owner-operated
and mainly rented. One opinion holds that the ownership of the
farm buildings should be regarded as decisive. What is true in
this view is that it is the ownership of the bulk of the capital
value of the farm rather than of the bulk of unweighted land
area that should count. Even if the problem is formulated in
this way, it would change very little of the judgement concerning
the Spanish plateau, where most farm buildings are simple and
have little capital value. It is difficult to avoid the impression
that the great importance of mixed tenures in Spain has led to
a certain under-estimation of the part played by tenancy in the
country. Also some data from Greece seem to indicate that
mixed tenures are underestimated in official statistics, which may
have led to an underestimation of the importance of tenancy [c].

Some regional data from the Netherlands also reveal an
astonishingly great importance for mixed tenures. In a certain
region, there were 40 mixed holdings as against 42 entirely
rented and 12 entirely owned [d].

It is in this context that the German and French figures on
leasehold and mixed tenures should be read. The German increase

for both may be true and result from the rural exodus, making still more farmers to rent land from urban relatives or from land-buyers who bought out the relatives. The change may however also, at least partly, be due to more and more exact registration of mixed tenures, in cases where only little land is rented. Evidence is available that rented land, in farms under mixed tenure, plays a rather important and probably increasing role in Germany [e]. In France, the registration of mixed tenures may be even less reliable than in Germany, and the whole phenomenon is likely to be underestimated. The fact that mixed tenures appeared to be far more frequent in the departments of Alsace-Lorraine than in any other region of France may thus derive at least partly from a difference in the statistical tradition. The method of ascribing the entire holding to the category of tenure that is dominant, as followed in the French census of 1946, clearly involves the risk of overestimating the farmers' ownership of their land, partly because of factors in rural psychology and partly because of statistical overlapping tending in the same direction [f].

As a conclusion it is thus appropriate to state that both the mixed tenures and, as a consequence thereof, tenancy, are under-estimated in most countries. Further, it may be stressed that the frequency of mixed tenures tends to weaken the independence of large strata of farmers. Regardless of whether a man rents 60 per cent or only 40 per cent of the land he runs, he will in both cases be utterly dependent on the rented land and the conditions of lease.

These considerations, together with what has been said in the preceding section of this chapter, lead to the conclusion that tenancy is of dominating importance not only in Great Britain and the Benelux countries, but also in France, Italy, Spain, and Portugal. Its importance in Germany and other countries where owner-operated farms predominate is greater than it might appear at first sight. It may, despite everything, remain of some importance in Eastern Europe. Even the large co-operative farms may sometimes represent instances of mixed tenure, as aforeseen by the Bulgarian statute on such farms [g].

LIMITATIONS TO THE RIGHTS OF OWNERS

(138) For decades, the legal and social content of land ownership in Europe has been undergoing profound changes, the outcome of which is a completely changed concept of both land
ownership and land tenure. The new concept differs radically
from the classical, Liberal (and Romanistic) concept, and in some
respects it is reminiscent of some of the concepts of Mediaeval
land law which we have briefly outlined at the beginning of this
chapter.

In a negative sense, these changes have mainly hit the landowner. His liberty to deal with his property as he likes is now
limited, and it becomes more and more difficult for non-farmers
to acquire agricultural land. Whatever the position of the owner
may be, his liberty to dispose of his property is now smaller
than it used to be.

In general, these new dispositions are in favor of the tenant
farmers, especially from the viewpoints of this book. Their
possible choice of action is however also limited in the purely
economic field as well as indirectly in some aspects of the land-
labor issue. We will here first focus attention on a set of rules,
old or new, that tend to limit the freedom of action of the
landowner (whether landlord or farmer). Those more directly
tending to protect the tenant farmer will be dealt with in a later
section of this chapter. For the moment, the main concern is
the tendency to preserve the agricultural enterprise as a legal
entity, that is, measures against subdivision of farms and in
favor of the farm as a legal unit.

(139) The idea that the agricultural holding might be preserved
by means of treating it as a legal entity is one of great practical
importance in modern economic and social policy. Despite this
it has so far seldom been pursued in a consistent and systematic
way. We are not here concerned with the mainly Romanistic
discussion whether the agricultural enterprise should be regarded
as a legal entity *in se*. The main result of that discussion, which
appears to be negative, is so much in accordance with our
positivist approach to legal phenomena as not to need direct
justification. Apart from the sometimes arbitrary definitions of
an agricultural enterprise, there are many examples of agricultural

enterprises that are too ephemeral to be legal entities[a]. Not the existence, but the need for legal preservation of the agricultural enterprise is the centre of the discussion. In this connection, we can only underline the view taken by A. FINZI, that positive law has to create new kinds of objects, in order to meet the needs of social utility[b].

In all this discussion, the concern is with agricultural holdings in the sense of the physical substance of farming enterprises. The units of agricultural property — the sum of land owned by one owner — are thus involved mainly when cultivated by one farmer as a unit. Inheritance rules on entailed estates and the like are in no way part of modern social policy but are rather objects for suppression. They have also by now virtually ceased to be of any importance in Europe.

(140) Most rules on indivisibility of farms have as their underlying practical reason the economic danger in treating parts of an agricultural enterprise as a mere sum of objects which can at any time be disposed of one by one. Other considerations, such as fiscal interests, or the special concerns of families or a familistic society at large are, regarded closely, mainly special consequences of this general principle, and so is the modern tendency towards large-scale planning of social economy.

The productive process of agriculture is not only to a large extent long-term, but also one for which interruptions may turn out especially disastrous. Unlike industrial manufacture, where work may be stopped and taken up again when it is suitable to finish the goods, agriculture's productive process goes on mainly within living plants and animals. Their growth has its optimum rhythm, reacting unfavorably against disturbances. This is so much the more important because of the length of the production cycle, which is seldom shorter than a year but often stretches over several years or decades. The risk of soil destruction also calls for a certain continuity in the way the land is being managed, if a capital asset with natural limits is not to be destroyed or diminished for the future. Farm buildings, finally, represent heavy investments which seldom can be adequately used for other purposes.

Breaking up of productive units, with their often carefully calculated equilibrium of land, buildings, dead stock and livestock, therefore often involves serious risks of capital destruction, detrimental not only to the holder and acting as a disincentive against the holder's capital formation. It may be to the detriment also, and under certain circumstances even more, of the holder's creditors, either private or public. As public creditors, we may here reckon the State, as creditor for taxes and services, and the whole Nation, as creditor for safe food supply from the farming class in exchange for the economic security provided by a modern society.

(141) Views opposite to those here referred to are also heard, though nowadays with less force than during the Liberal era, as arguments against an active land policy and its legal framework. In Germany, recently, there has been a discussion whether such a policy is in the whole compatible with civil freedom. Also the political struggle around the new legislation on lease contracts which filled much of Italy's political life as late as 1954 and 1955, is to a great extent about the basic principle of ownership rights. The Liberal and Romanistic concept of property is, of course, difficult to harmonize with coercive rules on the formation and subdivision of farm units. Even land fragmentation, which is rather generally condemned as one of the worst evils of agrarian society, is sometimes to some extent defended from the viewpoint that it would contribute to giving enterprising farmers a fair chance to improve their position, and to keeping a sound balance between capital and labor.

(142) Besides considerations of economic order, also the pressure of social unrest is a factor determining legal policy in this field. Both economic and social considerations are however always related to ideological concepts. In the ultimate analysis any policy implies a purely political valuation. Even to the extent that the arguments do correspond with rational factors of technical and economic order, or to obviously urgent social needs, they are likely to be more valid or less valid according to the conditions of the country. The decision, as to which considerations that should be preferred, is a matter of economic and social rather than of legal science. Even in this section, where the legal side of the institutional framework is viewed in a somewhat artificial isolation, it is however important to keep in mind the nature of the driving forces behind the different legal issues in the sphere.

(143) In the modern trend to shift stress from mainly private towards mainly public interests as guides for legal policy, a number of main lines can be distinguished by which the agricultural enterprises are protected from subdivision, and treated as legal entities. They represent different approaches and thereby reveal different kinds of interests involved. In due order, we will try to analyze:

a) Implicit rules of non-divisibility in the interest of private claims. Here the concern is not with the farming industry, and the protection therefore benefits the agricultural enterprise only inasmuch as it happens to coincide with the object of the claims.

b) Public control of land division. This negative issue is aimed at being to the benefit of the farming industry but has, in its bare form, limited effects, as regards the agricultural enterprises.

c) Undivided transition of farms when inheritance is to be divided (German *Anerbenrecht*, and similar institutions). This kind of rule concerns mainly owner-operated farms since tenancies are nowadays seldom protected to such a degree as to enable the heirs to divide them among themselves.

d) Homestead policy, which not seldom implies rules on complete indivisibility for the holdings created through that policy. By definition, such rules could affect a small part of the farming industry only.

e) Tenancy protection. Even this far-reaching type of regulation may in itself prove very incomplete as a protection for the agricultural enterprises, among other things because of the occurrence of mixed tenures.

f) Complete regulation of the formation of holdings (comprehensive land policy).

In this section, the four first types will be dealt with together with some aspects of the sixth type. Two other sections will try to deal with types e and f in a comprehensive way.

(144) The legislation of the Liberal era did not show much interest in the indivisibility of agricultural enterprises, since this was deemed to be mainly the affair of the parties concerned. However, the relations between these parties — as landlord and tenant, or as creditor and debtor — might call for restrictions in the freedom of the tenant, or of the debtor, as the case might be, in order to make easier the establishment of standard

contracts. Concern with the simplification of sales of real estate also contributed to creating a set of rules, with variations in most countries where such transactions are at all common, which virtually led to ascribing some kind of entity, if only for limited periods, to many agricultural enterprises.

The coherence between the elements that constituted an agricultural enterprise was strengthened through rules about fixtures and accessories. Not only buildings and trees, but in many instances also live stock and dead stock, and even seed and fertilizers "destined to the use of the farm" are counted as accessories to real estate and not as chattel.[a] From these rules others were easily derived, obliging the tenant farmer to maintain the holding and not to let its value deteriorate[b]. The increasing importance of invested capital in relation to the value of the land itself also tends to increase the importance of these rules.

On the other hand, the principle that all fixtures belong to the landlord has often acted as a powerful disincentive to the tenant farmer, and still does so in some areas of Southern Europe. There is a strong incentive to perpetuate lease contracts, but this is not the only solution. Rules on adequate compensation for improvements would do equally well, as in England and Sweden for a long time. The tradition that the rules on fixtures and accessories benefited landlords more than tenants has, however, formed an important part of the background to the modern impetus towards security of tenancy and towards peasant proprietorship.

This was the more so because the protection from subdivision here discussed referred only to the holding (the land rented under one contract), and not to the agricultural enterprise as such. And even the holding was only protected for the period of the lease.

Also the rules about an entire holding as security for debt have to some extent worked out as a virtual prohibition of subdivision of farms, even according to Civil Law only and long before public regulation of land division started or became effective. These rules, however, refer to units of property and thus touch the enterprise only insofar as both coincide.

As a whole, therefore, such rules have had the effect of slowing down somewhat the tendency to farm subdivision and un-economic units. They may also in many instances have strengthened the tendency to think about the farm as a coherent unit. But this alone would hardly have led to any really strong protection of agricultural enterprises.

(145) Excessive land fragmentation following upon unlimited freedom of land division is one of the classical cases where public regulation of private land has been contemplated rather early. Some features of this activity have been touched upon, in Chapter 2. Measures to prevent land fragmentation were in early epochs mainly rooted in the fiscal requirement of preserving the units paying land taxes. Nowadays comprehensive country planning, analogous to coercive planning of urban areas, also begins to play a part. In both instances, the starting point for negative regulations lies in the units of land registration. If they coincide with agricultural enterprises, the effect may be that of complete control of farm division. The most common case is, however, at least in most parts of Europe outside the USSR, that the cadastral unit is part of a holding only, often a very small part. This reduces the effect of such measures to that of slowing down farm subdivision and making its effect less destructive.

The weakest type of protection is thus that which prohibits the subdivision of individual plots below a certain minimum size. In order to be efficient, such rules require a good land register or, at least, a welltrained administrative service. An old Portuguese rule that individual parcels of land must not be subdivided below the size of a half hectare has obviously turned out to be inefficient [a]. In the framework of a farm structure where short-term leases and mixed tenures are dominating features, there was not very much to support the rule. A similar Bulgarian rule seems to have been somewhat more efficient, possibly because the pesant proprietors (there was not much tenancy in the country) counteracted the lack of a land register by their familiarity with local administration [b]. A similar rule has recently been at least contemplated in Greece as a measure to control land fragmentation.

In connection with modern consolidation activity, it has been observed more and more that consolidation ought to be complemented by rules limitating the freedom of land division, lest the result of the consolidations be undone relatively soon. The recent Spanish consolidation statute has thus enacted that minima

shall be established in each case below which the parcels laid
out at the consolidation must never be subdivided [c]. This statute
is also of interest because it identifies, in its Article 3, the minimum
plot in irrigated zones with the normal size of a family allotment
garden. The latter units, insofar as they have been covered by
consolidation schemes and subsequent registration of the results
thus become indivisible for the future. The corresponding French
statute, which is slightly prior to the Spanish one, does not
directly stipulate any minimum size of plot but states generally
that eventual subdivision of the plots created through consolidation must be authorized by competent authorities guaranteeing,
among other things, a good layout for the future [d].

Recently, the importance of consolidation of agricultural
enterprises has been increasing, since the attitude has changed
from stress upon property units to stress upon the enterprise. The
tradition of the 19th century was mostly concerned with the
consolidation of property units. The new French statute puts the
"exploitation" first, even if it also aims at bringing the property
units into rational shape. The Spanish statute, although later,
still talks about consolidation of property in the first place.

The recent German consolidation statute seems less concerned
with this problem. When most farms are owner-operated and a
great part of the rented land forms minor shares of the mixed
holdings, the separate consolidation of property units may be
less important [e].

Even though these regulations in connection with consolidation
legislation are interesting as expressions of changing attitudes in
favor of the agricultural enterprise rather than landed property,
they would not in themselves lead to indivisibility of the farm
units. Mere land division regulations could arrive at such a result
mainly in the case where the whole farm is registered as one
cadastral unit. Even here, the result would be most likely to
occur if the consolidation was radical, bringing together the land
of the farm in one single block or a few parcels only. On this point,
Scandinavian experience is instructive. Because of fiscal traditions, the farm became the registration unit. Consolidations in
the 18th and 19th centuries, on this basis, turned out to be a
success. The result was a dominating system of en-bloc holdings,
largely coinciding with the farm units. Indivisibility rules had

here their best chance to operate. Even in cases where the farm was still constituted of a modest number of separate plots, kept together as an hypothetical unit in the land register, this kind of unit proved to have a considerable psychological effect, so that renewed fragmentation was avoided. A regional exception to this rule in a province in northern Sweden, where the fiscal tradition was different and the 19th century consolidations failed, only underlines the conclusion[f]. In Denmark, the results of the consolidations have also been protected by the rule that no land subdivision could be given legal effect unless each of the resulting new farms got adequate farm buildings[g].

(146) The rule that a farm should be taken over by one heir only was, as already mentioned, widely spread before the French Revolution. Even since then, it has had much larger application in popular practice than in statute law[a]. The French Code Civil, in its original form, was not directly hostile to the practice of maintaining the farm undivided when inheritance was to be divided, but made this expressly dependent upon the guaranteeing of full compensation to the other heirs. Therefore it came in practice to act as an incentive towards increased subdivision and fragmentation of the land. Its revised form in France, introduced successively by statutes in 1938 and 1943, secures undivided transition of farms that do not seriously exceed the size of a family farm[b]. Legal development after the Revolution left the German-speaking countries as the classical ground of *Anerbenrecht,* or the rule that only one of the heirs takes over the undivided farm[c]. The rule became specially famous through its modification into the *Erbhof-system* in Germany in the thirties[d]. The abolition of the latter, after the war, left room for the reintroduction of *Anerbenrecht* in parts of Western Germany only. Eastern Germany seems to have avoided any similar institution. Rules of this kind are federal law in Switzerland, though with varying application in the cantons.

A similar regulation has recently been enacted in Czechoslovakia[e]. It may be seen as part of the Socialist regulation of rural economy but, since the other Eastern countries do not have such rules, it may be more appropriate to regard the Czechoslovak inheritance rule as inspired by the legal tradition from the period of Austrian domination.

The renewal of restricted inheritance in the Mediterranean countries will be mentioned in connection with their homestead policy. In the Scandinavian countries, undivided inheritance follows from the general prohibition of land division, but not from inheritance regulations, except in Norway as far as the *odelsret* is applicable [f].

(147) A special case of indivisibility of an agricultural holding is that of the Russian *dvor*. In Czarist time, it constituted a peculiar form of indivisible holding, belonging collectively to the family living on it or originating from it, thus even to such members of the family that had migrated from the land and desired to return to it. The land area of the *dvor* was subject to periodical changes, at least in the very numerous villages that were framed to the type of constitution known as the *mir*. These changes took place in order to adjust the size of the dvor, both according to the number of the people living on the dvor and to the number of people living in the whole village.

A vestige of this institution still exists in the Soviet Union. The buildings of the family household in the kolkhoz, with the live stock and dead stock of the household, form the *kolkhoznyĭ dvor*, which is a unit of individual property, to which the individual garden plot (generally not more than a half hectare) is assigned in perpetual usufruct (like the common kolkhoz land, these plots are formally State property). But this unit of individual property does not belong to any specific individual; it belongs to those living on it. Nobody can thus be said to be the heir of a defunct member of the dvor, since those surviving only remain in possession of the dvor as before. Russian doctrine expressly claims that the dvor is itself the *subject* (and not the object) of individual property [a]. This construction, though obviously determined by specific Russian traditions, at the same time arrives at avoiding the recognition of individual persons as subjects of property rights to means of production.

(148) The idea of creating a stratum of small indivisible family homes originated from a wish to meet the social needs of land reform without upsetting the bulk of the farming industry. At the same time the need was felt, when land was being allotted to people from the economically weakest part of rural society, to protect the new holdings from being broken up either through

division of inheritance or through execution of claims for debt. As far as the holdings created by this kind of policy remained a special stratum, with explicit or implicit rules that the new units should not be broken up, these measures did not directly contribute to solving the problem of farm indivisibility in general [a].

Even insofar as the homesteads were not from the outset protected against subdivision, they are now so in most countries, through general rules on land division.

Of a somewhat wider scope, from the point of view just examined, is the creation of new small holdings in Italy, Spain, and Portugal, where it may be seen as the first step towards a comprehensive land policy. This character is also underlined by the presence of parallel rules on model farms which are exempt from reform measures. At least in the two Iberian countries, rules are already in force to the effect that the holdings created by the colonization institutions shall remain indivisible family property [b]. The same intention can be credited to the makers of the Italian land reform, even though the long period of transition before the holdings are fully paid cause the point not to be very urgent. Because of general rules on security for debt, these new holdings cannot be either sold or divided over many years to come.

More important and comprehensive than these wide-spread rules limiting the owner's free disposition of his property are those aiming at protecting the tenant farmer against the landlord.

TENANCY PROTECTION

(149) Protection of tenant farmers by granting them long-term, life-time or even inheritable possession of holdings, is a method of preventing the breakup of agricultural enterprises which plays a different part in different countries, according to the part played by tenancy in each of them. The importance for farm indivisibility of such rules is further limited in countries where, as in France and Germany, a considerable part of the rented land is in holdings under mixed tenure. In Eastern Europe, the problem is nowadays very limited in scope. In the Soviet Union, it is non-existant, as far as individual farms are concerned. The collective farms may be said to be a kind of tenant holdings at

least from the formally legal point of view. Of course, their status contains many other peculiar features too.

Even apart from its importance for the indivisibility of farms, the protection of tenants is important for the tenant class itself and thereby for the stability of the farming industry. In this section, interest will be focussed upon tenancy protection as one of the factors which tend to shift decision-making in farming from the landowner to the tenant.

(150) Among the countries of the British Isles, Ireland was for long a battleground for fixity of tenure, and is now a country where for decades this claim has been realized. In contrast to this, Great Britain had only gradual development of protection for the tenant farmers. After World War II, very important improvements have taken place in the position of the tenants, through legislation from the years 1947–49[a]. At the same time as the period of lease was, formally, reduced to one year for all tenancy contracts, the tenants were granted prolongation of their original contracts for a practically unlimited period of years. This does not mean, however, an entirely rigid fixation of the existing pattern of tenures. On the contrary, the short period of lease offers the landlord the possibility that legal grounds may eventually occur for evicting the tenant at a shorter notice than is the case in most other countries.

To evict the tenant, the landlord must serve notice to quit 12 months in advance. The grounds for quitting must be stated in the notice, so that the tenant can see immediately what chance there is of protesting. If the tenant serves a counter-notice within one month after receiving the notice to quit, then the landlord's notice to quit is void and without any effect, unless the landlord obtains the consent of the Minister of Agriculture (or the Secretary of State for Scotland). The grounds he may then invoke are mainly such as the interests of town and country planning, allotment, agricultural education, certain very important interests of the landlord's own and, finally, certain kinds of bad husbandry on the part of the tenant. In the latter case, the tenant even loses his right to serve counternotice, unless he contests the validity of the ground stated. Thus the tenant farmer sits safe if he is a tolerably good farmer and nothing happens to bring public interest in conflict with his individual position. The main cases for eviction of tenants in Great Britain are thus now to be found in the framework of a comprehensive land policy.

(151) Also the new French tenancy statute of 1945 provides for automatic prolongation of the lease contract which is not even, as in Great Britain, on a year-to-year basis but for nine years at a time [a]. Thus, if there should be legal reason to evict the tenant, the landowner may have to wait longer for doing so than in Great Britain. There is one main exception to this rule: if the tenant failed to exercise his right of preemption, and the farm is then bought by another agriculturist who intends to run the farm himself. When the owner himself wants to take over the farm and manage it for his own account, he must wait until the lease expires, but if he sells it to a close relative with the view that this man should run the farm, the tenant must quit if he does not exercise the right of preemption.

There is a risk with this system that, since the far-reaching tenancy protection makes the situation of landlord less advantageous than it used to be, the number of sales may increase. This may diminish the security of the tenants [b]. Eventually, greater mobility in the farm pattern could be the outcome, which certainly was not the aim of this legislation.

On the whole, the right of preemption is regarded as one of the greatest safeguards of the tenant class. How far this really is so will be dealt with in a later section of this chapter. It has a great deal of bearing on the question whether an owner-operator really is safer and better off than a well protected tenant.

The recent French legislation also contains rules by which the contracts of sharecroppers are converted into regular lease contracts, which in turn will allow them to benefit from all the protection the holders of such contracts enjoy.

In Belgium, the old rules of civil law stated that the landlord might always evict the tenant in case of sale [c], but otherwise there were many protective rules. In 1951, a comprehensive statute was enacted which introduced quite as far-reaching protection as in the French statutes [d]. Even the continuation of the contract for the successors of a deceased tenant is provided for.

In the Netherlands, an elaborate system of tenancy protection has been developed step by step since 1937. Not only does the tenant in most instances have a right to have the contract prolonged, but any contract is subject to public approval and registration for validity, which guarantees that no unfair clauses are inserted. The effects of this kind of protection are especially important in a country like the Netherlands with its pronounced land hunger. One consequence will eventually at length be lower land values with subsequent shortage of capital for investments on the land [e]. On the other hand, it may be questioned whether there is not already some over-investment in Dutch land.

The Swedish rules on protection of tenant farmers are now so deeply incorporated in the general legislation on land policy that they are better dealt with in that context than here.

(152) If it can thus be said that in Western Europe, tenant farmers by now enjoy a far reaching degree of safety in the possession of the land they cultivate, the same can hardly as yet be said of Southern Europe.

Among these countries, protection of the tenants has reached farthest in Italy, where much of recent legislation has followed the French pattern. Since the war, all lease contracts have been collectively and compulsorily prolonged through annual statutes [a]. The protection is thus formally much more unsafe, even if it is certain that it represents the first stage towards more long-term protection. Since 1954, a new statute on agricultural leases has been discussed in the Italian parliament [b]. As a compromise solution, the proposal has proved one of the most controversial issues in modern Italian policy.

However, even protection of the existing contracts may not always mean a solution of the social problems of the countryside, unless the terms of the contracts are reformed too. Especially in southern Italy, lease contracts are often so little beneficial to tenants that prolongation may not mean any great advance. Many contracts are directly opposed to land inprovements on the part of the tenant, and security of tenure does not therefore set individual initiative free.

In Spain, tenancy protection is thus far limited to the small tenant farms only, while the larger remain unprotected [c]. This may involve the risk that the landlords will in the future prefer not to create any new contracts of the protected type but, on the contrary, shift as much as possible of their land to larger tenancies, to sharecroppping, or to own enterprise under hired managers. The latter seems to some extent to have taken place in France.

In Portugal, so far no tenancy regulation at all has come to disturb the classical pattern of Liberal freedom of contract between landlord and tenant. The high frequency of short-term leases and multiple-mixed tenancies, especially in the Northern parts of the country, does not at present allow any great stability to agricultural enterprises.

(153) In Eastern Europe, individual tenancies play an inferior role at present. The main case of tenancy is that of the collective or co-operative farms. Here, the question of fixity of tenure may play a role.

In the Soviet Union, the land of the kolkhozy as well as that of the individual *dvory* is, in legal theory, the property of the State. The latter puts the land at the disposition of the kolkhozy in proportion to membership and the needs of the members. The possession is of unlimited duration and free of charge[a]. The charges due by the kolkhoz to the State are not claimed as rent for the land but as taxes or as collective contributions to common welfare. This system seems to provide the kolkhoz, as long as it continues to exist with the same identity of organization, with full security of tenancy of the land it cultivates. When the organization of the kolkhozy is changed, as was to a large extent the case during the amalgamation movement around 1950, this is formally due to free decision of the membership. The fact that the whole movement was planned and directed by State organs does not enter into open conflict with this theory, because it is also supposed that the masses willingly follow the direction of the authorities.

A point of special interest as regards the kolkhozy is the rule that each one of the brigades in which their personnel is organized should always hold and be responsible for the cultivation of the same plots of land, together with necessary implements and draught animals, during at least a whole period of crop rotation[b]. Nowadays, after the merging of the kolkhozy, the brigades also have grown larger and often correspond each with one of the former small kolkhozy. Again, the land allotted to one brigade is often identical with the territory of the village where the members of the brigade live [c]. This will certainly lead to the result that the brigade continues to hold the same land without interruption for many successive rotation periods.

In other parts of Eastern Europe the land of the co-operative farms, for the most part, belongs to the membership. The State enters as owner of part of the land of the co-operative farm only inasmuch as it has contributed with land allotments from the State land fund. Since the members have formally the right to leave the co-operative farm and take with them the land they brought in, or a corresponding quantity, these co-operative farms cannot be said legally to enjoy security of tenure or protection of the integrity of the enterprise. In some instances, however, there may be rules stating that land that for one reason or another comes to belong to a non-member, is not for that reason to be handed over to the owner at once [d]. Owners who wish to withdraw their land from the co-operative farm may have to wait, and they may also have to be satisfied with land on the outskirts of the village territory, in order not to disturb the planned economy of the co-operative fields.

The importance of these features in the framework depends of course on the way in which they are applied. If it becomes politically easy to leave the co-operative farms, as in Yugoslavia in 1952–53, then the remainder of the farm may need all possible protection for the capital values it has already created. If the right to leave is formal only, then the co-operative farms are as safe as the kolkhozy in the USSR.

THE OWNER—TENANT DILEMMA

(154) The legal framework for land tenure is always more or less the expression of some kind of policy. The policy may be dominated by productivistic views, as seems actually to be the case in Great Britain and Sweden, or by social motives, as in Eastern Europe and in recent legislation in France and the Mediterranean countries. Different approaches compete, but in either case the question of decision-making is crucial. The content of the situation, for both owner-operator and tenant farmer, is largely a matter of how far they are allowed to decide themselves, and over what resources.

A main point in legislation and practice was for long the land-lord's right — and interest — to decide over the capital he brought into the enterprise of the tenant. In the first place he had contributed the land, more or less cultivated, but eventually also buildings and live and dead stock. The less the farmer contributed to this, the less, it was often thought, was he either capable of or interested in taking proper care of the productive resources unless he were forced to it by clauses in the contract. Especially during the early modernization drive, when crop rotation was introduced to replace the Mediaeval open field system in England, Scandinavia and northern Germany, binding clauses in the lease contracts were often necessary as a means of educating the tenant class. The fear of short-sighted exploitation is still alive in many areas and current discussion of the effects of actual tenancy legislation often returns to this issue.

As long as there was little concern with the social situation of the farming population, the issue might seem simple enough, at least in countries where landlords were educated and business-minded enough to try to make the most and best possible of their landed estates. Under full freedom of contract, land hunger forced the tenants to accept practically whatever clauses the landlords offered. It is too well known now that this did not meet with all justifiable wishes, not even all those of the Liberals themselves. Especially in the Mediterranean countries, many landlords fail to choose the most productive system of cropping. An improved practice of cultivation may increase the burden of management for the landlord without yielding a compensatory increase of income to the landlord. The precarious contract types that are still frequent in the area, and especially the share-cropping practices, witness this drawback of such a landlord system. So do also the many instances of sub-letting, sometimes with more than one middle-man between the landowner and those tilling the soil. Even in the British Isles, there long continued to be many instances of landlords far from acting for the benefit of the farming industry[a].

More important than this was the idea of social protection, especially north of the Alps. It was realized that the Liberal theory of freedom of contract was not so directly applicable when the parties did not, for economic reasons, enjoy the same degree of freedom of action[b]. Especially the right to the result of improvements made on the farm by the tenants proved to be crucial. Through his surplus labor, a family farmer can be expected to carry out more improvements on the land than any landlord is willing to pay for. Here too, the experience of the Mediterranean countries is especially eloquent. The principle that the best worker is he who works for himself was however observed earlier and its consequences were more fully recognized in Western Europe, already at an epoch when classical economics was in the making.

(155) It was on such grounds that Arthur Young laid down his famous statement on the superiority of the owner-operator over the leasehold system. It did not at first find any high degree of application in his own country, but it did so (or it happened to coincide whith what occurred anyhow) in Denmark in the 19th century. It was also held to be of importance in the kind of solution which the French Revolution gave or was thought to give to the land question in France. The same kind of views became of decisive importance for recent structural changes in Ireland and in the land reforms in Eastern Europe. In many cases, it was expected that the transition of the land to the ownership of those who cultivated it would provide a general solution of the land question.

The construction of the family farm as family property in the modern sense proved, however, to have a serious drawback. If each one of the heirs were to have his equal share in the inheritance, then the farms would be broken up too often, the land fragmented and farms turn out too small. The small peasants' ruin on the Balkans, imminent as it was in the thirties, is a modern illustration. In remote centuries in Western Europe, popular sentiment had come to regard the farm as something almost even more important than the farmer himself. It was for this reason that restricted inheritance had been brought about in the Late Middle Ages and later epochs. But undivided inheritance of the physical substance of the farm, as such, proved to be no solution under modern conditions. If the co-heirs were to be paid out by equal shares or at any rate by important sums in cash or goods, then each generation of those remaining on the farms might be contracting new debts and using up a lifetime's savings to pay them off rather than to invest in the farm. Capital flowed out from agriculture, where it had been created, to serve non-agricultural purposes[a].

Thus, the farm might remain undivided in appearance only. Economically, it was broken up by every generation. The value of invested capital matters as much, at least in modern times, as the capital value of the land. As a matter of fact, and even in defiance of the law, it has been extremely common in European peasant society to pay out the co-heirs at a lower rate or not at all. Both in Western Germany and in Switzerland, at present, the co-heirs are legally paid out according to the rental value of the farm instead of according to the sales value, which is commonly higher.

This kind of argument against the owner-operated farm as a socio-economic ideal has carried so much weight that it has been necessary to state, for instance, that the Danish freehold system did not suffer from economic crises any more than did farming in other European countries[b].

(156) If complete freehold did not give the solution desired, and restricted inheritance proved to be only a palliative rather than the solution to the problem of the integrity of the farm capital, then it might follow closely that tenancy is the best form of agricultural organization, a viewpoint not seldom advocated. The fact that the most advanced agriculture of France is in the north-western part of the country, where tenancy predominates, has been considered in conjunction with the fact that tenancy-dominated England has a prosperous agriculture[a]. Also in Germany, most of the tenancies are in the North, which is likewise the agriculturally most advanced part of that country. Since the tenant farmer is not concerned with paying out his co-heirs, or by preparing his successor to do so, he would be more interested in investing in farm equipment, provided he were sure to retain the value of these improvements. The validity of this viewpoint depends largely on the traditions and instincts of the farming community in question. If the tenant's greatest wish is to become owner, as seems to be the case for instance in Bretagne, then he may save money in order to buy land rather than invest it in the equipment of the farm. In such a case, and if there are tolerably good possibilities of

buying land, tenancy will barely prove superior to freehold as far as capital formation is concerned. Thus, the preemption right of the tenant might not be the ideal, but rather an efficient protection of his situation as a tenant. On the other hand, if he is too well protected, the situation may develop into another kind of ownership, something on the lines of Mediaeval divided ownership, and bring about the same drawbacks as freehold. The recent French legislation has been attacked on the ground that it would create a kind of *propriété culturale*, a form of secondary ownership, in the hands of the tenants. This might eventually be more to the benefit of the bad than of the good tenant[b].

(157) There is thus a contrast of views which regards now the landlord, now the tenant as especially interested in improving the farm or, conversely, as especially suspect of failing to do so or of dissipating the farm capital. Not only does the accruing of the tenant's investments to the landlord act as a disincentive to the former. Payment of exorbitant rents may also rob the land of its savings, as much as the paying out of co-heirs, or the selling of manure. The integrity of the farm as an equipped capital unit depends more on the economic application of the rules than on the rules themselves or the legal theory underlying them.

At first sight, for instance, it might appear as if a kolkhoz were completely protected against capital destruction, since neither land nor fixed equipment can be sold. But, if delivery quotas and the relationship between product prices and the prices of investment goods are disproportionate, then the savings of the enterprise may not even be sufficient for current repairs. Capital starvation may then hamper the development of the farm as much as any of the factors we discussed on either freeholds or tenant farms in capitalist countries.

The success of one or the other system of tenure therefore depends ultimately on economic policy. The conclusion, as far as legal theory is concerned, is merely the negative statement that the classical Liberal property concept does not seem to serve agriculture very well. But also the question of ownership versus tenancy depends essentially on the real socio-economic content of the régime under consideration. The concepts need be re-defined for future discussion.

(158) This apparent dilemma — the incompatibility of views held in different countries and regions — poses the question whether the form of tenure to some extent may depend on the natural conditions of various regions. Our knowledge of share-cropping especially in south-western France and in the Mediterranean countries indicates a connection with geography. It is often repeated that sharecropping represents the association of meagre land, of slow work, and timid capital[a]. It does not even appear as if the new legislation on transition from sharecropping to leasehold in France had been followed by any large-scale application[b]. At any rate, the stability in the geographical connection of sharecropping is remarkable, whether the explanation is to be found in the climate, in the general economic character of the region, or in the traditions of the population. Also a recent Spanish enquiry on land tenure indicates a distinct geographical localization of sharecropping in the most arid regions of the country, that is, in those regions where the farmer is more exposed to the risks of heavily fluctuating harvests. The men with large capital may be better equipped than the peasants to reap long-term profits[c]. If this is so, then Spanish sharecropping represents a kind of large-scale enterprise, comparable with those latifundia which are formally run by the owner, through a hired manager. The absence of a corresponding geographical concentration of owner-operators would then be explained by this category including both the latifundia and the small freeholds.

Even Italian experience points more or less towards similar conclusions, since sharecropping in that country has assumed different features in different parts of the country[d].

Conversely, it may be asked whether the freehold — the small-scale freehold of family size, as distinct from the capitalist enterprise — does not also belong to certain specific conditions of production, which are not the most remunerative; not to any specific type of climate and soil, but to some specific types of production, which depend on a conjunction of soil and climatic factors with technical development and economic conditions, among them the character of the market attraction. The fact that freeholds dominate in the meagrest parts of France and Germany may be interpreted in this way. It may be, for instance, that the dominance of tenancy in the most fertile regions is not in itself a test of the efficiency of the tenants, but rather demonstrates the difference in the interest taken by urban capitalists in buying land. Capital from outside is likely to be more interested in land from which some considerable rent might be taken, leaving small-scale owner-occupiers without competition in places where marginal return is small [e]. Even if this view be recognized as generally true, it is of course a relative truth. A multitude of other factors, among them the socio-economic past of the country or region, also contribute to the actual situation.

These "natural" differences can be supposed to have operated somewhat freely within the framework of a laissez-faire economy, and less so under the various attempts to direct the fate of rural society in the past. Modern policy claims to subordinate the whole farming industry to the needs of the nation. This is likely to make influences such as those just dicussed more difficult to trace. The underlying causes will however not be eliminated, but will continue to modify the results of uniformly applied policy measures.

ENTIRE SOCIAL CONTROL OF LAND USE

(159) What has been mentioned about the strong public influence on lease contracts nowadays in almost all countries of Europe is only one of the most important ways in which the State claims to decide what should be done with the nation's land. Even here, the motive is seldom exclusively one of social policy. A national land policy also aims at determining capital formation on the land, to make it develop as much as possible to the benefit of the community.

That modern social policy may lead towards a complete control of what is to be done with the land is a fairly old truth already [a]. An important impetus in that direction was given by World War I. Shortly after its end, Germany adopted rules implying control of all division of land over a certain low size level, in the interest of maintaining production [b]. Corresponding rules in Sweden had been in force since the beginning of the century. They started with the need to protect forests from wholesale destruction and, consequently, to protect farmsteads in the forest areas. The movement culminated, from the legislative point of view, in the Land Statute of 1927, making all land division depend on public consent [c]. Subsequent administrative legislation has developed these rules into a comprehensive system of constructive national land policy, especially since the last war. The task is to regulate the amalgamation of small farms into somewhat larger ones and to avoid this movement taking a direction deemed to be unsuitable for the country as a whole. Strong checks are laid on the freedom of landowners to do what they like with their land, but at the same time on leaseholders. The latter are not allowed to rent more land, or any other land, than is deemed suitable for the farming of the region. In Great Britain, the Agriculture Act of 1947 has laid down the foundations for a similar control of land use. This implies rather far-reaching possibilities for country planning by aid of expropriation or dispossession whenever necessary. The Act's definition of the "agricultural unit" not only reveals the new concept of legal unity of the farm, but at the same time how far the regulatory ambitions of government offices go. The "agricultural unit" is thus described as including, besides necessary buildings, also

"land falling within the definition in this Act of the expression 'agricultural land' which is in the occupation of one person, being land as to which the Minister is satisfied that having regard to the situation thereof and other relevant circumstances it ought in the interests of full and efficient production to be farmed in conjunction with the agricultural unit" (Art. 109 : 2)

Swiss development since the war equally implies a subordination of individual property rights under common welfare [d]. Since the war, also, French legislation and policy has tied the fate of the land more and more in the supposed interest of the whole nation [e]. Although some of the most far reaching coercive measures must not be applied in time of peace, the tendency has again been accentuated through the new expropriation statute [f]. The latter raises the problem of whether or not a comprehensive land policy will favor farm indivisibility. The same reasons that tend to prevent farm subdivision in the interest of individuals may have the opposite influence in those cases where public interest conflicts with private ones.

(160) As already mentioned, the trend has been less pronounced

in the Mediterranean countries than north of the Alps. Even
there, however, the tendency is clearly towards more and more
social control of land use. The land reform measures have so far
touched only limited sectors of the farming industry. In Italy
and Spain, however, the program, in principle, makes for complete
transformation of the agrarian structure which will be dominated
by small owner-operated farms, as has already been accomplished
in Greece. In the former countries, discussion has been concerned
with the damage caused when well managed large estates are
broken up through measures of land reform[a]. Consequently,
these enterprises, that is those among them that have made
heavy investments which can only show returns in the framework of large-scale agriculture, might well require measures to
protect their undisturbed existence, for very much the same kind
of reasons as underlie most measures to protect the indivisibility of
farm units. The reaction to these views is found in statutes
concerning "model farms" in Italy and Spain, which are exempted
from land reform measures[b]. Such exemption clearly implies
the idea that their owners or holders should continue to run them
as before, and not break them up or let them deteriorate. In
Portugal, by contrast, the operation of large farms is considered
satisfactory much more generally than in the other two countries, and the idea that they should not be broken up prevails
over the wish to create new small holdings.

(161) By contrast with these tendencies in the Western
countries, which may be described as various stages of "cold
socialism", there is the apparent lack of explicit regulations in
most countries in Eastern Europe, as far as control of land
division is concerned. At the same time, these countries have
generally more far reaching regulations as to what the farmers
should grow and produce than is the case in the Western countries. Apart from the complete land socialism in the Soviet
Union, Czechoslovakia seems to be the only one of the Eastern
countries that has enacted practically full social control of all
kinds of transactions with agricultural land, through recent
statutes on possession and inheritance of farm land[a]. We have
already mentioned the Austrian traditions in the Czech provinces
as being the partial background to this. For the prohibition
against selling farm land, the special demographic situation of

Czechoslovakia (especially in the Czech provinces) may also be responsible. In a country without land hunger, secret and un-authorized sale of land might undo the land reform and again create large private farms.

This kind of demographic problem barely concerns any other countries in Eastern Europe, apart from some Western districts in Poland, and Eastern Germany. The most important background to the apparently more liberal tendency in East European land division policy lies partly in the fact that maximum size of private landed property is rigorously limited. When, on the other hand, the ultimate goal of land policy is complete land socialism of the Russian model, it may also be felt to be unnecessary to make too many arrangements about the affairs of the small farms.

(162) The motive behind social land control is not only a wish to protect the tenants, or to maintain a sound equilibrium between capital formation and labor. The productivist view is encroached upon from two sides: the small-holding ideology, wishing to establish and maintain a broad stratum of inde-pendent small-scale farmers, and the collectivistic wish to organize farming into large units to as great a degree as urban industries.

The former, as in Belgium and Southern Europe, relies on individual and family welfare as the reason for restricting individual liberty[a]. The liberty of the few must be restricted in the interests of the liberty of the many. The latter too must be restricted in their freedom to divide inheritance and to break up farms in their lifetime, in the interest of the community and the system[b]. The co-operativist trend, as will be shown in the next chapter, only emphasizes the point. The outcome is a new concept of property: "Ownership is now regulated according to collective interest. It has ceased to be a private fact"[c].

Formally more radical, the Socialist approach tends to abolish private ownership or to make it entirely subordinate to co-operative use. Whatever the legal construction the aim is evident: to abolish *land value* and land rent (as the disturbing elements they often are). Only it is thereby overlooked that taxation and State deliveries at fixed prices may have very much the same kind of effect as land rent. At the same time, the

abolition of land value complicates the question of loans for
investments, which actually occur also in the USSR. Virtually,
both kolkhozy and dvory are owners, as much as both small and
large-scale farmers in other countries, where the risk of dispossession may be as great as in a Communist country. The term
"ownership" must not be taken to make any decisive difference.
Nor is the absence of free sale and free lease any longer a feature
peculiar to the Soviet Union. The difference between the societies
which are here compared lies in their political climate. This must
not prevent us from seeing the resemblance of the actual results
of different legal ideologies.

The outcome, in both East and West, is a new concept of land
ownership. In some respects, it brings to mind the Late Mediaeval
development, when feudal possession was crystallized into divided
ownership. The different drawbacks of various forms of land
ownership and land tenure systems all tend to make for this,
as it appears, inevitable solution: that the land be in safe
possession of those who work on it, for all productive purposes,
but not at their full disposition for sale and other aims alien to
the productive purposes of the land. The social purpose of the
land requires both that it should be treated as a special kind of
wealth (*Sondervermögen*, as a German term runs), and that the
integrity of prosperous productive units should be respected.
This is actually the case in most European countries, though in
varying degrees and not very consistently.

PUBLIC LAND AND PUBLIC TENURE

(163) Historically, the State has been, quantitatively, a great
landowner. State ownership has however mostly covered waste
or uncultivated land, and the cultivation of such land has in
most instances led to the creation of some class of State tenants,
who often became freeholders in course of time. Land rent and
tax could not always be clearly distinguished.

In the course of centuries, there were also many instances of
State land being identified with the land of monarchical families.
It is of special importance that in Czarist Russia, most of the
uncultivated land was held as property of the State or of the
Emperor. This seems to have strengthened the tendency to regard

the State, or its physical head, as responsible for the solution of the land question. The downfall of monarchies has in many cases contributed to enlarging the landed property of the State, as it did to a large extent in Russia. Recent political changes in Eastern Europe have also increased the area of land held as State property.

In Western and Southern Europe, as a whole, the State plays only a minor part as landholder. Excepting experiment stations and the like, agricultural land owned by the State is mostly let and does not have an important role in public land policy[a]. In Sweden, where for various historical reasons much land belonged to the Crown, most of it was let to tenants on long-term, often life-time and inheritable lease, and the tenants were encouraged to buy the land as freehold [b]. Nowadays, public ownership of land in England, Sweden and many other countries frequently occurs in connection with expropriation for country planning, though this is generally of a transitory character. There is scarcely any tendency to expand the landed property of the State.

The discussion on land socialism, which went on at the beginning of the century especially in England [c], has thus shown few signs of really changing the pattern of landowning and land tenure in Western Europe. The increasing trend to cold socialism, as outlined above, has made the idea of direct socialization of the land less interesting than before.

(164) In contrast to this, complete land socialism is the ultimate goal of land policy in the Soviet Union and Eastern Europe. The present division of the structure between collective and State farms is regarded as only a transitory stage on the road towards complete socialism.

The sovkhozy or State farms in the USSR had their strongest development in connection with the collectivization drive around 1930. In the late thirties, they declined slightly again. The following figures may be quoted in this connection [a].

The decrease was avowedly due to the failure of the institution to fulfill expectations [b]. The area figure, something close to 8 per cent of the total for the Union in 1938, is not very instructive in view of the great differences in value and fertility of the land. Some publications from the thirties refer to the regional

TABLE 27. *Development of State farms in the USSR 1928–1938*

	1928	1932	1938
Number of sovkhozy	1,400	4,337	3,961
Annual average of workers on the same	316,800	1,891,500	1,319,700
Sown area, hectares.	1,700,000	13,400,000	12,400,000
Tractors on the same	6,700	64,000	85,000

distribution in a way that is of interest here [c]. About half the sown area, or 6 million ha, was in grain sovkhozy. Among them, 93 farms with 1 million ha were in Ukraina, 67 farms with 1,7 million ha in Northern Caucasus, Crimea, and the Azov-Black Sea district, and 94 farms with 1.7 million ha sown area in the Saratov, Stalingrad, Middle Volga, and Cheliabinsk districts. Thus, 254 farms with some 4 million ha sown area were located in the semi-arid regions in the southern and south-eastern parts of the Union. Most of the remainder was in semi-arid regions in Asia. In the central, western, and north-western parts of the Union, the sovkhozy were mostly specialized in livestock, or of a mixed type.

Some further information, though incomplete, is available for the time around 1950 [d]. It is not clear whether the total number and area of the State farms have increased or decreased, but in any case new ones have been created in areas annexed to the USSR in connection with World War II. Examples from Russia and Ukraina indicate that most districts have some 10–20 such farms, but some regions much more. Some of the regions in Asia seem still to have more sovkhozy than the average for the Union, and it is known that the new land clearing projects in Siberia stick to this form of organization. A semi-arid region like the Astrakhan district is reported to have 15 per cent of its sown area in sovkhozy.

Looking at regions where livestock is the main activity of specialized farms, the 98 sovkhozy in Belorussia (1948) do not seem to exceed the average for the USSR. But Latvia's 58 sovkhozy (1952) is certainly above the average, and so are the 142 such farms in the Leningrad district (1953). The Carelian republic had 16 per cent of its sown area in sovkhozy, which also is probably above the average. An exceptionally great part

is played by the sovkhozy in the Kaliningrad district (northern
East Prussia), where there were 60 sovkhozy against only 152
kolkhozy (1950).

Despite their incompleteness, these data allow certain conclusions to be drawn. On the one hand, it appears as if sovkhozy
play a greater part in regions where large estates remained
important up to the revolution, as in the north-west. On the
other hand, it also seems as if sovkhozy had their greatest
quantitative importance in regions which are either semi-arid,
as well as being the scene of vast reclamation projects, or for
one reason or another suffer from shortage of manpower.

The latter feature — State farms as a solution preferred where
manpower is scarce — also seems repeated in Eastern Europe[e].
State farms reached a high percentage in Czechoslovakia (10 per
cent of agricultural area) and Poland (11, later 14 per cent of
agricultural area), that is in the two countries where the exodus
of the Germans had created a certain shortage of agricultural
manpower, at least under existing technical conditions. In
Hungary and Rumania, the proportion of State land rose
steadily during the collectivization drive around 1950, possibly
because of failures in the regular program of collectivization.
In Bulgaria, where collectivization is apparently very successful
and very little land has been expropriated, the proportion of
State land remained low. It did not rise very high in Yugoslavia
or Eastern Germany either.

These experiences seem to indicate that under present conditions
the State farm is an exceptional rather than a regular solution
even within the framework of Communist land policy. In so far
as it has been comprehensive, land socialism is up to now mainly
an affair of locally self-governing nuclei where the membership
and not the State takes the risk of management. This situation
indicates once more the role of the labor surplus.

(165) Discussion on communal and collective (or co-operative)
land tenure often tends to equate the two[a]. This may be convenient when dealing mainly with primitive societies, where a
collectivity for land holding or farming coincides with the social
nucleus corresponding to a civil community, and where the
common use of the land is closely related with other kinds of
common institutions. For the problems of modern Europe, on

the other hand, communal and collective tenure should be distinguished. It is a circumstance of some importance, in a modern society, whether rights in common land depend on membership in a civil community or are a consequence of the membership in a specialized group, organized for the purpose of collective or co-operative farming and existing independently of the civil community.

Identity between the civil (or tribal) community and a group for common land holding (and even common land use) was of course a normal feature also in Europe in remote centuries. Lingering remnants of this can still be found or were alive until recently in some backward parts of our continent. In the Portuguese mountains, examples can still be found where the dominating pastoral type of economy imposes not only communal ownership of the land but also a collective organization of land use [b]. Traces of similar institutions can be found here and there in the Mediterranean countries [c] and in the Balkans [d]. In the latter area, they are only vestiges of institutions once important, but still they play a part in the ideological background of the present collectivistic urge.

(166) The normal legacy of communal collectivism was, however, communal ownership of pastures, forests, and other extensively used land. This emerged, however, not only from the dissolution of primitive communities but also from the decay of feudal and quasi-feudal landlord systems. In countries where farm censuses are drawn up on the basis of total rather than agricultural area as the criterion for size classification, the presence of communal pastures sometimes causes the erroneous impression that they are "latifundia", where in fact they are a meagre and often not very important complement to the resources of small and medium-sized peasant farms.

Whatever the origin of the communal lands, they were often a source of conflicts between the small farmers of the village and some big landowner who claimed a right to the whole communal domain or some important part of it as a consequence of a feudal title. This type of conflict was frequent in 18th century France and formed part of the background to the agrarian unrest underlying the revolution. In the 19th century, victorious Liberal trends of thought often abolished the rights of the communities and dissolved the communal domains, which were eventually sold in the open market. It is nowadays often stated that the latifundia in the Iberian countries derived a considerable part of their land from such operations[a]. The analogous conflict made itself felt in connection with the liberation of the serfs in Russia and Rumania and elsewhere, since the landlords often retained as their individual property more land than they had been cultivating in their own management.

In the Scandinavian countries, large tracts of State or communal forests were divided and sold to individual settlers or forestry companies. In Norway, such subdivision is still held necessary for the development of forests on difficult sites[b].

In contrast to this kind of forest policy, communal pastures are regularly accepted as a normal feature of the agrarian structure, even in a country like the Netherlands[c]. In Switzerland, it is even in contemplation to expand common landowning on mountain pastures, and for that both civil communities and other corporations are under consideration[d]. Also in France, discussion is alive on what to do with the remaining communal lands[e].

Communal lands are really important in Italy where communities and, to some extent, specialized agricultural bodies own some 3 million hectares of land, most of which is under extensive use. Here too, the opinion seems now to prevail that the bulk of this land should continue to be used collectively[f]. More than half of this land is in the Alps, but there are important tracts of such land both in central Italy and in Sardinia.

Communal lands in the Mediterranean region are also connected with some of the earliest attempts at collective farming in Europe in modern time.

COLLECTIVE TENURE

(167) Some instances of collective farming in Spain are directly derived from old-style communal land tenure. In Extremadura, at least as late as around 1930, it was not infrequent that a large tract of land, even a whole civil community, belonged to a great number of peasants as shareholders. The shares (*maravedís* or *acciones*) were not equal but corresponded

to individually different rights in the undivided land. It was arranged that the shareholders worked for pay under a director for the common enterprise and afterwards received their shares in the net output according to the shares they held in the land [a]. Analogous institutions have been observed in other parts of Spain as late as in the forties [b].

Collective farms in Italy have a more modern character. The original idea was to rent land in common, above all in order to get rid of the extra burdens imposed by the system of sub-letting. The collectivity of farmers undertook to be the middle-man between the landlord and those actually cultivating the land. This idea was developed differently by co-operatives of Catholic and of Socialistic inspiration. The former divided the land between the members and managed it as small individual enterprises. The latter, in many cases, started managing the whole tract of land as a collective enterprise [c]. Most farms of the latter type are to be found in Northern Italy, though there are some cases in the South too. They are interesting for the fact that they have continued to exist during decades, and many of them still exist, although hardly any of the political régimes in Italy have been favorable towards them.

Of a different character are the collective agreements on labor which are in Italian called *compartecipazione* and have some features in common with large-scale sharecropping, though their independence from the landlord is unusually narrow [d]. It is sometimes discussed what really makes the difference between this form of organization and a kolkhoz [e].

(168) In other parts of Western Europe, collective farming belongs mainly to a quite recent development which attempts to benefit by the experience of Russian Communism in order to find new forms of organization [a]. Some intermediate forms will be discussed in the next chapter. It may be mentioned here that statutes on collective farms exist in Sweden and in France. In the former country, only a very few experimental examples have so far been put into existence, and the final outcome is not clear. At any rate, they are much smaller than in the Communist countries or even in Italy. In France too, collective farming seems to have been attempted rather on the scale of a few families than as a large-scale agrarian industry. Thus far, the idea has

been more a program than a solution in France[b]. The main hindrance to any appreciable extension seems to lie in the legal structure; a number of "sociétés de fait" do exist though little information is available[c].

(169) The development of the Russian kolkhoz will be dealt with more at length in Chapter 6. Its present organizational form, the "artel", is developed from one of the three forms existing in the twenties and represents an intermediary stage between the two others then existing. The lower of these forms, the "association" was deemed to be too little collective and the more advanced, the "commune", was reserved for the future as the final goal of Communist land policy.

Of the structure of the kolkhoz it may be said that legally it is co-operative and politically it is a State enterprise[a]. Formally, it is a self-governing body with the right to choose its own managers and to approve the plans of production. In practice, however, the kolkhoz is obliged to follow the guidance of the State in all important respects. The exercise of democratic rights within the kolkhoz therefore always runs the risk of entering in open or latent conflict with the directives of the State authorities and with the persons who are fully loyal to them. The co-operative character was stressed through the concession whereby the members retain a small patch of land each, together with certain small inventory and some livestock (the *dvor*, as described above). The tendency of actual policy is, however, to reduce or abolish these relics of individual farming. If and when the final stage of kolkhoz development is reached, the kolkhozy will be very similar to the sovkhozy. The problem of co-operation and of individual say in the management of the farm will then be the same as in urban-industrial enterprises.

Collectivization of Soviet agriculture had been almost completed before the outbreak of World War II. The number of private peasants remaining was given as 4.4 per cent of the peasant household (in 1939), holding 0.4 per cent of the sown area, which means that there should have been about 900,000 holdings on about half a million hectares of sown area[b]. Their location is not indicated in available sources, nor the number of their livestock. It is very likely that a great part of them were mainly stock-raisers in areas so thinly settled that it would have been technically very difficult to organize them as collective farms.

Even as regards the kolkhozy, there were many complaints during the thirties about violation of the collective principles of organization, especially in areas where rural settlement was dominated by hamlets and isolated farmsteads. After the kolkhoz mergers around 1950, the kolkhozy in the USSR are much larger, on average, than in any of the countries in Eastern Europe. Even now, however, their size must vary considerably from region to region.

Even after the war, there is seldom any indication that absolutely all land in a district was collectivized [c]. In Armenia, the kolkhozy are said to embrace 99.7 per cent of the peasant farms and 99.9 per cent of their sown area. In Azerbaïdzhan, the corresponding figures are 98.93 per cent of the farms and 99.2 per cent of the sown area. Thus, there must still exist some private farms here and there in the Caucasian mountains. In other districts, available data are less distinct and it cannot always be seen how much of the non-collectivized land really belongs to private farms and how much is in the individual garden plots of the kolkhoz members. In most districts, nothing is mentioned about the percentage of collectivization. This may mean that the private sector is nil or negligible, but this conclusion is not certain.

In the Western regions of the Union, collectivization was resumed after the war and had by the early fifties been pressed further than in any East European country outside the USSR. In Western Ukraina, 2/3 of the peasant farms were collectivized by 1950 [d], and later data for various districts indicate even higher rates. In Estonia, by the end of 1949, collectivization seems to have reached at least 4/5 of the peasant farms [e]. Also in Latvia, there seems to have been a high percentage of collectivization in the early fifties.

(170) Collectivization in Eastern Europe has had a more complicated history. The background in pre-war conditions was different from country to country, and the result of the collectivization drive in each of them turned out differently, both for this reason and because of different political stresses [a].

In the Balkans, Bulgaria and Yugoslavia had a special background for collectivization. This was not so much due to the famous *zadruga*, which was by then almost extinct and played the role of an ideological rather than a practical argument. On the other hand, traditions in the life of the Balkan Slavs which were remotely akin to the zadruga had kept alive a spirit of co-operation. Partly it was a habit of co-operation in critical labor operations in rush times, such as most primitive peasant societies have, and partly there was a tradition of forced work for public purposes [b]. In Bulgaria, these collectivistic elements were further developed through legislation in 1941 and 1943 [c]. The co-operative movement became involved and proved efficient for the purpose, since it had already organized a great part of the country's peasantry for various co-operative purposes, and also had started a small number of associations for agricultural work in common [d].

In this context, it is easy to understand why Bulgaria is the country in Eastern Europe where collectivization of agriculture has reached farthest [e]. Even if it has there come to include slightly more than half of the land of the country, this does not mean that all is in really well organized collective farms. Although Bulgaria, like the Soviet Union, has only one form of collective farm, many of these farms may be far from living up to their statute.

The same observation refers to other parts of Eastern Europe. Yugoslavia was at one moment the second most collectivized country in the area. Since the decline of the movement in 1952–53, this is no longer the case. Even before the decline, it was only in one region, in Macedonia, that co-operative farms were said to have included more than half of the land. This part of the country has traditions which are more akin with those of Bulgaria than is the case with the northern, formerly Austro-Hungarian parts of Yugoslavia. Here co-operative farms had quite a modest success, far below the average for Yugoslavia. It can be concluded from various information that part of the co-operative farms existing before the change of policy were little more than just brought into existence and actually had very few common functions [f].

In contrast to the USSR and Bulgaria, the other East European countries have favored a gradual transition from individual to collective farming. Data on the progress of collectivization, which will be discussed in Chapter 6, are not entirely conclusive as to the importance of collective farming, which in almost all cases is likely to lag behind the formal developments. However they are interpreted, it remains to state that large socialized enterprises do not dominate the farming industry in any of these countries. As late as in the early fifties, they had to rely essentially upon individual farms for their agricultural production.

These forms of organization on the borderline between co-operative and collective enterprise contribute to stressing the need to discuss the importance of co-operation in European agriculture. The following chapter will try to outline how far co-operation means only a modification of the underlying farm pattern, or a new type of management.

CHAPTER 5

AGRICULTURAL CO-OPERATION

CO-OPERATION OR COLLECTIVITY?

(171) Farm structure and land tenure, discussed in Chapters 3 and 4, represent labor organization in the traditional sense. So far, it has been simply assumed that each farm, large or small, was a productive unit by itself, and only the interchange of manpower between large and small farms was discussed. It was mentioned, however, that sometimes large farms may be composed of a number of co-ordinated cells, with some functions performed independently in each cell. This may of course be difficult to distinguish from a system where formally independent nuclei (small farms) have a set of functions or services in common. The problem may arise in a system of capitalist enterprise, as with certain share-cropping practices in the Mediterranean countries. However, most of these problems refer to the various forms of co-operation. Even when it does not include the work of primary production, co-operation may bind the participants so closely together that their real independence of each other becomes strongly reduced, and their whole pattern of management and decision-making becomes profoundly modified.

When primary production (agriculture in the narrow sense of the word), or part of it, is also subject to joint action, then the question may arise whether co-operating farms should still be regarded as independent enterprises, or as one single big enterprise. The large State farms in Eastern Europe, as well as many of the latifundia in the Mediterrranean world, are undoubtedly single large enterprises, even though their organization may embrace subordinated cells with a minor degree of local decision-making and self-management. The kolkhozy in the USSR, and the "higher" types of co-operative farms in Eastern Europe, are officially designed to be "large-scale enterprise in agriculture". From the management point of view, this is undoubtedly true. However, this management should, according to the law, obtain an important part of its instructions from the assembly of the membership rather than from decisions taken by the director or the managerial board. How far this is really so, will be of decisive importance for the real meaning of the terms "collective" and "co-operative" as applied to these farms. In the "lower" types of co-operative farms in Eastern Europe, and in certain forms of co-operative or collective farms developed in non-communist countries, the dependence of the constituent cells upon the managerial board is of a different nature. The question is then where the difference lies between collective and co-operative enterprise, which in turn raises the question how this difference may refer to the inter-dependency of farms under a system of general co-operation, and to the limitations on managerial freedom that are imposed by national economic policy.

(172) This distinction is essential, among other things because it is often held nowadays that co-operation would provide "the third solution" to most social problems, a solution that would be capable of bypassing the drawbacks of both capitalism and socialism [a]. It is no overstatement to say that there exists something that could be called a co-operative philosophy, claiming to be decisive for the future of human society. This is in many respects a fundamental issue when judging the structural differences discussed in this book.

According to generally accepted principles, co-operation means voluntary joint action between individuals, who do not thereby loose their individuality or freedom [b]. The co-operative organization remains their servant and not their master. Voluntary adherence and democratic management are the general criteria distinguishing co-operation from State and other public enterprise. Unfortunately, the degree to which these principles are in fact applied cannot be stated without a relatively deep insight into the internal affairs of each country and each co-operative organization. Formally, voluntary membership and democracy of management are guaranteed everywhere. The content of these terms is however not the same everywhere but varies with the political climate and the level of general development of the countries.

From a formal point of view, co-operation could scarcely be distinguished from collectivity on the basis of these criteria only. In agricultural co-operation, the issue is complicated by the fact that it is above all a matter of co-operation between producers, as producers. Even agricultural co-operation for the purchase of commodities has from the outset focussed interest on purchase of commodities to be used in the productive process of agriculture, rather than commodities for human consumption. By contrast with consumer co-operation, agricultural co-operation not only involves certain facets of the domestic economy of the members. Their enterprises, that is the very basis for their economic existence, are also involved to a greater or lesser extent.

Furthermore the question of capital organization will have a completely different significance than in consumers' co-operation. Formally, co-operation takes place between individuals rather than between their enterprises. A critical point will then be whether the individual farmer retains a greater or smaller share of his original managerial freedom. Certainly, there can also be co-operation between persons who hold in common one large farm, as is the case on collective farms in Italy and Sweden. This should be distinguished from the case where a co-operative society — a creamery, for instance — holds a farm and has it farmed on its account by a hired manager or a leaseholder, which is similar to factories and shops being owned by consumers' co-operatives. But in the former case it remains of importance, for instance, whether a member who leaves the co-operative enterprise can or cannot take with him his share of the land and establish himself as an independent farmer on it. It is also important whether or not the assembly of the membership is or is not its own managerial board. The degree to which the membership can go counter to the managerial board is also decisive. Finally, the degree to which both the membership and the managerial board are subject to regulations imposed by the State or other public authorities, as compared to the incidence of the same or similar regulations upon individual farmers, will raise questions relating to the difference between public and private enterprise.

Freedom to contract out of the co-operative farm, with the right to retain the individual share in the common land, is a principle inextricably connected with the idea of productive co-operation. This principle is also formally guaranteed in the statute for co-operative farms in Eastern Europe outside the USSR. In the collective farms of the Russian type, on the other hand, the case for retaining one's share in the land, does not arise since all land belongs to the State. In Italy and Sweden, the collective farms are primarily founded on rented land, held under one single collective contract. A member leaving the enterprise could not then possibly have any claim to the land or its equipment in kind, and only under certain circumstances to part of the value of the latter. In Italy, some collective farms have become owners of their land, and then the question of the divisibility of the land is likely to arise.

DEVELOPMENT AND GENERAL ORGANIZATION

(173) Co-operation in land improvement enterprises and in certain forms of processing of farm products is fairly long established. Examples can be found in the old French societies for cheese-making [a] and in various kinds of associations for drainage or irrigation [b]. Modern co-operation appeared as an invention of the latter half of the 19th century, partly in response to the search for viable forms of socialistic economic organization, partly as a reaction to the challenge of radical Socialism [c]. In agriculture, more often than in urban milieus, co-operation assumed a conservative character, and it showed more liability to associate with the traditional forms of a class society [d].

Agricultural co-operation in Europe has gained most of its importance during this century. As will be seen from the tables below, it was only in a few countries that it had already reached considerable importance around 1900. The credit co-operative movement, started in Germany by Raiffeisen and Schultze-Delitsch, was already promising by the nineties and achieved a dominating importance in Germany and parts of the Austrian empire during the first decade of our century [e]. It developed considerable importance also, for instance, in the Czech provinces and the Slovenian regions after the nineties [f], and reached Serbia in 1894 [g]. The famous Bulgarian credit co-operative movement had been initiated at an early date, as it appears independently of Western influence, and became equally of great importance after the nineties [h].

From somewhat different points of departure, the Belgian-Flemish "Boerenbond" was started early in the nineties as the first attempt to realize the new Catholic program for social action. Even by 1900, it had achieved only a small part of its later development, and thus belongs essentially to the 20th century [i].

(174) In Great Britain, which was in other respects the classical ground for co-operative ideas, agricultural co-operation did not begin to take definitive shape until after the close of the 19th century. It was then tried as one of the measures of reconstruction after the crisis of the nineties [a]. Even so, it proved a slow developer and, though far from negligible at present, it has not reached an importance comparable to those of some continental countries [b]. Irish rural co-operation was stimulated by the general movement to improve social conditions on the island and developed more rapidly than its counterpart in Great Britain. It drew some inspiration from the movement in Denmark, and was already of decisive importance in the years around 1900 [c].

Danish agricultural co-operation, which had already reached its dominating position around 1890 was indeed one of the earliest developed movements of its kind [d]. In the Netherlands, on the whole, agricultural co-operation grew to importance somewhat later [e]. In France, agricultural co-operation passed the first stages even later than in Great Britain. There is not yet any branch of activity where it dominates the situation in France as a whole. One of the most interesting of recent developments appears to be in common machine-owning [f].

In Southern Europe, agricultural co-operation has generally developed both later and more unevenly than in France. In Italy, it was for a long period influenced through being linked with the Fascist "corporative" organization of the country's economy; lately, it has become divided between influences of Socialist and Catholic origin [g]. Corporative organization and Catholic social policy have become linked together in the recent development of Spanish rural co-operation. This development has been spectacular since the forties, when there was created a common statute for harmonizing rural co-operation with other institutions in the Spanish State. Despite this, the movement is still far from being of dominating importance for the farming industry of Spain, and lags behind its counterparts in both France and Italy [h]. In Portugal, not even the corporative framework for economic life has provoked anything but scanty instances of effective agricultural co-operation [i] even though similar institutions had been far from non-existant in the country's past [j].

(175) In Eastern Europe, agricultural co-operation had an earlier development than in Southern Europe or even in France. Indeed, some of these countries belong to those earliest developed in the field. Credit needs in connection with measures of land reform and the establishment of new small holdings through purchase of land have been important incentives, besides all the difficulties normally facing a rural society of overcrowded small holdings [a]. Under the present political system, this factor is no longer effective, since there is little private capital left to borrow and almost all credit is public and subject to State regulations. In the Soviet Union, the co-operative movement was at an early date linked with the Socialist organization of the country's economy, in the framework of which independent co-operatives were not allowed to play the same role as elsewhere [b]. In other East European countries, co-operation has still retained more of its original importance than in the USSR, at least in all cases where agriculture is not yet collectivized. In Yugoslavia, rural co-operation has still very much the same kind of objectives as before the last war, even though the credit sector seems to have declined and societies of a "general-purpose" type dominate the picture.

(176) From the viewpoint of social organization at large, one distinction is essential: whether the primary organization is specialized or "general". The former used to be the case at the start of most co-operatives. The latter was the program in the Catholic-inspired Belgian Boerenbond, and it has come to be the main type in Great Britain, Italy, and Eastern Europe [a].

It has been pointed out that from the viewpoint of management of affairs, the specialized societies do better than the non-specialized ones, among other things because they can draw best on expert advice and need not take into account other branches of the same organization in their decisions [b]. It is therefore only natural that the specialized type was chosen spontaneously when the needs were clearly seen from the outset and those directly concerned felt themselves capable of tackling the problems. Danish co-operation, though founded on the principle of a village co-operative as the basic organization, has developed distinct branch organizations for a number of different activities. Swedish agricultural co-operation, on the whole, started with separate co-operatives for different types of activity and it was only relatively lately that the national organizations for each branch became united into a single over-all national agricultural co-operative organization, for the defense of the interests of the farming population as a whole. Even then, the local and regional entities were not merged but retained their independence vis-à-vis each other.

This was in countries with relatively high levels of popular education. The general-purpose societies, on the other hand, undertake to some extent to educate the agricultural population towards more co-operative-mindedness, and also in other directions. This was avowedly the case with the Belgian Boerenbond and is lately so in the Spanish "cooperativas del campo". In the land reform zones of Italy, where the need for education in favor of co-operation is evident and urgent, the obligation on settlers who receive land through the reform to belong to a co-operative for the next twenty years could scarcely refer to societies of other than the general-purpose type.

In the Balkans, generally also in the Mediterranean countries, the big villages tend to strengthen the case for general-purpose societies. In Scandinavia, dispersed settlement is likely to have had the opposite effect and encouraged the specialized type of organization. In Belgian Flanders, also an area of dispersed settlement, there was not this argument for the general-purpose societies, but the Church used the parish as the basis for its educational activity and the priest as the uniting link between co-operative activities of different kinds.

In Great Britain, none of these explanations apply. The general-purpose society is here rather a result of the late development of agricultural co-operation as a whole. Since one main type was prevalent — the sale-and-supply society, credit being available in the normal market — the few instances of other purposes often came to be associated with this main type of organization.

However, no classification can include all the confusing variety of co-operative societies [c]. Statistically, there is a considerable risk of error involved in any attempt to enumerate the co-operative societies and their membership. Double counting will often occur through the affiliation of different types of societies to each other and through the membership of the same persons in more than one society. The total number of both the co-operatives and their members may be over-estimated in countries with mostly specialized societies, as compared with those where general-purpose societies dominate. It is therefore safest not to attempt to draw any picture of "agricultural co-operation in general". Instead, we will try to assess the development and importance of some main branches.

The data collected on the following tables cannot claim to be exhaustive. As described in more detail in Appendix 6, they derive from various sources, among which are several special treatments of agricultural co-operation in individual countries. This type of literature may contain much more information, which it would take a very long time to exhaust.

CREDIT CO-OPERATION

(177) This form is the most important one in European agricultural co-operation, at least as far as importance can be expressed in terms of numbers of societies and members.

It is well known that agricultural credit has some peculiar features which make it difficult to organize under the liberal economic system. This is so at least in agricultural societies where population is dense in relation to productive resources and where, consequently, cultivation tends towards maximum intensity under prevalent technical and economic conditions. Credit for investment purposes will then be difficult to obtain, because the increase in land value is precarious and depends upon decreasing marginal increment. The financial weakness of European agri-

culture became a general feature in the late 19th century, when
for instance the German and Polish squires were about as heavily
burdened with debt as the small farmers in their countries. The
difficulty of capital supply was therefore more than simply a
consequence of overpopulation and farm structure. Private
banks generally found other investment opportunities more
rewarding. Agricultural credit, before it became organized in
public or co-operative channels, tended to be a system of private
usury which was not, of course, a long-term solution of the
problem of capital supply.

The situation was rendered still more precarious through the
seasonal character of many branches of agricultural production.
Especially in areas where grain production for sale is important
it was an embarassment that all the producers had their product
ready for sale at the same time. If many of them were harassed
by imminent rent and mortgage payments, their simultaneous
sales might depress the market so that an abundant harvest
turned out into almost the same disaster as a crop failure, from
the viewpoint of the farmers. Short-term credit to overcome
difficulties of this kind was in some instances an even more
urgent necessity than long- and medium-term credit for investments and improvements on the farms.

However it was viewed, the risk involved in credit to the farmers
was very much an individual one. The farmer did not have much
to offer as security, except his own ability to achieve the objects
for which credit was to be given. The situation called for
collective arrangements, where the risk of individual failure of
a few was counterbalanced by the soundness of the majority.
State intervention lay close at hand, though at that moment
nobody wanted it to any large extent. The farmers' capacity for
selfhelp and mutual help was heavily drawn upon and credit co-
operation often encouraged as the cheapest and, it was thought,
in the long run the soundest solution to the credit problem.

(178) Broadly speaking, credit co-operation may be said to
have a twofold origin, though the lines are not distinctly separated.
As indicated above, land reform measures in Eastern Europe
were a strong incentive to create special public credit arrangements. As is generally known, the liberation of the serfs in Russia
and the purchase of their land from the former estate owners led

to the organization of a special credit bank which for a long period gave to agricultural credit its special feature in that country. Somewhat less well-known, though of similar importance, were the special credit measures taken in other Eastern European countries under analogous conditions. These tended to encourage the establishment of credit co-operation, as in Hungary[a]. In these cases, the new stratum of small farmers was protected against their financial weakness. The Russian instance may however be quoted in addition as an example of supporting the landlords by paying them high prices for the land and thus overcoming their financial weakness with regard to their remaining estates. Bulgaria, where the movement was to some extent initiated already in the last years of Turkish rule, stands midway between the countries with movements caused by land distribution problems and those inspired by other, normal difficulties.

The organizational side of credit co-operation in European agriculture had its main inspiration in Germany, where Raiffeisen had first propounded the principle of unlimited mutual liability on a local basis. His influence went far beyond the boundaries of Imperial Germany, though in those early decades perhaps more in the Austrian monarchy than in any other country outside Germany itself. Even the first Belgian and Spanish credit co-operatives were designed as being of "type Raiffeisen" and this type soon became of first importance in most agricultural credit co-operation outside the British Isles. Here, credit co-operation remained secondary to other types of purpose and organization, which were largely moulded by the initiative of Sir Horace Plunkett, in connection with the reform and rehabilitation policy for Ireland.

The following two tables will give a broad idea of the development and importance of credit co-operation in most countries of Europe.

(179) The coverage of credit co-operation, judged by the number of societies compared with the number of communities appears to be high in Germany, Austria, Hungary, and most of the Balkans and Scandinavia. The coverage is complete also in the Netherlands but is incomplete in Belgium, where the Boerenbond is mainly confined to the Flemish parts of the country. It covers a minor part only of the country in France and even

TABLE 28. *Agricultural credit co-operation: number of societies at the following approximate dates*

Countries	Number of societies						Number of rural communities around 1950
	1900	1907/10	1920	1930	1937	1950	
England and Wales	—	20	18		12	19	
N. Ireland	} 261	} 112					
Eire							160
Norway					233	897	860
Finland	—	307	602	1,416	1,179	684	542
Sweden	—	—	113	117	816	631	500
Denmark			1,700		1,330		1,390
Netherlands	113	424	1,225	1,280	1,299	1,318	1,015
Belgium	266	286		1,139	1,165	776	2,666
Switzerland	25	108	271	516	640	912	
France	840	2,636	4,554	6,002	5,798	4,159	38,000
W. Germany	} 9,973	} 14,051	} 18,351	} 20,240	11,803 }18,121	11,201	24,175
E. Germany							9,775
Poland			1,479		3,736	927	
Czechoslovakia	1,347	2,201	4,393	5,419	6,080	3,508	15,093
Austria		1,500			1,839	1,763	1,506
Hungary	964		919	1,022	1,008	935	1,153
Rumania	256	2,410	3,476	4,810	4,638	3,504	
Bulgaria		617	838	1,552	1,899	3,152	
Yugoslavia		850		3,000*	4,283	1,160	4,050
Greece			77	2,150	4,327	4,873	
Italy		1,526	2,100	2,164	2,372	980	7,854
Spain	49		121			1,600*	9,210
Russia/USSR	745	3,400	14,768	8,400			

less in Italy and Spain. It is almost non-existant in Portugal and Great Britain.

On a membership basis, credit co-operation appears to cover the field rather completely also in Germany, Austria, the Netherlands, and much of the Balkans. Sweden and Switzerland have much fewer members in agricultural credit co-operatives than there are farmers. In Denmark, the membership is not available on the same basis as the number of unions and is therefore partly obscured. France, Southern Europe, and the British Isles show very much the same picture whether in membership or in the number of societies.

TABLE 29. *Agricultural credit-co-operation: Membership (000's omitted) at the following approximate dates*

Countries	1900	1907/10	1920	1930	1937	1950	Number of farmers around 1950 (thousands)
Norway					4	21	138
Finland	12	12	31	144	148	231	292
Sweden			5	13	93	142	318
Denmark			22		21		205
Netherlands . . .		60		223	214	232	247
Belgium				109	98		231
Switzerland . . .	2	7	22	45	60	95	188
France		117	241	471	589		2,500
Poland		225			816	233	
Czechoslovakia . .					1,441	950	
Austria					316	299	306
Hungary	194		275	399	422		
Rumania			788		905	986	
Bulgaria		40	75	223	217	905	
Yugoslavia. . . .					215		2,800
Greece					194	750	1,000*
Italy		150	200	152	482	250	
Russia/USSR . .		264	1,500	9,523	4,675		

(180) This difference in structure and coverage has a twofold background. In Great Britain, agricultural credit was to be had on commercial terms and did not require special provision to the same extent as on the continent. French farmers also, on the whole, had more land and a better chance of accumulating savings than was the case in most other Continental countries. This however only partly explains the incomplete coverage of credit co-operation in that country; partly it is due to the same causes as have hampered the development of other branches of co-operation in France[a]. Lack of co-operative spirit has probably been more important in this connection, and the same factor is at least apparently responsible for the even weaker development in the Mediterranean countries[b].

In Central Europe, and in most of Eastern Europe including the Balkans, there has, on the contrary, been a steady, rather quiet development of credit co-operation. The movement started by Raiffeisen and others (for instance, FR. V. KAMPELÍK in the Czech provinces) here came to be the basis for the whole movement of agricultural co-operation. The steady spread of the movement has of course been disturbed by periods of agricultural crisis, as for instance during the thirties in Bulgaria [c]. An example lying between the patterns of Southern and of Eastern Europe is the movement in Greece. Here the efforts of reconstruction and agricultural expansion in the twenties prompted a sudden and succesful build-up of credit co-operation, in reponse to the services offered by the State bank for agricultural credit [d].

A promising development in Russia was interrupted during the revolution. The pre-war position was a long way from being regained when the collectivization drive started around 1930 [e]. The first five-year plan foresaw renewed development in this field, intended to surpass the achievements of 1916 [f]. It is not clear how far this goal was achieved before all kinds of co-operative activity were absorbed in the kolkhoz organization.

(181) Nowadays, agricultural credit is to a large extent institutionalized and State supported in most European countries. This is so not only in the Soviet Union, where the whole movement, and practically all important allocations of investment funds, are directed by the State [a]. Virtually the same is true about all the East European countries, including Yugoslavia. There is extensive State direction of agricultural credit in the Scandinavian countries, Germany, Greece, and Italy, and credit for investment purposes is equally supervised by the State in the United Kingdom.

Although important parts of the original mission of an expanding credit co-operative movement can thus be said to have been accomplished in most of Europe, the importance which the movement has had for the development of agricultural co-operation as a whole must not be overlooked. The Raffeisen principle of unlimited mutual liability strengthened the solidarity of the farming class, and credit facilities broadened the scope for development in various directions. The road was cleared towards processing and marketing activities which, along with other forms of co-operation, were to modify the significance of traditional farm structures.

These reflections tend to strengthen the impression that credit co-operation will still have an important mission to fulfil in Southern Europe.

SUPPLY, MARKETING, AND PROCESSING

(182) While credit co-operation met with needs that were rather peculiar to the agricultural sector of the economy, the co-operative organization of purchases and sales in agriculture had much in common with the urban movement of consumers' co-operation. In Great-Britain, the country of origin of the latter, this branch of agricultural co-operation is also the most developed — indeed, the only well developed branch of agricultural co-operation in that country. Since the early thirties, part of the functions of marketing and processing co-operatives have been organized on a nation-wide scale in the United Kingdom through the marketing boards for some of the most important kinds of agricultural products.

The following two tables (30 and 31) represent an attempt to assess the general quantitative importance of this kind of agricultural co-operation. The field is vast and not very clearly defined, but in many instances no better data were obtainable. In some instances, the figures may represent the total of agricultural societies in the country, except those included under specialized headings in the various sources. It has thus not been possible to avoid all double counting. The figures should therefore be read as merely indicative.

Nor are the data always comparable within the same country. Development trends too are thus only broadly indicated and no exact conclusions can be drawn as to details.

(183) Supply and sales co-operation on the whole developed somewhat later than credit co-operation, and still has not got as far in general coverage. Yet it may be said to have developed very much on the same geographical and social lines. The main exception to this rule is in the British Isles, where supply and sales co-operatives are the core of agricultural co-operation[a]. The late development in Great Britain may to some extent be due to lack of incentive in a country where some of the peculiar economic difficulties of agriculture were less accentuated than

TABLE 30. *Supply and sales co-operatives (without further specification) number of societies around each of the following years. (For number of communes around 1950, see Table 28)*

Country	1900	1907/10	1920	1930	1937	1950
Great Britain . .	9	131	1,558		482	471
N. Ireland . . .	} 92		141	100	39	17
Eire			1,114	585	93	74
Norway		227	963	2,240	1,763	2,096
Sweden		1,211	1,376		1,662	
Denmark . . .	911		1,792	1,903		
		685		500	1,119	1,284
Belgium	730	1,523		1,370	1,391	1,323
Switzerland. . .		566			1,100	
France				17,500	20,673	5,472
W. Germany . .	} 1,115	} 3,846	} 22,552		11,774	10,861
E. Germany . .						
Poland			400*		3,573	
Czechoslovakia .					1,475	
Austria.					143	200
Hungary	267		1,956		1,482	
Rumania			2,820		1,699	
Bulgaria			621	1,030	1,624	
Yugoslavia . . .				1,500*	2,183	9,000
Greece					758	2,250
Italy	50	620	1,113	618	830	
Portugal			121			
Russia/USSR . .	334	2,500	20,000	78,064		

on the Continent. An indication of this is the fact that agricultural co-operation developed a little faster in Wales than in England and somewhat more in the poorer than in the richer parts of the principality [b]. Although rural co-operation in Ireland has had a stronger and more many-sided development than in England, there also the supply and sales branches were among the most important [c].

This type of co-operation has also played an important part in the Belgian Boerenbond. In tables 30 and 31, the number of societies and membership figures are those for the Boerenbond as a whole. It may be noted that this movement covered practically all of the Flemish parts of the country. The 1147 Flemish communities almost all have a co-operative, while less than

TABLE 31. *Supply and sales co-operatives (without further specification): Membership (000's omitted), around each of the following years. (For number of farmers around 1950, see Table 29)*

Country	1900	1907/10	1920	1930	1937	1950
Great Britain . .	2	15	215		139	230
N. Ireland . . .	} 12		26	20	6	
Eire			158	100	21	
Norway		13	34	250		
Finland				61	64	83
Sweden		77	81	90		136
Denmark . . .			170			
Netherlands . .		60		65	134	145
Belgium	52			134	126	
Switzerland. . .		45			100	
France				1,000	1,753	
Poland				250*	438	
Czechoslovakia .					334	
Hungary			900		636	
Rumania			210		199	
Bulgaria				119	176	
Yugoslavia . . .						5,200
Greece					18	
Italy	8	129	350	500	800	
Portugal			2			
Russia/USSR . .		290	1,500	8,508		

200 co-operatives take care of the 1500 communities of Walloon Belgium[d].

In France, this type of co-operation is not only less developed than credit co-operation, but also covers only a minor part of the country. For South European developments, the information available is ambiguous and not always reliable. Though far from negligible in importance, Spanish rural co-operation seems at some epochs to have developed mushroom organizations of little vitality[e].

In more than one of the East European States, development is difficult to trace because of the mixed set-up of organizations deriving from different States in the past, as is the case in Yugoslavia[f], or belonging to different nationalities within the same State, as in Czechoslovakia and Poland.

(184) If it can be said that both credit and sales-and-supply co-operation corresponded essentially to modern problems facing the farming community in a changing world, it is equally true that co-operative processing of products is not so new. Joint action in processing for sale has had forerunners at very early dates. This appears to have occurred, as a rule, when a specialized and standardized commodity was being prepared for distant markets, as certain qualities of wine and some makes of cheese. When European agriculture, especially during the latter half of the nineteenth century, was gradually linked up with commercial markets and became more and more dependent upon them for its survival, the tendency to standardize products was of course strengthened. On this point, it is instructive to note that dairy co-operatives have had an earlier development than the general societies for sales and supply. Their early growth was often rather spontaneous and occurred at least in many instances without any direct impulse from the ideological movement to create a spirit of co-operation. In fact, they came to be one of the first big successes of the co-operative movement. By now, they have achieved a more complete coverage than most other branches, as will be seen from Tables 32 and 33.

The coverage is very close to being complete in Eire, the Scandinavian countries, the Netherlands, Switzerland, and Austria, that is in most of the important dairying countries. It was extensive also in Hungary, at least immediately before the last war. It had little significance in Great Britain and had only a very partial coverage also in Germany. In the former country, the milk marketing boards fulfil part of the functions of a central co-operative union since a couple of decades. In France, the coverage appears to be very incomplete indeed, even if it is taken into account that dairying is not of importance in all parts of the country. The latter circumstance also serves as a partial explanation for the weak development of dairy co-operatives in most of Southern Europe, even if it is not by any means the full explanation. The argument works the other way around also, and developing dairy co-operatives would certainly be one of the most efficient means of promoting the dairy industry in these countries.

(185) Some other branches of processing co-operation have

TABLE 32. *Dairy co-operatives: Number of societies at each of the following dates. For number of communities around 1950, see Table 28*

Country	1900	1907/10	1920	1930	1937	1950
Great Britain . .	—	13	13			11
N. Ireland . . .		} 288	} 339		55	21
Eire					229	192
Norway		51		80	168	502
Finland	—	343	434	697	670	414
Sweden	430	550	592	715	862	
Denmark . . .	1,056	1,157	1,335	1,338	1,417	1,309
Netherlands . .	416		438	438	496	920
Belgium	356			213	169	
Switzerland. . .	1,459		2,651	2,816	3,800	3,079
France	2,200				2,213	
W. Germany . .	} 1,917	} 2,373	} 3,305	} 4,587	6,926	5,657
E. Germany . .					} 8,798	
Poland					1,560	
Czechoslovakia .					500	
Austria.						1,274
Hungary	246	587		243	947	
Bulgaria		10			38	
Yugoslavia . . .					200	
Greece					77	
Italy		138	324	427	2,130	
Spain						33

developed later and none has yet achieved a coverage comparable to that of the dairies. Slaughterhouse and livestock co-operatives have a high coverage only in Scandinavia and Switzerland, and only in Denmark and Switzerland was this development early. Even in a country like the Netherlands, this branch was still in its initial stages in the inter-war period[a].

The co-operatives for processing winegrapes and horticultural products are probably still less advanced than those for processing livestock products, even if the coverage is more difficult to judge in view of the restricted geographical and numerical representation of these branches of production. In 1937, France had over a thousand winegrowers' co-operatives with some 150,000 members, which represents at least a substantial proportion of the industry. Germany, at the same date, had almost 500 societies with some 25,000 members, which is probably a higher

TABLE 33. *Dairy co-operatives: Membership (000's omitted) around each of the following dates. For number of farms around 1950, see Table 29*

Country	1900	1907/10	1920	1930	1937	1950
Great Britain . .	—		1			3
N. Ireland . . .		} 41	} 50		9	
Eire					55	50
Norway					70	111
Finland	—	33	46	75	76	77
Sweden			58	106	156	259
Denmark . . .	140	157	180	189	Z90	180
Netherlands . .			100		130	
Belgium	25			35	35	
Switzerland. . .		22		103	117	
France.					280	
Poland					642	
Czechoslovakia .					90	
Hungary	27	56		50	110	
Bulgaria					3	
Yugoslavia . . .					17	
Greece.					1	
Italy		10		237	240	

proportion of the industry in that country. In other countries, only small numbers of winegrowers were thus associated, e.g. in Italy only 16,000 in about 200 societies. The horticultural industry was co-operatively organized to a large extent in the Netherlands, and the same movement was important in Switzerland and Germany.

Although the wine industry to some extent was already co-operatively organized a very long time ago, its coverage in the Mediterranean countries is still small, as in Spain for instance [b]. The explanation is partly that so much of Spanish grape production is in large-scale agriculture, where the individual producer has resources enough to process his own produce.

Despite analogous preconditions, the olive oil industry appears to have been organized in co-operative plants to a higher degree than wine production, both in Spain and Italy [c].

CO-OPERATION ON MEANS OF PRODUCTION

(186) The co-operatives for land reclamation and land improvement are old and well-known. Especially in the Netherlands, Belgium, north-western Germany, land reclamation and land protection along the low shores of the North Sea have for many centuries enforced a comprehensive discipline among neighbors near and far. For instance, in Prussian legislation relating to Schleswig-Holstein and Oldenburg, there are important regulations in support of societies of a co-operative character, organized for the control of water and drainage[a].

In Southern Europe, large-scale irrigation has also for many centuries prompted the organization of co-operative associations. For instance, in the Spanish *huertas* on the Mediterranean coast, the *"sindacatos de riegos"* possess an important disciplinary power over the distribution of irrigation water among their members[b]. Modern Spanish co-operation statistics list 42 irrigation co-operatives, 11 of which are in the province of Valencia, corresponding to some of those old syndicates; another 15 are in the province of Valladolid, in the northern part of the plateau and may be recent creations[c].

(187) In contrast to these old types of co-operatives, those specializing in machine-owning are recent, for obvious reasons. For the appreciation of their importance, it is a difficulty that their size and character is extremely variable, from loose associations of two or three neighbors who own some big machine in common, to large-scale establishments serving one or more whole communities. The position becomes even more complicated through the occurrence of hire of machinery services against payment, either by farmers for their neighbors, or by machine-stations.

The latter feature is of growing importance in some countries in Western Europe, on a capitalistic basis. It is however the dominating form of agricultural machinery administration in the Soviet Union and most countries in Eastern Europe. In these countries, only the State owns big agricultural machinery to any large extent; hence co-operative activity of this kind is practically excluded.

As far as available statistics cover the field, co-operative machine-owning is perhaps most developed in France, where there existed something between six and seven thousand such associations, with 200,000 members, in the early fifties.[a] In Western Germany, this form of co-operation has contributed substantially to the mechanization of small farms, partly through the combination of draught cows and co-operatively owned tractors.[b]

In the Netherlands, threshing machine associations had shortly after the war risen to 373 societies with 11,500 members[c], which was still only a small proportion of the possible coverage. At the end of 1950, there were over 400 machinery societies covering an area of almost 300,000 hectares. It was calculated that these associations cut down the expenditure for capital equipment on the farms served by them by at least one-fifth[d]. The same report also holds that co-operatives of this type function best if they are small; they did not seem to pay if they were so large as to be run by a hired manager.

This was mainly to a service for small farmers. Whenever a farm is large enough to possess a complete set of the essential machinery itself, it tends to do so rather than rely upon co-operative action, since the latter necessarily limits the availability of the machines to each particular member. In the UK, about 50 pools of this kind were formed in 1943 and 1944, but only few among them survived until the late forties, presumably because supply of machinery became plentiful again[e].

In Southern Europe, in connection with the measures of land reform and domestic colonization, the State does some of the procurement of agricultural machinery and thereby encourages co-operation in the field of machine-owning[f].

JOINT CULTIVATION

(188) Farming within the framework of co-operative institutions is a fairly old idea which has had little success on the whole[a]. This is generally held to be due to the fact that such farms are not co-operative just because the landlord happens to be a co-operative association. As agricultural enterprises, they are exposed to very much the same difficulties as private farms.

Actually, some enterprises of this kind do exist in the British

Isles. In 1948–49, they covered some 38,000 acres, most of which was in central and southern England and in Scotland[b]. There are some examples in Eire too; it is sometimes suggested that they might play the role of "model farms", promoting the advancement of the industry and the education of the small farmers towards applying modern techniques[c].

(189) In quite another way, the idea of joint action has penetrated into the sector of small farming. It was repeatedly found that the weak bargaining position of small tenants against their landlords could be strengthened if the tenants co-operated over their lease contracts. This was the starting point for co-operative farming in Italy, as will be described in the next paragraph. Similar forms also occurred in other countries. For instance, in Rumania there existed at some time in the twenties more than 600 societies for common land lease, with some 43,000 members[a].

A kind of group holding or corporate ownership of allotments by local associations has been long established in England and is fairly wide-spread, especially in areas where the urban co-operative movement is strong. Until recently, the Allotments Advisory Board encouraged this form of land holding, though it has lately tended to prefer public ownership of allotments[b].

Another kind of small-scale group holding is being introduced in the Italian land reform zones, where the allotments for agricultural workers are being grouped by five (the so-called *quote*, five of which equal a full-scale farm according to the land reform scheme) and are equipped for joint operation in many respects.

(190) Though not in itself a measure of joint cultivation, co-operative land holding is the starting point for some of the most interesting spontaneous instances of co-operative farming. A case of this kind was the Russian *artel* in the pre-Communist period, which was essentially founded on the idea of common land holding rather than ownership of the land. This became the starting point both for the experiments in common farming in the twenties and for the present kolkhoz.

A similar movement was originated in Italy as an attempt to escape the exactions of the middle-men between landlords and tenants. The first collective farm with this intention was formed around 1900. Despite the unfavorable attitude of the government, there were in the early thirties about 400 such societies with some 45,000 members, cultivating about a quarter million hectares all of which were not, however, under joint cultivation[a]. In the early fifties, Italy had a total of 787 co-operatives of various kinds for common cultivation, cultivating over a million hectares, of which 585,000 hectares were actually under joint cultivation, while the common business of the remainder was more limited.

Also the recent Swedish statute on co-operative farming envisages only renting (especially of public land) as the basis for joint cultivation. The few existing co-operatives of this kind in the country are founded on that basis.

(191) All these instances — the Russian kolkhoz, the Italian co-operative leasehold farm, and the Swedish experimental co-operatives for joint farming — mean, in substance, the joint or co-operative holding of one single unified enterprise. Discussion on joint farming in other countries is not always quite clear, but the prevailing idea seems rather to be the successive amalgamation of a group of primarily independent small farms, by their assuming more and more functions in common. This is also the main line of action in most of the countries in Eastern Europe outside the USSR, where the various "lower" and "higher" types of co-operative farms are intended to bring about a gradual amalgamation of the small enterprises into big ones. A similar line of argument is encountered in France and Germany, for instance, where it is suggested that far-reaching co-operation should be capable of doing away with all the disadvantages of small-scale farming[a].

This approach to joint cultivation is fundamentally different from that of the unified big enterprise run by a co-operative. If the starting point is the small farm, the shortcomings of which are remedied through joint action wherever useful, the final outcome is not an entirely unified big enterprise but something else, a new form of agricultural organization. This was the way in which the Balkan countries were by themselves slowly approaching the group farming idea. As touched on in Chapter 4, Bulgarian co-operation especially had already begun to exhibit instances of joint cultivation before the war[b]. The present attempts at

new forms of organization in Yugoslavia, after the abandonment
of the first coercive collectivization drive, tend to approach
again the idea of grouping small individual farms together for
the purpose of joint action in all operations that are most
profitable on a large-scale basis but retaining other functions on
the private and small-scale basis.

CO-OPERATION VERSUS COLLECTIVITY

(192) The material discussed in this chapter may justify some
reflections of a systematic nature. Co-operation and collectivity
are too often confounded. In reality, there is a distinct difference,
though with numerous aspects.

In Western and Southern Europe, co-operation in agriculture
has been and is still essentially a spontaneous popular movement
for the care of common interests felt to need joint action. The
reaction to actual needs has seldom been immediate. Even in a
situation where the need for co-operation is obvious, it generally
takes at least a generation to bring it into effect, just as with
most branches of technical extension and general education.
The movement indicates that there has been a great need for
activities such as credit, processing of products for sale, marketing
and the purchase of investment goods, that is, on the whole,
for the contacts with the non-agricultural sectors of the economy.
In the field of primary production, co-operative activities are
so far tentative and cannot yet be said to have given any decisive
answer as to the nature of the needs of the future.

In Eastern Europe, including the Soviet Union, similar lines
of development have recently been channelled into wholesale
State plans for the organization of the farming industry. The
coercive rules thus applied do of course diminish the general
interest which the experience of these countries might have, since
the measures were not always those which corresponded to the
needs felt by the farming population. But the way in which co-
operation is brought about is not necessarily decisive for the
outcome of the movement. Distinct differences may be traced
between various forms of organization, which in their turn have
effects both on the economic success and the social pattern of
the farming community.

(193) There may be co-operation between men and between enterprises. The men may be those who run a farm in common, or they may run different farms and co-operate without being joint producers, or they may belong to other industries. A farm owned by a co-operative (a creamery, for instance) belongs to "the co-operative sector" from the viewpoint of the general economic structure of society as a whole. From the viewpoint of the farming industry, however, it has all the characteristics of an individual farm.

The small individual farms which co-operate only in their contacts with the other sectors of the economy may, as far as these contacts are concerned, function as one single enterprise, if the main features of their economic policy are laid down in the framework of their organization. In a country like Sweden, for instance, one may say that the whole farming industry functions in many respects as one single big enterprise for the whole country. The effects of price policies jointly agreed make themselves felt in the decision-making of the individual farmer. The recommendations on changes in sowings and other production measures which the over-all organizations issue as consequences of these policies are followed generally enough to justify the judgement that the industry is jointly planned.

When the small farms go a step further in common action and perform some operations of cultivation jointly, this does not necessarily mean any change of principle. As long as each farm retains its independence in important sectors of work, it also remains a distinct enterprise and thus retains the specific advantage of the small farm, that is the elasticity of its labor organization.

A co-operative farm of the Italian type is still a kind of co-operative, even if the farm is unified. The farm is collective, but the membership is co-operative. The decisive characteristics are on the one hand unified action, on the other hand the co-operative character of the association, i.e. voluntary membership and democratic management through the membership itself rather than through a managerial board or by outside authorities.

The Russian kolkhoz, in theory, was meant to be very much the same: a co-operative association cultivating a collective farm. Whether the membership is co-operative or not in practice is a question which depends largely on the definition of voluntariness and on the capacity of the membership to take decisions which are essential for its own well-being. When there is no real choice, most people are likely to accept, "voluntarily", the inevitable. In a Western society where the whole industry is thoroughly organized and the co-operative general organizations negotiate with the State, the individual farmer may also find his choice limited in some respects. The loss of some liberties is then compensated by the increase in security. There is always a vast series of possible variations in the life of the individual producer to make his own decision-making an essential factor in what happens to him economically.

The kolkhoz membership, on the other hand, is not a co-operative for the reason that its local decision-making on how the farm should be managed is severely restricted, not only through the model statutes but also through successive directives from State authorities. The individual kolkhoz member can improve his individual economic status by working harder and in as close conformity as possible with the rules laid down by the management of the farm. In this respect he is in the same position as a hired worker. But, except for the limited sphere of freedom left in the *dvor* (which is not co-operative), he cannot by his own decisions concerning the productive process make any essential change in the collective product of the farm, from which he draws according to his share in the work.

(194) Economically, the difference between co-operation and collectivity would make itself felt especially through the labor organization. The collective farm of the Russian model will, as shown above, have all the shortcomings of the labor organization of a large farm. As long as small farms in co-operation are not entirely merged, they are likely to retain the specific advantage of small farms in this respect. Even when the farm is unified but the membership is still a co-operative association with a decisive say in its own affairs, some of the small farmers' interest in their own production may be preserved, if the co-operative rules are well devised.

Theoretically at least, a balance could be found between those operations which are best carried out on a large scale and those where the careful and interested work of independent individuals gives the best result. The contrast between individual and joint action is only apparently a dilemma; in reality it is a scale with two poles which could be brought to harmonize. Where, on the other hand, all essential productive functions are made collective, and the membership reduced to a collective of workers who receive a kind of salary, then the specific psychological incentive of individual farming must be lost and the members are likely to react very much as do hired farmhands on large plantations. The effects are strongest in livestock husbandry, and the most salient failures of Soviet agriculture are also in this sector.

These observations must not conceal the fact that also other forms of collective decision-making may have the effect of strangling progress, in agriculture as well as in other branches of the economic life. Also in Western societies, a limit may some day be found beyond which national planning and tax systems together produce the same kind of effects as the comprehensive regulation of kolkhozy through model statutes and production directives.

(195) From the viewpoint of social structure, two main types of society could be the outcome of different forms of joint action in agriculture. One is a society of farmers who are each others' equals, equipped with a stratum of organization specialists recruited from their own ranks and hiring certain expert assistance from outside. The other is a technocratic hierarchy, close to the pattern of a centrally operated factory.

This difference would of course seldom be absolute. In practice, all kinds of transitional forms would occur, and no type of society could be expected to remain absolutely immobile. In both directions, the difference is likely to lie more in the political climate of the country and in the general way in which the rules are applied than in the rules themselves. This is what makes it so difficult to apply the definitions attempted above, but this is also why it is necessary to keep the definitions clear so that they can be reconsidered again and again.

CHAPTER 6

LAND POLICY

(196) The preceding chapters have attempted to describe some main features of the institutional framework of agriculture in Europe. The aim has not been merely descriptive but also to view the structure in relation to economics and policy, as a help or a hindrance for agricultural society and its objectives. Indications of actual and recent policy have therefore been given as appropriate, in order to help the reader to grasp the implications of each of the structural features described.

We are satisfied that no historical analysis can result in an exhaustive "explanation" in the sense of a complete analysis of causes and effects. Yet it appears that European experience in the land question can be made more understandable and more useful if land policies are put in relation with the structures these policies refer to and the spontaneous development of these structures. The different attempted solutions are likely to tell us how the main problems were viewed by those responsible for the policies. The success or failure of the solutions attempted will to some extent indicate whether these ideas were realistic or not. In the ultimate analysis, the lesson is likely to be that certain conditions are basic necessities for the farming industry.

Once the basic necessities of a given situation are known, future policies will have to accept either that the natural impediments to a given policy are too expensive to overcome, and hence abstain from it, or also to pay the price for disregarding them. Seemingly, the political choice may not be any easier because more facts are known. At any rate, the responsibilities will be more clearly outlined.

(197) Some of the deliberate ideological trends underlying recent land policies are relatively easy to describe. The French

Revolution in itself exhibited contrasting tendencies, but its main outcome in the field of agrarian policy was the realization of Liberal theories. Individual initiative was to be set free and landed property freely disposed of. From this original standpoint, which was only formally unequivocal, both agrarian industrialism and family farm policy could develop under the pressure of various incidental circumstances.

More distinct in its outlines was the claim of the early Socialist movement, continued by Communism. Exploitation of man by man should be abolished; everybody should work only for himself and for the community, nobody was to work for the profit of any other individual. This, it was originally thought, could only be realized if small production was abandoned and agriculture organized as large enterprise and socialized, on lines analogous to those of urban industries. It was when practical solutions began to be necessary that the line of Socialist discussion was divided and many adherents of the movement found that what was claim for large-scale farming was not borne out by practical experience.

The chief instrument of the Conservative response was, above all, the new Catholic social program, from the nineties onwards; the family was to be strengthened as an independent social cell, primary in relation to both the State and society at large; ethical and traditional values of Western society would be best protected if the family continued to be the basic entity of economic life.

From the viewpoint of social policy, the main division of opinion was over the question whether those working on the land should be made to live like wage-earners or continue as independent small entrepreneurs. The Conservative view, often independently of the Catholic Church, frequently associated itself with economic ideas emanating from the Physiocrats or the social romanticism of the 18th century, with the contention that peasant society is the true prototype of human society. The theme became infinitely varied, from idealistic radicalism down to nationalistic militarism, expecting more and better soldiers from a sound and prolific countryside.

(198) Underlying these social motives there were of course, though not always consciously, economic realities, which are

now beginning to attract primary attention. The modern productivist arguments are based on either maximum production or cheap production, according to the commercial interests and security necessities of each country. Rural over-population, on the other hand, was not so significant in the local self-supporting economy of past centuries. It then made itself felt as temporary food shortage in frequent years of crop failure. Hunger and disease then reduced the population of each region, when existing resources could not support it under the technique prevailing, and thus re-established the threatened balance between land and people. Modern development of medical science, together with a new concept of the responsibility of governing bodies for plague control, has set free an unparalleled increase in rural population. At the same time, the new economic framework gave the problem of rural over-population quite a new meaning.

Gradually, peasant society was brought into economic dependence on the urban sector of the economy. Whether they wish it or not, peasants are now definitely deprived of their millennia-old capacity to satisfy all their needs by themselves. The trend is inexorably towards increase of primary agricultural production at the same time as the farming community is stripped of more and more of its old economic functions outside agriculture in the narrow sense of the word. The fact that agriculture was much oversupplied with manpower had scarcely been felt before, except in cases of extreme monoculture in some regions. In the framework of a self-supporting economy there was always something to do, some handicraft to exercise, and scarcity of material was compensated by more detailed and artistic elaboration of each object.

The disproportion between manpower and productive resources began to make itself felt in bargaining with urban industries. The latter produced on a large scale and at prices that made the products of rural craftsmen luxury commodities. By stages specialization progressed from clothing and metal work to primary processing of raw textiles, and further to dairying and baking. At the same time, urban industries avoided, by and large, obtaining more manpower than they could use. Those really unemployed were at each occasion squeezed out of active production, with the result that they returned to the countryside from which they had migrated and again increased the numbers of underemployed farming population.

The faster rural population numbers increased, the more the bargaining position of the farming sector deteriorated. It was this basic situation of overcrowding that political theories and practices tried to remedy. The formulas for social organization applied were, in each case, intended to last, if not for eternity, at least for any foreseeable future.

In each case, the solutions can be said to have been founded on some kind of previous experience, either the remote phenomena of the self-supporting rural households of the pre-industrial era, or the nearer events of still immature forms of industrial production and of agricultural production in transition. The differences between manufacturing and agricultural production thus tended to be overlooked, and especially the difference in the manpower situation. The real significance of the situation was difficult to grasp because the situation was new. Agrarian society on the threshold between self-sufficiency and market dependency was a new thing which had never before been under observation. Its problems could scarcely have been judged realistically at once.

LAND REFORMS AND HOMESTEAD POLICIES

(199) The claim that the land should be given to those who work on it has many aspects, even apart from the historical arguments that were many times advanced as pretexts, or the national sentiments involved[a]. The claim appealed to the individualistic feelings of farmers, but at the same time to the class feelings of landless or otherwise poor people among the farming population. On the one hand, the urge for land reform was radical in its immediate scope, by threatening the privileges of large landowners. On the other hand, it was conservative in the more remote perspective in the intention to establish a broad stratum of well-to-do individual farmers as a stabilizing force in the social and political life of the country.

(200) Under conditions of urgent social pressure, two basic situations might provide different starting points for a re-

distribution of the land. One is that where most land is tenanted. Here, the program to make the tenants safe on their holdings, and eventually to make them owners, clashed mainly with the class interests of the landlords, involving also financial difficulties of compensation if the land reform were to avoid a violent break in the established legal tradition. This was the dominating situation on Ireland, and in part of the Balkan countries as successors to the Turkish empire.

The other situation is where the landlords keep all or most of their land as large-scale productive units under their own direct or indirect personal supervision. This was frequently so in Hungary, parts of the Austrian monarchy, and Southern Europe. Land reform would then mean not only a big change in the social setup but also in the economic structure of the country's agriculture. The class interests of the landlords then mobilize economic arguments in their support, claiming that land reform would reduce production or make it more expensive.

More frequently, the two situations occurred together. The landlords kept part of their land as large-scale agricultural enterprises under their own supervision and let the rest. Part of the rent of the tenants was in the form of work on the estate. Even if this was not formally regulated, the tenancies might be so small as to make work on the estates a necessary source of additional income for the tenants. The former was the classical case in Mediaeval feudal Western Europe, and instances of the latter continued to exist in many regions where the French Revolution had formally done away with even the remainders of feudalism. Such was the case in Denmark and northern Germany until early in the 19th century. The peasants then received land, in north-eastern Germany in a very piece-meal way, in Denmark throughout most of the 19th century in stages, so that the estate system was almost entirely abolished. This was also the case of Russia before 1861, when the peasants' part of the land was allotted to them, and in parts of Poland and the Balkans until even later. In these areas, therefore, the land reform tended to consist of two main phases. The first one was to liberate the already established small tenants from the burden of their rents and obligations towards their landlords. More difficult and controversial was the breaking up of the large estates.

(201) In the countries of Southern Europe, with their many regional contrasts in stages of development, various combinations of these problems could be found over the period here discussed. For the most part, the solutions are still pending.

In Western Europe, as already indicated, the whole series of problems were already mostly over by the beginning of this century. Formal tenants had become owners on a large scale through the French Revolution and other developments, such as those already mentioned in Scandinavia. Although tenancy remained a frequent feature in parts of the Continent (and also in some Swedish regions), deliberate land policy has not aimed at any profound change of the land pattern in these countries. Measures of economic support, and settlement schemes on a modest scale have aimed at preserving rather than expanding the independent farmer class in these countries. The main instances of large-scale land reform in Western Europe were the changes brought about in Ireland and Finland.

(202) The Irish land reform, which was partly continued into our century, was largely for the rehabilitation of a congested area, connected with strong national resentment against outside domination. Irish misery came acutely to the notice of the outside world during the great famine in 1848. Although whole-sale emigration has contributed more than anything else towards establishing reasonable proportions between land and manpower in Ireland, the measures of reform in the sphere of agrarian structure have formed the main content of agrarian policy in the country. The problem of overpopulation was also a consideration in the attempts to bring relief to the most congested areas, a process which is not quite finished yet.

The Irish tenants' claim for "the three f's" — fixity of tenure, fair rent, and free sale — implied a profound modification of the agrarian structure. Even though ownership was not generally claimed from the outset, the three f's would yet virtually mean ownership, and the landlords were then to retain at best the capitalized value of the fair rent. The claims were to a great extent already realized during the last decades of the 19th century through legislation from 1881 onwards[a]. Provision came to be made also for tenants to purchase the land they cultivated, by aid of public loans. Over the period of 70 years the Land

Commission worked in Ireland, it advanced 130 million pounds to 450,000 tenant farmers to purchase holdings covering 15 million acres (6 million hectares). Out of this, 2 million acres were untenanted land which the landlords had held themselves and was now divided [b]. The fact that all land subject to some kind of agricultural use in Ireland amounts to about 19 million acres may give an idea as to the scope of these measures.

Despite all this public aid, not all the new owners proved capable of coping with their task. During the struggles of the thirties, new expropriations were carried out, including land belonging to "new landlords" who had bought it up from unsuccessful small farmers. It was even talked about the recurrence of tenure problems within fifty years [c].

Untenanted land was taken over mainly in the twenties, after the purchase of tenanted land had been completed and the new State became responsible for the socio-economic problems of the countryside. At that stage, about 1,2 million acres of such land was allotted, creating some 25,000 new holdings with about half a million acres and improving some 53,000 existing holdings through enlargement or rearrangement [c]. It was estimated that, by 1952, there were still some 25,000–30,000 families in congested areas in need of re-settlement or enlargement of their holdings. Thereafter, the whole problem of the congested areas would be definitely solved. This would require the migration of some 6,000 farmers from the congested areas so that the land surrendered by them could be used to enlarge the holdings of those remaining. One "congest" migrated would solve the problems for four or five remaining "congests" [d]. It may of course be questioned whether this solution is not closely related to the actual situation of technology and economy. The present congested areas would probably not have been considered as congested at all according to the standards of the 19th century. This is a question of the degree to which there is a surplus population which, relatively speaking, is probably more urgent now than fifty years ago, if the differences in available technique are taken into account.

(203) In Great Britain, the absence of any urgent pressure of unemployed or underemployed population on the land was probably one of the real reasons why interest in land questions

came to be focussed around landlord-tenant relationships and very little was done as regards re-distribution of the land or the creation of new holdings. The long series of Land Acts provided the tenants with more and more protection. To begin with, they were granted security of full compensation for improvements on the holding, until the movement gradually culminated in the far reaching protection of the tenants, as discussed in Chapter 4 above.

Even though "land reform" on a broader scale was scarcely considered by those responsible for policy, there existed despite this a tendency to try and solve social emergency problems through the establishment of small holdings. This solution did not belong to the program of any particular political party, and the lack of consistency between these measures and policies in other fields seems to have long passed unobserved [a].

British land settlement policy tended to create new tenanted holdings rather than freeholds. The first Small Holdings Act, in 1892, was only permissive in character and had very little practical consequences. Under the Small Holdings and Allotments Act, 1908, and the Land Settlements (Facilities) Act, 1919, 29,500 holdings were created with altogether 438,000 acres of land [b]. This appears to have implied considerable financial disbursements by the State [c]. The succeding acts before the last war, as well as the special provisions for veterans from World War I, had even less effect. As far as England and Wales are concerned, pre-war policies had therefore only added minor features to the agrarian structure [d]. They are however likely to have contributed to the slow decrease in the size of holdings visible up to the early thirties. In Wales, where this kind of activity may have been deemed a little more important than in England, the movement created about 2,500 small holdings with 66,000 acres of land, which is about $2\frac{1}{2}$ per cent of the land of Wales [e]. The total number of holdings, large and small, is about 300,000 in England and 60,000 in Wales.

In Scotland, between 1886 and 1943, 5,224 new holdings were created and 5,197 already existing were enlarged, covering 102,000 acres of arable land and 763,000 acres of pastures [f]. The net result has, however, been even more meagre than indicated by these figures. It is stated that the total number of holdings increased less than by the number of new small holdings thus established, and that there was even a slight decline in the total number of small holdings[a]. A spontaneous movement of concentration in the structure of holdings has outbalanced the efforts of settlement and colonization.

The foundation of new small holdings in the United Kingdom has not been abandoned after the second world war, but the scope and character of this policy has changed in important respects.

(204) Land distribution and settlement problems in Scandinavia assumed essentially different features in three main regions. In Denmark and southern Sweden, settlement is relatively old and the social history had many features in common with central Europe. In the central and northern parts of the peninsula, a considerable part of the settlement is of recent origin and peasant farming was dominant, partly because of the poor character of the area. In Finland, similar conditions had been prevailing up to the 16th century, but thereafter a great number of estates had been organized.

In Sweden, it was a centuries old tradition to encourage land clearing on forests in public ownership. This procedure increased the taxable stratum of farms and therefore it was deemed to be profitable to the Crown, even though the land was generally given to the farmers in full ownership. This policy is one of the main reasons why freehold came to be the dominating tenure condition in the country, and especially so in the northern parts where the land clearance movement has continued until recently.

In the middle of the last century it was realized that this policy was to some extent abused as a pretext for the penetration of private capitalist forestry enterprises in the vast areas of public forest. A reaction against the liberal forest policy made itself felt towards the end of the century. The reaction was caused partly by fear of quick exhaustion of the forest resources and eventual deterioration of the climate, partly by concern for the farming population. The wish to maintain and strengthen the peasantry in the traditional sense was rather general in Europe at the epoch. Also in Sweden, measures were introduced for the creation of new homesteads[a]. Well established prohibitions on subdivision of farm land were abolished, and a special service

instituted to promote homestead colonization. The general
impact of the latter on the farm pattern of country has not been
very great on the whole. The policy to encourage land division
was reversed after some time and successive measures to restrict
the freedom to divide land culminated in a statute of 1927 under
which land division was entirely controlled by State institutions.
Since the last war, homestead colonization also has been abandoned.

(205) Though historically a country of peasant freeholds, Finland had become dominated since the reformation by an estate
system. The secession of Finland from Sweden and its association
in personal union with the Russian empire had only sharpened
this trend, since much land clearance was done on the fringes
of the estates, resulting in tenanted small holdings. At the
beginning of this century, therefore, Finland showed some of the
typical features of East European countries and the situation
called for a land reform.

A radical land policy was embarked upon under the new
constitution of 1905. The conditions of tenancy were improved,
and preparations made for a thorough revision of the land
structure. In 1918, the independent Finnish State enacted a
statute on liberation of leaseholds and dependent crofts. By the
end of 1922, some 50,000 such places had been transformed into
independent farmsteads. In 1921, other statutes were enacted
on the liberation of leaseholds belonging to the State or to
ecclesiastical institutions, and on the colonization of State forest
land. Finally, in 1922 the Lex Kallio introduced public measures
for establishing entirely new farmsteads, not exceeding 20 hectares
of arable land[a]. By 1928, a profound change in the agrarian
structure had already been brought about. The number of
independent farmsteads has been more than doubled; up to 1935
it was even quadrupled. The distribution of land on various
size-classes of holdings was entirely changed in favor of small
and medium-sized holdings[b]. Most of the difference in farm
structure between 1901 and 1951 depends upon these reform
measures in the twenties and thirties. To what extent spontaneous
colonization, independent of public aid, might have contributed
to the change, is difficult to say. The relative abundance of
virgin soil for land clearance gave this land reform a broader
scope than was possible in most other countries at the same epoch.

The second war again left Finland with grave problems of social land distribution. A farming population of a quarter million from the ceded Carelian area had to be settled, and at the same time many ex-service men wanted land as a way of life. Modernized technique made many of the old farms appear too small. The basis of the new reform was a Land Expropriation Act, of 1945, according to which all landowners had to surrender part of their land, though on a varying scale. A minimum farm size was established, below which existing farms should not be reduced. Unlike the post-war land reforms in Communist countries, the Finnish reform provided for indemnification of former owners [c].

Most of those who applied under the Land Expropriation Act, had obtained land before the end of the forties, either under the provisions of the Act or by voluntary sales [c]. By the end of 1951, the whole land reform had touched about 1.9 million hectares and created 50,000 new holdings. Most of this increase took place in the size-classes between 2 and 10 hectares; the size-class between 10 and 15 hectares increased a little, while the number of holdings over 15 hectares diminished. The average size of holding was reduced from 10.6 to 8.9 hectares [d]. Most of the changes in farm structure between 1941 and 1951 must be ascribed to this reform.

(206) While peasant liberation in Denmark had been mainly accomplished during the 19th century, the continued pressure of a rapidly increasing population, together with a wish to diminish overseas emigration, inspired interest in smallholdings' settlement late in the nineties. A Small Holdings' Act was passed in 1899, encouraging the establishment of co-operative associations for purchase of estates to be divided among the members. Up to 1919, some 9,000 holdings had been created this way, partly financed by public loans. In 1919, three further Land Acts were passed, providing for the sale of glebe lands, the conversion of fiefs, entailed estates, and feoffments held in trust, into free estates. Further, conditions were stipulated for the sale of public land [a]. The immediate results of this legislation were, however, not very speedy being on a scale similar to the results of the previous legislation [b].

Danish agrarian policy in this century has therefore not brought about any profound changes in the holding structure of the country, even if it has contributed to increasing the part played by small farms. The considerable change in the holding structure shown in Chapter 3 will therefore partly have to be interpreted as the consequence of spontaneous land subdivision.

(207) In countries like the Netherlands, Belgium, and Switzerland, the farm structure had for so long been dominated by small farms that the idea of a land reform was scarcely conceivable in terms of a redistribution of land. The immediate need was to improve tenure conditions, especially in the two former countries, where tenancy was important. The goal of making tenants safe in possession of their holdings has also been realized step by step, as shown in Chapter 4. In the Netherlands, a considerable amount of new holdings have been created in land reclaimed from the sea, and the planning of the new regions as viable tracts of country is famous.

In Belgium, the farms are as a whole even smaller, and a redistribution policy was even further out of the question. [a] On the contrary, as in some other Western countries, the problem of small holdings has often been viewed differently: it was feared that rural exodus could lead large strata of the people to lose contact with the land. More specifically, the Catholic social program, with its recommendation that as many as possible should be holders of independent pieces of land, has largely inspired the Société Nationale de la Petite Propriété Terrienne (SNPPT). This movement has, between 1935 and 1951, established about 14,000 small holdings (part-time holdings), varying between 8 ares and 3 hectares [b]. This certainly is still only a small fraction of all smallholdings existing in Belgium. However, the movement has been continued with a somewhat enlarged scope recently. A special statute in 1949 has granted the society considerable financial means for buying up land between 1950 and 1955, with a view to create 3,000–3,500 new smallholdings per year. An ambitious program aims at reclaiming some 280,000 hectares of cultivated land, though over a much longer period.

Swiss economic policy has in general aimed at preserving the farming class of the country. The disparities between world market prices and domestic costs of production for agricultural products are specially great in this case, and unprotected agriculture would soon be faced with a crisis that would lead to extensive farming and concentration on much fewer and larger holdings. The reasons for protecting the farmers were strengthened by the emergency during World War II. Large-scale reclamation and land improvement schemes, generally known as Plan Wahlen, both expanded the cultivated land of the country and increased the number of holdings. Although no farm census has been taken since 1939, the impression is that the slow process of concentration upon somewhat fewer and larger holdings, which went on between 1905 and 1939, has continued over the forties. The difficulties of making small farms viable have thus probably not been entirely overcome, despite all public assistance. However, the traditional policy of preserving the peasantry as a numerous class of independent enterprisers is continued in recent legislation [c].

(208) France offers one of the least impressive examples of active land policy in Europe. The myth about the great changes brought about by the great Revolution helped to lessen public interest in the issue. The stagnant population situation also contributed to divert public interest from the disparities in the distribution of French land. Furthermore the real development during the first decades of this century probably pointed in the same direction although this development cannot have been very clearly conscious. As we showed in Chapter 3, large farms declined over much of the period, except in the Mediterranean departments.

The policy of the 19th century has, characteristically, reinforced the small property so that it might support the large property, as part of a harmonious social system [a]. For a long period, however, there were merely words and no action in this policy. It was therefore only in the nineties, under the impact of the Catholic social program, that attempts were made to legislate in favor of indivisible family holdings. This initiative did not reach the stage of legislation until 1909 [b]. The material results following upon this legislation were also extremely meagre, and seemed to show that the legislator had confused the interests of the farmers with those of homestead owners in the suburbs of Paris [c].

Since World War II, French land policy has taken a more distinct shape. The main outcome has been protection of tenants,

who have also got the right of preemption, if their holdings are
to be sold, as discussed in Chapter 4. This is in substance a kind
of land reform policy. The land pattern which was aimed at is
indicated in the new rules for indivisibility of farms on inheritance:
a farm should not be divided if it is not too large to be con-
veniently cultivated by the farmer and his family, if necessary
with the aid of one or two hired persons [d]. The definition of the
family farm has thus been put rather high, where landhungry
Eastern Europe would already talk about "kulaks". This policy
is however clearly hostile to large-scale enterprise in agriculture.
The question is whether the preemption right given to the tenants
has not counteracted the general intentions of the new land policy.
It appears as if many landowners, rather than rent out their
land, try to keep as much as possible of it untenanted and
cultivated through a hired manager, who is not legally a tenant.

The productivist view, strongly advocated by one side in
current discussion in France [e], has so far been overshadowed by
the social motive of protecting the farming class. Post-war
changes in the farm structure are not yet known, but a farm
census is scheduled to take place early in 1956.

(209) A movement to create homesteads on the family farm
level was started in Prussia in 1886. The motive was not so much
general social or economic utility as a wish to strengthen the
German element in some eastern provinces, where an increasing
influx of Polish farmhands seemed to threaten the Germanic
character of large districts [a]. This movement has to some extent
contributed to diminishing the importance of large estates in
eastern Germany. As far as national policy was concerned, the
movement did not reach its goal. On the contrary, a Polish
countermovement managed to settle a large number of farm
families. The land held by Polish farmers increased more than
the land held by German farmers. This countermovement also
contributed to modifying the East German farm structure in
favor of family farms.

Thus far, the movement only emphasizes the unsoundness of
the East German estate system. Since much land was sold to
Poles, who operated without State support and in competition
with the German colonization movement, the latter can scarcely
be said to have brought about very much greater changes than

those which would have come about spontaneously. On the other
hand, the powerful class interests of the Junkers rather tended
to make the dissolution of large estates slower than it would
have been by itself, under economic influences only.

During the first world war, the need was felt for settlement
of ex-servicemen, and legislation to this effect was enacted in
1916[b]. Because of the way the war ended, there was very little,
if any effect at all.

Immediately after the war, the problem of agricultural
colonization was taken up again. Germany still had problems
deriving from surplus population on the countryside, and it was
still held that part of the problem should be solved through
expansion of the class of landowning farmers and smallholders.
This view the German Social Democrats also shared; having
been led to abandon the claim for immediate land socialization,
they concluded that small family farms were the most practicable
ad hoc solution[c].

The new legislation, issued in 1919, was not exclusively
political in scope. It was also based on detailed economic considerations, formulated by the author of the first Statute,
Professor SERING[d], who advocated medium-sized farms as not
only socially but also economically superior to large estates. As a
matter of principle, this legislation was not confined to the
eastern regions with their large estates, but was applicable to
the whole Reich. However, in its practical application it became
another attempt to reform the East German farm structure.

This legislation envisaged both clearing of peatbogs and waste
land, and redistribution of State domains and private large
estates[e]. The former measures might, if efficiently applied, have
yielded considerable areas for colonization, especially in Bavaria,
East Prussia, Brandenburg, and Pomerania. However, in these
very regions, no land clearance was undertaken at all during the
twenties. In all other regions only very modest areas were cleared
during the same period. In the thirties, land clearance was again
taken up, though the movement did not even procure enough
cultivated land to balance the simultaneous losses through road
construction, town expansion, and military establishments.

State land was to be available for redistribution as the leases
duly expired. However, this regulation was not fully applied

and many State domains were leased afresh. During the twenties, some 50,000 hectares became available, most of it in Prussia and Mecklenburg [f].

The redistribution of private estates was specially important shortly after the end of World War I because of the influx of refugees from the areas ceded to Poland. Many of these were the same families who had been settled under the legislation of the eighties. A special statute was issued in 1923 for the re-settling of these refugees in eastern areas that had remained German [g].

The total area for redistribution under both Statutes (1919 and 1923) was about $1\frac{1}{2}$ million hectares. Not very far from half of this area was in regions that are now Polish, and most of the remainder is in present Eastern Germany. Schleswig-Holstein and Hannover were the only West German regions where any considerable areas were considered in this connection (70,000 and 20,000 hectares, respectively). Up to 1928, about one-fourth of the redistribution program had been fulfilled, with about the same territorial distribution as the total plan. If continued at about the same pace, the original program might have been fulfilled, early in the forties in a few regions, but in most regions only in the sixties of this century, and in some regions not until even later [h].

The most important effect of these redistribution measures was, as far as area is concerned, the foundation of new holdings. For the over-all distribution of size-classes of holdings, the enlargement of existing holdings is somewhat more impressive. About 20,000 new farms were created, most of them in Prussian territories. Some 175,000 existing holdings were enlarged, of which about 125,000 in Prussia, but also over 20,000 in Hessen, where some 7,500 hectares were distributed among them [i].

These measures have contributed to the changes in farm structure between 1907 and 1939, which were quite sizeable in Eastern Germany. These changes were, however, on the whole considerably wider in scope than the land clearance and distribution measures, and most of them therefore must have taken place spontaneously. This conclusion refers especially to Eastern Germany.

(210) The second World War has again brought the land question under discussion in Germany and land reform measures

have taken place in both Eastern and Western Germany. The former has had all the characteristics of a radical left-wing reform aimed at turning the whole farming class into small landowners and doing away with the large estates completely. It will be further discussed in a later section of this chapter.

The West German reform, in fact, had to start from a farm pattern which was not very different from that established in Eastern Germany as a result of the last reform. It follows directly that no very radical change of the structure could be brought about. The settlement of the refugees from the Eastern regions was therefore formulated as a long-term program, to take place as farms became free when their occupiers left them for other occupations. Up to 1955, about 55,000 new holdings had been created, including 35,000 for refugees. Of this total, 9,500 were created in 1954 alone, which indicates a certain speedup of the program. Another 31,000 existing small holdings had been enlarged, including 6,500 in 1954. Out of the 55,000 new holdings, about 7,000 were farms, 600 market gardens, 10,500 homes for farm and forestry workers, 20,000 part-time farms, and 16,000 belonged to other categories.

Along with this policy of strengthening and broadening the stratum of small and medium-sized farms, public discussion has been increasingly concerned with the usefulness of the methods chosen[a].

(211) The whole of southeastern and adjacent parts of central Europe had until relatively recent times belonged to the two empires of Austria and Turkey. The basic land problems had to a great extent been conditioned — or were believed to have been so — by the impact of the rule of these two States.

The Habsburg monarchy has not enjoyed a very good reputation for democratic traditions, and claims for a different social order on the countryside were an inevitable part of the urge for an integrated modernized society[a]. This urge has to some extent clouded the picture of the social land distribution in the core of the Austrian countries which nowadays are the republic of Austria. The fact is that the farm structure in these regions, even at the beginning of the century, was very close to what it is at present. Expressed in weighted figures, this structure is not too different from that of Western Germany. The illusion about

Austria as a country full of large estates may to some extent
have been caused by the traditional system of farm classification
according to total area. Despite the more instructive data that
are nowadays available, this illusion seems to persist [b]. Reform
measures to some extent undertaken in the twenties [c] did not
change the structural picture very much. At present, since
Austria has become an industrial country concerned about rural
exodus and abandonment of farms in the Alps, land policy
concentrates on supporting existing small farms rather than
creating new ones [d].

(212) The eastern component of the dual monarchy had land
problems of quite another kind. Unlike Austria, these problems
were most acute in the center, in the Magyar regions.

Large quasi-feudal estates had been established as a consequence of the leadership of the nobles in the long drawn-out
wars against the Turks, which did not cease to be a practical
justification until the 19th century. The liberation of the serfs,
in response to the political unrest of 1848, created a stratum of
owner-operated small farms, but at the same time a great part
of the large estates were consolidated in the hands of the high
nobility, partly even in the form of entailed estates. The highly
aristocratic pattern of the country was closely linked to the
nationalistic and centralistic policy of the Hungarian crown and
long barred any attempts at progressive land reform. The
precipitate measures taken by the short-lived Communist régime
of Bela Kun, after World War I, made it easy for the reactionary
government that took over to make the idea of a radical land
reform look mainly destructive.

The reform measures which despite everything took place in
the twenties, in response to a widely held opinion that something
should be done, embraced mostly the establishment of very small
holdings. These were on the whole too small to be viable as
independent family enterprises, they were rather part-time
holdings for agricultural workmen. The resulting modification
in the farm pattern touched about one-tenth of the agricultural land of the country. The changes shown in Chapter
3 are partly due to subdivision of large estates (of some importance already around 1900), partly to differences in the statistical basis [a].

Hungary was thus a country where large estates played a leading part as late as during World War II.

(213) From the two halves of the dual monarchy, Czechoslovakia inherited contrasting elements in its farm structure.

In both main parts of the country, the traditional classification of holdings according to total area contributed to overstating the importance of large holdings. Unlike Hungary, both Slovakia and the Czech provinces have much mountainous forest and grazing land, and much of this' was organized as "compossessorates", communal property. These "holdings" largely distort the picture of the land distribution and still do so, because they are now organized as a small number of State holdings. The distribution of agricultural land was much less extreme than in Hungary, though large farms played a somewhat greater part than in Austria. The fact that fragmentation of small and medium-sized holdings is an almost omnipresent feature indicates the dominance of these categories of holdings.

The land reform undertaken in the twenties was of much the same magnitude as in Hungary, affecting a little over one-tenth of the agricultural land of the country. Part of the large farms were broken up, but not all of them. The new holdings created were however larger and more viable than in Hungary. This type of reform did not satisfy the most radical claims but at the same time it was open to conservative criticism on economic grounds [a].

The relatively levelled out structure that was inherited, and the low pressure of population recently, restricted the scope for a radical land redistribution in Czechoslovakia after World War II.

(214) Rumanian land problems derived partly from the estates of local nobility in the old Principalities, and partly from the landlord-tenant relations in the Transsylvanian districts taken over from Hungary. During the inter-war period, Bessarabia also entered as a component in the Rumanian equation, introducing elements of Russian experiences.

The land problems of the Principalities derived from the government of a local feudal aristocracy. These were not Turks, nor even too closely dependent on the Turkish monarchy, but for centuries they had taken advantage of their leading position to exercise far-reaching authority over the peasantry. The end of the 19th century and the beginning of the 20th witnessed a continuous struggle between landlords and peasants. Successively, the latter were made independent, first through abolition of rents on their holdings and their establishment as freeholds, and later through breaking up of the large estates. The latter operation ought to have taken place during the twenties but in fact it was only partly accomplished[a].

As shown by the tables in Chapter 3, the Transsylvanian regions at the beginning of the century already had a farm pattern which was not very different from the present one. The main problems lay in the rights of landlords over tenants on uncertain conditions. The liberation of the latter and their establishment as freeholders was to a great extent part of a struggle between nationalities.

The accession of Bessarabia to the Rumanian State at the end of World War I helped to make land policy more radical. The process was simultaneous with the radical changes in Russia, which also had advanced further towards a complete land reform than had Rumania before World War I.

(215) Yugoslavia emerged as a succession State to Austria, Hungary, and Turkey, and inherited some of the problems of all three. The core of the country, Old Serbia, had been delivered from the Turkish rule at such an early date that all traces of landlord domination had been wiped out long before the expansion of the State into Yugoslavia. In fact, the old Kingdom of Serbia had no problems of land reform in the sense of breaking up large estates or regulating unsatisfactory tenancy conditions. The problems were those of rapidly increasing population in a community of small farmers.

In the regions taken over from Turkey, the rights of the Turkish landlords over their small tenants needed only be abolished; the picture was already dominated by small holdings. This applies both to Macedonia and the Kosmet District, conquered in 1912, and to Bosnia and Hercegovina, where Austria had exercised sovereignty since 1878.

Among the areas that had belonged to the Austrian crown lands, both Slovenia and Dalmatia were also already dominated by small farms, like most of modern Austria. It was thus mainly in the previously Hungarian regions, in Croatia and Vojvodina, that land redistribution was required[a], and these were the scence of the most important reform measures in the twenties. This partly runs counter to the fact that these were the regions where population pressure was least acute.

The dominant structure of small farms thus established was not tested as to its economic viability in the long run. At the eve of the second war, many small holders were close to ruin, only avoided by the inflation that extinguished the debts of the peasants.

(216) The independent Bulgarian State took over from the Turkish régime a structure similar to that of southern Yugoslavia. There were almost no large estates farmed as large enterprises, but only landlords with the right of receiving rents from the peasants. In fact, the Turkish landlords never owned their estates with full property rights. They were a kind of vassals to the Turkish crown, while their land belonged to the State. The new State therefore could take over the same rights and only needed to dispose of them to make the peasants into rent-free owners[a]. This main reform had already been carried out a couple of decades before the beginning of this century and corresponds to what happened in Serbia at an even earlier stage.

Since then, only minor changes have been made to this main result, through more recent land reforms. One was undertaken in the twenties, another after World War II. None of them touched more than a small fraction of Bulgarian land. The subdivision of farms through inheritance in the often large families has been much more important for the changes in farm structure over the period here studied.

(217) Among the Turkish succession States, Albania was liberated last. Having been a Moslem part of the empire, it long retained more inherited features in social life than other parts of the Balkans.

Around 1930, however, a land reform was planned and an Italian expert was asked to study the conditions and design proposals for the reform. On the basis of his memorandum, legislation was enacted[a]. The measures there envisaged were not implemented to any appreciable extent. The main reason was the resistance offered by the owners of large estates, and their domination of the country therefore continued until World War II.

(218) The Greek State that was created through the war of liberation in the 1820's, covering a much smaller territory than modern Greece, from the outset became a country where small owner-operated peasant farms dominated. The landlords had been Turks or their allies, and the leading class of the new State was more interested in trade than in agriculture. Spontaneous liberation and successive legislation up to the 1880's confirmed the peasant character of Greek agriculture. In lately liberated Thessalia, the estates of Turkish landlords were left intact until the 1920's [a]. The accession of Macedonia and Thrace through World War I meant a further increase of the large estates. The population transfers that were connected with the final peace treaty burdened the country with an additional 1 million inhabitants, the majority of whom were peasants. For the settlement of this mass, no other possiblity seemed to exist except a radical land reform. This reform, largely carried out during the twenties, affected about 40 per cent of the agricultural land of the whole country and brought about a profound re-modelling of the farm structure in all the northern parts of the country [b]. Following this operation, Greece is as much dominated by small farms as any of the other Balkan countries. However, to a minor extent some large estate managed to survive, as it seems partly through obstruction of the reform measures. The residuum was affected by continued reform measures after World War II.

(219) While Italy is over and over again cited as a classical country of fedual (or, better, quasi-feudal) landlordism, it appears to be insufficiently observed (at least outside Italy) that this kind of statement is partly out of date. Even late in the 19th century, the statement was true mainly about southern and part of central Italy and about the Islands. Even in these regions, the structure has slowly changed towards more and more independent peasant farms.

Most governments since the unification of the country have discussed a redistribution of landed wealth, but not very much was actually achieved. Those attempted at the beginning of the century failed, as it seems, because they were too sudden, without taking into account the need for improvement of the land and education of the population. The result was therefore a re-construction of the large estates.

More important than these attempts at land reform was the spontaneous transfer of land from absentee landlords to small peasants, a movement that went on over the whole period. The movement was specially fast in the twenties. The post-war drive for social reform made many landlords, especially small urban savers who had put their money in land, willing to sell rather than risk dispossession. According to a special enquiry, more than a million hectares passed into the hands of small farmers during a decade [a].

Also the Fascist régime, in its efforts for "inner colonization" contributed somewhat to expansion of small-scale farming. The aim was not to expand peasant ownership; certain tenancy forms of Central Italy were introduced, in Sardinia and Sicily for instance, and no radical scheme to do away with the estate system was brought forth [b].

(220) In Spain, especially on the vast plateau lands in the interior, the distribution of land has been a grave social and economic problem for centuries [a]. The discrepancies were aggravated during the 19th century, when large tracts of Church and Communal land were turned into private estates [b]. Any discussion of the Spanish land problem is made difficult because of the huge differences in the value of the land in various regions which obviously exist but are not easy to describe in exact terms. The cadastre system has also sometimes caused confusion, because the cadastre units have been taken as indicators of the degree of concentration in the property structure, which they are only in a very imperfect way [c].

The need for a reform of the land distribution has made itself felt throughout this century and aroused a great number of enquiries even before World War I [d]. During the twenties, a certain amount of inner colonization was undertaken. Around 1930, there was an attempt at a radical land reform, accompanied by a flood of enquiries and pamphlets on the problem [e]. Little statistical evidence is available to show how far these measures were put into practice before they were stopped through the civil war and, finally, undone through the action of the new régime.

The latter, however, could by no means let the problem alone but had to try and cope with it in its own way, as will be described in a later section of this chapter.

In Portugal, there was very little action throughout the period. The measures that have finally been taken to some extent have the character of a pilot reform and will also be treated in the section on policies after World War II.

(221) As a summary, it may be stated that of the countries that had any land reform or far reaching schemes of land redistribution between the beginning of the century and the outbreak of World War II, only a few redistributed a really considerable part of the agricultural land. The coverage of redistribution was about 40 per cent in Greece and of a similar magnitude in Finland. It ought to have been between 25 and 30 per cent in Rumania, but the entire program was probably never accomplished. In Eastern Germany, Poland, Czechoslovakia, and Hungary, the coverage was of the magnitude of 10 per cent, in Yugoslavia about 5 per cent. It was only about 2 per cent in Bulgaria, and in none of the countries of Southern and Western Europe, except Ireland, did the changes brought about politically cover more than a fraction of the land of the country.

The farm structure tables in Chapter 3 show the differences in the background. Even in the thirties, the Balkans were a group of countries where the farm structure was dominated by small holdings. Hungary, Poland, and Eastern Germany, to some extent also Czechoslovakia and Rumania, were the countries in Eastern Europe where the land reform could still be of any size. It will be useful to recall this when post-war policies are discussed.

RUSSIAN LAND REFORM EXPERIENCES AND
SOVIET COLLECTIVIZATION

(222) The liberation of the serfs in 1861 had apparently reduced the size of the estates of the nobles. In fact, it strengthened them and made them economically viable for another period of existence. The peasants were to have received only the same land as they had already been cultivating for their own needs, and sometimes they did not get even that. In exchange for the labor service to which the estate owners had no longer any claim, they obtained considerable financial support through the payment the

peasants had to make for their land. A special Agricultural Bank was organized for the purpose [a].

The estate owners thus got capital for fresh investments, while the peasants had to use their savings to amortize the purchase debt. This undoubtedly underlies much of the apparent superiority of the estates as compared to the peasant farms during the following decades. Despite this, the estates of the nobility continued to shrink throughout the period after 1861. These losses, which to a great extent must have been due to lack of economic capacity among the nobles, went half to peasant owners and half to urban capitalists [b]. The land bought by the latter was for the most part let to peasant leaseholders, as was also the case of much of the land that continued to belong to the nobles.

Large-scale farming in Russia was therefore already a lost cause by the beginning of this century. It was in this situation that Prime Minister Stolypin decided to organize the Russian peasantry according to Western European standards, as independent smallholders rather than as shareholders in a loosely organized village community. By all the evidence, a movement of this kind was already under way. The model was sought in the transformation of Scandinavian agriculture a century earlier [c].

(223) The Bolshevik revolution owed a considerable part of its initial success to social unrest on the Russian countryside. The main background to that unrest was the land hunger of a rapidly increasing farm population in a country where most of the good land was already occupied by somebody. The resources remaining for re-distribution were already small, except in Belorussia and the Baltic countries. This fact seems to have escaped most of those who discussed the land problem. Especially the peasantry seemed to believe that the Tsar had at his disposition unlimited resources of land for redistribution among peasants with too little land, if he only had good counsel. Their belief was to some extent shared by the revolutionary politicians, who did not always realize that the vast Crown lands were mostly barren or otherwise unsuitable for cultivation under existing conditions [a].

By giving its sanction to the many seizures of property that occurred during most of 1917, against the will of the Menshevik

government, the Bolsheviks succeeded in rallying great masses
of peasants to their cause. In doing so, they not only helped do
away with the remainder of the estate system, but also secured
the support of the broad masses of "village poor" against the
well-to-do farmers (the "village rich" or "kulaks").

(224) Among the territories of the Tsarist empire which during
the inter-war period belonged to other States, the old Kingdom
of Poland, together with adjacent parts of Belorussia and Ukraina
had to a great extent undergone the same development as
Russia herself. Most of the large estates had been broken down
and replaced by a broad stratum of small peasant farms. This was
in strong contrast to the regions which Poland took over from
Germany. In the latter areas there existed, between the not
too large estates and the numerous smallholdings, also an
important stratum of middle-sized farms. The regions taken over
from Austria, *i.e.*, Galicia, showed very much the same structure
as the formerly Russian regions.

The Polish land reform in the twenties was a compromise
between divergent interests and, in fact, was only partially
carried out [a].

Within the Rumanian State of the inter-war period, Bessarabia
played a similar role. The fact that there had been to a great
extent a levelling out of the farm structure in favor of small farms
in this rich agricultural region contributed to make the policy
of Rumania itself more radical.

The most original development was in the Baltic countries.
During the Tsarist period, in the territories corresponding to
Estonia and Latvia, large estates had dominated the situation
more than in any other part of the empire. The estate-owning
German nobility enjoyed special consideration from the Russian
crown, ever since it helped the Tsar to conquer the region in the
18th century. Modern Lithuania, like adjacent Belorussia, was
also influenced by the German colonization, though to a lesser
degree than the northern Baltic regions. The estate system there
survived less than in the latter region, but more than in most
other regions of the empire. The Stolypin reform had some
impact also in the Baltic area, though less than elsewhere.

The new Baltic republics had thus to cope themselves with the
inequality of the land distribution, which was also regarded as a

remnant of foreign domination. Early in the twenties, all three
countries carried out land reforms which were radical in the
sense of doing away with the estate system. Unlike most other
countries in Eastern Europe, this could be done on the basis of
a relatively high hectarage per man. A dominant stratum of
relatively large peasant farms was created, large enough to
allow the farmers to employ those remaining landless[b]. These
land reforms are known to have been the background for some
of the most remarkable agricultural progress in inter-war Europe.

(225) As the ultimate outcome of six decades of successive
developments, Russia had in the early twenties a structure of
peasant farms, most of them very small. During the period of
war communism, the village communities were brought to life
again even where they had been abolished by the Stolypin reform
or fallen into desuetude independently. With the NEP-period,
the communities once again lost control of the peasant masses.
The small farms silently emancipated themselves, and the
resultant structure had much in common with that of the
Balkan countries.

It does not seem to have been explored how far this broad
mass of small peasants was an active political force in the USSR
of the twenties. It is very clear that it did not serve the goals
of a rapid industrial build-up which the régime aimed at. During
the period of war communism, when farm prices were unrealistic,
the cities had been almost starved through lack of food deliveries.
During the NEP-period, the industrial build-up was to some
extent hampered by the high prices for food in urban areas,
tending to slow down the formation of fresh industrial capital.
If industrialization was to be rapid, the régime could not afford
to pay the real costs of food production.

The collectivization drive during the first five-year plan
(1928–1933) therefore deliberately aimed at forcing the peasants
to make deliveries below the real costs of production. Stalin
advanced the argument that the industrialization of England
in the 19th century was based on exploitation of colonial peoples,
that of Germany on the great tribute paid by France after 1870.
For the USSR, Stalin says there is

"only one way to develop industrialisation and that is by means
of savings within the nation. The sources of wealth are, first, the

working class, which creates the real values and operates industry and, second, the peasantry. With the peasantry, our policy takes this form: The peasantry pays to the State not only the direct and indirect taxes but *overpays* through high prices for industrial articles. Furthermore, the peasantry *does not receive the entire price* for the agricultural products. That constitutes an additional tax on the peasantry. It is a kind of tribute, kind of overtax, which we must take temporarily"[a].

The implementation of this program through the collectivization of most agricultural resources in the USSR is too well known and has been described too often to need a new description here[b]. The main features of the process, before the last war, can be resumed in this table, quoted from an official source[c].

TABLE 34. *Collectivization in the USSR 1918–1939*

	1918	1920	1930	1934	1937	1939
Number of kolkhozy (thousands).	1.6	57.0	85.9	233.3	243.7	241.0
Number of households in the kolkhozy (millions)	0.02	1.0	6.0	15.7	18.5	19.3
Per cent collectivization of peasant households	0.1	3.9	23.6	71.4	93.0	95.6
Per cent collectivization of sown area	..	4.9	33.6	87.4	99.1	99.6

As discussed in Chapter 3, the kolkhozy were of very uneven size. In the post-war years, when there was a drive to enlarge them, it was avowed that also their organization was often less collective in practice than in theory throughout the thirties and the war years.

In contrast to the kolkhozy, the sovkhozy were already from the outset really gigantic enterprises. In addition to being a kind of experiment stations, often specializing in one single branch of production, they were intended as the real model for the development of the kolkhozy[d].

(226) After the last war, consolidation of the kolkhozy was resumed to make them correspond closer than before to their role in Communist society. One of the most important long-term goals was formulated as "the liquidation of the animosity between town and countryside", that is between urban and rural workers[a].

A main result of the consolidation measures was the enlargement of the kolkhozy, even though some traditional differences between various parts of the country subsisted [b]. As discussed in Chapter 1, the simultaneous goal of changing the settlement pattern into a system of agro-towns has been only partly successful. The isolated farmsteads and the small hamlets have probably disappeared in most regions, but medium-sized villages have survived to a great extent as semi-independent nuclei within the same kolkhoz.

Along with these external changes went the attempt to bring about a higher degree of consolidation in the economic system of the kolkhozy. The private garden plots, which are still said to produce about one-tenth of Soviet agricultural production, are regarded as a concession for the time being, to disappear when the "higher" stages of Communist development are reached. The kolkhoz mergers, and especially the attempts to change the settlement pattern, seem to have been a starting point also for attacks on the garden plots [c]. Even though the discipline in observance of the kolkhoz statutes is likely to have been strengthened, there is little evidence that the dvor-system has been seriously changed [d].

(227) A special feature in post-war land policy of the USSR is the treatment of the regions taken over from the neighbors.

The Baltic States were completely incorporated in the Union. The bourgeois farm structure of these countries, which corresponded largely to what the Russians call "kulak" farms, was of course the first to be done away with. Soviet land policy therefore started with a radical re-distribution of the land, intended to create more or less the same pattern of farms as had preceded the kolkhozy in Russia. Farms larger than 30 hectares disappeared and the number of farms increased considerably, though not overwhelmingly. Only the very smallest units, those below 1 hectare, diminished both in number and area, while the category between 1–5 hectares remained stable in number and increased in area [a].

After some preliminaries soon after the war, the real collectivization drive started in 1949. In 1950, the new kolkhozy were already largely amalgamated into larger ones, even before the primary phase of collectivization was finished [b]. To some extent private farming seems to have survived until the early fifties, but by 1953 the private sector was of very small importance [c].

In the other areas taken over from neighboring States, that is in the western parts of Belorussia and Ukraina, and the largest part of the republic of Moldova, the farm pattern had not previously been dominated by medium-sized holdings to the same extent as in the Baltic States, but showed more of the typical East European smallholdings, together with some surviving estates, mainly in the territories taken over from Poland. Despite this, collectivization of these districts did not include the majority of the land until around 1950, and the whole movement was not completed much sooner than in the Baltic countries[d].

POST-WAR POLICIES IN EASTERN EUROPE

(228) The revolutions occurring all over Eastern Europe after the second war brought as the first fruit in the field of land policy a radical re-distribution of land, intended to create a stage where all who worked on the land owned some patch of it, and nobody worked for other individuals[a].

The degree to which such a scheme had any impact was of course dependent upon the structure existing before. In Bulgaria, Rumania, and Yugoslavia, only a few per cent of all the land was re-distributed, because there was little to re-distribute. Even so, some of it came from dispossessed German-speaking elements rather than from big landlords, at least in Yugoslavia. In Eastern Germany, Poland, and Albania, something like one-fourth of the land was re-distributed, and this came to a considerable part from large estates. In Poland, however, much of it was taken from exiled Germans, and the same is to a great extent true of Czechoslovakia, where almost half of the land is reported to have been re-distributed[b].

(229) It will be seen from these data, compared with those on pre-war reforms that most of the land in Eastern Europe has been formed into small peasant farms independently of reform measures during this century. The liberation of the Balkans and the more or less spontaneous transition of land from large-scale to small-scale farming has played the leading part, and the reforms have precipitated a development which was under way by itself, as well as removing artificial hindrances to it, e.g.

those deriving from class interests of big landowners in Hungary and Poland.

Part of the expropriated land, however, remained public property in Poland, Yugoslavia, and Eastern Germany, as also most of the expropriated forests in Czechoslovakia.

In the Balkans, only Albania had preserved part of the large estates of the 19th century. In the northern group, the changes in Czechoslovakia would have been of the same magnitude as in the inter-war period, if the expellee land could have been kept outside the calculation. The same would probably be true of Poland. This is why the holding structure has not been more radically changed, especially since part of the expropriated land remained in large enterprises, those of the State. Only in Hungary, the reform meant a really spectacular breaking up of large estates. In this country, on the other hand, relatively many large peasant farms were retained, and relatively much land remained rented.

(230) The viability of the new farm patterns has never been tested under a policy aiming at its maintenance in the long run. The obvious intention underlying the reform, even though often denied for the moment for reasons of political opportunism, was the creation of collective farms on the Russian pattern. As in Russia in the twenties, the problem was to furnish growing industrial cities with cheap food and at the same time to prevent a new social differentiation on the countryside.

The creation of the many very small farms made even more acute than before the difficulties felt in the twenties and thirties, when the small holdings had tended to provide merely for the physical subsistence of the holders. The primitive and stagnating small farms in the thirties had at least two good features, from the viewpoint of the urban classes. One was the tendency for food prices to be low in the not very well organized competition between the many small producers. The other was the growing tendency for many peasant farms to be ruined, presumably in the first line those which were least viable economically. The amalgamation of these farms into larger ones had already started to some extent before the war, and only war-time inflation rescued the indebted peasants for the time being.

Both these ways towards a progressive economy were however

blocked in the post-war period, for ideological reasons. The source of abundant and cheap food supply could be re-created, it was thought, through one of two alternatives: considerably increased productivity or forced deliveries. It was thought easiest to bring about both these on State and collective farms.

The way in which small farmers were now burdened with delivery quotas even to some extent caused them to be reluctant to cultivate all available land. The normal tendency to land hunger has thus been strangled, especially in Eastern Germany, Poland, and Czechoslovakia. The latter country, as shown in Chapter 4, even enacted regulations to prohibit the unauthorized relinquishing of land ownership.

(231) These developments may to a varying degree have contributed to speeding up the process of collectivization of agriculture so as to carry it through at an earlier stage of socialist development than that reached by the USSR around 1930. From the viewpoint of general development, most of the areas now discussed were undoubtedly far ahead of what Russia had reached in the twenties. Whether this was helpful or not to collectivization is a question which cannot be treated regardless of how the collectivization was implemented. At any rate, collectivization advanced more slowly and unevenly than it had done in the Soviet Union. It is still far from achieved. The contrast to those regions that were attached to the USSR after the war is especially striking. The following table gives some main features of what happened up to the early fifties[a].

The data in the table refer to the end of each year, unless otherwise indicated. The data on Czechoslovakia refer only to types II, III, and IV, type I being considered too little advanced to introduce in the progress reports. On collectivization in Albania only scanty and inconsistent information is available. Yugoslavia will be treated in a later paragraph.

(232) The slow and uneven growth of collective farming is only partially revealed by these figures, because it would be too complicated in a comparative survey to show the distribution by various types of co-operatives and the progress of each. To some extent the establishment of new co-operative farms may have meant the construction of an empty façade. The pace with which they have been filled afterwards with the kind of life

TABLE 35. *Progress of socialist agriculture in Eastern Europe*

Country, Date	Number of co-operative farms	Peasant farms per co-operative	Per cent of agri-cultural area socialized		
			In co-opera-tives	In State Farms	Total
E. Germany					
1951.	..	..	..	..	5.1
Nov. 1952	1,335	10	1.7	5.2	6.9
Mid 1953.	5,000	29	12.2	5.2	17.4
Poland					
April 1949 . . .	60	18	0.1	..	..
1950.	2,199	44	2.3	11.0	13.3
1953.	7,300	50	6.4	14.5	20.9
Czechoslovakia . .					
1950.	3,760	..	15.4	8.8	24.2
1952.	7,835	..	32.6	10.9	43.5
Hungary					
1949. . . . , ,	1,500	30	3.1	4.1	7.2
1952.	5,315	60	22.8	11.1	33.9
Rumania					
1948.	377	50	0.1	..	..
1949.	1,952	52	1.0	3.6	4.6
Mid 1953. . . .	3,980	75	6.9	13.6	17.5
Bulgaria.					
Sept 1944	28	60	..	..	..
1947.	549	80	3.8	..	..
1952. . , . . .	2,747	212	60.5	2.5	63

they were intended for, is even more difficult to say anything about. The same observation also refers to the transitions from "lower" to "higher" types of co-operative farms.

The early fifties were marked by a certain slowing down in the collectivization drive. Some reasons for this can be learned from official statements. In Poland, after an allegedly quick development of co-operative farms in 1951[a], Deputy Prime Minister Hilary Minc gave a speech (October 9), stating, among other things, that:

"agriculture has not developed at the same speed as industry, which is fatal, as the speedy increase of industrial workers requires more food supply... Bad wheather has sharpened the situation, but the main cause lies in the capitalist structure of petty farming, giving way for too much fluctuations.

Despite this, industrialization cannot slow down.

But collectivization, how desirable it is, cannot be speeded up: industrial production must increase first, and the financial strength of the State too. The mental disposition of the peasants must be radically changed, they must understand and accept, and really be able to manage the collectives..." [b].

In Czechoslovakia, it was stated in 1952 that

"In spite of these good initial successes in the building and strengthening of the cooperatives and their progress to higher types, there are a whole series of shortcomings. The cooperative farming does not make use of all its great possibilities and therefore Czechoslovak agriculture lags behind the increasing tempo of the growth of the Czechoslovak industry...".

As a conclusion, a broad campaign is proposed for the recruitment of new members to the existing co-operative farms, as well as for the foundation of new ones [c].

In Hungary, the incapacity of agriculture to meet production expectations caused a self-critical appraisal in 1952, stating that collectivization had been pushed too far without awaiting the necessary internal development of the rural community [d].

The policy change in Rumania came in the fall of 1953, with the announcement of the new production plan. As an emergency measure, considerable concessions were given to the private farmers [e].

In Bulgaria, the country where collectivization had been pushed farthest in the countries outside the USSR, doubts began to be officially expressed in the first half of 1954 as to the efficiency of the system [f]. There is, however, no question about partially going back, as in Hungary.

Eastern Germany was the last country in which collective farming was introduced. As late as in the fall of 1951, such a policy was not in mind [g]. The movement was not launched until July 1952, and was immediately followed by many instances of farmers abandoning their land. Already in the summer of 1953, a standstill of the movement was ordered, though partly recalled in the fall of the same year [h].

In all these countries, there were renewed collectivization drives in the middle fifties. At least in Czechoslovakia, the effect is reported to have been considerable.

In Yugoslavia, a country where at a certain moment collectivization had reached farther than in any of the other countries except Bulgaria and the USSR, a change in policy occurred earlier than elsewhere and was more lasting. The new policy was made public in the fall of 1951 and was partly carried out during 1952. Among other things, it had been realized that part of the existing co-operative farms were "passive", *i.e.* they existed mainly on paper without having too many practical functions *i*. With the re-established freedom of the peasants to leave and to dissolve co-operative farms, more than half went out of existence. Certainly all the "passive" ones were dissolved, which may have made the change smaller in reality than it was formally. On those which continued to exist, new forms of organization were attempted, which was said to mean that "co-operative" rather than "collective" principles were to be applied. However this dogmatic difference is judged, it is obvious that the change meant the introduction of much more self-government in the remaining co-operative farms than there had existed before. After some time, the greater confidence in the new style of these farms made itself felt through a trend to return to them or even to found new ones, even if this was no longer official policy *j*.

(233) The arguments for and against different approaches to collectivization quoted above cover in substance some of the underlying practical reasons. One motive for not speeding up the movement too much may have been the discouraging experiences of the USSR in the early thirties, when hasty collectivization caused enormous losses of material values. The post-war situations of most Eastern European countries contained so many elements of emergency, and Communist power had been so recently established, that such a rapid shift was not desired. The need to await more machinery and more technical development cannot have been decisive by itself, since the Soviet Union had not waited for such reasons. The obvious reason for the delays is the resistance from broad strata of the peasant population. That the same is true about the policy change in Yugoslavia is also obvious.

From a general viewpoint not very much can be learned from these experiences, except the negative indications as to the harm that can be done by a policy which does not correspond to the sentiments and wishes of those it directly concerns. The degree of success of collective farming in Eastern Europe does not indicate the usefulness or uselessness of the method of collective or co-operative farming. The method of implementation, by its implications on national and local policies overshadows the real issue. The co-operative farms of Yugoslavia, as also those of Italy, may afford really useful indications, when they have existed under their new form for a sequence of years and been tested in competition with the private farms. In other countries, the conditions for such competition are arranged by the policy-makers to such an extent that their experience has not much positive value.

WESTERN POST-WAR POLICIES

(234) The last post-war period has brought to maturity some trends in the land policy of the countries of Southern and Western Europe which were to some extent alive or at least in the making in the inter-war period. Neo-conservative and neo-liberal trends of thought have had to contend both with legacies of old-styled land-reform programs and with the tendency to think of the social order of the countryside exclusively in terms of quantities and prices.

The new program of the Catholic Church on social questions had been set out already in the nineties. Because of some ambiguity in both social and technical aspects, it came to influence practical policy mainly when Catholic governments in power found themselves faced with emergency situations[a].

In countries where there are no urgent problems but where the prospect of further industrialization of agriculture has aroused emotional resistance, the vestiges of a romantic view of the land have eventually emerged as neo-Liberal views. It is claimed that the peasant farm has an inborn capacity to survive as a social form, if it is only left alone free from regulation by the State, because it corresponds to basic needs of the human nature[b].

Purely economic views, holding that agriculture can reach its proper position in an integrated society only if it conforms to the economic necessities of maximum productivity, have conditioned actual policy in some countries and been prominent in public discussion in a few more.

(235) The post-war land reform in Italy had a practical background which included a rich experience of success and failure.
It was established expert opinion that mere re-distribution of
the land would not serve in a country like Italy, because the land
of the large estates was too often such as to call for land improvement before it could be intensively cultivated[a]. The bitter
experiences of the beginning of the century had inspired the
land policy of the Fascist régime, which concentrated upon land
improvement but distrusted the capacity of the farmers to
stand by themselves. New leaseholds and an elaborate system of
guidance was thought more important than education in independence and co-operation.

The new land reform policy goes counter to this approach.
A mere land improvement scheme would, it is argued, affect
material values only without improving the personal situation
of those working on the land. The small men of the countryside
should be given the chance to act on their own responsibility.
The double approach, technical and human, gave the formula
of the new reform program as *bonifica-riforma*[b].

This new program concerns primarily the latifundia, the bulk
of which it is the intention to transform into small peasant
farms. It is concerned with them because they are the main
source for expansion of the rural wealth of Italy, the man-made,
highly productive land. The land which is already highly
productive, and that which is deemed likely to remain forever
of low fertility, are not considered suitable for re-distribution
to the same extent. A compromise has been sought between the
need for a social reform and the necessity to leave high-productive
enterprises undisturbed.

The application of these principles of the land reform should,
one might think, cover also the many small farms under various
forms of leasehold or sharecropping. These people are already
established as more or less independent producers, and no harm
would be likely to be caused if they were made either owners or
at least tenants under permanent contracts. This has been
contemplated but no final settlement of the question has been
reached thus far. The resistance to granting the tenants the same
kind of protection as they have in France comes from the
Liberal side. One argument is that the notion of property must

not be made void of content. Such an argument could as well be
advanced against the whole land reform, where landlords are
being dispossessed against cash indemnity. At the same time
it is often argued that the sharecroppers are not independent
producers but act as subordinate elements in a productive
process directed by the landlord. This argument appears to
amount to a productivist reason against the extension of a reform
which otherwise is supposed to increase production.

On the other hand, productivist considerations have caused
exceptions to be made to the reform measures in the cases of a
few very well-run large estates, which are to continue to exist
as model farms[c]. Further, the so-called "cascine" on the Po
plain are also exempted from reform measures, because no
further intensification is held possible under any other form of
tenure.

(236) An attempt at social reform in the countryside was made
in Spain by the present régime at the end of the civil war. It was
further pursued after World War II and represents a kind of
compromise between the Italian land policies of the Fascist
period and at present.

The main principles for this action are laid down in a Statute
of December, 1939[a]. It is underlined that the political doctrine
of the new State gives its agrarian policy firm principles, and
reference is made to opinions expressed by Primo de Rivera and
Franco. Colonization in large zones is declared to be a vital
interest of the nation, and it is deplored that this enterprise
has been hampered for decades, not only by rightful interests of
rural capitalism, but also by other interests, labelled as "bastard"
ones. Colonization schemes should be directed not only towards
the vast marsh zones where irrigation can be introduced with
great profit, but also towards such zones as a whole where big
enterprises could be undertaken under public management. The
aim should be both increase of production and the creation of
many thousands of new family farms as a valuable backbone
for the defence of the country.

The primary concern is thus with increasing production, and
the present owners are apparently to be left alone in so far as
no important increase in production could be brought about
through a change of structure. It is, however, foreseen that in

many instances there could be improvement even without
important investments, through the higher intensity of cultivation on peasant farms. For this reason, certain articles in a
Statute from the twenties, on subdivision of large estates, are
still in force [b]. For the implementation of all this reform legislation, a Statute of 1946 [c] lays down the main lines of action. The
principle for expropriation is that there must be a public interest
in the measure [d].

How this conflict between competing ideas comes to work in
practice depends on the outcome of the internal struggles between
various trends of the régime. The colonization law can be used
for consolidating much of the existing large estates but also as
an instrument for far reaching reforms. The Catholic wing is
more radical in practical application than the government and
regards the present reform measures as the first step towards the
realization of a society where small independent family enterprises are dominant as recommended by the social encyclicals.
Co-operation between the small owners should give them the
advantages of large scale enterprise, a solution independent of
both capitalism and socialism [e].

The limited scale on which the reform has been implemented
thus far has prevented this conflict from flaring up. Until the
early fifties, only a very small part of the land of Spain had been
subject to reform measures. The reason seems to lie in the lack
of funds and of skilled personnel [f]. For this reason too, it is
difficult to judge the real intentions of the régime. There is the
same ambiguity in practical implementation as in the laws on
which it is based.

(237) Even less impressive are the pilot attempts at inner
colonization in Portugal. As in Spain, this policy was inaugurated
before the war, and there are few signs that it is to be speeded
up. Underlying this action is a somewhat different concept of
the Catholic social policy, with more stress upon maintaining
the existing order. New small holdings are planned mainly in
areas where cultivation has been non-existant or much neglected.
If the limited scope is taken into account, this ideological
approach has much in common with that of the Italian post-war
reform [a].

(238) In most of Central and Northern Europe, the immediate

post-war approach to land problems has been mainly one of
direct continuation of former policies to strengthen the small
peasant farms and broaden their scope. Dutch policy in this
sense on the new polders is a direct consequence of the constantly
high population pressure. At the same time, the economic
inadequacy of small holdings on the sandy soils is a matter of
much concern.

The French tenancy reform, as described in Chapter 4, was
intended to strengthen peasant farming and weaken land
capitalism. The degree of success of this policy is not quite clear.
Recent attempts at a re-orientation of the economy of the country
rather tend to favor amalgamation of small farms into larger ones [a].

West German land policy in the immediate post-war years,
was, through the pressure of numerous refugees, to seek ways of
further increasing the number of family-sized farms, as
touched on in a preceding section of the chapter. Recently,
public discussion has begun to doubt the wisdom of this policy
in the long run [b]. In a situation where traditional demographic
incentives towards smallholding policies have lost much of their
weight, part of Western Europe is on the threshold of a policy
shift, the direction of which is not yet visible.

Thus far, it is mainly in the U.K. and Sweden that a policy
of favoring small farms for their social value has been deliberately
abandoned and the productivistic criterion has become dominant
in land policy.

(239) In the United Kingdom, the new orientation of land
policy is productivistic in a double sense. The last war and
experiences following it caused more stress to be laid on home
production of food. At the same time as the creation of new small
holdings acquired a new kind of interest, when intensification
of cultivation was desired, the new approach to employment
questions made the official policy incompatible with economic
needs, in so far as it abstained from consideration of social needs:

"... the publicly-owned smallholdings must be made an integral
part of British agriculture. They must be regarded, not as sometimes
has happened in the past, as something artificially grafted on to the
industry, but as fully economic units with their own particular
problems and requirements arising, from their size and the special
functions they are intended to perform...".
"It will also be noted that the duty of Smallholdings Authorities

is limited to the extent to which smallholdings can be provided without detriment to the general interests of agriculture... The creation of smallholdings ... will ... necessarily involve the acquisition and sub-division of larger farms ... Developments on these lines will tend to alter the present balance between larger and smaller holdings ..." [a].

Further on in the same report one learns, *i.a.*, that the upper limit for new smallholdings is 50 acres, and that the holdings were normally to be established as providing full-time employment for their occupiers.

In Scotland the parallel discussion was even more concerned with former policies intended to prevent rural exodus. These by and large had admittedly failed. For the future, it was even considered that individual family farming should be encouraged mainly in regions where animal husbandry was the dominanting feature, rather than the regions where large-scale mechanized farming is possible [b].

(240) In Sweden, there was an even more marked shift in land policies after the war. Rural exodus and urbanization had gone on at an unusually high speed during the thirties and forties, and the former policy of founding smallholdings, apart from having little success, did not seem of immediate interest to anybody. The long-term program laid down after the war therefore envisaged that the farming population should gradually be brought to enjoy the same level of living as urban workers and craftsmen. If this were to be brought about without burdensome subventions to the farming industry, a considerable amount of technical rationalization would be necessary including the concentration of the industry on fewer and larger units. This will lead unavoidably to abandoning the meagre soil which is now often cultivated in the forest areas, but which would better be used for forestry [a].

On the whole, this planned amalgamation of holdings is to be implemented by public land planning boards, which in certain cases even are authorized to dispossess present owners. In general, it is planned to take advantage of amalgamation possibilities as and when small holders shift occupancy for normal reasons. In the southern and central parts of the country, holdings with less than 10 hectares are considered "marginal" and bound to disappear (except of course those with specialized production). Holdings between 10 and 20 hectares of arable land

were regarded as "basic" when the program was drawn up in
the forties, which means that the amalgamations would tend in
the first place to create new units of this size. It is already being
discussed whether this size is not too small for the future. In
the forest areas of northern Sweden, even holdings with less
than 10 hectares of arable are considered desirable in the long
run, because their farming is mainly a subsidiary source of income along with forestry work.

The data from the 1951 farm census indicate that actual
development is as desired. A strong spontaneous trend undoubtedly draws in the same direction as policy. How far the latter has
contributed to speeding up and regulating the movement cannot
be judged at present.

LAND REFORM AS A PROPAGANDA THEME

by

KARIN DOVRING

CHAPTER 7

LAND REFORM AS A PROPAGANDA THEME

A study in Quantitative Semantics

THE COMMUNICATION OF IDEAS

(241) The question of land and labor has also left its mark in modern political propaganda, where it shows up as a demand for land reform. It is based on the need of food, a value common to the whole world. This value is its own justification by its elementary necessity. But there agreement stops. Even at this stage the demand for food production clashes with social and political interests in the world, since that very demand immediately has bearings on relations between different classes in a society and makes the organization and relation of land and labor a burning question not only for those immediately concerned, the farmers and agrarian experts. As a consequence of this social significance of the problem, the field is open to the different ideologies and systems trying to influence the relation between land and labor.

The self-evident need of food makes it certain that attention will be paid to the problem. Land reform in modern propaganda therefore does not need to attract attention, often the first requirement in a modern propaganda or advertising campaign. Here its communicator can go directly ahead with seeking the interest of his public.

It is true, however, that even so the attention area of the public on "how to get food", is shaded with different nuances according to who the public is, and according to technical conditions in the particular society, which will be even more stressed in the interest area. If the attention area takes the need of food as a self-evident value, the interest area, through the claim for land reform will give opportunity to a more sophisticated interplay between the public's and the communicator's immediate perhaps prejudiced interests, their social predispositions, experiences and training. Once these divergencies between the common attention area and the limited interest area have arisen, they crystallize the type of task, not only for politicians and technical experts on agrarian reforms, but for anybody wanting to teach or know how the problems are to be solved.

(242) The demand for knowledge is a modern claim, the more pronounced the more unbiassed a society wants to be. Mental and technical communication among societies of the world today makes that demand world-wide. As regards land reforms, the topic itself is already a problem of international status. The different languages for communicating international ideologies to different nationalities complicate the task of the authorities of any society in communicating with the particular individual and the masses on problems important to all.

It is known that decision-making in modern societies, how to solve a practical social problem, is anticipated and followed by mental communication between the authorities of a society and the society members at large[a]. The task of preparing for land reform, however, is not expressed in a technical manual. This is, in fact, the final step of a long decision-seeking process; of meetings at a high level among politicians and among technicians; more information meetings among different classes of the population at large; legislation procedures and all the communication media anticipating them, and so on. Any modern communication channel, from broadcasting and speeches through pamphlets and newspapers to movies and television, can be and are involved in this. The justification of reforms, the needs and wants, the demands for land and labor and social justice, the sanctions of valid laws, the fundamental ideology or ideologies that dominate the basic values in a particular society, the expectations from certain solutions, technical development or under-development, everything is thrown into the preparation for the important change in the social life. The controversial topic, whether to do a reform and how to do it, is confronted by a probably doubtful public with different predispositions and with its interest area limited by its actual attention. How to guide actual attention to the problem into interest in a desired direction and to certain decisions in recommended ways is the problem for the authorities when meeting the public. Or, perhaps more adequately expressed, for the particular communicators of the authorities' opinions who are called propagandists. The opportunity to make reforms is namely the making of minds to wanting reforms. And the battles for minds and their decisions are therefore the necessary company to any attempts at making reform and at doing it successfully. Which is a natural consequence of the functional structure of any human society, where mental contacts and appeals aimed at keeping together individuals in communities and interest groups have been significant and fundamental features since the first human beings built a society.

(243) It is clear that all this mental activity may have a more or less disastrous effect upon the real, technical or factual contents of the presentation of the proposed reform. It may lead to the result that the presentation of the technical facts necessary for the solution of the practical problem may be neglected on behalf of the manipulation of ideological appeals. The linguistic skill displayed by the communicator has given him reputation as an artist, caused problems to grammarians meeting phenomena not described in their grammars, and has had effects on the public not always aforeseen by politicians or sociologists trying to see what causes what [a].

The same things have to be said to and the same final decisions made by different kinds of people. To speak to legislators, or to speak to agricultural workmen about the same thing, is not always to express oneself in the same way. The way in which the same thing is said is a question of the level of the public. The demand for knowledge makes our age an invitation to propaganda [b]. That is, the communicator must manipulate the themes and symbols describing the actual topic in a way that the public believes that it understands. The themes and symbols for the subject-matter discussed must consequently be connected with themes and symbols and values well known to the public's daily life in its society. Thus the communicator is given further opportunities for ideological appeals in disseminating facts on the subject-matter. At the same time he must be aware of the fact that the limited attention area of his public decides what he must pay attention to; his own purpose decides how to guide the particular attention to a certain interest area. And here the skilful communicator turns propagandist when he tries to influence the interests aroused in favor of certain decisions, understandings, and attitudes of his public [c]. An attentive public may ask for nothing but facts, and real facts, in the information issued by the communicator. But the dissemination of facts is not merely an attempt at giving knowledge. Questions of time and space often make it a problem of chosen facts. Consequently, even "mere facts" can give opportunity for an ideological bias [d].

Any information can thus become a complicated communication process, where the expert on the particular topic, owing to lack of ability to communicate or to the political structure of his society, is not successful in reaching informative contacts with a public that for political, economic, or intellectual reasons is not always prepared immediately to meet expert knowledge. This lack of equilibrium in the relation between the attentive public and the experts is one feature that prepares the way for ideological makes-up in information. That is why the task of giving information on any subject matter is often handed over to the skilful communication expert who is above all able to communicate with different publics but is not always a thoroughly informed expert on the topic he speaks about, or believes in what he says.

(244) All this gives rise to the natural question from the public: Who is speaking? Which circles or interests does he represent? This is a question that many communicators and their sponsors, to put it mildly, do not like. However, it is the only safeguard an attentive public has, meeting the communicator already in the attention area. Of course, it is a useful question for analysts of information too. Political scientists and sociologists in our days have stressed the need to map out the different ideological languages in a society, on a small scale or a worldwide one. Ideological languages which pervade the ordinary languages are built of concepts, and use ordinary linguistic means in a daring new way. It has been observed that any ideology in our world of today and of yesterday has its own ideological vocabulary, which it uses as soon as it tries to influence a decision on any topic under debate [a]. The Second World War made investigations of these ideological languages necessary in order to catch the real

meaning of messages from the enemy [b]. But such investigations have far more important aspects than that of mapping out hostile messages. Peaceful information among different nations, societies, and individuals, is founded on and aimed at understanding. Without thorough understanding of one another's ideological vocabulary this peaceful information will be difficult to obtain. The question who is speaking, is therefore a question of the ideological home of the communicator, of his education and training, the ideological language he speaks, and thus which interest group he represents when he tries to influence his public [c].

(245) In the claim for land reform we meet all the communication difficulties we have glanced at above. Scanning the headlines of the documents we shall examine here, the public might expect that land reform or social relationships connected with it would be the main topic of their contents, while the agrarian expert might look for valuable solutions of problems on his own field. Whether these natural expectations are met by the documents, may be discovered by a close examination of what they say.

After the Second World War the agrarian question appeared as topic for debate even in Europe. The quantity of material from this debate is large. A fascinating investigation might be to follow the agrarian question in its ideological aspect in all the available communication channels of several nations after the Second World War; in documents issued by responsible politicians, in newspapers and periodicals, on movies, in television, in pamphlets and posters, at meetings, and so on. This would be a lifetime's work for several scientists, or a research project at large for an ambitious modern university. For a chapter with only the modest ambition of showing what was said when something was done or not done, as described in the previous chapters of this book, there must be a choice of adequate material for investigation.

(246) The natural question from the public; Who is speaking, leads us to enquire as to responsibility, knowledge and significance in the stream of words on land reform after the Second World War. For many centuries, Europe has been the battlefield for different ideologies fighting for power over minds and decisions. It would be irrational to believe that the claim for land reform is the only one free from this aspect. In principle, it would be

helpful to assume that this demand is only one of the many social fields today where the mental appeal of an ideology supports a specific society by determining the spiritual approach to technical and human problems and by influencing the decisions on any part of human life. Thus, if the quest for responsibility gives us national material issued by responsible statesmen of different nationalities, competing international ideologies should display the supranational aspects of the demand, if this is not already inherent in the subject.

Thus, to quote an illuminating example founded on the speaker's own experience, when Prime Minister Chervenkov of Bulgaria speaks about the necessity of rural reforms in his country, he does so aware of his own national responsibility as premier and administrator of Bulgarian land policy. But he is also an exponent of a supranational ideology whose roots in the past are talked of as if they were still living so frequently that a comparative investigation of older ideological statements on the subject has become necessary. This case is not the only one that has caused "prolonged interview" with the past. Guiseppe Medici, head of the Ente Maremma, professor of agricultural economics and later Minister of Agriculture in the Scelba government, is one of the experts on his subject. Nevertheless, his policy is not a creation of his own. He is an exponent of a party policy whose stress on the family and individual property is close to the Social Encyclicals of the Vatican. These documents with their claim to authority at any time that the social order impinges on the moral order, add new aspects to the issue by looking upon the individual and the social problems *sub specie aeternitatis* and making the individual's dignity as a human being a justification of his right to property. By these examples we can already see how ideologies penetrate the concepts actually under discussion in land reform. It is a logical consequence of the struggle for minds that when we choose material to investigate, we look first for the ideologies and then for their temporary national exponents.

(247) On a world-wide scale, political scientists of our days speak about a bipolar ideological world. Europe is not an exception to this rule [a]. The examples we have chosen from European countries where the question of land reform is a burning problem, stress this bipolarity.

We have already mentioned Italy as one of the battlegrounds for land reform. We have introduced Giuseppe Medici as an agrarian expert and at the same time a politician and, so far as we can judge from his document, an outstanding communicator. "Il contratto con i contadini", printed in Rome in 1953, is a speech given by Mr Medici at Cerveteri, on the Maremma north of Rome, on February 3 the previous year to an attentive public of land-hungry farmers [b].

Also of interest in this connection is the justification for the Italian land reform bill, published in a special number of the review "L'agricoltura italiana", where the Italian government itself, in "La relazione ministeriale", officially presents the reasons and necessities for an Italian land reform [c]. The ideological tenor of these documents is supported by the Vatican Encyclicals which, here as elsewhere in the world, try to penetrate the basic concepts of any topic where the social order impinges on the moral one; that is, in any human relationship where human dignity and individual life clash with the social environments [d]. As examples of these aspects we have looked at the great social Encyclicals of the Vatican, that is "De rerum novarum" of 1891, "Quadragesimo Anno" 1931, and a Pentecost message of Pope Pius XII in 1941 also dealing with the questions of labor and land and the human relationships involved [e].

(248) If the Vatican sponsors the ideological views of Catholic social life, Lenin supports his followers in the same all embracing degree. We have spoken about Vulko Chervenkov, Prime Minister of Bulgaria, a well-trained Communist for many years, educated in the Soviet Union. There is nothing in his life that foreshadows any special interest in agrarian questions.

The contribution he has given us is a report delivered on April 5, 1950. It deals with "Tasks of the co-operative farms". The report was printed in Sofia, after delivery at the Second National Conference of Co-operative farm representatives [a]. This indicates that at least some of the audience were experts skilled in the topic. At that time, Mr Cherkenkov was Secretary of the Central Committee of the Bulgarian Communist Party. His ideological origin is also expressed in several quotations of Lenin and other sponsors. Our investigations on statements of Lenin on the question of land and labor stress this relationship. Lenin is here represented by: "Small production in agriculture", "The peasantry and the working class", "Child labor in peasant farming", "Messrs Bourgeois on 'toiler' farming", "Speech delivered to delegates from the Committees of poor peasants of the Moscow region on the 8th of November 1918", "Policy towards the Middle Peasantry, Resolution adopted by the Eight Congress of the R.C.P. (Bolsheviks), on 23rd of March in 1919". This latter theme was also the topic of his Speech for a Grammophone Record on "The Middle Peasants" [b].

(249) The German contribution "Auf dem Wege zur Kolchose" claims to be a presentation of the practice of this ideology. It evaluates the theme in a sub-title: "Die Sowjetisierung der Landwirtschaft in der Sowjet-zone". The document is issued by the Bundesministerium für gesamtdeutsche Fragen in 1952 [a]. "Land reform in Hungary", by András Sandór, is an official statement that rejects the "feudal past" of Hungary and supports a Hungarian new deal so as to obtain a place in the new world growing up around Hungary [b]. The French document we have chosen is a speech on "Démocratie à la terre" by the Socialist Tanguy-Prigent who was Minister of Agriculture in the first French government after the Vichy régime. His background as farmer's son from Bretagne has directed his attention to the psychological problems of the agricultural population as an obstacle to democracy on the land in post-war France [c].

(250) All these documents have two things in common. First, they are regarded as responsible statements justifying agrarian policy in practice in the respective countries after the Second World War. Secondly, they claim to deal with agrarian or social questions, but at the same time they are all living statements of current ideologies in conflict today. These two aspects result in a complicated communication process which it may have a certain interest to clarify so as to see what is said in public.

At the beginning of our chapter we said that the demand for land reform based on the self-evident value of food, was already the object of attention everywhere. We also said that the competing ideologies in Europe made it reasonable to appreciate that it was not merely technical information we could expect to meet in the discussion on land reform. The communicator, or better the propagandist, has for centuries had experience of using people's need of values, and the demands based on them, to influence public minds and decisions in certain directions. Is it possible for the public, or for an analyst of propaganda, to see through the technique of the communicator in his manipulating of the themes and symbols which stand for values and demands so as to give them his own ideological make-up?

(251) The question: who is the communicator, is a natural attempt to discover his ideological home and his specific use of language. As we said above, this question is often the public's only protection against an official pronouncement. Then the public is left to its attention, interest, opportunity to get influenced, to understand or not to understand, and to the skilful communicator able to use all this lack of equilibrium in the communication process. The public sometimes has the impression that there is something more or something else than the literally expressed purpose that the communicator is aiming at, something difficult to catch. But lack of time and training make the doubtful stop wondering and forget about it. Till the day comes when the "sleeper" effect that psychologists have observed comes to a head. And the public, forgetting whom the message came from, expresses as its "own", convinced opinions concerning controversial problems those which the communicator himself a long time ago tried to give his public when he spoke about the same topic, or a related one, or quite another one[a]. This process scientists have paid attention to recently. But the phenomenon is as old as the communication process itself and used by every successful propagandist since the very beginning. That is why interest in influencing children is so high in different ideologies. The child is more likely not to be able to ask for the ideological bias of a communicator, or at least is more likely uncritically to accept the ideological authority with confidence. Only later, with maturity, are some people apt to be critical in asking for the background of a communicator. It is in the frame of such a maturation process that it is convenient to discuss and try to apply some methods which are suitable for the propagandist's own working approach in public messages.

These methods, it must be stressed, do not aim at replacing the impressionistic interpretations of a message which anybody can freely obtain. They try, however, to expose some aspects of the communication process which have been useful to communicators at the expense of the public and sometimes at the expense of the value under debate. In 18th century Sweden, the Orthodox Lutheran State Church tried, at first instinctively and then consciously, to apply such methods when it attempted to make a detailed analysis of those propagandists who were softening its tenets. It was at once answered by these same propagandists who tried similarly to lay bare how many and which were the values used in the propaganda and counterpropaganda [b]. These attempts are examples of the fact that as soon as evidence is required of what really is said, an impressionistic view is not satisfying. Human wellbeing must rely upon something else than an impression. In consistency with this, the Supreme Court of the United States and the Department of Justice, have applied these methods during the Second World War as a way of disclosing subversive propaganda against the country and of exposing the ideological background of some disturbing elements, thereby establishing a new technique of evidence in legal procedure [c]. This use might give the impression that these methods are especially fit for condemning people and preventing freedom of speech. But their use by authorities against subversive elements is in fact of less importance than their use to exculpate people from accusations of belonging to a certain ideology, accusations that are often based on impressionistic and arbitrary opinions. And all this is of far less importance than their significance in the presentation of different ideologies' propaganda which at last contributes to understanding different ideological languages. Which in its turn might give people the opportunity of free and conscious choice of what ideology they want to belong to, or to reject, or to get rid of altogether [d].

(252) These methods, which have been called Quantitative Semantics, give close attention to certain significant aspects of a propagandist message [a]. As applied to a particular material it might seem to be only a new technique. Closer scrutiny of the nature of any propaganda will prove that the relation of quantity in what is said, is deeply rooted in the nature of any message, that is, its contents. Skilful communicators aware of the value of their own particular message, have pointed out the difference between true and false as gradual. The false message may

contain certain elements of truth or have a character of half-truth [b]. This quantitative concept – it is to be stressed that figures are only the most known means of presentation of quantitative concepts – how much of the values that is allowed in a new message, is the basis for creating new opinions, new meanings of words, symbols, and themes, and new attitudes of a public which is under exposure to a quantitatively colored presentation of the original message and thereby a wholly new or a partly new message. Manipulation of the quantity is the basis of a propagandist's work. His play with words, figures, concepts, contexts, themes, symbols, values, demands, and needs depends on his freedom to use the quantity. These aspects have given birth to the methods used in this chapter to analyse the claims for land reform. The experience of communicators is as old as human society itself. The work of the propaganda analyst is very young, based as it is on the general requirement for knowledge based on evidence. It has to be developed by case studies and by experiments so as at last to be able to show and keep up with the quantitative function of a message.

(253) The material on claims for land reform exhibits some problems even on a quick glance at the documents. Its international aspects are already evident through the different languages of the statements. Some of these difficulties are solved by responsible editors themselves who, aware of the interest of the topic to an international public, have translated the documents into a world wide language. This is the case of the statements from the Vatican, of Lenin, of Chervenkov, and of Sandór. The French and German documents have relied on the currency of their languages. We have chosen to let them stay so because this will give us an opportunity to see how international concepts are dressed up in a certain tongue without losing their original meaning. The Italian documents, the speech of Medici and the ministerial introduction to the Land Reform Statute, have been translated by us into English.

Looking for the documents' treatment of the demand and value under discussion, we go to the documents directly. We want a survey of the way in which land reform is handled in responsible statements, and we want to know what the texts themselves tell us about it before we make the survey.

CATHOLIC LAND REFORM DOCUMENTS

(254) It would be irrational to neglect the fact that the religious institutions are the oldest experts on human relationships and the relation between different social classes. Approaching the Vatican documents we therefore look upon them in their function as sponsors of a practical agrarian policy after the Second World War and as a justification of this policy. Which values do the documents deal with, which values do the texts identify as belonging to the ideology and its program, which values are rejected and which claims and demands have been put or rejected? And, at last, what is the tendency or tendencies of all these approved or rejected values and demands? And, having clarified this, which of all these values, demands, and tendencies are followed, rejected or neglected in other responsible documents of followers and opponents?

Rerum Novarum, the Social Encyclical of the Vatican in 1891, is already a much studied document. Its successor, the encyclical Quadragesimo Anno in 1931, stressed the great importance of Rerum Novarum and its influence in practically all fields of social and human life. It is thus the call from the encyclical of 1931, and later affirmations of the same thing we follow when seeking Vatican influence on ideas concerning the relation between labor and land as expressed in demands and symbols of identifications and rejections. The quantitative enumeration of these demands and symbols makes the survey possible.

In its English edition, Rerum Novarum numbers about 14200 words. Thorough readings of the text give us 3718 symbols. These symbols are, as usual with the written word, associated with their context. "Human dignity", for instance, is a symbol. The literal or conceptual context of this symbol or its synonyms gives it a positive or a negative value. By the frequency of its occurrence, a symbol can dominate the text and give the text a certain meaning. With less frequency, the meaning of the text is modified. In a positive, or negative, or neutral context, the particular symbol derives a certain meaning which can influence or modify by the frequency of its occurrence [a]. This interplay may give an analyst headache, a grammarian trouble, or confuse

the public in its understanding of what is said, if not ideologically
trained in a certain direction. On a world-wide scale the ideological predispositions are not always the same. To the communicator, however, this ambivalent interplay of usage and meaning
in values and symbols is useful and necessary for what he says.
To the propagandist who is trying to influence our decisions on
values under discussion, this instability of meaning in a word or
concept or symbol is the opening which language itself offers for
guiding his public on the road he desires.

(255) Political scientists have described our world as societies
built on different values, where human life and endeavor is
explained as a differential rate of identification with some of
these symbols, rejection of others, and demands for something
else [a]. The lacking equilibrium of these developments makes the
frequency of their occurrence a significant quality of a particular
society and makes its most frequently used symbols a key for
communicating with it. This configurative way of looking upon
and analyzing a society and its communication is strongly supported by any propaganda message, no matter what the actual
topic is. In order to influence and get adherents, a communicator
must always appeal to values to be identified with, something has
to be rejected and something demanded so as to change or to
reinforce present conditions. The symbols he uses for this purpose
can be identifications with the person of the speaker, with the
particular ideology he represents and its values, or with the
program this ideology claims. A program derives from the
demands made by the particular ideology. And it depends on the
success of the ideological program whether the demands are
already realized identification symbols or whether they are still
in contention to be included in the future in the identification of
the ideology. In our present material there are already trends
which indicate that the more totalitarian a particular ideology is,
the more identification symbols are used and the more difficult
it becomes to discern between symbols used as identifications
and those used as demands. There are also trends in our material
that make us ask whether facts, symbols, or neutral statements
without any indication of preference or rejection, are likely to
show up in a message where everything is inflammatory, designed
to influence the decisions of the audience.

(256) Returning to Rerum Novarum, investigation of the meanings of the symbols shows no less than eighteen themes. How the symbols making these themes are dispersed over the text by their frequency and function, we can see in Table 36. The technically more detailed way of making such an analysis and its problems are described in a forthcoming book. It might be sufficient here to say about the technique used in analysing the documents in this chapter, that every symbol is built up of its context and its function. This determines the volume of the symbol and its positive or negative value and direction in the text. Exhaustive analysis of the text is aimed at. Each time a symbol appears, literally or synonymously, it has been recorded with a reference making it possible to find it again in its place in the text. Thereafter, different symbols, according to function, have been gathered into themes[a]. It is also this function which has given them their positive or negative value and thereby the positive or negative treatments of the themes, viewed from the opinion of the communicator. For the sake of surveyability, it has been necessary to unite the themes growing up from the symbols with related themes, where the original themes built nuances within the main theme. The table in Appendix 7 is here presented as an example of a phase of this process, but the procedure as a whole has been applied to all the material. This is the background to the final survey of all the documents, where the main themes of the different statements are compared in order to show the difference or uniformity in the propaganda. It is evident that all the research behind these surveys could give rise to a prolonged and detailed description of the style in which values and concepts are expressed in different propaganda. But for the purpose of this chapter we have to limit ourselves to the intention to lay bare how many and which concepts, values, demands, and their symbols are used in certain authoritative documents in order to influence the public opinion on a certain debated controversial demand.

(257) Looking at the table on the Vatican document of 1891 we get a clear picture of the quantitative relation between the eighteen themes at attention. The document is as we know a theological statement aimed at influencing the mental approach to social questions. For our purpose here the theological aspects

TABLE 36. *Symbols in the Vatican encyclical of 1891*

Groups of symbols on values	Main direction (Favorable or Unfavorable)	Identifications	Demands	Resistance	Total
Man as a social being . . .	F	544	122	74	740
State, its function in society	F	275	77	78	430
Approved unions	F	255	62	26	343
Authority of Church . . .	F	211	19	20	250
Real remedy	F	190	80	43	313
Labor remuneration- possession (see below) . . .	F	72	31	6	109
Moral justice	F	144	38	24	206
Lawful order	F	134	40	30	204
Labor remuneration-possession, by Nature . . .	F	216	4	4	224
Authority of God	F	119	4	14	137
Socialists, injustice	U	92	2	150	244
Attention to the problem by Us	F	58	18	16	92
The proletariat's misery . .	U	47	—	88	135
Condemnation of Capitalists	U	40	10	92	142
Changes and unstability on earth	U	25	—	40	65
Non-approved unions . . .	U	20	—	27	47
Address of the message . .	F	19	—	—	19
Supplies of the earth . . .	F	17	—	1	18
Sub-total Favorable	F	2,254	495	336	3,085
Sub-total Unfavorable . . .	U	224	12	397	633
TOTAL		2,478	507	733	3,718

serve as a justification for the interference of the Vatican in social problems. The rich nuances of the theological themes in the document that our research on symbols and their quantitative relationship has discovered, we must consequently leave aside and here only point out that the symbols for the Authority of God and that of the Church can be comprehended by the demand: Give heed to the laws and judgments of Christ as represented by the Church. As we see in the table, the importance of the social question is noticed. The message is directed to the Vatican hierarchy, the clergy and their followers living on this earth, which is unfavorably described as a place of unstability and conflicts, even though the 40 negative symbols for this bad earth are modified by 17 others describing earth as an abundant storehouse. This is the frame of the message.

Most attention, almost 20%, is devoted to man as a social being.

The quantitative relation of the symbols of identification with certain values, of the symbols of demands, and of the symbols of resistance, give a nuanced picture of the quality of this man and the society he ought to create. This can be comprehensively presented as follows:

544 symbols of identification:

Humanity, individuals' relation, personality, human dignity, mercy	260
Rights of God in a society, just and right, lawful, necessity . . .	106
Family, paternal authority, the future from the past	80
Workmen, his wages, daily labor, the poor, rest from work . . .	56
Employers, the rich, wealth, private property.	42
	544

The kind of troubles this society meets is described by 74 negative symbols:

Labor as a painful expiation of sin, work cursed	44
Corrupting influences, passions, want, misery	30
	74

In consistency with this, 122 demands ask for better conditions:

Hold private property, sufficient wages, rest, religion	58
Right to marry, free action, love God, fellowman, Church . . .	54
Housework to preserve woman's modesty, wellbeing of family .	10
	122

Already by this theme we see that the intensified kind of attention which usually is expressed as interest, is focussed on man as an individual whose chief role in his society is that of the head of his family. The stress on Religion and Church as respected social institutions already has a long perspective in the light of the authority of God and Church. In fact, the high frequency theme of man as a social being gives us already in principle the kind of society the Vatican document identifies as its own, the troubles it condemns, and the demands it makes. The other themes in the attention area only evaluate by their frequency further aspects. Thus, among troubles to be condemned are themes on, not only the misery and hard conditions of the proletariat, but also the Socialists and their irreligious unions which make use of this evil. Another aspect of the misery of the prole-

tariat are the greedy Capitalists. A comprehensive picture of
these social evils is not different in kind to the one that we already
have of the social problems. Values worth identification facing
the attacks of Socialists and their unions are expressed by 112
symbols altogether:

Public well-being, Catholic societies, charity, remedy, religion   45
Employer, the rich, wealth, private property, wages to dispose .   42
Hard pressed people, the poor, the workmen, all classes   21
Natural right   4
                                                                _____
                                                                 112

The disturbing Socialists, their work, their unions, are described
by 177 negative symbols:

Crafty agitators, sedition, futile, ridiculous equality   60
Transferring property to the community, force workmen   45
Threaten the existence of family life, system of State organized
    relief, contrary to natural rights, harmful to Religion   39
Class naturally hostile to class, Socialists, strikes   33
                                                                _____
                                                                 177

The two demands that are made in this connection go to the core
of this struggle by suggesting a modified intervention from the
State "to see that each obtains his own". The limited action that
is expected from the State introduces the particular concept of
the State put forward by the document. Before treating this we
have, however, to conclude our survey of the social evils by
meeting the greedy Capitalist. His very existence in a society
threatens 40 symbols worth Vatican identification:

Workmen's earnings, their dignity as human beings   24
Humanity, justice, anger of Heaven   16
                                                             _____
                                                              40

92 symbols give a condemnatory description of this Capitalist
at work:

Greatest inhumanity, rapacious usury, profit out of the needs of
    another, defraud anyone of wages, cruelty, grasping speculators   77
Enormous fortunes of individuals, concentration of so many
    branches of trade in the hands of a few individuals   15
                                                                _____
                                                                 92

7 demands ask him to refrain from cutting down workmen's
earnings while 3 menace him with the strict account that he must
give in the life to come.

The natural result of all this evil is the misery of the proletariat. 47 symbols express the Vatican's identification with the suffering ones and the kind of help they need:

Poor workers, those in labor and grief, powerless multitude, wage
   earners 43
Charity, love   4
                                                           47

88 negative symbols describe the kind of the misery:

Working men, wage earners, fooled, empty promises, unprotected   47
Work too hard, hours of labor too long, slavery, grasping
   employers 26
Strikes, irreligious associations, unresigned poverty 15
                                                           88

No demands are made in this connection. This would be surprising if we do not consider that the described conditions of misery are results of other powers in society to which, as we have seen, demands to improve conditions are already put. This description of the social evil serves in fact to stress the necessity of demands already made.

We referred above to the limited interference of the State in times of need. The State is the subject of high frequency of attention with over $11\frac{1}{2}\%$ of the symbols. It is the theme which by frequency is closest to man as a social being. The concept of the State that is valuable to the Vatican, is however more sophisticatedly described than that of the Socialist state. Worth identification in the State are:

State authority, assistance, administration, all classes 143
Private societies, religious orders, the Gospel, Thomas of Aquin   67
Man as individual, mutual rights, family life as a part of the
   Commonwealth, interests of the poor, the working people . . 51
The rich, lawful owners, private owners 14
                                                       275

This description already permits large limitations of the 143 symbols for State authority by identifications with private societies, mutual rights, and family life as living independent components. The limitation of the State authority is also made clear by the symbols attacking this concept of the State as well as disease menacing it:

Undue interference, depriving the private owner more than just   36
These disturbers (Socialists), strikes   20
Misery, wage earners, no resources of their own   13
Violation, (Capitalistic) wealth   9
                                                                 ——
                                                                   78

Also the demands are intended to limit action by the State, well understood to be a potential danger to the Vatican State concept, unless it uses its power to build up a society where the human individual is the most important component. A point of view already expressed by the frequency of attention symbols, the symbols for the human individual in society being 72% more frequent than those of the State. To realize this State concept 77 symbols demand:

Strict justice, do not disturb the individual and the family . . .   28
Harmony, agreement, public welfare, private property, especially
    care for the wage earners   26
Save the workmen from the disturbers (Socialists)   16
Defend the religious associations but do not interfere   7
                                                                   ——
                                                                     77

Moral justice and lawful order are concepts already appearing as necessary conditions for the State. They are evaluated by further identifications:

Human law, civil law, sanctity of justice   82
Every class, mutual relation, duties, common good, peace,
    morality   63
Working population's spiritual and mental interests, the poor   52
Masters, the wealthy, private property, ownership, lawful owner 36
Eternal law of God, rights of Church, idea of futurity, natural law 33
Family life   6
Wages, right use of money   6
                                                                 ———
                                                                 278

The importance of these values is evaluated also by negative symbols of the two themes.

Rob citizens of their rights, use money as one pleases   54

78 demands claim maintenance of this peaceful position:

Peace and good order, high standard of morality, religion obeyed,
    family life in accordance with God's law, strict justice   32
Results of labor belong to him who has labored, private property   29
Keep the multitude within the line of duty, respect every man's
    dignity, never injure capital, never engage in riot, have nothing
    to do with men of evil principles, carry out honestly and well   17
                                                                    ——
                                                                      78

Experience of human life indicates that such a society is a Utopia. This is also realized by the Vatican that suggests remedy for that. It is under the aspect of reality we now look for concrete suggestions to cure all the social evils described and to build up a society in which they are missing. A way to this new society are the unions between employers and workers. 255 symbols describe the qualities of these means for help:

Religious orders and instruction, societies for mutual help, Church	158
Strictest honesty, mercy, piety, relief, care	43
Christian workmen, interests of wage earners	34
Labor benefited to the community at large	15
Employers, masters	5
	255

The bad conditions which justify these unions are expressed by 26 negative symbols. 19 refer to death, sickness, and destitution of means, whereas 7 mention false teaching and irreligious societies. The 62 demands for improving the Vatican unions claim:

Unity of purpose, more effective administration, harmony of action, the State watching, not interfering, funds for help . .	53
Look first and before all to God, religious instruction	9
	62

The religious element of the unions is stressed but detailed instructions are lacking. In general, the program of this Vatican document gives more guidance to action along certain lines than instruction of what to do to solve the practical problem. The same is the case as regards the theme on "Remedy for social ills". The identification symbols stress the lines we already know:

Assistance of religion and Church, Christian morality, charity	70
Human race, class to class in friendliness, duties to each other	43
Practical solutions mentioned by principles	39
Christian workmen, conditions of the working people, families	21
Private property, Catholics well off	17
	190

The threats to such a general remedy are expressed by 43 negative symbols:

Main tenet of Socialism, community of goods, strike 26
Lust of possession, worldly pride, immoderate love of self, leave
   out the Church 17
                                                43

80 symbols demand the application of this remedy and the defeat
of the resistance:

Refute false teaching, obey the precepts of the Church, bind class
   to class, spirit of justice, all human means must conspire . . 62
Safeguarding the interests of wage earners, content with frugal
   living, inviolability of private property 11
Look at the world as it is, look elsewhere for a remedy 7
                                              80

This moral aspect of the evils of the world, of the remedy for
these evils that we have now observed significant to the Vatican
concept of a society, also gives the justification to the important
question of labor. The interplay among duties to work, rights to
wages and to possess the results of labor is justified by man's own
nature and moral qualities distinguishing him from beasts and
animals. Values worth identification on this field, paid attention
to by 333 symbols, are 288:

Private ownership, natural right of man, disposal of remuneration,
   free to work, dictate of nature, man's nature 140
Man's labor necessary, his personal attribute, remunerative labor,
   sustain his life, honorable employment, the poor 92
Material well-being, wealth, stable and permanent possession,
   for advantage in time to come, cling to the country where they
   were born 56
                                          288

10 negative symbols indicate the contrary concepts such as
excessive taxation, deal with property as they please and disobey
the dictate of nature. 35 demands want to realize the high respect
for work as a means of supporting life and getting property:

Free to work, to accept, not chained by extensive taxation, at his
   own disposal, private property, capital cannot do without labor
   nor labor without capital, right to possess, enough remuneration 28
Labor nothing to be ashamed of 7
                                          35

(258) This is the content of the Rerum Novarum as shown by
the quantitative relation of the values and concepts it offers for

the interpretation of its opinion and for the solution of the conditions of labor. Table 36 gave its attention area and the kind of themes this attention caused. If we look closely at the quantitative relation among all these symbols that build up the themes, we shall see how the attention is distributed and intensified into interest. The degree of interest in different values of positive and negative color determines the frequency of occurrence. The program for a society approved by the Vatican shows up in the demands that are made. Their very contents and the quantitative distribution among them also give guidance on the further distribution of Vatican values in communication with different publics on questions on labor and relationship among different classes.

(259) The concepts of the Rerum Novarum have been the topic for many studies. According to his ideological and cultural predispositions every interpreter has tried to evaluate the message of the social encyclical. Due to these predispositions of intellectual training and temporary circumstances, the results of the reading of the Rerum Novarum showed divergencies and caused many debates. Forty years later, the Vatican issued another social encyclical presenting the Vatican's own interpretation of the values of the Rerum Novarum. This encyclical, the "Quadragesimo Anno", was published in 1931. The literature on the field presents it as a document of "social reconstruction". The encyclical itself has a solemn approach to its topic. It celebrates an anniversary with impressive congratulations on the importance of the Rerum Novarum in the social life. This approach gives an atmosphere of power and success to the elites backing this program and is likely to be understood as such by the public at large. It is, however, realistic to ask whether the message of the Quadragesimo Anno really is a story of success or whether it has a more qualified meaning for the clergy to whom it is immediately addressed.

The idea of a comparison between the two encyclicals was obvious and was already applied in 1931 by a blackfriar, as to the coincidence of some themes [a]. An investigation of the quantitative relationships of the values and concepts which the Quadragesimo Anno introduces as its own, condemns, or demands, will give some aspects of the further communication of the ideas of the Rerum Novarum as well as answer our question as to the intention of the message.

TABLE 37. *Symbols in the Vatican encyclical of 1931*

Groups of symbols on values	Main direction (Favorable or Unfavorable)	Identifi-cations	Demands	Resistance	Total
Authority of Church . . .	F	458	83	47	588
Congratulations on Rerum Novarum and its benefits	F	294	18	26	338
Real remedy	F	270	114	57	441
Injustice	U	251	10	502	763
Man as a social being . . .	F	227	64	52	343
Approved unions	F	215	30	18	263
Attention to the problem by Us	F	214	42	35	291
Justice	F	197	70	26	293
The social question	F	195	7	66	268
Labor, remuneration-possession	F	193	46	24	263
State, its function in society	F	191	40	43	274
Conditions of change on earth	U	171	—	159	330
Authority of God	F	128	6	6	140
The right to property . . .	F	111	19	12	142
Lawful order	F	90	31	7	128
Address of the message . .	F	59	—	—	59
The Capitalist	U	50	—	106	156
The proletariat's misery . .	U	38	—	43	81
Active resistance	F	18	9	7	34
Non-approved unions . . .	U	—	—	6	6
Sub-total Favorable. . . .	F	2,860	579	426	3,865
Sub-total Unfavorable. . .	U	510	10	816	1,336
Total		3,370	589	1,242	5,201

(260) These comments on the Rerum Novarum fall into 20 themes with about 18900 words covering 5201 symbols, as shown in Table 37. It is a consequence of the explanatory nature of the Quadragesimo Anno that the significance of the earlier message is emphasized. As ever, the authority of God and Church justifies the Vatican's interference in social questions. It is true that the Rerum Novarum has already pointed out the way. But changes of time and new needs as well as misunderstanding by both Catholics and non-Catholics have made a new encyclical necessary. Over 6% of the symbols at attention deal with this unfavorable theme of changes. Of these 330 symbols, 159 describe this evil: spirit of socialistic and revolutionary agitators, class warfare, mutual hatred, paganism, liberalism, unemployment, Capitalistic regime, concentration and accumulation of power, despotic

economic domination, directors of invested funds, the two armies on the labor market. Among them are 33 symbols applied to the victims of these evil powers: the poor and the oppressed laborers. These bad conditions menace 171 symbols for concepts worth identification and support: not only the victims we have just mentioned, but also the two classes in a society as well as the agricultural classes. Further, the human dignity, economic conditions, peace, justice, modern machinery, dictates of the conscience, Our pontificat, and Leo XIII. No demands are made. But the menacing development is immediately opposed by $20\frac{1}{2}\%$ of the total symbols which emphasize not only the authority of God and Church, but also the importance of the Rerum Novarum, another aspect of the power and wisdom of the Church. In consistency with this, even the theme of Attention to the problems turns out to deal more with clerical symbols than the relation between the different classes on the labor market. 170 symbols identify the problems at attention as encyclical letters, Catholic doctrine, true sense of Leo's teaching, the Catholic world, reform of Christian morals. Only 44 symbols refer to the social order, ownership, civil authority, capital, labor, the working classes and the many young wealthy men studying social problems. The 42 demands on this topic are related to this quantitative interest. 38 of them claim reform of morals, more precise application of Leo's doctrine as well as answers to the doubts the Rerum Novarum has caused. Only 4 symbols ask for an examination of the nature of Socialism, for an exposure of the root of the present social disorder, for an "arraignment" of modern economics. The 35 symbols describing resistance are variations of those evils. Whether this quantitative interest is significant to the whole document and to what extent, we can see by studying the different themes at attention. The quantitative relationship of different aspects within each theme is specially useful in this connection.

The clerical power confronting modern times has increased its old social experience by the mere existence and supposed benefits of the Rerum Novarum. A closer examination of the congratulations on this encyclical gives us the Vatican impression of the achievement of the Rerum Novarum in the social life.

Symbols worth identification:

Magna Charta of social order, truly Christian social science . . . 122
Numerous organizations, mutual assistance, truly Christian work-
   men, conditions of the workmen improved, their true dignity . 72
Catholic Church, instructions of the Holy See. 51
The whole human race, rulers of the leading nations 43
Associations among farmers and other of the humbler classes . . 4
Particular regard to women and children. 2
                                                 294

This result of the Rerum Novarum is menaced by:

Socialist organizations, liberalism, internal strife, misery   26

The 18 demands ask for action to insist on the authority of the
Gospel, and to apply the doctrine of the Rerum Novarum
according to the mind and instructions of the Holy See. To the
"man as a social being" living in this society, are applied over
$6\frac{1}{2}\%$ of the total number of symbols.
Values worth identification on this topic are:

God the Creator, individual and social character of man, moral 89
The mass of the poor, wage earners, fathers, mothers, family,
   human dignity of the workingmen, position by Divine providence 54
Twofold character of ownership, two classes, capital, labor . . 34
The state, government, public institutions of the nation . . . 26
The richer class, employers, obligations of superfluous income . 17
Agricultural classes 7
                                               227

52 symbols threaten this kind of society and show up as ruin,
ignorance, unfavorable surroundings, conditions of the economic
world, unemployment, human frailty and temporal upheavals.
64 demands make us understand that this society, despite the
great influence of the Rerum Novarum, still is more a goal than
a fact and claim human dignity, protection of labor, rejection
of class warfare and ask for charity, common good, and fulfilling
of duties. Here as in the Rerum Novarum, means to maintain this
desirable society are lawful order, justice, the State, approved
unions, real remedy. New is the appeal to active resistance and
fight against those who menace the ideals of the Rerum Novarum,
whereas the defence of the Right to property, already deeply
involved in the social concept of the Rerum Novarum has here

turned out to be an important theme of its own. The social question, the theme of labor-remuneration-possession, complete the picture of the society favored by the concepts of the Vatican. A survey of these themes gives us their real interests.
Symbols of identification:

Real remedy: Leo XIII, Christian truth whole and entire, social peace, Church 163
Just share, civil authority, social, economic progress, common good 54
Dense masses of young workers 34
Employers, the rich, others in power 19
                                                        270

Approved unions: Interests of employers and employees, labor contracts, all groups. 104
Our predecessor, precepts of Church, Catholic unions, Catholic workingmen, religious purposes 75
Neutral trade unions, labor unions, justice, common good, freedom 24
Associations of employers 8
Associations among farmers 4
                                                        215

Justice: Social and individual character of labor, just freedom of action, right distribution of property, charity, common good 162
Catholic members, their conscience, Church. 35
                                                        197

The State: Power, civil authority, administration, friend of private owners, public well-being, private prosperity 121
The richer class, property owners, right of private property . . 28
A graded hierarchial order 19
Leo XIII, God, moral law 16
The mass of the poor, wage-earners 7
                                                        191

Lawful order: Social justice, charity, juridical order, laws, labor 48
Church, Catholic principles in social and economic matters . . 42
                                                        90

Right to property: Right to property, ownership, individual and social characters, given by nature, God's will, proper use . . 97
Leo XIII, Guidance and direction of the Church 14
                                                        111

Labor-remuneration-possession: Capital, human wealth, save
  money, living sparingly, increased wages, certain modest
  fortune, moderate ownership, mutual harmony, his labor an
  alliance between his toil and his neighbor's property, capital
  cannot do without labor nor labor without capital, strict
  justice 171
Natural law, God's will, Leo XIII, Christian charity. 15
The employer, develops the wealth of the society 7
                                                        193

The social question: Rerum Novarum, Chair of Peter, Chief
  guardian of religion, Church highest authority on earth, right
  solution of different problems. 87
Employers, the rich, capital, private ownership, right to
  property. 49
The workingmen, the poor, Christian workingmen, associations,
  foundation of social laws, religion, duties, morality 42
Sociological students, legislators, the State, mankind 17
                                                        195

As we see the picture is filled with clerical symbols, no matter
which topic that is actually at attention. The symbols expressing
resistance to this clerical society are of course colored by this
specifice view of the world and are negatively described thus:

Real remedy: Growing ranks of revolutionaries, envy, hatred,
  away from God. 44
Socialists, tenets of mitigated Socialism, unjust claims . . . , 10
The rich and those in power, negligence 3
                                                        57

Approved unions are resisted in 18 symbols by organizations of
Socialists and Communists, strikes, lockouts and the difficulty
to form Catholic unions. Even the theme of Justice is menaced
by 26 expressions for Socialists and their erroneous doctrines, as
well as class warfare and the uncontrolled use of wealth. The
State is menaced by results of its own activity. 43 symbols speak
about bureaucratic character, exhausting the means of individuals,
crushing taxes, abolishing private initiative and ownership,
Liberalism and individualism. The Lawful order is in danger by
the conflict between classes for economic supremacy, in 7 symbols;
the Right to property is threatened by 12 symbols evaluating
the confusion between the right to property and its proper use.
24 symbols describe individualism and collectivism as well as

propertyless wage earners as negative to the realization of the Vatican concept of Labor and remuneration. The topic of the Social question mirrors by 66 negative symbols the dangers already encountered: Socialism, grievously harmful to the working class, Liberalism, hard-heartedness of employers, general indifference. 9 of these 66 symbols emphasize that it is false to believe that economic science and moral discipline are distinct and alien. These great dangers justify the many demands for bettering conditions and launching a program. Solutions of the social question are put forward in the following demands on the different topics we have already introduced:

Real remedy: Christian social doctrine, stern insistance on moral law, mutual co-operation, social peace, preach the Christian truth, convince Socialists, spiritual exercises, Christian harmony, charity 105
Wealth distributed that the common good of all be promoted, uplifting the proletariat, wage earners attain property . . . 9
114

Approved unions: Peaceful collaboration of the classes, founding associations with Christian social doctrine, common interests 25
Regression of Socialists' organizations, strikes, lockouts forbidden 5
30

Justice: Wage-contract modified, contract of partnership, just wage, reform society according to the mind of Church, each class receive its due share, commutative justice supported by Christian charity 49
Respect justice and equity, obey the precepts of the Church, Catholic members full freedom to follow their consciences . . 21
70

The State: Public well-being, private prosperity, protect the rights of individuals, special regard for the needy, wage-earners 24
A graded hierarchial order, healthy economic co-operation, moral 16
40

Lawful order: Reform of manners, God the first and supreme end, Catholic principles, co-operation of all men of good will, justice 31
Right to property: Respect the possession of others, everything having its proper owner, right of property distinguished from its use 19
Labor-remuneration-possession: Not forbidden to increase fortune in a lawful and just manner, respect the laws of God and the right of his neighbors, human dignity in labor, certain moderate ownership, due consideration for the double character,

individual, social of capital and labor, right order in applying
natural resources to human needs, alliance between toil and
property   46
The social question: No solution apart from the intervention of
religion and the Church   7

The quantitative relationship of the attention area on all
these topics agrees with the picture we already obtained from
the theme of the importance of the Rerum Novarum as a social
doctrine as well as the kind of society it designs around man as
a social being. The interest focussed on the different aspects of
this society, expressed by the quantitative occurrence of certain
values, can also be observed.

Directly unfavorable themes cover over $25\frac{1}{2}\%$ of the whole
attention area. This is a remarkable trend in the light of the
presentation of all the benefits due to the Rerum Novarum and
the strong attention to divine and clerical power with $20\frac{1}{2}\%$ of
the total symbols. We have even observed how and to what
extent this attention to the clerical power and its precepts for
mankind is intensified into interest on all social topics at the
expense of suggestions for practical solutions of actual social
problems.

Obviously, there remain still evils calling for this strong
attention. These are described as injustice, conditions of change
on earth, the Capitalist, the proletariat's misery, non-approved
unions. The topic of changes on earth we have already evaluated.
Symbols worth Vatican identifications as being menaced by
these bad themes are dispersed thus over the rest of the topics:

Injustice: Church, true social authority, moral law, social justice 136
Social and public aspect of ownership, just wage 76
Proletariat, harassed workingmen, human dignity 26
Weakness of women, mothers of families, children.   8
Wealthier classes, the rich, employer   5
                                                              ———
                                                              251

The Capitalist: Laborer, sufferings of disinherited, welfare of
   their souls, clearly just demands, wages, religion, human
   dignity 50
The proletariat's misery: Immense number of propertyless wage
   earners, immense army of hired rural laborers, moral of workers,
   family life, proper observance of the holy days 36
Virtue of girls and women   2
                                                              ———
                                                               38

Highest hostility is reserved for the non-approved unions whose nature is so foreign to any Vatican value that there is nothing in these unions which the Vatican can identify as its own. The whole phenomenon as such is a menace to the Vatican society. Under negative symbols describing topics unfavorable to this Vatican society, these non-approved unions are represented by 6 symbols as organizations of Socialists and of Communists. Other negative symbols are:

Injustice: Socialism, Cultural S., Religious S., Christian S., no place for true social authority, a certain element of truth, loss of human dignity, abolition of private property, class warfare, all means of production to the State, hostility to Christian religion, false liberty, spread their false doctrines, society on Socialistic principles 170
Selfishness, greed, paganism, violation of justice by Capitalists   81
Doctrines of rationalism, Liberalism, some form of collectivism, international imperialism in financial affairs, where a man's fortune is there is his country, individualism   72
Bolshevism, Communism, fear nothing, merciless class warfare, most violent opposition to the Christian faith, extinction of ownership, bloodshed, destruction of all society, inhuman . .   72
Grave injury to our predecessor, Church favors the rich   52
Superabundant riches of the fortunate few, unjust claims of capital, economic dictatorship, no regard to human dignity, private profit   36
Insufficiency of the fathers' salary, abuse children, women . .   19
                                                                  ———
                                                                  502

The Capitalist: Capital, capitalists' excessive advantages, lower or raise wages unduly, left the laborer the barest minimum . 100
Church accused of taking sides with the wealthy, break God's law   6
                                                                  ———
                                                                  106

The proletariat's misery: Multitudes of workingmen, hired rural laborers, propertyless wage earners, hand-to-mouth uncertainty, disgraceful housing conditions, obstacles to the family life, no hope of ever obtaining a share in the land, perils to moral .   38
Superabundant riches   5
                                                                  ——
                                                                  43

Only ten demands – on the theme of injustice – are made. Their contents, however, in fact sum up what the whole thing is about. Oppose with all our strengh these bad conditions in the present society, reform it and enforce moral law. There is no reason to become Socialist. That is the message which sums up the particular interplay of symbols we have already observed. And in accordance with this the favorable theme of the appeal to Active resistance against evil, is launched. 18 symbols of identification speak about valiant courage and good soldiers of Christ who are able to face stern combat. 7 symbols for danger indicate the menace to this fight for God in society by losing heart and being children of this world. There are 9 demands to the hard fighting soldiers of Christ: Spare no labor, take more courage, oppose. No victory is mentioned here.

It is evident that despite all the importance claimed for the Rerum Novarum and the benefits due to it, resistance has grown great during the forty years. That the Church now not only has to fight against social evils from the time of the Rerum Novarum and new evils of modern times and new social developments. But she is also obliged to emphasize the importance of her own program to a degree that limits her interests in the social question to expressing divine and clerical values on most topics and to the condemnation of certain social evils that are in the highest degree opposite to her concept of a right social order. Her recognition of the growing opposition to her program can also be observed in the list of those to whom her message is addressed. Patriarchs, Primates, Bishops, Venerable Brethren, Our beloved sons and children, all the faithful of the Catholic world that are assured of "special affection of our heart" and "paternal affection" cover most of the 59 symbols that indicate the right milieu of the appeal to urgent action in approved directions in a darkening world. Despite the solemn, impressive celebration of the "Magna Charta of social order" the Quadragesimo Anno presents an ideology and a social program fighting for its existence in a world growing more dangerous, hostile, or indifferent every year.

(261) The Second World War gave a new impulse to clarify the Vatican standpoint on the relation between labor, property, and human beings. The need to build up a new world after the War and awareness of its task of persuasion made the Vatican refer to the social concepts from the Rerum Novarum and the Quadragesimo Anno in a Pentecost message in 1941.

This text is a short message of about 4800 words with a total of 1420 symbols. The symbols cover 16 themes. Some of them coincide with those of the earlier encyclicals as we can see by comparing Table 38 with those preceding, especially from a glance at the different topics at attention. This message is conveyed in a modern communication medium. Aware of this, the communicator pays more attention to his radio public than his predecessors even by the names he gives his audience. Venerable brethren is here succeeded by "Dear children of the whole world" (35 symbols). The reason for the message is expressed in 5 symbols presenting wants, injustice, passion, and disorder, as threatening the "lawful order" of the world. The exhortatory purpose of the message is represented by 2 symbols of demand. The dangerous present time also dominates the theme of conditions on earth as well as that of its supplies even though the latter is a favorable aspect of the future. The authority of the Church and that of God are as usual held to justify interference in social questions. The authority of Church and God is in fact more stressed here than in the Rerum Novarum where the divine authority symbols were almost $10\frac{1}{2}\%$ of the whole symbol mass, whereas the directly corresponding symbols in 1941 cover 20% of the total concepts.

TABLE 38. *Symbols in the Vatican message of Pentecost 1941.*

Groups of symbols on values	Main direction (Favorable or Unfavorable)	Identifi- cations	Demands	Resistance	Total
Authority of Church . . .	F	162	30	24	216
Man as a social being . . .	F	158	75	10	243
Congratulations on Rerum Novarum	F	110	24	20	154
Labor-remuneration- possession	F	61	18	1	80
State, its function in society	U	60	33	13	106
Attention to the problem by Us	F	59	32	22	113
Authority of God	F	57	12	2	71
Justice	F	57	32	2	91
Lawful order	F	37	21	5	63
Address of the message . .	F	35	2	.	37
Real remedy	F	31	10	12	53
Approved unions	F	24	3	5	32
Injustice	U	21	9	81	111
Conditions of change on earth	U	12	3	12	27
Moral justice	F	11	2	—	13
Supplies of the earth . . .	F	8	2	—	10
Sub-total Favorable. . . .	F	810	263	103	1176
Sub-total Unfavorable. . .	U	93	45	106	244
TOTAL		903	308	209	1,420

This can be interpreted as evidence of increasing public doubts as to this justification of authority, that the times are unfavorable for this particular ideology since its authority has to be stressed to such a degree. It is also an indicator as to the kind of public. Dear children of the whole world might have more doubts and unfaithful reactions than the chosen public of "Venerable brethren". This tendency to assert ideological authority has also influenced the theme of attention to the social problem and the kind of troubles it gives rise to; 22 symbols evaluate negatively the whirlwind of the Antichristian, the non-Christian spirit, conflict and misery. These evils menace the 59 identification symbols on the same topic overwhelmingly described as encyclicals, church, our redeemer, moral principles and the past as the guide for the future. The 32 demands put in this connection underline the problem at attention as a clerical question, not social in its deepest meaning: keep alive the message of Rerum Novarum, do not slow up, do not get depressed, organize the new order.

Corresponding to this clerical grip of the social problem are the symbols on the authority of the Church, the demands it makes and the troubles it meets. The 42 demands on divine and clerical authority comprehend the program: Convince all, moral obligation to co-operate, religious and moral scope, duty to make an authoritative pronouncement on the social question. That is, the social problem at attention has been evaluated as a moral problem supported by divine and clerical authority.

In consistency with this call for moral-religious influence on the social field, it is not surprising that the congratulation on the existence and results of the Rerum Novarum occupies a high attention with almost 11% of all symbols. This reference back to the Rerum Novarum is another way of expressing the authority of the Church which furthermore adds to the explicit references already made to the divine authority. Speaking about the Rerum Novarum, 110 symbols of identification evaluate it as:

Epochmaking social encyclical of Leo XIII, Magna Charta of Christian social endeavor, powerful influence, amount of well-being 92
Workers, their families, the weak, the dispossessed   12
Commemorative encyclical Quadragesimo Anno 6
                                                          110

Groups and values negative to this or by their needy conditions a danger to the society of the Rerum Novarum are described by 12 symbols as agricultural and middle class, workers, and by 8 symbols as passion, disorder, and world hurricane. The demands are in accordance with this picture. 11 symbols commend commemoration and praise of the encyclical, 9 ask for improvement on the material and spiritual lot of the worker and the agricultural class, 4 claim reconstruction of a new social order.

If we sum up the contents of the themes we have just evaluated we shall find that those aiming at recalling divine and clerical authority and the beneficient results of their work, embrace no less than over 31% of the whole mass of symbols. The stress on authority is obvious and goes far beyond the $10\frac{1}{2}$% and the $20\frac{1}{2}$% that the Rerum Novarum and the Quadragesimo Anno respectively devoted to divine and clerical authority. This aspect of the Pentecost message which does not appear in the attention area but only when attention is intensified by its frequency into an interest tells us the intention of the message. The power of the Church is of great interest in a social message to "the whole world".

Here as well as in earlier social messages from the Vatican, high attention is paid to Man as a social being. 158 symbols of identification describe the kind of society that is desirable under the care of the clerical authority:

Family, general well-being, moral virtue, liberty, personal dignity	71
Private property, homestead of one's own, emigration, migration	36
Church, Rerum Novarum, faithful Christians, God	27
The State, moderating social authority, nation, social life . . .	24
	158

10 kind of difficulties are noted, as needs of the poor, corruption, thickly inhabited countries. There are 75 demands for the realization of this desirable society. The way to it is described by 42 symbols that ask for the good of the family, formulate the idea of homestead and consider the use of material goods. 21 symbols emphasize the moral obligation to co-operate, the personal duty to labor and the right to organize it. 12 symbols claim the Church's duty to form consciences. A comparison between this picture of 1941 and those of the earlier messages is enlightening as regards

the ideas of 1891 that have or have not been communicated to the world of 1941.

This Christian society is menaced by injustice. That is according to the Vatican:

Danger of the materialist Socialism conception, fatal inconse-
quences of economic Liberalism, society an end in itself, man has
no other life beyond this, private property void of significance,
taking from the family freedom to family life, injustice . . . 42
Struggles, anti-Christianism, misery, passion, corruption 23
Indifferent, silent onlooker (that is the Church) 16
                                                                 ——
                                                                 81

The 21 favorable values directly threatened by this are Christian life, perfection of the family life, just distribution of goods and private property. In close connection with this there are 9 demands for just distribution of goods, co-operation and exercise of personal rights and duties. This concept of injustice, however, which turns out to be a continuation of the call to fight against socialism and liberalism already present in the earlier encyclicals, is not the only danger. The Rerum Novarum had a positive State concept of its own. The concepts of injustice now indicate that the State has meantimes become a real menace against the State concept of the Vatican. The view on the State is now negative. Symbols worth identification within this topic are

Private property, free reciprocal commerce of goods, increase
welfare, common good, the good of the family 28
Public authority, legitimate and beneficial interference 19
Natural order deriving from God, rights of human person . . . 13
                                                                 ——
                                                                 60

Negative symbols speak in this connection about a state with extensive power (13), but in addition there are the symbols for the concept of the State as a threat evaluated above as existing evils and injustice.

In accordance with this the demands also stress the need for the values which were a part of the positive State concept of the Rerum Novarum and ask for the good of the family and moral obligation with 11 symbols, while 6 reject extensive state power. 16 permit intervention in the field of labor by the State but require also respect for the personal character of labor.

The real remedy for all these evils are Lawful order, Justice, and Approved unions. These four themes manipulate several common symbols, where lawful order and justice serve as the conditions for the very remedy of which approved unions among employers and workmen are one of the healthy means. The symbols of identification on these topics are thus distributed:

Lawful order: Natural law and order, moral, use of money,
    property. 20
Church guardian of supernatural Christian order, Leo XIII . . 17
                                              37

Justice, Moral justice: Goods created by God for all men, personal
    right of all to use, organize labor belongs above all to the
    people immediately concerned 30
Personal duties and rights, family life, peace, justice, dignity,
    every man gifted with reason 23
Indisputable competence of the Church, God, due worship . . . 15
                                              68

Remedy: Three fundamental values of social and economic life 18
The Divine Heart, We 13
                                            31
Approved unions: Catholic unions, Rerum Novarum, associations,
    individuals, free organization, centers for reciprocal help . . 16
Agricultural and middle class, workers, their families, well-being 8
                                            24

The dangers to these values are, to Lawful order: the blind interplay of force and weakness, in 5 symbols. To Justice: suppression, with 2 symbols. To the application of Remedy: injustice, solely material calculation, hardpressed, which is evaluated in 12 symbols. And to the Approved unions, with 5 symbols: injustice, want and disorder. The demands for keeping lawful order, justice, for applying remedy and for getting along with the unions are together 68. Speaking about lawful order 21 of them claim a new social order, ask for security of private property and the formation of conscience. The topics of justice lead to 34 demands:

Right to worship, right of the family to vital space, right to
    organize labor, proper personal development 18
Right to make use of the material goods, scope of the national
    economy correctly considered. 16
                                            34

10 symbols demand further instruction in the remedy and in moral principles, and the approved unions give rise to 3 demands for defence.

All these themes are, however, only the circumstances under which the question of labor, remuneration and possession is to be solved. This theme is by the frequency of its identification symbols the fourth topic in the attention area, as shown by Table 38. To the Rerum Novarum it was a main topic for identification, the second after man as a social being. It is in accordance with the clerical stress of the message of 1941, that several themes of divine and clerical authority by their frequency occupy the attention around the high-frequent "man as a social being" and the problem of his labor, remuneration and possession. The view of labor and solutions of its problems uses the following identification symbols:

National economy, product of men who work together in the community of the State, general well-fare, healthy liberty, private property conduce to the good of the family, land as the holding on which the family lives and gets satisfied	30
Labor personal and necessary, free organizations	19
Natural order deriving from God, nature herself closely joined private property, teachings from Rerum Novarum	12
	61

18 demands want to secure the material conditions in which the individual life of the citizens may fully develop, to conduce to the good of the family and private property. Only 1 obstacle is mentioned: continual exactions in goods and blood.

(262) The fine nuances in coping with the values and their quantitative relation, the coincidences or the gaps among the different Vatican messages, can be seen by an attentive observer. How a practical Catholic politician, expert on land reforms and farming, evaluates his ideological background when he communicates with land hungry farmers educated in this very ideology, is exemplified by Mr Medici. How a Catholic government justifies a land reform before a whole population of land hungry farmers and proletarians, rich owners and landlords, is clarified for us by "La relazione ministeriale", published in 1951.

This document represents the last stage in a long public com-

munication process on a debate on land reforms. It is the example
of a communication document in one of the most powerful
situations possible for it: a justification of a bill which has
practically already been accepted, where most demands can be
freely identified with successful values. When we consider its
contents we have consequently to bear in mind its definite
character; that it has been anticipated by a long struggle for
minds and decisions and is by its success supposed to be the
basis for the new communication process when the bill is applied
in practical life. It is in the light of this that its treatment of
positive or negative values is to be considered; for instance, its
small attention to opponents still existing and its favorable view
of all the many problems to be solved do not absolutely indicate
a totalitarian grasp of the problems. In a society of different
competing wills it may be more realistic to see it as a summing
up of modifications and demands already manipulated at earlier
stages of communication among the different interests in the
society. The communicator is a speaker for a government of
members of the Italian party "Democrazia Cristiana". From
the Vatican's social encyclicals we know the guiding values for
acceptance or rejection by faithful Catholics in social questions.

TABLE 39. *Symbols in the "Relazione ministeriale" 1951*

Groups of symbols on values	Main direction (Favorable or Unfavorable)	Identifi- cations	Demands	Resistance	Total
Government's version . . .	F	342	44	43	429
Characteristics of the Ex- propriation.	F	321	14	7	342
Improvement of the land, the Reform	F	217	72	11	300
Remedy	F	129	6	23	158
Land Reform.	F	119	26	14	159
The problem of the ,,Cascina'' (certain big landed pro- perties)	F	100	25	42	167
Purpose of the land reform	F	82	31	12	125
Charges of the reform . . .	F	70	5	—	75
Duties of land reform offices	F	56	13	4	73
Opponents of the land reform.	U	46	—	67	113
Sub-total Favorable. . . .	F	1,436	236	156	1,828
Sub-total Unfavorable. . .	U	46	—	67	113
TOTAL		1,482	236	223	1,941

It would be useful however to assume that despite the probable summing up of the earlier discussions on land reform, the élite in power has in the end to put its own seal upon the evolution of a decision for which in theory and practice it will be responsible, and looked upon as responsible. The document has consequently most interest in our chapter as a reply to the question of whether or how a certain ruling élite can put its own ideological seal on a document that is the result of a long struggle of communication among different wills; or whether and in what degree the powerful élite with all the resources of a society at its disposal cares to penetrate social problems with its own ideological concepts.

(263) Table 39 gives us the attention area of the document. The statement embraces about 10200 words in Italian. In English it has about 11000 words and 1941 symbols. The document is not very clear in its Italian version and therefore difficult to translate. The outcome of our investigation is the following: The ten themes in the attention area illustrate the powerful situation of the document. The necessary institutions in a society to make a land reform feasible are here put at the disposal of the communicator. The 342 symbols of identification speaking about the government's official version of the reform are, in consistency with this, stressing the lawful aspect of the reform, the approval of the Senate, and statistical reports (155), while 62 symbols refer to identifications with values such as all workers, agricultural class, independent owners, and independent small farmers. A further 61 symbols assess the reform of landed property as a limitation of property, fair social conditions, or care for the possession of the landed property, labor and production. The rest of the symbols describe the criteria for expropriation, a main instrument of the reform, as quantitative, selective and not qualitative or depending on the size of the landed property submitted to the reform. 44 demands are put on this topic embracing 8 claims for the content of the law to be easily understandable; 14 demands ask for mechanical methods in the reform, which has a bearing on the identification symbols of quantity and selection. Juster distribution is also asked for, as well as employment. First expropriation of the land and then transformation of it, common contribution to the common good, social improve-

ment of the working groups in the farming; limit the big landed property, protect the small and middle-sized landed property, are claims interpreting the rest of the 44 demands.

Negative values menace in 43 symbols this picture of a small-farm-property society. Among them are old laws, density of the agricultural class, workers in dependent positions, overtaken by the demand for tax, false critics, collective use. As we can observe, there is already in the version the Government proposes a conden-sation of Vatican values supporting a society of small owners with farms fit to developing family life. Moderation in this principle of approval of the small-sized property is caused in practice by the "Cascina" enterprises, a topic with symbols which stress the unfortunate necessity of accepting these big agricultural enterprises. On this topic appear 100 identification symbols:

Application of the law, obligatory improvements of land, variation of the procedure, Cascina, small individual landed property. 49
Progress of agriculture, an own home, many children, education . 42
Reduction of the volume of the landed property, expropriation 9
                                                                100

The Cascina offer not only serious problems from the viewpoint of correct ideology. There are also practical problems expressed by 42 symbols:

Conditions of the farmhands' tenements, bad painful sight of a grey life, insufferable ways of living, tuberculosis, consumption 30
Big enterprises not always favorable to the development of farming property, Diminution of production 12
                                                                 42

Some of the demands made in this connection may be seen as a consequence of the call for human dignity by the Vatican:

Improvements of the tenements, new buildings, increase the number of permanently employed laborers, promote the progress of agriculture. 20
Necessary works without diminishing the production 5
                                                                 25

Not only the Cascina, favorably described as a result of the document's character as an exposition of the law, give hints of several remaining problems. The topic on opponents of the reform reflects the fierce opposition that gave trouble during earlier communication stages of the debate. An opposition which probably still is a danger. Consistent with this viewpoint the communicator presents the identification values he feels are still menaced:

The recipients, farmers, best production, expropriation.   28
Justice, principles, sanction, the bill, law.   12
Middle sized landed property, small farm property   6
                                                                     ———
                                                                      46

No demands are made but 67 symbols describe the kind of the opponents and their works:

Mere speculation to harm the farmers, economic ruin, economically
    strong groups, excessively great gains at the expense of the
    recipient, delay   38
Many attempts to get the reform going astray, individual judg-
    ment, subjective, older systems, reform at the expense of the
    middle sized landed property   29
                                                                     ———
                                                                      67

The other themes at attention are further developments of the government's version of the kind and evolution of the land reform. Among the organs for the reform most attention is paid to the Expropriation, even explicitly stated as the first step to going ahead with a land reform. The identification symbols stress the lawful aspect of the reform:

The law, bill, statistics, Istituto Nazionale di Economia
    Agraria, the reform, facts, justifications,obligatory improvement
    of land, due of giving up the land, expropriation of land,
    reduction   168
Gradual progression, mechanical operation, compensation,
    calculation   99
Owner of the land, farm families, employment, increased
    production   54
                                                                     ———
                                                                      321

14 demands are for understanding of practical modifications: Not to be uniform, exceptions necessary, not diminishing production. This modification is made necessary by 7 symbols for

troubles as uniform procedure of execution, unemployment, unreliability of statistics, as well as expropriation charges. The
expenditure for the reform is, however, a subject favorably
treated; 70 symbols describe it as necessary in the identification
with organs of the reform, improvement of land, colonization
and distribution to the farmers. Easily passed over are the 5
demands referring to the charges: A financial claim which is not
urgent, which gives a favorable outlook intensified by the lack
of negative symbols. The topic of land reform and the improvement of land manipulate in their own way the symbols we already
know. If we present here the quantitative relationship within
the topics on the purpose of the reform and the remedy offered,
we in fact also give a condensation of the method of dealing with
land reform, its reform offices, and the improvement of land.
Identification symbols on Purpose of the land reform:

Protection of the new small farm property, distribution of the
  landed property, economic measure of size, professional unions   34
Reform operation, state, law, contracts, farmers, new owners   28
Psychology of the farm population, individual right to landed
  property, ingenious work of the farmers, products   20
                                                                 ——
                                                                 82

Values worth identification as Remedy:

Small farms, new family farms, middle size landed property
  increased considerably, modern technique, methods, highest
  possible productive and economic procedure, best conditions
  of life and work to the working masses, corresponding to
  developments in Italian agriculture   95
Farmers, owners, pioneers for technical progress, working masses   23
Big landed property under certain conditions   11
                                                                 ——
                                                                 129

The 37 demands on these two topics make the program for the
new land reform:

Purpose of the reform: Reduction of the too great differences in
  the division of landed property, great increase of the small farm
  property, economic and not a physical measure of size   18
Low moderate rent, payment during 25 years, testing period,
  State to control the allotments, not represent a mere
  speculation.   13
                                                                 ——
                                                                 31

while 6 demands for remedy require intensive transformation on behalf of the working masses. There are troubles ahead before this program is carried out. 35 symbols evaluate them on the two topics:

Purpose of the reform: Mere speculation to harm the farmers, high price of acquisition, excessive great gain 12
Remedy: Big landed property, Cascina, existing small tenancies 16
Influence of unknown factors, primitive conditions, conditions of nature, dwelling far away 7
                                                                                         ‾‾
                                                                                         23

That is, the ideological home of the document is evident. The justification for its demands appears to be eager care of the individual male farmer, his workplace and land, his home and the raising of his own family. No comments in the statement tell us whether his country has land enough for this family program for the masses. Reference is, however, made to the unreliability of the statistics available.

(264) Mr Medici's speech in February 1952 to land hungry farmers at Cerveteri embraces about 6100 words in Italian. In English it is about 7100 words and a symbol mass of 2021. In his function as the head of the Ente Maremma, a government office for the implementation of the land reform, the speaker had to explain to his public the kind of relation existing between this office and its work and the farmers who had recently got land with the beginning of the land reform. The legal expression of this is the contract made between this office and the new owners. This contract is at attention in the speech and is one of the means used to impart to the whole land reform certain ideological directions.

The symbols in the speech of Medici make 9 themes, as shown in Table 40. Close psychological contact is from the beginning expressed by 349 symbols of identification of the communicator with his public:

You, (we), dear friends, farmers, peasants, put to your service, your duties, technical capacities, your patience, your income, farms 290
Recipients of allotments, lawful new owners, possessors, honest people, know to judge by themselves, work regularly, cease to be a daylaborer 47
Those who for personal disaster are not able to pay the rent 12
                                                                                         ‾‾
                                                                                         349

TABLE 40. *Symbols in the Speech of Medici 1952*

Groups of symbols on values	Main direction (Favorable or Unfavorable)	Identifi- cations	Demands	Resistance	Total
Address of the message . .	F	349	4	17	370
Land	F	287	76	45	408
Confidence.	F	265	106	50	421
Authority behind the land reform.	F	224	5	.	229
Labor	F	172	50	27	249
Sincerity.	F	76	25	14	115
Distrust	U	65	8	52	125
Opponents of the land reform.	U	29	4	58	91
Old land reforms	U	7	.	6	13
Sub-total Favorable. . . .	F	1,373	266	153	1,792
Sub-total Unfavorable. . .	U	101	12	116	229
TOTAL		1,474	278	269	2,021

The authorities behind the land reform, however, are not blind to the existence of other kinds of publics. 14 symbols describe the dishonest individual who sells materials, misuses confidence and is in general unwise and 3 symbols present salaried people as obstacles to the land reform. In consistency with this are the desirable qualities of the public: Wants to have land, work, live on it in peace (4). The authority behind the land reform introduces itself with 224 symbols of identification as:

I, President of the Ente Maremma, We of the Ente with the
 contract, possibility to punish, our duty 209
Created by Parliament, put to your service, Land Reform Bureau   15
                                                            ─────
                                                              224

Nothing negative or dangerous threatens the existence of this legal enterprise, but its duties are emphasized by 5 demands where the possibility to prevent or punish is stressed. The land reform itself in the relation to Labor gave 172 symbols of identification:

Expropriation, small rent, lay way plan, small indemnity,
 machines in production, very strong increase of production,
 transport 74
Concrete immediate help, co-operative union, your duty, farmers 41
The Ente Maremma, you, we, I, me 40
Contract, statute, private property, individual social order, lawful   17
                                                                ─────
                                                                  172

Obstacles for Labor are:

Heavy work, tiresome walk, little and bad cultivation, errors   21
Working as a day-laborer not a way of growing rich, taxes, debts   5
Great absentee property   1
                                                            ‾‾
                                                            27

50 demands on the topic emphasize fulfilment of your duties, more production, small payment, indemnity and expropriation with 34 symbols, easy circulation by modern means of transport with 10 symbols, and the last demands evaluate principles of private property and initiative in 6 symbols. All this Labor is concerned with production on the Land, another important aspect of the work on land reform, represented by 287 symbols of identification:

Your farms and land, land reform a fact and success, expropriate
   the land from the big landowner, small farmers' property, basis
   of a modern equilibrated and civilized society, fine houses,
   machines, selected seed, much higher production, peasant,
   honest workmen, farmers 179
Transformation of agriculture, allotment of land, rights, fulfilment of reciprocal duties, interest of the whole people, contract   88
Professors of agriculture, Ente as aiding authority.   20
                                                                  ‾‾‾
                                                                  287

Difficulties for the successful use of land are evaluated by 45 negative symbols:

Large estates, big landowners, payment of indemnity   17
Meager and scarce land, dead forest, destruction   15
Only make chattering, leaving farmers without means of production   13
                                                                  ‾‾
                                                                  45

There are 76 demands for better conditions:

Respect for the contract, create small farmers' property, defend
   the great majority of honest peasants, their rights to receive
   land as property and work on it, reciprocal duties   47
Grow more and more productive   21
Large estates ought to be expropriated, maintain the work of
   reform.   8
                                                                  ‾‾
                                                                  76

All these positive values are threatened by three things. Old land reforms resulting in nothing have left scars on people's minds. They have added to their distrust of the new land reform and have given arguments to the opponents of the reform. These three themes menace above all the following identification symbols:

Distrust: Right of the farmers, their land, people in all classes 31
We of the Ente, the contract, statute, norms 24
Reform, allotments, prescribed rent, price so low, machines . . 10
                                                      65

Old land reforms: Farmers, guidance, allotments of land, State   7

Opponents of the land reform: Respect, law, control from the State, contract, the Ente, reform, allotment of land, small lots of land, new small land owners, just, confidence, no luxury 29

Distrust is a bad relationship between the authority behind the new land reform and the agricultural population. 52 symbols describe this:

Only to attract votes, trap contract, delay, distrust 24
Make bad use of land, purchased on loan and sold them again in the night, enemies of the reform, machines creating unemployment 12
Class hatred, anemia of the will, the worst of all social ills . . . 11
The State the worst of all proprietors, deaf and cruel   5
                                                      52

6 symbols for the State's former negligence under the old land reforms support the arguments of the opponents. And the opponents themselves are:

Dishonest individuals, idlers, playing a lord, chattering, try to create confusion, sold the plot of land, bad use, false land reforms 44
The old owner, large estate, enemies of the reform, the extreme right, the extreme left, usury 14
                                                      58

Facing all these difficulties, it seems natural that the call for confidence in the land reform and in its sincerity occupies a high degree of attention. No less than $26\frac{1}{2}\%$ of the total symbols treat these themes. Supporting this is further the more than 11% of the symbols for the authority responsible for the reform. Worth confidence are:

The contract, honest, land reform, transfer from the too rich to
    those who own nothing, technical assistance, increase income,
    sound, equilibrated society, respect of law, private property
    and initiative, lawful owner, agreement with the farmers, freely
    accepting, cordial collaboration, mutual confidence 180
We of the Ente, its authority and duty 46
Laborious farmers who pay conscientiously. 31
Fighting hatred among classes and individuals 8
                                                            ─────
                                                              265

The reasons for sincerity are evident:

Contract honest, respect statute, frank, truth, sincere, honest
    farmers as voluntary recipients of land, their duties, reform,
    sound enterprise 42
We of the Ente, duties to fulfil 34
                                                            ─────
                                                               76

Accusations of lack of sincerity are refuted as well as those of
lack of confidence. 64 symbols express the obstacles the authorities have to face, speaking about confidence and sincerity.

Confidence: Your distrust, selling the piece of land they received,
    those who regard with sympathy the Russian experiment . . 16
Deluge of words, useless words, fib, nonsense, errors 14
Personal disaster, great absentee property, serious needs . . . 8
Hatred among classes and groups 6
We are those who claim the rent, trap contract 6
                                                            ─────
                                                               50

Sincerity: Misuse confidence, bad use, sick enterprise, trap
    contract 14

The importance of these two themes is stressed by the frequency
of demands evaluated with 131 symbols.

Confidence: Cordial collaboration, demonstrate with facts, advance
    unanimously, tolerance, fighting class hatred, agreement with
    farmers 62
Ente's duty to fulfil, your economic conditions improved, ever-
    more productive agriculture, modern machinery. 44
                                                            ─────
                                                              106

25 symbols demand sincerity:

Respect for the contract, correspond to the truth, make you to
    expend less and less, make you earn more and more, reciprocal
    duty, the Ente has possibility to punish 25

(265) Comparing the tables on the attention area of the
Vatican with those on the attention area of the Medici speech,

it is not difficult to see the coincidence in the ideological approach. Confidence in clerical, paternal authority has with Medici been transmuted into confidence in the authority behind the land reform, that is the Ente, Parliament, and sincerity of the intention to make the reform. Almost 38% of the total symbols deal with this appeal to confidence in Authority. The call for confidence is powerfully supported by the 370 symbols which pay attention to the address of the speech. You, my dear friends, honest farmers, these expressions give a touch of intimate chat that stressess the reciprocal confidence. Altogether, this atmosphere of friendly authority sincerely discussing common interests with dear friends, will cover more than 56% of all the symbols. Within the frame of this heart-to-heart atmosphere, which the communicator tries to create, the "facts" are to be discussed. The question of land and labor, the reform and its legal expression, the contract, are at stake. The concept of the State, the claim for the right of the individual, private property, negativism against the too rich, the stress on the lawful owner and respect for the law, the care for those who own nothing, are among the concepts the Vatican made its own. A comparative glance at the different documents will disclose more common symbols which definitely conform to the Vatican ideal for a society: small holdings, small lands where the family can be supported. The obstacles to Medici's picture of a balanced law abiding society, are mentioned, but not overwhelmingly. Over 11% of the total symbols concern these difficulties, but of those, over 6% are expressed as misunderstanding and distrust between the two parties concerned. The Medici document is an act of persuasion where the values significant in the Vatican program are launched as solutions of the questions of land and labor. The request for belief in what has happened and will happen, the notice of obstacles without stressing them, present a certain kind of ideological modification which is not unusual, especially when an ideology meets the technical reality in societies where everybody's opinion and mind is cared for, at least during the communication process. The degree and kind of this modification, as compared with the Vatican hierarchy's precepts of remedy for the evil, can be noticed by the quantitative analysis above. The manipulation and function of the common key symbols of, for instance, private

property and the individual's value and dignity and equivalents
for that are also of interest in this connection.

COMMUNIST LAND POLICY

(266) With Lenin, we are back to a militant ideology not yet
bothered by technical developments and obstacles. Such a stage
indicates a primitive society. But it can also be a sign that this
particular ideology is not yet in a position to make the reforms.
The seven documents by Lenin we have mentioned above,
introduce such topics as "small production in agriculture",
"the peasantry and the working class", "child labor in peasant
farming", "messrs bourgeois on toiler farming", "policy towards
the middle peasantry", "middle peasants", and a "speech held
before the delegates from the committees of poor peasants of the
Moscow region". That is, these texts deal with land and labor in
agriculture.

Lenin's approach is still that of the oppositional élite. He
speaks to a people which is the victim of certain social evils. His
picture of a society where these evils have disappeared presents,
as usual in a communication process, positive values of identifications, demands to make and evils to condemn. The seven
statements embrace about 8700 words in English, with a symbol
mass of 1560. The nine themes arising from the symbols on this
one topic of land and labor in agriculture, despite the many
headings, pay the greatest attention to the victims of the Capitalist at work on land and labor, as shown by Table 41, that is
$52\frac{1}{2}\%$ of the total symbols. These victims are in principle the
whole nation but, for the moment, special attention is paid to
those who work on the land. The revolution has brought its fight
to victory in the cities and among the industrial workers. But
these workers are only one part of the suffering proletariat. The
exponent for this new ruling élite of proletarians is the Communist Party. The Communist Party knows that city workers
are not the only proletarians. The task ahead is consequently to
see to what degree the Communist Party can help its suffering
brethren in all nations. The identification symbols of the topic
will clarify who the Communist Party is, a presentation that, as

TABLE 41. *Symbols in the Lenin documents*

Groups of symbols on values	Main direction (Favorable or Unfavorable)	Identifi- cations	Demands	Resistance	Total
Communist Party identical with workers, Socialism and middle peasants . .	F	171	22	30	223
Victims of Capitalism on the land	U	85	11	164	260
Victims of Capitalism on labor	U	188	6	365	559
Solutions of the social question: labor	F	220	75	{ 58	374
Id., land.	F	14	7		
Approved unions	F	23	20	.	43
Peasants' qualities	F	25	—	6	31
Foreign changes	U	4	3	12	19
Land	F	31	9	11	51
Sub-total Favorable. . . .	F	484	133	105	722
Sub-total Unfavorable. . .	U	277	20	541	838
TOTAL		761	153	646	1,560

will be shown, will have a bearing on the whole program of these statements [a]:

Communist Party, identical with workers, Soviet Union, Socialism, middle peasants, Marxists, peasants 152
Communists, government as agency 19
                                            171

The evils which have hitherto prevented this union are

Bourgeoisie, exploit the labor of others, capital, Capitalists, domination of the Kulaks, parasites, ruin, our Tsar, enemies of the people, landlord, yoke of exploitation 30

The demands are close to the declaration of identification:

Wrench the mills, factories from Capitalists, the means of production the property of the whole people, reconstruct agriculture on Socialist lines, organization 14
Agreement with poor and middle peasants, fight against kulaks   8
                                            22

Already by the demands we can observe that many of the values there described should in a peaceful community function as the

identification of those in power. All these values, normally a part
of the action area or the aggregates of the ruling élites, are here
still battlefields for demands and claims. The struggle for power
in the particular society is obviously still going on.

If we thus get the identification on the Communist Party,
the next step is to describe the victims of its enemies. Victims of
Capitalists on land are presented by 85 symbols identifying the
victims and their conditions as objects for the concern of the new
élite:

Wage workers, proletarians, small poor peasants, very needy
  peasants, wage labor, small production, land proletarian,
  communal farming, peasant associations 65
Proletarian farm, tiny plots of land, peasant farm, child labor,
  middle peasant 20
                                                               ‾‾
                                                               85

The Capitalist is at work on all these fields:

Bourgeois, toiler farming, parcellised dwarf farms, proletarian
  and small peasant farms, small poor peasantry, Capitalist
  relationship in agriculture, Capitalist farm, narodniki, Capitalist
  prosperity, big peasants, the small group at the top, laborer
  farm, exploitation of female labor, exhaustion, private property 121
Subsidiary earnings, exploitation of child labor, big Capitalist
  farms, the Landlord, his land, basis of exploitation, concentrated in single hands, small scale farming, kulak domination,
  ruin 43
                                                               ‾‾‾
                                                               164

The 11 demands are for study of the facts and practical work:

Not force the peasants, equal divisions nonsense, solution is
  social cultivation of land, communes, peasant associations   6
Examine statistics on farms of various size, prove that toiler
  farming is petty-bourgeois-capitalist-farming, compare, learn 5
                                                                 ‾‾
                                                                 11

Even the process of labor, however, is a victim of the Capitalist
as well as the laborers themselves. Victims and needs worth
identification are:

Middle peasants, wage labors, small farmers, subsidiary occupations, sell their labor, masses, peasant farming, small
  production, child labor, male and female, young workers, masses
  of the toilers into wage workers, masses of rural population,

proletariat, wage labor in agriculture, hire themselves out, workers of mill, poor peasants, farmlaborer, people, Soviet government 188

No less than 365 symbols describe this destructive power and its work:

Kulaks, exploiting peasantry, imperial war, exceptional wealth during war, bourgeoisie, yoke of capital, profit from labor of others, economic disruption, position of middle peasant extremely grave, private property in land, all forms of Capitalism, insignificant minority, working to death his (the peasant's) children, profit, grow rich, individual lines, employ labor of others 200
Capitalist production, feudal big landowner, transformation of masses of toilers into wage workers, female labor 124
Employment of wage labor in peasant farming, principal symptom of Capitalism 41
                                                                          ———
                                                                          365

The demands mix claims for facts with attacks. 4 ask the kulaks not to profiteer, and 2 want to examine statistics. The problems are obviously overwhelming, and solution of the social question urgent. Speaking about labor, the solution can be identified as:

Communist, city workers, middle peasants united against Capitalists and kulaks in large scale enterprises on land, communal principles in agriculture, peasant proletariat joining class struggle, wage workers, small producers, peasantry, intelligent workers. 122
Communist Party, government with middle peasant, comradely relations, alliance, agreement between workers and middle peasants 98
                                                                          ———
                                                                          220

These symbols of identification sometimes appear as so Utopian that it would be convenient to speak about their demanding aspects in a struggling social program. They also touch the question of land and the identification symbols of that topic:

Soviet farms, peasant land tenure, comradely relationships between Communist workers, middle peasants, Socialism, social cultivation of land, October revolution identical with non-exploiters, fight in the country district 45

The obstacles to the solutions are due to

Kulaks, yoke of capital, exploitation of wage labor, bourgeoisie,
    aversion of the middle peasants to innovations, absolute
    hopelessness of the position of the small producers in Capitalist
    society, exploitation of child labor, parasites, sabotages, wilful
    damage, Capitalists, rich exploiters   58
Landlord, his land   11
                                                            ———
                                                             69

75 demands are for the solution of the question on labor thus:

Collaboration, Soviet workers, understanding middle peasants,
    correct policy, moderately conducted, harmful haste, agree-
    ment, careful attention to peasants' need.   31
Duty to comradely relationships between middle peasants and
    the Soviet government, voluntary alliance, confidence, merge
    poor peasants with Soviet, consolidate, not leave peasants,
    plan for reformation, new elections, introduction of communal
    principles in agriculture, organize, carry out into practice,
    fight against kulaks, expropriate, large scale enterprise . . .   26
Exposure of the Capitalist, open the masses' eyes, joining the
    proletarian struggle, organization, class struggle, wrest
    bourgeoisie, explain, try to test, study, seek for data   18
                                                                  ———
                                                                   75

The claims which directly concern the land are:

The whole land to the peasants, success of Socialism, struggle
    in the agricultural districts, conquest of land, independent
    action, way of escape from ruin and kulak domination,
    solution   9
Systematization of peasants' land tenure, improving the land of the
    peasant, model fields, comradely relations   7
                                                                ———
                                                                 16

Certain aspects of the solution of the social question indicate
that recommended unions may be a means of tightening the
relations between the Soviet government and the peasants. 23
symbols are worth Communist identification:

Soviet government, agricultural communes of middle peasants,
    poor peasants, Soviet farms, co-operative associations, volost,
    Soviet Union   23

In this connection the theme on the quality of the peasants is
interesting. Its full significance derives from the qualities of the
Communist party and its government that have already been
described:

Middle peasants identical with the worker, non-capitalist,
  non-exploiter, a worker 18
We and the social cultivation on the land will be appreciated by
  the peasants later 7
                                                             ———
                                                              25

The unions mentioned above are evidently a part of a future
world where the capitalist elements are liquidated, since no social
evils are mentioned as threatening their existence. This aspect is
furthermore stressed by 20 symbols which demand on their behalf:

Encouraging, assistance, carried into effect, co-operative
  associations, associations, agricultural communes 12
Peasants to join, own free will 8
                                                             ———
                                                              20

Closer to contemporary reality, however, seem to be the social
features of the peasants. The identification of the peasant with
the worker still invites the attacks of existing social ills:

Exploit the labor of others, live on the labor of others, private
  property, capitalism 6

Of course, there exists another world beyond this one, a world
however to which only small attention is paid for the moment.
Symbols applied to this theme are not much more than 1% of
the whole symbol mass. The outlook on this foreign world is
negative. The values worth identification in that world beyond
the limits of Russia are "our brothers(!) abroad" (4 symbols)
who are the victims of the social evils of this particular world,
appraised as foreign imperialism, especially in Germany and
Great Britain (12 symbols). The demand in this context is hopeful
to the Brethren abroad and horrifying to foreign imperialists:

Watch for the Russian Bolshevism 3

(267) The slogan for unity of all proletarians is nowadays a
common fund of knowledge. Originally expressed by the Communist Manifesto in 1848 as a rallying call to its adherents, it
evoked a wide response from the very beginning. It might seem
to kill all theories on the great importance of the quantitative
relations of values in propaganda by its immediate success as a

slogan. The frequency of its literal occurrence is not overwhelming in Lenin, the most outstanding exponent for the ideology of the Communist Manifesto. For instance, the slogan itself is not mentioned at all in speaking about land reforms and human relations on the land. A glance at the above symbols will, however, soon make clear that this literal and formal view of what is frequent gives a wrong impression of the real contents of a message, whereas the search for the function of used symbols and values of a text – that is, symbols literally, synonymously or equivalently expressed – guides us to the expressed intention and contents of a message. And, no less important, it tells us how a slogan is born or created. Some slogans seem to be a bolt out of the blue. But in fact, there is deliberate work behind every product of genius. Limiting ourselves to the topic here, we can already see in all the themes treated that the symbols above by quantity and function identify proletarians as workers, Communists and suffering peasants. So also does the call to unite in one front these different strata which by social conditions and experience of suffering belong to one social group. In the fight for revolution and a new world where this group claims to be the ruling élite, already the identification of Communists-workers-peasants is in itself a call to unite all proletarians, its importance expressed by the high frequency of its occurrence. The resistance of the temporarily ruling élite to this identification only makes the call more urgent and is stressed by the demands, as we have seen, for a worker-peasant dominated society, on land organized as a community's large scale enterprise in agriculture or, to use the more ideological name, Soviet farms. Thus, the whole contents of the message prepare the public for the formally more elegant appeal that makes the public, as it seems, suddenly surrender to a slogan. A further investigation of other topics treated by Lenin will also show a tendency of the message to prepare the public for the appeal of the famous slogan. And Lenin is not the only propagandist manipulating symbols of different topics for one single purpose, suddenly showing up in one single statement evoking a wide response in positive or negative directions. This manipulation of symbols for one unifying purpose is in fact a key to understanding propaganda. The public has been prepared already before, by the message as a whole, and looks upon the

slogan as the positive or negative manifestation of what it
"always" has feared or hoped. The slogan is the single word,
concept, or statement which sums up at the same time the purpose
of a certain message and the public's ideological, social, and
psychological preparedness to accept or reject it [a]. The comparatively scanty appearance of slogans in many communication
processes is obviously not due to lack of purpose in the message
or in the public's will to receive a message condensed into a
single response-evoking statement, but to the communicator's
lack of will or ability to display the whole purpose and trend of
his message in the spotlight of public opinion.

To call for unity of all proletarians in a society where only a
few know what the communicator is speaking about is a task of
propaganda. This asks for identification or rejection of the values
under debate, before the public is mature enough to keep up
with the purpose launched as a statement or slogan. This preparation process of the public is related to that of the "sleeping
effect" we referred to above. The public is not always conscious
of what is going on. The fact that a public really responds to a
statement indicates the public's preparedness for the message.
The quantity and the intensity of occurrence of the concealed
appeals condensed into a single public statement, word, or
concept with the same meaning as that of the appeals, make the
slogan. There are of course communication processes where the
slogan is the first statement to appear. But it is a question of
order in the process. What is called variation of the theme always
follows the first slogan to appear, and is of the same kind and
function: to support the slogan, to explain it and to make its
meaning familiar and response-evoking to the public. It is then
a question of the communicator's judgment whether he wants
the supporting communication process to be a preface or an
epilogue to a slogan, depending on how much the ideological and
social structure of his audience is already prepared for the values
he calls attention to, identifies, or rejects by his appeal. The more
need there is to call identification symbols to the attention of the
public, the more intensified must a message be. To Lenin it was
important to clarify the identity of Communists as workers and
poor peasants. His presentation of this identity was so intensified
that it in fact functioned as demands and turned out to be the

only theme of his symbols and message in the seven documents. In consistency with this, the new society he wanted to build on the land also was colored by his identifying demand. And the claim for land reform grew to a demand for industrial enterprises in agriculture where the worker could feel at home even when occupied with cultivating the land. This new society would in its turn give the peasants feelings of identification with the worker, and so on.

(268) Lenin is always quoted by his followers, even as regards land reform. We have seen that Lenin was not at all an expert on agrarian questions. His dealing with land reform was intended to prepare minds to desire changes and reorganization of society in certain directions. The structure of his society made it necessary to deal with the topic of land as an opportunity for supporting identification with the revolution. The barrier did not separate town and country any more, but two classes living everywhere, that is, the workers and the employers. This effort at identification also functions as a justification for the class struggle, a value, as we observed, which was rejected by the Vatican and its followers, but which turns out to be a key symbol in a Communist society.

This society is the distant goal of the Hungarian document on "Land reform in Hungary". A new world is growing up around Hungary after the Second World War. It is high time therefore to change the pace to catch up with new developments, the document says in presenting the land reform of 1945. This will to change and the existing difficulties are an enlightening example of an exercise in self-criticism. This is expressed by about 5800 words manipulating 902 symbols, as shown in Table 42. 40% of the total symbols are applied to the land reform. Exponents of the new order are the new owner, a result of the land reform, and the progressive intellectuals, an outcome of propaganda. These two themes take more than 7% of the attention symbols. The hopeful aspect is however, as is natural in a document of self-criticism, shadowed by dark spots from today and yesterday. These dark spots occupy over $45\frac{1}{2}$% of all attention symbols and are Feudalism, Capitalism, and Enemies of the new State in general. A nuance of this darkness is the class struggle, a favorable topic paid attention to by more than 7% of all the symbols.

TABLE 42. *Symbols in "Land reform in Hungary" by Sandór, 1947*

Groups of symbols on values	Main direction (Favorable or Unfavorable)	Identifi-cations	Demands	Resistance	Total
Land reform	F	184	92	85	361
Feudalism	U	59	3	221	283
Class struggle	F	36	13	15	64
The new owner	F	26	9	15	50
Capitalism	U	19	2	67	88
Progressive intellectuals . .	F	7	2	6	15
Enemies of the new State	U	6	6	29	41
Sub-total Favorable. . . .	F	253	116	121	490
Sub-total Unfavorable. . .	U	84	11	317	412
TOTAL		337	127	438	902

Starting with the problem of land reform, we look for facts in accordance with the subtitle of the document and meet the following identification symbols:

Democratic transformation, distribution of land, radical land reform, completely changed social structure, small-holding policy, justice, peasants, general well-fare, higher standard of life, agrarian proletariat, peasant property, peasants 120
Local co-operative society, liberation, measure of importance to Hungary's continued existence 64
                                                                    184

These facts or values are met by resistance as the outcome of old errors and social conditions:

Large estate system. 52
Ruin, disaster, difficulties, serious drought 22
Feudalism, Fascism, traitors, collaborationists, moral arguments 7
Fresh growing in the numbers of the agrarian proletariat . . . 4
                                                                    85

92 demands show that the claim for land reform is part of a future program, not a finished work:

Dividing up the land, remodelling on democratic principles, cessation of the estate system, continuance of three categories of large estates, allocation to agricultural people, to farmer-owner whose occupation is agriculture, only as much land as he and his family can manage to work, necessary to reorganize

agricultural production, competent agricultural scientists,
agrarian problem the country's most burning question, land
reform as a necessity of foreign policy   76
Doing away with feudalism, Fascist confiscated property return,
go into possession of the local co-operative society   16
                                                               ⎯⎯
                                                                 92

Already now, the symbols give a very mixed program of agrarian
policy. The demands make clear that the most important and
decisive steps on the new way are still ahead, a feature that is
natural in a document of self-criticism. The realization of this
planned reform is menaced by Feudalism, Capitalism, and
Enemies of the new State in general. They immediately threaten
identification symbols as, speaking about Feudalism:

Population, landless peasantry, agrarian proletariat, new owners,
co-operatives, serfs, slaves (results of the Capitalist against
peasantry)   59

or, speaking about Capitalism:

Peasant, agricultural laborers, serfdom, mass poverty, reform   19

or about Enemies of the new State:

New order, peasant local co-operative societies   6

The evaluation of this Feudalism fills 221 symbols:

Estate owners, numerically small ruling class, Feudalism, clans,
vassals, clergy, Church, vast manorial estates   92
Land reform as a tool of feudal-capitalism, unfair distribution,
slavery of the serfs, bondage, great masses in abject destitution   86
Hungary as the scene of war, imperialism, colony of Austria,
Fascism   28
Economic crises, permanent uncertainty, social, economic draw-
backs   15
                                                               ⎯⎯
                                                                221

Capitalism and its work appear thus:

Bourgeoisie, moral arguments, opponents to the land reform,
Capitalist lines, terroristic methods, counter-revolution, big
estates, aristocracy   56
Serfdom, mass poverty, famine   11
                                                               ⎯⎯
                                                                 67

Enemies of the new State are represented by:

Traitors, collaborationists, war criminals, foreign citizens, feudal
    powers, Fascists, profiteers, imbeciles 21
Agitation, neglect, wilful sabotage   8
                                                                  29

The remedy for all that social evil is demanded by 11 symbols.
On Feudalism: Relieve the hardship, 3 symbols. On Capitalism:
Higher wages, better living conditions, 2 symbols. On Enemies
of the new State: Property taken from them, rejection, withdrawal, 6 symbols. That is, the explanation of Hungary's need
of land reform with the features the symbols mentioned, lies in
its historical and social conditions, not in the new ruling élite in
Hungary, the party name of which is not mentioned. The self-
criticism is obviously wide and extensive, since it refers to the
old self of Hungary, not so much to the new élite that is asking
for new conditions. Since the old Hungary naturally is not able
to defend itself after its defeat, the mistakes are overwhelming
and the task for the new élite important. That is what the symbols
tell us.

    Among this new élite are the progressive intellectuals who also
have a task to fulfil in creating the new Hungary. 7 symbols
identify them as a worthy group of intellectuals of peasant stock.
The destructive power opposite them 6 symbols describe as
intellectuals in general as well as "economic arguments" and
want of sympathy. In consistency with the intellectual topic the
2 demands ask for propaganda of the land reform. This propaganda, which is the task of the intellectuals of "peasant stock",
has a bearing on the class struggle which, as we observed with
Lenin, is a means for creating the new society. Values to identify
with this struggle are:

Agrarian proletariat, serf, peasantry, Communist government,
    industrial workers, political organizations 24
Fight, organize, strikes, rebellious spirit   8
Distribution of land   4
                                                                  36

Destructive to this class struggle are the "liberation with a certain
sum of money" as well as poverty-stricken millions, emigration

and "constabulary estates" (15 symbols). The call for action is
intensive:

Struggle for life, organize, protect, defend their rights   13

   This self-criticism of the past, the problems arising on realization of the land reform, the frequent descriptions of the destructive powers of today and yesterday, the class struggle even
with the help of certain progressive intellectuals — all this aims
at helping the new owner who is the obvious result of the reform
that still is more of a program than a fact. The owner and his
conditions cause 26 identification symbols. 13 of them refer to
himself, 9 to the new order, freedom, political ripeness, training
courses and the Ministry of Agriculture; 4 mention small holders,
landless claimant peasantry and agricultural laborers. His own
new position is still very delicate. He suffers from the general
hardships evaluated by 11 symbols, and is attacked by feudalism,
4 symbols. The demands closely refer to this. But at the same
time there is even at this stage of Communist policy in agriculture
an obvious trend of claims by the new élite concerning production
and organization on the new owner's land. 5 symbols want him
to concentrate on arriving at maximum results, and 4 symbols
permit him to sell his land solely with the approval of the
Ministry of Agriculture.

   Thus, the symbols show that the self-criticism is directed
against the old part of the national self, still existent as social
ills. The claim for land reform is a demand for the future. The
new land owners showing up here and there as symbols of its
very beginning need protection – it is realized – but are at the
same time immediately met by demands from the new élite and
its State. The symbols expressing foreign policy as justification
for the social changes on the land give the key to the ideological
home of the communicator and the new order. The comparison
with Lenin is given. If Lenin's agrarian policy was making minds
to wanting reforms, by identifying workers and suffering
peasants, the Hungarian program on land reform displays some
of Lenin's concepts much modified by their symbols and their
quantitative relationships. Their communication turns into an
apology for the modified thoughts on land reform. A land reform
which embraces ideas that might be more at home in other

ideological movements than that sponsored by Lenin. This fact as well as the frequent apologies expressed as criticism of the old self, and the necessity to consider existing practical conditions is here, as in the Medici speech, a reason for modification of the original ideology. The collectivization stage of Communist land policy, though not explicitly mentioned, is implied in the State demands on the new owner, and waits its turn just round the corner.

(269) Closer to the Lenin ideas on land and labor is the picture of the collectivization stage of land reform drawn by the Bulgarian Prime Minister, Vulko Chervenkov, in his speech to the delegates at the Second National Conference of co-operative farm representatives in 1950. As we have indicated, Mr Chervenkov was then secretary of the Central Committee of the Bulgarian Communist Party. It is also of interest that Mr Chervenkov is responsible for the administration of the Bulgarian land policy. So far as his biography is known, there is no mention of agricultural training.

TABLE 43. *Symbols in the Speech of Chervenkov, 1950*

Groups of symbols on values	Main direction (Favorable or Unfavorable)	Identifications	Demands	Resistance	Total
The Communist State, its policy	F	970	20	1	991
The task ahead	F	444	256	45	745
Co-operative farm as a fact	F	408	116	20	544
Character of accepted model statute	F	167	101	19	287
Confidence in victory	F	166	4	9	179
Social nature of the co-operative farm	F	135	6	17	158
Self-criticism	F	116	21	12	149
Democracy's enemies	U	65	36	175	276
Greetings	F	60	3	.	63
Rural economy	U	59	27	43	129
Heroes of labor	F	47	11	.	58
Class struggle	F	44	21	38	103
Doubts of the agrarian reform	U	23	1	5	29
The intellectuals	F	19	4	—	23
Sub-total Favorable	F	2,576	563	161	3,300
Sub-total Unfavorable	U	147	64	223	434
TOTAL		2,723	627	384	3,734

About 16200 words describe the new agrarian society. 3734 symbols manipulate the values involved. 14 themes is the outcome, as shown by Table 43, and with more details than usual in the Appendix to this chapter. $26\frac{1}{2}\%$ of the total symbols deal with the Communist State and its policy. This authority is aware of the "task ahead". In consistency with this, symbols giving attention to the task are the next big group covering almost 20% of all symbols. With the exception of a certain resistance to the land reform by "Democracy's enemies", doubts of the reform by hesitant farmers, and practical difficulties due to the backwardness of the rural economy, the other themes represent variations on and more detailed descriptions of the two main themes of Communist authority and its task. Resistance to taking the new path is expressed by more than $11\frac{1}{2}\%$ of all the symbols. This figure is not high, and from the viewpoint of propaganda in general, it is of course more convenient to pass over the resistance as smoothly as possible in front of a public which the communicator wants to involve and inspire in favor of the "new path" of life. To pay great attention to resistance is a privilege reserved for the faithful at intimate meetings.

The values worth identification by the communicator and his ideology are gathered under the title Identification symbols. The negative values which resist them give rise to the caption "The Capitalist at work". The claims forming the social program on land are expressed by the symbols of demands. In Appendix 7 we find presented the quantitative relation and the function of the symbols. This appendix demonstrates a significant step in the kind of analysis that lies behind the treatment of all the documents analyzed in this chapter. This approach is founded on the propagandist's own method of working with values before his public. It is only in consistency with the propagandist's carelessness of the temporary form of the values that no philologist looking at the grammatical form or the historical background of word creation has succeeded in exposing the purpose of a propagandist's message.

The first stage of the analysis, as we said above, picked up the symbols in their context. Each was recorded with reference to the place where it could be found in the text. The next step was to assemble the symbols according to their functions which gave the categories of meaning composed of literal symbols for a particular meaning as well as their synonyms and equivalents. It is to be stressed that the search for the values and concepts that are used in propaganda aims at exposing these concepts' function, not their forms from different aspects of traditional academic science.

The step we mentioned above, to assemble symbols according to their functions, constructing categories of meaning broadening into main themes, is here presented by the table of the Chervenkov values. A comparison with the symbols of Lenin and his treatment of them gives the kind and degree of Chervenkov's loyalty to his ideological sponsor and is a commentary for the reader. It will be enough here to point out that the Communist State identifies the "task ahead" as "New Socialist reconstruction of the village". The means to this is the "accepted model statute" which is the "spontaneous" work of Government and people, prescribing the lines for this Socialist reconstruction. Co-operative farms in Bulgaria are facts with a certain social character. But of course, there are still problems to be solved. The difficulties are presented under the symbols for the work of Capitalism in different aspects. Despite the resistance to be met, the self-criticism, the class struggle, and the intellectuals – these latter by symbols mostly described as specialists – together give a strong confidence in final victory for the Socialist society where the Heroes of Labor comprehend both the ideology and its successful application to land and labor. The greetings from the authorities to the public are consequently optimistic and in agreement with the program. It is also a result of this atmosphere of success that the hesitant doubtful farmer is regarded with indulgence and understanding, even though the subject itself is negatively treated. Such a successful program and régime can afford patience with the slow-minded. Even here we can recall the Lenin concept of the nature of the peasants.

(270) The practical result of such an ideology applied to land and labor in an old, cultivated area, is what the German document wishes to communicate to people everywhere, but above all to the population of Western Germany. It is called "Auf dem Wege zur Kolchose". As we have already mentioned, it is produced by the Bundesministerium für gesamtdeutsche Fragen, in 1952.

Its sub-title, "Die Sowjetisierung der Landwirtschaft in der Sowjetzone" underlines the topic. About 11900 words in German manipulate 1701 symbols for the subject at attention, as shown by Table 44. The greatest attention is paid to two themes, "Sowjetisierung" and Land Reform in Eastern Germany. Over 35% of the total symbols deal with the "Sowjetisierung", and almost 34% with land reform in Eastern Germany. That adds up to more than 69% of the total attention. As usual in propaganda, some sub-themes support the main themes' approach to the problem by evaluating the topic[a]. Old Russia and the Communistic agrarian revolution under Lenin-Stalin are here shown to be the models for the process of Sovietization and of land reform in East Germany. German Soviet collaborators are the tools used for this action, looked upon with disgust by the communicator. The enemies of the Soviet Union, and Germany itself, give hope that there is a remedy for the social evil.

The communicator behind this document is aware of the "Übersetzer-deutsch" and the "Terminologie der sowjetzonalen Machthaber", a function of language that has been the daily experience of the communicator and the man in the street, but not always understood by philologists. When studying the German document, we have to bear in mind the inverted relationship between positive and negative values. Concepts overwhelmingly described in the Communist statements as worth identification, or condemnation as the case may be, here appear inversely as values significant to a detested and destructive enemy, or as dear values menaced by this particular power. The statement is also an example of the relative unimportance of the precise linguistic form for manipulating international values of positive or negative color in the disseminating of a certain message. The feelings, negative or positive, and the practical results and ideological colors that the symbols of the international message are able to evoke in different languages, is a problem for everybody interested in studying the relation between form and content. It turns out, however, more a question of the relation between the ideological predispositions and social conditions of the public than to its formal linguistic predispositions. Even in this connection, socio-psychological research on reactions and attitudes of the public is important for clarifying the responses to basic values and symbols in every nation [b]. The result of such research can, of course, be used by the communicator as a reliable

TABLE 44. *Symbols in the pamphlet "Auf dem Wege zur Kolchose", 1952*

Groups of symbols on values	Main direction (Favorable or Unfavorable)	Identifications	Demands	Resistance	Total
Land reform in Eastern Germany	U	129	3	446	578
Sovietization	U	111	3	484	598
Enemies of the Soviet Union	F	63	—	19	82
Germany	F	50	—	11	61
Remedy	F	22	25	8	55
Communist agrarian revolution under Lenin-Stalin	U	21	—	88	109
Old Russia	U	13	—	85	98
German Soviet collaborators	U	6	—	114	120
Sub-total Favorable	F	135	25	38	198
Sub-total Unfavorable	U	280	6	1,217	1,503
TOTAL		415	31	1,255	1,701

addition to the instinctive knowledge he already has of his public. It can however also lead him to make disastrous mistakes in communication, if he uses the results under other conditions or with different tacit assumptions than those to which the results apply. That is, reactions and attitudes of Main Street are not always to be expected in Bangkok or Rome, even though the same values and symbols are used in the communication. On a world-wide scale, the communicator must first thoroughly study the ideology of the particular society he wants to reach, and how much and in what way it uses symbols which are particular to it or common to the whole world. The material that can be investigated for this purpose is more often documents of various kinds, literature and newspapers, than human beings. Knowing the ideological language, the communicator knows the key to different doors in the society he wants to contact. Considering the particular topic he wants to communicate for the moment, and the contemporary social conditions of the particular community, he has a greater chance to contact the mass of his public on a world-wide scale than speaking from his own ideological conditions and tacit assumptions. The German document is in

fact a description of the results of uninformed foreign communication, with disastrous practical consequences.

(271) 415 symbols express identification with values menaced
by the new ruling élite. 31% of them are applied to the land
reform in Eastern Germany. It is worth noting that some of
these values are expressed by the very symbol the enemy has
created for attacking these values. The grammatical forms of
the words are derived from their context, but are not always
consonant with their psychological function, thereby illustrating
our experience of propaganda at work.

Symbols of identification on Land reform:

Hochentwickelten deutschen Landwirtschaft der Sowjetzone,
  Reaktionäre, westlich eingestellten "Mitarbeiter", bewährte
  Fachleute, dass Können der Bauern, Kenntnis der deutschen
  Verhältnisse, Bedürfnissen der einzelnen Wirtschaft, Boden-
  und Klima-Verhältnisse, Produktion 76
Altbauern, Mittel- und Grossbauern, privaten Bauerntums,
  Kulaken, Freier Bauern, Landarbeitern, Bevölkerung,
  Deutsche für Deutsche Interessen, ohne ideologische Befangen-
  heit, Persönlichen Interessen, Rentabilität 53
                                                              129

These positive values are menaced by no less than 446 negative
ones:

Maschinenausleihestationen, MAS, Mord am Siedler, auf Kosten
  der Qualität, die von den Sowjets durchgeführte Bodenreform,
  demokratische Form, schematische Verteilung, Chaos der Plan-
  wirtschaft, eine Reihe Zwangwirtschaft, Ablieferungssoll, Ver-
  drängung der Kulaken, Volkseigene Güter, Verschuldigung,
  von Rentabilität keine Rede 208
Staatsbürokratie, Regierung der Deutschen Demokratischen
  Republik, Funktionäre, sowjetzonale Presse, Kulturabteilung,
  Befreiungstat, von politischen Erwägungen geleitete Personal-
  politik, Terminologie der sowjetzonalen Machthaber, kalte
  Kriege, linientreuen Kommunisten, Aktivisten, Helden der
  Arbeit, Taktik, sowjetische Übersetzerdeutsch 145
Bauernflucht, Unterstützung der Neubauern, Kollektiv, Kolchose,
  Produktionsgenossenschaften, Kolchosknechte, herrenlosen
  Flächen, Kontrolle seiner Arbeit, vorfristige Termin zum
  Gesetz erhoben, spontane Kundgebung, freiwilligen Wettbewerb,
  fortschrittliches Gepräge 65
Ganz im Sinne der Sowjets, getreue Kopie, Lenin, Stalin 28
                                                              446

All these evils cause 3 demands for "Reform in den uns Deutschen von früherher bekannten Sinne" as well as for free farmers. Thus, the land reform is shown to be part of the ideological struggle. The attempt of ideology to conquer social life as a whole is described by a symbol we already know from the land reform theme: sovietization. This symbol has 484 variations, negatively presented. Values menaced by these and favored by the communicator are

Bevölkerung der Zone, Bauern, Kulaken, Kinder der Mittel- und
    Grossbauern 58
Wiederaufbauwillen, reaktionäre Überbleibsel, Landwirtschaft
    der Zone, natürlicher Arbeitslauf eines landwirtschaftlichen
    Betriebes 48
Religiöse Gedanken, persönliche Freiheit, Sicherheit 5
                                                 111

whereas the 484 negative symbols are composed of:

Kommunistische Theorie, Partei, Diktatur, Infiltration, Politische
    Diffamierung, Kindern in die FDJ gezwungen, allgemeine
    Unsicherheit, Aktivisten, Helden der Arbeit, Roten Kloster,
    Sowjetpropaganda, Sowjetische Übersetzerdeutsch, Kultur-
    abteilung, Stalin-Schüler, DDR, Netz von Funktionären, li-
    nientreuen Kommunisten, Politik alles zu durchdringen,
    SED-Presse, Aufbau des Sozialismus, Kontrollieren ist besser
    als Vertrauen, Planwirtschaftssystems, Bauernflucht 242
Befreiung, spontan, freiwillig, Zwang, fortschrittlich, Verhaftung,
    Schau-prozessen, Klassenkampf, Verdrängung der Kulaken,
    Staatsbürokratie, Sowjetisierung, MAS, Verwaltungsapparat,
    sowjetzonale Wissenschaft 172
Not, Aderlass, namenloses Elend, endlose Transporten nach dem
    Osten, freien Bauern Kolchosknechte, verboten vom herren-
    losen Land zu sprechen 36
Genau wie in der UdSSR, Lenin, Stalin, Lyssenko, russische
    Sowchose 34
                                                 484

3 demands condemn the economic aspect of this sovietization and are only footnotes to the pages describing the social difficulties under the new élite. The description of something as a social ill, supports here as everywhere in a propaganda text the final demand. We shall return to that later.

The enemies of the new rulers are favorably treated, evaluated by 63 symbols of identification:

Mittel- und Grossbauern, jeder Kulak, Sabotage, Kriegsverbrecher,
   privaten Bauerntum, nicht Einhaltung der Termine, vergeht
 · sich gegen der Solidarität   47
Fachleute, westlicher Einstellung, reaktionäre retardierende
   Verwaltung   16
                                                           ———
                                                             63

which are viewed by 19 symbols as dangerous to the Sowjetzone,
das System, the Musterwirtschaften and the Ansehen der DDR.
The communicator makes no demands.

   The new ruling élite is backed by the traditions of Old Russia,
by examples from the Communist agrarian revolution under
Lenin and Stalin, and supported by German Soviet collaborators.
The outlook on these three themes is unfavorable and occupies
over 19% of the whole attention. Values accepted by the communicator and rejected by the new élite in the topic of Old Russia
are

Freie Bauern auf freier Scholle . . . . , ...   13

in the topic of Communist agrarian revolution under Lenin and
Stalin:

Privateigentum, kapitalistische Wirtschaft, das russische Volk   21

on German Soviet collaborators:

Interessen der Bauern, Bevölkerung der Zone   6

The work of the new élite and its background are evaluated by
287 negative symbols of which 85 describe Old Russia as a
country of landhungry farmers, strongly communistic already
in the beginning due to certain social conditions on the land and
without understanding of the value of private property. 88
symbols describe the agrarian revolution under Lenin and Stalin
as a "zwangsweisen Einführung der Kolchosen", and as stages
of violence, revolution, and the carrying out of party programs
despite the resistance from the farmers. "Vernichtung" and
"allgemeiner Chaos" is the description of the result of the revolution on the land. The last 114 symbols stand for the German
Soviet collaborators and their work:

SED-Presse, Politbüro der SED, politische Massen-Organisati-
    onen, Regime 79
Kulturleiter, Opportunisten, linientreue kommunistische junge
    unerfahrene in Russland ausgebildete Stalin-Schüler 28
Aderlass, abgesetzt, verhaftet 7
                                                              ———
                                                              114

No demands are made immediately. But the themes which describe the remedy for the social ills, and mention Deutschland
as a justification for this remedy, are in fact the demands of the
whole document, as we can see by the relation between the
different symbols above and their functional meanings. If we
note that hardly 7% of the total attention is applied to these
themes, we have not got the whole story. We have also to observe
that the intensified attention to the different aspects of the
symbols by their frequency turns into an interest that makes the
plea for "Freie Bauern" and a free Germany a tendency of the
whole statement. The figures on these two themes should therefore be considered together with the earlier quantitative relationships in the document.
Germany, 50 symbols of identification:

Heutige Deutschland, Industriestaat, westlichen Welt 25
Hochentwickelten deutschen Landwirtschaft, Wohlhabenheit
    unserer Bauern, Ordnung, Sauberkeit, Vergleich zwischen
    Sowjetpropaganda, Wirklichkeit und eigenen Verhältnissen . 25
                                                                ———
                                                                50

Remedy, 22 symbols of identification:

Ungeteilte Freiheit, Menschen, Deutsche, Bauern der Sowjetzone,
    Bauern im Westen, moralische Unterstützung, Widerstand . . 22

The new élite negative to all these symbols appears in 19 values:

Germany: Sowjetpropaganda, Rauberei, Aderlass 11
Remedy: Kommunistische Infiltration, Parteidiktatur, Angst,
    Tod 8

No demands are made on the Germany topic but 25 call
    for Remedy:

Ungeteilte, Freiheit als Menschen, freie Bauern 13
Schauen nach dem Westen, Erwarten, Widerstand, Unterstützung 12
                                                              ———
                                                              25

This description of an ideology and its policy on land and labor is the reverse of the picture drawn up by Lenin and his modern followers. It would be useful to compare not only the symbols used by the German document with those used by Lenin and his followers, but also this document and its concepts with the communicator's own ideological sponsors'. Such a comparison would give, among other things, information as to whether or how the Soviet German Communists follow their ideological sponsors. It would also tell which are the values prized by the communicator and his ideological sponsors that are menaced when Communist policy faces other ideologies in practice. This will be illustrated by our final survey in some degree. But a better opportunity to see the interplay of politics is offered by the different ideologies' mass of symbols as a whole.

*A MODERATE SOCIALIST SOLUTION

(272) It was only at the end of the Second World War that France adopted a conscious policy on agrarian questions. The scars of the war and the Vichy régime were still fresh, when the new Statutes on agricultural leases were proposed in 1945 and 1946. The politician responsible for this attempt was the Socialist

TABLE 45. *Symbols in the speech of Tanguy-Prigent, 1945*

Groups of symbols on values	Main direction (Favorable or Unfavorable)	Identifi- cations	Demands	Resistance	Total
Land reform	F	185	184	34	403
Problems of today	U	129	48	150	327
We Socialists.	F	115	35	11	161
L'épuration	F	33	24	18	75
Confidence in victory . . .	F	20	5	.	25
La coopération	F	19	25	9	53
Opponents of the Socialists	U	19	6	61	86
Le remembrement (consolidation of fragmented land)	F	16	20	2	38
Qualities of the peasants .	F	14	.	15	29
L'épargne (Saving thrift) .	F	9	9	—	18
Sub-total Favorable. . . .	F	411	302	89	802
Sub-total Unfavorable. . .	U	148	54	211	413
TOTAL		559	356	300	1,215

Tanguy-Prigent, a farmer's son from Bretagne who was Minister of Agriculture in the first free government. In substance, this legislation was a kind of land reform. The speech Tanguy-Prigent gave on "Démocratie à la terre" aimed at preparing minds for the social change and at justifying the legislation presented some months later.

The document embraces about 5600 words with 1215 symbols, as shown by Table 45. Most attention is paid to the theme of Land reform by over 33% of the total symbols. The topic is favorably treated. Problems to be solved are described with negative symbols, which may be a natural approach under the adverse circumstances reigning. They cover almost 27% of the total sum. The problems at attention, however, are further blackened not only by the existence of Opponents of the Socialists but also by the theme of l'Epuration which intensifies attention to the point of interest in the problems. L'Epuration is favorably described by the communicator. Nevertheless, its very existence retards and is therefore a negative factor in the execution of the land reform. Thus, the symbols negative to the interest in land reform cover more than 40% of all concepts. The figure of confidence in victory for the new social program is not high in the attention area, only 2%. But this pessimistic outlook is modified by belief in "We Socialists" and flattery of the heroic peasants, which two together will be able to succeed in making even the Epuration a part of social progress. These themes cover almost 24% of the total attention. They are further supported by the favorable themes of l'Epargne, la Co-opération, and le Remembrement, as opportunities for making land reform feasible. The finer nuances of the relationships among these different symbols derives from numerous variations in their presentation. But here as elsewhere in this chapter we have to limit our presentation to comprehending the results of the function of the symbols. On the topic of Land Reform we obtained the following values of identification:

Nos institutions, intérèts de profession agricole, les paysans, petits propriétaires, ouvriers agricoles, vieux travailleurs, grands problèmes 131
Démocratie à la terre, fermiers, réformes de structure, village   28
Paris, notre industrie, les jeunes, la nation, librement   26
                                                                    ———
                                                                    185

These values are menaced by 34 concepts of social evils:

Hommes de Vichy, système autoritaire, spéculation sur la terre,
  calamités 23
Inférieur à personne, toujours compter sur l'Etat 6
Division en petites fermages, dualité pénible 5
                                                                ————
                                                                 34

The demands for land reform yet not executed are expressed by
184 symbols:

Démocratie à la terre, réformes de structure, réelles en profon-
  deur, distribuez généreusement, financé plus démocratiquement,
  améliorer les conditions d'existence à la campagne, un projet
  de réforme du statut de fermage-métayage, réaliser un tel programme de transformation de l'agriculture, réformes économiques 102
Sécurité, stabilité inconnue, minimum de rémuneration, assurances
  sociales obligatoires, rendre au paysan la fierté de son métier,
  maintenir les jeunes à la terre, droit d'appartenir au parti de
  votre choix 47
Nécessité. 24
Supprimer la spéculation, exclusion des hommes de Vichy, de
  ceux qui ne sont pas agriculteurs 11
                                                                ————
                                                                184

As we observed above the Problems of today in this social field
are many. Directly menaced by them are the following identification symbols:

Vie matérielle, progrès, les paysans, ces jeunes, France, nos
  colonies 75
Parti socialiste, gouvernement 29
Capacité de l'épargne paysanne, prix des produits, salaires . . 17
Les ouvriers, ceux qui ont de petits salaires, consommateurs . . 8
                                                                ————
                                                                129

150 symbols for troubles:

Misère paysanne, complex d'infériorité, dégout de la ferme, trop
  tard 64
L'état de production, écrasé par la concurrence étrangère, politique
  des prix, bataille économique 53
Occupation, Vichy, la guerre 24
L'exode rural, l'hiver extrèmement dur 9
                                                                ————
                                                                150

48 demands emphasize by 36 symbols that it is up to Us to
construct the new society of tomorrow, to instruct the farmers,
to revalorize the prices in agriculture. The last 12 symbols are
accusations of lacking interests in the young among the farmers.
"Appartient à nous" is a demand given value by the theme of
We Socialists in 115 symbols of identification:

Nos socialistes, mes camarades, le seul parti, Je, notre devoir,
    propagande, recrutement, librement 80
Ouvriers, paysans, le parti des travailleurs de la terre, des usines,
    agriculteurs, campagne, la jeunesse paysanne, les jeunes
    ouvriers 22
Politique des prix, ministère de l'agriculture 13
                                                              115

These values are menaced by 11 negative symbols as "Séparer en
désaccord" and "danger de compromettre la monnaie" which
make necessary 35 demands for action: "Dénoncer tous les sabo-
tages" (15), "recrutement plus intense" among the young
peasants and workers for the Socialists (11), and "revisée la
question des prix agricoles" (9). Because of the Qualitities of the
peasants, this need for action will be easy to meet. In flattering
the peasants 14 symbols of identification express also a particular
aspect on the farmers as suppliers of food to the towns. The
difficulties encountered by these peasants while supplying the
townpeople during the War are described by 15 symbols whose
qualities stress the heroic work of the peasants under conditions of:

Fausse monnaie, surenchère, circonstances tentatrices 10
La famine, dommages, ces années difficiles 5
                                                          15

Of course, there are no demands to put in this connection except
the general claim of the document itself for a land reform to
improve the conditions of the peasants.

The kind of difficulties encountered by the peasants indicates
the necessity for purification, "L'Epuration", of all subversive
elements. 33 symbols worth identification are especially menaced
by subversive factors:

Nous, France, le bonheur de posséder un toit 15
Raisons, preuves, moyen d'y rémédier 9
Majorité de résistance, déportés 9
                                                          33

Expressions for subversive elements and activity are

Sabotage, critique, manque d'épuration, la guerre, Vichy . . .   13
Déporté, tombé, souffert   5
                                                                          18

The demands justify action against those subversive elements
still active:

Poursuivre notre oeuvre d'épuration, exclusion des hommes de
    Vichy   13
Un devoir de justice, preuves   11
                                                                          24

These subversive elements also show up among the Opponents
of the Socialists and their social program on land. Values menaced
but worth identification on this theme are expressed by 19
symbols covering such concepts as France, nos richesses, notre
travail, and la terre, as well as profession agricole, socialisme,
and libération. 61 symbols described the Opponents at work as:

Entreprise de trahison, spéculation, enrichissent scandaleusement,
    marché noir, capitalistes, grands banquiers, trusts, grandes
    industries, extérieurs à la profession agricole   35
Règne de Vichy, nos adversaires, occupation   23
Ce fossé (within the Socialist party itself)   3
                                                                          61

6 demands direct action to

Chasse aux trusts, supprimer, démontrer, condamnés, plus efficace   6

Practical means to reach favorable results in solving the problems
are saving thrift, co-operation, and "remembrement", that is the
consolidation of fragmented land. 44 concepts on these themes
function as symbols of identification:

Le remembrement: Remembrement, travail agricole, excellents
    résultats, collectivement   16
Saving thrift: L'épargne, paysans honnets, jeunes ménages . . .   9
Co-operation: Coopération, nouveau statut, equipement moderne,
    économie coopérative   19

"Remembrement" encounters two kinds of troubles described in
2 symbols as "morcelées, droits d'ainesse" thereby calling at-

tention to the social aspect of the land. Saving thrift shows no difficulties, whereas Co-operation in 9 symbols demonstrates the negative results of the splitting ("éparpillement") of co-operatives, and the war. 54 symbols claim the effectiveness of the means we have expressed by the three themes above. Thus, for the "remembrement": Utiliser collectivement, moyens d'empècher les fermes morcelées, with 20 symbols. For Saving thrift "Possibilité de se reéquiper" with 9 symbols, and for Co-operation the necessity for "coopératives sincères" with 20 symbols and for educating the farmer with 5 symbols.

Confidence in the success of this program covers, as we said earlier, only 2% of the attention area but is intensified by confidence in Socialism and in certain qualities of the peasants. No symbols for difficulties appear in this theme, but 20 symbols are worth identification:

Nous, nos fédérations 10
Politique de réalisations, socialistes, contact étroit avec la
    réalité. 6
Ouvriers, paysans, jeunesse 4
                                                             ——
                                                             20

5 demands refer closely to these identification symbols:

Capables de réaliser 3
Doivent peupler nos (:socialistic) sections 2
                                                             ——
                                                             5

This theme of confidence in victory is more important than might be assumed at a first reading. A comparison between the quantitative relation among the symbols of the theme and the kind of symbols will prove that belief in success is expressed by a program that takes farmers, workmen, and youth, as well as close contact with reality, into consideration as a Socialist field for action. The Socialists are the only party mentioned in this connection. A glance on the other themes of the message gives the same picture. That is, the theme of confidence in the victory of the program is deeply rooted in all the symbols manipulated in the document and is a summing up of the concepts earlier used. As we see, no resistance to the program is summed up in the theme of confidence. In the light of this we have to look deeper

than the attention area. The interest area, where the symbols
and themes at attention are intensified by their quantitative
relation proves that all the values worth identification, or expressing demands, indicating confidence in success, appear
everywhere with great frequency in the document. That is,
studying them we have to keep in mind that it is not the 40%
of resistance we mentioned above that the communicator counts
upon for the future. It is on the contrary all the symbols deemed
worthy of victory and appearing everywhere in the message,
that show that he believes in final victory over the difficulties. As
we observed, most parts of this resistance are specified in the
problems to be solved. It is also a consequence of this that they
are not even worth mentioning under a successful aspect.

TENDENCIES OF COMMUNICATION

(273) Summing up the results of our investigations and
referring to the questions we put in the beginning of this chapter,
we feel that the expert on agrarian reform has to look elsewhere
than the communication process of his topic to discover solutions
for the theoretical and practical problems on his field. We are
not even sure that the attentive public is pleased if it expected
land reform to be a main topic throughout the documents. However, that is what responsible communicators have given the
public in justifying their treatment of land reform and the
relation between different classes. Freedom of speech has made
this communication feasible. Where the free word did not
convince the public, other kinds of public powers have aided in
making the public at least attentive to the message. Another
aspect of freedom of speech is the public's opportunity to consider
what is publicly said, what kind of concepts are offered to their
minds and how. This chapter is an application of that opportunity.

(274) Surveying the documents there are two questions that
might help to an understanding of the tendencies of the messages.
Is there any remarkable difference of the proportions among
symbols for identification, demands, or resistance in the particular statements? And, can we trace any tendency of the documents'
dealing with the favorable and unfavorable aspects on the
symbols? Expressed numerically as a percentage of all the at-

tention area of the documents, we get the following picture in reply to our first question:

TABLE 46

Document	Symbols of Identification	Demands	Resistance	Total
Vatican 1891	66,7	13.6	19.7	100
,, 1931	64.8	11.3	23.9	100
,, 1941	63.6	21.7	14.7	100
Italian Bill	76.3	12.2	11.5	100
Medici	72.9	13.8	13.3	100
Lenin	48.8	9.8	41.4	100
Sándor	37.4	14.1	48.5	100
Chervenkov	72.9	16.8	10.3	100
Bundesministerium .	24.4	1.8	73.8	100
Tanguy-Prigent. . .	46.0	29.3	24.7	100

Before commenting on this picture, we can also look at the tables that will answer our second question. The percentage figure still relates to all the symbols in the documents:

TABLE 47

Document	Favorable symbols	Unfavorable symbols	Total
Vatican 1891	83	17	100
,, 1931	74.3	25.7	100
,, 1941	82.8	17.2	100
Italian Bill	94.2	5.8	100
Medici	88.7	11.3	100
Lenin	46.3	53.7	100
Sándor	54.3	45.7	100
Chervenkov	88.4	11.6	100
Bundesministerium	11.6	88.4	100
Tanguy-Prigent.	66	34	100

The distribution of favorable and unfavorable symbols in the categories of identification, demands, and resistance give further enlightment. The percentage now relates separately to each main part of the documents in the following table:

TABLE 48

Document	Symbols of identification		Demands		Resistance	
	F	U	F	U	F	U
Vatican 1891	91	9	97.6	2.4	45.8	54.2
,, 1931	84.9	15.1	98.3	1.7	34.3	65.7
,, 1941	89.7	10.3	85.4	14.6	49.3	50.7
Italian Bill	96.9	3.1	100.0	—	70	30
Medici	93.1	6.9	95.7	4.3	56.9	43.1
Lenin	63.6	36.4	86.9	13.1	16.3	83.7
Sándor	75.1	24.9	91.3	8.7	27.6	72.4
Chervenkov	94.6	5.4	89.8	10.2	42	58
Bundesministerium . .	32.5	67.5	80.6	19.4	3	97
Tanguy-Prigent . . .	73.5	26.5	84.8	15.2	29.7	70.3

Table 46 makes clear that the statements by strong powers, as for instance the Vatican, Medici, and Chervenkov, give rise to a high percentage of identification symbols in the attention area. The powerful position of the Italian Bill has a special background as we already know. The German document is here as always of a certain interest because of its inverted character. Resistance finds there expression in the identifications of the enemy in power.

When making demands, those in power do not pay much attention to their task. It seems as if they were more attentive to their own values than to putting forward demands on the social question indicated in the titles of their statements. A public may ask whether these ideologies, introducing themselves as powerful, really are interested in doing much about the burning question of land and labor.

Resistance to the particular program, according to the documents, is also represented by comparatively low figures. Chervenkov counts upon the least resistance, even less than the Italian Bill. But Medici and the Vatican also present resistance to their ideas as very weak in comparison with identifications and demands. As we have discussed earlier when speaking about these statements, this bias might depend on the particular public to whom the communicator wants to appear as if mastering the situation. The Vatican documents illustrate this, where the older, dealing with a chosen public of indulgent "Venerable Brethren" pay more attention to resistance than the Vatican statement of 1941; this has, as we know, a mixed world wide audience and had therefore to pass over resistance more quickly. In this table we obviously get the picture the communicator wants to give his public of himself and his ideological institution.

This is the case also with weaker groups such as Lenin, Sándor, and Tanguy-Prigent. As regards Lenin, we have already stated that his identification symbols, as a result of his lack of practical background, often served as demands for the future, thereby increasing the formal figure of obvious demands. The resistance Lenin expects is great. The number of identification symbols heads those of resistance by only a few per cent. It is an ideology fighting for its life with dim prospects of realizing its program. Sándor, one of his late followers, has experience of a similar situation. Looking at the relation between his identification symbols and those of resistance, we find the latter evidently higher. The figures for demands are not overwhelming. This relationship makes us suspect that in the present situation there is not much for Sándor and his ideology to be identified with since he is not interested in presenting himself and his identifications as a strong convincing power. Evidently, his real identifications are somewhere else than what he actually pays attention to, judging by the attention paid to the resistance he calculates.

Every propaganda message has to convince the public to certain opinions or attitudes to the value under debate. A logical consequence of this is that the communicator presents himself or his program with strong and attractive and "just" power, and describes the resistance as small, or at least unjust and immoral. This feature has been clearly observed in the propaganda during warfare and times of tension[a]. In fact, what a particular communicator favorably describes as moral, strong, and attractive in a message, has proved his ideological home, even though it was not known originally. This way of exposing the sources of different propaganda is not only useful in time of war. The categories of moral and immoral, strength and weakness in a message give a deep insight into the function of any topic category aiming at convincing a public. Sometimes, this psychological function of militant ideas is overlooked, and it is stated that "at the present time, content analysis should employ the categories most meaningful for the particular problem at hand: and relatively specific and concrete categories are often the most meaningful" [b]. That would be right, if the particular problem at hand only treated relatively specific and concrete categories. That is, in our present case, if the categories of land and labor were the overwhelmingly meaningful concrete categories in the material. We have, however, already seen that propaganda messages use every value under debate to impress a certain desired ideology on the public mind. This communication process which colors with ideology meaningful categories of the subject matter, is the very propaganda process. To lay bare the relatively specific and concrete categories of a text is, as regards propaganda messages, only to take the first steps of the analysis. To analyse propaganda is to go further and see how these concrete categories are manipulated, by the frequency of their occurrence in the text, to tendency and bias of the message and to psychological functions that turn out to meaningful common denominators fit for any content launched in a propaganda campaign. But this aspect is not clear without considering the role of the ideology as the most important component in content analysis, at home as tacit assumptions and abroad by taking account of the foreign ideology involved.

Tanguy-Prigent uses more identification symbols than Sándor. The high percentage of demands, however, makes us understand that he fights for a program. He appreciates that there is resistance as well as Lenin, but the clear difference between identification symbols and demands we missed in Lenin is here a fact. Tanguy-Prigent is evidently more in power than Lenin in his society. The figures for demands and resistance tell, however, that even Tanguy-Prigent has great difficulties to overcome. This is such an evident fact that it cannot be denied in public.

(275) Table 47 on the distribution of favorable and unfavorable symbols gives some clues as to the color of the communicator's attention. The optimistic outlook is evident when the Vatican and its followers as well as Chervenkov present themselves to the large public as powerful. The German document is as usual a mirror of a negative élite in power and the communicator himself as extremely powerless. Lenin, even by his treatment of favorable and unfavorable concepts, still pays more attention to the negative factors than the positive ones he represents and fights

for. Sándor is the one closest to the Lenin approach here, whereas Tanguy-Prigent, despite all resistance, prefers to pay more attention to positive concepts. An approach that already in the attention area echoes our remark on the overwhelmingly optimistic belief in victory as a trend significant of Tanguy-Prigent's interest.

(276) Table 48 finally gives a picture of the relationship between the positive and negative features in the three main aspects of the different messages. The Vatican and its followers as well as Chervenkov identify themselves to an extreme degree by favorable symbols. This selfcongratulatory attitude is followed in more or less modified form by the other documents. The unfavorable symbols evidently serve to limit the boundaries of this self which is in such a high degree identical with positive values.

The demand symbols throughout the statements indicate that the favorable aspects of a demand are necessary psychological conditions for its success. The relationship to the quality of the particular power seems to be of less importance. Noticeable is the case of Lenin with his clear awareness of the negativism around him even when he puts forward his program. A program that, as we recall, embraced also groups still hesitant and doubtful of him. The identifications made by Lenin, Sándor, and Tanguy-Prigent stress their similar psychological and political situations, which we have already characterized as those of still weak and struggling powers, deeply aware of resistance.

It is not only noticeable that this resistance is great, but the use in overwhelming degree of negative symbols to describe the kind of opposition gives a touch of bitterness to the view of the enemy and involves a calculation of the real power of the opposition. The case of the Vatican document of 1931 is here enlightening. Its powerful approach to the public in the attention area is here diminished by the highly negative appraisal of its opponents. Its situation suddenly appears to be as precarious as that of Lenin and others, and forecasts its real interest, as shown when we studied the document earlier. The case of Chervenkov is also remarkable. This strong power might be expected to show a more positive approach to the defeated enemy. It may be that the intensification of negative attention to resistance involves a realization of dangerous opponents, suppressed in the communication but nevertheless existing in the mind of the communicator.

In general, we find that situations of social tension, of post-war uncertainty, or of revolutions, stress the opposition as something in overwhelming degree bad and immoral. The degree to which such an approach is characteristic of the more powerful communicators is worth further enquiry as well as the degree of the use of favorable symbols characterizing the communicator as identical with something good and strong.

(277) As we indicated above, there are trends in our material that imply that the communicators care more for a certain ideal of society than for providing for practical arrangements. Leaving the attention area of the statements and asking for the communicator's interest, we have to look for his use of symbols which not only by their literal or equivalent and synonymous appearance but also by their frequency and function build up a certain theme or category of a topic. We can call this phenomenon intensified attention or, more commonly, interest or tendency.

The titles of the documents indicate a claim for land reform or at least for interest in social problems. Already the claim for a reform or a change gives information on existing conditions, looked upon as more or less bad. These are in this connection, with one exception, of less interest than the positive new conditions the communicator is interested in building up. What is he interested in? What is the tendency of his message?

The positive concepts to be found throughout the documents pour out into two main categories. One is land reform, or guidance for the solution of the social question. It would be justifiable if this question with all its aspects were the main topic or even the sole topic for these agrarian and social reformers. In the light of this, it is remarkable that this main topic has a strong competitor in the communicator's interest: the various aspects of the authority which he claims to have when communicating with his public. Schematically, counted in per cent on all the contents of the different documents, it can be presented thus:

TABLE 49

Document	Theme	%
Vatican 1891	Social question: (theme built up of Man as a social being, Approved unions, Real remedy, Labor-remuneration-possession, id. justified by Nature, Supplies of the earth)	47.0
	Authority, sponsoring this program: (theme built up of God, Church, State, Moral justice, Lawful order, Attention to the problem by Us, Authority meeting the Address of the message)	36.0
	Negative symbols (expressing problems to be solved)	17.0
	Total	100.0
Vatican 1931	Social question: (Man as a social being, Approved unions, Real remedy, Labor-remuneration-possession, Right to property, Social question)	33.1
	Authority, sponsoring this program: (God, Church, Rerum Novarum, State, Justice, Lawful order, Attention to the problem by Us, Authority meeting the Address of the message, Active resistance)	41.2
	Negative symbols	25.7
	Total	100.0
Vatican 1941	Social question: (Man as a social being, Approved unions, Real remedy, Labor-remuneration-possession, Supplies of the earth)	29.4
	Authority, sponsoring this program: (God, Church, Rerum novarum, Moral, Justice, Lawful order, Attention to the problem by Us, Authority meeting the Address of the message)	53.4
	Negative symbols	17.2
	Total	100.0
Italian Bill	Land reform: (Expropriation, Improvement of land, Remedy, Land reform, Cascina, Purpose of land reform, Charges of the reform)	68.3
	Authority, sponsoring this program: (Government's version, Duties of land reform offices)	25.9
	Negative symbols	5.8
	Total	100.0
Medici	Land reform: (Land, Labor)	32.5
	Authority, sponsoring this program: (Confidence, Sincerity, Authority, Meeting the Address of the message)	56.2
	Negative symbols	11.3
	Total	100.0
Lenin	Land reform: (Land, Labor, Approved unions, Peasants' qualities, Solution)	32.0
	Authority, sponsoring this program: (Communist Party)	14.3
	Negative symbols	53.7
	Total	100.0

Document	Theme	%
Sándor	Land reform: (Land reform, New owner).	45.6
	New authority, sponsoring this program: (Progressive intellectuals, Class struggle)	8.7
	Old authority - negative(Feudalism, Capitalists, Enemies of the new State)	45.7
	Total	100.0
Chervenkov	Land reform (The task ahead, Co-operative farms as a fact, Character of accepted model statute, Social nature of the co-operative farm)	46.5
	Authority, sponsoring this program: (Communist State and its policy, Confidence in victory, Self-criticism, Greetings, Heroes of labor, Class struggle, Progressive intellectuals)	41.9
	Negative symbols	11.6
	Total	100.0
Bundes-ministerium	Land reform: (Land reform)	34.0
	Authority, sponsoring this program: (Sovietization, Lenin, Stalin, Old Russia, German Soviet collaborators)	54.4
	Positive symbols (inverted negative symbols).	11.6
	Total	100.0
Tanguy-Prigent	Land reform: (Land reform, Co-operation, "Remembrement", Saving thrift, Peasants' qualities)	44.5
	Authority, sponsoring this program: (Socialists, Confidence, ,,Epuration")	21.5
	Negative symbols	34.0
	Total	100.0

The interest in consolidation and increase of the ruling élites' power (or their defeat in the German document) is evident. The Italian Bill is the only statement that can afford to neglect it, as we recall. In the other documents land reform is a main topic of the whole interest area but only by reason of its connection with authority. The negative social conditions would be disastrous to the realization of the reform unless backed by authority, as we see in Lenin. The authority of the élite is consequently described as the only way in which to make progress. The opportunities for ideological and political interference in the social problem are here put in their proper light. And so is the necessity of the public's asking about the ideological home of the communicator.

(278) Not only by speaking about problems, but also by silence about them is it possible to give a message a particular bias or

tendency and to influence the public's mind and decisions when communicating controversial values. Speaking about land reforms, there are social problems of significance that the communicators avoid or mention only incidentally. Such a question is the female labor force in agriculture. The small attention to the problem sometimes comes up for self-criticism. Communication for decision-making is evidently an affair for male human beings, when it is a question of land reform and the relations between social classes. Agrarian overpopulation, in fact basic to all land problems, is another problem that suffers from the same lack of attention by the communicators. The incidental mention of the earth as an abundant storehouse, and of the overpopulation problems as solved by emigration, only serves in the communication to justify this silence. In other cases, the common problems under debate, the condemnation of certain phenomena point to the contemporary evil. The remedy indicated is however overshadowed by propaganda for the doctor and for the ideological circles to which he belongs.

CONCLUSIONS

(279) In this analysis of structural features in European agriculture, interest has been focussed upon the relation between land and labor. This relation was found to be essential for the development of the structure of farms and of the related factors of the type of settlement, land fragmentation, land tenure, and agricultural co-operation.

The analysis in Chapter 3 shows that there has been a distinct connection between the demographic development and the changes in farm structure. Rapid demographic increase in Eastern Europe precipitated a subdivision of farm land even independently of the land reforms. A similar development had taken place in Western Europe in much earlier epochs. In recent times, stable or declining numbers of farm population were reflected in considerable immobility in the farm structure. In Southern Europe, the subdivision of land went on without being too much observed in the zones of intensive cultivation, while the latifundia could maintain themselves in zones where the natural conditions were not favorable for smal-lscale farming.

Factors in the economy of farming also contributed to both kinds of result. The pressure of industrial markets in Western Europe caused concentration on livestock and other intensive branches of agricultural production, with much stress on work by the individual for his own benefit. This is what really has preserved the family farm structure where 19th century economists had expected rapid industrialization of agriculture. In Eastern and Southern Europe, population pressure was too high to allow the expenditure necessary for large-scale mechanization, and small-scale farming got an even stronger hold except in areas favorable to specialization on very extensive methods of production.

The other structural features analyzed have followed the same main trend as the farm structure. Villages were gradually dissolved into scattered settlements where conditions allowed increasing efficiency of labor, but in heavily over-populated areas the incentive was weak in this direction unless the cultivation of the land was so highly intensive as to require the constant presence of the farmer on the land. Fragmentation went on and increased recently in regions where population pressure made the waste of manpower it causes to be of no concern. Land consolidation closely follows the occurrence of the need to save labor. Land tenure conditions have become stabilized insofar as the need for continuity of farming called for concessions to those who work on the land. Agricultural co-operation, though less directly connected with population pressure, has answered the needs of agriculture where it was developing towards higher specialization in densely settled areas but failed to get a hold both where excess of labor was not combined with a progressive development of specialized farm production and where many farms were large enough to take care of their own interests individually.

(280) To these various trends of a spontaneous character, land policies have tried to react in order to influence development. The observation of these attempts leads to the general conclusion that land policy has more often been a failure than a success. Any attempt towards formulating a "general" program of land policy is therefore an utterly difficult task.

Western countries tried to stop the rural exodus by colonization policy; the rural exodus continued and was even accelerated. Eastern countries tried to remedy the evils of rural over-population by radical land reforms; population increase continued and over-population remained unremedied. Western countries sought to strengthen small and discourage large farms; farms have continued to grow larger spontaneously, where conditions allowed the trend to manifest itself. The Soviet Union tried to discourage the familistic society by creating large-scale, highly mechanized agriculture; the response was a drive towards over-intensification in the cultivation of the small family gardens and neglect of the collective sector, with overt failure of the livestock industry, and hidden failures in crop production, as the consequence.

This double set of failures has its background in the failures to see the real content of some basic trends of development. To some extent the misjudgement depended upon the fact that a changing Europe produced problems not covered by any previous experience. The rural exodus engendered a fear that the country-side would become depopulated; the measures adopted were therefore directed against the spontaneous development. Collectivization was equally inspired by a fear that the peasantry would use its economic position to exert pressure on the growing urban markets which needed food at low prices; the measures introduced tended to reduce the initiative of the food producers and thereby strangled the development towards a more complete food supply.

The analysis of land reform propaganda in Chapter 7 has further revealed a leading feature which could not have been shown clearly without quantitative analysis. Besides being interested in social reform, the propagandists for such reform have also all of them paid overdue interest to strengthening the power of their own ideological circle and the organizations representing it. The high frequency of symbols glorifying the powers backing the orator or governed by him, and of those condemning the opposite side as such, reveal the degree to which the problems of social reform are linked with those of political and ideological power. Which of the two aims is the primary concern of those acting on an issue is decisive for their capacity to grapple with the practical problems.

(281) If, instead of being inspired by fear or by concern for the power of their own ideology or power organization, the politicians had been more inspired by curiosity as to the real content of the socio-economic processes, the attempts to cope with essentially new situations could have been made with more success. Two main sets of facts could then have been established to form the focus of attention. One is the demographic process which conditions the development of labor supply in relation to the work to be done in agriculture in a modern world. The other is in the scale of varying necessities inherent in the technical side of farming at various stages of development and in various types of specialization.

The most suitable type of farm can be decided empirically in each case. It is the type which under given conditions makes the most rational use of all production factors, including the human factor in the broad sense of the expression. The practical answer will be different under different types of farming, and also at different levels of intensity. Maximum absorption of existing manpower is a primary goal when the possibilities for employment in other activities are scarce or difficult to arrange for the existing farm population. A full-scale use of invested capital becomes more essential when much is invested, which tends to be the case mainly when manpower is not abundant and cheap.

The judgements underlying land policies in various countries have interpreted some of these things differently, because the goal of policy was not identical. Large-scale farming has been defended from the viewpoint that it provides more net increment. This is the leading advantage for those who reap that increment, if they are landlords in a capitalistic country or the government in a socialistic country. Small-scale farming, it has often been feared, would tend to reduce production, as might happen in the initial phases of some land reforms but, above all, it tended to increase local consumption and make less food available for the towns and the export markets. It is thereby often overlooked that the loss for the latter means a gain for the farming class, and that the increase in their food consumption may mean an asset for the future, a factor which increases the capacity of the agricultural population to develop and integrate in the life of the country.

This reflection does not add up to an argument in favor of land reform and a structure of very small farms under all conceivable conditions. It does so under certain specific conditions which are at present very wide-spread both in Europe and in other parts of the world. This is why the conclusions from Western Europe in the last decades cannot be used as a pattern for judging the conditions in Eastern Europe or Asia or Latin America. The conclusions one may draw from the development of Western Europe in the Middle Ages, or at the eve of the French revolution, are a more appropriate, though very imperfect, guide to understanding what is going on in the under-developed countries now.

The land problem is not one problem but many problems, they are as many as the agrarian situations which exist or have existed. It follows from this that a successful land policy cannot be too much fettered either by the experience of the past or by abstract theory. The future will show gradual changes in the problems of the socio-economic organization of the land, continuing as long as human technique develops and as long as we are at all dependent on plant and animal production for our food. Only attentive and as far as possible unbiassed study can help us to cope with this renewed challenge. If this is to be done with some success, the ideologies must be kept at bay. Their influence will have to be reduced to the narrow space left for choice when the necessities of the farming industry, as a component of an integrated society, have been clearly outlined.

APPENDICES

SOURCES AND METHODS FOR THE SETTLEMENT MAP

The median figures represented on the map refer to total agricultural population. The discrimination of agricultural and non-agricultural population is available in the local detail of the census materials only from Hungary and Eastern Germany. In all other countries, the medians for total rural population have been reduced proportionately to the ratio between rural and agricultural population. This procedure risks to some extent to over-estimate the size of agricultural villages, but this is largely compensated by the fact that agglomerations of an urban character, where the majority of the population belongs to non-agricultural occupations, are not included in the area for which the computation is made. The "agrotowns" in some Southern areas are on the other hand included among the agricultural settlement.

The results thus obtained are, of course, reliable mainly in their broad features, and details should be read with caution. For the calculations here presented, administrative subdivisions have been followed. For reasons obvious in connection with a survey like this one, the administrative units are generally on the provincial level, and sometimes even larger subdivisions have had to be accepted as basis. It has not been possible to make the distribution to correspond with homogeneous geographical regions. Contrasts occurring at short distances are therefore largely hidden.

In many instances it might have been desirable to calculate more fractiles, *e.g.* quartiles. In regions where the settlement consists of a combination of large rural centers and scattered farms, the median values may represent a size of village which is of rare occurrence. It would however not have been possible to represent further detail on map. Whether the median size of village is in practice frequent or not, the median size at any rate represents the average situation as regards the distance factor and related factors.

In the following, details of methods used and results found are given for each country, listed in alphabetical order.

ALBANIA. A population census was taken in 1930 but never published (cf *South-Eastern Europe. A political and economic survey*, ed. by The Royal Institute of International Affairs, London 1939). M. Urban, *Die Siedlungen Südalbaniens* (Öhringen 1938), has analyzed the data of this census with regard to the southern half of the country. There were in this part 1,636 localities, out of which 300 had less than 100 inhabitants each, 1,063 had between 100 and 500, 208 between 500 and 1,000, 60 between 1,000 and 5,000, and 5 over 5,000 inhabitants. If the latter five are reckoned as urban settlement, then the median among the rest will fall close to 500. But according to the quoted author, pp 95 sqq and 107, many of these localities were not nucleated but were districts with scattered settlement. It is therefore certain that the median should have been below 400. On the other hand, the part played by nucleated villages in many parts of the area makes it unlikely that the median were under 200. The category 200–400 was therefore inserted on the map. The analogy with neighbouring parts of Greece and Yugoslavia allowed the same category to be interpolated for the northern part of Albania as well.

The low quotient of agricultural land per man working in agriculture indicates that the Albanian villages cannot be very large, as measured in cultivated area. When rough grazings and waste mountain land are included, some of them may cover a considerable area.

AUSTRIA. The main sources are the *Volkszählungsergebnisse 1951* (Wien 1952), and *Verwaltungsatlas auf statistischer Grundlage* (Wien 1952). Medians were calculated for each of some 80 "politische Bezirke". In the following, indication is given of the maxima and minima between which these medians range in each of the "Bundesländer". To these are added calculated values for the extension of village territories, both in all land put to agricultural use and in arable land. It has also seemed interesting to add the figures for average size of "ortschaften" according to the population census of 1900 (*Die Ergebnisse der Volkszählung vom 31 Dezember 1900*... Wien 1902–03, H. 2). Although the concept is different and also includes the towns, a certain resemblance can be traced with the medians from 1950.

Bundesland	Median of village size in 1950			Average size of "Ortschaft" in 1900
	In agricultural population	In land put to agricultural use	In arable land	
Niederösterreich	125– 450	500–1,500	300–1,100	765
Oberösterreich	Under 100	300	Under 100	133
Steiermark	150– 400	500–1,200	300– 800	354
Kärnten	100– 150	700	300	128
Salzburg	100– 200	800–2,000	400–1,000	255
Tirol, Vorarlberg	100– 400	1,200–7,000	700–2,500	427
Burgenland	350–1,150	800–1,700	500–1,200	..

Cf also A. Klaar, "Die Siedlungslandschaften Niederösterreichs", *Aufbau* (Wien) 1949, pp 178–188.

BELGIUM. The main source used is the 1931 population census, *Recensement général au 31 décembre 1931*, T. 1 and 5. The census gives data only for communities, not for individual settlements. Approximate medians for size of village have been calculated by combining the census data with the indications on the general character of the settlement in each region contained in M. A. Lefèvre, *L'habitat rural en Belgique* (Liège 1926).

Province	Medians of village size		
	in agricultural population	in agricultural area (hectares)	in total area (hectares)
Antwerpen	300	400	900
Brabant.	300	400	600
West-Vlaanderen.	Under 100	Under 100	About 100
Oost-Vlaanderen	Under 100	Under 100	About 100
Hainaut.	100	300	450
Liège	100	300	550
Limburg	300	450	900
Luxembourg	125	475	900
Namur	100	450	900

The area figures are based on the 1950 census of agriculture, *Recensement général de l'agriculture 1950*, in the preliminary results issued in November 1950, and *Annuaire de statistique* 72, 1952.

BULGARIA. The main source is the *Recensement de la population 1934* (Sofia 1935). Total rural population was about 4.8 million and the agricultural population about 4.4 million. The medians for rural population could thus be reduced by about one-tenth to approach medians for agricultural population. For the then existing seven districts (*oblast*), the following medians were found.

Burgaz.	1,000	Sofia	950
Vratza	2,200	Stara-Zagora	950
Plovdiv	1,550	Shumen.	1,350
Pleven	1,400		

For southern Dobrudsha, recent census returns are lacking. For this area, therefore, the same category was adopted, by interpolation, as in the surrounding regions of both Bulgaria and Rumania. On the map, also the districts of Sofia and Stara-Zagora are represented by the category 1000–2000, because they are so close to it that it seemed safer to adopt only one representation for the whole of Bulgaria except Vratza.

According to the statistical yearbooks from the early forties, the quotient of agricultural land was very close to 1 hectare per person of the agricultural population. The size of median villages may thus be assumed to be of a similar magnitude in hectares as in inhabitants.

Interesting information on a somewhat earlier stage of development can be drawn from the *Statistique de la propriété foncière pendant l'année 1908*, Vol. 2, (Sofiia 1920). Already then, most of the Bulgarian villages included more than 50 holdings and many had more than 100 or even 200 holdings, and thousands of hectares of cultivated land. Small hamlets are also registered separately but were of small importance.

CZECHOSLOVAKIA. The main source for population data has been the census of 1930, *Recensement de la population de la république tchécoslovaque, effectué le 1er décembre 1930*, T. 1, (Prague 1934), 2:2 (Ibid. 1935). For the Western provinces, medians drawn from this source can be compared to average size of "Ortschaft" in the Austrian census of 1900, as in Austria. Area figures were taken from the statistical yearbook of Czechoslovakia for the year 1938.

Part of the country	Median of agricultural population	Total village area corresponding thereto	Arable land per village, Id.	Average size of "Ortschaft" 1900
Bohemia	285	850	430	500
Moravia-Silesia	420	1,100	600	800
Slovakia	725	1,875	700	..

For the country as a whole, the result has had to be generalized on these main parts only. For Slovakia, it can be checked on the basis of small districts, from two sources. One is the *Lexikon obcí Slovenskoj republiky* (Bratislava 1942), the other the *Recensement de la population, de la propiété foncière et du cheptel, en 1938, dans la zone Nord recouvrée*... (Publications statistiques hongroises, N.S., Vol. 108, Budapest 1939). The result obtained from these two sources, with a somewhat different procedure, gave essentially the same picture of the settlement structure and one which is well in accordance with the generalization for the whole of Slovakia that was found according to the first source used for the entire republic.

See also A. Prokeš, "Ueberkommene Siedlungsformen", *Die sozialökonomische Struktur der Landwirtschaft in der Tschechoslowakei*, red. V. Brdlík (Berlin 1938), pp 53–86.

DENMARK. The well known fact that Danish agricultural settlement in modern time has essentially the form of isolated farmsteads can easily be studied on the ordnance survey map. Cf also, for instance, K. Skovgaard, in *FAO Agricultural Studies*, 11 (Rome 1950), p. 50.

ESTONIA. As well as in the other Baltic countries, agricultural settlement in Estonia became to a great extent re-grouped into isolated farmsteads in connection with the land reform in the twenties. Even so, the background was one of relatively scattered settlement, as in the neighbouring Russian district of Pskov. No special enquiry has therefore been necessary to state that the median was safely below 100, at least until a few years ago.

FINLAND. The fact that Finnish agricultural settlement is essentially constituted by isolated farmsteads is well known in historical and geographical literature and can also be studied on the ordnance survey map. Even formerly nucleated villages in the Baltic coastland have to a great extent become dissolved in connection with reallotments and consolidations of land.

FRANCE. The main source for population data has been the population census of 1946. In this source, figures are given for total population in each community, and also a separate figure for the part of this population that does not live in the commune centre but in peripheral settlements, the *écarts*. These data could be combined with the coefficients for dispersion and concentration of settlement which are given in the *Atlas de France*, on the basis of the formula of DEMANGEON. By calculating the formula in the inverse sense, medians could thus be established for rural population, which have thereafter been reduced in accordance with the proportion found between rural and agricultural population in each department. Figures for the characteristic size of village territories have thereafter been calculated on the basis of the data on agricultural land contained in the agricultural census of 1929. The following values were thus established for each department.

Department	Village median		Department	Village median	
	In agricultural population	In agricultural land		In agricultural population	In agricultural land
Ain.	45	120	Hérault	680	1,450
Aisne	125	550	Ille et Vilaine	40	225
Allier	50	225	Indre	45	275
Alpes (Basses)	45	300	Indre et Loire	45	175
Alpes (Hautes) . . .	50	200	Isère	35	100
Alpes-Maritimes . . .	315	500	Jura	100	400
Ardèche.	50	100	Landes	45	70
Ardennes	160	1,000	Loir et Cher	45	175
Ariège	60	250	Loire	35	90
Aube	135	350	Loire (Haute)	50	150
Aude	275	600	Loire-Inférieure . . .	80	80
Aveyron	50	150	Loiret	85	375
Belfort	110	400	Lot.	55	150
Bouches-du-Rhône . .	40	80	Lot et-Garonne . . .	55	175
Calvados	35	150	Lozère	55	300
Cantal	40	170	Maine-et-Loire . . .	45	150
Charente	40	125	Manche.	40	100
Charente-Maritime . .	45	150	Marne	145	750
Cher	60	350	Marne (Haute). . . .	100	600
Corrèze	40	100	Mayenne	45	150
Corse	180	700	Meurthe-et-Moselle . .	80	400
Côte d'Or	100	600	Meuse	80	500
Côtes du Nord	30	70	Morbihan	35	65
Creuse	40	150	Moselle	100	500
Dordogne	50	200	Nièvre	35	200
Doubs	95	450	Nord	160	425
Drôme	40	125	Oise	120	525
Eure	50	250	Orne	35	150
Eure et Loire	85	450	Pas-de-Calais	135	350
Finistère	40	70	Puy-de-Dôme	50	125
Gard	290	700	Pyrénées (Basses) . .	65	175
Garonne (Haute) . .	45	175	Pyrénées (Hautes) . .	145	400
Gers	50	200	Pyrénées-Orientales .	400	650
Gironde.	45	80	Rhin (Bas)	240	500

Department	Village median		Department	Village median	
	In agri-cultural population	In agri-cultural land		In agri-cultural population	In agri-cultural land
Rhin (Haut)	180	425	Sèvres (Deux)	50	175
Rhône	40	80	Somme	125	600
Saône.	95	400	Tarn	45	160
Saône-et-Loire. . . .	45	150	Tarn-et-Garonne . . .	50	150
Sarthe	40	150	Var	350	800
Savoie	55	150	Vaucluse	50	100
Savoie (Haute). . . .	40	100	Vendée	70	200
Seine.	..	..	Vienne	45	175
Seine-Inférieure . . .	75	250	Vienne (Haute) . . .	40	125
Seine-et-Marne . . .	100	475	Vosges	125	275
Seine-et-Oise	125	425	Yonne	115	650

Among general literature on French rural settlement, see especially A. Demangeon, "Types de peuplement rural en France", *Annales de géographie*, 48 (1939), pp 1–21; P. de Saint-Jacob, "Le village: les conditions juridiques de l'habitat", *Annales de Bourgogne* 13 (1941), pp 169–202, *idem*, "La banlieue du village", *ibid.*, 18 (1946), pp 237–350. Cf also J. Nicod, "Problèmes de structure agraire en Lorraine", *Annales de géographie* 60 (1951), pp 337–348.

GERMANY. The post-war censuses have been drawn up according to somewhat different principles in Western and Eastern Germany. In the latter, the census of 1946 gives separate data for agricultural population in each commune. On the basis of this, medians could be estimated, for each *Landkreis*, by aid of ordnance survey maps. For Western Germany, the census of 1950 gives even less support to the calculation of medians of agricultural population. The publication for the whole Federal Republic gives only totals for each commune, without any occupational distribution at this level of geographical breakdown. Medians for rural population, estimated with the aid of map studies as in Eastern Germany, were thereafter converted by aid of the proportions of agricultural to rural population in large districts. This procedure was applied in Niedersachsen, Hessen, Baden-Württemberg, and Bayern. In Schleswig-Holstein, Nordrhein-Westfalen, and Rheinland-Pfalz, on the other hand, publications issued especially for these Länder give details for each village and hamlet which are of the same nature as the materials available from southern Europe and allow the same kind of calculations. These publications are *Verzeichnis der Gemeinden, Ortschaften und Wohnplätze in Schleswig-Holstein nach dem Gebietsstand vom 1. Januar 1953 und dem Bevölkerungsstand vom 13. September 1950* (Kiel 1953); *Amtliches Verzeichnis der Gemeinden und Wohnplätze (Ortschaften) in Nordrhein-Westfalen*, (Beiträge zur Statistik des Landes Nordrhein-Westfalen, Sonderreihe Volkszählung 1950, H. 2, cf also H. 5a); and *Volkszählung am 13. September 1950*, 12, "Die Wohnbevölkerung", 13, "Die Berufszählung" (Statistik von Rheinland-Pfalz, Band 12–13).

The medians found can be thus generalized by Länder (on the map each small district has been marked with the median found):

Schleswig-Holstein	100–650	Baden-Württemberg	300–500
Niedersachsen	300–700	Bayern	300–600
Nordrhein-Westfalen		Brandenburg.	200–500
Landesteil Nordrhein	50–300	Mecklenburg	200–500
Landesteil Westfalen	125–550	Sachsen-Anhalt	150–600
Rheinland-Pfalz	75–475	Thüringen.	100–500
Hessen	200–300	Sachsen.	200–800

Because of the double hypothesis underlying the computation in most German regions, corresponding figures for the size of village territories cannot be calculated with any great accuracy. The following estimates may give an idea as to the variations that are likely to occur.

Länder	Village size in	
	Total area	Arable land
Nordrhein-Westfalen, Rheinland-Pfalz	300– 600	100–200
Rest of Western Germany.	500–1,200	200–400
Eastern Germany	500–1,000	200–500

Cf also W. Christaller, "Eine neue Karte der ländlichen Siedlungsweise im Deutschen Reich", *Zeitschrift für Erdkunde*, 5 (1937), pp 734–737 (based on the census of 1933); *idem, Die ländliche Siedlungsweise im Deutschen Reich und ihre Beziehungen zur Gemeindeorganisation,* (Stuttgart & Berlin 1937); P. Hesse, *Grundprobleme der Agrarverfassung* (Stuttgart & Köln 1949); K. H. Schröder, "Die geographischen Grundlagen der Bevölkerungsverteilung im südwestlichen Deutschland", *Württemberg-Hohenzollern in Zahlen,* 2/3 (1948), pp. 81–88; Fr. Huttenlocher, "Funktionelle Siedlungstypen", *Berichte zur deutschen Landeskunde,* Band 7 (1949), pp 76–86, and A. Sievers, "Der Einfluss der Siedlungsformen auf das Wirtschafts- und Sozialgefüge des Dorfes", *Berichte über Landwirtschaft,* N. F., 29 (1942), pp. 1–52.

GREECE. The calculation of village medians was made on the basis of the population census of 1928. Partial data from the census of 1950 have become available later, for some districts. A repeated calculation on the basis of these showed essentially the same settlement situation as in 1928. The following results are entirely from the former source.

Aitolia kai Akarnania .	475	Ioannina	325	Prebeza	475
Argolis kai Korinthis .	625	Kaballa	1,350	Rhethymne	250
Arkadia	575	Kerkyra	600	Rhodope	550
Arte	550	Kefallenia	275	Samos	850
Attike kai boiotia . . .	1,475	Kozane . , , , , , ,	650	Serrai . . . . . , , ,	1,000
Achaia kai Elis	500	Kyklades	300	Trikkala.	675
Drama.	1,200	Lakonia	450	Phthiotis kai Phokis .	600
Evros	725	Larisa.	725	Phlorina.	675
Evboia.	625	Lassethioi	425	Chalkidike	625
Zakynthos	500	Lesbos	575	Chaniai	200
Eraklion	450	Messenia	600	Chios	850
Thessalonike	900	Pella	700		

The quotient of arable land is close to 1 hectare per person among the agricultural population. On the whole, therefore, village territories as calculated in arable land will be of the same magnitude as in population. If total area of the villages is considered, including rough grazings, then many of them must embrace tenths and even hundreds of square kilometers, although the scale will then vary much more than in the figures above.

HUNGARY. The *Recensement général de la population de 1930* (Publications statistiques hongroises, N.S., Vol. 83, 86, 95, 96), gives not only full specification of the rural population in all populated sites, however small they are. At the same time, it also gives a separate figure for the agricultural population of each village, hamlet, or isolated farmstead. In this case, therefore, the calculation of village medians of agricultural population can be made without using any hypotheses.

It may be mentioned that the total population figures for each district do not seem to have undergone any important change as late as in 1941; see on the census of that year L. Thirring, "Les résultats provisoires du recensement exécuté en Hongrie en 1941", *Revue hongroise de statistique* 19 (1941), pp 155–187. As late as in 1949, total population had changed relatively little.

The medians calculated for 1930 are as follows. Area figures have been calculated from the sources mentioned in Appendix 3.

District	Village median		
	In agricultural population	In total area	In arable area
Dunantul:			
Baranya	500	2,000	1,300
Fejér	975	4,000	2,900
Györ, Moson és Pozoni	825	3,100	2,150
Komárom és Esztergom	850	3,900	2,300
Somogy.	700	2,650	1,500
Sopron	775	2,400	1,575
Tolna	975	3,350	2,400
Vas	500	1,800	1,100
Veszprem	575	2,500	1,450
Zala	525	1,725	800
Alföld:			
Bács-Bodrog	1,700	5,700	4,500
Békés	2,800	8,500	6,800
Bihar.	1,525	5,300	3,800
Csanád, Arad és Torontál	1,725	4,800	4,100
Csongrád	1,325	4 400	3,100
Hajdu	4,250	13,700	8,850
Jász-Nagykun-Szolnok	2,400	8,100	6,300
Pest-Pilis-Solt-Kiskun	1,150	4 000	2,500
Szabolcs és Ung	1,100	3,200	2,450
Szatmar, Ugocsa és Bereg.	925	2,950	2,200
Eszak:			
Abauj-Torna	450	1,900	1,050
Borsod, Gömör és Kishont	925	3,700	1,900
Heves	1,675	5,200	3,100
Nógrád és Hont	600	2,500	1,300
Zemplén	900	3,100	1,750

Cf also L. Thirring, "Accroissement, densité et agglomération de la population dans les comitats, villes autonomes et régions de la Hongrie"/in Hungarian/, *Magyar statisztikai szemle* (1932), pp 1–16; A. N. J. den Hollander, "Het ontstaan der "tanya"-vestiging in de Groote Hongaarsche laagvlakte", *Tijdschrift van het K. Nederlandsch aardrijkskundig genootschap*, R. 2, Vol. 43:2 (Mar 1946), pp. 146–203, with rich bibliographical references; *Struktur und Verfassung der ungarischen Landwirtschaft* (Budapest 1937), especially p. 67 on "engineer villages"; I. Takács, "Die wirtschaftlichen und sozialen Folgen der Wiederbesiedlung der ungarischen Tiefebene im 18. Jahrhundert, Tanyasiedlung", *Ungarische Jahrbücher* 13 : 1/2, pp. 106 sqq. See also P. George, "Les transformations des campagnes hongroises", *Annales de géographie* (1951), pp. 199–209, on the recent plans for a regulation of agricultural settlement in Hungary.

ICELAND. The well-known character of Icelandic rural settlement, including almost nothing but scattered farmsteads, is mentioned, for instance, in the official yearbook *Iceland* (1946), p. 88.

IRELAND (EIRE). The main source has been the *Census of the population of Ireland 1951*, Vol. 1 (Dublin 1952), pp 18 sqq. It is there noted that "town and village population" includes all persons living in all villages down to the smallest "cluster of 20 houses or more". The latter means that practically all persons living in villages larger than 100 inhabitants are included among "town and village population".

Total town and village population was less than half the total population of Eire, or 48,4 per cent. The proportion varies from 66.3 per cent in Leinster to 19.7 per cent in Ulster. Because a considerable part of this "town and village population" must be urban, it can be concluded that the agricultural population mainly lives in settlements with less than 100 agricultural inhabitants. About half of the population of Eire is agricultural.

Essentially the same conclusions can be drawn on the basis of the *Census of Ireland, 1901. General topographical index to the townlands and towns of Ireland.* (Dublin 1904), which also includes Northern Ireland. This material also reflects the inherited organization of the countryside in small hamlets rather than in nucleated villages.

Cf also C. S. Smith, "A new deal for the Irish peasant", *The Farmer's Weekly* (London 1952), pp. 55–57.

ITALY. Medians of agricultural population have been calculated on the basis of the population census of 1936. Calculating medians of rural population was relatively easy, since the results are already summed up in size-classes of settled localities in the census publication. Urban agglomerations (except the agro-towns in the South) were taken out of the picture and medians were interpolated in the remaining material. The distribution between agro-towns and other urban agglomeration was made on the basis of the data on occupational distribution in the localities in question. The medians for agricultural population have thereafter been reduced in accordance with the ratio of agricultural to rural population in each province.

The corresponding data for area — both total and cultivated — were calculated on the basis of the *Catasto agrario* of 1929. Cultivated land in this connection means the item "seminativi e colture legnose" in the tables of the Catasto agrario.

In the following table, the provinces are listed in the same order as they have in the census publication, *i.e.* grouped into larger regional units and arranged in alphabetical order within each. The Istrian provinces are also included here, because the calculations for them gave interesting possibilities for checking against Yugoslav sources from the last years.

Provinces	Village median		
	In agricultural population	In total area	In cultivated area
Alessandria	150	300	200
Aosta	150	400	50
Asti	85	70	50
Cuneo	70	125 .	50
Novara	300	525	175
Torino	150	300	100
Vercelli	225	525	250
Genova	50	50	15
Imperia.	225	300	90
La Spezia	150	175	50
Savona	85	175	50
Bergamo	325	135	125
Brescia	325	400	175
Como.	175	250	50
Cremona	475	425	350
Mantova	65	60	50
Milano	425	425	350
Pavia	325	350	275
Sondrio.	250	600	30
Varese	250	425	125
Bolzano	60	300	20
Trento	300	800	75
Belluno.	150	375	25
Friuli (Udine)	225	575	200
Padova	40	25	20

Provinces	Village median		
	In agricultural population	In total area	In cultivated area
Rovigo	60	50	25
Treviso	50	50	25
Venezia	50	25	25
Verona	60	50	50
Vicenza	50	50	25
Carnaro (Fiume)	250	700	50
Gorizia	150	350	25
Istria (Pola)	75	150	50
Trieste	175	375	75
Bologna	65	75	50
Ferrara	65	50	50
Forli	35	25	25
Modena	50	50	25
Parma	50	75	50
Piacenza	50	75	50
Ravenna	65	50	50
Reggio nell'Emilia	50	50	25
Arezzo	60	75	50
Firenze	50	50	25
Grosseto	325	1,250	700
Livorno	350	525	175
Lucca	50	50	15
Massa e Carrara	125	150	25
Pisa	75	100	50
Pistoia	40	40	15
Siena	65	150	75
Ancona	65	50	50
Ascoli Piceno	65	50	50
Macerata	65	75	50
Pesaro e Urbino	50	75	50
Perugia	60	100	50
Terni	60	100	50
Frosinone	65	50	25
Littoria (Latina)	75	100	50
Rieti	200	450	200
Roma	1,750	3,750	2,100
Viterbo	1,750	3,600	2,650
Aquila degli Abruzzi	1,200	2,100	750
Campobasso	1,750	2,400	1,800
Chieti	450	400	300
Pescara	65	50	50
Teramo	65	50	50
Avellino	950	775	500
Benevento	750	700	525
Napoli	2,300	1,000	750
Salerno	900	950	425
Bari	13,400	11,700	5,100
Brindisi	6,300	7,300	6,900
Foggia	7,800	16,500	11,000
Ionio (Taranto)	5,700	9,200	6,900
Lecce	3,650	3,500	3,100
Matera	4,800	14,500	7,600
Potenza	2,100	4,200	1,900
Catanzaro	2,150	2,550	1,350
Cosenza	1,300	1,950	875
Reggio di Calabria	1,200	950	525
Agrigento	9,000	10,200	9,000
Caltanissetta	11,200	15,000	13,800
Catania	6,100	6,000	4,750
Enna	8,000	15,300	12,500
Messina	1,000	875	500
Palermo	4,900	6,100	4,700
Ragusa	5,100	5,900	5,700
Siracusa	9,300	14,200	12,700
Trapani	5,300	6,000	5,150
Cagliari	1,950	6,700	2,650
Nuoro	1,800	8,200	1,500
Sassari	1,050	4,550	950

Cf also N. Mazzocchi-Alemanni, "Insediamento umano, bonifica e riforma nei territori latifondistici", *Atti della XII riunione della Società Italiana di economia, demografia e statistica*, Vol. 4 (1950), and T. Storai de Rocchi, *Guida bibliografica allo studio dell'abitazione rurale in Italia* (Firenze 1950).

LATVIA. For the same general reasons as in Estonia, rural settlement in Latvia must be assumed to have included more dispersed than nucleated settlement, at least since the land reform in the twenties. This conclusion is supported by S. A. Udachin, *Zemel'naia reforma v Sovetskoi Latvii* (Riga 1948), especially pp 141 sq and 322 sqq.

LITHUANIA. Essentially the same conditions as in Estonia and Latvia made also the rural settlement of Lithuania to be essentially of a dispersed character. This impression is already supported by the population census of 1923. A relatively rich literature gives account of different stages in the development of Lithuanian settlement.

H. Mortensen, *Litauen, Grundzüge einer Landeskunde* (Hamburg 1926), pp 104 sqq, shows that in some regions, isolated farmsteads were not the result of modern developments but inherited from remote ages. W. Essen, *Die ländlichen Siedlungen in Litauen* (Leipzig 1931), Textband, p. 83, shows the dissolution of nucleated villages in many areas in modern time, as a result of a deliberate policy. On the historical background, see also W. Conze, *Agrarverfassung und Bevölkerung in Litauen und Weissrussland* (Leipzig 1940), especially pp 18 and 53 sqq.

LUXEMBOURG has not been investigated separately. On the map, medians have been interpolated in accordance with surrounding parts of Belgium, France, and Germany.

NETHERLANDS. Medians of agricultural population were derived from the population census of 1947: *12e volkstelling, Annex woningtelling, 31 mei 1947*, (Utrecht 1952). Corresponding figures for village areas were calculated on the basis of the agricultural census of 1950, *Landbouwtelling 1950* (Utrecht 1952). The following values were found, by provinces.

Province	Village median		
	In agricultural population	In total agricultural area	In arable land
Groningen	325	450	300
Friesland	300	450	50
Drenthe	300 .	425	200
Overijssel	40	60	20
Gelderland	40	40	15
Utrecht	325	375	50
Noordholland	500	475	150
Zuidholland	550	425	125
Zeeland	375	525	375
Noordbrabant	375	400	200
Limburg	250	275	150

H. J. Keuning, "L'habitat rural aux Pays-Bas", *Tijdschrift van het K. aardrijkskundig genootschap*, Vol. 55 (1938), p. 636, notes the modern trend towards increased dispersion of rural settlement.

NORWAY. The essentially dispersed character of Norwegian rural settlement is well known from general literature on the country. See especially *Økonomiskgeografisk atlas over Norge ...* utarb. ... P. Nissen (Kristiania 1921), p. 43.

POLAND. The great changes in territory and administrative divisions of
Poland makes it difficult to establish the settlement map here on the same basis
as in other countries. No post-war census is available to give the detail of the
present settlement situation. A combination has had to be made of information
from various older sources, with all the reservations this procedure calls for.

Data for the central, eastern and southern parts of modern Poland have
been based on the population censuses of 1920 and 1930; for the western parts,
taken over on a preliminary basis from Germany, medians have been constructed
on the basis of the German census of 1939, following the same general procedure
as in most regions of Western Germany.

The Polish census of 1920 gives tables on size-classes of villages, very much
like the Italian census of 1936 does. On the basis thereof, medians for rural
and agricultrual population were deducted according to the same principles
as in most other countries. These medians have thereafter been adjusted upwards
on the basis of the population data of 1930, assuming largely the same kind of
distribution as in 1920.

These medians, roughly representing the pre-war situation, are better than
nothing. With reference to the present situation, they give mainly a vague
indication on the material recent settlement policy has had to start from and
probably not entirely managed to get free of.

The territorial division of Poland thereby followed was that in the Agricultural Statistics, 1947 (*Statistics of Poland*, Ser. D, No 11). The subdivision
again became altered, especially in the western parts of the country, around
1950. On the district basis, the following medians were found (the districts of
1947 having been brought together by combining data on their components
in the sources used; figures representing agricultural population):

Kraków	800	Warszawa	200	Wrocław	300
Kielce	300	Lublin	425	Szczecin	250
Łódz	200	Rzeszów	1,200	Poznań	225
Bydgoszcz	225	Katowice	350	Olsztyn	150
Białystok	225				

Atlas statistique de la République Polonaise (Warszawa 1930), in its Table 2,
summarizes the data on village size in the census of 1921, and thereby indicates
an over-all median of a little over 400 at that time.

Concentration indices, similar to those of Demangeon, have been calculated
and published by J. Pawlowski and A. Czekalski, "L'habitat rural en Pologne",
Comptes rendus du Congrès International de Géographie (Warsaw, 1934), T. 3.

Especially interesting for the historical background is S. Szulc, *Appréciation
des données statistiques relatives á l'état de la population de l'ancien Royaume de
Pologne* (Warszawa 1920), pp 183 sqq, showing a clear predominance of small
villages over both large villages and dispersed settlement forms. If medians were
calculated on the basis of this material, they would certainly be considerably
below 500 in all districts with the possible exception of the district of Lublin.

Cf also B. Zaborski, *Über Dorfformen in Polen und ihre Verbreitung*, übers. v.
F. Schmidbauer (Breslau 1930).

PORTUGAL. Detailed figures for agricultural population were taken from the
census of 1940. Figures for cultivated area cannot be obtained except for the
country as a whole and even so, they are partly based on estimates. The size
of village territories has therefore had to be expressed only in total area, based
on data borrowed from E. A. Lima Basto, *Inquérito económico-agrícola.* (Lisboa
1935), Table 12 in the appendices. According to the same author, p. 27, most of
the land in Portugal is productive in one way or another. The figures for village
size in total area should therefore not exceed those in useful area very much,
except in mountain districts like Bragança and Castelo Branco.

| District | Village median | | District | Village median | |
	In agricultural population	In total area		In agricultural population	In total area
Aveiro	100	150	Leiria	125	200
Beja	400	3,000	Lisboa	150	300
Braga	40	50	Portalegre	475	3,100
Bragança	250	1,400	Porto.	60	75
Castelo Branco. . . .	375	1,550	Santarem	225	725
Coimbra	125	250	Setubal	200	1,300
Evora	375	3,000	Viana do Castelo . .	50	75
Faro	150	500	Vila Real	200	500
Guarda	250	900	Viseu	150	350

The general character of Portuguese settlement can also be studied on a map called *Distribuição da população de Portugal*, elaborated under the direction of O. RIBEIRO and on the *Carta corográfica de Portugal*.

From detailed maps, as well as from various special treatments on the subject, it can be seen that Portuguese settlement has recently tended to become more and more dispersed. This impression is largely confirmed by an enquiry included in the 1911 census: *Censo da população de Portugal ao 1º de dezembre de 1911*, P. 6, "Censo das povoações" (Lisboa 1917). If medians of villages are established on the basis of this source, they almost always turn out somewhat higher than on the basis of the 1940 census.

In southern Portugal, the medians tend to conceal the contrast between very large villages and scattered farms around them; in fact, the median is here an abstract expression and there are not many villages on the magnitude it indicates.

RUMANIA. For most of the Rumanian territory, village medians have been calculated on the basis of the 1941 census: *Recenseământul general al României din 1941, 6 aprile, Date sumare provizorii* (Bucureşti 1944). The figures for rural population have been checked against those of 1948, according to A. Golopentia and D. C. Georgescu, "Populatia Republicii Populare Române la 25 ianuarii 1948, Rezultatele provizorii ale recensământului" *Probleme economice*, Nr 2 (1948). This publication shows that in most districts there were only small differences between the figures from the two censuses. The ratio between agricultural and rural population was found separately for each district, through a comparison between the latter census and the agricultural census of 1948: A. Golopentia and P. Onica "Recensământul agricol din Republica Populara Română, 25 Ianuarie 1948, Resultate provizorii", *Probleme economice*, 3 (1948).

Because of the smallness of the districts, the medians were introduced on the map with some generalization. For the districts which were ceded to Hungary when the 1941 census was taken, and later restored, medians have been constructed by means of interpolation, on the basis of the values for surrounding districts in both Rumania and Hungary. The medians found were within the limits shown below; corresponding village medians for agricultural area have been calculated, with even more generalization, on the basis of data in the agricultural census of 1948.

| Group of districts | Village median | |
	In agricultural population	In agricultural area
Moldova Carpathians	900–1,200	900
Muntenia and Oltenia Carpathians	600–1,500	900
Seret- and Prut-valleys	775–1,900	1,500
Bucovina	1,600–2,600	1,500
Transylvanian Plateau	950–2,300	1,500
Danube and Tisza valleys	950–2,500	2,500
Dobrogea	1,300–1,775	3,000

SPAIN. The medians for agricultural population are founded on the population census of 1940. For the area medians, area figures were taken from the statistical yearbook of Spain, 1950 (data referring to 1948).

Province	Village medians		
	In agricultural population	In total area	In arable and horticultural area
Alava	200	575	225
Albacete	1,550	8,450	4,750
Alicante	1,050	1,650	875
Almería.	800	2,500	1,100
Avila.	875	2,650	1,225
Badajoz	2,450	9,700	4,275
Baleares	950	2,550	1,325
Barcelona.	850	950 .	550
Burgos	300	1,250	725
Caceres.	1,700	8,200	2,550
Cadiz	3,200	7,300	2,800
Castellón	2,150	5,600	2,400
Ciudad Real	5,500	32,000	14,700
Cordoba	4,850	11,700	7,100
La Coruña	75	100	50
Cuenca	1,050	6,875	2,725
Gerona	200	400	225
Granada	1,400	3,000	1,700
Guadalajara.	475	2,100	1,025
Guipuzcoa	325	525	150
Huelva	1,925	9,100	1,900
Huesca	400	3,650	950
Jaén	3,800	9,200	5,200
León	375	1,125	425
Lerida	625	3,750	1,400
Logroño	950	2,850	1,125
Lugo	75	150	50
Madrid	2,400	6,250	2,950
Malaga	2,050	3,450	1,700
Murcia	1,625	3,925	2,450
Navarra	800	3,300	1,250
Orense	150	225	50
Oviedo	75	175	50
Palencia	525	2,525	1,725
Pontevedra	100	75	50
Salamanca	625	2,350	1,350
Santander.	300	525	75
Segovia.	475	1,875	1,250
Sevilla	4,750	12,800	8,050
Soria	325	2,350	650
Tarragona	1,200	2,875	1,050
Teruel	725	4,750	1,300
Toledo	1,325	3,400	3,100
Valencia	3,700	5,150	3,225
Valladolid	900	2,950	2,525
Vizcaya.	150	225	50
Zamora.	350	1,125	725
Zaragoza	1,300	5,000	2,400

In cases like Murcia, where a great many villages belong to an urban commune, it has been important to count these villages separately, despite their administrative ties to the city. From the viewpoint of our enquiry, Murcia is *not* a huge agrotown; the most distant village within the territory of the city is situated at 25 kilometres from the nucleated urban center, which includes only a minority of the population of the administrative city.

See also, for instance, G. Niemeier, *Siedlungsgeographische Untersuchungen in Niederandalusien* (Hamburg 1935), p. 25, where it is mentioned that in this area, there is generally one nucleated settlement on every 130 square kilometers (13,000 hectares); thus, the average distance between these centers is about 11.5 kilometers. Most of the population of the area, or 86,7 per cent, lives in 242 nucleated settlements, and only 13.3 per cent in dispersed settlement.

SWEDEN. The 1950 census of population in Sweden is the first of its kind to give account of the character of the settlement, by containing data on agricultural villages with more than 200 inhabitants. For assessing the situation in various parts of the country, a combination was made between the data published thus far, part of the unpublished primary returns, and the settlement map by G. ENEQUIST in *Atlas över Sverige*. This enquiry made clear that dispersed settlement, in the sense of this book (medians under 100 inhabitants of agricultural population) dominates in almost all regions of the country. The exceptions are part of Dalarne, the coastward parts of Norrbotten, and, possibly, the island of Öland. In no district the median was found to be over 200.

SWITZERLAND. As in parts of Germany, the village medians have had to be estimated on the basis of medians for communes (calculated from data in the population census of 1941). From these, village medians were approximately constructed by aid of the map communicated by CH. BIERMANN, in the *Comptes rendus du congrès international de géographie* (Warsaw, 1934). The following values were thus found:

Under 100, in Aargau, both Appenzell, Luzern, St Gallen, and the Alpine parts of Canton Bern;
150 in Solothurn, Thurgau, Ticino, and the Jura part of the Canton Bern;
200 in Basel-Landschaft, Neuchâtel, Nidwalden, Obwalden, Schwyz, and Zug;
250 in Glarus;
300 in Fribourg, Genève, Graubünden, Schaffhausen, and Vaud;
400 in the central parts of Canton Bern;
450 in Zürich;
500 in Valais.

Cf. also E. Winkler and others, *Das Schweizer Dorf* (Zürich 1941).

U.S.S.R. For most of the territories of the Soviet Union, the most recent census material which is available in detail is that of 1926. Although this is a quarter of a century before the time the map should refer to, there are sufficient reasons for believing in the survival of the main features of this settlement structure to include these data on the map. In the census of 1926, the calculation of medians for rural population has been facilitated by the fact that those who made and published the census were interested in this feature; even more than in the Italian census of 1936, the tabulations make it easy to interpolate the medians. At this time, furthermore, most of the rural population was agricultural, so that the reduction of the medians for rural population into medians for agricultural population is a safer operation here than in most other cases. The census itself has made the distinction between urban and rural settlement. This distinction was not based only on the size of the places, but also on qualitative criteria in their general character and occupational composition. Especially in the southeast there are many big agricultural villages which are greater than the smaller cities.

For the territories taken over by the Soviet Union from Germany, Poland, and Czechoslovakia, the medians have been calculated in the same way as described under each one of these countries. The Baltic countries have been dealt with separately, in the alphabetical list of countries above. Formerly Rumanian Bessarabia (now parts of Moldova and Ukraina) has been supposed to have medians between 1,000 and 2,000 agricultural inhabitants, in analogy with surrounding parts of Ukraina and Rumania. This assumption is justified by data in a publication called *Dicţionarul statistic al Basarabiei* (Chişinau 1923). Although based on Russian census returns from the period around 1900, it claims to have been brought up to date.

The following medians were found, by large districts and autonomous republics (ASSR) respectively.

RSFSR:

Arkhangel'sk	175	Vologda	175
Komi	350	Severo-Dvina	175
Karelskaia ASSR	100	Leningrad	150
Murmansk	125	Novgorod	175
Pskov	75	Cherepovetsk	150
Briansk	600	Smolensk	175
Vladimir	350	Ivanovo	150
Kaluga	300	Kostroma	125
Moskva	250	Nizhegorod (Gor'kiĭ)	650
Riazan	950	Tver (Kalinin)	200
Tula	425	IAroslavl'	125
Voronezh	1,850	Kursk	1,225
Orel'	500	Tambov	1,650
Orenburg (Chkalov)	825	Penza	1,550
Samara (Kuĭbyshev)	1,600	Tatarskaia ASSR	875
Ul'ianov	1,700	Chuvashskaia	625
Astrakhan	1,225	Kalmytskaia	350
Saratov	1,550	Volga-German ASSR	1,825
Stalingrad	750	Votskaia ASSR	300
Viatka (Kirov)	150	Mari ASSR	300
Ural'	550	Bashkirskaia ASSR	600
Krymskaia ASSR	300	Dagestanskaia ASSR	600
North Caucasus	3,000		

Within North Caucasus (small districts):

Armavir	5,600	Shuchtinsko-Donetskiĭ	750
Don	3,150	Adygeĭsko-Cherkesskaia	1,050
Maĭkop	4,500	Kabardino-Balkarskaia	2,700
Stavropol'	5,600	Severo-Ossetinskaia	3,150
Taganrog	850	Chechenskaia	950
Donets	550	Ingushskaia	1,975
Black Sea distr.	625	Karachaevskaia	3,150
Kuban	8,500	Cherkesskaia	1,350
Sal'skiĭ	4,500		
Sunzha	3,600		
Terskiĭ	4,950		

Ukraina:

Polesskiĭ	1,225	Volynia	1,110
Pravoberezhnyĭ	1,700	Lwow	1,300
Levoberezhnyĭ	1,475	Tarnopol	1,400
Stepnoĭ	1,650	Stainislawow	1,450
Dnepropetrovskiĭ	1,700	Uzhgorod	1,450
Gornopromyshlennyĭ	1,000		

Transcaucasia:

Azerbaĭdzhan	525
Armeniia	950
Gruziia	750

Belorussia:

Minsk	225	Polotsk	175
Bobruisk	400	Rechitsa	650
Borisov	275	Slutsk	500
Vitebsk	125		
Gomel'	700	Wilno	175
Kalinin	325	Białystok	225
Mogilev	400	Nowogrodek	250
Mozyr	425	Poleskie	600
Orsha	300		

All these districts are those mentioned in the sources used. Much of this administrative subdivision has been changed later. For close comparisons with modern conditions, it would therefore be necessary to reconstitute the present subdivisions from the small districts mentioned in the sources.

For the development that may have taken place later, it is of interest to have the general demographic trends in mind. Some data from the 1939 census are included in the *Sotsialisticheskoe stroitel'stvo Soiuza SSR (1933–38 gg), Statisticheskiĭ sbornik* (Moskva & Leningrad 1939), others in B. Plaetschke, "Ergebnisse der vorjährigen sowjetrussischen Volkszählung", *Petermans geographische Mitteilungen* (1940). There had taken place a decrease in rural population of a few per cent, reflected by a change of the same order of size in the RSFSR, but the decrease was much greater in Ukraina (to 83.5 per cent of the 1926 figure), and a weak increase in Belorussia and a strong one in the Caucasian and most of the Asian republics.

Area medians were calculated on the basis of data referring to 1939, taken from the *Sotsialisticheskoe sel'skoe khoziaistvo SSSR (1939)*, which also has data on kolkhozy etc. However, the administrative divisions have already changed in many cases, and some estimations have had to be made. The following data have been calculated (village medians in area of sown arable land):

RSFSR:

Arkhangel'sk	100	Saratov		2,250
Voronezh	2,250	Stalingrad		2,175
Ivanovo	200	Tula		600
Kirov	125	IAroslavl'		100
Kursk	925	Bashkir	ASSR	900
Moskva	150	Kalmuk	„	600
Orel	900	Komi	„	150
Riazan	1,050	Dagestan	„	350
Smolensk	175	Karel	„	35
Tambov	1,400	Crimea	„	850
Chkalov	5,000	Mari	„	350
Vologda	100	Volga German		6,150
Gor'kiĭ	675	Udmurt	„	575
Kalinin	150	Mordvin	„	800
Kuĭbyshev	1,925	Tatar		1,250
Leningrad	100	Chuvash	„	550
Murmansk	50			
Penza	1,975	Northern Caucasus		2,700

Belorussia	250
Ukraina	1,800
Azerbaĭdzhan	400
Armeniia	600
Gruziia	375

On sown areas at this time, see also *Posevnye ploshchadi SSSR* (Moskva 1938). On Russian settlement before the collectivization of agriculture, see A. A. Kofoed, *Russkoe zemleustroĭstvo* (Sankt Peterburg 1914); A. I. Gozulov *Morfologiia naseleniia, Opyt izucheniia stroeniia osnovnykh svoĭstv nasleniia Sev. Kav. Kraia po dannym trech narodnykh perepiseĭ – 1926, 1920 i 1897–gg* (Rostov na Donu 1929), describing the huge villages in Northern Caucasus; and IA. Kis'liakoŭ, *Pasiolki (Optimum terytorii i efekt zemleŭparadkavan'nia)* (Minsk 1928; with a summary in local German), showing the attempts of the rural engineers of the twenties to solve the settlement problems along lines which implied less centralization than later Soviet policy.

On Soviet settlement policy during and after the collectivization, see B. Plaetschke, "Beseitigung der Einzelhöfe und Streusiedlungen in der Sowjetunion", *Zeitschrift der Gesellschaft für Erdkunde zu Berlin* (1940),pp. 204–210; V. Ivanov, "La reconstruction et la transformation des agglomérations rurales en U.R.S.S.", *Problèmes économiques* (Paris 1949), No 101, pp 20 sq; and A. Pavlov, "Le regroupement des kolkhoz", *Etudes soviétiques* (Paris 1950), No 28, Aug., pp 72 sqq. Cf also article by N. Khrushchev in *Pravda* (Moskva 1950), Apr. 25.

UNITED KINGDOM. For Northern Ireland, no special enquiry has been necessary' since that area obviously has essentially the same settlement structure and settlement history as Eire, as shown, *i.a.*, by the census of 1901, quoted above under Ireland. Cf also J. M. Mogey, *Rural life in Northern Ireland* (London 1947), p. 15, stating that the old hamlets – which were only small clusters of houses – have gone and that isolated farmsteads are now the dominating feature.

For England, Wales, and Scotland, the census returns on population refer only to "civil parishes". On the basis of such data in the 1931 census, which was the latetst available with such detail when the research was made for the map, medians for rural population could be calculated for the civil parishes. This, as a rule, does not reflect the settlement pattern. On the other hand, in areas where the civil parishes are small, their size indicates the possible maximum for the size of villages. This is the case in some of the counties where other sources show that village settlement still prevails, and in these cases the medians for civil parishes could be assumed to be only a little higher than the village medians. The median for civil parishes lies below 200 in Rutland, and below 300 in Anglesey, Huntingdon, Pembroke, Chester, Westmorland, Devon, Hereford, Lincoln, Radnor, Northampton, Northumberland, Oxford, Suffolk, and Yorkshire East and North. Most of the designations on the map have however been founded on the maps in *The Land of Britain*, by L. Dudley Stamp and others, which indicate the degree of dispersion of settlement as a whole. These maps show that dispersed settlement is prevalent in a great many English and all the Welsh counties, as well as in most of Scotland. A number of counties in eastern England have been shown as having medians between 100 and 200, because on the one hand the maps show that nucleated villages still play a considerable part, while on the other hand the medians for civil parishes are too low to allow the hypothesis of the median for agricultural settlement to lie over 200 inhabitants. Only two counties near London may eventually be assumed to have medians over 200, but this detail it was not possible to represent on the map.

The relative smallness of English villages is to some extent due to the fact that the agricultural population of the country is less dense than on the Continent. In Wales and Scotland the dispersed character of agricultural settlement is largely an original feature, but in part at least of western and central England, old nucleated villages have declined; see, *e.g.*, M. W. Beresford, "The lost villages of Mediaeval England", *The Geographical Journal* (1951, June,) pp 129–149.

See also B. M. Swainson,"The dispersion and agglomeration of rural settlement in Somerset", *Geography* (1944); H. E. Bracey *Social provision in rural Wiltshire* (London 1952); F. H. W. Green, "Rural and coastal settlement in the Moray Firth Lowlands", *Scottish Geographical Magazine* (Edinburgh 1936), and *Scientific Survey of South-Eastern Scotland* (Edinburgh 1951), p. 135.

YUGOSLAVIA. In continuation of a relatively long statistical tradition, the Yugoslav population census of 1948 gives figures for the population of every settled point, including hamlets and isolated farmsteads. Medians for rural population calculated on the basis thereof could be converted into medians for agricultural population with relatively great certainty, because the proportion of agricultural population is high outside the towns. Area medians have been estimated on the basis of the current data on land such as quoted below in Appendix 3. The following values were found for population and area medians.

Region	Village median	
	In agricultural population	In agricultural land
Old Serbia	900	900
Vojvodina	2,600	5,000
Kosmet District	600	500
East Croatia	600	1,000
West Croatia excl. Istria	150	250
Istria	75	100
Slovenia	200	350
Bosnia-Hercegovina	600	1,000
Macedonia	600	1,000
Montenegro	200	500

On the history of Serbian settlement, see above all the publication series called *Naselja*, published by the Serbian Academy of Science, in a large number of volumes over a long series of years. For Croatia and Vojvodina, see Fr. Vaniček, *Spezialgeschichte der Militärgrenze* (Wien 1875), giving account of the foundation of big villages on the Danube plain as part of the defense plans of the 18th century.

SOURCES TO TABLE 1

AUSTRIA. The estimates for the table are founded upon the opinions of local experts as expressed directly to the author.

BELGIUM. The number of plots of land in each size-class is indicated in the agricultural census of 1950. On the basis of this, the following structural data have been derived.

Size of holding, ha	Of all holdings, each size-class has		Of holdings 1 hectare and over, each size-class has	
	Per cent of area	Per cent of plots	Per cent of area	Per cent of plots
– 1	5.7	28.2	—	—
1– 3	9.6	16.2	10.4	22,2
3– 5	11.0	13.9	11.7	19.4
5– 10	22.5	20.6	23.8	29.1
10– 20	24.5	14,5	25.5	20.4
20– 30	10.3	3.7	11.1	5.1
30– 50	7.4	1.8	7.9	2.4
50–100	6.6	0.9	7.2	1.1
Over 100	2.2	0.2	2.4	0.2
TOTAL.	100.0	100.0	100.0	100.0

The percentage of area and plots obviously lie closer to each other at the median of size of holdings (10.3 hectares) in the latter series than in the former.

Cf. A. Martens, "L'étendue moyenne des pieces de terre par provinces", *Sillon belge* (Bruxelles 1952), Vol. 22, (1952) No 510, p. 9.

BULGARIA. The main source available is the farm census of 1934. On the basis of its data, it could be estimated that most of the land in Bulgaria would be in need of consolidation. At present, the land in need of consolidation should be somewhat more than the private sector, since it cannot be assumed that all the co-operative farms have solved the consolidation problem in their villages.

On the basis of the 1934 census, it can also be noted that fragmentation then touched mainly the arable land. The average number of plots per farm was much lower in the meadows and only in the highest size-classes was as high as 5 per farm. The number of plots of vineyards and horticultural land seldom was over 2 per farm.

Cf also the *Statistique de la propriété foncière*.... (Sofia 1908), and the farm census of 1926. It appears as if fragmentation were slowly increasing; the total number of plots in arable land was 5.5 million in 1897, 6.9 million in 1908, and 10.1 million in 1934. Cf also N. Kondov, "Promeni v razmera i razdrobenostla na Bulgarskoto stopanstvo", *Narodno stopanstvo* (Sofia 1946), No 1, pp 32–45; the total number of plots was 11.5 million in 1926, 11.9 million in 1934, and 12.2 million in 1946 (on a somewhat expanded territory). In any case, the increase in the number of plots cannot be said to be superior to the increase in the number of farms, so the number of plots per farm may not have changed much.

CZECHOSLOVAKIA A. Öhm, *Scelování pozemků jako účinný prostředek k odstranění všech nedostatků a závad dnešního nezdravého rozdělení půdy a tím zajištění pevné výrobní základny* (Brno 1931), gives figures for the total number of plots:

Bohemia, Moravia, and Silesia	18 million
Slovakia	17 „
Carpatho-Ruthenia	4 „

Total 39 million plots, of which 35 million in the present territory of Czechoslovakia. Dividing the total holding area with this number, the average size of plot is calculated to 0.36 ha. A number of maps give model examples of bad layout. A table is given (pp 42 sqq) of consolidation activities in Moravia-Silesia over the period 1892–1930. 251 communities were consolidated, including 144,000 hectares of which 112,000 were touched by the consolidations. This land belonged to 36,000 owners, and 334,600 plots were reduced to 72,000. 75,000 kilometers of borderlines were reduced to 16,000 km, and thereby 4,680 hectares of land were recovered, which is 4.17 per cent of the area touched by the consolidations. 97 of these communes were consolidated before World War I and 154 in the twenties.

More or less the same information is also communicated by A. Krčmár, "La ricomposizione della proprietà fondiaria nella repubblica Cecoslovacca", *Rivista del catasto e dei servizi tecnici erariali* (Rome 1938), No 2. An example is quoted of a farm of 14 hectares that had 845 plots of land.

Partly the same basic data are also communicated by V. Brdlík, *Die sozial-ökonomische Struktur der Landwirtschaft in der Tschechoslowakei* (Berlin 1938), pp. 98 sqq. More than 70 per cent of all farms had more than 5 plots, 45 per cent over 10 plots. It is stressed that fragmentation was worse in Slovakia than in the Czech provinces. The average distance from the farmstead to each plot (of arable land and meadow) is said to be about 1 kilometer in Bohemia, 1.25–1.40 km in Moravia-Silesia, and about 1.6–2.3 km in Slovakia and Carpatho-Ruthenia.

As regards the need of consolidation, V. Novák, *Úkoly pozemkových úprav zvláště scelovacich v CSR* (Prague 1933), estimates it to 75 per cent. Even a late writer, V. Fábry, *Agricultural laws of the Czechoslovak Republic* (Prague 1949), p. 23, indicates that in Bohemia only, over 2 million ha were in need of consolidation. The estimate in the table has tried to take into account the impact of the State and collective farms; the older structure data may be regarded as basically characteristic of the remaining private sector.

DENMARK. The consolidations of the 19th century did away with most of the fragmentation in Denmark and left very little to be done in this respect, as far as the standards of that century are decisive. Some places will however still need a better layout. More important for the estimate is the fact that Southern Jutland, which was integrated into Denmark in 1920, has a considerable amount of its land in fragmented villages in need of consolidation.

FRANCE. The available basic data on French land fragmentation are from 1891, as still quoted in *Le remembrement rural en France* (Paris, Ministère de l'agriculture, 1951). At that time, the total holding area of 52 million hectares was divided into 151 million cadastre plots and 62 million "îlots de propriété", the latter being most close to the concept of "fragment" in comparable sources from other countries. The latter concept gives an average size of plot of 0.85 ha, and an average of 18 plots per landowner. The average size of an îlot de propriété varied from 0.20 ha in the department of Meuse to 17.4 ha in the Landes; it was, for instance, 0.36 ha in Puy-deDome, 0.65 ha in the Marne, 0.80 ha in Drôme, 1.6 ha in Gers, and 4.2 ha in Morbihan (Bretagne). In a group of some 20

departments around Paris and in the East and North the average size was below
1 ha, in most of these departments about 0.6; in the West and the Center, it
varies between 1 and 5 ha; in the South West, except the Landes, it is less than
2 ha, and in the Rhône valley less than 1 ha.

Cf also Fr. A. Sargent, "Fragmentation of French land", *Land Economics*
(Madison 1952), pp 218 sqq, and J. M. Schmerber, *La réorganisation foncière en
France, Le remembrement rural* (Paris 1949).

FINLAND. The estimate is founded on data communicated by K. U. Pihkala
and S. Suomela, "Land fragmentation and measures of consolidation in Finland",
International Journal of Agrarian Affairs (Oxford 1952), No 4, pp 15 sqq.

GERMANY. Basic data on land fragmentation in Western Germany are contained in the *Statistik der Bundesrepublik Deutschland, Bd 21, H. 2, Grössen- und
Besitzverhältnisse der land- und forstwirtschaftlichen Betriebe, Ergebnisse der
landwirtschaftlichen Betriebszählung vom 22. Mai 1949* (Wiesbaden 1951), Table
24. Regional tables for each of the *Länder* and the larger administrative sub-
divisons show that fragmentation is worst in Rheinland-Pfalz but important also in Bayern, Hessen and Baden-Württemberg, and less so, though
far from non-existant, in Nordrhein-Westfalen, Niedersachsen, and Schleswig-
Holstein. These observations are on the whole in accordance with observations
made in the twenties and thirties. The latter have also been unanimous in
stating that fragmentation was of limited importance in most of the areas that
are now Eastern Germany. See, for instance, H. Deck, *Die Entwicklung der Grundstückszusammenlegung seit der Stein-Hardenberg'schen Reform* (Bleicherode am
Harz 1939), and K. Sperber, "Stand und Entwicklung der wirtschaftlichen
Umlegung der Grundstücke in der Rheinprovinz", *Berichte über Landwirtschaft*,
N. F. Sonderheft 123, p. 51.

Map examples of fragmentation in north-western Germany before the consolidations of the 19th century are communicated by O. August, "Umkreis von
Halle um 1840, 1820 und vorher", *Petermanns geographische Mitteilungen* (1952),
pp. 232 – 244 and Plates 23 and. 24

Calculations of the economic effect of fragmentation, based on German material, have been attempted by H. G. Bohte, *Die Bodenzersplitterung und ihr
Einfluss auf die betriebswirtschaftlichen Verhältnisse in Deutschland* (Kiel 1928),
especially p. 132, where the need of consolidation in Germany is estimated at
$5^3/_4$–6 million ha, and H. Priebe, *Landarbeit heute und morgen* (Hamburg and
Berlin 1953), p. 67.

GREECE. The agricultural census of 1929 also gives data on land fragmentation. At that time, the 3.88 million ha agricultural area (excluding the rough
grazings) were divided into 5.35 million plots on 953,000 farms, which indicates
an average size of plot of 0.72 ha, and an average number of plots per farm of
5.6. The average size of plot was about 0.5 ha on the islands, close to the national
average in Thrace, Macedonia, and the Peloponnesos, somewhat larger in
Central Greece and Epirus, and over 1 ha in Thessalia. These data give only
a vague impression of the fact that fragmentation is a problem above all in the
old Kingdom and much less so in the regions annexed at later stages.

The latest Greek farm census, of 1950, which is still unpublished, also contains
data on fragmentation, indicating an even smaller average size of plot and an
even higher number of plots per farm.

Some inside glimpses can be seen from special literature as, for instance,
A. A. Diamantopoulos, *Ē pedias tou Mornou* (Athens 1940), p. 36, N. E. Aivalio-
takis, *O kampos tēs Messenias kai ai oreinai lekanai avtou* (Athens 1942), p. 93,
where division of inheritance is indicated as the main cause of fragmentation,
idem, Ai oreinai lekanai Pheneou-Stymphalias (Athens 1941), p. 39, and N. I.
Anagnostopoulos, *O kampos tōn Serrōn* (Athens 1937), p. 79.

G. Xenos, *To agrotikon ktēmatologion tēs Ellados* (Athens 1935), p. 10 sq, states that the worst stages of fragmentation may lead to abandoning of cultivation of small plots at great distances from the village center.

HUNGARY. *Publications statistiques hongroises*, N.S. 99, "Les conditions de la propriété foncière en Hongrie dans l'année 1935" (Budapest 1936), gives data on land fragmentation: 9,56 million ha farm land were divided into 6.42 million plots with an average size of 1.44 ha (which includes pasture land). The average was 1.16 ha in the areas west of the Danube, 1.27 in the northern region and 2.14 on the vast plain in the south-east (Alföld). Of 1.9 million holdings, almost half the number were en-bloc holdings and only a little over half the number was divided into two or more plots. Because of the settlement system, with the huge villages dominating the picture, the need for consolidation may have been greater than these figures seem to indicate.

The post-war land reform is likely to have increased the importance of land fragmentation, but the collectivization is likely to have done away with some part of it again.

IRELAND. C. S. Smith, "A new deal for the Irish tenant", *The farmer's weekly* (London 1952), pp 55–77, mentions as a not quite unknown feature that single pieces of unfenced land are scattered over many miles and yet farmed by the same owner. Although there are no statistics on Irish fragmentation, it seems not to be entirely non-existant.

ITALY. The estimate in the table is founded on data in Fr. Simonatti, "La ricomposizione delle proprietà frammentate", *Rivista del catasto e dei servizi tecnici erariali* (Rome 1937), pp 606 sqq, especially p. 622. A cadastred area of 19 million hectares was then divided into 6.4 million ownership units and 33 million plots, thus averaging 0.6 ha per plot and close to 6 plots per ownership unit.

See also G. Medici, "Il numero degli articoli contenuti nei ruoli delle imposte e la statistica della proprietà fondiaria", *La riforma sociale* (1930), p. 333, underlining that often more than one ownership unit belongs to the same owner.

Italian literature on fragmentation includes several theoretical treatments. Among articles dealing with concrete cases, see U. Sorbi, "La ricomposizione della proprietà frammentata e dispersa in Italia" *Rivista di economia agraria* (Rome 1951), pp 83 sqq; *Il riordinamento fondiario del Bacino Planais* (Udine 1947); and R. Vazzoler, *Il riordinamento fondiario in Istria* (Parenzo 1939). Cf. also U. Sorbi, "Land fragmentation and dispersion in Italy", *International Journal of Agrarian Affairs* (Oxford 1952), pp 44 sqq.

NETHERLANDS. *Landbouwtelling 1950*, Table 7 (pp 40 sq) shows the total number of plots to be 1.07 million, covering 2.34 million ha. The average number of plots is highest on farms over 100 hectares, where it is 7.1; next comes the size-class 10–20 ha, with 5.1 plots as an average per farm. The specification by size-classes also shows that 82 per cent of all farms have less than 5 plots each. The official estimate, that something between 40 and 50 per cent of all Dutch land was in need of consolidation, must therefore include all land where some kind of improved layout is desirable.

See also M. J. Boerendonk, "De verkavelingstoestand der Nederlandse land-bouwbedrijven (Census 1950)", *De Pacht* (The Hague 1951), Vol. 12, pp. 354 sqq, and A. Rienks, "Reallocation of land in the Netherlands", *International Journal of Agrarian Affairs* (Oxford 1952), pp 33 sqq.

NORWAY. Th. Grendal, "Utskiftningen", *Tidsskrift for skogbruk* (Oslo 1947), pp 145–148, stresses that the absence of a comprehensive land register makes it difficult to estimate the need for reallocation of land. The problem does not so much concern arable land or the meadows in the prevailing system of isolated farmsteads, but is of importance with regard to forests and rough grazings.

Cf also K. J. Moen, *Hovedtrekk i den norske jordutstykking* (Skien 1938).

POLAND. *Statistical yearbook of Poland* (1948), p. 42, Table 2 H, describes recent consolidation activities. Up to January 1, 1948, 299 villages had been consolidated in the present Polish territory, including 72,000 holdings and 328,000 hectares. The movement was most important in Kielce, and next in other old Polish areas, but very little was done in the areas recently taken over from Germany. The latter may be due to the fact that this land, when reallotted to new Polish holders, did not become fragmented from the outset. The estimate in the table has taken into account the degree of fragmentation in surrounding parts of Germany and Czechoslovakia; there are good reasons to think that the southern Polish provinces, *i.e.* part of formerly Austrian Galizia, are about as fragmented as Slovakia, while the old Polish provinces are something in-between these regions and the not very fragmented East German regions. The degree of recent collectivization has also been taken into account, but its success seems to have been greatest in the Western regions, where there was not so much fragmentation.

PORTUGAL. The main source for knowledge of fragmentation in the whole of Portugal has thus far been the taxation statistics, as published in the special yearbook of financial statistics and, in abbreviated form, in the *Anuario estadistico*. About 1950, there were some 12 million ownership lots, averaging a little more than 0.25 ha and about 25 plots per farmer, the latter being counted in the population censuses. The number of ownership lots can be shown to have increased steadily over at least 80 years, except in the latifundia districts, where the opposite is true; thus, the characteristics of the main parts of the country have been more and more sharpened, a sign of continuing disintegration. See the map by A. de Amorim Girão, "Divisão de propriedade rústica", *Biblos* (Coimbra 1951).

This kind of data, however, tend to overestimate the problem, since there may be more than one ownership lot lying together and farmed together in the same operational holding. The first Portuguese farm census, taken in 1952–54, shows considerably fewer plots and, consequently, fewer per holding also. Even so, the need for consolidation must be very great in the northern and central parts of the country, and not entirely nonexistent in the South either. In many areas of Portugal, moreover, it is frequent that trees belong to other persons than the land, and even that the same tree belongs, *pro rata parte*, to several owners. From all these considerations, it could be estimated that the need for consolidations in Portugal is relatively greater than in most if not all other European countries.

RUMANIA. The average size of plots is derived from the 1948 farm census, A. Golopentia and P. Onică, "Recenseământul agricol din Republica Populară Română 25 Ianuarie 1948, Rezultate provizorii", *Probleme economice* (București 1948, March). The need for consolidation has been estimated taking into account the impact of collectivization.

SPAIN. *Estadistica de propietarios de fincas rústicas de España, Resumenes globales y generales rectificados de las 50 provincias* (Madrid 1951), p. 11 states that there were almost 5 million plots in irrigated land, over 24 million in unirrigated cultivated land, and 6.7 million in forests and rough grazings, total 36 million plots, with an average size of 0.34 ha in irrigated land, 0.92 ha in unirrigated cultivated land, and 3.35 ha in forests and rough grazings. The average size of plot in irrigated land varied from 0.05 ha in the province of Murcia to 2.44 ha in the province of Cádiz; in unirrigated cultivated land the variation goes from 0.07 ha in the province of Pontevedra (Galicia), to 3.7 ha in Granada (Andalucia); and in forests and rough grazings from 0.32 in Pontevedra to 50,45 in the province of Jaén (Andalucia).

From this material it can be concluded that the need for consolidation is great in large parts of Spain. Cf. also *El parcelamiento de la propiedad rústica en España* (Madrid 1952, Instituto de estudios agro-sociales).

SWEDEN. Most land in Sweden that was once in need of consolidation was reallocated in the course of the 19th century. There are scattered exceptions to this rule here and there in the country, but in the province of Dalarne, the whole action essentially failed, because the villages were larger than in most other parts of the country, the holdings smaller and of less importance in a remote province where other industries at an early date began to play a role for the population, and the fragmentation was unusually grave.

A pilot enquiry in some parishes in central Sweden showed that, even in the fully consolidated areas, it is not infrequent for a farm to include 3–5 plots of arable land and meadows. The future need for reallocation in most parts of the country is derived more from general considerations of the geometry of layout than of the number of plots.

The estimate for the table took mainly in account the exceptions from the 19th century consolidations, while the future considerations of a better layout were not included in that estimate.

SWITZERLAND. The most recent basic information on Swiss land fragmentation is in the agricultural census of 1939. Half of all the farms had less than six plots each; at the other end of the scale, there were a few thousand farms which had more than 50 plots each.

Comparison with the *Ergebnisse der Eidg. Betriebszählung vom 9. August* 1905 Band 2 (Schweizerische Statistik, 168), p. 82* sq indicates that the average size of plot was then somewhat larger; however, the method of calculating does not seem to have been entirely the same.

See also *FAO Agricultural Studies*, 11, pp 78 sqq, where an official account is given of the problem, founded upon the 1939 census. Other studies on Swiss consolidation are J. Heuser, "Der Einfluss der Güterzusammenlegungen auf Rohertrag und Produktionskosten landwirtschaftlicher Betriebe", *Agrarpolitische Revue* (Zürich 1949), pp 194 sqq, and A. Hüni, "Der Einfluss der Arrondierung auf die Betriebsergebnisse, "*Schweizerische landwirtschaftliche Monatshefte* (Bern 1941), pp 209 sqq.

UNITED KINGDOM. *National Farm Survey of England and Wales, A Summary Report* (London 1946), pp 35 sqq, shows that about $^1/_4$ of all holdings were constituted by more than one plot of land, and that there were many instances of bad layout. No estimate as to the need for consolidation could however be made on this basis, since the requirements for a good layout seem to have been put higher here than is usual on the Continent.

Cf also R. McG Carslaw, "Size of fields in the Eastern counties of England", *The Farm Economist* (Oxford 1933), No 2, pp 36 sq, and W. H. Long, "Size of fields in Devon", *The Farm Economist* (Oxford 1935), No 11, pp 224 sqq.

YUGOSLAVIA. Because of the absence of a complete cadastre system, the estimate for the table has had to be founded on a combination of various published sources and the opinions of local experts communicated directly to the author.

See, at first hand, L. Fritscher, "Agrarverfassung und agrarische Umwälzung in Jugoslawien", *Die agrarischen Umwälzungen im ausserrussischen Osteuropa*, hrsg... M. Sering (Berlin & Leipzig 1930), pp 276–340, especially p. 293, where it is stated that the formerly Austrian countries of Slovenia and Dalmatia belong to the worst fragmented rural areas of Europe. Even trees were reported sometimes to belong to more than one owner, as in Portugal. It is added, p. 298, that fragmentation was a grave problem throughout Croatia.

Map examples of fragmented villages in Slovenia can be studied in Sv. Ilešić, *Sistemi poljske razdelitve na Slovenskom* (Ljubljana 1950).

The degree of fragmentation in Bosnia-Hercegovina can to some extent be grasped by data communicated by D. Bajalica, "Reorganizacija pasivnih zadruga Bosne i Hercegovine", *Socijalistička poljoprivreda* (Beograd 1952), pp 59 sqq: examples were found of a *zadruga* (co-operative farm) of 700 hectares divided in 4,400 plots of land, etc.

For the estimate in Table 1, the impact of collective and State farms has been taken into account.

SOURCES AND METHODS USED FOR TABLE 3

The figures referring to the years around 1950 are derived either from the yearbooks of FAO or from national statistics. In some countries, special estimates were necessary in order to make the figures as comparable as possible. The manpower figures referring to the years around 1930 are partly derived from national statistics and partly borrowed from H. Böker, "La diminution de la population active dans l'agriculture", *Revue internationale d'agriculture* (Rome, IIA, 1942), pp 385E–447 E. In some instances adjustments had to be made for subsequent changes of boundaries. These adjustments have, as far as possible, been made on the basis of detailed regional figures but, where such material was lacking, estimates have been made. The same refers even more to the figures for both manpower and agricultural land in the years around 1900, where rather extensive research was necessary in order to reconstruct figures referring to the present territory of each country.

In cases where no exact data were available on agricultural land around 1900, it was supposed that the 1950 figure is usable, since the concept of "agricultural land" here includes rough grazings.

Some information on the land-labor relationship can also be drawn from a publication called *European conference on rural life 1939, Technical documentation, Population and agriculture with special reference to agricultural overpopulation* (Geneva, League of Nations 1939, official no: C. 18 M. 10. 1939. Conf. E. V. R. 6).

In the following, details are given of the computations underlying the figures of Table 3.

ALBANIA. The area figure given in the FAO yearbook has been accepted as an approximate estimate. D. Zavalani, "Die landwirtschaftlichen Verhältnisse Albaniens", *Berichte über Landwirtschaft* (Berlin 1938), N. F., Sonderh. 140, p. 56, indicates 1,363,000 ha, out of which 1,027,000 ha grazings. *South-Eastern Europe, A political and economic survey* (London 1939, The Royal Institute of International Affairs), p. 151, gives figures totalling 1,123,000 ha agricultural land. S. F. Burenko, "Novoe administrativno-territorial'noe delenie Albanskoï Narodnoï Respubliki", *Izvestiia vsesoiuznogo geograficheskogo obshchestva* (Moskva 1952), pp 53 sqq, states that sown area has increased from 221.000 ha in 1938 (the figure given by Zavalani was 236 000) to 362,000 ha in 1951.

The manpower figure for 1950 is equally borrowed from the FAO yearbook. The figure for 1900 is an estimate on the basis of the Turkish population census of 1910, details of which are discussed below under Greece. The population figure as in 1930 is constructed by means of interpolation between the figures for 1900 and 1950 and should be read as a rough estimate.

AUSTRIA. Area and manpower figures referring to 1950 are taken from the censuses of 1951.

The population figure referring to 1930 is that given by the German census of 1939.

For both area and manpower data referring to 1900, a combination had to be made of partial data in Austrian and Hungarian sources. Out of Tyrol, it was supposed that half of it went to Italy, and of Steiermark 30 per cent were supposed to have gone to Yugoslavia. Burgenland was constituted by fractions of the Hungarian comitates of Moson, Sopron, and Vas; these fractions have been estimated in accordance with the procedure indicated below under Hungary. Area and manpower figures, except for Burgenland, were taken from "Ergebnisse der landwirtschaftlichen Betriebszählung vom 3. Juni 1902", *Österreichische Statistik*, 83 (Wien 1909), p. xv, 38.

The details indicate that the increase in hectares per man is distributed over all the old Austrian Länder, while Burgenland, like Hungary, has been rather stationary in this respect.

BELGIUM. The area figure for 1950 is that of the agricultural census taken in 1950, while that referring to 1900 has been borrowed from *Exposé de la situation du royaume de 1876 à 1900*, Vol. 3 (no year indicated), p. 23 sq, to which the agricultural areas of Eupen and Malmédy have been added from German sources.

The manpower figure for 1900 is that given in the statistical yearbooks from the years following 1900. The census of 1910 indicates 442,000. The figure for 1930 is that given by BÖKER, and that for 1950 by FAO.

The Belgian statistics on agricultural manpower are not quite consistent from time to time, as can easily be shown by comparing the census returns from 1910–30 and 1930–50. The apparent changes are due not only to a strong rural exodus but also to the use of different concepts for the delimitation of the industries and for defining unemployment. The factual development does not seem to have been very well explored; cf R. Grooten, "L'évolution de la population active agricole et horticole en Belgique depuis 1856", *Revue de l'agriculture* (Bruxelles 1951), pp 426–441, where the official figures are accepted as true, by and large.

Cf. also I. Frost, *Agrarverfassung und Landwirtschaft in Belgien* (Berlin 1909).

BULGARIA. The present territory of Bulgaria includes, besides the same territory as in 1900, also certain regions in the South which became the final gain from Turkey through the Balkan wars. These latter territories also belonged to Bulgaria in the inter-war period, when southern Dobrudsha belonged to Rumania. Both for 1930 and for 1900, the statistics have therefore to be adjusted to correspond to the present territory.

A tolerable estimation of the population of the southern territories could be made on the basis of the Turkish population census of 1910 (cf below under Greece). The agricultural area was estimated by deducting southern Dobrudsha from the Bulgarian territory before 1912, and thereafter deducting the remainder from the Bulgarian territory in the inter-war period. The following sources were used at these calculations: *La population en Bulgarie d'après le recensement au 1 janvier 1888, 1 janvier 1893 et 31 décembre 1900*, (Sofia 1907); the population censuses of 1910 and 1920; *Statistique de la propriété foncière pendant l'année 1908*, Vol 3, (Sofia 1921); *Statistique agricole, Ensemencements et récoltes 1935/36* (Sofia 1938); the farm census of 1934, and the statistical yearbook 1942 (with census data from 1934).

For 1950, estimates given by FAO and ECE were used. For 1930, the manpower figure has been interpolated between the census returns of 1926 and 1934, assuming the same rate of growth every year; to this was added a figure for southern Dobrudsha, estimated from the Rumanian census returns 1930 for the districts of Caliacra and Durostor.

The area statistics of 1908 also includes figures for 1897, giving a total of agricultural area as 4.4 million ha, including rough grazings, as against 5.1 million in 1908, also including rough grazings. The estimate of 5.5 million ha represents an interpolation between these plus an allowance for the southern districts, calculated as indicated above.

CZECHOSLOVAKIA. For the Western provinces, figures for agricultural area in 1896 and males active in agriculture in 1902 were derived from the Austrian farm census of 1902, deducting the later Polish part of Cieszyn. For Slovakia, the computation was made on the basis indicated below under Hungary. The manpower figure from 1930 is derived from the census of that year. For 1950, estimates made by FAO and ECE have been used in conjunction with the *Manuel statistique de la républizue tchécoslovaque*, 1938. Other sources consulted are V. Brdlík, *Die sozialökonomische Struktur der tschechoslowakischen Landwirtschaft* (Berlin 1938), showing, p. 109, that the distribution of capital and production was slightly different from the distribution of area among the size-classes of farms, and H. Böker & F. W. v. Bülow, *Die Landflucht in der Tschechoslowakei* (Rom 1935).

DENMARK. *Statistisk Tabelvaerk*, R. 4, Lit. A, "Tabellariske Oversigter over Folkemaengdens Fordeling... den 1ste Februar 1890" (København 1893), reckons only the heads of family as active population, so that aiding family members are reckoned as passive population. The total number of males dependent on agriculture was 463,000, but this, obviously, includes also those not in working age. *Statistisk Tabelvaerk*, R. 5, Lit. A, Nr 5, "Befolkningsforholdene i Danmark i det 18 Aarhundrede (København 1905), p. 170, gives figures based on a broader concept of active population; the total for heads of family and employees is 337,000 males active in agriculture, to which an allowance should be added of 21,000 for southern Jutland, according to German sources. *Statistisk Tabelvaerk* (5 C 4, 1861–1907), and *Anvendelsen af Landbrugsarealet* 1912–1928, give the following figures for total agricultural area:

1861.	2,444,000 ha
1901.	2,917,000 „
1919.	2,906,000 „
1920.	3,172,000 „

where the figure for 1919 excludes and that for 1920 includes southern Jutland. To the figure from 1901, a corresponding allowance has been added on Table 3, drawn from German sources.

Cf also E. Jensen, *Danish agriculture, Its economic development* (København 1937).

ESTONIA. The inter-war figure for manpower is that given by the latest statistical yearbook, referring the figure to 1934. On the basis thereof, and of the contemporary figure for agricultural land, the estimates for 1950 have been made. The estimates for 1900 are based on the same sources as for Russia (see under USSR).

Cf also T. Sinberg, "Das Siedlungswesen in Estland", *Siedlung und Siedlungspolitik in den Ländern Europas*, bearb, v. R. Stegemann & Fr. Schmidt, (Berlin 1939), pp 99 sqq.

FINLAND. *Aperçu de la population de la Finlande au 31 décembre 1900...* (Helsinki 1905, Suomen virallinen tilasto, 6 Väestötilastoa, 37), gives figures on active males in agriculture which must be much too low, because aiding family members are excluded. On the basis of the general age-distribution in rural communities, it could be estimated that out of a total of 784,000 males dependent on agriculture, 465,000 were between 15 and 65 years old. Deducting 10 per cent for ceded Carelia, we arrive at approximately 420,000 active males in agriculture on the present territory of Finland.

In Finland, agricultural land could not be supposed to have remained without important changes over this period, since there has obviously been a great deal of land clearance from forest area and peatbogs. H. Paavalainen, *Om landthushållningen och åtgärderna för dess främjande åren 1908–1910 med beaktande af utvecklingen under senaste årtionde* (Helsingfors 1914), p. 63, gives as for 1901 the figures of 1,568,000 ha arable land and 1,281,000 ha meadows, together

2,849,000 ha agricultural area. Again deducting 10 percent for the ceded territory, we obtain approximately 2.6 million ha as by 1901.

The figures for 1930 and 1950 have been borrowed from current statistics. The manpower figure for 1930 has also been adjusted downwards by 10 per cent.

FRANCE. The manpower figures are those of the population censuses taken in 1896, 1931, and 1946, the figures on agricultural land are derived from the agricultural censuses of 1892 and 1929, the latter giving the most recent figures referring to all agriculturally used land in France. To the figures from 1896 and 1892 have been added figures for Alsace-Lorraine, borrowed from the German agricultural census of 1907.

Smaller inadequacies in the early population returns have recently been corrected in an article by Mme Cahen, "Evolution de la population active en France depuis cent ans d'après les dénombrements quinquennaux", *Etudes et conjoncture, Economie française* (Paris 1953), pp 230–288, where corrected numbers for active males in agriculture are communicated on p. 146 sq. It becomes clear that the figures barely allow us to follow any real changes that may have taken place during the latter half of the 19th century, because the changes in definitions and methods are probably greater than the real changes. It is from World War I and onwards that the diminution of agricultural manpower can be seen clearly. The returns from 1906 onwards are also adjusted to the definitions used in the most recent census. Because the difference is modest and adjusted data are not available by department, we have used the uncorrected figures throughout this enquiry.

See also R. P. Allo, "Enquête sur la mobilité des familles paysannes", *France, Ministère de l'agriculture, Revue, Etudes et Monographies,* (Paris 1949), pp 18 sqq, and A. Demangeon & G. Manco, *Documents pour servir a l'étude des étrangers dans l'agriculture française* (Paris 1939), showing, *i.a.,* that current opinions on the large-scale replacement of the French population through Italians and Spaniards in some regions are largely due to impressionistic over-estimation.

GERMANY. The statistical yearbook of Western Germany gives figures for agricultural area and manpower for both Western and Eastern Germany and Saar, and also figures for 1939 adjusted to the present territorial subdivisions; for this reason, these data were used for representing the inter-war situation (around 1930) on Table 3. Regional details have also been taken from the West German population census of 1950, the West German agricultural census from 1949, and the East German population census of 1946. The figures from the latter source, however, represented an immediate post-war situation and have therefore been adjusted by aid of data in the West German yearbook and estimates made by ECE.

The figures referring to the beginning of the century have been taken from the German agricultural census of 1907.

In using this source, a great many territorial adjustments were necessary. From the Western parts of the country, Alsace-Lorraine was added to France, Eupen and Malmédy to Belgium, the districts (*Landkreise*) of Aabenraa, Haderslev, Sønderborg, and half Tønder to Denmark (as approximately corresponding to Southern Jutland). Among the eastern parts of the old empire, East Prussia has been entirely divided between Poland and the Soviet Union. Under Polish rule, though according to two different kinds of legal status thus far, are the the entire old *Regierungsbezirke* of Breslau, Oppeln, Posen, Bromberg and Marienwerder, further Regierungsbezirk Liegnitz with the ecxeption of the *Landkreise* Rottenburg, Hoyerswerda and half Görlitz, and about half Regierungsbezirk Frankfurt/Oder.

The Saar territory has been reconstituted by adding together the *Landkreise,* and fractions of such, that are included in the present Saar (which is larger than the Saar territory of 1919–35). Also the present *Länder* of Western Germany, and the *Länder* existing in Eastern Germany at the end of the forties, have been reconstituted by adding together the territories equivalent to them.

See also H. Böker & F. W. v. Bülow, *The rural exodus in Germany*, (Rome 1933); S. H. Palmer, "Die Eingliederung heimatvertriebener Landwirte im Zusammenhang mit der Landflucht in Westdeutschland, *Institut für Raumforschung, Information*, 1951, Apr. 9; T. Oberländer & others, *Die Eingliederung der Heimatvertriebenen Landwirte in die westdeutsche Landwirtschaft* (Hannover 1952), and H. Priebe & K. Kündiger, "Der Arbeitskräftebesatz der deutschen Landwirtschaft", *Agrarwirtschaft* (Hannover 1952), pp 269 sqq. The most recent phases of rural exodus in Western Germany can be seen from official figures in the *Statistischer Monatsbericht des Bundesministeriums für Ernährung, Landwirtschaft und Forsten*, June 1955, p. 50.

GREECE. The figures from Greece in 1950 and 1930 are those communicated by the FAO yearbook and current statistics. Regional details in the agricultural census of 1929 do not reveal any significant regional differences in the quotient of land per man. The data on rough grazings are however of low reliability.

The calculation of areas and population as by 1900 was more complicated, since large parts of Greece were then still under Turkish rule. Most of the data can be found in Greek sources from 1911–13: *Recensement agricole de 1911* (Athens 1914): *Statistique annuelle de rendement agricole ... des nouvelles provinces de la Grèce*, Année 1914 (Athens 1916), and *Dénombrement des habitants des nouvelles provinces de la Grèce de 1913* (Athens 1915). Population data for the exact territory that finally remained Greek can also be checked through a comparison between two Turkish sources: *Empire Ottoman. Ministère des finances. Bulletin annuel de statistique... 1326 (1910)*, Année 2 (Constantinople 1913), and *Population de la Turquie... d'après le recensement du 28 octobre 1927* (Angora 1928). Another Greek population census was taken in 1920/21, before the great population exchange with Turkey, following the Lausanne treaty. A comparison between these various sources for the population numbers in directly comparable territories (Crete, the Aegaean islands, and Macedonia by and large) makes evident that the Turkish population census of 1910 was of reasonable accuracy. From the viewpoint of the critical appraisal of the sources, it is specially interesting that while the Turkish census only publishes provincial totals, the following Greek census also gives population numbers for each village; the latter source cannot therefore be founded on the former, and the reasonable coincidence of the data of these two censuses taken independently of each other increases the trustworthines of both.

For this reason, the Turkish population figures from 1910 have been split up on the territories that ultimately went to each of the succession States: Greece, Albania, Yugoslavia, Bulgaria, and modern Turkey. A careful examination of the general demographic trend in each of these countries has been the basis for an extrapolation back to 1900. Obviously, the population increase has been slower among the Greeks than among the Slavonic populations. The agricultural population has thereafter been calculated on the basis of the same proportions as are known somewhat later from each country. For Greece, it becomes evident that most of the increase in manpower that occurred over the period described here depends on the influx of refugees from Asia Minor and the regions around the Black Sea, and rather little on natural increase.

On the contrary, the Turkish figures on agricultural area are rather fanciful and cannot be brought into any degree of accordance with other and better documented information. For 1900, therefore, Table 3 gives rough estimates, based on the assumption that no great changes could occur over the period, when rough grazings are included in the concept of agricultural land.

After the last war, the Greek territory has again increased somewhat by the accession of the Dodecanese Islands. See D. Papasarantopoulos, "Prooptikē tēs georgikēs exelixeōs tēs Dōdekanēsou," *Bulletin agricole* (Athens 1953), pp 96 sq, showing that the agricultural area of the islands (in the sense of this enquiry) is something around 150,000 ha.

HUNGARY. Since 1919, Hungary has not had any lasting territorial changes of a size making adjustments of older statistics necessary. The figures for 1930 and 1950 therefore regard the same territory and are derived from current statistics, and FAO and ECE estimates.

Reconstructing present Hungary from data referring to the period around 1900 was more complicated. The basis for computing agricultural manpower is the census of 1900, "Dénombrement de la population des pays de la Sainte Couronne Hongroise en 1900", P. 10, *Publications statistiques hongroises* N. S. Vol. 27 (Budapest 1909). For the breaking down of these figures on the territories of the succession States, including present Hungary, there was a special difficulty in the fact that the new boundaries cross old administrative subdivisions in almost as many cases as was ever possible. For estimating the fractions of the divided comitates that went to each State, percentages of ceded territories published in the Hungarian statistical yearbooks in the early twenties have been used, in combination with the maps in *Hungary before and after the war in economic-statistical maps*, ed. by A. E. Illés & A. Halász (Budapest 1926). The census identifies the population of working age as the age-strata between 15 and 59 years; 6 through 14 years of age are shown to be school ages.

For the whole of the old Kingdom of Hungary (without Croatia-Slavonia, which was another kingdom under the same crown), the census indicates a total figure of active males in agriculture of 3,61 million. Of this figure, 1.4 million comes to Hungary, 316,000 to Yugoslavia, 59,000 to Austria, 581,000 to present Czechoslovakia, 143,000 to USSR (Czechoslovakia in the inter-war period), and 1.1 million to Rumania (600,000 in Transylvania and 500,000 in the Tisza valley).

Area figures are also given in the same publication as the population census, Vol. 9, and in some special publications on the entailed estates. Unfortunately, these area figures are not very precise, and it was therefore safest to suppose no change to have taken place over the period, for the same reasons as in the Balkans.

IRELAND (Eire). The manpower figure for 1900 has been constructed by adding together data in the *Census of Ireland, 1901*, regarding Leinster, Munster, Connaught and three counties of Ulster (Cavan, Donegal, and Monaghan). In the same way, the area figure for 1900 has been calculated on the basis of the *Agricultural Statistics of Ireland with detailed report for the year 1900* (Dublin 1901). In all area figures from Eire, rough grazings are excluded, which makes some difference in the comparison with Northern Ireland, where the areas of rough grazings can be estimated by aid of recent figures.

ITALY. U. Giusti, *Caratteristiche ambientali italiane agrarie, sociali, demografiche 1815–1942* (Roma 1943) contains data on manpower and land as far back as to 1861; it resorts that the quotient of land per male active in agriculture was about 4 hectares at that time.

The manpower figure for the beginning of the century has been taken from the census of 1901. The corresponding area figure is drawn from G. Zattini, *Superficie e popolazione del Regno d'Italia* (Roma 1913), p. 19, with addition of the areas taken over from Austria and not again ceded to Yugoslavia. The data for 1930 and 1950 are taken from current national statistics, the former with deduction of the territory ceded to Yugoslavia.

Regional details are not yet fully available from the population census of 1951. The following table will however give some idea of the regional distribution and its changes.

Region	Agricultural area, 000 ha		Active males in agriculture, 000	
	1900	1950	1901	1936
North	7,020	7,190	2,825	2,679
Center	3,760	3,862	1,159	1,180
South.	6,120	5,551	1,710	1,554
Islands	4,560	4,024	875	803
ITALY	21,460	20,626	6,570	6,215

The slight increase in manpower in Central Italy may depend upon the colonization scheme on the Pontinian fields. Otherwise it is striking that, when only unweighted hectarages are taken into account and the fertility of the soil and the development of crop yields left out of sight, the not very spectacular improvement in man-land ratio should have been about the same in southern as in northern Italy.

LATVIA. The inter-war manpower figure is derived from national statistics and refers to 1935. The figures for 1900 are taken from the same sources as for Russia, while those referring to 1950 have been estimated in connection with the estimates for the Soviet Union as a whole.

LITHUANIA. The figure for manpower in inter-war years is based upon the national census returns of 1923, giving a total of 513,000, to which an allowance was added for the part of the Vilnius district which was assigned to Lithuania after World War II. The figures for 1900 are derived from the same sources as were used for Russia, and those referring to 1950 have been estimated in the same way as for Latvia.

LUXEMBOURG. Area figures for 1898 have been taken from *Grossherzogtum Luxemburg, Publikationen der ständigen Kommission für Statistik*, H. 14 (1907), p. 12. The manpower figure for the year 1900 has been taken from *Publications de la Commission permanente de statistique*, Fasc. 2, "Etat de la population dans le Grand-Duché d'après les résultats du recensement du 1er décembre 1900" (Luxembourg 1903), p. 205.

NETHERLANDS. *Bijdragen tot de statistiek van Nederland*, N. V. 12, "Uitkomsten der beroepstelling... (31/12) 1899" indicates 513,000 active males in agriculture, including 22,000 fishermen. *Jaarcijfers voor het Koninkrijk der Nederlanden, Rijk in Europa*, 1901 ('s-Gravenhage 1902), p. 136, gives the figure of 2,116,000 ha agricultural area, as against 2,044,000 in 1891, and 1.896,000 in 1833.

NORWAY. *Norges officielle statistik*, Vol. 145, "Jordbrukstaellingen i Kongeriket Norge 30 september 1907", H. 7 (Kristiania 1911), p. 3, gives area figures according to another system than later sources:

Arable land.	247,192	ha
Cultivated meadows	493,491	„
Horticultural land.	10,054	„
Natural meadow, as "inmark"	361,210	„
(Sub-total	1,111,947)	„
Harvested meadows on mountains etc. . .	268,244	„
Rough grazings	993,244	„
TOTAL	2,373,500	„

The sub-total indicates the figure which is comparable with later classifications. In the classification now used, agricultural area is returned only when on "inmark" (within fence, or equivalent), with addition only of such mountain meadows as have been harvested or are for harvesting in the census year. The rough grazings, as well as distant meadows not harvested for hay in the census year are now included either among forest land or (more frequently) among waste land. For the sake of homogeneity within the Scandinavian group, the recent classification has been adopted for the figures in the table. The low quotient of land per man resulting from this is however to a considerable extent due to the exclusion of the rough grazings.

Folketaellingen i Norge 1 december 1910, H. 4 (Kristìania 1913), p. 20, gives a total of 305,000 adult males active in agriculture and related industries, thereof 16,000 active in forestry and 50,500 in fishing. Many of the latter are more independent of the farming industry than is the case in many other countries, even though part of them may hold an intermediary position here too.

POLAND. *Statistics of Poland*, Ser. D, No 11, "Agricultural statistics 1947" (Warsaw 1949), Table 6, p. 10, gives figures for the present territory of Poland referring to 1931/38, derived from Polish and German sources from the inter-war period, also separately for former and recovered territories. In our enquiry, these figures for agricultural area have been supposed to correspond closely to the areas available in post-war Poland; the official figures for 1946 and 1947 obviously represent an only incomplete recovery and also an only incomplete registration, in the immediate post-war period. The figures given in the *Statistical News of the Central Statistical Office* (Warsaw 1951), Year 24, No 2, p. 7, are already considerably higher than those from 1946 and 1947, and rather close to the interwar figures. This justifies the use of the latter, also in the regional breakdown.

Agricultural area around 1900 has been computed on the basis of the German agricultural census in 1907, the *Annuaire statistique de la République Polonaise*, Année 1, 1920/22, T. 1, Table 19, p. 53 sq (including data derived from Russian sources from around 1900), and the Austrian farm census of 1902. Cf also *Statystyka Polski* 12:5, containing a farm census for the former Austrian parts of the country, taken in 1921.

Active males in agriculture around 1900 have been calculated on the basis also of the German farm census of 1907 and the Austrian one of 1902, and S. Szulc, *Appréciation des données statistiques relatives à l'état de la population de l'ancien Royaume de Pologne* (Warszawa 1920), Tables IX, X, and XIV.

The regional breakdown has been made in accordance with the subdivisions indicated on *Agricultural statistics 1947*. When distributing the manpower figure on the districs, it was hereby assumed that total active males in agriculture (3.45 million) were equally distributed among rural population (15.9 million in 1949); a percentage of 21.7 was thus applied uniformly to the figure of rural population for each district. This assumption is probably not entirely correct, and especially in highly industrialized Silesia it is probable that the share of the rural population that belongs to agriculture is in reality lower than the all-over average would indicate. The real number of agriculturally active males was probably only 1 or 1.1 million in the Western parts, and correspondingly higher in the center.

The following figures were thus computed.

District	Agricultural land, 000 ha		Active males in agriculture, 000		Hectares per man	
	1897/1907	1949	1897/1907	1949	1900	1949
Warszawa	1,974	2,098	330	395	6.0	5.3
Łódz	1,532	1,461	285	284	5.4	5.1
Kielce	1,203	1,241	235	289	5.1	4.3
Lublin	1,823	1,974	290	302	6.3	6.5
Białystok	1,241	1,469	195	167	6.4	8.8
Olsztyn	1,252	1,201	140	86	8.9	14.0
Gdańsk	677	709	100	84	6.8	8.4
Pomorze (Bydgoszcz)	1,426	1,388	190	183	7.5	7.6
Szczecin	2,101	1,819	230	117	9.1	15.5
Poznań	2,500	2,678	360	346	6.9	7.7
Wrocław	1,665	1,564	260	229	6.4	6.8
Sląsk (Katowice)	1,009	951	225	375	4.5	2.5
Kraków	1,086	1,091	285	344	3.8	3.2
Rzeszów	1,275	1,220	420	248	3.0	4.9
TOTAL	20,763	20,864	3,545	3,450	5.9	6.0

In the adjustment of older statistics to the subdivisions of 1949, small inadequacies have been unavoidable. The fact that the quotients of land per man following from these reconstituted figures show a considerable continuity over the former State boundaries, strengthens the confidence in the result. The following may be quoted to show how similar the results are in districts including territories from more than one former administration:

	Land per man according to various sources:		
	Polish (Russian) 1897	Austrian 1902	German 1907
Białystok	6.4	—	6.6
Pomorze (Bydgoszcz)	6.6	—	6.5
Poznań	5.6		5.9
Sląsk (Katowice)	3.4	3.9	4.0
Kraków	3.9	3.8	—

See also S. Szulc, article in *Problèmes démographiques de la Pologne*, Sér. C., fasc. 51 (Warsaw 1936), and G. Frumkin, "Pologne, Dix années d'histoire démographique", *Population* (Paris 1949), Oct.-Déc.

For older area statistics, see also *Stosunki rolnicze Królestwa Kongresowego, Zbior wiadomości o stanie i warunkach rozwoju rolnictwa na ziemach Królestwa Polskiego*, ed. S. Janicky, S. Rosinsky & F. Ubysz, (Warszawa 1918), pp 33, 262 sq.

PORTUGAL. The area figures are based on the estimates given by A. E. Lima Basto, *Inquérito económico-agrícola* (Lisboa 1935), T. 4, pp 25 sqq. Given the low reliability of these estimates, it has not seemed adviseable to suppose any distinguishable development of the agricultural area over the period. It is known that a great deal of land clearance was made in the South in the last quarter of the 19th century, but most of this can be supposed to have been done around 1900.

The manpower figures indicate a complicated development, an impression which is probably to some extent due to the use of the different statistical criteria:

Region	Active males in Portuguese agriculture (000)		
	1900	1930	1950
North	660	587	679
South	332	380	470
Algarve	61	62	74
Atlantic Islands	95	93	107
TOTAL	1,148	1,122	1,330

Under reservations for the impact of different statistical criteria, the following reflections may be made. Population pressure in the regions of intensive small-scale farming in the North, in Algarve, and on the Atlantic Islands, was already high at the beginning of the century. For the time being, it was eased through overseas emigration. The decrease in agricultural numbers caused thereby has however largely been compensated by continued demographic increase over the last two decades, when emigration does not appear to have had the same effect, so that the numbers active in agriculture now are close to, or even higher than, they were at the beginning of the century. In Southern Portugal, the land clearance boom around 1900 may not have had its full effect on the demographic development until in the course of the first of quarter of this century, hence the physical possibility for an increasing population even recently. It is known that very few people emigrate from southern Portugal, and this seems to be so still now, despite the fact that population pressure on the land must now be considerable. In the south, the increase in numbers active in agriculture is on the magnitude of 50 per cent, thus on an "east European" level. The disintegration of the country appears clearly.

In case the numbers were understated in 1900, the above conclusions would be even more stressed as regards the North, while those on the South would be somewhat weakened; under the opposite assumption, the opposite modifications would be true. In case the numbers are understated in 1950, the conclusion on the South would be even more stressed etc. On the whole, the differences within the country are too great to depend solely on differences in the statistical criteria.

Cf. also O. Ribeiro, "Deslocamento da população em Portugal, Programa de um estudo", *Revista da faculdade de letras*, (Lisboa 1940–41).

RUMANIA. The post-war figures are borrowed from the FAO yearbook and estimates made in ECE. The manpower figure for 1930 is derived from the census of 1930, deducting the figures for Bessarabia, northern Bucovina, and southern Dobrogea (the districts of Caliacra and Durostor).

For the figures referring to the period around 1900, a combination has been made of data from Rumanian, Hungarian and Austrian sources.

L. Colescu, *Analiza resultatelor recenseământului general al populatiei Romaniei din 1899* (București 1944), pp 31 sqq, indicates that total population of the Old Kingdom was 3.7 million in 1859 and 5.7 million in 1899; of these totals, rural population would have been 3.2 million in 1859 and 4.6 million in 1899. It is further shown (p. 56) that the sex proportion was 98 females to 100 males; thus the male rural population in 1899 should have been about 2.34 million. Of these, 56.7 per cent were in the age-strata 16–65 years, in 1899, which gives a total of 1.33 million males in the working ages in the rural population. In such a structure as that of Rumania at that date, a certain part of the agricultural population actually lived in towns. This should by and large compensate for the fact that there were some non-agriculturists among the rural population. The number of active males in agriculture in the Old Kingdom around 1900 may therefore be estimated at $1^1/_3$million.

The Hungarian census of 1900, quoted above under Hungary, shows that about 630.000 males active in agriculture lived in the Transylvanian regions, and 480,000 in the counties and parts of such which add up to the Rumanian region of Tisza valley, together 1.1 million.

The Austrian census of 1902 indicates that there were 159,000 active males in agriculture in Bucovina. Of these, the number living in the region which is still Rumanian can be estimated at 90,000.

The total of these three figures can be rounded to 2,540,000.

For the area figure around 1900, the Hungarian and Austrian sources quoted above under these countries, have been used in conjunction with a publication called *Agricultorii și repartizareă pământului cultivat in 1913*, (București 1915). The information found in these three sources justify the assumption that the agricultural area of Rumania, including rough grazings, has not changed much over the period here studied. The early sources, on the other hand, did not make it possible to assess the small changes that may have taken place. For this reason, the actual figure was retained also as an estimate for the agricultural area around 1900.

SPAIN. While this country has not had any changes of boundaries over the period, there are difficulties in defining agricultural area. Spanish agricultural statistics accept the fact that the same land is often used for different purposes and consequently give separate figures for various land categories which together add up to more than the real total of areas. This procedure is of course useful from many points of view, especially on land under intensive cultivation cropped more than once. As regards the vast areas of land under very extensive use, on the other hand, the double reckoning of the same land both as forest and rough grazing creates an illusion as to the extension of grazings in comparison with other countries. The figures given in the FAO yearbook, of some 42 million hectares of agricultural land, corresponds to the total of all land used for cultivation or grazing and leaves over as forest area only areas which are not grazed at all.

The *Anuário estadístico de las producciones agrícolas*, 1949 (Madrid 1951), gives the following breakdown of grassland:

Meadows	1,222,000 ha
Pastures	9,001,000 „
Low forests	6,282,000 „
"Encinar", etc.	3,316,000 „
Pine forests.	2,392,000 „
Other high forests	1,107,000 „
Total grassland	23.321,000 „

The last three items give a total of 6.8 million ha of real, high forest which should at all events be reckoned as woodland and not as grassland. The two first items, on the other hand, totalling 10.2 million ha, are not at all forest land but must be reckoned to the agricultural area. The only doubt thus refers to the category called "low forest". It should be observed that the value of the production per hectare of this land is extremely low; in other countries, this land, or most of it, would be classified either as waste land or as "productive uncultivated land". Such is certainly the case in both Portugal and Italy. For the sake of comparability with these countries, we therefore prefer to exclude these "low forests" from the agricultural area.

From the total for "agricultural area" in the statistical yearbooks around 1950, or 42.9 million ha, we should therefore deduct about 13.1 million ha, leaving 29.8 million ha as agricultural area according to our definition. For the country as a whole, the figure could better be rounded to 30 million ha, an estimate to be used over the whole period. When making the same estimates by regions, the total of the figures for the latter will differ somewhat from the rounded total of 30 million ha.

Figures for active males in agriculture have been borrowed from the population censuses. The subdivision of the country in provinces appears to have remained essentially the same over the period. For the year 1900, the figure for active males in agriculture is to some extent an estimate. The total of the categories that should add up to "active males in agriculture" would amount to 4.52 million, but this also includes the whole of an item called "jornaleros, braceros, peones, destajistas" (day-laborers, etc), given on p. 217 in the census publication. Of the figure given for this item, some 200,000 must belong to non-agricultural occupations. The corrected total will then be approximately 4.3 million, and the difference has been proportionately distributed over the provinces and regions.

By main regions (groups of provinces), the following table can be given to show the variations in manpower and man-land quotient.

Region	Agricultural area 000 ha	Active males in agriculture			Hectares per man		
		1900	1930	1950	1900	1930	1950
Galicia	1,114	485	394	582	2.3	2.8	1.9
Cantábrica (Atlantic)	1,277	290	209	257	4.4	6.1	5.0
Ebro Valley	4,264	445	370	442	9.6	11,5	9.6
Cataluña and Baleares	1,083	345	300	300	3.1	3.6	3.6
Levante (Mediterranean)	2,240	500	426	544	4.5	5.3	4.1
Andalucía	5,441	850	897	1.092	6.4	6.1	5.0
Northern Plateau	5,465	580	457	599	9.4	12.0	9.1
Southern Plateau	8,861	720	669	881	12.3	13.2	10.1
Canary Islands	374	85	53	131	4.4	7.1	2.9
TOTAL	30,119	4.300	3.775	4,828	7.0	8.0	6.2

Both the national totals and some of the regional figures suggest that the statistical definitions may not have been exactly the same. However, the development in Andalucía shows anyhow an even rise in numbers seeking employment in agriculture, and this result is in accordance with the fact that this region was one where political unrest was especially strong in the early thirties and where the call for land reform seems to have met with specially favorable attention.

Another way of measuring the regional distribution of agricultural wealth in Spain is offered by the figures given by the recent agricultural yearbooks for the total value of agricultural production (gross value in pesetas) in each province Simplified on some main regional subdivisions, these figures give the following picture of output per man, in 1950.

Region	Total value of production, million pesetas	Active males in agriculture, 000	Value per man, pesetas
North (Galicia and Cantábrica).	5,544	839	661
Ebro Valley	3,498	442	791
Levante and Cataluña (incl. Baleraes)	8,410	844	996
Andalucía	6,815	1,092	624
Plateau (Meseta)	11,965	1,480	808
Canary Islands	1,253	131	956
TOTAL	37,485	4,828	776

The figures tend to reveal the favorable position of the Mediterranean regions and the unfavorable situation not only in Andalucía but also in the Northern regions with their dominating structure of small family holdings. However, these figures for value of gross output are of course only a rough indicator.

In contrast to Italy, cadastre values are not available for making over-all estimates of the value of land in Spain. Most of the work done on the cadastre in the forties is described in an official publication called *Memoria sobre los trabajos realizados por los Servicios de Catastro de la Ricueza Rústica e de Valoración Forestal, publicado por la Dirección General de Propriedades y Contribución Territorial, del Ministerio de Hacienda,* (Madrid 1949). At this moment, there remained a considerable part of the work to be done on the cadastre, and only examples are furnished as to the variations in the value of land. Some of these may be quoted. Horticultural land varies from 1,000 to 6,000 pesetas taxed revenue per hectare; irrigated land used for growing cereals from 400 to 2,200; irrigated olive plantations from 90 to 1,400; irrigated citrus plantations from 200 to 5,000; land used for rice growing from 100 to 1,700; land used for growing sugar cane from 250 to 4,000; unirrigated land used for growing cereals from 6 pesetas to 1,460; unirrigated olive plantations from 25 pesetas to over 800; vineyards from 22 to 3,800; and fruit plantations from 90 pesetas to 2,500 per hectare. All this only shows the marginal values available for taxation. The value relations in the hands of the farmers are likely to be different and in most cases not quite so striking as shown by these figures.

Further indications on the value of Spanish land are found in the *Boletín de estadística*, issued by the Instituto Geográfico y Cadastral from 1915 onwards.

For the demographic impact of emigration to Latin America, see for instance M. Gonzales-Rothvoss y Gil, *Los problemas actuales de la emigración española* (Madrid 1949), especially p. 21, where it is stated that emigration in this century culminated in 1912, with 200,000 emigrants. Figures for net emigration (that is, minus those who returned) are available only from 1916 onwards. For the period 1916–48, there was a net emigration of 228,000, most of which was before the civil war.

Cf. also J. Redondo Gomez, *El paro agrícola en España* (Madrid 1948); J. E. Molins, *El abandono de la tierra en España: la población y el grande y el pequeño riego* (Barcelona 1927); and M. Fuentes Martiañez, *Despoblación y repoblación de España 1482–1920* (Madrid 1929).

SWEDEN. Both area and manpower figures are borrowed from current national statistics. Agricultural area does not include rough grazings, since such land is not returned separately but is included either with forest or waste land.

On early phases of demographic development, see N. Wohlin, *Den svenska jordstyckningspolitiken i 18: e och 19: e århundradena* (Stockholm 1912).

SWITZERLAND. The figure for active males in agriculture around 1900 refers to 1910 and is borrowed from the population census of that year: *Résultats du recensement fédéral de la population du 1er décembre 1910*, Vol 3. The figure appears to have been higher in 1900; the agricultural census of 1905 gives a higher total (432,000), though probably on the basis of a somewhat different definition: *Schweizerische Statistik*, 168, "Ergebnisse der eidgenössischen Betriebszählung... 1905", T. 2, p. 29*.

The figure for agricultural area in 1900 is that given by the official statistical yearbook for that year.

UNITED KINGDOM. The *Statistical Abstract for the United Kingdom... 1900–1914*, p. 308 sq, indicates a cultivated area of Great Britain of 32,437,000 acres in 1900, and 32,287,000 in 1905. Permanent pastures are reckoned as excluding heath and mountain land. Areas under woods, coppices, and plantations are given only for 1905, 2,768,000 acres. The *Agricultural Returns for Great Britain... 1900*, p. 2 sq, gives a figure for cultivated area (total acreage under crops and grass, including bare fallow) equalling that of the first source. Of this total, each of the countries had as follows:

England	24,714,000 acres
Wales	2,824,000 „
Scotland	4,899,000 „

For Northern Ireland, returns relating to 1900 are available in the *Agricultural Statistics of Ireland, with detailed report for the year 1900* (Dublin 1901), though net of rough grazings. For the six counties of Antrim, Armagh, Down, Fermanagh, Londonderry and Tyrone, the areas under crops, meadows, grass, and fallow amount to a total of 2,688,400 acres, or 1,084,780 hectares. A comparison with actual proportions between rough grazings and other land underlie the estimate of 1,200,000 hectares of agricultural land in Northern Ireland in 1900.

Also the estimates for the countries of Great Britain include allowances for rough grazings, calculated on the basis of more recent sources.

The figures for active males in agriculture are derived from the population censuses of 1901, 1931, and 1951. As elsewhere, these figures include population engaged in fishing. The latter are a considerable proportion in Scotland (27,000 out of 197,000 in 1901).

See also *Report of the Agricultural Research Tribunal, 1924,* giving a critical appraisal of the manpower figures.

For Northern Ireland, no population figure seems to be available later than that from 1926. This figure is reproduced as representing the situation close to 1930, while the figure for 1950 is estimated on the basis of the assumption that decrease has went on at the same rate as between 1900 and 1920.

USSR. For the estimation of agricultural area and manpower in the Soviet Union, special difficulties arose for several reasons. One is in the necessity to combine information derived from Russian, Austrian, Hungarian, Polish and Baltic sources. Another is in the scarcity of available official statistics from the Union since the end of the thirties. One more difficulty lies in the frequent changes of administrative boundaries. In view of the fact that most data referring to 1950 are rather unprecise estimates, it has not seemed worthwhile to make even those exact reconstructions of present administrative subdivisions for earlier dates that are possible through re-combination of data for small administrative units. On the table, therefore, only a rough correspondence between areas at 1900, 1926, and 1950 is represented.

For agricultural areas in 1900, the *Ezhegodnik Rossii 1905 g* has been used, in conjunction with the uncomplete agricultural census of 1917: *Résultats par districts du recensement agricole et foncier pour toute la Russie de 1917* (Moskva 1923), and the *Statisticheskaia svedĕniia po zemel'-nomu voprosu v Rossii* (St Petersburg 1907). The reconstruction of the agricultural area refers to the year 1905 but cannot differ much from that of 1900. The importance of the census of 1917 in this connection is that it contains figures not only for sown area and total area, but also for arable land, horticultural land, meadows and pastures; despite their uncompleteness, these data have been valuable as a check on other calculations.

The total found for the whole of European Russia has thereafter been increased by figures referring to Carpatho-Ukraina (from Hungarian sources), northern Bucovina (from the Austrian census of 1902), and eastern Galizia (from the same source).

The total thus found cannot differ very much from the present agricultural area. The spectacular increase in sown area since 1917 must derive, for the most part, from ploughing up of grassland and from restricting the practice of fallowing. There has also been a considerable amount of land clearance, especially through draining of swamps. N. Anisimov, *Razvitie sel'skogo khoziaĭstva v piatoĭ piatiletke* (Moskva 1953) p. 97 gives the following data for the whole Union (in thousand hectares)

Type of improvement	1917	1929	1937	1940
Irrigated land	4,080	4,470	5,620	6,150
Drained swamps	1,200	2,050	3,450	5,710
Total improved land . . .	5,280	6,520	9,070	11,860

However, no data indicate how far this refers to the European regions, nor how far the drained land was or was not included among agricultural area before the draining.

The theory that agricultural area around 1950 does not differ radically from that around 1900 can to some extent be checked by aid of official data, contained in the second edition of the *Bol'shaia entsiklopediia.* For Ukraina, the special volume on the Soviet Union (1946), gives the territory (post-war) as 576,000 square kilometers, of which arable and horticultural land should be "over $^2/_3$",

that is not very much less than 40 million hectares. Adding allowances for
meadows and pastures, we seem to arrive at a figure close to that found for 1900
by combining Russian, Austrian and Hungarian sources. In the whole of this
calculation the Republic of Moldova is included in Ukraina because a separate
calculation on behalf of it referring to 1900 and 1926 would be difficult. For
Moldova, the encyclopedia indicates an agricultural area of 2.9 million ha.

For Belorussia, the encyclopedia gives the figure of 207,600 square kilometers
as total area, out of which the categories adding up to our concept of agricultural
area should be togheter 53.1 per cent, or 10.8 million ha. This figure also falls
rather close to the estimate made for the year 1900.

For the various regions of the RSFSR, the figures are necessarily less precise,
because the coincidence of administrative divisions over time has been reconstructed in a very rough way only, and also because the boundary between
Europe and Asia has not always been exactly the same. As far as possible,
individual departments have been checked by aid of the data in the encyclopedia.

As regards manpower, the estimates have had to be made independently for
each of the years appearing in the table. For 1900, an interpolation was
made between population data referring to 1897 and 1905, both communicated in the
Ezhegodnik Rossii for 1905; the result was thereafter converted into "active
males in agriculture" on the basis of manpower data referring to 1897 in the
Statisticheskaia svědeniia po zemel'nomu voprosu v Rossii (St Petersburg 1907).
The latter source only gives figures for males active in agriculture 20 years of age
and over, which is of course too narrow a definition, especially in a population
with so high a birthrate and so low average life expectations as the farm population of Russia at that time. Between 1897 and 1905, the average annual growth
was 15.6 per cent of the figure for 1897. The total population of European Russia
as in 1900 may be estimated at 100 million, out of which 20.6 million males active
in agriculture, 15 years of age and over (extrapolated on the basis of the age
distribution in rural districts). To this should be added, from sources outside
the Russian empire:

Carpatho-Ruthenia	153,000
Eastern Galizia	1,106,000
Northern Bucovina	60,000
Northeastern East Prussia	150,000
TOTAL	1,470.000

To the total of 22 million thus found should also be added 1.2 million for
Transcaucasia, which was then reckoned to Asia, plus about $1^1/_2$ million for the
southern and most extensive part of Northern Caucasus, which was by then also
reckoned as part of Asia.

The total estimate may be rounded to 25 million.

For the year 1926, it is considerably easier to reconstruct the manpower in
the present territory of the Soviet Union, above all since the official census of
that year seems to be of acceptable quality. To the figures it gives, considerable
additions had to be made derived from the censuses of the Baltic States, from
Czechoslovak and Rumanian sources, and an estimate for some parts of Ukraina
and Belorussia, based on the Polish census of 1931.

For 1950, finally, the starting point was an estimate by ECE referring to
that year, giving active males in agriculture as 29 million in the whole of USSR.
On the basis of this estimate – unfortunately not very precise in itself – a calculation was made in order to show what part of this number that may live in
the European part of the Union. This was done by taking the same proportions
between rural population of the various districts as shown in the available data
from the population census of 1939. First, from the estimate of 29 million, the
numbers referring to the territories integrated in the USSR after 1939 was
deducted. The remainder was proportionated, as indicated, on the various parts
of both European and Asiatic USSR; to the latter, the figures referring to those

Western areas that were integrated in the Union after 1939 were added anew. This is why the agricultural population of Ukraina does not appear to have dropped quite so much as one might have expected; the Western parts of the country had,at least in the late forties, a much denser agricultural population than old Ukraina after the dramatic thinning in the thirties. A certain dimiuntion in Belorussia may to some extent depend upon the net deficit resulting from the population exchange between the USSR and Poland after World War II.

YUGOSLAVIA. The figures for 1950 are derived from the FAO yearbook and national statistics. The manpower figure for 1930 is also derived from national statistics, plus an allowance for Istria, derived from Italian statistics.

For the figures referring to 1900, a combination had to be made of data from Serbian, Austrian, Hungarian, and Turkish statistics.

Annuaire statistique du Royaume de Serbie, Année 9, p. 126, gives figures for active males in agriculture, 20 years of age and over, for 1900. This number was 472,000, while the males living from agriculture and being under 20 years of age were 585,000. In a demographic situation like this one, the strata between 15 and 20 years of age must play a considerable role. Estimating the number of active males in agriculture, 15 years of age and over, at 600,000, is certainly not too high. *Statistique du Royame de Serbie*, T. 16 (Belgrade 1900). "Recensement de la terre cultivée... 1897", p. xxiv, gives arable land as 1,021,144 ha, meadows and pastures 652,270, vineyards 68,330, and orchards 97,971 ha, together 1,839,715 ha. Cf *ibid.*, p. 364 sq, where the total of "cultivated land" is given as 2.53 million ha, but this includes both 481.000 ha forests and 208,000 ha "non-cultivated agricultural land", which leaves over the same total as according to the first quotation.

The Austrian farm census of 1902 gives figures corresponding to Slovenia (adding the whole of Krain and Görz and 30 per cent of Steiermark): 1,836,000 ha productive area, whereof 1,004,000 ha agricultural area and 832,000 ha forest. The number of active males in agriculture is given as 256,000, out of which 221,000 over 16 years of age.

The Hungarian population census of 1900 indicates the number of active males in agriculture in the comitates (and parts of such) corresponding to Vojvodina as 316,000, in Croatia-Slavonia plus Fiume as 626,000 to which should be added 226,000 for Istria and Dalmatia from the Austrian census. For the same reasons as discussed under Hungary, agricultural area has here had to be supposed to be approximately the same as now.

For the southern regions, estimates were made on the basis of the Turkish population census of 1910 (cf above under Greece). For the elaboration of the proportions between the different areas, also the Yugoslav population census of 1921 was used: *Résultats définitifs du recensement de la population du 31 janvier 1921* (Sarajevo 1932).

On the basis of these various data and estimates, the following, though incomplete, regional table has been drawn up:

Region	Active males in agriculture, 000		Agricultural land, 000 hectares		Hectares per man	
	1900	1950	1900	1950	1900	1950
Slovenia	222	174	1,000*	968	4.5	5.6
Croatia	852	706	3,500*	3,421	4.1	4.8
Vojvodina.	316	328	1,860*	1,863	5.9	5.7
Old Serbia	600*	960	1,840	3,096	3.1	3.2
Kosmet District	100*	160	..	422	..	2,6
Bosnia-Hercegovina	400*	477	1,604	2,469	4.0	5.1
Montenegro	50*	72	..	525	..	7.3
Macedonia	150*	226	..	1,119	..	4.9
YUGOSLAVIA	2,690*	3,104	..	13,882	..	4.5

The total national estimates shown in Table 3 represent a somewhat less exact assessment of regional resources as at 1900; it was thereby assumed, *i.a.*, that most of the apparent increase in agricultural area in Serbia and Bosnia-Hercegovina depends upon another principle of enumerating rough grazings that were probably used even at the beginning of the century.

On the general lines of demographic history in Yugoslavia, see M. Mirković, "Struktura poljoprivrede Jugoslavije", *Socialni arhiv* (Beograd 1941), pp 7 sqq; cf *idem, Ekonomika agrara FNRJ* (Zagreb 1950), p. 26.

On the most recent developments, see M. Ban, "O poljoprivrednom stanovništvu", *Statistička revija* (Beograd 1953), pp. 331 sqq, showing that the spectacular recent decline in agricultural population (between the censuses of 1948 and 1953 population dependent on agriculture should have declined from 70.5 to 59.7 per cent) is to a large extent due to different statistical definitions. If the definitions of 1948 had been applied in the 1953 census, then the percentage would have been 64 in the latter year. Most of the difference regards the registration of female workers and of persons out of work.

LABOR RESEARCH USED OR DISCUSSED IN CHAPTER 3

When using labor norms for different parts of the agricultural production, which can be found in agricultural literature from various countries, it is a basic rule of some importance that a coherent set of norms, experienced in a concrete situation and covering large parts of the productive process in a country's agriculture, should be preferred to compilations of norms from different sources. In many instances, it is a matter of judgement whether a work operation should be ascribed to one or another branch of agricultural production. Deep ploughing, manuring etc. can be ascribed to the preceding or to the following crop, but they could as well be referred to the whole production cycle, that is to all the crops grown between two such operations. Care of manure belongs to some extent to livestock husbandry but partly to crop production, etc. Some operations, such as drainage, fencing, repair of tools and machinery etc., cannot at all be ascribed to any particular branch of production but can only be described as belonging to the farming activities in general. Many enquiries on agricultural labor make special allowances for "maintenance work", which may be expressed as a certain percentage of total labor expenditure or as a certain number of days per hectare. It is inevitable that the relative part played by such work increases when mechanization and other measures of modern rationalization diminish the total volume of work required for many operations in agricultural work; the maintenance operations are generally not so dependent on season and weather as the field operations, and therefore not so much is done to mechanize them, and at the same time the increased use of machinery increases the scope for this kind of work. Thereby it is sometimes overlooked that work on the maintenance of machinery partly plays the same role as the work formerly done to maintain draught animals. When it comes to analysis of the productivity of labor, the latter branch is of course not a branch of production but part of the work done for other branches of production.

In this enquiry, the last step towards productivity analysis is not yet taken. Draught animals are therefore here reckoned as "branches of activity", and "maintenance work" is defined as work for which no distinct norms have been available.

If, on the other hand, a norm series were constructed by picking out one norm here and another there, one would risk either to overestimate or to underestimate the total need for labor, because some of the partial operations which add up to the norms for each branch of production might then be counted either twice or not at all. As a whole, it is here assumed that each coherent set of norms, communicated in one source, refers to a concrete situation and has been experienced on the basis of the distribution of the work done on the various branches of production. The exception should be the not very numerous cases where the norms have been found by means of direct time-studies. The latter is at any rate a complicated affair, since it would then be easy to overlook or to overestimate the importance of the frictional loss of time in starting and stopping the work of the day, or of certain small partial operations.

In the cases where only very uncomplete data are available from a country, it has therefore seemed safer to take over a whole series of norms from a country with a similar technical level than to try and construct a non-empirical series by picking together data from national and foreign sources. Certain use has also been made of the possibilities to check the results by using more than one source reflecting similar situations.

From this general viewpoint it has seemed too risky, at least at present, to try and construct any kind of general "European normal" series of norms. Conditions are too different in various countries, e.g. in England and Italy, to make it possible to use any of them as "normal average". Instead of constructing an average European series, it seemed safer to use the American standard as a common measure in order to make all European countries directly comparable. The fact that American agriculture is on the whole less intensive than European agriculture is in this connection of limited importance, since the difference between American and European labor standards is least in the most intensive branches of production and the theoretical application of American norms on European production patterns does not change the latter.

AMERICAN STANDARD. The American labor norms used for the whole of Europe are those communicated by R. W. Hecht and G. T. Barton, "Gains in productivity of farm labor", USDA Technical Bulletin, No 1020 (Washington 1950), referring to the period 1945–48 (p. 11, Table 3, cf also pp 70 sq; for livestock, p. 79, Table 36). Even later data are available (in typescript), but the series 1945–48 was preferred in this connection, because it also relates to other data which are not yet available in published form for later years. Among other things, this procedure made it possible to derive norms for some items not directly mentioned in the list of labor norms, above all fruit and vegetables and livestock other than milk cows. On the basis of the data for total labor consumption in US agriculture, it was also found that maintenance work should amount to about 17½ per cent of the total for other work.

Supplementary information was drawn from "Mechanization in Agriculture as a Factor of Labor Displacement", Monthly Labor Review (Washington 1931), pp 1–33, especially p 28 (labor norms for fruit production).

AUSTRIA. The same norms were used as for Western Germany.

BELGIUM. The basis is the series of labor norms communicated by A. G. Baptist & H. Waterschoot, Etudes de la petite exploitation agricole, 2, "Le travail" (processed, 1950). The norms, expressed in man-hours per hectare under crops and per animal, respectively, are as follows:

Wheat, oats, mixed grains	136.49	Potatoes	504.50
Rye	119.66	Rutabagas	183.00
Barley	141.10	Turnips and Swedes	130.00
Pulses, rapes	300.00	Meadows for hay	73.00
Chicory	178.00	Milk cows	208.00
Hemp	341.00	Other cattle, 1 year of age and over.	78.00
Flax	249.50	Calves	52.00
Hops	2.353.75	Sows with litter	208.00
Tobacco	2.206.00	Pigs for fattening	52.00
Sugar beets	394.00	Sheep and goats	12.49
Fodder beets	463.50	Poultry	3.9

A labor norm for pastures, 124 hours per hectare, was disregarded in this enquiry, since it seems to suppose permanent watching of small herds on unfenced grazings.

The labor year in the quoted study was calculated at 3,120 hours. When using this norm series, we have applied the same labor year. The allowance for maintenance work was fixed at 15 per cent, in analogy with British labor norms representing a similar though somewhat higher level of mechanization.

Cf also the brief review given by BAPTIST in the Monographies sur le bien-être rural en Belgiques (Bruxelles 1951).

Bulgaria. The calculation of labor consumption in the thirties has been founded on norms contained in M. P. Vitanov, "Trudoemkost'ta na někoi zemědělski kulturi i kulturni vidove", *Zemědělsko-stopanski vǎprosi* 1 (Sofia 1936). The norms are given as days' work per decare under crops, together with per cent distribution on male and female labor. In the following, the decares are converted into hectares:

Crop	Labor days per hectare	Thereof, as per cent	
		Male labor	Female labor
Wheat	46.7	61.52	38.48
Barley	41.8	53.26	46.74
Oats	29.4	65.57	34.43
Mixed grains.	39.8	58.39	41.61
Maize.	75.0	44.36	55.64
Vetches	15.9	84.63	15.37
Beans.	109.8	36.48	63.52
Sunflower	98.1	42.87	57.13
Potatoes	97.4	49.44	40.56
Fodder beets	99.2	49.46	50.54
Vegetables	43.5	80.66	19.34
Natural meadow	12.5	78.87	21.13

The seasonal distribution is also shown (p, 12), indicating no field work at all in December, January and February, and not very much in March, October and November either.

In our enquiry, further norms, for tree-crops, certain very intensive crops like tobacco, and livestock, were supplied mainly from Greek sources (see below under Greece), since the general level of efficiency seemed to be close to that prevalent in Greece. The allowance for maintenance work was fixed at 6 per cent, in analogy with Italian norms on a similar level.

On the basis of these norms, calculations were made in the thirties of the agricultural surplus labor in Bulgaria. P. P. Egoroff, "Die Arbeit in der Landwirtschaft", *Die sozialökonomische Struktur der bulgarischen Landwirtschaft*, hrsg. v. J. St. Molloff (Berlin 1936), calculates that crop and livestock production and maintenance work should add up to a total labor consumption of 355 million man-days. The population active in Bulgarian agriculture was calculated to be the equivalent of 1.944,000 males, and the useful year, when sundays and holidays are deducted, to 290 days. Thus, 564 million labor days would be available and only 63 per cent employed (pp. 152 sq).

Czechoslovakia. The only labor enquiry available from Czechoslovakia seems to be that presented in *Produktionsbedingungen, Organisation und Ergebnisse landwirtschaftlicher Betriebe in der Tschecoslowakei (Durchschnitt der Jahre 1926–1930)*. *Verarbeitung der Erhebungsergebnisse landwirtschaftlicher Betriebe*, hrsg. . . . V. Brdlík (Prague 1935). The method here applied is simply that of assuming all employed labor to be fully employed, which tends to conceal all the problems of underemployment. The results indicate an average labor consumption of 114 days per hectare of agricultural land (122 in the Western Provinces and 102 in Slovakia), which is far more than indicated by any known labor norms in Southern or Eastern Europe. The average is as high as 211 days per hectare on holdings under 2 ha, but on large holdings over 100 ha the average is still as high as 64 days per hectare.

V. Brdlík, *Die sozialökonomische Struktur der Landwirtschaft in der Tschechoslowakei* (Berlin 1938), p. 155, refers to the above quoted enquiry as the only one existing.

Because labor norms properly speaking could not be traced, West German norms were applied in the Western Provinces and Hungarian ones in Slovakia.

Denmark. Labor research representing Danish standard before tractors came into general use are published in *Undersøgerlser over landbrugets drifts-forhold, Periodiske beretninger*, 5, "Arbejdsforbruget i danske landbrug 1946—49" (København 1950).

This enquiry is founded on studies on 20 middle-sized peasant holdings farmed under conditions held to be normal in the country; the farmers themselves were participating in the work, though with one or two full-time hired hands and some extra hands in rush seasons. Labor consumption was computed in man-hours and horse hours. Women hours were counted as $^3/_4$ of man-hours, and child hours as $^1/_2$ of man-hours. Piecework for which no indication was available as to the time it consumed was converted into hours worked on the basis of the wage paid for the work. Total labor consumption for the main branches of work was indicated as follows:

	Hours per hectare		As per cent of total	
	Sjaelland	Jutland	Sjaelland	Jutland
Crop production	139.1	134.9	43.0	44.6
Livestock production . . .	144.7	128.5	44.8	42.5
Other agricultural work .	25.9	25.9	8.0	8.6
Non-agricultural work . .	13.6	13.1	4.2	4.3
TOTAL.	323.3	302.4	100	100

The distribution of labor consumption over the 52 weeks of the year is also indicated, showing peaks in the third week of August and the last week of September, with 8,8 and 8,7 hours per hectare respectively (on Sjaelland), and the lowpoint in the last week of December with 4,1 hours per hectare.

Labor norms for the most important individual crops are given as follows:

Hours per hectare/year	Sjaelland	Jutland
Autumn grains.	130.1	84.9
Spring grains	101.8	89.7
Swedes	376.0	313.8
Sugar beets (for fodder) .	403.3	371.5
Potatoes	557.8	452.5
Temporary grass	37.0	85.5
Permanent grass	10.3	6.4

The rush seasons for each crops are also shown: 12–17 hours per hectare on grains during some weeks of August, and over 20 hours per hectare a week on beets in June and potatoes in April.

Cf also *Thirty years of farm accounts and agricultural economics in Denmark 1917–1947* (København 1949).

The efficiency level represented by the above quoted norms falls very close to that of contemporary Swedish norms referring to farming without tractors. On the other hand, mechanization has advanced quickly in Danish agriculture since the quoted norms were elaborated. It has therefore seemed advisable to base the calculation of labor consumption in Danish agriculture on corresponding Swedish norms referring to agriculture with large use of tractors, as discussed below under Sweden.

Eire. The same norms were used as for the United Kingdom.

Finland. Some norms were experienced as early as in the first years of this century, indicating still an efficiency level not very much higher than that of primitive farming in Eastern Europe. J. Enkell, *Om arbetsintensiteten å*

Mustiala egendoms åkercirkulationer, 2, (Helsingfors 1908), p. 124, gives the following norms in man-days per hectare:

Rye	12.87–18.20
Barley	24.90
Oats	18.95–24.03
Root-crops	74.85
Hay-crops	4.69–12.97
Fallow	26.98–64.29

The publication series *Investigations on the profitableness of agriculture in Finland* (text in Finnish and Swedish), does not furnish detailed norms for each branch of production but only figures for total labor consumption per hectare of reduced arable land; see its year 25 (1936–37). Female work has been reckoned as $\frac{2}{3}$ and child work as $\frac{1}{3}$ of the work of adult males. The number of reduced man-days per hectare (10 hour days) averages about 40 per hectare, varying from 85 on small holdings to 29 on large farms. In January, the average was 3–4 days per ha, in July-August 5–7. All work was included, except household work done by the farmer's family. Year 39 (1950–51), p. 50, indicates that regular agricultural work, expressed in man-hours per hectare of reduced arable land averaged 357, varying from 567 on small holdings to 254 on large farms.

Because specified norms were not available for measuring the real consumption of labor on different stages of intensity, the Swedish norms for nonmechanized farming (from 1939) were applied.

FRANCE. From the country itself only incomplete data are available. Norms for a few crops are communicated in an article by J. Darnis in the *Revue de l'Economie contemporaine* (Paris 1951, Sep), p. 24, quoting an unpublished enquiry by J. VOCHELLE. The series of interest here is that for non-motorized farming, since the degree of mechanization was not high in France in the forties. The following shows that the level was slightly lower in efficiency than the German norms for animal-drawn implements:

	hours per hectare
Wheat	107
Oast	116
Rapes	242
Sugar beets	456
Potatoes	549
Sown hay	229

The same observation is applicable to incomplete data in the *Bulletin de la Confédération générale de l'agriculture, Divison de la rentabilité* (Paris 1951, Nov), pp 30, 32.

On the basis of these observations, it seemed advisable to found the calculation of labor consumption in French agriculture referring to the structure data from 1942–46 and global data from 1950 on the coherent norm series communicated by Priebe as referring to Continental farming without motorization ("Gespann-geräte", see below under Germany).

To this series was added a norm for vineyards drawn from an enquiry regarding Languedoc: "Une enquète sur le temps de travail et les frais de production de la viticulture dans le Languedoc", *Etudes et Conjoncture, Economie Française*, (Paris 1953, Jan-Feb), pp 37–62. On the basis of a large material it was shown that labor consumption per hectare under vines varied between 150 and 700 hours, with a weighted average of 400 hours. Since the season useful for vineyard work is about 1600 hours per year, the result is that a man could not cope with more than 4 hectares under vines. Farms with more than 30 hectares under vines were not included; otherwise the average might have turned out even lower. Cf R. Dumont, *Voyage en France d'un agronome* (Paris 1951), p. 365, estimating at $3\frac{1}{2}$–4 hectares the vineyard area that could keep a man fully employed during the part of the year when this work goes on.

A norm for orchards was conjectured in analogy with that for vineyards and the proportions between both that are known from other countries.

Calculations were also made for a number of main regions in France, the composition of which is described in Appendix 5. In those where up to all evidence mechanization of agriculture has gone farthest, norms for "partial mechanization" were used alternatively. The result is as follows:

Region	Active males in agriculture, 000		Number of man-years needed according to		Per cent employment		American standard	
	1946	1946 + 20%	No moto rization	Partial moto- rization	a	b	man- years needed (000)	per cent employ- ment
East	253	304	405	314	133	103	131	43
North	596	715	822	633	115	89	253	35
Alsace-Lorraine . . .	112	134	136	107	101	80	50	37
North-Center	635	762	842	..	111	..	254	33
Bretagne	428	514	508	391	99	76	165	19
Center-SW	1,016	1,219	1,152	..	94	..	390	32
Center-SE.	469	563	392	..	70	..	147	26
Landes	127	152	105	..	69	..	56	37
Alps	29	35	35	..	100	..	16	46
Corsica	32	38	22	..	58	..	11	29
Mediterranean	325	390	246	..	63	..	162	42
FRANCE	4,022	4,826	4,664	4.239	97	88	1,635	34

The fact that some regions appear to suffer from shortage of manpower indicates that the whole level is slightly too low. This leads to the conclusion that there must be a real labor surplus in some parts of France, especially in the South. The calculation according to American norms indicates the relative changes in labor consumption by regions that may follow upon progressive mechanization.

GERMANY. For the weighting of productive resources in Germany and some other countries, the basis is in the norm series given by H. Priebe, *Landarbeit heute und Morgen* (Hamburg & Berlin 1953), p. 68, corresponding to four different stages of technical development. The series for "partial mechanization" was used in Germany, Austria, the Western provinces of Czechoslovakia, and alternatively for some regions of France. The series for "animal drawn implements" was used for France as a whole, with the additions mentioned above.

The norms had first to be raised in accordance with PRIEBE's own indications regarding manuring and "general work on arable land". The norms for livestock were accepted, despite the fact that their assessment according to their value as "livestock units" led to relatively high norms for some categories; the detailed figures are in this case barely usable for productivity analysis, even if the result is acceptable for our analysis of labor surpluses. The high norm for "grazing under supervision" was disregarded for the same reason as in Belgium: this method of grazing is rather an expression of the existence of the labor surplus than an inevitable necessity. Finally, the unusually high allowance for "various agricultural work", which was put as high as 80 hours per hectare of agricultural land, was equally disregarded, since it would lead to the acceptance of too high labor consumption standards on large farms with much land under relatively extensive use. Instead, the British principle of adding 15 per cent for maintenance work was applied also on these norms.

Further indications of the labor consumption in German agriculture under various conditions are given by Wunderlich in the *Mitteilungen der Deutschen Landwirtschafts-Gesellschaft*, H. 40 (1953), pp 1022 sqq, stressing, among other things, that merely 40 per cent of all agricultural work is done in the fields. The norms he communicates (prepared by LENZ & KRÜGER) indicated a rather high degree of mechanization; per livestock unit, the norm is 120 hours, as against 300, 230, 170 and 110 respectively for the four alternatives of PRIEBE (the two last being partial and complete motorization). For general farm work, only 28 hours per hectare are allowed, as against 80 according to Priebe.

Cf also L.W. Ries, *Die Arbeit in der Landwirtschaft*, 2. Aufl. (Stuttgart 1950), and G. Blohm, article in *Handbuch der Landwirtschaft*... 2. Aufl., Bd 5, pp 567 sqq.

GREECE. A complete set of norms is communicated by Chr. Evelpidēs, *Ē georgia tēs Ellados* (Athens 1944), p. 30, which was used here because it covers the whole field of Greek agriculture and has also been used by the author for a comprehensive calculation of labor consumption in the country's agriculture (ibid., p. 26). Slightly different norms have been made available in late years from the Greek Ministry of Agriculture, although not quite so complete as those communicated by Evelpides.

The norms are given as days per stremma ($^1/_{10}$ of a hectare) under each crop, and per head of each kind of livestock, respectively. Converting the stremma into hectares, we present the material as follows.

Crop	Norms according to Evelpides			Norms according to the Ministry of Agriculture		
	Male work	Female work	Total	Male work	Female work	Total
Small grains	23	3	26	19.7	6.7	26.4
Maize	17	33	50	34	33.6	67.6
Rice	38	75	113	55.8	35	90.8
Pulses	21	60	81	26.4	46.6	73
Potatoes	47	85	132	97.5	125	222.5
Melons	34	67	101	124.2	103.1	227.3
Vegetables	37	105	142	124.2	103.1	227.3
Tobacco	171	157	328	111	120	231
Cotton	28	90	118	38.5	80	118.5
Sesame	28	20	48	34	33.6	67.6
Other industrial crops	36	10	46	..	..	..
Cultivated hay	25	5	30	25.5	20	45.5
Alfalfa	58	—	58	54.9	30	84.9
Meadow hay	15	—	15	14	2.3	16.3
Grapes for wine	60	15	75	85	30	115
Sultanas	190	120	310	135	72.5	207.5
Currants	85	60	145	113	46.5	159.5
Olives for oil	23	20	43	20.6	37.5	58.1
Table olives	32	27	59	20.6	37.5	58.1
Citrus fruits	140	20	160	83.4	32.5	115.9
Apples and pears	67	65	132	28.3	47.5	75.8
Figs	11	110	121	20	20	40
Carobs	33	20	53	..	..	..
Mulberries	26	20	46	..	..	..
Almonds	23	15	38	..	..	..
Horses, and mules	9	9	18	22,5	11	33.5
Asses	—	4.5	4.5	4.5	4.5	9
Cattle: Cows	15	15	30	} 15.5	15.5	31
Cattle: Other	7.2	7.2	14.4			
Sheep	4.3	—	4.3	4.5	—	4.5
Goats	3.6	—	3.6	4.5	—	4.5
Pigs	—	12	12	2.0	4.5	6.5
Poultry	—	1.2	1.2	—	0.67	0.67
Beehives	—	1.1	1.1	..	..	..
Silk worms, per 80.000 cocoons	30	30	60	..	..	..

The Ministry indicates the labor need on silk cocoons as $0.364 + 0.47$ days per kilogramme, and adds an allowance of 5 million man-days and 5 million woman-days for "other crops" (than those for which norms are specified). The Ministry also adds an allowance of 5 million man-days for forestry work (as against 9,1 million man-days and woman-days, estimated by Evelpides, p. 26).

The differences between the two sets of norms do not always draw in the same direction. Applied to the actual agricultural resources of Greece, they give a global figure for labor need which is of the same magnitude in both cases. For eventual future research in differential productivity of labor, the choice between different norms must be studied carefully.

Some further information on labor consumption in various branches of Greek agriculture are included in F. Altsitzoglos, *Oi Giakades kai o kampos tēs Xanthēs* (Athens 1941), pp 376 sqq, showing large individual variations according to various geographical and structural conditions.

HUNGARY. Labor norms for Hungarian agriculture around 1930 have been published by B. Reichenbach, *Mezögazdasági üzemtan* (Budapest 1930), cf also eeM. Matolcsy, *A mezögazdasági munkaélküliseg Maggyarországon* (Budapest 1933), p. 10. The norms are given as labor days per cadastre yoke (0.575 hectare), and heads of livestock per man. The norms are as follows:

Crop	Days per yoke	Days per hectare	Kind of livestock	Heads per man
Grains	8¼	14.9	Horses in stable	6–10
Potatoes	23	40.4	Young horses	20–25
Fodder beets	30	52.6	Grazing horses	40–50
Other root crops . . .	20	35.0	Herds of horses, grazing . . .	250–350
Meadows	8	14.0	Sows	16–20
Vineyard . . . . ⅰ ⅰ ⅰ	120	210.5	Pigs for fattening	120–140
Maize	22	38.6	Meat pigs	150–250
Sugar beets	40	70.2	Milk cows	10–14
Tobacco	160	280.7	Young cows	14–16
Rotation hay	9	15.8	Calves	20–24
Grazing	1	1.8	Young sheep	120–250
Garden	35	61.4	Mother sheep	150–200

The norms are given in labor days, which are reckoned to be longer in the summer than in the winter; coefficients are indicated for the conversion of female and child work into male labor days. The counting of long labor days in the summer may to some extent explain the low labor norms for grains. Actually, a higher norm is indicated considerably later, in an article by A. Mód in *Statisztikai szemle* (Budapest 1953), giving 114 hours per yoke under wheat in 1951 and 94 in 1952 (which means 198 and 163 hours per hectare, respectively). A similar notice is included in *Mezögazdasági statisztika* (Budapest 1952), p. 145, where the figures are 120 and 100 hours per yoke (209 and 174 hours per hectare). The norms indicated for 1951 in both sources fall close to what is experienced in Latvia and Russia in the twenties, and to what PRIEBE gives as "hand-tool" norm for grains. It would, therefore ,probably be more adequate to reckon with 20 than with 15 days per hectare under small grains.

On the other hand, the norm for vineyards is unusually high. Various conceivable modifications would lead to about the same total amount for labor consumption, when applied on Hungarian agricultural statistics. Here as elsewhere, the proportions between the norms for each branch of production will become critical when it comes to analysis of the productivity in each branch of production. For this enquiry, it has seemed safest to accept the norm series as it stands.

The appropriate level of maintenance work appears here to be 10 per cent, in analogy with regions in Italy at about the same level of technique and intensity.

The article of MATOLCSY also refers to labor needs in forestry work, indicating 0.4 days for cutting and 0.2 days for transporting one cubic metre of wood, plus a rather low allowance for forestry maintenance work, so that total labor consumption would be substantially below 1 day per cubic metre.

The norms from about 1930 have been used in Hungary rather recently for calculating the labor surplus in the country's agriculture. J. Nádujfalvy, in the *Revue hongroise de statistique* (Budapest 1947), p. 323, states that in 1930, the total need of labor in Hungarian agriculture was estimated at about 360 million labor-days per year. At the same moment, the available labor force might have produced 471 million labor days; the surplus manpower should then have been 24 per cent of the total available. According to fresh estimates, on a slightly different basis, the annual labor need as in 1947 should have been 338 million days out of an available total of 441 million, thus still a surplus of 23.1 per cent. A. Mészáros, "A mezögazdasági termelés munkaeröszükséglete", *Statisztikai szemle* (Budapest 1952), pp 285–295 uses the same basis for an assessment of the level of employment in Hungarian agriculture. The total need of labor is calculated at 340 million labor days, out of 644 million that could be obtained from the population occupied only in agriculture, resulting in an employment level on the magnitude of 50 per cent only. Female labor is here included to a higher extent than supposed in our enquiry. It is stressed that the grave problem of underemployment continues to exist despite the recent agrarian reforms and the start made towards socialized agriculture.

ITALY. The computation of labor needs in Italian agriculture is in principle based on G. Orlando, "Metodi di accertamento della disoccupazione agricola italiana", *Rivista di economia agraria* (Rome 1952), and unpublished labor norms underlying the same. Cf also G. Medici & G. Orlando, *Agricoltura e disoccupazione* (Bologna 1952), and *Indagine sulla stagionalità del lavoro e sul grado di impiego dei lavoratori in agricoltura*, (Roma 1953).

The first mentioned enquiry by ORLANDO deals primarily with owner-operated and leased farms, while the sharecropped farms are excluded. The averages per hectare shown for each region and each homogeneous zone cannot therefore be extended to all land in the region or zone, because the sharecropped land may have structural peculiarities affecting the over-all average. An independent calculation has therefore been made for this enquiry, based partly on norms communicated by Orlando in the quoted article but partly on unpublished norms available in the Istituto Nazionale di Economia Agraria. From these norms, which refer to provinces or parts of such, weighted averages were constructed, based on the quantitative data by provinces included in current agricultural statistics. This material cannot be published here in full, for reasons of space. Figures derived therefrom and adapted for the Iberian countries are shown below, under Spain. The norms for crops are available both for provinces and for homogeneous agricultural zones, the latter as defined in the *Annuario dell' agricoltura italiana* (Roma 1950), pp 372 and 82* sq. Such "homogenized" norms were used for corresponding zones in the Iberian countries. For crops in Italy, and for livestock in all three countries, weighted averages for Italian regions (Piemonte, Liguria, etc) were calculated, out from the provincial norms, especially for this enquiry.

NETHERLANDS. This country is among those where research on agricultural labor has been made with considerable energy in late years. Despite this, a comprehensive material of labor norms representing normal conditions in all parts of the country does not seem to have been published. A. Maris, *Enkele aspecten van het kleine-boerenvraagstuk op de zandgronden* (Assen 1951), gives labor norms for the main kinds of crops and livestock on small holdings on the sandy soils of the Netherlands, p. 105, with details of the seasonal distribution of work in each branch of production. These norms are hardly applicable to Dutch agriculture as a whole, because they are so high as to suggest a very low degree of mechanization. The norms are given in "standard hours" per hectare under each crop and per head of each kind of livestock. 250 hours per ha under grains, 500 for peas, 600 for maize, 700 for most root crops, 215 for grassland, 275 for milk cows, and 4 per head of poultry, is a scale which recalls to mind the norms of countries and epochs where the plough was almost the only animal-drawn implement and most of the work was done by aid of hand-tools. Results of calculations on the basis of these norms are set forth in A. Maris, C. Scheer, & M. A. J. Visser,, *Het kleine-boerenvraagstuk op zandgronden* (Assen 1951).

The method of the "standard hours" is presented by E. W. Hofstee, "Die Normalarbeitsstunden-Methode", *Zeitschrift für das gesamte Siedlungswesen* (Bielefeld 1952), together with results of the method from a horticultural region in the Netherlands.

Global indications of the total expenditure for labor in agriculture are given, expressed in guilders per hectare of agricultural land, in G. M. Hoornsman & P. M. van Nieuwenhuizen, "Gemiddelde uitkomsten van een aantal groepen bedrijven over 1947–48 tot met 1950–51", *Bedrijfseconomische mededelingen... Landbouw economisch instituut*, No 9 (The Hague 1952). The figures include both family and hired labor. The expenditure varies between 360 and 470 guilders per hectare on livestock farms, between 320 and 450 guilders on arable farms, and between 540 and 620 guilders on mixed farms in the size-group 7–15 hectares.

For the computation in our enquiry, the Belgian norm series was applied in the same way as in Belgium. The result seems to justify the choice, since the medium-sized and large farms appear to have neither surplus nor shortage of labor, when compared to their actual labor-force. The figures on the latter are taken from the agricultural census of 1950, p. 13, where males, 15 years of age and over are counted as 1 unit, females and children as $^2/_3$ unit, and the labor year as 310 days, especially for the conversion of casual labor into full labor years.

NORWAY. Since no set of norms for labor requirements in individual branches of production seem to have been published from Norway, the same set of norms was applied here as in Sweden (see below).

Global calculations of the consumption of labor per hectare are available in "Regnskapsresultater fra norske gårdsbruk", *Undersøhelser over jordbrukets driftsforhold* 25, 38 etc. (Halden 1933, 1947, etc.). The number of man-hours consumed per hectare of agricultural land (under the definition of the Norwegian agricultural statistics) is indicated as follows.

Region	1932/33	1945/46
Østlandet	610	530
Trøndelag	580	530
Vestlandet	1,050	940
Sørlandet	1,020	790
Nordland	600	900
Fjellbygder	740	780
TOTAL	600	650

For 1945/46, figures are also given separately for some main size-groups of holdings:

5–10 ha	650
10–20 ha	570
20–30 ha	500
Over 30 ha	390

The result of our weighting by Swedish labor norms indicates an average labor need of slightly less than 500 hours per hectare.

POLAND. Because no separate indications of labor consumption in Polish agriculture seem to have been published from the country itself, a series was chosen which ought to represent conditions similar to those in Poland before any appreciable mechanization was introduced in the country: the Latvian labor norms, published in A. Fridbergs & J. Skuja, *Rentabilité de l'agriculture en 1935/36, 1936/37 et 1927/37* (Riga 1939). These norms represent the experience of ten years' investigations, and separate data are also given by provinces, substantially though not overwhelmingly different. The following three sets may be quoted, out of which the last one has served in this connection (expressed as days per hectare or head):

Branch of production	1927/32	1932/37	1927/37
Total agricultural land	28.51	32.05	30.18
Rye	24.8	26.7	25.6
Winter wheat	23.9	26.1	25.1
Spring wheat	16.6	19.6	18.5
Barley	14.8	16.6	15.6
Oats	13.2	14.4	13.8
Peas	16.7	16.9	16.7
Potatoes	59.6	65.7	62.2
Root crops	95.4	104.9	99.5
Clover	6,07	6.01	6.04
Flax	48.3	61.3	54.7
Gardens	25.6	33.0	29.3
Meadows	5.4	5.8	5.6
Cattle	30.5	30.5	30.5
Sheep (1 year of age and over)	5.9	4.7	5.4
Pigs (per 100 kg pork produced)	14.0	11.7	12.7
Poultry.		c:a 1 day per head	

The general level is obviously similar to what PRIEBE indicates for "hand tools". In the preconditions of the Latvian enquiry, female labor plays about the same role as male labor and in Latvia, at that time, there appears to have been a certain shortage of manpower; see P. Starcs, "The shortage of agricultural labour in Latvia", *International Labour Review* (1939), pp 768 sqq, stating even so that there was a certain labor surplus on small farms.

The application of these labor norms in Poland understates the labor surplus (and overestimates the level of employment) for two reasons: one is in the fact that female labor actually plays a much greater role than the 20 per cent allowance supposed in our enquiry for the sake of comparability; the other is in the impact of recent mechanization and other modernization measures, which ought to have lowered the real need of labor.

PORTUGAL. From this country, incomplete indications on the need of labor are available from certain limited regions. The main reason why these cannot be used is that they are too little representative for the country as a whole, and no elements are at hand for calculating weighted averages. The data thus far available are however of interest as indicators of the general level of efficiency and intensity in various parts of the country.

E. A. Lima Basto, *Inquérito económico agrícola* (Lisboa 1936), p. 394, gives norms for the most important field crops: wheat 51 days per hectare, maize 39, potatoes 94. The time to be spent in wheat production is distributed as 20 female labor-days in March and the rest as male labor, mainly in June-July, to a small extent in November. The first item evidently represents weeding (manually, as can frequently be seen in the fields in Portugal in the spring). The 27 days of male labor corresponds to what is reported from Greece, Latvia, etc.

H. de Barros, *Economia agraria*, Vol. 1 (Lisboa 1948), quotes norms produced by a special enquiry organized by the Cadastre office in three municipalities in different parts of the country (expressed in days per hectare):

Crop	Mogadouro (Trás-os-Montes)	Mafra (Estremadura)	Vidigueira (Baixo Alentejo)
Garden.	221	840	..
Potatoes, unirrigated	74	197	..
Wheat, land of 1a quality.	..	53	44
Id. 2a land	36	..	31
Maize 2a land.	..	49	..
Oats 3a land	..	..	11.
Rye 3a land	19	..	..
Barley 4a land	..	18	..
Natural meadow 1a land	27	..	..
Id. 5a land	2	..	..
Vineyard, 1a land	76	112	100
Id., 2a land	..	86	..
Olives, 1a land	46	..	73
Id. 3a land	20	..	23
Orchards	..	125	..
Oak forest	..	..	4

It is noted that all these data refer to individual plots and not to entire farms. The grading of the land is that of the Cadastre office. The first of the three regions is in the meagre mountain landscape of the north-east, the second belongs to a region of mixed structure near Lisbon, and the third to the extensive plains of "latifundia" farming in the South.

Aguçadoura. Estudo económico-agrícola (Lisboa 1944), also quotes isolated instances of labor norms from different parts of the country, expressed as total labor need per hectare of farm land (p. 168):

	man-days
Region of Barroso (Montalegre)	45
Region of Alvão (Vila Pouca d'Aguiar)	80
Campina da Idanha	120
Colónia agricola do Sabugal	31
Peninsula of Sebúbal (irrigated land only)	235
Same region, mixed irrigated and unirrigated land.	50
Colony of Pègões	30
Pliocene zone south of Tejo (large farms)	5
Same zone, medium-sized farms	15
Same zone, small farms	89
Zone of Agouçadoura, sandy soil only	320
Same zone, both sandy and normal soil	500

The norms are mostly derived from the colonization activities of the Junta de Colonização Interna and its pilot colonies. The zone of Agouçadoura is on the coast north of Porto and represents one of the most labor-intensive forms of land use in the country.

These norms, however incomplete they are, lead to the conclusion that the general level is similar to that of Italy. For our enquiry, we have therefore used Italian norms adapted in the same way as for Spain, applying to northern Portugal the same norms as for the Northern zone of Spain, for southern Portugal except Algarve the same as for the Spanish plateau, and for Algarve the same as for the Mediterranean zone in Spain. The regional detail can be observed in full only in the thirties ,while regional data on land use are not available for earlier epochs and regional figures for livestock as yet not available for the years around 1950.

SPAIN. As in Portugal, only incomplete data are available on labor needs in various branches of production. E. G. Ayau, *Importancia del coste de la vivienda rural en la economia de las explotaciones familiares de los nuevos regadíos* (Madrid 1947), p. 51, refers to a limited set of crops and only under the conditions of irrigation and maximum intensity of cultivation, which causes the labor requirements to be rather high: 45 days per hectare under barley, 71 days for maize, 105 days for potatoes, 115 days for sugar beets, 54 days for beans, and 80–150 days for various garden crops. There are hardly any of the Italian homogeneous zones that reach such high average requirements (except for garden crops), but none of these zones include only irrigated land.

On the contrary, it is possible that Spanish agriculture on the whole in certain respects is less intensive and therefore requires somewhat less labor per area unit of some important crops than is the case in Italy; we will comment upon this aspect below. There could barely be any radical difference in the general level of efficiency. The adaptation of Italian norms for calculation of levels of employment and labor surplus in Spanish agriculture does not therefore represent a very bold assumption.

For our enquiry, Spain was divided into six zones, each being a group of "agricultural regions", the latter defined as in recent official statistics. Our zones are as follows:

I	North	Galicia, Asturias-Santander, and Vascongadas.
II	Mediterranean	Cataluña y Baleares (without the province of Lérida), plus Levante (without the province of Albacete).
III	Ebro Valley	Aragón, Rioja y Navarra, and the province of Lérida
IV	The Plateau	Leonesa, Castilla la Vieja, Castilla la Nueva, Extremadura, and the province of Albacete.
V	Andalucía	Andalucía Occidental and Andalucía Oriental.
VI	Canary Islands	Canarias.

The Italian regions and zones from which norms were borrowed to weight the resources in these Spanish regions are as follows:

Spanish zone	Corresponding Italian regions (for weighted average of livestock norms) and homogeneous zones (for crop norms).
I	Piemonte; zones III and IV (hillside areas in Northern Italy).
II	Campania; zones XIII and II (intensive areas in Campania, and Liguria).
III	Apulia; zones VIII and IX (extensive capitalistic agriculture in Central and Southern Italy).
IV	Calabria; zone X (the latifundia under peasant farming in Southern Italy and on Sardinia).
V	Sicily; zones XI, XIII, and XIV (zone XI, Sicilian latifundia under peasant farming, for most crop items; zones XIII and XIV, zones of intensive agriculture in Campania, and in other parts of Southern Italy, for norms on certain intensive crops).
VI	Same as for II.

The combination of norms found for each of these five alternatives is as follows, expressed in labor-days per hectare under crops, and per head of livestock, respectively.

Branch of production	I	II, VI	III	IV	V
Small grains.	37	33	34	26	25
Maize	63	55	45	43	38
Rice	97	97	75	60	60
Pulses	35	32	25	27	28
Tobacco	130	175	170	170	180
Beets.	66	83	69	54	83
Hemp	79	115	57	60	115
Flax and cotten	56	68	58	59	54
Flaxseed	35	35	32	32	30
Rapes and sunflower	32	32	45	32	32
Ricinus and groundnuts	61	60	63	55	34
Potatoes	63	67	47	57	58
Family garden, unirrigated	217	224	218	80	80
Industrial garden, irrigated	504	354	261	265	250
Tomatoes	110	107	86	97	94
Vegetables in the open	80	103	88	75	65
Flowers.	650	350	368	440	440
Temporary grassland	22	20	15	15	16
Permanent grassland, unirrigated	27	13	10	12	10
D : o, irrigated	36	39	23	30	39
Vineyards.	145	119	130	101	122
Olives	70	54	40	40	35
Orchards	156	103	58	71	62
Citrus plantations	..	125	115	90	115
Nuts and almonds	66	40	35	31	35
Chestnuts.	20	21	20	21	16
Nurseries	666	400	350	305	250
Mulberry plantations	5	5	5	5	5
Horses	19.6	19.6	15.2	18.6	12.8
Cattle for work	15.2	15.1	12.4	16.1	11.2
Cattle for milk	21.8	18.6	12.3	17.0	11.4
Cattle for fattening	11.3	10.8	12.2	9.0	11.3
Pigs	7.0	6.3	5.9	8.3	5.5
Sheep	3.6	3.6	3.0	4.3	2.9
Goats	3.3	3.7	3.1	4.1	3.2

In the cases when the items of Spanish (and Portuguese) agricultural statistics did not coincide with those of the Italian statistics, weighted averages were calculated in order to find out the appropriate modifications to apply to the norms.

The published material from Spain includes the regional detail of the occupational distribution of the population according to the latest census, of 1950: *Censo de la población de Espana... 1950*, T. 2 (Madrid 1954). For this reason, the regional results can be presented in full. The following table shows the calculated labor requirement in each of the six regions in 1920, 1930, and 1950, the manpower existing in the same years (active males in agriculture, raised by 20 per cent), and the level of employment that would follow if all the assumptions we made were true.

Regions	Calculated need of labor, 000 labor years			Manpower available, active males in agriculture raised by 20 per cent, 000			Per cent employment		
	1920	1930	1950	1920	1930	1950	1920	1930	1950
I.	497	457	416	869	724	1,007	57	65	41
II	714	812	706	946	871	1.013	75	93	70
III.	409	437	422	526	444	530	78	98	80
IV.	1,383	1,529	1,467	1,552	1,351	1,776	89	113	83
V.	542	575	570	1,027	1,076	1,310	53	53	44
VI.	40	30	44	77	64	157	52	47	28
TOTAL	3,585	3,840	3,625	4,997	4,530	5,793	72	85	62

The apparent shortage of labor on the plateau in 1930 may to some extent be due to the fact that the Italian norms for vineyards are probably too high; the vast vineyards in New Castilla are to a great extent large-scale enterprise and can barely spend so much labor per hectare as is usual in most Italian regions. A further explanation is in a much greater use of female labor than supposed in our enquiry and, to some extent, in the use of migrating labor. The latter factor diminishes the regional contrasts somewhat, though barely in any decisive way. The high norms applied and the actual use of female labor only makes the lack of employment in Andalucia and the Northern regions so much the more striking.

It is also interesting to note that, apart from the Canary Islands where very special conditions seem to be decisive, there is a vague correlation with the product values per man shown above in Appendix 3 (under Spain): Andalucia and the Northern regions are on a considerably lower level than the rest of the mainland.

SWEDEN. For crop production, separate sets of norms are available from the late thirties and from the middle forties. The former are published in G. Ringborg *Arbetsförbrukning och rationalisering i jordbruket. Promemoria rörande jordbrukets produktionskostnader för olika produktionsgrenar* (processed, 1939), and relate to agriculture without tractors but with the full set of horse-drawn implements (including, for instance, reapers and binders) which were generally in use at that moment; the level of mechanization corresponds to what Priebe labels "Gespanngeräte". The author stresses that the distribution of total work in agriculture on its various branches of production is to a considerable extent arbitrary. This paper also contains norms for livestock production.

G. Larsson, *Inflytandet av avståndet från brukningscentrum till inägojorden på arbetsbehov, driftsformer och driftsresultat* (Stockholm 1947), pp 213 sqq, communicates norms experienced in the middle of the forties, and representing three different stages of mechanization. The method of splitting the total work done on the farm on various branches of production is not the same as in Ringborg, primarily because systematic time-studies are the basis of Larsson's enquiry.

Livestock norms are also referred to in L. Hjelm & A. Persson, *Köttproduktionens ekonomiska förutsättningar* (Stockholm 1951). Finally, summary norms for crop and livestock production have been used by L. Gustafsson, *Arbetskraften som produktionsfaktor i svenskt jordbruk* (Uppsala 1949), expressly for lack of anything more precise; his main source seems to have been Ringborg or some similar enquiry. All the norms are given as hours per hectare and per head of livestock, respectively.

Branch of production	Ringborg	Larsson horse-drawn implements	Larsson half-mechanization	Larsson tractor transports	Gustafsson	Hjelm-Persson
Spring grains	87	59.76	40.03	35.72	70	..
Autumn grains	150	40.21	35.0	30.0	90	..
Pulses	170	..	..	..	..	..
Potatoes	465	352.08	264.80	262.32	400	..
Sugar beets	710	..	..	..	680	..
Root crops for fodder	465	386.71	350.53	335.74	400	..
Industrial crops and vegetables	270	..	..	..	..	..
Green fodder	135	63.05	43.75	39.50	..	..
Leys for hay	90	26.32	26.32	22.45	60	..
Leys for grazing	50	16.95	16.95	16.95	..	..
Green fallow	—	24.13	8.92	8.92	..	..
Black fallow	—	46.55	17.87	18.21	..	..
Common work on arable land	—	45	45	45	45	..
Meadows	20	..	..	..	30	..
Rough grazing	5	..	..	..	..	..
Work horses	225	..	..	..	..	..
Young horses	90	..	..	..	..	..
Milk cows	160	..	..	..	140	160
Young cattle	47	..	..	..	..	35
Pigs	31	..	..	..	35	..
Sheep and goats	10	..	..	..	..	..
Poultry	5	..	..	..	..	..

The consistency of these norm sets can be shown in their application. As mentioned under Denmark, the two sets of Swedish norms for agriculture without tractors give only slightly different global results when applied on the Danish agricultural statistics, and the result of corresponding Danish norms applied on the same material lies in between the two results according to the two sets of Swedish norms. The same observation can be repeated when Swedish norms are applied in the United Kingdom, and British norms in Sweden.

In this enquiry, the "half-way mechanized" norms were used for crops in Sweden, Norway and Denmark, the norms "without tractor" in Finland. The livestock norms from the enquiry of Ringborg were applied in all four countries, since no later material indicates any important change. Allowance for maintenance work was at the rate of 15 per cent of the total.

UNITED KINGDOM. English standard of labor norms is relatively well known. The set contained in the official *Farm Management Handbook* has been published, with a few additions, by W. E. Jones, *Assessment of the farmers resources* (processed; a lecture held at Reading, 22/3 1954). Further, E. Sturrock, *Efficiency in the use of farm labour* (Paper presented at the Training Course on Farm Planning and Budgeting Services in Farm Management Advisory Work at St Patrick's Hall, University of Reading, England, on March 24th, 1954; processed), gives virtually the same set of norms, although computed in a slightly different way, on the basis of "work units" of 8 hours each. Similar norms are also published by W. H. Kirkpatrick, "The seasonal distribution of farm labour requirements", *University of Cambridge, Department of Agriculture, Farm Economics Branch, Report No 17.*

For this enquiry, the series published by Jones has been used for the weighting of land and livestock in the United Kingdom and Ireland. This includes the allowance of 15 per cent to be added, to the sum found on the basis of the individual crop and livestock norms, for general and maintenance work on the farm.

U.S.S.R. From the Soviet Union, a complete set of official norms is available for the main branches of livestock production. For crop production, there is relatively much material to be had from the twenties, before mechanization started, while only scanty and partly inconsistent information is available on labor requirements under the conditions in the forties and fifties.

The livestock norms are included in a circular from the Supreme Soviet in April, 1948, and published in the *Spravochnik predsedatel'ia kolkhoza*, 3 ed. (Moscow 1948). Although these norms were issued in connection with an effort at increasing productivity in the kolkhozy, they are only slightly higher than those in vigor the year before; see, for instance, the *Kolkhoznoe zhivotnovodstvo* (Moscow 1947). The norms are formulated as the number of heads of each kind of livestock to allocate to each full-time worker in the livestock farms of the kolkhozy.

Horses	10–12
Horses on grazing	20–25
Milk cows	8–14
Grazing cattle	30–50
Calves	20–25
Bulls for breading	3–4
Sheep	100–200 plus extra manpower for shearing wool
Sows with litter	7–8
Young sows	10–12
Chicken	500
Ducks	300
Geese	100
Turkeys	100
Young chicks	800
Young ducks	400
Young geese and turkeys	300

The norm for milk cows is similar to that experienced in Latvia in the twenties and thirties and in Greece in modern time. Its validity in the Soviet Union is further stressed through an article by N. Petrov in the *Sotsialisticheskoe sel'skoe khoziaistvo* (Moscow 1953), p. 35, where it is stated that — under very advanced and mechanized conditions of work — a team of two milkmaids should be fully employed by taking care of 26 cows. The level was not very different in Belorussia in the twenties. IA. Kis'liakoǔ, *Pasiolki* (Minsk 1928), says that 18–22 days' work were needed per year and per head of cattle. This is lower than the actual norm for milk cows, but includes also young cattle and work oxen.

For crops production, the last quoted author also gives two sets of norms, experienced in the Belorussian districts of Kalininshchina and Babruǐshchina. They are interesting among other things because of their resemblance to the general level of the Latvian norms we applied in Poland. Some alternatives are given to show what happens when the size of the plot varies.

Crop	Days per hectare	
	Kalininshchina	Babruǐshchina
Rye, up to 1 ha	28	28
Rye, 1–1.5 ha	25	23
Rye, over 1.5 ha	20	23
Spring wheat, 0.2 ha	28	36
Spring wheat, over 0.2 ha	28	26
Barley, 0.7 ha	27	36
Barley, over 0.7 ha	26	36
Millet	28	36
Oats, up to 0.5 ha	18	21
Oats, over 0.5 ha	18	17
Buckwheat, up to 1 ha	17	21
Buckwheat, over 1 ha	15	17
Summer rye	28	28
Potatoes	58	60
Potatoes, over 0.5 ha	54	57
Flax	92	110
Clover	18	18
Vetches	23	25
Garden	107	100
Hay	9	14

With reference to Russia, a series of labor norms was published in the review *Na agrarnom fronte* (Moscow 1927), No 4.

days per des'iatina (à 1.09 ha)

Grains	17
Maize	35
Sugar beet	138
Potatoes	75
Cotton	140
Flax	85
Hemp	105
Sunflower	35
Tobacco	212
Machorka (local tobacco)	141

On a similar level are also a few norms communicated by M. Latsis, *Agrarnoe perenaselenie i perspektivy bor'by s nim* (Moscow-Leningrad 1929), p. 57:

days per hectare

Rye	21.6
Oats	14.7
Potatoes	76.4

The last quoted author concludes that 5–6 hectares should give adequate employment to a man. The result of his enquiry is (pp 58, 60) that 20–24 million workers could be adequately employed, out of the 40 million actually available at that date.

Modern Soviet literature on labor norms is rich, but there are not many statements directly on the labor requirement in each branch of production. M. I. Tikhomirov, *Normirovanie truda v MTS i kolkhozakh* (Moscow 1938), p. 176 sq, indicates norms for various partial operations, from which comprehensive norms for entire crops might be concluded, if the practices of Soviet farming were known in detail.

Some data are available with reference to grain production. P. Golubkov, "Voprosy razvitiia sel'skoge khoziaĭstva SSSR v piatoĭ stalinskoĭ piatiletke," *Voprosy ekonomiki* (Moscow 1953), pp 41–56, says that the labor requirement was 20.8 days per hectare under grains in the twenties, on individual farms, then was reduced to 12.3 days on the first kolkhozy, and to 10.5 on the kolkhozy in 1937. The same information is repeated by I. Anisimov, *Razvitie sel'skogo khoziaĭstva piatoĭ piatiletke* (Moscow 1953), p. 133. The *Bol'shaia éntsiklopediia*, in the special volume on the Soviet Union, in its article on Ukraina, says that in the steppe regions of that country, the most far reaching measures of mechanization were to have reduced the labor requirement in wheat production to 2.5 days per hectare.

The savings of labor requirements through mechanization are dealt with by A. Kuropatkin, *Voprosy ékonomiki sel'skokhoziaistvennogo truda v SSSR* (Moscow 1952), pp 276 sqq. The following savings should have been achieved in some of the key operations:

Ploughing	2.1 – 2.2	days per ha less than before
Harrowing	1.16	„ „ „ „ „ „
Spring sowing.	1.69	„ „ „ „ „ „
Grain harvesting		
without combines . . .	4.09	„ „ „ „ „ „
with combines	13.74	„ „ „ „ „ „

Adding up the gain through all of these operations (all of which are applicable on grain production) and including the gain of time through combine harvesters, one arrives at a total gain per hectare under grains of 18–19 days. Deducting this from the norm indicated for the twenties in other articles, there cannot be much more left than the 2.5 days the *Bolshaia éntsiklopediia* indicates for Ukraina.

How far these improvements have penetrated into practice is indicated by the *Sel'skokhoziaĭstvennaia éntsiklopediia*, T. 3 (Moscow 1953), p. 192. Its is stated that on the kolkhozy, the MTS perform 96.1 per cent of the ploughing, 75 per cent of the sowing, 62 per cent of the grain harvesting (with combines), 81.1 per cent of the harvesting of sunflower seed, 27.8 per cent of the hay harvesting, 30 per cent of the silage work, and 33 per cent of the processing of flax. *Ibid.*, p. p. 246, it is stated that ploughing, sowing and harvesting are almost 100 per cent mechanized in Western Siberia, the Volga regions, Northern Caucasus and Crimea, though only so to 85.8 per cent in the Krasnodar district and to 87.1 per cent in the district of Chkalov, still in the eastern part of Russia. These various data indicate a considerable regional differentiation. At least as late as by 1950, the degree of mechanization must have been substantially lower in the European parts of the Union than in the USSR as a whole. Mechanization had advanced most in the areas of extensive grain production.

Some indications are also available as to what ratio of land to the workers is considered normal. V. Peremykin, in the *Sotsialisticheskoe sel'skoe khoziaĭstvo* (Moscow 1953), dealing with the Krasnodar district, says that 19 hectares per worker would be appropriate, under conditions of advanced technique and relatively much industrial crops and other labor consuming branches of production. The author states that there was a certain labor surplus in the area. M. Mikhaĭlov, "Proizvodstvennye brigady v ukrupnennykh kolkhozakh Voronezhskoĭ oblasti", *Sotsialisticheskoe sel'skoe khoziaĭstvo* (Moscow 1951), pp 37–44, shows that in this region, the number of hectares per man varied from 4 to 10.5 according to the different kolkhozy. It is striking that among the draught animals of the field brigades, there were almost always more oxen than horses, which indicates frequent occurrence of slow work operations. Even so, the ratio of draught animals to the manpower is not very high.

An official manual, *Voprosy organizatsii kolkhoznogo proizvodstva*, ed. 2, (Moscow 1946), p. 126 sqq, warns against relying too much upon the availability of machinery; the capacity of the machines must not be reckoned with in full, otherwise some unexpected and lengthy repairs may spoil the whole harvest plan.

These various indications show that Soviet agriculture is likely to have gained considerably in efficiency since the twenties, but also that, on the other hand, the present over-all efficiency must be considerably lower than the American standard of 1945–48. For the livestock industry, we have of course taken the official norms of the 1948 decree as the basis of our computation. For crop production, it proved impossible to assess the present over-all efficiency. Therefore, the computation was essentially based on the Russian and Belorussian indications from the twenties, supplemented by some norms from countries on an essentially similar level of agricultural technique. Because of the great possibilities for early mechanization, the norm for grain production was reduced to the half in Ukraina, thus applying there the 10.5 days-norm that must have been general in the late thirties. This computation shows a level of employment which is likely to be approximately true with reference to the livestock industry but is certainly too high to the extent it depends on calculations referring to crop production. The level of efficient employment (in the sense of this book) ought thus to be considerably lower than the $\frac{2}{3}$ we arrived at. On the other hand, the parallel computation according to American standard serves, here as elsewhere, more as landmark for direct comparison than as a description of the state of facts. The two extremes give the scope for possible interpolations.

The livestock figures taken into account are those published in 1953, in N. Anisimov, *Razvitie sel'skogo khoziaĭstva v piatoĭ piatiletke*, (Moscow 1953) and, after him, by KHRUSHCHOV in the great September speech. The figures on crop areas are those of the plan target figures referring to 1950; this also ought to have lead to a certain overestimation of the level of employment. Regional livestock figures were found by a combination of both these sources of information.

YUGOSLAVIA. Although enough material was not found to make a global calculation of the labor requirements in this geographically rather heterogeneous country, some indications may be quoted because they are of interest for the discussion on the reliability of other data used.

F. Uratnik, "Poljedelska proizvodnja in potrošnja živil v luči primerjalne statistike", *Ekonomska revija* (Ljubljana 1952), pp 234–254, discusses the possibilities of increasing labor productivity and communicates some labor norms, p. 244 (hours per hectare)–:

Maize	549–606
Wheat	180–400
Potatoes	450–600
Hay	160–240
Vegetables	770–900
Vineyard	2,800

The level is essentially the same as that experienced from the Alpine regions of Italy; the regions are geographically similar, but the national authors discussing them have not known each other's material.

D. Regan, *Radne norme i obračun zarade u seljačkim radnim zadrugama* (Zagreb 1950), and S. Lazarov, *Normite vo selanskite rabotni zadrugi* (Skopje 1952) give detailed norms for partial labor operations, the former with reference to Croatia and the latter for conditions in Macedonia. Some comprehensive norms for individual crops can be concluded from the material indicating, *i.a.*, that there are many similarities in the labor requirements in Yugoslav Macedonia and in Greece.

FORESTRY LABOR is in most cases not mentioned in studies on agricultural labor. A questionnaire was therefore prepared and sent to experts in a number of European countries, most of which kindly answered the questions.

Forestry labor cannot be supposed to be directly correlated to the area under productive forest, since the productivity of such area varies in a way which is likely to provoke greater variations in the labor requirements than is the case with any variations in the crop practices. The questions were therefore formulated in terms of output rather than area. Three main questions were asked:

a) How much timber can a man fell during a full labor day?

b) How much timber can be transported per man per day, the distance the timber is normally transported by the personnel in the forest (especially the farmers felling their own timber)?

c) How much maintenance work is normally done per area unit, for instance per 100 hectares of productive forest?

To the first question, the Swedish reply stated that fellings per day could be assessed at $1-1\frac{1}{2}$ cubic meter per day in thinning operations, but about 4 m³ in normal, final, fellings. Total weighted average of all fellings might indicate 3.25 m³ per day, under optimal conditions. Because of variations in weather conditions, actual fellings might be about $2\frac{1}{2}$ m³ of coniferous wood and 2 m³ of birch wood.

The Finnish reply refers to O. Makkonen, *Practical application of the results of time studies in logging* (Helsinki 1950), p. 61, according to which a daily performance could be some $2\frac{1}{4}-5$ m³ of coniferous and about 4 m³ of birch wood.

From Denmark, the anwer was that about 3 m³ per day was considered normal.

The Norwegian reply indicates that the output of an efficient labor day could vary between $1\frac{1}{2}-3.3$ m³.

From W. Germany, 3 m³ per day was said to be a rough assessment of normal felling per day.

The Swiss reply equally indicates 2–3 m⁶ as a normal performance per day in logging.

The Italian reply indicates a variation between 1.6–5 m³ per day. Since charcoal making is an important industry in Italy, it is noted that 10 hours per quintal of charcoal is considered normal for this kind of work.

The reply from Yugoslavia states that 3 m⁶ per day is a normal performance in that country.

To question 2, on the importance of transport work, the Swedish reply indicates that on snow, 10 m³ could be transported 3 km in a day, 8 m³ 5 km. When there is no snow, the performance could be half as much.

From Finland, it is communicated that on distances up to 1 km, a man can transport 17.4 m⁶; on a distance of 7–8 km, 6.2 m³, etc.

The Norwegian reply says that when there is snow, 5–6 m³ per day can be transported up to 5 km; on the same distance, a tractor could drag 25–30 m³.

The Danish reply says that with horse transports up to 5 km, 5–8 m³ can be transported a distance of 5–10 km, $3\frac{1}{2}-5$ m³, at 10–20 km $2\frac{1}{2}-3$ m³ per day. With lorries, the performances at the same distances might be 10–15, $8\frac{1}{2}-12$, and 6–8 m³, respectively.

From Switzerland, 5–10 m³ per day is said to be a normal performance by a two-man team.

The German reply says that 6–10 m³ per day is a normal transport performance and adds the suggestion that the farmers carry out about half the transports of timber and fuel felled by them in their own forests.

The Yugoslav reply indicates $2\frac{1}{2}$ m³ per day as normal transport performance, and equally says that the peasants themselves transport about half their fellings.

To question 3, on maintenance work, the Swedish reply says that, when everything is included, it may be said that the production of 1 m³ wood requires 1 laborday (including felling, transport, and maintenance work). About $\frac{3}{4}$ of this goes to felling and transport and $\frac{1}{4}$ to maintenance work.

The Finnish reply says that maintenance work alone requires about 1 labor day a year per hectare under productive forest.

The Norwegian reply is rather detailed on this point, stating that the performance in thinning operations (inasmuch as they are not included among felling operations) amounts to 0.4 ha per day; in planting, 0.1 ha can be made per day, in sowing 0.15, and in all other kinds of maintenance work 0.30 ha per day. As a total assessment, it is said that 1,000 ha require 1147.8 days' work per year for all kinds of work together. This figure seems however to be based on figures for annual removals which are considerably lower than those communicated to FAO, and should probably be corrected by adding the felling of fuelwood used on the farms.

The Danish reply estimates total labor requirements on State forests at 5 days per hectare and suggests that on farms forests, the total annual work per hectare does not exceed 3 days. It is indicated that the work on the State forests to some extent is encumbered by performances in the interest of urban public using the forests as recreation area.

From W. Germany, 40 days per 100 hectares under forest is given as a rough assessment of labor needs in maintenance work.

The Swiss answer says that 132 labor hours per hectare is a normal total for all kinds of forestry work. This figure, which is extremely high, includes all the time spent under difficult transport conditions in the mountains.

The Italian reply does not think feasible to assess the amount of labor required for maintenance operations.

From Yugoslavia, details are given of planned plantations and maintenance operations, totalling 5.2 million days' labor in the country.

In the above quoted material of labor norms from Hungary, also some indications of forestry labor were included; MATOLCSY says that for the production of 1 m³, 0,4 days are spent in logging and 0.2 days in transport. No mention is made of maintenance work. It is quite likely that labor requirements are lower than elsewhere in Hungarian forests, part of which are on rather plain ground. If the data are slightly underestimated and an allowance is made for maintenance work as in the Swedish reply, the total requirements may be between 0.8–1 day per m³.

Actual Soviet practice reckons with 0.6 m³ as a normal output of timber per day (including strictly all work done for this production) which should, however, in a near future be improved to 0.9 m³ per day.

Despite all variations it can be stated that for work under similar conditions, most of the contents of the replies is fairly consistent. The Swedish rule, 1 labor day per m³ produced, can be accepted as a rough average. In the Scandinavian countries, when all fellings are included, the average annual output is about 2 m³ per hectare of productive forest. For our enquiry, it was therefore accepted as a general rule that, in countries where the average output does not depart too much from 2 m³ per hectare, 20 hours or 2 days were reckoned as normal requirement per hectare of farm forest; in countries where the output differs substantially, corresponding corrections were made. This rule seems to be accurate enough for an assessment of the role of forestry labor in relation to the farming population. It is of course not precise enough if interest were to be focussed specially on the forestry industry itself.

SOURCES AND METHODS, AND SOME DETAILED DATA, ON THE ANALYSIS OF FARM STRUCTURES.

Current farm censuses used for the analysis of farm structures are to a great extent the same as have been already quoted in Appendix 3. For data referring to 1950, some unpublished information was obtained through FAO. The following will serve to illustrate and complete the calculations presented in the latter part of Chapter 3.

AUSTRIA. The farm censuses of 1902 and 1951 can be compared if Burgenland is deducted from the figures of the latter. The areas included in each sizeclass in 1902 can be roughly estimated on the basis of probable average sizes in each size-class.

Size-class, ha	Number of holdings, (000)		Area of the holdings, (000 hectares)	
	1902	1951	1902	1951
–0.5	59	..	15	..
0.5–2	113	94	115	111
2–5	93	91	325	308
5–20	141	142	1,500	1,544
20–100	63	59	2,250	2,032
Over 100	6	6	3,150	3,445
TOTAL.	475	..	7,345	..
Sub-total, 0.5 ha and over	416	392	7,330	7,440
Sub-total, 2 ha and over .	303	298	7,215	7,329

The totals 1951 including Burgenland can be seen from the farm census. In 1902, half Tirol and $^7/_{10}$ of Steiermark are reckoned to belong to modern Austria.

For modern structure research, cf. A. Steden, "Die landwirtschaftlichen Betriebsformen der Bundesländer Österreich, Salzburg, Tirol und Vorarlberg", *Bodenkultur* (Wien 1951), pp 17–36.

BELGIUM. Farm structure data referring to 1895 were taken from *Exposé de la situation du Royaume de 1876 à 1900* (Bruxelles, *s.a.*), p. 58sq, those referring to 1950 from the farm census of that year.

BULGARIA. Farm structure data referring to 1908 and 1934 were derived from the sources quoted in Appendix 3; in both cases, the data include only private farms but exclude public lands, which tends to overestimate the role of small farms somewhat. Summary farm structure data referring to 1946 were taken from *Zycie gospodarcze* (Warsaw 1951), p. 937.

CZECHOSLOVAKIA. The early structure data were obtained from the Austrian census of 1902 (with deduction of Polish Czieszyn), and the Hungarian farm data from 1900 (see below under Hungary). Data referring to 1930 are derived from the farm census of that year: *Landwirtschaftliche Betriebszählung der Czechoslowakischen Republik*, T. 1, (Prague 1935). The structure as in 1949 is rendered in accordance with the pre-census returns of that year by L. Stejskal, "Programme of the Census of Agricultural Holdings in 1950", *Statistický Zpravodaj* (Prague 1950), p. 46, in comparison with such of 1930. The 1950 census itself does not seem to have been published. The data in the quoted article include details for the Czech provinces and Slovakia. Those for the whole republic give the following comparative picture:

Size-class, ha	Number of holdings 000		Area of the holdings, 000 hectares		Per cent distribution 1949	
	1930	1949	1930	1949	Number	Area
–0.5	261	297	70	84	19.7	0.7
0.5–1	178	192	133	147	12.7	1.3
1–2	240	207	359	317	13.7	2.7
2–5	404	351	1,357	1,240	23.3	10.6
5–10	240	255	1,697	1,881	16.9	16.0
10–20	141	159	1,963	2,215	10.6	18.9
20–50	57	35	1,603	1,033	2.3	8.8
50 and over	15	11	5,044	4,810	0.8	41,0
TOTAL.	1,536	1,507	12,227	11,729	100.0	100.0

The impression of rather modest changes in the structure is repeated both in the Czech provinces and in Slovakia.

Cf. also L. Malassis, "Les principaux types d'entreprise agricoles et leur évolution en Tchécoslovaquie", *Revue du Ministère d'agriculture* (Paris 1950), pp 103–112.

DENMARK. Farm structure data referring to 1901 were borrowed from J. Warming, *Danmarks Statistik*, (Copenhagen 1913), pp 188 sq; cf also *Statistiske Meddelelser* (Copenhagen) 4–16–6 and 4–21–4, and *Statistisk Tabelvaerk* (Copenhagen) 5 E 3, p. 16, containing land assessment data from 1904.

EIRE. From *Agricultural statistics for Ireland with detailed report for the year 1900* (Dublin 1901), data were regrouped so as to correspond with the present division into Eire and Northern Ireland. Thereby the figures on occupiers were preferred to those on holdings, since a farmer may occupy more than one "holding", and the former are those which correspond closest to the concept of operational holding.

FINLAND. For the year 1896, summary farm structure data were estimated on the basis of figures in the *Annuaire statistique pour la Finlande*, Année 21, (Helsinki 1900), p. 28 sq, referring to landed property units (most of which were actually farms), classified according to area of arable land:

Over 100 ha 2,694
25–100 ha 22,172
5–25 ha 60,676
Under 5 ha 32,162
TOTAL FARMS 117,704
Crofters 71,577

To these data can be added some information in G. Grotenfelt, *Landtbruket i Finland, En öfversikt* (Helsingfors 1896), especially p. 26 and 57, including the figure of 900–950 thousand hectares as the total of arable land in the country at that time. The crofts can be supposed to have averaged about 1 hectare of arable land each, and by aid of a rough estimation of the possible averages in the size-classes under 100 ha, the share of arable land of the large holdings could also be roughly estimated.

FRANCE. The differences in definition of the holdings in the French farm censuses have made difficult a direct comparison of the structure in order to show the development over the period, as shown in F. Dovring, "Les recensements agricoles français", *Bulletin mensuel de statistique, Supplément trimestriel* (Paris 1955, Apr.-Jun) (cf also note 98 a to Chapter 3). In a forthcoming article, the author will show that the main features of the structure in 1892 can be explored by means of an enquiry on the department level, exploiting the incidences of various formal and real changes that can be shown in the material. The structural changes are presented below, expressed as fractiles of farm area, by a number of main regions (the same as in Appendix 4).

Region	Year	1	2	3	4	M	6	7	8	9 decile
Alsace-Lorraine . . .	1907	1.6	3	4	6	8	11	17	30	80
	1929	1,7	3	5	7	9	13	19	34	120*
East	1892	6	12	20	26	36	51	89	230*	550*
	1929	8	15	22	29	38	50	69	100	170
	1942	11	19	26	34	44	56	75	105	190
North	1892	6	11	18	26	37	55	101	195	400*
	1929	7	13	18	23	31	41	80	180	250*
	1942	11	16	22	29	38	50	72	110	200
Center-North	1892	6	12	19	27	42	71	140	375*	800*
	1929	6	11	17	23	32	44	64	105	210
	1942	9	15	20	27	35	46	60	86	155
Bretagne	1892	4	7	11	15	20	25	34	50	350*
	1929	5	8	10	12	15	18	21	25	34
	1942	6	9	11	14	16	19	23	29	37
Center-South-West . .	1892	5	9	14	19	26	34	50	101	300*
	1929	6	9	12	16	20	26	34	46	75
	1942	9	12	16	20	24	30	38	48	75
Landes	1892	5	11	18	25	36	53	110	250*	500*
	1929	6	11	17	23	31	42	60	100	230
	1942	8	11	16	23	32	46	74	155	280
Center-South-East . .	1892	3	6	8	12	17	23	33	58	280*
	1929	4	6	8	11	14	18	27	41	81
	1942	5	8	9	13	16	21	27	41	81
Alpes	1892	5	11	18	27	42	100	300*	700*	1500*
	1929	8	14	21	32	49	73	114	208	600*
	1942	10	17	25	38	54	76	112	177	300
Corsica	1892	6	11	17	27	100	300*	600*	1200*	2300*
	1929	6	10	18	28	50	88	190	540	2200*
Mediterranean region .	1892	4	8	14	24	40	74	160	400*	1200*
	1929	4	7	11	19	32	63	117	250	600*
	1942	5	9	15	25	45	73	131	255	600*

The grouping of departments into regions is as follows:

Alsace-Lorraine	Bas-Rhin, Haut-Rhin, Moselle.
East	Ardennes, Aube, Côte d'Or, Marne, Haute-Marne, Meurthe-et-Moselle, Meuse, Haute-Saône, Vosges, Yonne.
North	Aisne, Calvados, Eure, Manche, Nord, Oise, Orne, Pas-de-Calais, Seine, Seine-Inférieure, Seine-et-Marne, Seine-et-Oise, Somme.
North Center	Allier, Belfort, Cher, Doubs, Eure-et-Loire, Indre, Indre-et-Loire, Jura, Loir-et-Cher, Loiret, Maine-et-Loire, Mayenne, Nièvre, Saône-et-Loire, Sarthe.
Bretagne	Côtes-du-Nord, Finistère, Ille-et-Vilaine, Loire-Inférieure, Morbihan.
South West Center	Ariège, Aveyron, Cantal, Charente, Charente-Maritime, Corrèze, Creuse, Dordogne Hante-Garonne. Gers, Lot, Lot-et-Garonne, Lozère, Basses-Pyrénées, Hautes-Pyrénées, Deux-Sèvres, Tarn, Tarn-et-Garonne, Vendée, Vienne, Haute-Vienne.
Landes	Gironde, Landes.

South East Center   Ain, Ardèche, Drôme, Isère, Loire, Haute-Loire, Puy-de-Dôme, Rhône, Savoie,
                     Haute-Savoie.
Alpes   Basses-Alpes, Hautes-Alpes.
Corsica   Corse.
Mediterranean region Alpes-Maritimes, Aude, Bouches-du-Rhône, Gard, Hérault, Pyrénées-Orientales,
                     Var, Vaucluse.

In addition to some historically and geographically individualized regions like Bretagne, Alsace-Lorraine and Corsica, the grouping of departments into main regions has been done by combining the dominating land tenure situations and the general level of land values. The regions appear to be sufficiently homogeneous for the purposes of this enquiry.

Cf. also M. Augé-Laribé, *La politique agricole de la France* (Paris 1950), p. 477; E. Weill-Raynal, "La répartition des terres en France, légende et réalité", *Etudes et conjoncture, Economie française* (Paris 1948, Oct.–Dec.), pp. 61–76, and the redactional comments to the same article, *ibid.*; and, finally, the article in *Revue du Ministère de l'Agriculture* (Paris 1951, Mar), p. 59.

GERMANY. Both for Western and Eastern Germany, and for each of the *Länder* existing in the late forties (later abolished in Eastern Germany), the farm structure tables of the census of 1907 were for this enquiry broken down to correspond with the actual territorial subdivisions.

For the present territory of Western Germany, the following structural figures were found:

Size-class, hectares of agricultural land	Number of farms, 000	Agricultural area of the same, 000ha
0.05–0.5.	1,163	181
0.5–2	700	766
2–5	627	2,026
5–20	591	5,689
20–100	116	3,923
100 and over	3	656
TOTAL.	3,200	13,241
Sub-total, 0.5 ha and over	2,037	13.060

For the present territory of Eastern Germany, the following figures were found:

Size-class, hectares of agricultural area	Number of farms, 000	Agricultural area of the same, 000ha
0.05–0.5.	437	87
0.5–2	256	253
2–5	134	475
5–20	168	1,703
20–100	55	2,048
100 and over	7	2,165
TOTAL.	1,057	6.731
Sub-Total, 0.5 ha and over	620	6,644

The detail by *Länder* do not show sufficiently great deviations in the trend from that of the two main parts of Germany to justify the inclusion of these tables in this comparative survey of Europe. As an example, the fractile breakdown can be shown from two of the West German Länder and the Saar.

		1	2	3	4	M	6	7	8	9 decile
Niedersachsen	1907	4	6	9	13	17	23	31	43	80
	1949	4	7	11	14	19	24	31	42	64
Bavaria.	1907	4	6	8	10	13	17	21	29	42
	1949	4	6	8	10	12	16	20	27	40
Saar	1907	1.2	2.2	3	5	6	8	10	14	20
	1948	1.0	2.0	3	4	6	7	10	13	20

The regional differences in structure are important enough, but the rate of change does not vary in any important way.

Details on recent changes in Eastern Germany can be seen in the *Statistisches Jahrbuch der Bundesrepublik Deutschland*, 1953 showing, *i.a.* that much of the land reform in Eastern Germany took place between 1946 and 1951.

On the long-term changes in Western Germany, see also *Vergrösserung landwirtschaftlicher Kleinbetriebe* (Agrarsoziale Gesellschaft e.V., processed, 1954 Apr) showing, *i.a.*, the development of holdings between 2 and 5 hectares since 1882.

Cf also L. Deczyk, "Betriebsgrössenstruktur der deutschen Landwirtschaft (in Westdeutschland unterblieb die Bodenreform)", *Deutsches Wirtschaftsinstitut, Berichte* (Berlin 1950, Sep); G. Jensch, "Die Verschiebung der landwirtschaftlichen Produktion bei Betriebsgrössenänderungen", *Berichte zur deutschen Landeskunde* (Leipzig & Stuttgart 1950), pp 48–53; H. Regenspurg, "Die zweckmässige Siedlungsgrösse in Ostpreussen", Berichte über Landwirtschaft" (1942), pp 593–640, commenting on the increase of middle-sized holdings.

GREECE. In addition to the census of 1929, preliminary data from the farm census of 1950 were obtained through FAO.

HUNGARY. The farm structure in 1900 has had to be estimated on the basis of the "Dénombrement de la population des pays de la Sainte Couronne Hongroise en 1900, P. 9, Conditions de la propriété bâtie et foncière", *Publications statistiques hongroises*, N.S., Vol. 18 (Budapest 1907).

The introduction to this publication strongly warns the reader that the figures do not represent a farm census. As a complement to the population census, landed property has been enumerated, not where the properties are situated but where the owner or holder resides. The geographical distribution of holders therefore does not reflect that of the holdings. As an example, the apparent great concentration of landed property in Budapest is mentioned.

These remarks have their full significance with regard to big estates which were farmed as large-scale enterprises by absentee owners. They can not, on the other hand, be too disturbing on the impression of the regional distribution of small and medium-sized holdings, farmed by their owners or held in lease. Their holders are bound to live on the holding or in its neighbourhood, and the mass of such holdings are therefore no doubt registered where they were situated. Thus, the columns, for owner-operators, holders in usufruct, leaseholders, and sharecroppers, give us the framework of the holding structure in the lower and medium-sized strata of holdings. These figures are available by comitates. In each comitate, the balance of the area must belong to large estates, and this can therefore be estimated, when an estimate has been made of the land belonging to the lower size-classes, on the basis of their probable average size. It has, therefore, seemed interesting to split up the figures on the territories of the various succession States. In doing so, the same approximative procedure was followed, with regard to comitates divided by present State boundaries, as described in Appendix 3.

With regard to the large holdings, some further information was drawn from two publications issued in the mid-nineties, one dealing with State property and the other with communal property and entailed private estates. The former, *A kincstari, közalapitvanyi tovabba az egyhazi és szersztetesi nagyobb birtokok területének és mivelési agak szerinti megoszlasanak kimutatasa* (Budapest 1895), shows that the State, other public bodies, and the Churches, together owned 4.73 million cadastre yokes (à 0.575 ha), which was 9.6 per cent of the then Hungarian territory; in the agricultural area, the share held by these public owners was only 6.1 per cent. The latter publication, *A hitzbizományi valamint a köszségi és közbirtokossági birtokok területének és mívelési ágak szerinti megoszlásának kimutatása* (Budapest 1894), dealing with entailed estates and with various categories of communal property, shows that about $^1/_3$ of the land of Old Hungary was subject to some kind of restricted circulation, while $^2/_3$ could be sold and bought freely. On pp 67 sqq, a list is given of estates over 6,000 yokes, most of which were forest estates, especially in Transylvania and Slovakia, but even on the Alföld (the great plain in south-eastern Hungary) some estates had many thousand yokes (Zenta 14,388, Szeged-Tapén 19,782). On pp 75 sqq, as an appendix, a list is given of estates between 1,000 and 6,000 yokes showing, i.a., that out of 220 such estates only 13 had more than 1000 yokes of arable land each.

By aid of these various indications, the farm structure in present-day Hungary has been estimated as in 1900. Bringing in the corresponding figures from the farm census of 1935, we obtain the following comparative table.

Size-class, in cadastre yokes (à 0.575 ha) of total farm ar	Number of holdings, 000		Area of the same, 000 yokes	
	1900	1935	1900	1935
−1	209	558	75	198
1–5 . . . . . ./.	358	484	900	1,225
5–50	324	446	4,530	6,248
50–100	12	16	780	1,102
100 and over	10	13	9.700	7,259
TOTAL.	913	1,517	16,000	16,033

The most recent structure data available are those returned through the agricultural questions on the questionnaire of the population census of 1949. The report on this census, *Az 1949 évi népszámlálás*, 2. "Mezögazdasági eredmények" (Budapest 1950), shows that the enumeration was one of operational holdings and can be interpreted as such. See also P. George, "La transformation des campagnes hongroises", *Annales de géographie* (Paris 1951), pp 199 sqq.

ITALY. The only available farm census is that of 1930, which contains only a few specifications and does not make possible any weighting of the size-classes. The wide diversity in the fertility and value of farm land in Italy makes unweighted structure figures rather uninstructive. A kind of complement is in the statistics on landed property units, as published, for instance, in the *Annuario statistico dell' agricoltura italiana*, 1947–50, pp 43 sqq (referring to 1946). The basic classification is according to total area here too, but there is a second classification according to taxable revenue ("Reddito imponibile"), which gives a better idea of the land structure than the unweighted hectare figures, even if it is true that the weighted figures are not comparable with those we have computed from other countries, on the basis of labor requirements. The property units have been registered separately within each community, so that vast landed domains scattered over many communities are counted as several smaller properties. This, of course, makes the picture of the property structure more akin to the farm structure, even if it is by no means identical with the latter.

Cf G. Medici, *Land property and land tenure in Italy* (Bologna 1952), where the property statistics, with the classification according to taxable revenue, is used as the best means to describe the land structure of Italy.

NETHERLANDS. For the comparison with the structure presented by the 1950 census we have chosen the 1910 census, because this is the first of a series of consecutive censuses with comparable classification. Older census figures, as those for 1900 available in the *Jaarcijfers* for 1901, are based on a slightly different criterion.

See also A. Groenman, "Hoe zijn de kleine boerenbedrijven ontstaan?", *Tijdschrift voor economische geoggraphie* (1946), pp 296 sqq, stressing that the smallholdings of the size between 1–5 ha reached their maximum in 1921, and that a certain concentration of the holding structure made itself felt already in the thirties; and C. Rietsema, *Agrarische bedrijfsvormen in Hollands noorderkwartier*, (Assen 1950).

NORWAY. "Jordbrukstellingen i Kongeriket Norge 30 september 1907", *Norges officielle statistik*, 145, H. 3, p. 28, gives the size classification according to cultivated area, which is a criterion slightly narrower than that used in the most recent census, of 1949.

POLAND. For the eastern parts of Poland, corresponding to the old Kingdom of Poland ("Congress Poland"), the farm structure as in the nineties has been reconstructed on the basis of data in the *Stosunki rolnicze Królestwa Kongresowego, Zbior wiadomości o stanie i warunkach rozwoju rolnictwa na ziemach Królestwa Polskiego*... ed. S. Janicky, S. Rosińsky, F. Ubysz (Warsaw 1918). Separate data are given pp 31 sqq and 40, on the structure of small holdings in Russian *des'iatiny* (à 1.09 ha), and on large estates on Polish *Morgen* (à 0.56 ha). There were also some 800,000 ha public lands, but since no breakdown on size-classes is available for them, the computation had to be made on the assumption that they were distributed over the size-classes on the same pattern as the private lands. For the private holdings, the following distribution of farm land on size-classes was found (in 000 ha):

–2.18 ha	275
2.18–5.46 ha	1,200
5.46–21.85 ha	5,000
Over 21,85 ha	600
168–560 ha	1,200
560–1.680 ha	1,700
Over 1.680 ha	1,400
TOTAL	11,375

For the western regions, data were derived from the German farm census of 1907, with additional data on Polish Czieszyn from the Austrian census of 1902. The distribution of agricultural land on the size-classes was found to have been as follows (in 000 ha):

–0.5 ha	64
0.5–2 ha	238
2–5 ha	569
5–20 ha	2,514
20–100 ha	2,618
Over 100 ha	3,757
TOTAL	9.760

For the southern parts of Poland, finally, that is the western part of Austrian Galizia, structure data have been derived from the Austrian farm census of 1902, in the same way as for Austria and western Czechoslovakia. The distribution of area on the size-classes had to be estimated, since only farm numbers are indicated in the census. The following distribution was found (in 000 ha):

–0.5 ha	10
0.5–1	40
1–2	150
2–5	600
5–10.	500
10–20	200
20–50	100
50–100.	75
Over 100	500
TOTAL	2,175

Detailed data can also be shown for districts and parts of such, but putting together data derived from the various sources on behalf of parts of the same district, or on behalf of the whole country, is not feasible, since the criteria were different. Especially in eastern Poland, it would be a disadvantage to adapt the system to the western and southern figures where the highest size-class is "over 100 ha".

An attempt at classifying farms according to their available labor force (not according to labor requirements) was made by Cz. Nowakowski & W. Ponikowski, *Zagadnienie podziału gospodarstw włościańskich na klasy wielkości według stosunków pracy* (Warsaw 1936), with stress upon the proportions between family labor and hired labor.

For the farm structure in 1949, data were borrowed from the *Rocznyk statystyczny*, 1949, p. 53, showing separate size-classifications for private and State (and other public) farms. There were some private farms over 50 ha, and some public farms under 50 ha, but since most land in the public farms was in farms over 100 ha, and the private farms under 50 ha covered some 89 per cent of the total farm area, the construction of one single set of structure figures does not involve any hardy hypothesis.

PORTUGAL. The only existing farm census is that of 1952–54, carried out in three parts. The farm structure is indicated only by numbers of farms in each size-class, but no direct figures are given as to the distribution of the area. The size-classification is according to arable land, and there are many size-classes, which makes it relatively easy to estimate the distribution of arable area.

As regards the development of the farm structure since 1900, very little information is available. The land fragmentation data quoted above in Appendix 2 are only indicative and do not allow any strong conclusions. It can only be stated that the characteristic regional differences in farm structure are inherited from a remote past, but the rate or even the direction of modern development cannot be outlined.

Some individual instances are known when large estates have been broken up into small holdings by voluntary sale of the landowners; see, for instance, *Parcelamento das herdades do Montinho e Gramacha* (Lisboa 1938), pp 9 sq, showing parcellization to some extent already around 1900 and finished in 1920: 894 hectares were divided into 304 plots and distributed to 219 families. The new holdings were too small to be the only means of income for the families of agricultural workmen who bought them. The parcellization led to a certain intensification of the cultivation, though at a modest scale since no new irrigation was introduced at the moment of parcellization. Similar experiences are held forth in *Parcelamento da herdade da Tôrre* (Lisboa 1938).

Cf also E. de Castro Caldas, *O problema sociológico das formas de exploração da propriedade rústica em Portugal* (Lisboa 1947).

RUMANIA. Farm structure in the Old Kingdom, referring to 1913, is computed according to the *Agricultorii și repartizarea pamântului cultivat în 1913*, (Bucureşti 1915), which also has figures for property distribution in 1896, 1902, and 1905.

For the Transylvanian plateau and the Tisza valley, structure data were calculated on the basis of the Hungarian population census of 1900, in the same way as described above under Hungary. These regions were already then much more dominated by small holdings than was then the case with the central Hungarian regions; consequently, the result is less uncertain here. The distribution of the area on the size-classes was estimated on the basis of the probable average size of holding within each size-class; since number of holdings in each size-class was not very different from the structure in modern time in this area, there is no great difference possible in the distribution of areas either.

Also the Austrian farm census of 1902 shows for Bucovina only a small number of large farms but a great mass of small holdings, most of them owner-operated.

The Rumanian farm structure as in 1948 was derived from A. Golopentia & P. Onică, "Recenseământul agricol din Republica populară Româna, 25 Ianuarie 1948, Rezultate provizorii", *Probleme economice* (Bucureşti 1948 Mar). The geographical subdivision still makes it possible to distinguish the Old Kindom as identical with five of eight zones, Bucovina as one and the formerly Hungarian regions as two.

SWEDEN. The farm structure as in 1900 was derived from *Statistisk Årsbok*, 1911, Table 56, p. 51, where some elementary data are given as referring to the year 1900. As in Finland, a special category of smallholders in dependent position (corresponding to "crofters") is mentioned outside the size-classified structure and must be supposed to have had a very small average size in arable land. Because the classification criterion is arable land, the distribution of this area could be estimated with tolerable certainty. On the other hand, only a few size-classes were mentioned, and because of this, the fractile values should be read as roughly estimated.

The latest farm census, of 1951, has been used through the preliminary figures published in *Statistisk Tidskrift* (Stockholm 1954–55).

On the reliability and comparability of the census data over the last decades, see K. Lindman, "Antalet jordbruk av olika storlek och arealen åkerjord enligt 1951 ars jordbruksräkning", *Statistisk Tidskrift* (Stockholm 1954, Oct), pp 450–460.

SWITZERLAND. Farm structure data are available according to farm censuses in 1905 and 1939, but the development over the last decade cannot yet be described. The fact that the farm structure is despite everything concentrating towards somewhat larger holdings is stated by F. T. Wahlen, "Landwirtschaftliche Weltprobleme", *Agrarpolitische Revue* (Zürich 1953), pp 198 sqq.

UNITED KINGDOM. The structure of holdings in England and Wales became known in outline with the so-called New Domesday Book in 1875. A statement of the number of agricultural holdings of various size-classes, and of the acreage of each class of holdings, is included in G. C. Brodrick, *English land and English landlords* (London 1881), p. 500, referring to the years 1875 and 1880. The following figures may be quoted therefrom:

Size-class of holdings, acres	Number of holdings,		Acreage of the same, 000 acres	
	1875	1880	1875	1880
50 acres and under	333,630	336,149	4,182	4,177
50–100	54,498	54,369	3,958	3,941
100–300	65,766	66,373	11,184	11,400
300–500	11,678	12,071	4,360	4,516
500–1000	3,955	4,170	2,568	2,702
1000 and over	473	506	585	644
TOTAL.	470,000	473,638	26,837	27,379

From the 20th century, structure data are obtainable in the annual agricultural statistics; the special figures for 1950, classified according to area including rough grazings, were taken from the preliminary publication of World Census data in the *Monthly Bulletin of Statistics*, of FAO.

The long-term trend in the development of size of holdings has been treated for England and Wales as a whole, by D. K. Britton, "Are holdings becoming larger or smaller?", *The Farm Economist* (Oxford 1950), pp 188–197. An article analyzing some regional trends is under preparation jointly by Britton and Dovring.

Cf also A. W. Ashby & I. L. Evans, *The agriculture of Wales and Monmouthshire*, (Cardiff 1944), p. 93 sq, on the concept of "holding" as deviating from that of the agricultural enterprise, which may include more than one holding. – For Scotland, figures may also be obtained from *Land settlement in Scotland, Report by the Scottish Land Settlement Committee* (Edinburgh 1945), showing that, between 1913 and the early forties, the number of holdings had increased much less than the number of holdings established by the Committee, and also that there had been a slight decline in the number of small holdings. The same view is even more stressed in *Scotland's marginal farms, General Report* (Edinburgh 1947).

For Northern Ireland, figures referring to the year 1900 were derived from the same source as for Eire. In this case also, the figures referring to occupiers were preferred to those referring to "holdings". The classification should be according to the total area of the farm land, but no mention is made of rough grazings. For 1950, approximate figures were derived from the preliminary World Census figures in the *Monthly Bulletin of Statistics* of FAO, by making subtractions of the returns for Great Britain from those for the U.K. This operation gave the number of holdings in each size-class; the area distribution was thereafter estimated on the basis of probable average size in each size-class.

U.S.S.R. For some parts of Ukraina, which at the beginning of the century belonged to the Austrian monarchy, farm structure data can be obtained from the farm census of that country in 1902. For most of the Soviet Union, farm structure data properly speaking are not available until 1926, when the structure of farms shows almost only small and very few medium-sized farms, while the State and collective farms then existing were the only large farms. For the beginning of the century, some indications can be derived from the statistics on landed property, especially as regards the structure of peasant farms in various parts of the country. Even so, it must be kept in mind that the real importance of small-scale farming was already much greater than the figures indicate, since large parts of the big estates were let out to peasants, and this movement went increasing during the decade following the compilation of the data.

The statistics on landed property is available through two publications, the *Statistika zemlevladeniia 1905 g, Svod dannykh po 50-ti guberbiiam Evropeĭskoĭ Rossii* (S.-Peterburg 1907), and the *Kizdaniiu 'Statisticheskaia svedeniia po zemel'nom voprosu v Rossii'* (S.-Petersburg 1907).

The properties are distinguished as *krest'ianskaia nadel'naia*, or peasant property held as shares in village land following the liberation of the serfs, and *chastnaia*, or fully individual property, most of which belonged to noblemen or urban capitalists. The former was mainly small and the latter mostly big property, and a different scale of size-classes was therefore used for each. There were however very few holdings and very little land in the size-classes common to both categories, so that it was not very difficult to construct one single set of size-classified properties in each region.

The peasant properties added up to some 135–140 million desiatiny (à 1.09 hectare), out of which about 80 per cent or 110 million were agricultural land, and 55 per cent, or 76 million, were arable land. The category of individual property included 101 million desiatiny, out of which just over the half, or 51 million, were agricultural land, and one-third, or about 34 million desiatiny, were arable land. Public bodies also owned immense tracts of land, but it can be shown that almost all of it was forest or waste land, to a great extent located in the northern regions. Agricultural area in public property may have amounted to some 15 million desiatiny, whereof perhaps 10 million arable land. To the extent they were cultivated, these public estates were generally let to peasants, and it will therefore not be necessary to consider them when discussion is about the degree to which large farms still existed.

Size classification is given in total area only. Adding up the peasants and the individual property (part of which also belonged to peasants), this already leads to some overstatement of the relative importance of large properties, since the average value of their land must have been considerably lower than was the case with the peasant properties, as shown by the above figures on the proportion of agricultural and arable to total area in each of the two categories. With these reservations, the following table can be drawn up to show the fractile values of the property structure as in 1905, for the European part of the Tsarist empire and for some main regions within the same. The fractiles are expressed in hectares.

Region	1	2	3	4	M	6	7	8	9
Total Russia, excl. Northern Region	7	10	14	20	37	103	550	1,900	10,000
Baltic Region	30	38	47	78	1,170	2,200	3,600	6,000	9,500
Lake Region	9	12	17	31	150	550	1,500	4,300	13,000
Lithuanian-Belorussian Region	9	11	16	27	160	650	1,800	4,600	14,000
Central and Middle Volga Regions	6	8	9	11	15	52	270	850	4,000
Black Soil Region	6	8	9	11	13	17	115	550	2,600
Ukraina	5	7	10	14	30	105	700	1,600	4,000
Volga and Volga-Don Regions	11	15	19	25	39	80	400	1,500	4,000
Rostov District (Northern Caucasus)	32	37	42	45	51	62	82	125	400

The size-classification already indicates that the large estates had their stronghold in the north-western regions, above all the Baltic countries, but also in Belorussia and the regions around S.-Peterburg. The Northern Region has been excluded, because many properties there included vast tracts of forest and waste land, which would give a false impression of the importance of these estates. Already in the regions of the Black Soil and Central-Middle Volga, peasant property is dominating and in the Rostov district there was almost nothing but peasant property on the vast, semi-arid lands which were then mostly used as grazings.

For early Soviet views on this epoch, see for instance A. Gaĭster, *Sel'skoe khoziaĭstvo kapitalisticheskoĭ Rossii, Ch. 1, Ot reformy 1861 g. do revoliutsii 1905 g.* (Moscow 1928).

YUGOSLAVIA. For Slovenia, Croatia, and Vojvodina, farm structure data were derived from the Austrian and Hungarian censuses described under Austria and Hungary. For Old Serbia, the *Statistique du Royaume de Serbie*, T. 16, (Beograd 1900), give figures from an agricultural census taken in 1897, on numbers of owners of cultivated land, by size-classes. Since there was very little leasehold in the country, this may be taken as being close to the real farm structure. The distribution of area had to be estimated on the basis of probable averages, which could be done with tolerable certainty since there were nine size-classes and most farms were small. Structure data from Bosnia-Hercegovina, referring to the year 1906, are given by O. v. Frangeš, *Die sozialökonomische Struktur der jugoslawischen Landwirtschaft* (Berlin 1937), p. 149. Comparing these data with those on private farms according to statistics of 1949, one finds that the number of farms under 2 hectares is almost unchanged, those between 2–10 hectares are almost doubled in numbers, and those over 10 hectares are reduced to ¾ of their number in 1906.

From Montenegro, the Kosmet District, and Macedonia, no early structure data seem to be available.

The present farm structure was derived from the *Socialistička poljoprivreda* (Beograd 1952, Jan), compared with the *Statistički bilten*, Ser. B-III, Year 3 (Beograd 1952, Jul), Table 7, p. 34 sq.

APPENDIX 6

SOURCES OF THE TABLES ON CO-OPERATION

A basic difficulty for these tables has been that of avoiding double counting. The over-estimation of the number of societies and members is probably most important in the table on "general" sales-and-supply societies, because over-lapping of activities and double membership is likely to be frequent there. The risk is relatively small in specialized branches like dairy co-operation but there, on the other hand, a certain risk exists for under-estimation, because some activities of the kind may be carried on also in societies of a less specialized character which are not therefore included in the statistics on dairy co-operatives.

Instead of the years 1910 and 1940, the period 1907/10 and the year 1937 were chosen, because more information could be made available in this way.

In addition to data found in current national statistics of a number of countries, the following sources have been used.

a. For information on many countries:

Annuaire du mouvement coopératif international, 1–2 (London 1910–13).

Year Book of Agricultural co-operation, 1927 sqq.

"Co-operative societies throughout the world: Numerical data", *International Labour Review* (Geneva 1939, Aug-Sep).

La coopération agricole, 1, (Rome 1931), with data on Germany, Belgium, Denmark, Eire, France, U.K., Hungary, Italy, Netherlands, Switzerland, and Czechoslovakia.

Co-operative action and rural life, Survey prepared by the Co-operation service of the International Labour Office (Geneva 1939, League of Nations, European Conference on Rural Life, 1939, C.I.M.I. 1939, Conf. E.V.R. 2), especially pp 9, 19.

"ILO Directory on co-operatives", *International Labour Review*, also available as reprints.

Report on the proceedings of the... Congress of the International Co-operative alliance... 1902 and later.

b. National monographs:

Bulgaria: P. Kiranov, *Kooperatsiiata v Bulgariia* (Sofia 1928).

Czechoslovakia: *Třicet let české zemědělské družstvení práce* (Prague 1928).

Denmark: H. Ravnholt, *The Danish co-operative movement* (Copenhagen 1947).

Finland: *Andelsvärksamheten i Finland 1910*, 2, "Statistik" (Helsingfors 1913).

Germany: *Genossenschaftskataster für das Deutsche Reich, Die eingetragenen Erwerbs- und Wirtschaftsgenossenschaften am 1. Januar 1903...* (Berlin 1906).

Netherlands: *The co-operative movement in the Netherlands*, (The Hague 1947).

Sweden: *Kooperativ verksamhet i Sverige åren 1911–1913* (Stockholm 1918), and subsequent annual reports under similar titles.

U.K. and Eire: *Agricultural co-operation...* with an introduction by Sir Horace Plunkett... (London 1925).

U.S.S.R.: V. P. Miliutin, *Kooperatsiia v SSSR za desiat let* (Moscow 1928); *Vsia kooperatsiia v SSSR, Spravochnik ezhegodnik* (Moscow 1928); E. M. Kayden & A. N. Antsiferov, *The co-operative movement in Russia during the war* (New Haven 1929).

APPENDIX 7

ANALYSIS OF THE CHERVENKOV SPEECH *

Identification symbols 2723

Communist State and its policy *970*

Work on co-operative farms, 205.
The co-operative, the correctness of it, 120.
Socialism as large scale economy in the village and a nation's economy as a whole, 67.
Comrade, teacher, leader, Dimitrov, Stalin, Lenin, Marx, Engels, 63.
State, a powerful means for building of socialism, 50.
New type of rural economy, large scale agriculture, a road for development of rural economy to Socialism, rural economic artel, agricultural artel, 46.
Party, we as leaders, our correct policy, planning, 43.
The Soviet Union as a mighty supporter and founder of the kolkhozes and socialism, 43.
The statute, 42.
Government, solid, socialistic democratic Ministry of Agriculture, 37.
Work on farms as synonymous to co-operation and meetings, 36.
Industry as a means of socialisation, increasing importance in the reconstruction of rural economy, 28.
Brigade, working peasant, poor and middle peasant, 25.
Communist party in its mass, Bolsheviks, 25.
Economically correct planning, payment organization, income, 24.
Workers' class, 21.
Leadership of Bulgarian Communist Party, 16.
Collective economy in rural economy, 15.
Our conference, important, 14.
People's democracy and council, 8.
Proletariat, revolution, 8.
Correct path, 6.
Right to private property in a restricted way, 6.
Agreeing cheers, 6.
Productive co-operation, 5.
Correct estimation of labor, 5.
Machine hire depots, 4.
Bulgarian Agrarian National Union, 2.

The task ahead *444*

Co-operative farms, life, members, movement, 105.
Workers and peasants, aided by our policy, large economic scale agriculture, a rich life, alliance between workers and peasants, system of contracts, 84.
We, 39.
After the examples of the Soviet Union and its kolkhozes, 37.

* The analysis of this document was finalized in March 1955.

New socialist reconstruction of village, transformation of rural economy, production, 33.
Strict large-scale rural economy, mass transmission, organization of labor, experienced cadres, 31.
Bulgarian Communist party, conference, 29.
The way out, success, 21.
The State and government, 20.
Model statute, 13.
Collective farms, labor, rural economic policy, 12.
Our five-year plan, 7.
Peasants joining co-operative farms, their own free will, 5.
Private auxiliary farms, right to private property, 5.
Nationalization of land, 3.

Co-operative farm, its property, movement, members, discipline, general meetings, developments, 171.
Great success, overfulfilled the plan, 51.
Organization, distribution of land, large farms, economic units, new form of large-scale production in rural economy, 43.
Communist government, State, fulfilment of obligations on time, 32.
Machine-hire depots, use of modern agrotechnical science, better life to the peasants, 25.
Peasants, women, youth, 23.
Permanent production brigades in agriculture, 17.
Statute, basic norms, 14.
We, 9.
Planning necessary, 7.
Systematic participation of the Soviet Government in the construction of the kolkhozes, 5.
Subject to socialisation, socialism, construction, road to socialism, 4.
Voluntary unions of peasants, means of production and labor, 4.
Only correct path, 3.

Co-operative farms, their members, discipline, co-operative democracy, 92.
This new basic model statute, 34.
Document of greatest significance for the socialist rural economy, 15.
Obligations of the State, 7.
Member, every poor and middle peasant, men, women, youth, 6.
Production brigades, cadres, 5.
Welfare of the peasants and their families, 5.
Use of the kolkhoz experience of the Soviet Union, 3.

Members, constantly growing, voluntarily, persuasion, propaganda, 31.
Co-operative farms, movement, members, 25.
Communist party, we, government, comrades, 21.
Tremendous influence, securing well-fare, cultural life, greater income, producing accumulating, 20.
Thousands of peasants, broad masses of poor and middle peasants, 19.
Remarkable success, victory, 17.
Socialist system in the village, 8.
State agricultural farms, machine-hire depots, 6.
Model statute, 6.
Identification with the Soviet Union and its kolkhozes, 5.
Correct path, 5.
The value of youth, 3.

Social nature of the co-operative farm 135
    Co-operative farms, members, movement, land, 27.
New form of economic organization, socialism in labor, proper principles 25.
    We, working class, peasantry, 14.
    Public labor, public property, State property, 14.
    Society, co-operative farm as a political instrument, 10.
    Kolkhozes, 10.
    Agricultural artel, 9.
    The collective, its members' property, private auxiliary farms, 6.
    Large-scale high-productive agricultural economy in our village, 5.
    Machine-hire depots, 5.
    Dictatorship of the proletariat, revolution, 5.
    Identification with the Soviet Union, Lenin, 5.

Self-criticism. 116
    Co-operative farms, their members, 30.
    We, I, 27.
    Comrades, delegates, 20.
    Model statute, basic law, 9.
    Communist party, government policy, 9.
    Women, youth, 7.
    Large-scale co-operative farming, new type of rural economic enterprises, 4.
    Brigades, 4.
    My duty, must, 3.
    Gross errors corrected, 2.
    Principles of voluntariness, 1.

Enemies of democracy 65
    Co-operative farms, discipline, movement, 18.
    Poor, middle peasants, greater majority, 13.
    We, 9.
    Majority of women, youth, co-operative members, 8.
    People's democratic rule, socialism in industry, in farms, principle of voluntarism, 6.
    Urban population, army, industry, free citizens, 5.
    New statutes, planning, organization, 4.
    Well-to-do life for the majority of peasants, 2.

Greetings 60
    Greetings, cheers, Stalin, Stalin, Stalin, comrades, applause, Long live, 60.

Rural economy 59
    We, our, 34.
    Socialist reconstruction of our rural economy, enlargement, 19.
    Peasants, 6.

Heroes of labor 47
Women, youth, the most valuable heroes on the co-operative farm, 24.
    Heroes, members of the co-operative farms, 21.
    Stalin, Dimitrov 2.

Class struggle. 44
    Restricting policy, progressive income tax, revolutionary vigilance, 10.
    Liquidate, drive out, take away, 9.
    Class struggle acute, sharp, 8.
    Co-operative farms, 7.

Leadership in our country, 6.
In the hands of the State, People's property, 4.

Doubts of the agrarian reform *23*
Pondering peasants, poor and middle peasants, private farmer, 16.
Co-operative farming, new method, 7.

The intellectuals *19*
Specialists, 11.
Intellectuals, intelligent workers, people's intelligentia, 4.
Working class, militant alliance of workers and peasants, 4.

Symbols for demands 627

The Communist State and its policy *20*
Immediate exemplary fulfillment of all obligations to the State, 10.
Correct organization of the labor, its payment, organization, 7.
Central higher school for leading co-operatives' members, similar country school, 3.

The task ahead *256*
Propagate, convince the peasants, voluntary entrance in the co-operative farms, main task, 52.
The need of industry justifies the developing of agriculture, industry, need of 66, 2 per cent more shoes, 39.
Point out the task, problems, questions, find a correct solution, the way, path, road, 38.
Work correctly organized in the collective farm, principle for payment, remuneration of labor, working days, 18.
Organization of large scale agriculture along Soviet lines, appeal to Stalin for help, publicity, 17.
Securing rich life to peasants, over-production, 15.
Developing machine-hire depots, industrialization of agriculture, apply agricultural science, 15.
Transformation of a large scale economy, 15.
Building of Socialism, socialistic reconstruction of rural economy, 12.
Workers, Communists, government, party support of the policy to the peasants, 7.
School for training of qualified quadres, 7.
Unite, build, 6.
1950 years' plan, 5.
Satisfactory scale for land-rent, 4.
Liquidation of, thrust out Capitalists, 4.
Draw the youth into production, 2.

Co-operative farm as a fact *116*
Correct estimation, organization of labor, paying days, 44.
Suggesting, planning, accounting, example of the Soviet Union, 31.
Aid must be given to co-operative farms, 17.
Introduction of correct crop rotation, 7.
Immediate exemplary fulfilment of obligations to the State, 6.
Securing victory over the kulaks, the backwardness, 5.
Difficulties to be solved, 3.
More women to leading positions in agriculture, 3.

Character of accepted model statute *101*
Outlining tasks as organizations, overfulfilment of production, conditions for membership, economic planning, management, obligations to the State, 56.

436 APPENDIX 7

Backwardness of rural economy, private property of land, 18.
Difficulties, obstacles, 14.
Poverty, poor peasants, 5.
Capitalistic elements in the village, 4.
Renting out, sale of land, 4.

Co-operative farm as a fact **20**
Difficulties due to different contributions, 6.
Devaluation of the working day, 4.
Poverty, poor peasants, 4.
Errors, 3.
Backwardness of rural economy, 2.
Kulak, 1.

Character of accepted model statue **19**
Rent, its payment, right to private ownership, 11.
Kulaks, exploitation ,persons undermining co-operative discipline, 7.
Poor, middle peasants, 1.

Confidence in victory **9**
Drought, difficulties, 6.
Private ownership of land, 3.

Social nature of the co-operative farm **17**
Absolute rent, exploitation, 9.
Hiding place for every kind of counter-revolutionary activities, 4.
Capitalist principle, 2.
Contradiction, cause of internal strife, 2.

Self-criticism **12**
Incorrect attitude toward representation of women, 4.
The rent, 4.
Errors, 4.

Enemies of democracy **175**
Undermining, wrenching activities of co-operative farm and new rural
economy, 30.
Capitalism, big landowners, Capitalist enterprises in the village, 29.
Present backwardness of rural economy, small farming, great lag in our
rural economy, 23.
Poverty, ignorance, misery, mass ruination of the peasants, 22.
Mistakes, droughts, 19.
Increase of private property elements, 14.
Enemies of working class and peasantry, counter-revolution, White
Guard men, 12.
Kulaks, 12.
Exploit the labor of others, 8.
Underestimation of women, 6.

Greetings (not applicable here).

Rural economy **43**
Dominance of private small backward primitive agricultural production,
25.
Backwardness of our rural economy, lagging behind, 16.
Non-capitalist economy, the crossroad between capitalism and socialism,2

Heroes of labor (not applicable here).

Class struggle. *38*
    Kulaks, big landowners, 12.
    Capitalist elements, 11.
    Resisting rapidity, hostile activities, agitators, 11.
    Cause of internal strife, 4.

Doubts of the agrarian reform *5*
    Private farmers, poor middle peasants, 5.

The intellectuals (no references)

NOTE

It may be convenient to recall some points earlier mentioned in our discussion:
The titles, as for instance "The Communist Party and its policy", indicate the treated subject-matter.

On any subject-matter, the communicator manipulates three kinds of symbols:
    1. Symbols of identification, that is, values dear to the communicator (his party, ideology, or program). As normal in human speech, these values can appear in debating any issue. It is therefore entirely wrong to interpret the identification symbols only as synonyms of the subject-matter debated for the moment.
    2. Symbols of demands, that is values, positive or negative, demanded by the communicator on any issue, independently of their positive or negative direction in the text.
    3. Symbols of resistance, that is, values rejected by the communicator (his party, ideology, or program), appearing on any debated issue. It is therefore too narrow, and misleading, to interpret symbols of resistance merely as synonyms and equivalents for the actual enemy and his activity.

Note also that the same words and expressions may be quoted more than once in the analysis above, according to their double or multiple function in the context.

In the discussion about qualitative and quantitative analysis of texts, there are two fundamental differences overlooked. One difference is relative whereas the other is absolute. The relative difference refers to the intensity with which every phrase is submitted to separate analysis. In the quantitative analysis, attention is not permitted to be unevenly dispersed and focussed longer on certain statements than others. This difference is relative because also the quantitative analyst has to interpret the text and therefore risks adding some of his own bias into the interpretation of each single phrase.

The absolute difference, on the other hand, is in the way of weighting the separate components of the material analysed. The qualitative analyst is the subject of his own bias not only in the interpretation of every separate phrase but also in the weighting of their relative value to the interpretation of the whole message. In the quantitative analysis, the interpretations in detail of every single statement are mechanically added together in such a way that the value which is given to different tendencies of the message becomes independent of the tendency of the temporary interpreter. The result of the measurement is likely to represent the average of the public's possible interpretations.

Sometimes, content analysts discern between "analysis a priori" of a content and "analysis a posteriori". The first is understood as mere symbol analysis of a message whereas the second is grasped as an analysis of themes in a text. This discrimination is confusing since all themes are built up of symbols whose direction and function in the text at last make them themes indicating the tendency of the message. That is, when recording the themes we have to sum up the functions of the symbols which build up the themes.

NOTES

INTRODUCTION

6a. L. Febvre, *Combats pour l'histoire*, (Paris 1953), p. 20, a lecture held in 1941.

7a. D. Mitrany, *Marx against the peasant* (London 1951), p. 12 sq.

CHAPTER 1

12a. M. A. Lefèvre, *L'habitat rural en Belgique*, (Liège 1926). Similar observations can be made, for instance, in many areas in Western Germany, and also in Northern Portugal.

13a. Out of date, though still frequently quoted, is M. Meitzen, *Siedlung und Agrarwesen der Westgermanen und Ostgermanen, Kelten, Römer, Slawen* . . . 1–3 (Berlin 1895–1905). Variations of the same method are found in A. Gradmann, "Das mitteleuropäische Landschaftsbild nach seiner geschichtlichen Entwicklung", *Geographische Zeitschrift* (1901), pp 361–377, 435–447; *idem, Das ländliche Siedlungswesen des Königreichs Württemberg* (Stuttgart 1913); and R. Martiny, "Die Grundrissgestaltung der deutschen Siedlungen", *Petermann's geographische Mitteilungen*, Erg.-H. 197 (Gotha 1928). Cf also P. Lauridsen, "Nogle Oplysninger og Bemaerkninger om danske Landsbyer", *Aarbøger for nordisk Oldkyndighed* (Copenhagen 1896), and W. Uhlemann, "Gegenwartsaufgaben vergleichender Siedlungsforschung auf deutschem Volksboden", *Deutsche Siedlungsforschung, R. Kötzschke zum 60 Geburtstag* (Leipzig & Berlin 1927).

13b. See, e.g., M. Le Lannou, *Pâtres et paysans de la Sardaigne* (Tours 1941), pp 271 sqq, and a number of modern French and Swedish studies in human geography.

13c. One of the broadest collections of empirical material of this kind is the *Naselja*-series, published since some decades by the Serbian Academy of Science in Belgrade and still continued. An individual example is in P. Zryd, *Grafenried zur Zeit der Dreifelderwirtschaft* (Bern 1940).

14a. W. Christaller, *Die ländliche Siedlungsweise im Deutschen Reich*, (Berlin 1937), especially p. 7.

14b. A. Demangeon, "La géographie de l'habitat rural", *Annales de géographie* (Paris 1927), pp 1–23, 97–114. Bibliography of settlement studies in M. Terán, *Habitat rural* (Zaragoza 1951).

14c. The formula, and one attempt to modify it, were applied on the settlement maps in the first edition of the *Atlas de France*. Cf O. Ribeiro, *Aglomeração e dispersão do povoamento rural em Portugal*, (Lisboa 1939), advancing criticism on the formula.

14d. The Polish contribution was published in the *Proceedings of the eighth International Congress of Geography* (Amsterdam).

14e. See, e.g., the settlement map in the *Atlante fisico-economico d'Italia* (Milano 1940), map prepared by R. Biasutti.

14f. *The Land of Britain*, by L. Dudley Stamp and others (London 1936 sqq).

15a. French *village* and *hameau*, German *Dorf* and *Weiler*, in Russian *seló* and *derevnia*, in Serbian *selo* and *zaselak*, in Bulgarian *selo* and *mĕsta*; in Spanish *pueblo, aldea, pueblecito, aldehuela, cortijo*, etc., and in Portuguese *aldeia, monte, lugar, lugarejo, casal*, and *quinta*. For Italian reseach and terminology, see T. Storai de Rocchi, *Guida bibliografica allo studio dell' abitazione rurale in Italia* (Firenze 1950).

442

15b. The separate Croatian edition of the population census of 1947 has its predecessors in V. Sabljar, *Miestopisni riečnik kraljevinah Dalmacije, Hèrvatske i Slavonie, Orts-Lexikon der Königreiche Dalmatien, Kroatien und Slawonien...* (Agram 1872), referring to 1866; *Pregled političkogo i subdenoga rezdieljenja Kraljevinah Hrvatske i Slavonije i uredjenja upravnih obcinah*, (Zagreb 1877), and analogous publications from 1889 and 1892. This tradition has largely determined the terminology of actual classification of settled places.

16a. An exception is in the early Bulgarian land statistics (see Appendix 1 under Bulgaria).

16b. An attempt towards mathematical analysis in H. de Barros Bernardo, *Monografía de Sesimbra, Estudo geo-económico do concelho*, (Lisboa 1941), p. 121.

17a. Similar views in W. Christaller, *Die ländliche Siedlungsweise im Deutschen Reich*, (Berlin 1937), pp 10 sqq, proposing the following system of size groups:

Isolated farmsteads etc., up to 15 inhabitants;

Farm groups and small hamlets, 15 to 70 inhabitants;

Large hamlets and small villages, 70 to 200 inhabitants;

Normal villages, from 200 to 600 inhabitants;

Large villages (or, church villages), from 600 to 1.600 inhabitants, normally 800–1,000;

"Market villages", or "Central Places", 1,600–4.500 inhabitants.

Places over 4,500 inhabitants should be reckoned as towns.

19a. Early Soviet settlement policy was favorable to the creation of hamlets, see IA. Kis'liakoŭ, *Pasiolki*, (Minsk 1928). The decree on abolition of isolated settlements was commented upon by N. Khrushchiov, in *Pravda*, April 25, 1950. Cf also A. Pavlov, "Le regroupement des kolkhoz", *Etudes soviétiques* (Paris 1950, No 28), pp 72 sqq. Partial survival of hamlets is witnessed by map examples published in *Ob ulushchenii sel'skokhoziaĭstvennogo ispol'zovaniia zemel necher-noziomnoĭ polosy evropeĭskoĭ chasti SSSR* (Moskva 1952), pp 122 sqq.

19b. S. A. Udachin, *Zemel'naia reforma v Sovetskoi Latvii*, (Riga 1948), p. 329, cf pp 141, 322 sqq.

20a. A. Demangeon, "La géographie de l'habitat rural", *Annales de géographie* (Paris 1927), pp 1–23, 97–114.

21a. *E.g.*, G. Lindgren, *Falbygden och dess närmaste omgivning vid 1600-talets mitt*, (Uppsala 1939), and S. Dahl, *Torna och Bara* (Lund 1942).

21b. S. A. Udachin, *Zemel'naia reforma v Sovetskoĭ Latvii* (Riga 1948), pp 141, 322 sqq; H. Mortensen, *Litauen, Grundzüge einer Landeskunde* (Hamburg 1926), pp 104 sqq; W. Essen, *Die ländlichen Siedlungen in Litauen* (Leipzig 1931), p. 83, Cf also V. Jungfer, "Die Siedlungen in Litauen", *Siedlung und Siedlungs-politik in den Ländern Europas*, bearb. v. R. Stegemann & Fr. Schmidt, (Wien & Leipzig 1939), p. 231, footnote 1. H. Łowiański, "Przyczynki do kwestii najstarzych kształtów wsi Litowskeij", *Ateneum Wileńskie* (Vilno 1929), pp 293 sqq, and W. Conze, *Agrarverfassung und Bevölkerung in Litauen und Weissrussland* (Leipzig 1940), pp 18, 53 sqq.

22a. J. M. Mogey, *Rural life in Northern Ireland*, (London 1947), p. 15; cf C. S. Smith, "A new deal for the Irish farmer", *The Farmer's Weekly* (London 1952 Feb), pp 55–57.

22b. A. W. Ashby & I. L. Evans, *The agriculture of Wales and Monmouthshire* (Cardiff 1944), p. 7.

22c. M. W. Beresford, "The lost villages of Mediaeval England", *The Geographical Journal* (London 1951, Jun), pp 129 sqq.

22d. A. Demangeon, "Types de peuplement rural en France", *Annales de géographie* (Paris 1939), pp 1–21, and *idem, Problèmes de géographie humaine* (Paris 1942), p. 191; P. Veyret, *Les pays de la moyenne Durance alpestre* (Grenoble 1944), p. 524.

22e. M. Rochefort, "La pénétration des capitaux bourgeois dans la campagne autunoise: ses conséquences sur l'habitat et la structure agraire". *Etudes rhodaniennes* (Lyon 1950), pp 249–266, A. Durand, *La vie rurale dans les massifs volcaniques des Dores, du Cézallier, du Cantal et de l'Aubrec* (Aurillac 1946), pp 434 sq, and M. Le Lannou, *Pâtres et paysans de la Sardaigne* (Tours 1941), pp 222 sqq, 271 sqq.

22f. J. Keilling, *Les conséquences sociales du progrès technique dans le milieu agricole* (Paris 1950). In the opposite sense, showing maintenance of village settlement, J. Nicod, "Problèmes de structure agraire en Lorraine", *Annales de géographie* (Paris 1951), pp 337–348.

23a. See, e.g., G. Medici, *Land property and land tenure in Italy*, (Bologna 1952).

23b. M. Le Lannou, *Pâtres et paysans de la Sardaigne* (Tours 1941), pp 141 sqq.

23c. A. de Amorim Girão, *Geografia de Portugal* (Porto 1941), pp 258 sqq, *idem, Geografia humana* (Coimbra 1946), pp 194 sqq, and O. Ribeiro, *Aglomeração e dispersão do povoamento rural em Portugal* (Lisboa 1939).

23d. H. Hopfner, *Die ländlichen Siedlungen der altkastilischen Meseta*, (Hamburg 1939), pp. 106 sqq, especially p 115. Cf also G. Niemeier, *Siedlungsgeographische Untersuchungen in Niederandalusien* (Hamburg 1935), pp 25 sqq, and B. de Quirós, *Los reyes y la colonización interior de España desde el siglo xvi al xix* (Madrid 1929).

23e. A. de Amorim Girão, *Geografia de Portugal* (Porto 1941), pp 258 sqq.

23f. H. J. Keuning, "L'habitat rural aux Pays-Bas", *Tijdschrift van het Koninklijk aardrijkskundig genootschap* (Leiden 1938).

24a. J. Pawlowski & A. Czekalski, "L'habitat rural en Pologne", *Comptes rendus du Congrès International de Géographie* (Warsaw, 1934), T. 3.

24b. The evidence is in the population census. Cf below, note 25 (c), and Appendix 1 under Hungary.

25a. Above all, the Serbian *Naselja*-series. Cf also J. Cvijić, *Balkansko poluostrvo* (Zagreb 1922), pp 316 sqq, O. v. Frangeš, *Die sozialökonomische Struktur der jugoslawischen Landwirtschaft* (Berlin 1937) p. 232, O. Jaranoff, "Die Siedlungstypen in der östlichen und zentralen Balkanhalbinsel", *Zeitschrift der Gesellschaft für Erdkunde* (Berlin 1934), H. 5/6, pp 186 sqq, especially the map, p. 189, I. Batalkiev, "Geschichte der Besiedlung und die Siedlungsformen in Bulgarian", *Die sozialökonomische Struktur der bulgarischen Landwirtschaft*, hrsg. v. J. St. Molloff, (Berlin 1936), pp 37–47. Cf also M. Urban, *Die Siedlungen Südalbiens* (Öhringen 1938), and A. Melik, "Kmetska naselja na Slovenskom", *Geografski Vestnik* (Ljubljana1 933), pp 129–165.

25b. I. Batakliev, *op. cit.*, especially the maps, Tafel 5–6.

25c. L. Thirring, *Struktur und Verfassung der ungarischen Landwirtschaft*, (Budapest 1937), p. 67; *idem*, article in *Statisztikai szemle* (Budapest 1932), pp 12 sqq; I, Takács, "Die wirtschaftlichen und sozialen Folgen der Wiederbesiedlung der ungarischen Tiefebene im 18. Jahrhundert, Tanyasiedlung", *Ungarische Jahrbücher* (Berlin 1933), p. 106; N. J. den Hollander, "Het ontstaan der "tanya"-vestiging in de Groote Hongaarsche laagvlakte", *Tijdschrift van het Koninklijk Nederlandsche aardrijkskundige genootschap* (Leiden 1946), pp 146–203, and *idem, Nederzettingsvormen en -problemen in de Groote Hongaarsche laagvlakte, een Europeesch "frontier"-gebied* (Amsterdam 1947).

27a. S. A. Udachin, *Zemel'naia reforma v Sovetskoĭ Latvii* (Riga 1948), pp 322 sqq.

28a. Cf above under 16 (a).

32a. A. P. Takes, *Bevolkingscentra in het oude en het nieuwe land* (Alphen aan den Rijn 1948), pp 11 sqq, describes the system of settlement on the new polders:

A-kernen, villages of less than 2,000 inhabitants, with houses for agricultural workmen, retail shops, etc;

B-kernen, small towns with some 5,000 to 15,000 inhabitants, and

C-kernen, towns with over 25,000 inhabitants.

Cf also H. van der Weyde, "Trennung von Wohnungsbau und Landesplanung in Holland", *Institut für Raumforschung, Information*, (1951, Jan 29), J. Godefroy, *Enkele arbeidsproblemen van de Wieringermeer* (1941), and *De verspreiding van de*

444 NOTES

bevolking in de Wieringermeer, Nota van de Directie van de Wieringermeer, (1946, Mar).

32b. G. Larsson, *Inflytandet av avståndet från brukningscentrum till inägojorden på arbetsbehov, driftsformer och driftsresultat* (Stockholm 1947); E. Carlegrim, *Fastighetsstruktur, arbetskostnader och driftsform* (Nyköping 1952, mimeogr); H. Priebe, *Landarbeit heute und morgen* (Hamburg & Berlin 1953), p. 60 sq; idem, "Zur Frage der Gestaltung und Grösse des zukünftigen bäuerlichen Familienbetriebes", *Berichte über Landwirtschaft* (Hamburg & Berlin 1942), pp 485–592: at least one-third of the land should be in the immediate vicinity of the farm center, maximum distance to the rest not more than 1,500 metres. Cf also IA. Kis'liakoŭ, Pasiolki (Minsk 1928). A similar conclusion was communicated to the author in Belgrade on behalf of planning of State farms.

34a. N. E. Aïvaliotakis, *O kampos tēs Messenias kai ai oreinai lekanai avtou* (Athens 1942), p. 93, and idem, *Ai oreina lekanai Feneou-Stymfalias* (Athens 1941), p. 39. Cf also N. Altsitzoglos, *Oi Giakades kai o kampos tēs Xanthēs* (Athens 1941), p. 372.

34b. D. Bajalica, "Reorganizacija pasivnih zadruga Bosne i Hercegovine", *Socijalistička poljoprivreda* (Beograd 1952, Mar), p. 61.

34c. G. Xenos, *To agrotikon ktēmatologion tēs Ellados* (Athens 1935), p. 10 sq.

35a. N. Mazzocchi-Alemanni, "Il 'borgo' e la riforma agraria", *Italia agricola* (Rome 1948), recommends dispersed settlement in combination with two kinds of centers: *borghi di servizio*, and *borghi residenziali*.

35b. For instance, the settlement of Pègões, south of Lisbon, established by the Junta de colonização interna.

36a. A. P. Takes, *Bevolkingscentra in het oude en het nieuwe land* (Alphen aan den Rijn 1948); cf note 32 (a) above.

36b. H. Farner, "Betriebswirtschaftliche Auswirkungen der Umsiedlung bei Güterzusammenlegungen", *Agrarpolitische Revue* (Zürich 1949), pp 192–194; H. Hochstetter, "Flurbereinigung und Landtechnik", *Landtechnik* (1951, Nov), pp 711 sqq.

36c. H. Frank, "Das Bauen von Dörfern", *Neues Bauerntum* (1940), pp 225–233.

36d. H. Priebe, "Der neue Hof im neuen Dorf", *Neues Bauerntum* (1940), pp 220 sqq.

36e. *Smallholdings, First report of the Smallholdings Advisory Council...* (London 1949), in its § 53, p. 15 sq, recommends grouping of settlement only when this is not detrimental to agriculture, "but where the village type of development does not meet farming needs, alternative lay-outs with adequate communications can be devised so that the sense of community is not sacrificed".

38a. O. E. Heuser, "Entwicklungsmöglichkeiten der landwirtschaftlichen Betriebsorganisation", *Berichte über Landwirtschaft* (Hamburg & Berlin 1952), pp 86 sq, recommends the village community as the basis for productive cooperation.

38b. "Statuts-modèles de la ferme coopérative... bulgare", in V. Tchervenkov, *Les tâches des fermes coopératives* (Sofia 1950), p. 119, art. 1, speaking about "Les paysans laborieux du village de... district de... s'associent bénévolement pour constituer une ferme coopérative..."

38c. P. George, "Les transformations des campagnes hongroises", *Annales de géographie* (Paris 1951), pp 199–209, especially p. 208 sq: "'Centres agricoles' et urbanisme rural. Le Ministère de la Construction a établi des plans d'une nouvelle répartition de la population rurale... Le village-type susceptible d'être équipé de façon complète au point de vue scolaire, sanitaire, culturel, d'être pourvu comme une ville de canalisations d'eau, d'égouts d'électricité... est le gros village de 6,000 à 8,000 hab., possédant éventuellement des installations industrielles élementaires de traitement des produits agricoles... Plus d'une centaine de centres agricoles doivent être aménagés au cours du quinquennat 1950–1954..."

38d. S. A. Udachin, *Zemel'naia reforma v Sovetskoĭ Latvii* (Riga 1948), pp 322 sqq, 336 sq.

38e. *Sbornik rukovodiashchikh materialov kolkhoznomu stroitelstva*, (Moscow 1948), pp 680 sq.

38f. M. Gendel'man, "Vnutrikhoziaĭstvennoe zemleustroĭstvo kolkhozov s neskol'kimi naselennymi punktami, (Na primere kolkhozov stepnykh raionov USSR)", *Sotsialisticheskoe sel'skoe khoziaĭstvo* (Moscow 1952, Mar), pp 38–46: up to 7 settled points in the same village could be tolerated in some concrete instances in Ukraina. A balance is sought between the need for concentration and the distance factor. The standpoint of early Soviet research was different, as illustrated by IA. Kis'liakoŭ, *Pasiolki (optimum terytorii i éfekt zemleuparadkavan'nia)*, (Minsk 1928), pp 119–121, discussing maxima of distance and territory which are much smaller than those of the enlarged brigades described in the article of Gendel'man.

CHAPTER 2

42a. *Statistiques et études financières*, Supplément statistique N:o 4, (Paris 1949), pp 648 sqq, and J. Chombart de Lauwe, "Le cadastre et la statistique agricole", *Revue du Ministère de l'agriculture* (Paris 1947, May), pp 109–114. Cf also Th. Dreux, *Le cadastre et l'impôt foncier*, (Paris 1933); E. Michel, "Questions immobilières et livre foncier", *Société de statistiques de Paris, Journal*, (Paris 1940, No 2), pp 28–37, and *idem, Questions immobilières et livre foncier* (Paris 1939). – The list of documents in the French cadastre is as follows: *le plan cadastral*, a map showing the boundaries of all parcels of land; *le registre des états de sections*, a list of the parcels in each section of the map with names of the actual owners of each parcel; and *la matrice cadastrale*, a list of all landowners showing which parcels of land belong to each of them. It is only here that changes are currently registered.

43a. L. Einaudi, *La terra e l'imposta* (Torino 1942), especially pp 293–306, "Proposta di una immaginaria unità catastale di stima"; cf also an article by G. Boaga in the *Rivista del catasto e dei servizi tecnici erariali* (Rome 1951), pp 12–25, and another by M. Tofani in the *Giornale di agricoltura* (Rome 1950), p. 6. Further information on the Italian cadastre may be drawn from A. Messedaglia, *Il catasto e la perequazione* (Bologna 1936), and A. Grandi, "Il catasto geometrico particellare", *Rivista del catasto e dei servizi tecnici erariali* (Rome 1938). The list of documents in the Italian cadastre is basically the same as in France, only the list of owners has been divided into two parts, *il registro delle partite* and *la matricola dei possessori*.

43b. *Ministerio de hacienda. Dirección general de propriedades y contribución territorial. Servicios de la riqueza rústica y de valoración forestal. Memoria sobre los trabajos realizados por estos servicios durante los anos de 1944 al 1948* (Madrid 1949), representing an enlarged version of a similar publication in 1946, covering the years 1944–45. Cf also Z. Salazar Monliaa, *Valoración agrícola y catastro*, 3. ed. (Madrid 1950), F. Pou Pelaez, *El catastro desde el punto de vista fiscal y como defensa de los intereses agrícolas* (Madrid 1943), and G. García-Badell, El catastro de la riqueza rústica en España (Madrid 1943).

43c. A. Viriato da Fonseca, "O cadastro predial rústica no Baixo-Alentejo", *Boletim do Instituto Geográfico e Cadastral* (Lisboa 1934), pp 171–181, and L. de Pina Manique, "Notas sobre o concelho de Cuba", *ibid.*, pp 183–208; cf also G. A. Pery, *Estatística agricola do distrito de Beja*, P. 1 (Lisboa 1883).

44a. *Güthes Grundbuchordnung für das Deutsche Reich...* 5. Aufl., bearb. Fr. Triebel, Bd 1 (Berlin 1929), pp 80 sqq; cf also the separate *Grundbuchordnung* (for Eastern Germany), (Berlin 1950).

44b. G. Xenos, *To agrotikon ktēmatologion tēs Ellados* (Athens 1935), with maps and examples of cadastre documents, pp 34 sq. Cf also *Nomos yp'arith. 478/1943* Statute on the cadastre), and *Agrotikos kōdix* art. 190, pp 116 sq.

44c. H. Demelius, *Österreichisches Grundbuchsrecht* (Wien 1948); cf also *Der österreichische Grundkataster* (Wien 1948).

44d. L. Kamilo, "Osvt narzvitak katastra u Jugoslaviji", *Geometarski igeodetski glasnik* (Beograd 1935).

44e. L. Dikoff, "Die rechtliche Lage des Landbesitzes vom Standpunkt des Erb- und Sachenrechtes", *Die sozialökonomische Struktur der bulgarischen Landwirtschaft*, hrsg. v. J. St. Molloff (Berlin 1936), p. 98.

44f. "Statuts-modèles de la ferme coopérative", in V. Tchervenkov, *Les tâches des fermes coopératives* (Sofia 1950), p. 120 sq: "Art. 6. La réception des terres entrant dans la ferme coopérative s'effectue par la commision de la propriété foncière basée sur le travail, prévue dans l'art. 13 de la Loi sur les fermes coopératives et l'art. 11 du règlement sur le régime foncier des fermes coopératives. Chaque parcelle de terre est reçue d'après les dimensions indiquées dans les registres fonciers du conseil populaire ou après arpentage. L'acte de réception mentionne: les dimensions de toute la superficie, d'après les espèces de cultures; les dimensions des différentes parcelles, ainsi que la qualité de la terre par catégories, d'après l'ordre établi dans le règlement sur le régime foncier".

44g. Before 1917 only very uncomplete land registers existed; see E. S. Poliuta, *Osnovy zemel'nogo katastra* (Voronezh 1926), pp 24 sqq. On the present *shnurovaia kniga* and other actual land registration practices, see the "Arr. N. 1192 approuvant le livre foncier des kolkhozy, le livre foncier du Gouvernement pour l'enregistrement des terres et le règlement relatif au réviseur-arpenteur de l'U.R.S.S., 19/10 1939", *Sobranie postanovlenii i rasporiadenii* (Moscow 1939, Dec 4), N. 57, texte 577; *Spravochnik predsedatelia kolkhoza*, 3. ed., (Moscow 1948), and the *Bol'shaia Sovetskaia èntsiklopediia*, 2 ed., under *zemel'naia registratsiia* and *zemel'naia shnurovaia kniga*.

45a. V. Pedersen, *Matrikelvaesen* (Copenhagen 1951), especially p. 166 on the concepts of "main holding" consisting of one or more plots of land, and "free land" which may be separated from the "main holding". Th. Grendal, "Utskiftningen", *Tidsskrift for skogbruk* (Oslo 1947), pp 145–148.

45b. J. J. Wontner, *A guide to land registration practice, 6. ed.*, (London 1951); E. Dowson, "Land surveying: the conversion of the fiscal into a proprietary register", *Royal Institute of Chartered Surveyors, Journal* (London 1949), pp 408–429; J. Fr. Garner, *Local land changes* (London 1952); I. Finlay, *Scotland* (London 1945), on the deposition of all land tenure or transfer deeds in the Register House in Edinburgh.

46a. J. Chombart de Lauwe, "Le cadastre et la statistique agricole", *Revue du Ministère de l'agriculture* (Paris 1947, May), pp 109–114.

46b. G. García-Badell, "Estudio sobre la distribución de la extensión superficial de la propiedad agrícola en España entre las diferentes categorias de fincas", *Estudios geográficos* (Madrid 1946), pp 171 sqq, especially p. 176: "La voz 'parcela' no es equivalente a ‚finca', ya que ésta es la extensión continua o discontinua de propiedad de un solo dueño, que puede estar comprendida en un solo linde o en varios lindes. A cada una de las partes en que por la discontinuidad de los linderos queda dividida una finca, se le llama parcela en el catastro· Solamente una parcela equivale a finca cuando ésta se encuentra bajo un mismo linde.

No hay tampoco que confundir en la interpretación de las cifras la parcela con la subparcela... En definitiva, pueden considerarse equivalentes las voces ‚finca' y ‚parcela' en los cultivos intensivos, y casi equivalentes en los demás cultivos; pero no en los aprovechamientos de la producción espontanea, en los cuales la finca suele estar constituida por diferentes parcelas".

46c. *Wijhe, Een economisch-sociographisch onderzoek, door het Economisch Technologisch Instituut voor Overijssel en het Landbouw-Economisch Instituut* (1951, Sep., processed), p. 7: "als een kavel wordt beschouwd een stuk grond, dat geheel omgeven is door land van anderen. Een perceel is een stuk land, dat wordt begrensd door greppel, sloot, heg of wal". The former concept corresponds directly to that recommended in the FAO Program for the World Census of Agriculture in 1950.

47a. The table has also been published, based on the preliminary draft to this book, in: *European Agriculture, A Statement of Problems*, E/ECE/175 (Geneva 1954, Feb), p. 20. A few changes have been brought into the definitive version owing to further information.

49a. M. P. Vitanov, "A study of the relation of labor to distance of fields from farmsteads in Bulgaria", *Bulletins of the Department of Agricultural Economics, Faculty of Agriculture and Forestry, University of Sofia* (Sofia 1936), especially pp 35 and 55 (Table 17), and *idem, Der Wert der Arbeit die man für die Überwindung der Parzellenentfernung vom Wirtschaftshofe bei gewisse Getreidekulturen Bulgariens gebraucht* (Sofia 1937), p. 14 (both in Bulgarian, with summaries); cf also G. Larsson, *Inflytandet av avståndet från brukningscentrum till inägojorden på arbetsbehov, driftsformer och driftsresultat* (Stockholm 1947); F. Laur, *Landwirtschaftliche Betriebslehre* (Aarau 1938), p. 124, and M. Tcherkinsky, "The problem of the consolidation of agricultural holdings in Europe", *Monthly Bulletin of Agricultural Economics and Sociology* (Rome, IIA, 1942, Mar), pp 59 E sq.

53a. *Revue de l'agriculture* (Bruxelles 1953), p. 542.

53b. E. Grass & A. Münzinger, "Die Flurbereinigung in Süddeutschland, ihre Geschichte und ihr Stand am 1. Januar 1935", *Berichte über Landwirtschaft*, Sonderh. 123 (Hamburg & Berlin 1936), pp 25 sqq, recommending "Güterzusammenlegung" as superior to "Flurbereinigung".

53c. Especially instructive is the case of Yugoslav Vojvodina, where the rectilinear land layout from the 18th century has proved useful as a framework for modern large-scale agriculture. – For the legal conditions in some countries, see W. Schaumann, *Die Landesplanung im schweizerischen, englischen und französischen Recht* (Zürich 1950).

53d. *National Farm Survey of England and Wales, A summary Report* (London 1946), pp 35 sqq.

54a See, *e.g.*, F. Dovring, "Etudes sur le cadastre médiéval en Suisse romande", *Revue d'histoire suisse* (Zürich 1950), *idem*, "Contribution à l'étude des villages Normands au Moyen en Age" *Annales de Normandie* (Caen 1952), *idem*, "Le problème du manse dans le Sundgau", *L'Alsace et la Suisse a travers les siècles* (Strasbourg 1952), P. Zryd, *Grafenried zur Zeit der Dreifelderwirtschaft* (Bern 1940), and E. W. Hofstee & A. W. Vlam, "Opmerkingen over de ontwikkeling van de perceelsvormen in Nederland", *Boor en Spade* (1952), pp 194–235.

54b. F. Passino, "Frazionamento della proprieta e colonizzazione in Sardegna" *Bonifica integrale* (Rome 1932, May), pp 45–49, showing the correlation between "il flagello particellare" and the distance factor.

54c. Cf also the article "Resultaten van verkaveling in gevaar?" *De Landbode* (Meppel 1950, Apr).

55a. K. Skovgaard, "Consolidation of agricultural land in Denmark", *International Journal of Agrarian Affairs* (Oxford 1952, May), pp 9 sqq; cf *idem*, article in *FAO Agricultural Studies*, 11 (Rome 1950), pp 43 sqq, stating that the process was essentially completed before 1835.

56a. H. Deck, *Die Entwicklung der Grundstückzusammenlegung seit der Stein-Hardenberg'schen Reform* (Bleicherode am Harz 1939), especially the tables, p. 51, and the comments to them, pp 57 sqq. Some examples of village plans in northern Germany before the consolidations are shown in an article in *Petermann's geographische Mitteilungen* (Gotha 1939), pp 1–18, Maps 1–6. Cf also Fr. Ertl, *Die Flurbereinigung im deutschen Raum* (München 1953).

56b. E. Grass & A. Münzinger, "Die Flurbereinigung in Süddeutschland", *Berichte über Landwirtschaft* Sonderh. 123, (Hamburg & Berlin 1936), and K. Sperber, "Stand und Entwicklung der wirtschaftlichen Umlegung der Grundstücke in der Rheinprovinz", *ibid.* See also T. Miller, *Grundlagen des ländlichen Siedlungswesens*, 3. ed., (Weimar 1948).

56c. See the Swiss contribution in *FAO Agricultural Studies*, 11 (Rome 1950), pp 78 sqq, an official study based on the census of 1939, showing, *i.a.*, the increase in net average return per hectare of the land through consolidation; from 1941 to 1946, 123,000 hectares were consolidated, reducing 400,000 plots to 120,000.

56d. A. Rienks, "Reallocation of land in the Netherlands", *International Journal of Agrarian Affairs* (Oxford 1952, May), pp 33 sqq; J. A. Eshuis, "Grosszügige Zusammenlegung von Grundstücken, westliches Maas- und Waalgebiet", *Wasser und Boden* (1950, Aug.); J. H. Bouwman, "Ruilverkaveling in de tuinbouw", *De Tuinbouw* (Amsterdam 1950, Nov.).

56e. *Le remembrement rural en France* (Paris 1951).

56f. F. van den Abeele, "Le projet de loi belge sur le remembrement", *Revue de l'agriculture* (Bruxelles 1948), pp 871–889.

57a. *El parcelamiento de la propidad rústica en España* (Madrid 1952).

57b. See the statute in the *Ephēmeris tēs kyvernēseos tou Vasileiou tēs Ellados*, 30/9 1949, No 234 and 31/12 1949, No 364.

58a. V. Brdlík, *Die sozialökonomische Struktur der Landwirtschaft in der Tschechoslowakei* (Berlin 1938), pp 98 sqq, q120 sq, and A. Krčmár, "La ricomposizione della proprietà fondiaria nella repubblica Cecoslovacca", *Rivista del catasto e dei servizi tecnici erariali* (Rome 1938); cf also V. Fábry, *Agricultural laws of the Czechoslovak Republic* (Prague 1949).

58b. C. A. Koefoed, *Comasarea proprietatiei agricole* (Iaşi 1939).

58c. See, for instance, D. I. Toscheff, "Grundstückzusammenlegung und Siedling in Bulgarien", *Die sozialökonomische Struktur der bulgarischen Landwirtschaft* (Berlin 1936), pp 191–196.

58d. *Ob ulushcheniiu sel'skokhoziaistvennogo izpol'zovaniia zemel' nechernoziomnoǐ polosy evropeǐskoǐ chasti SSSR* (Moscow 1952), pp 121 sqq, with instructive map examples.

61a. J. Röhner & J. F. Wander, "Die Hälfte der Arbeitszeit unproduktiv", *Landtechnik* (Wolfratshausen b. München 1951, pp 564–567); *Confédération générale de l'agriculture, Divison de rentabilité, Bulletin*, 13 (Paris 1951, Nov), p 34; cf also E. Grass & A. Münzinger, "Die Flurbereinigung in Süddeutschland", *Berichte über Landwirtschaft*, N.F., Sonderh. 123 (Berlin 1936), p. 38.

61b. A. Hüni, "Der Einfluss der Landverteilung auf die Betriebsergebnisse", *Schweizerische landwirtschaftliche Zeitschrift* (Zürich 1941), pp 713–718: the tables show "good" conditions on farms with only 5–11 plots of land per farm, "intermediary" conditions on farms with 10–23 plots each, and "bad" conditions on farms with 19–71 plots. A. Studler, "Güterzusammenlegungen im Kanton Aargau", *Festgabe Ernst Laur* (Brugg 1937), p. 302, stating that consolidations led to saving of 20 to 40 per cent of the work time; E. Näf, "Die Wirtschaftlichkeit der Güterzusammenlegungen mit spezieller Berücksichtigung der Verhältnisse im Kanton Zürich", *Schweizerische landwirtschaftliche Monatsschrift* (Bern 1929), reckons with 10 to 30 per cent time-saving.

61c. Cf W. C. Visser, "Gedachten en getallen over de geldelijke gevolgen van ruilverkavelingen", *Landbouwkundig Tijdschrift* (The Hague 1950, Dec) p. 12.

61d. *Verslag van de Centrale Cultuurtechnische Commissie en van de Cultuurtechnische Dienst over 1950* (processed, pp 142, maps), p. 9: since 1924, 42,850 ha have been reallocated in the Netherlands, thereof 11,150 ha up to 1940 and 23,776 ha up to 1945; p 11 shows that from the decision to the final execution there was seldom less than a year, often 1½–2 years, sometimes many years (up to 8 or 9); table 3 shows that by then, 67 reallocations had been finished while 62 others were in process, covering 268,983 ha. – Cf also L. H. Bouwmann, *Ruilverkaveling* (Utrecht 1951).

61e. K. Beilner, "Der ‚Flurkrebs' und seine Behandlung", *Agrarische Rundschau* (Wien 1950/51), pp 34 sqq; *idem*, "Neue Wege der Grundstückszusammenlegung", *Agrarische Rundschau* (Wien 1952), pp 57 sqq; cf N. Donner, "Die Entwicklung der agrarischen Operationen in Österreich", *Hochschule für Bodenkultur in Wien, Jahrbuch* 1948 (Wien 1949), pp 294 sqq, and O. Schiller, *Mittel und Wege einer beschleunigten Flurbereinigung und Reform der Flurverfassung* (Stuttgart 1949).

61f. M. Kühner, "Feldbereinigung oder Raumgestaltung, besonders bei Grossgemarkungen?" *Zeitschrift für Raumforschung* (Bielefeld 1950), pp 342–348; *idem*, (ed.) *Landesgestaltung* (Minden-Westf. 1950); O. E. Heuser, "Entwicklungsmöglichkeiten der landwirtschaftlichen Betriebsorganisation", *Berichte über Landwirtschaft* (Hamburg & Berlin 1952). Cf also the recent Swedish contributions to country planning technique and science: K. D. Myrbeck, "Den förvandlade byn", *Lantmannen* (Stockholm 1946), pp 759 sqq; C. G. Berg, "Försök att förbättra fastighetsbildningen i Norrland", *Lantmannen* (Stockholm 1945), pp 1003 sq; E. Carlegrim, *Fastighetsstruktur, arbetskostnader och driftsform* (Nyköping 1952, mimeogr.), pp 34 sqq; S. Kihlberg, "Redefinition of farms in Sweden", *International Journal of Agrarian Affairs* (Oxford 1952, May).

62a. "Flurbereinigungsgesetz vom 14. Juli 1953", *Bundesgesetzblatt* I Nr 37, vom 18. Juli 1953; cf the issue in *Ministerialblatt des Bundesministeriums für Ernährung, Landwirtschaft und Forsten* (Bonn 1953, 22/7).

62b. The basic French legislation on consolidation is in a law of March 9, 1941, and a decree of January 7, 1942, both validated by an ordnance of July 7, 1945; see *Le remembrement rural en France* (Paris 1951). Cf also J. Auboyer-Treuille, "Remembrement rural", *Revue de législation agricole* (Paris 1950, Nov-Dec), pp 218 sq, J. Roche, "Important aspects of land consolidation in France", *Conference of world land tenure problems, Proceedings* (Madison, Wis., 1951), Vol. 1 pp 336–345, and M. Poirée, *Réorganization foncière et remembrement de la propriété rurale* (Paris 1951).

62c. On the Austrian statute, see K. Beilner, "Neue Wege der Grundstückszusammenlegung", *Agrarische Rundschau* (Wien 1952),... 57–66; The Dutch Statute is the *Ruilverkavelingswet* of 1951, Jan 19; the Belgian Statute was issued in 1949, May 4, cf F. van den Abeele, "Le projet de loi belge sur le remembrement", *Revue de l'agriculture* (Bruxelles 1948), pp 871–889, and *Monographies sur le bien-être rural en Belgique, élaborées en vue d'une conférence europénne pour l'étude du bien-être rural* (Bruxelles 1951), pp 188–197.

62d. Greek Statute in the *Ephēmeris tēs kyvernēseos tou Vasileiou tēs Ellados* (Athens 1949), Sep 30, No 234, and Dec. 31, No 364, Cf E. Papageorgiou, "Fragmentation of land holdings and measures of consolidation in Greece", *Conference on World Land Tenure Problems, Proceedings* (Madison, Wis., 1951), Vol. 1, pp 350–355. – Spanish consolidation statute of 1952, Dec. 12; *Concentración parcelaria* (Madrid 1952), including the text of the statute and two ministerial speeches held before the Cortes regarding this statute.

63a. F. H. v. Babo, *Betriebswirtschaftliche Grundlagen der Flurbereinigung* (Stuttgart 1951); C. Morel, "Indiscutable supériorité de remembrement sur le regroupement cultural", *Génie rural* (Paris 1950), pp 144–146; K. Beilner, "Neue Wege der Grundstückszusammenlegung", *Agrarische Rundschau* (Wien 1952), pp. 57–66; H. Hoechstetter, "Flurbereinigung und Landtechnik", *Landtechnik* (Wolfratshausen bei München 1951), pp 711–715. A slightly different approach in F. T. Wahlen, *Unser Boden heute und morgen* (Zürich 1943), pp 204 sqq, stressing the need for rationalization of farm size structure at the same time as consolidation is undertaken.

For East European lines of action, see V. Tchervenkov, *Les tâches des fermes coopératives* (Sofia 1950), pp 119 sqq (model statutes of the cooperative farms, p. 124, art. 12), cf *Državen Vestnik* (Sofia 1941, Jun 13) and *Annuaire International de législation agricole* (Rome 1942); A. Krekmanov, *Komasazijata na zemt našija stopanski zhivot* (Sofia 1942); K. Juva, "Le remaniement parcellaire comme base pour la mécanisation dirigée de l'agriculture", *Ceskoslovenska akademia zemědědelska, Věstnik* (Prague 1947), pp 399–409. See also *Dziennik Ustav* (Warsaw 1948, Apr 22), N 21, poz. 144, re-enacting consolidation legislation from the twenties and thirties, and the Hungarian consolidation decree of 1949, Aug. 30, published, *i.a.*, in *Problèmes économiques* (Paris 1949, Nov 9).

63b. IA. Lovkov & M. Gumerov, "Ukrupnenie melkikh kolkhozov i rabota MTS (po materialam MTS Moskovskoĭ oblasti)", *Sotsialisticheskoe sel'skoe khoziaĭstvo* (Moscow 1950, Dec.), pp 32–41, especially pp 34 sq.

CHAPTER 3

64a. See R. W. Hecht & G. T. Barton, "Gains in productivity of farm labor", *USDA Technical Bulletin*, No 1020 (Washington, D.C., 1950, Dec), and the manpower figures in the *Statistical Abstract of the United States* for the same period.

66a. C. Nawratzki, *Bevölkerungsstillstand als Wirtschaftsproblem unter besonderer Berücksichtigung der Landwirtschaft* (Berlin 1930), pp 87 sqq, showing the difference in trend of development of manpower when female workers are included and stressing the lack of comparability of data on female manpower. See further H. B. Krohn, "Die Produktivität in der Landwirtschaft im europäischen Vergleich", *Berichte über Landwirtschaft* (Hamburg & Berlin 1954).

71a. *Report on the decline of the agricultural population* (Board of Agriculture and Fisheries, Cf 3,273).

72a. A. Demangeon & G. Manco, *Documents pour servir a l'étude des étrangers dans l'agriculture française* (Paris 1939).

72b. C. Nawratzki, *Bevölkerungsstillstand als Wirtschaftsproblem* (Berlin 1936), p. 95.

73a. H. Böker & F. v. Bülow, *Die Landflucht in der Tschechoslowakei* (Rome 1935), pp 177 sq. However, the first table, relating to "active population, both sexes" may lead to some overestimation of the trend.

73b. *Manuel statistique de la République tchécoslovaque* (Prague 1940), p. 20.

73c. Reproduced in the *Statistisches Jahrbuch für die Bundesrepublik Deutschland*, as late as in 1953.

73d. S. Szulc, art. in *Problèmes démographiques de la Pologne*, Sér. C, fasc. 41 (Warsaw 1936); cf Appendix 3, under Poland.

78a. See, for instance, H. Böker & F. v. Bülow, *The rural exodus in Germany* (Geneva 1933), pp 5–15 and same authors, *The rural exodus in Czechoslovakia* (Geneva 1935), pp 5–9. – In the opposite sense, for instance, *Population and agriculture, with special reference to agricultural overpopulation* (Geneva 1939, League of Nations, European Conference on rural life 1939, Contribution by the International Institute of Agriculture), and O. v. Frangeš, *Die Bevölkerungsdichte als Triebkraft der Wirtschaftspolitik der südosteuropäischen Bauernstaaten* (Jena 1939).

78b. *Labour problems in agriculture* (Geneva 1950, International Labour Conference, 33rd session, Report 6), discusses "surplus manpower", although only in very broad terms. See also A. W. Ashby, "Planning Welsh agriculture", *Welsh Housing and Development Year Book* (1934), pp 5 sqq, stressing the economic disparities between town and countryside as an argument against any further increase in agricultural population.

78c. C. Clark, *The conditions of economic progress* (London 1951), and E. M. Ojala, *Agriculture and economic progress* (Oxford 1953).

80a. W. E. Moore, *Economic demography of Southern and Eastern Europe* (Geneva 1945). Almost the same scale is used in Hungary, according to *Mezögazdasági statisztika* (Budapest 1952), p. 29, where arable land is taken as = 1, horticultural land = 4, vineyard = 5, meadow = 0,5, pasture = 0.2 and orchard = 8.

Cf also P. Starcs, "The shortage of agricultural labour in Latvia", *International Labour Review* (Geneva 1939), p. 771, using the following scale: arable = 1, meadow = 0,4, pasture = 0.2.

80b. J. Klatzmann, "La classification des entreprises agricoles suivant leur importance économique", *Bulletin de la société française d'économie rurale* (Paris 1952, Apr), and "Valeurs vénales des terres labourables et herbages 1950", *Revue du Ministère de l'Agriculture, Etudes et Monographies* 67 (Paris 1952). See also R. Dumont, "La propriété agricole", *Revue du Ministère de l'Agriculture* (Paris 1952).

80c. See the references in Note 43 (a), above.

81a. P. A. Linehan, J. Lowe & R. H. Stewart, "The output of pasture and its measurement", *Journal of the British grassland society* (Aberystwyth 1946), pp 1–29, *ibid* (1947), pp 145–168, and *ibid*. (1952), pp 73–98; M. E. Castle, "Grassland production and its measurement using the dairy cow", *ibid*. (1953), pp 195–211: in output of milk, c:a 4,500–5,500 lbs per acre should be normal. A similar method has been used in Norwegian agricultural statistics to assess the production from the rough grazings. Cf also T. W. Evans, *Land potential* (London 1951), p. 72, pointing out that permanent grass is a kind of monoculture.

83a. R. W. Hecht & G. T. Barton, "Gains in productivity of farm labor", *USDA Technical Bulletin*, No 1,020 (Washington, D.C., 1950).

83b. *L'organisation scientifique du travail en Europe* (by N. M. Tcherkinsky, Rome, IIA, 1931), pp 1 sqq, 13 sqq, Cf also L. W. Ries, *Die Arbeit in der Landwirtschaft* (Stuttgart 1950); G. Preuschen, *Bauernarbeit die sich lohnt* (München 1950); E. Mejer, *Agricultural labour in England and Wales* (Loughborough 1949); M. Noilhan, *Les agriculteurs sont-ils des gaspilleurs de main-d'oeuvre?"* (Paris 1950).

83c. See, for instance, P. Maslov, *Perenaselenie russkoĭ derevni* (Moscow & Leningrad 1930); M. Latsis, *Agrarnoe perenaselenie i perspektivy bor'by s nim* (Moscow & Leningrad 1929); L. E. Mints, *Agrarnoe perenaselenie i rynok truda SSSR* (Moscow & Leningrad 1929); P. P. Faĭngluz & M. A. Potapov, *Normirovannie truda v sel'skom khoziaĭstve* (Moscow & Leningrad 1930). For recent references, see Appendix 4, under the U.S.S.R.

93a. F. Dovring, "Betriebsgrösse und Arbeitsbesatz", *Agrarwirtschaft* (Hannover 1955), p. 103.

93b. See table in Appendix 4, under France.

94a. The French and German farm censuses, for instance, have put much stress on this point, trying to illustrate the size of farm by classification according to the number of persons employed. Cf H. Priebe & K. Kündiger, "Der Arbeitskräftebesatz der deutschen Landwirtschaft", *Agrarwirtschaft* (Hannover 1952), pp 269–272.

95a. The concentration index was developed mathematically by C. Gini, *Indici di concentrazione e di dipendenza* (Torino 1922), especially pp 16 sqq. The most important attempt at applying this theory on farm structures is G. Loyo, *La concentración agraria en el mundo* (Mexico City 1933), especially p. 41. Cf also C. Gini, *Intorno alle curve di concentrazione* (Madrid 1931), and the redactional article "A propos de la répartition des terres en France, La notion de concentration économique", *Etudes et conjoncture, Economie française* (Paris 1951 Sep-Oct), pp 72–77. See further A. Bilimovič, "Die vergleichende Untersuchung von Agrarstrukturen," *Weltwirtschaftliches Archiv* (Münster 1939), pp 493–522, arriving at materially the same result as Loyo though without quoting him or Gini, and stressing the need for strictly comparable staitstics; A. H. Maunder, "Size and efficiency in farming" *University of Oxford, Occasional papers in agricultural economics*, 4, (Oxford 1952), pointing to a correlation between efficiency and size of farm only in some types of farm; F. Schaad, *Die Entwicklung der landwirtschaftlichen Betriebsgrössen und die Strukturwandlungen in der Agrarverfassung Westeuropas* (Bern 1953, processed), with almost no statistical treatment of the subject.

98a. F. Dovring, "Les recensements agricoles français", *Bulletin mensuel de statistique, Supplément trimestriel* (Paris 1955, Apr-Jun). Some minor details in this article have turned out inexact because the review did not enter all the author's corrections to the proofs in the printed version. – The author prepares a further analysis of the French farm censuses, *i.a.* in order to show the main features of the real development in the farm structure since 1892; results from this enquiry are included in the table in Appendix 5, under France.

98b. D. K. Britton & F. Dovring, "Where are holdings growing larger?" (forthcoming).

102a. *European agriculture, A statement of problems*, E/ECE/175 (Geneva 1954), p.57.

103a. The idea to measure farm size in terms of labor economy was in a sense put forth already by H. Passy, *Des systèmes de culture en France et de leur influence sur l'économie sociale* (Paris 1852), seeking the criterion in the farm implements and their use. Cf M. Augé-Laribé, *Grande ou petite propriété?* (Montpellier 1902), pp 11 sq, 81 sqq. A further step was taken by R. Enkell, *Om arbetsintensiteten à Mustiala egendoms åkercirkulationer* (Helsingfors 1908), followed by E. Höjer, *Undersökning av det större och det mindre jordbrukets produktion* (Stockholm 1919), although still on the basis of a very small empirical material.

103b. E. W. Hofstee, "Die ‚Normalarbeitsstunden'-Methode, Untersuchung über die Feststellung der zweckmässigen Grösse landwirtschaftlicher Familienbetriebe", *Zeitschrift für das gesamte Siedlungswesen* (Bielefeld 1952, Jul).

103c. F. Dovring, "Betriebsgrösse und Arbeitsbesatz", *Agrarwirtschaft* (Hannover 1955), pp 100–105.

106a. The weighting of manpower was done on the basis of the indications in H. T. Williams, "Changes in the productivity of labour in British agriculture", *Journal of the agricultural Economics Society*, Vol. 10, fasc. 4. (Reading 1952).

107a. F. Dovring, "Betriebsgrösse und Arbeitsbesatz," *Agrarwirtschaft* (Hannover 1955), p. 102.

108a. *ibid.*

108b. The breakdown of manpower figures on the size structure of holdings was borrowed from the *Annuaire statistique de la France*, "1952, édition de 1953" (Paris 1953), p. 84. The casual laborers were assumed to belong almost exclusively to the higher size-classes of holdings.

111a. In this sense, the chart in E. W. Hofstee, "Die ‚Normalarbeitsstunden'-Methode", *Zeitschrift für das gesamte Siedlungswesen* (Bielefeld 1952, Jul), quoting also an American enquiry from South Dakota. See further Th. J. Platenburg, *Kleine boeren in Nederland* (Hilversum 1942), p. 74: the problem of the smallholdings is essentially a demographic one; *Confédération générale de l'agriculture, Division de la rentabilité, Bulletin*, No 13,"Les conditions de la prosperité de l'exploitation agricole" (Paris 1951), with charts, pp 18 and 47; "Une enquête sur le temps de travail et les frais de production de la viticulture dans le Languedoc", *Etudes et conjoncture, Economie française* (Paris 1953, Jan-Feb), pp 37–62; E. Weill-Raynal, "La répartition des terres en France: légende et réalité", *ibid.* (1948: Sep-Dec), pp 61 sqq, still defending the classification according to total area of the holdings; against the latter, the redactional article, *ibid.* (1951, Sep-Oct), pp 62–67, advances the need for qualitative criteria, although without developing the idea. – N. Visocchi, "Indagini sull'ampiezza del podere in Toscana", *Rivista di economia agraria* (Rome 1948), pp 358–403, calculates the ratio of labor forces to the land and establishes formulas on a high mathematical level. He arrives at the result that "The causal complex consists of the labour requirement per hectare, the degree of regularity in the annual distribution of labour, and the composition of the family labour units" (summary, p. 403). Fr. Acquaviva, "Occupazione di nuclei familiari nel piano di Salerno", *ibid.*, pp 404–413, states that only very few families approached 100 per cent employment, and many had only a little more than 50 per cent, despite the high level of intensity in the cultivation of the area.

111b. Modern literature on the problem of the best size of farm is very rich. See, for instance, A. Münzinger, *Der Arbeitsvertrag in der bäuerlichen Familienwirtschaft* (Berlin 1929); H. Krüger, "Die Betriebsgrössenfrage aus arbeitswirtschaftlicher Sicht", *Zeitschrift für das gesamte Siedlungswesen* (Bielefeld 1952, May), pp 87–89; H. Priebe, "Zur Frage der Gestaltung und Grösse des zukünftigen bäuerlichen Familienbetriebes in Grossdeutschland", *Berichte über Landwirtschaft* (Hamburg & Berlin 1942), pp 485–592, especially p. 580 sq, stating that the upper limit for the family farm should be about 20 hectares; *idem, Wer wird die Scheunen füllen? Sozialprobleme der deutschen Landwirtschaft* (Düsseldorf 1954), pp 315 sq, defending a mainly liberal approach to the problems of the farm structure; W. Söder, "Das Arbeitsjahr des Bauern", *Journal für Landwirtschaft* (Berlin 1936), pp 97–187; H. Noilhan, *Techniques industrielles, techniques agricóles* (Paris 1948); M. Tcherkinsky, "The economic importance of the various size groups of farms in European agriculture", *Monthly Bulletin of Agricultural Economics and Sociology* (Rome 1943, IIA, Jan-Feb), pp 1–30, 47–70; E. W. Hofstee, "De sociale positie van de agrarische bevolking, in verband met de arbeidsproductiviteit in de agrarische bedrijven van verschillende grootte", *Friesch landbouwblad* (Leeuwarden 1950), pp 124 sq, 140 sq; A. Maris, C. D. Scheer & M. A. J. Visser, *Het kleine-boeren vraagstuk* (Assen 1951); C. Rietsema, *Agrarische bedrijfsvormen in Hollands noorderkwartier* (Assen 1950); W. C. Visser, "De samenstelling van productiviteitsschattingen op grond van vruchtbaarheidskenmerken", *Landbouwkundig tijdschrift* (The Hague 1949), pp 321–335; F. Bogusławski, "The influence of family labour on the structure of small holdings", *Rocznik nauk rolnicza i lesnych* (Poznań 1947), pp 199–234; W. Schramm, "Measures of the best size of farm", *ibid.*, pp 403–414; D. I. Ticulescu, *Evaluari şi cubaje agricole* (Cluj 1946); *idem, Lotul tip economice* (Bucureşti 1943); *Aguçadoura, Estudo económico-agrícola* (Lisboa 1944).

112a. F. Dovring, "Betriebsgrösse und Arbeitsbesatz", *Agrarwirtschaft* (Hannover 1955), p. 102 sq. The fact that the output figures are based on the calorie values of the products is largely compensated by the fact that the labor requirement is higher on those products where the price is higher per calorie unit. Lower yields on small than on large holdings are shown, for instance, by the Finnish Census of Agriculture 1950, Vol. 1 (Helsinki 1954), p. 129: the yields were highest on the large holdings, of all important crops except the potatoes, where the peak is in the middle-sized holdings and the large ones are below average.

113a. P. P. Egoroff, "Die Arbeit in der Landwirtschaft", *Die sozialökonomische Struktur der bulgarischen Landwirtschaft*, hrsg. J. St. Molloff (Sofia 1936), p. 152 sq.

116a. L. Thirring, "Les rapports entre les professions et la fécondité des mariages d'après une statistique hongroise", *Congrès international de la population, Paris 1937, T. 5, Démographie statistique, Etudes spéciales: natalité, nuptialité, mortalité*, (Paris 1938), pp 113–124, especially pp 120, 122 sq. Cf also M. Kaprzac, "Family limitation in Poland", *Population* (London 1935), pp 24–60, and S. Szulc, "Research on differential fertility in Poland, *Population* (London 1935), pp 14–35.

116b. *Résultats statistiques du recensement général de la population... 1946, Résultats par départements* (Paris 1952), Table IV, 2, a, "selon le nombre d'enfants survivants d'âge inférieur à 14 ans" (in each department volume).

116c. *Recensement général de la population en 1930, P. 4, Les professions* (Budapest 1936), Table 7, pp 154 sqq.

116d. L. Stengel –v. Rutkowski, *Die unterschiedliche Fortpflanzung, Untersuchung über die Fortpflanzung 20,000 thüringischer Bauern* (München & Berlin, 1939), pp 63 sqq: since 1905 there has been no appreciable difference.

116e. A. Münzinger & W. v. Stauffenberg, "Der Kinderreichtum der bäuerlichen Familien Württembergs", *Berichte über Landwirtschaft* (Hamburg & Berlin 1938), pp 1–40. Cf also H. I. Herpel, "Zur Frage des Nachwuchses landwirtschaftlicher Familien", *Journal für Landwirtschaft* (Berlin 1936), showing a slight tendency towards greater families among farmers whose main occupation was outside agriculture.

CHAPTER 4

123a. Cf W. Stark, *Ursprung und Aufstieg des landwirtschaftlichen Grossbetriebs in den böhmischen Ländern* (Brünn 1934).

123b. A. Gurland, *Grundzüge der muhammedanischen Agrarverfassung und Agrarpolitik, mit besonderer Berücksichtigung der türkischen Verhältnisse* (Dorpat 1907). The main conclusion, summarized p. 84 sq, is that the land system in the Turkish empire was not feudal, not even in the sense this term may have had in 19th century Europe, since the peasants owed only rents in cash or kind but no personal service to the landlord. From Bartholdi, *Geschichte Griechenlands*, p. 3, Gurland quotes the statement that the Greek *rajah*, under the rule of the Turkish landlords, enjoyed more of the fruits of his work than did many Polish peasants at a much later date.

127a. In this sense, still M. Sering & C. v. Dietze, (ed.), *Die Vererbung des ländlichen Grundbesitzes in der Nachkriegszeit* (München & Leipzig 1930), T. 3, p. 4.

128a. L. Dikoff, "Die rechtliche Lage des Landbesitzes vom Standpunkt des Erb- und Sachenrechtes", *Die sozialökonomische Struktur der bulgarischen Landwirtschaft*, hrsg. v. J. St. Molloff (Berlin 1936), p. 97.

131a. See G. C. Brodrick, *English land and English landlords, An enquiry into the origin and character of the English land system, with proposals for its reform* (London 1881), pp 156 sqq:

"In default of authoritative statistics, the loosest conjectures were long current respecting the distribution of ownership caused by these divergent tendencies towards aggregation and subdivision. It was confidently stated, for instance, that whereas in the latter part of the last century this country was divided among 200,000 landowners, it had come to be divided among no more than 30,000. No proof was thought necessary to support the former assertion; the latter was supported by a proof, which, on examination, turned out to be perfectly worthless... until the year 1875 it was regarded as open to doubt whether the whole body of English landowners, properly so called, amounted to 30,000 or 300,000.

"The appearance of the ‚New Domesday Book', as it was called, was the first step towards a thorough investigation of this question, which it ought to have set finally at rest. It purported to show that England and Wales, exclusive of the metropolis, was divided in 1874–5 among 972,836 proprietors in all... Of these proprietors, however, no less than 703,289, ... were returned as possessors of less than one acre each. The aggregate acreage and gross estimated rental of the 269,547 proprietors owning one acre and upwards were stated as follows.... (a table, excluded here) "This return, prepared by the Local Government Board, was represented as no more than "proximately accurate", and a very cursory inspection sufficed to disclose errors of detail so numerous and important as to cast suspicion even upon its proximate accuracy. Further analysis has amply confirmed this suspicion...

p. 163: "In other words, the names of dukes are repeated 5.6 times, those of marquises 3.7 times, those of earls 3.3 times, and those of viscounts and barons 2.5 times. The Duke of Buccleuch alone counts as fourteen landowners, in respect of as many separate estates in England and Scotland ... Altogether, the 525 members of the peerage stand for upwards of 1,500 "owners" in the New Domesday Book..."

Partly on the basis of J. Bateman, *Great landowners of the United Kingdom*, Brodrick arrives at an approximate classification of the land ownership in England and Wales, referring to 1875, p. 187:

No. of owners	Class	Extent in acres
400	Peers and Peeresses	5,728,979
1,288	Great landowners	8,497,699
2,529	Squires	4,319,271
9,585	Greater Yeomen	4,782,627
24,412	Lesser Yeomen	4,144,272
217,049	Small Proprietors	3,931,806
703,289	Cottagers	151,148
14,459	Public bodies	1,443,548
..	Waste land	1,524,624
TOTAL 973,011		34,523,974

On Eastern Germany, see J. Conrad, in *Jahrbücher für Nationalökonomie und*

Statistik (Berlin 1888), p. 149, with comments in the same sense as Brodrick's on England.

On Italy, at a recent date, see A. Serpieri, *La struttura sociale dell'agricoltura italiana* (Roma 1947), and M. Rossi-Doria, "Problemi del lavoro in agricoltura", *Annuario dell'agricoltura italiana* (Roma 1950), pp 369–404, especially p. 377, giving the percentages of farms operated by their owners, and by aid of hired managers, respectively, which were 37.2 and 10.9 per cent in Italy as a whole, but 80.4 and 2.2 per cent in the Alpine mountains, 15.2 and 13.3 in the recently improved areas of the Po delta, etc.

131b. Fr. de Cárdenas, "Del estado de la propiedad territorial en España durante la edad media", *Revista de España* (Madrid 1872); P. Carrión, *Los latifundios en España* (Madrid 1932); J. Gaviga, "El reparto de tierras en España", *Sitzungsberichte des Seminars für europäische Geographie* (Würzburg 1932): G. García-Badell, *El régimen de la propiedad de nuestro suelo agrícolo y el problema de los minifundios* (Madrid 1941); *idem*, "Estudio sobre la distribución de la extensión superficial y de la riqueza de la propiedad agrícola en España entre las diferentes categorias de fincas", *Estudios geográficos* (Madrid 1946), pp 171 sqq; *Estadística de propietarios de fincas rústicas de Espana, Avance referido al primer semestro de 1947* (Madrid 1948 sqq). Cf also G. Moreno, *Los minifundios y los cotos acasarados* (Vitoria 1951).

131c. *Publications statistiques hongroises*, N. S., Vol. 18, "Dénombrement de la population des pays de la Sainte Couronne Hongroise en 1900, 9me partie, Conditions de la propriété bâtie et foncière" (Budapest 1907).

133a. *Norges offisielle statistikk*, XI. 103 (Oslo 1952), pp 50 sq.

133b. Thus, L. García de Oteyza, "Los regímenes de explotación de suelo nacional", *Revista de estudios agro-sociales* (-Madrid 1952, Oct-Dec), pp 49–62; also the French farm censuses of 1882, 1892, 1929, and 1946.

133c. See, *e.g.*, *Norges offisielle statistikk*, VIII. 188 (Oslo 1932), pp 83–100, and *ibid.*, XI. 103 (Oslo 1952), pp 48 sqq.

133d. See the early Russian property statistics, as quoted in Appendix 5, under U.S.S.R.

133e. F. Dovring, "Les recensements agricoles français", *Bulletin mensuel de statistique, Supplément trimestriel* (Paris 1955, Apr-Jun).

133f. For instance, *Les diverses formes du métayage, Vol. 1, Rapports, avis et études de synthèse* (Paris 1953, Conseil économique, Etudes et travaux), in the general report (by J. Milhaud), seems to have overlooked the basic impossibility to compare the figures on land tenure in the various farm censuses. It is stated, p. 9, that the sharecropping were to have diminished considerably in some departments, for instance in the Landes, where a decline from 590,000 ha in 1929 to 208,000 ha in 1946 should mean a diminution by 65 per cent, and in the Basses-Pyrénées and the Cher, by 60 and 57 per cent respectively. In fact, the census figures do not at all support any such conclusions, as will be seen from the following figures:

Landes	in 1892 117,000	hectares of total	230,000	under "métayage"		= 51%;
"	in 1929 590,000	"	"	"	820,000	"	"	= 72%;
"	in 1946 208,000	"	"	"	341,000	"	"	= 61%;
Cher	in 1892 158,000	"	"	"	533,000	"	"	= 30%;
"	in 1929 220,000	"	"	"	635,000	"	"	= 35%;
"	in 1946 96,000	"	"	"	441,000	"	"	= 22%;
Basses-Pyrénées	in 1892 50,000	"	"	"	293,000	"	"	= 17%;
"	in 1929 180,000	"	"	"	600,000	"	"	= 30%;
"	in 1946 73,000	"	"	"	394,000	"	"	= 18%:

Since the coverage of the censuses is different as regards area, the figures hardly prove anything at all. In 1892, no forest area was included in the breakdown on modes of tenure; in 1929 all private forests were included, while in 1946 in principle those forests should be included which belonged to the farms enumerated, which means much less than in 1929. In the departments of Landes and Basses-Pyrénées, where the figure of 1892 is lower than any of those following, it may be that nothing at all happened, and the development may even be contrary to what the percentages indicate. In Cher, it is clear that there has been some decrease in the métayage since 1892, but if this happened before or after 1929 cannot be settled on the basis of the published statistics. Especially in the department of the Landes, the importance of forest area in connection with the métayage is made clear by R. Courregelongue, "La condition juridique du gemmeur", *La semaine juridique* (Paris 1947, Oct 2), also reproduced in Vol. 2 of *Les diverses formes du métayage*, pp 280–292: the dominating industry of the department is the winning of turpentine, which is to a great extent carried out under a type of contract which is generally classified as a kind of sharecropping.

137a. L. García de Oteyza, "Los regímenes de explotación del suelo nacional", *Revista de estudios agro-sociales* (Madrid 1952, Oct-Dec), pp 49–62: Up to that date, the only available figures relating to the distribution of the main types of tenure were those in G. García-Badell, "Estudio sobre la distribución de la extensión superficial y de la riqueza de la propiedad agrícola en España entre las diferentes categorías de fincas", *Estudios geográficos* (Madrid 1946, May), based on cadastre data available in 1930 and covering only some 40 per cent of the Spanish territory. Recently, as shown in the article of García de Oteyza, the Instituto de estudios agro-sociales has carried out an enquiry, by means of questionnaires to be filled in by the provincial agricultural bureaus. The following figures were found (p. 53), expressed in hectares of cultivated land (and here rounded to thousands):

Region	Owner-operated	Share-cropped	Under leasehold		Total
			Protected	Not protected	
Andalucía Occidental	1,579	211	169	430	2,389
Andalucía Oriental.	1,254	184	178	398	2,015
Castilla la Vieja	1,823	105	398	238	2,564
Castilla la Nueva	2,468	265	310	497	3,540
Aragón.	1,098	185	67	110	1,459
Levante	1,143	967	116	269	2,494
Leonesa	1,095	15	156	269	1,536
Cataluña y Baleares	699	419	110	74	1,302
Extremadura	1,200	458	29	485	2,172
Rioja y Navarra	373	55	81	54	562
Galicia	407	66	130	2	606
Vascongadas	89	1	53	3	146
Canarias	107	39	6	10	162
Asturias-Santander.	77	2	49	1	129
TOTAL	13,411	2,972	1,851	2,841	21,076

The same figures are thus converted into percentages:

Andalucía Occidental	66.1	8.8	7.1	18.8	11.3
Andalucía Oriental.	62.2	9.2	8.8	19.8	9.5
Castilla la Vieja	71.1	4.1	15.5	9.3	12.2
Castilla la Nuvea	69.7	7.5	8.8	14.0	16.8
Aragón.	75.2	12.7	4.6	7.5	6.9
Levante	45.8	38.8	4.6	10.8	11.8
Leonesa	71.3	1.0	10.2	17.5	7.3
Cataluña y Baleares	53.7	32.2	8.4	5.7	6.2
Extremadura	55.2	21.1	1.4	22.3	10.3
Rioja y Navarra	66.3	9.7	14.4	9.6	2.7
Galicia	67.3	11.0	21.4	0.3	2.9
Vascongadas	60.6	0.5	36.5	2.4	0.7
Canarias	66.2	24.0	3.4	6.4	0.8
Asturias-Santander	60.0	1.7	37.8	0.5	0.6
TOTAL	63.6	14.1	8.8	13.5	100.0

García de Oteyza stresses the fact that sharecropping ("aparcería") is regionally concentrated: half of it is in seven provinces. Referring to M. Torres, *Teoria de la politica social* (Madrid 1949), pp 249 sqq, and C. Tames, "Bosquejo del clima de España peninsular", *Boletín del Instituto de Investigaciones agronómicas* (Madrid 1949, Jun), it is shown how the climate influences the distribution of the modes of tenure: sharecropping is most important in provinces where the climate is arid ("seco y arido"), while leasehold is most widespread in regions of a semi-arid character ("preponderantemente seco"), according to Table 2, p. 57. – The number of farmers is calculated, pp 58 sqq, to 3,739,150 individuals. This number does not include those proprietors ("empresarios") who cultivate their land through sharecroppers. The distribution on the main tenure categories was found to be:

Owner-operators	2,102,950	= 56.25%
Sharecroppers	460,400	= 12.31%
Protected leaseholders	816,600	= 21.84%
Non-protected leaseholders	359,200	= 9.60%

The average size of holding is indicated to be 7.8 ha for non-protected leaseholders, 6.46 ha for sharecroppers, 6.19 ha for owner-operators, and 2.21 ial for protected leaseholders. Regional detail is given in Table 3, p. 60, while Table 5, p. 62, contains provincial figures both for distribution of area and number of holdings for the modes of tenure.

137b. H. Hopfner, *Die ländlichen Siedlungen der altkastilischen Meseta, Ein Beitrag zur Siedlungsgeographie Zentralspaniens* (Hamburg 1939), especially pp 140 sq: "Der Bauer bestellt dabei zum geringsten Teil nur Eigenland, sondern hat in der Regel noch eine Anzahl von Feldern gepachtet. Kleinbauern (Gütler) und Landarbeiter haben manchmal überhaupt keinen Besitz, sondern nur Land in Pacht. Die Gemischtbetriebe (Eigenland/Pachtland) überwiegen auf der ganzen Meseta bei weitem (ca 80 per cent), sind über 90% in den Provinzen León, Palencia, Burgos und Valladolid vertreten, d.h. als in der Hauptsache in den Landstrichen Altkastiliens, in denen ein zahlreiches Kolonat fehlt und in denen neben den Bauern zum grossen Teil auch die Landarbeiter Bodenbesitz aufweisen. Die bäuerlichen Betriebe, die sich nur auf Eigenland stützen, betragen z.B. in den Provinzen Valladolid und Zamora noch nicht 5%... Andererseits zählen die reinen Pachtbetriebe im zentralen Altkastilien höchstens 10%..."

For this information, Hopfner quotes statistics available in the local administrations. The enquiry presented by García de Oteyza (see preceding note) seems to have distributed the mixed tenures on the main categories.

137c. Chr. Evelpides, *Ē geōrgia tēs Ellados* (Athens 1944), p. 25, footnote 2, states that out of 954,000 holdings, 768,900 were owner-operated, 55,860 rented, 31,500 sharecropped, 12,130 under *emphyteusis* (very long-term leasehold), and 51,750 under unknown tenure status. This picture may be representative above all as regards those parts of the country where the land reform had been carried out after World War I. For the Old Kingdom, on the other hand, the picture is obscured through the occurrence of mixed tenures, as shown even clearer in the agricultural census of 1950. Some regional enquiries may also be quoted on this point. A. A. Diamantopoulos, *Ē pedias tou Mornou* (Athens 1940), p. 32 sq, states that considerable portions of the land were held by people residing outside the parishes under review, much of which was leased to local residents with some land of their own, in many cases. Similar conclusions can also be inferred from N. E. Aïvaliotakis, *O kampos tēs Messenias kai ai oreinai lekanai avtou* (Athens 1942), pp 92 sq, and *idem, Ai oreinai lekanai Feneou-Stymfalias* (Athens 1941).

137d. D. H. Franssens, *Een onderzoek naar de toestand van de landbouwers in Rump en Gellicum* (Wageningen 1950, processed), p. 13 sq, with an attempt to weight the land simply by counting the horticultural land thrice.

137e. H. Krause, "Pachtland und Betriebsgrössen, Reichsgebiet", *Berichte über Landwirtschaft* (Hamburg & Berlin 1937, Bd 21), pp 733 sqq, and *idem,* "Pachtland und Betriebsgrössen, Landschaftliche Unterschiede", *Berichte über Landwirtschaft* (Hamburg & Berlin 1938, Bd 22), pp 252–280. In both articles, it is shown that the leased land has had considerable importance for the changes in the size structure of holdings. A set of maps shows that in north-western Germany (including Schleswig-Holstein, Mecklenburg, Provinz Sachsen, and Anhalt), and in the Rheinprovinz, leased land amounts to some 15–27 per cent of the area of all holdings above 0.5 ha, which is considerably over the average for the Reich. Southern Germany, and the regions east of the Elbe, on the whole, were considerably below the average. In some parts of north-western Germany, the small holdings below 5 ha rented more than half of their land. On the other hand, the gradual increase of medium-sized holdings, between 10–20 ha, to a great extent depends upon increasing importance for mixed tenures; even though leased land is only $1/7$ of the area of these holdings, only half of them are purely owner-operated, without any leased land. The decline of large holdings is also shown to have meant above all a diminution of leased land in these holdings. Thus, it is stated as a conclusion, the leased land represents the most dynamic element in the development of the size structure of holdings (p. 263 sq, 1938).

137f. F. Dovring, "Les recensements agricoles français", *Bulletin mensuel de statistique, Supplément trimestriel* (Paris 1955, Apr.-Jun).

137g. "Statuts-modèles de la ferme coopérative", in V. Tchervenkov, *Les taches des fermes coopératives* (Sofia 1950), pp 119 sq.

139a. Many holdings in Southern Europe, under mixed tenure, are so unstable that they cannot possibly be legal entities. The question then arises what degree of stability would be necessary to qualify a holding as such an entity. – Another difficulty in the defining of agricultural enterprises is in the various instances of sharecropping and co-partnership. In Italy, at least part of the sharecropped holdings are counted as owner-operated, *i.e.* operated by the landlord rather than by the sharecropper. See, for instance, M. Rossi-Doria, "Considerazioni circa il carattere dei contratti di compartecipazione e di colonia parziaria nel Mezzogiorno d'Italia", *Rivista di economia agraria* (Rome 1948) pp, 318–333. Cf also M. R. Savatier, *La distinction entre métayage et salariat* (Paris 1948); A. Prax, "Métayage et société", *Progrès agricole et viticole* (Lyon 1951), pp 246–250; L. H. Thiney, "Le métayage est-il une société?" *Revue de législation agricole* (Paris 1951), pp 43–45; A. Seiquier-Velasco, "La dirección de cultivo en las aparcerias", *Boletín de la Cámara oficial sindacal de la provincia de Murcia* (Murcia 1950, Dec), pp 6–8. Even the distinction between leasehold and society may sometimes arouse doubts, in case the landowner wants to escape the legal regulation of leasehold; see A. N. Houwing, "Pacht of maatschappij?", *De Pacht* (The Hague 1951, May), pp 130–140. – In all these cases, then, the question would arise where the limit goes between different agricultural enterprises, both in the case that two or more persons are partners with regard to one enterprise or group of such, and in the case when one person commands or is partner in more than one enterprise. The Italian distinction between *mezzadria appoderata* and *mezzadria non appoderata* is instructive in this respect. Consequently, an agricultural enterprise can be a legal entity only inasmuch as positive law defines it as such.

139b. A. Finzi, "Diritto di proprietà e disciplina della produzione", *Atti del primo congresso nazionale di diritto agrario* (Firenze 1936).

144a. French C.c. 522,524: includes livestock, straw, and manure. German BGB 94–97: distinction between "Bestandteile" and "Zubehör". Italian C.c. 812: Land and buildings, trees, etc; 817–818 on "pertinenze"; cf also 816 on "universalità di mobili".

Swedish Statute of 1875 on real estate: includes a limited set of fixtures; attached chattel is not dealt with here but treated separately in the rules on tenancy.

The rule of English Common Law was that *quicquid plantatur solo, solo cedit* (what is planted on the land accrues to the land).

144b. French C.c. 1821 (undiminished inventory), 1824 (manure is inventory, not part of the holder's profit).

Italian C. c. 1640–1642.

German GBG 582 sqq.

Cf also B. W. Adkin. *A handbook of the law relating to Landlord and Tenant*, 12 ed. (London 1947), pp 219 sqq, giving account of a secular development tending to improve the tenant's position with regard to improvements brought about by himself, and pp 280 sq, especially on agricultural holdings; M. de Juglart, *Exploitation rurale* (Paris 1949), p 24, stating that a new owner of an estate is bound by the debts of the estate. This, and parallel rules elsewhere, merely prevents the debtor from breaking up an indebted estate, but it does not prevent the creditors from doing so, in case they take over the estate. In the same sense, *e.g.*, the German rules of BGB 98, 314, 926, 1,120. The holding has almost always been protected against the tenant.

145a. L. de Pina Manique, *A fragmentação da propriedade rústica* (Lisboa 1935).

145b. L. Dikoff, "Die rechtliche Lage des Landbesitzes vom Standpunkt des Erb- und Sachenrechtes", *Die sozialökonomische Struktur der bulgarischen Landwirtschaft*, hrsg v. J. St. Molloff (Berlin 1936), p. 98. However, the minimum limits were rather low: 0.3 ha in arable land, 0.2 ha in meadows, 0.1 ha in vineyards and rose-plantations.

145c. *Ley de 20.12.1952 sobre concentración parcelaria*, Art. 9. On the family gardens (*huertos familiares*), which are only part-time holdings, although as such of considerable importance, see the *Fuero del Trabajo*, art. 5:4, and the pamphlet *Huertos familares para campesinos* (Madrid s.a., c:a 1950, Instituto Nacional de Colonización, Ser. 3, No 5).

145d. *Loi du 9 mars 1941.*

145e. "Flurbeireinigungsgesetz vom 14. Juli 1953", *Bundesgesetzblatt*, I, (Bonn 1953, 18/7).

145f. Cf C. A. Ramberg, article in *Lantbrukstidskrift för Dalarne* (Falun 1952), pp 87–95.

145g. N. Skovgaard, in the *FAO Agricultural Studies*, 11 (Rome 1951), pp 52 sq.

146a. A. Durand, *La vie rurale dans les massifs volcaniques des Dores, du Cézallier, du Cantal et de l'Aubreo* (Aurillac 1946), pp 149 sqq; J. Baert, "Deling van grond bij boerennalatenschap" *De Pacht* (The Hague 1949), pp 134–152; A. W. Ashby & I. L. Evans, *The agriculture of Wales and Monmouthshire* (Cardiff 1944), p. 85. On the general development of inheritance rules in recent years, see M. Tcherkinsky, "The evolution of the system of succession to landed property in Europe", *Monthly Bulletin of Agricultural Economics and Sociology* (Rome, IIA, 1941, Jun).

146b. French C.c. 832; cf Greek C.c. 1889, still providing for only facultative indivisibility, which cannot have had great effect in a poor peasant society where little more than the land is available to divide between the heirs. Cf also C.V. Noilhan. "Une évolution de la législation française en faveur de l'indivisibilité de l'exploitation agricole", *Académie d'agriculture de France, Comptes rendus* (Paris 1951, Apr. 11), pp 249–253, also printed in the *International Bulletin of Agricultural Law* (Rome 1945), pp 94–98.

146c. On the geography of *anerbenrecht*, see W. Henkelmann, "Grundstückszusammenlegung und Erbrechtsreform", *Deutsche Agrarpolitik im Rahmen der inneren und äusseren Wirtschaftspolitik*... hrsg Fr. Beckmann, H. Bente & B. Harms (Berlin 1932), Vol. 1, pp 601–612; E. Grass & A. Münzinger, "Die Flurbereinigung in Süddeutschland", *Berichte über Landwirtschaft* (Hamburg & Berlin 1936), Sonderh. 123, p 33 and the map facing p 49; and W. Hartke, "Zur Geographie der bäuerlichen Liegenschaften in Deutschland", *Petermann's Geographische Mitteilungen* (Gotha 1940), pp 16–19 and Plate 3.

146d. E. H. Kaden, "The peasant inheritance law in Germany", *Iowa Law Review* (Iowa City 1934–35), pp 350–388.

141e. Statute of 1947 3/7, No 139; cf A. Bedřich, "A propos des questions de la propriété agricole et sa protection", *Bulletin de droit tchécoslovaque* (Prague 1952, Dec. 1), p. 332. For older Czechoslovak law, see Fr. Kubec, "Besitzwechsel", in V. Brdlík, *Die sozialökonomische Struktur der Landwirtschaft in der Tschechoslowakei* (Berlin 1938), pp 111–118, stating that the Imperial Austrian statute on *anerbenrecht* of 1889 had been followed up through a regional Statute for Bohemia in 1908 and homestead legislation in the twenties; actually, this does not seem to have had any effect in Slovakia in the inter-war period.

146f. J. Skeie, *Odelsretten og aseteretten* (Oslo 1951).

147a. *Sovetskoe grazhdanskoe pravo*, red. D. N. Genkin (Moscow 1950), Vol. 1, pp 340 sq, Cf the Constitution of the Soviet Union, Art. 7, and V. Gsovski, *Soviet Civil Law* (Ann Arbor 1948), Vol. 1, pp 773 sqq.

148a. *Reichsheimstätten-Gesetz*, of 1924 18/1. Cf M. Sering & C. v. Dietze (ed.), *Die Vererbung des ländlichen Grundbesitzes in der Nachkriegszeit* (München & Leipzig 1930), Vol. 3, pp 4 sq with note 7; *Smallholdings, First Report of the Smallholdings Advisory Council* (London 1949); *Land Settlement in Scotland , Report by the Scottish Land Settlement Committee* (Edinburgh 1945); D. Arnskov, *Smallholdings in Denmark* (Copenhagen 1924); *Loi de 12/6 1909 sur la consommation d'un bien de famille insaississable*; cf M. Augé-Laribé, *La politique agricole de la France de 1880 a 1940* (Paris 1950), pp 89 sq.

148b. Spain: *Ley sobre colonización y distribución de la propiedad de las zonas regables*, of 1949 21/4.

Portugal: *Regulamento de Lei No 2,014, Aproveitamento de terrenos pela colonização, Decreto No 36,709 de 5 de Janeiro de 1948*, in its Divisão 3, stating that the owner may decide which of the heirs is to take over the entire holding, but admitting that the holding may remain undivided family property, held by all the heirs in co-ownership. Thus far, this legislation only regards the holdings created by the Junta de colonização interna.

150a. *Agriculture Act 1947*, Art. 31, now partly superseded by *Agricultural Holdings Act, 1948;* for Scotland, the *Agricultural Holdings (Scottland) Act, 1949.* For comments, see, *e.g., Jackson's Agricultural Holdings* (1949).

151a. *Loi du 13/4/1946*, superseding a provisional statute of 1945 17/10.

151b. R. Savatier, article in *Semaine Juridique* (Paris 1948), 2, 4420: "Le désir de donner la terre à celui qui le cultive l'emporte sur celui d'assurer au fermier une exploitation durable"; cf also P. de Felice, "Vers des nouvelles modalités du droit de reprise", *Nord agricole* (Lille 1951, May 11), p. 7.

151c. Belgian C.c. 1743, 1748; cf the Statute of 1929, Mars 7, § 3.

151d. Statute of 1951, July 7; cf W. G. A. Lammers, "De gewezigde Belgische pachtwetgeving", *Landbouwwereldnieuws* (The Hague 1952, Jan) pp 53–57.

151e. See M. J. Boerendonk, *Farm tenancy policy in the Netherlands* (The Hague 1950).

152a. *Gazzetta ufficiale* (Rome), Serie speciale, 1944, 24/6, No 36; 1945 2/5, No 53 (valid for the period up to the end of war conditions); 1947 3/5, No 101; 1948 20/8, No 193; 1949 7/7, No 153; 1950 26/7, No 169; 1952 12/7, No 160, Cf *Provvedimenti in materia agraria... Legislazione aggiornata al 1 guigno 1953...* (Milano 1953), pp 3–43.

152b. A. de Feo, "I patti agrari", *Notiziario C.G.I.L.* (Rome 1954), pp 107–110, with text of the project of Statute, pp 111–117.

152c. Cf L. García de Oteyza, "Los regimenes de explotación del suelo nacional", *Revista de estudios agro-sociales* (Madrid 1952), pp 49–62.

153a. Constitution of the Soviet Union, artt. 6–8; *Ustav sel'skokhoziaïstvennoï arteli* (Moskow 1935), st. 2, stating that the land must not be sold or leased. Cf N. D. Kazantsev, *Stalinskiï ustav sel'skokhoziaïstvennoï arteli – osnovoï zakon kolkhoznoï zhizni* (Moscow 1951), pp 36 sqq.

153b. *Ustav sel'skokhoziaïstvennoï arteli*, st. 13. That the rule was often violated is made clear by the claims for a stricter compliance set forth in a party resolution in 1947 (Kazantsev, as quoted in the preceding note, p. 62), and in a government decree in 1948 (printed, i.a., in the *Spravochnik predsedatel'ia kolkhoza*, 3 ed., Moscow 1948, p. III).

153c. M. Gendel'man, "Vnutrikhoziařstvennoe zemleustrořstvo kolkhozov s neskol'kimi naselennymi punktami", *Sotsialisticheskoe sel'skoe khoziařstvo* (Moscow 1952, Mar) pp 38–46.

153d. Thus, the Bulgarian statute which is among the most radical ones: "Statuts-modèles de la ferme coopérative, adoptés par la Deuxième Conférence nationale des fermes coopératives...", in V. Tchervenkov, *Les tâches des fermes coopératives* (Sofia 1950), pp 119 sq, in its art. 4: in case cooperative land were inherited by a non-member, this heir would have to await the expiration of a three-year period before he could take over the land.

154a. A. W. Ashby & I. L. Evans, *The agriculture of Wales and Monmoutshire* (Cardiff 1944), p. 93, describing how many landlords owning land in Wales did nothing to improve the holdings – and were often considered good landlords because they charged low rents for land kept in a poor state of equipment.

154b. Cf V. A. Dicey, *Lectures on the relations between Law and Public Opinion in England during the nineteenth century* (London 1905, re-ed. 1924. Behind the Agricultural Holdings Act lies the idea that social protection must be combined with the restriction to the freedom of contract in order to guide classes of the society "who though not in any strictness incapable of managing their own affairs, are, in the opinion of the legislature, unlikely to provide as well for their own interest as can the community".

155a. A. W. Ashby & I. L. Evans, *The agriculture of Wales and Monmouthshire*, (Cardiff 1944), p. 85.

155b. K. Skovgaard & A. Pedersen, *Survey of Danish agriculture* (Copenhagen 1946), pp 35 sq: Against the wide-spread belief that tenancy should be more advantageous from the viewpoint of capital supply (to working capital), the dominating freehold system in Denmark is held forth as a piece of practical evidence of the contrary: not even during the crises of the 1880'ties, 1890'ties or 1930'ties was the confidence in the freehold system shaken earnestly, and Danish agriculture is said not to have suffered any more than did agriculture in other countries.

156a. Fr. Houillier, "Les modes de faire-valoir en France, L'importance économique et sociale du fermage", *Agriculture pratique* (Paris 1951, Sep), pp 415–418.

156b. P. Caziot, *La valeur de la terre en France*, 3 éd, rev., (Paris 1952), pp 27 sqq; af also P. Voirin, "La propriété dite culturale dans le nouveau statut français du fermage", *Legislative information* (Rome, FAO Legislative Service, 1950, Sep), pp 115–124.

158a. Fr. Houillier, "Les modes de faire-valoir en France, Le métayage", *Agriculture pratique* (Paris 1952, Jan), pp 11–14. This author stresses the localization of the sharecropping in the south-western departments and its character of relatively large family enterprise, and tries to defend it as a tolerably good solution for the region. Cf also H. de Farcy, "La répartition des modes de faire-valoir en France", *Revue de géographie de Lyon* (Lyon 1951), and *Les diverses formes de métayage, 1, Rapports, avis et études de synthèse* (Paris 1953). On the latter, see also above, note 133 (f).

158b. Cf M. Andrault, article in the *Revue de législation agricole* (Paris 1951, Sep-Oct), estimating that the instances of transition from sharecropping to leasehold have been few and have generally taken place amicably, more often at the request of the landlord than because the sharecropper took any initiative.

158c. L. García de Oteyza, "Los regimenes de explotación del suelo nacional", *Revista de estudios agro-sociales* (Madrid 1952), pp 49–62. Cf also M. García Isidro, "Contratos de aparceria: el célebre articulo 7° de la ley de 1940" *Agricultura* (Madrid 1951, Feb), pp 70–74, and P. Gonzalez García, "Algo sobre arrendamientos rústicos", *Ceres* (Valladolid 1951, Jun), pp 31–33.

158d. M. Rossi-Doria, "Considerazioni circa il carattere dei contratti di compartecipazione e di colonia parziaria nel Mezzogiorno d'Italia e i modi di una loro regolazione", *Rivista di economia agraria* (Rome 1948), pp 318–333. The main point, according to this author, is the question whether the so-called mezzadrias in the South of Italy do correspond to what is generally understood as mezzadria or sharecropping. The success of any attempt to regulate these contracts would, in the opinion of Rossi-Doria, depend on an appropriate understanding of their nature, among other things because the contracts in question are not uniform, which seems to be unfavorable for the attempts towards a unique solution to apply to all of them. The analysis gives the result that these southern mezzadrias are rather a kind of leasehold than of sharecropping, in many cases at least, while they in other cases are some kind of hire of labor force.

158e. Thus at least in the Po valley; but also instances such as the port-wine district in northern Portugal, and the Spanish *huerta* on the Mediterranean coast, would probably justify analogous conclusions if the property and tenancy structures were better known.

159a. C. v. Dietze, H. C. Taylor, M. Ezekiel, and others, "Land tenure and the social control of land", *International Conference of Agricultural Economists 1938* (London 1939), pp 118–196; M. Tcherkinsky, *The land tenure systems of Europe* (Geneva 1939, League of Nations Publications, European Conference on Rural Life, Official No: C. 19. M. 11 1939 Conf. E.V.R. 7).

159b. G. Prawitz, *Jordfrågan* (Stockholm 1951).

159c. *Agriculture Act 1947*, Art. 109: 2. Analogous rules on expropriation on the ground of bad management are found in most countries, see, for instance, Italian C.c., Art. 838, Cf also J. R. H. Roberts, "Compulsory acquisition of land by public authorities". *Public administration* (London 1946), pp 176–181.

159d. O. Howald, "Das neue Bodenrecht", *Agrarpolitische Revue* (Zürich 1949, fasc. 4), pp 121–128; *idem,* "Das neue schweizerische Landwirtschaftsgesetz", *Agrarische Rundschau* (Wien 1952), fasc. 8, pp 9–18; O. Kauffmann, *Die Neuordnung des Landwirtschaftsrechtes* (Zürich & Strasbourg 1952, reproducing two articles in the *Agrarpolitische Revue*).

159e. C. V. Noilhan, "Une évolution de la législation française en faveur de l'indivisibilité de l'exploitation agricole", *Académie d'agriculture de France, Comptes rendus* (Paris 1951, Apr. 11), pp 249–253.

159f. *Loi 53–683*, of 1953 6/8. Cf the pessimistic comments by J. Playeth, "La loi foncière est votée", *L'agriculture pratique* (Paris 1953) pp 509–512.

160a. A. Serpieri, "Imprese contadine e non contadine nell'agricoltura italiana" *Rivista di economia agraria* (Rome 1951), pp 71–82.

160b. Italian Statute, No 841, of 1950 21/10, Cf L. Gui, "Le prime sei aziende modello", *Agricoltura* (Rome 1952, May), pp 5–8. – The Spanish statute is the *Ley de explotaciones agrarias ejemplares*, of 1952, 14/7; cf A. Leal García, "La ley de explotaciones agrarias ejemplares", *Revista de estudios agro-sociales* (Madrid 1953, Apr. - Jun.).

161a. Statute of 1951 11/7, No 5, *Receuil des lois* (Prague), on sales and lease of land; and Statute of 1947 3/7, on farm inherentance. Cf A. Bedřich, „A propos des questions de la propriété agricole et sa protection", *Bulletin de droit tchécoslovaque* (Prague 1952, Dec), p. 332.

162a. "Leggi di riforma fondiaria e provvedimenti connessi", including a number of statements of this legislation, published as a special issue of *L'agricoltura italiana* (Rome 1951); "Ley de colonización de grandes zonas", *Boletín oficial del estado* (Madrid 1940, 25/1, No 25), stating in the preamble that the foremost aim of the measures is increase of production; social values are also taken into account, though on the second plane. Cf E. Gomez Ayau, in the *Revista de estudios agro-sociales* (Madrid 1952), p. 32; L. Quartín Graça, *Subsidios para uma politica agraria* (Lisboa 1949).

162b. B. Rossi, "Il fondamento giuridico del limite alla proprietà", *L'agricoltura italiana* (Rome 1950), pp 169–171; A. Ballarin Marcial, "El sentido humano del nuevo derecho de la agricultura", *Arbor* (Madrid 1953), pp 481–500; J. L. del Arco, "La nouvelle loi espagnole concernant l'enterprise agricole familiale", *Agrarpolitische Revue* (Zürich 1953).

162c. G. Costanzo, "The small holdings: its creation and its problems", *Monthly Bulletin of Agricultural Economics and Sociology* (Rome, IIA, 1943), pp 81–115.

163a. H. Campion, *Public and private property in Great Britain* (London 1939).

163b. "Statens utarrenderade domäner arrendeåret 1910–1911", *Kungl. Statistiska Centralbyrån, Statistiska Meddelanden*, Ser. A, Vol. 1:2 (Stockholm 1913), Table 1, p. 38: in 1910/11: 1,993 leased holdings, including 90,000 hectares of arable land, 25,000 ha meadow and 80.000 ha forest, against 2,118 holdings, and somewhat larger areas too, in 1907/08. – On the important public forests in Sweden, see the official series, *Kungl. Domänstyrelsens förvaltning, Skogsväsendet...* 1911/12 sqq, later changed into *Sveriges officiella statistik, Domänverket* (annual issues). In 1949, the property of the Swedish State included 109,000 hectares of arable land and meadow, 4.1 million ha forest and 1.6 million ha wasteland, together 5.8 million ha land and 220,000 ha water.

163c. A. E. Davies & D. Evans, *Land nationalisation: the key to social reform* (London 1921); R. A. Price, *Public freeholds* (London 1944); L. B. Powel, *The land: State or free?* (London 1946); R. G. Proby, "The future of private land-owning", *Central Landowners' Association, Journal* (London 1949), pp 75–82. Cf also "The control of land use in the United Kingdom of Great Britain and Northern Ireland", *International Bulletin of Agricultural Law* (Rome, IIA, 1946), pp 58–65.

164a. I. Matveev, "Proizvoditel'nost truda v sovkhozakh", *Planovoe khoziaïstvo* (Moscow 1939), p. 100; cf A. Vucinich, *Soviet economic institutions, The social structure of productive units* (Stanford 1952), p. 100.

164b. J. Stalin, *Problemy leninizma*, 11 ed. (Moscow 1943), pp 485–486.

164c. *Sovkhozy k xv godovshchine oktiabria, Sbornik pod redakciei* A. P. Teriaevoї (Moscow 1932); *Sovkhozy, VII Vsesoiuznom s'esdu sovetov Narodnyї kommissariat zernovykh i zhivotnovodcheskikh sovkhozov SSSR 1935* (Moscow 1936).

164d. In the *Bol'shaia Sovetskaia Èntsiklopediia*, 2 ed., by mid-1955 published up to "Pol'..."

164e. *European Agriculture, A Statement of Problems*, E/ECE/175 (Geneva 1954), p. 57. On State farms in Albania, see *Probleme economice* (Bucharest 1950, Feb), pp 143 sqq.

165a. Thus, G. Clauson, *Communal land tenure* (Rome 1953, FAO Agricultural Studies, No 17).

165b. J. Días, *Vilarinho da Furna, Uma aldeia comunitaria* (Porto 1948), dealing with a case of accentuated "vida comunitaria" which is in this village better preserved than in most other villages, as a consequence of the still mainly pastoral character of its economy. This village appears to be almost a kind of self-supporting petty State, managing its own affairs largely according to local customs.

165c. J. Costa, *Colectivismo agrario en España*, 2 ed. (Madrid 1915); cf also M. Le Lannou, *Pâtres et paysans de la Sardaigne* (Tours 1941).

165d. R. Belitch, *La propriété foncière en Yougoslavie* (Paris 1930).

166a. See, for instance, J. M. Zumalacárregui, *Ensayo sobre el origen y desarrollo de la propiedad comunal en España hasta el final de la Edad Media* (Madrid 1903); L. Carretero y Nieva, *Las comunidades castellanas en la historia y en el estado actual* (Segovia 1922); R. Altamira, *Historia de la propiedad comunal* (Madrid 1927).

166b. P. Gronset, "Stölshamnene våre, Utskifting må til", *Norsk landbruk* (Oslo 1944), pp 144 sq; on communal pastures in Norway, see H. Slogedal, article in *Tidsskrift for det norske landbrug* (Oslo 1948), pp 4–13.

166c. W. H. Ubbink, "Schaarweiden", *De Pacht* (The Hague 1951), pp 162–180.

166d. *Bundesgesetz über die Erhaltung des bäuerlichen Grundbesitzes*, of 1951

12/6, especially art. 17. Cf also O. Kauffmann, *Die Neuordning des Landwirtschafsrechtes* (Zürich & Strasbourg 1952).

166e. A. Durand, *La vie rurale dans les massifs volcaniques des Dores, du Cézallier, du Cantal et de l'Aubrec* (Aurillac 1946), pp 130 sqq, deals with communal collective property inherited from Mediaeval communal usufructs by appointment of the landlords. It often became divided during the Revolution and later, but there are still important remainders which are the focus of a vivid discussion in recent years. Durand holds (pp 145 sq) that communal property might in many cases to best advantage be maintained and developed to the benefit of the whole region, despite the experience which seems to indicate that communal land is in a poorer state of cultivation and maintenance than private land.

166f. G. Medici, "Proprietà collettive, demani, usi civici", *Rivista di economia agraria* (Rome 1948), pp 303–317. When land is subject to collective usage rights, it is a basic distinction whether the land belongs to a community, an association, or a private person. Some of these rights have their origin in the Antiquity, others in the Middle Ages.

Legislation on the subject has on the whole been hostile to these collective rights. This was so especially in the 19th century, but is still the case in the latest Statute, No 1,766 of 1927 and subsequent regulations referring to it. The remaining instances of collective rights over private property regard only some 200,000 or 250,000 hectares, and with regard to these rights, the law aforesees successive abolishment of collective rights, eventually cession of part of the land in question to the community holding the usage right to the whole, or by introduction of an emphyteutic (perpetual) rent.

Much more important are the collective properties of communities or associations, covering more than 3 million hectares, or one-tenth of the surface of Italy. The land is mostly low-productive forest and pasture land but does even so represent considerable values. To a great extent, this land is not suitable for cultivation and its use is most rational in large coherent units. They are of importance not only in the Alpine communities but also in Central Italy, above all in the so-called *università agrarie* (collective ownership associations) in Lazio, and also in the South (especially on Sardinia).Cf also G. Cassani, *I dominii collettivi, la colonizzazione agricola e le partecipanze* (Bologne 1894); M. Volpe, *Note sui pascoli alpini de proprietà sociale indivisa del mandamento di Chiavenna* (Rome 1912); A. Cencelli, *La proprietà collettiva in Italia* (Milano 1920); A. Sertoli, article in the *Rassegna economica della provincia di Sondrio* (Sondrio 1952), pp 9 sq.

167a. A. Leal García, "Modalidades de la propiedad immobiliaria en la provincia de Cáceres", *Boletín del instituto de reforma agraria* (Madrid 1934, Jun), stressing that Spanish legal science had not yet arrived at a consistent definition of this form of ownership.

167b. R. García Redruello, "Derecho rural consuetudinario; las ,suertes' como forma de propiedad colectivizada en el agro español", *Surco* (Madrid 1947), pp 29 sq.

167c. P. Benassi, *Affittanze collettive* (Torino 1920), partly referring to G. Raineri, *Le affittanze collettive in Italia* (Piacenza 1906). Benassi, pp 43 sqq, mentions that the first experiment in collective leasehold was made as early as in 1886, in land belonging to the city of Ravenna; this case was still in function in 1920. A few more attempts were made during the last decade of the 19th century, but the movement got considerable significance from about 1900, when the "Società dei probi contadini di Castel Cerreto e Battaglie" in Lombardy created a whole movement for collective renting of land. In 1906, there were 108 collective holdings scattered over Northern Italy and Sicily; in 1920, they were more than 200, despite the unfavorable effects of the war. Part of these collectives were of Catholic inspiration and aimed merely at a collective rent contract but developed individual small-scale farming. Another part is Socialistic and runs the land collectively. It is added, p. 53, that part of these collectives also took up various co-operative activities. Examples of statutes for collectives are quoted, pp 101 sqq.

167d. G. Pesce, *La compartecipazione collettiva nell'azienda agraria* 2 ed, (Rome 1937), with the statutes for "patto di compartecipazione generale familiare e collettiva", and "patto di mezzadria collettiva", both from January, 1932. They represent an attempt at formally doing away with the system of hired hands by replacing it with a kind of sharecropping, though with very little freedom of action for the workers; the landlord, in each case, were to remain the director of the enterprise. Among other things, the collectivity of workers was also supposed to take care of their own unemployed.

167e. M. Montanuccio, *Kolkhoz e mezzadria* (Rome 1945).

168a. *Joint Farming Co-operatives, A preliminary survey* (Geneva, ILO 1949); H. F. Infield, "Cooperative farming in the world today", *Cooperative living* (Poughkeepsie, N.Y., 1949, Spring); H. F. Infield & J. B. Maier, *Cooperative group living: an international symposium on group farming and the sociology of cooperation* (New York 1950).

168b. G. Gojat & M. Tournier, "L'application des principes communautaires à la répartition des terres communales", *Diagnostic économique et social, Economie et humanisme* (Paris 1951, pp 291–294, discussing the principle "to each according to his needs" in connection with redistribution of land etc.

168c. P. Coutin, "Les exploitations agricoles en France", *Revue de l'action populaire* (Paris 1951), pp 583 sqq, especially pp 587, 594.

169a. Above all, the *Spravochnik predsedatel'ia kolkhoza*, 3 ed. (Moscow 1948), including most of the relevant legal texts; cf A. Vucinich, *Soviet economic institutions* (Stanford 1952), pp 57 sqq, and P. Honigsheim, "The roots of Soviet rural social structure: where and why it has spread," *Agricultural history* (Washington D.C. 1951), pp 104–114.

169b. *Spravochnik predsedatel'ia kolkhoza* (Moscow 1948), p. 4.

169c. Data in the *Bol'shaia Sovetskaia Éntsiklopediia*, 2 ed.

169d. P. Adamenko, "Sel'skoe khoziaĭstvo zapadnykh oblasteĭ Ukrainy na putiakh kollektivizatsii", *Sotsialisticheskoe sel'shoe khoziaĭstvo* (Moscow 1951), pp 57–61.

169e. E. Jaska, "The results of collectivization of Estonian agriculture", *Land Economics* (Madison, Wis., 1952, Aug), pp 212–217.

170a. For the background, see D. Warriner, *Revolution in Eastern Europe* (London 1950), chapters 7 and 8.

170b. O. v. Frangeš, "Agricultural labour communities in south-eastern Europe", *Monthly Bulletin of Agricultural Economics and Sociology* (Rome, IIA, 1941), pp 22–32.

170c. *Ibid.*, pp 25 sq.

170d. I. Balev, *Zěmědělskoto stopanstvo i kooperativnata obrabotka na zemiata* (Sofia 1940), p. 45; N.I. Kanev, *Kooperativno obrabotvane na zemiate i natsionalen stopanski plan* (Sofia 1939); M. Genovski, *Obsrtvenost i kultura* (Sofia 1939), pp 202 sq.

170e. Figures on collectivization in agriculture in *European Agriculture, A Statement of Problems*, E/ECE/175 (Geneva 1954), p. 57; on the low degree of collectivization in Albania, see article on Albanian agriculture in *Interagra* (Prague 1952), pp 264 sq. For details on the movement in Eastern Germany, see the article "Kolchosen in der Sowjetzone nach russischem Vorbild", *Zeitschrift für das gesamte Siedlungswesen* (Bielefeld 1952), pp 141–143.

170f. For instance, D. Bajalica, "Reorganizacija pasivnih zadruga Bosne i Hercegovine", *Socijalistička poljoprivreda* (Beograd 1952, Mar), pp 59 sqq.

CHAPTER 5

172a. See, for instance, G. Fauquet, *Le secteur coopératif, essai sur la place de l'homme dans les institutions et de celles-ci dans l'économie*, 2 ed. (Bruxelles

1935). Among the followers of the Catholic social encyclicals, see, *e.g.*, *La obra cooperativa agraria en España, Lecciones pronunciadas en el Cursillo de formación social agraria para sacerdotes, celebrado en Pamplona del 4 al 13 de agosto de 1948* (Madrid 1949). Cf also L. Valko, *International handbook of cooperative legislation* (Washington 1954), and the *Papers on agricultural advisory service in various countries* (Bonn 1951, Conference on agricultural extension, Bonn, Germany, December 1951).

172b. See A. Thomas, *The relation between the different forms of co-operation* (Report submitted to the 11th Congress of the International Co-operative alliance, 1924), and *Co-operative organisations and post-war relief* (Montreal 1943, ILO, Studies and reports, Ser. H. No 4). – Communism, at least in the early twenties, did not regard co-operation as an alternative to socialism but rather as a very imperfect stage on the road towards socialist development which was bound to disappear or to become merged into the general social structure when socialist society reached its maturity; on this point, see *The co-operative movement in Soviet Russia* (Geneva 1925, ILO, Studies and Reports, Ser. H, No 3), pp 1 sqq.

173a. See article by L. Tardy in *La coopération agricole* (Rome, IIA, 1931), pp 167 sqq.

173b. Thus the Dutch and German land reclamation societies, the Spanish and other South European irrigation societies, etc.

173c. Cf E. Vandervelde, *La coopération neutre et la coopération socialiste* (Paris 1913). On early manifestations in this sense, see E. A. Pratt, *Agricultural organisation* (London 1914), pp 2 sqq.

173d. J. Gaumont, *Histoire générale de la coopération en France* (Paris 1923), Vol. 2, pp 568 sqq.

173e. On Austria, see *Mitteilungen aus der Statistik der landwirtschaftlichen Genossenschaften in Österreich, hrsg im Auftrage des k.k. Ackerbauministeriums von dem Allgemeinen Verband landwirtschaftlicher Genossenschaften in Österreich* (Wien 1910–12), Vol. 1–2, especially Vol. 1, pp 262 sq, with figures on co-operatives as in 1907.

173f. *Třicet let české zemědělské družstveni práce* (Prague 1928), p. 102; M. Vučković, *Zadrugarstvo juce i danas* (Beograd 1945), p. 56.

173g. M. Vučković, *Zadrugarstvo*, p. 61.

173h. A. Tschakaloff, "Die Verschuldung der bulgarischen Landwirtschaft" *Die sozialökonomische Struktur der bulgarischen Landwirtschaft*, hrsg. v. J. St. Molloff (Berlin 1936).

173i. P. Vanderdael, *Le boerenbond belge, Soixante ans d'activité, 1890–1950* (Louvain 1950), with figures on the development of the movement, p. 51.

174a. A. W. Ashby & J. Morgan Jones, "The agricultural movement in Wales", *Year Book of Agricultural Co-operation in the British Empire* (London 1928).

174b. M. Digby, "Agricultural co-operation in England and Wales", *Agriculture* (London 1954, Apr), pp 26–29.

174c. H. Plunkett, *Ireland in the new century* (London 1904).

174d. A. Freyer, *Den danske Andelsbevaegelse* (Copenhagen 1929).

174e. *League of Nations, European Conference on Rural Life, National Monographs drawn up by Governments, The Netherlands* (Geneva 1939, C. II. M.S. 1939, Conf. E.V.R. 4), p. 27. Cf also H. v. Haastert & G. W. M. Huysman, *Veertig jaaren landbouwcredit onder leiding van de coöperatieve Boerenleenbank te Eindhoven 1898–1938* (Eindhoven 1938).

174f. "Situation des coopératives agricoles agréées au 15 février 1952", *Revue du Ministère de l'Agriculture* (Paris 1952, Jun), pp 149–151. On early French developments, see article by L. Tardy in *La coopération agricole* (Rome 1931), Vol. 1, pp 167 sqq. An historical outlook on French agricultural cooperation, together with analysis of its present legal structure, in J. Rozier, *Les coopératives agricoles* (Paris 1952). See also E. M. Owen, "Co-operative mechanisation in

France, the Netherlands, and England and Wales", *The Farm Economist* (Oxford 1949), pp 93–96.

174g. See G. Acerbo, *La cooperazione agraria in Italia* (Piacenza 1932), and A. Serpieri, article in the *Rivista di economia agraria* (Rome 1951), pp 103–114.

174h. *Unión Nacional de cooperativas del campo, Memoria; Ejercicio 1950* (Madrid 1951), and *La obra cooperativa agraria en España* (Madrid 1949), most of which is reprinted in *Las organisaciones cooperativas en la teoria y en la practica* (Madrid 1951), especially the contribution by V. Puyal, trying to trace urban co-operation back to national issues, in an historical outlook; agricultural cooperation, at any rate, took its start with the establishment of a co-operative wine-cellar in 1900 and a credit co-operative type Raiffeisen in 1901. From the first legal statute, in 1906, the "social-Catholic" trend of thought began to exercise its influence.

174i. E. A. Lima Basto, *Inquérito económico agrícola* (Lisboa 1936), Vol. 4, pp 283–300, gives account of rural co-operation as it existed in 1933–35 and stresses its extremely scarce occurrence and weak importance. The point is being stressed anew, pp 433 sqq, together with a mild wish for more co-operation in the future, despite the enormous apparent difficulties. See also E. Martinez de Bujanda, "Corporative organisation of agriculture in Portugal", *Monthly Bulletin of Agricultural Economics and Sociology* (Rome, IIA, 1938), pp 78–86; A. Ramos de Paula Coelho, *As cooperativas na economia corporativa portuguesa* (Coimbra 1944); and J. Ribeiro Teixeira, "The corporative organisation in Portugal", *International Bulletin of Agricultural Law* (Rome 1945), pp 22–30.

174j. R. de Moraes Soares, "Celleiros communs, Noticia historica", *Boletim do Ministerio das obras publicas, commercio e industria* (Lisboa 1855), reprinted separately (Lisboa 1898).

175a. *Rural credit and co-operation in Hungary* (Budapest 1913, Publications of the Royal Hungarian Minister of Agriculture).

175b. *The co-operative movement in Soviet Russia* (Geneva 1925, ILO, Studies and Reports, Ser. H, No 3).

176a. M. Digby, "Agricultural co-operation in England and Wales", *Agriculture* (London 1954, Apr.), pp. 26–29.

176b. G. Fauquet, "The diversity of co-operative institutions and their classification", *International Labour Review* (Geneva 1939), pp 435–458.

178a. *Rural credit and co-operation in Hungary* (Budapest 1913).

180a. See M. Birou, "XXXIIIme Congrès National de la Mutualité de la Coopération et du Crédit Agricoles à Lyon", *Progrès agricole et viticole* (Lyon 1951), pp 311 sqq; L. Fondard, "Le crédit agricole", *Bouches du-Rhône-agricoles* (Marseilles 1951), pp 16 sq; R. Cercler, "La coopération agricole et la politique du crédit", *Nouvelle revue contemporaine* (Paris 1952, Nov).

180b. A. Basevi, "A special co-operative credit section of the National Labour Bank in Italy", *Review of international co-operation* (London 1951, Jul), pp 169–173; C. Lopez del Haro, *Movilización de la propiedad rustica y el credito rural…* (Madrid 1931); *Unión Nacional de cooperativas del campo, Memoria: Ejercicio 1950* (Madrid 1951), pp 19 sqq; *La obra cooperativa en España* (Madrid 1949), pp 99 sqq: S. Iroz, "Sistema y funcionamiento de una Caja Rural", showing this part of the movement to be founded essentially on the principles of Raiffeisen.

180c. R. L. Vorkapitch, *Le crédit agricole en Yugoslavie* (Paris 1930); A. Tschakaloff, "Die Verschuldung der bulgarischen Landwirtschaft", *Die sozial-ökonomische Struktur der bulgarischen Landwirtschaft* hrsg. v. J. St. Molloff (Berlin 1936), pp 180 sqq.

180d. K. Leontides, "Ekthesis epi tēs en Elladi askoumenēs agrotikēs pisteos", *Bulletin agricole* (Athens 1953, Direction des recherches agricoles), fasc. 6, pp 38 sqq.

180e. V. P. Miliutin, *Kooperatsiia v SSSR za desiat let* (Moscow 1928), p. 130.

180f. *Vsia kooperatsiia SSSR, Spravochnik i ezhegodnik* (Moscow 1928), p. 826.

181a. S. S. Nosyrev, K. A. Miseiuk & M. V. Sidelnikov, *Kreditovanie sel'khozbankom kolkhozov i sel'skogo naseleniia* (Moscow 1950).

183a. M. Digby, "Agricultural co-operation in England and Wales", *Agriculture* (London 1954, Apr), pp 26–29: the most important branch of "single-purpose" societies were those for eggs.

183b. A. W. Ashby & J. Morgan Jones, "The agricultural movement in Wales", *Year Book of Agricultural Co-operation in the British Empire* (London 1928), p. 2.

183c. L. Smith-Gordon & L. C. Staples, *Rural reconstruction in Ireland, A record of co-operative organization* (London 1917).

183d. P. Vanderdael, *Le Boerenbond belge, Soixante ans d'activité* (Louvain 1950), p. 51.

183e. J. Costa, *Colectivismo agrario en Espana* (Madrid 1898, 2 ed. 1915). – *Unión Nacional de cooperativas del campo... Memoria; Ejercicio 1950* (Madrid 1951), pp 9 sq.

183f. M. Vučković, *Zadrugarstvo juce i danas* (Beograd 1945), pp 51 sqq: the first co-operative in present Yugoslavia was a credit society in Ljubljana in 1856, of the Schultze-Delitsch type. See also P. Rastovčan, *Pravo zemljoradničkih zadruga* (Zagreb 1950), and S. Dolfe, *Prva doba našega zadružništva* (Ljubljana 1945).

185a. *The co-operative movement in the Netherlands* (The Hague 1947).

185b. *Unión Nacional de cooperativas del campo, Memoria: Ejercicio 1950* (Madrid 1951), pp 25 sqq: 193 co-operative wine-cellars in 22 provinces, processing 1½million hectolitres of wine.

185c. *Ibid.* p. 27: 419 co-operative oil presses in 29 provinces (olive oil is not produced in all the 50 provinces). – G. Vagliasindi, *La cooperazione applicata alla olivicoltura e all'industria olearia* (Rome 1911); G. Nicosia, *Cantine sociali e cooperazione vitivinicola*, 2 ed., (Rome 1935).

186a. P. A. Tönnesmann, *Das Recht der Bodenkulturgenossenschaften in Preussen* (Berlin 1933).

186b. A. Lopez Gomez, "Riegos y cultivos en la huerta de Alicante, Evolucion y estado actual", *Estudios geograficos* (Madrid 1951), pp 701 sqq.

186c. *Unión Nacional de Cooperativas del campo, Memoria; Ejercicio 1950* (Madrid 1951), p. 32.

187a. "Situation des coopératives agricoles agrées au 15 février 1952", *Revue du Ministère de l'agriculture* (Paris 1952, Jun), pp 149–151, mentioning 6,653 "coopératives de service"; E, M. Owen, "Co-operative mechanisation in France, the Netherlands, and England and Wales", *The Farm Economist* (Oxford 1949), pp 89–93; F. Bourget, "Les coopératives d'utilisation de matériel agricole (C.U.M.A.)", *Agriculture* (Paris 1953, May), pp 145–148: before the last war, there were some 3,000–3,500 such societies, most of them merely for common use of threshing machines; in 1940, they were 8,000. A certain setback occurred when machine supply became more abundant; an enquête in 1953 showed that still more than 5,000 existed, with more than 35 per department in most departments, and more than 100 in each of a number of departments in the West and the adjoining Central parts (Sarthe, Charente, Vendée, Isère). It is estimated that by then there existed some 6,000–6,500 such co-operatives, with about 200,000 member farmers and owning 7,000 or 8,000 tractors, 3,000 threshing machines and 1,000 combine harvesters.

187b. A. Münzinger & others, *Bäuerliche Maschinengenossenschaft Häusern, Ein Versuch genossenschaftlicher Dorfgemeinschaft* (Berlin 1934); O. Schiller, "Experiences in operation of farm machinery cooperatives in Germany", *Proceedings of the World Conference on Land Tenure Problems* (Madison, Wis., 1951), Vol. 2, pp 3–8, mentions some examples of joint machinery use in connection with attempts at common crop rotation as a means of overcoming the drawbacks of land fragmentation without land consolidation; but these attempts do not appear to have been very successful. See also H. Priebe, *Landarbeit heute und morgen* (Hamburg & Berlin 1953), pp 46 sq.

187c. The cooperative movement in the Netherlands (The Hague 1947); see also E. M. Owen, "Co-operative mechanisation in France, the Netherlands, and England and Wales," The Farm Economist (Oxford 1949), pp 89-93.

187d. C. D. Scheer, "The Dutch experience with machinery co-operatives", Proceedings of the World Conference on Land Tenure Problems (Madison, Wis. 1951), Vol. 2, pp 14-16.

187e. E. M. Owen, "Co-operative mechanisation in France, the Netherlands, and England and Wales," The Farm Economist (Oxford 1949), pp 89-93.

187f. Statute of 1950, 12/5, No 230, Art. 22; cf. e.g. La riforma fondiaria in Maremma (Rome 1953), pp 106 sqq, and G. Medici, "La cooperazione agricola nelle zone di riforma fondiaria", Rivista della cooperazione (Rome 1951). – "Synoptikē ekthesis pepragmenōn tmēmatos Geōrgikōn Mēchanōn kai Ypēresias Mechanikēs Kalliergeias..." Bulletin agricole (Athens 1953), fasc. 6, pp 1 sqq. – Unión Nacional de cooperativas del campo, Memoria: Ejercicio 1950 (Madrid 1951), pp 31 sqq; Temas de cooperación agrícola (Madrid 1951), pp 45 sqq.

188a. E. David, Sozialismus und Landwirtschaft, 2 ed. (Leipzig 1922), pp 483 sqq. – Report on the proceedings at the fifth Congress of the International Co-operative Alliance. (London 1902), p. 43: between 8,000 and 9,000 acres were under co-operative cultivation in Great Britain (in 1901), but the results were not held to be promising.

188b. La cooperazione in cammino (Rome 1953, Confederazione cooperativa italiana), pp 124 sqq. – Report of the 81st annual co-operative Congress... (Manchester 1950), p. 447.

188c. J. Johnston, Irish agriculture in transition (Dublin & Oxford 1951), pp 125 sqq.

189a. ILO Directory on cooperatives (Geneva), for 1924.

189b. Allotments, Report of the Allotments Advisory Committee to the Minister of Agriculture and Fisheries, respecting amendments of existing allotments legislation (London 1950), pp 16 sq.

190a. The ILO Directory indicates, as in 1930, that the "Federazione Nazionale Fascista delle Cooperative tra lavoratori agricoli" included 414 societies with 75,000 members. Cf also, for instance, O. Schiller, article in Agricoltura italiana (Rome 1951, Feb), pp 70 sqq; R. Vittorangeli, La cooperazione agricola coltivatrice (Reggio Emilia 1928); W. D. Preyer, Die Arbeits- und Pachtgenossenschaften Italiens (Jena 1913); A. Brizi, article in the Rivista di economia agraria (Rome 1948), pp 230-238.

191a. A. Poulain, "Les sociétés d'exploitation agricole", Revue hebdomadaire de l'Académie Française agricole (Paris 1952), pp 286 sqq, followed by notes by A. Toussaint & J. Ferté, ibid. – R. A. Lacan, "Les actions d'apport et l'enregistrement", Revue de législation agricole (Paris 1951, Mar), p. 47; P. Lemasson, "Les coopératives d'exploitation en commun", Mon village (Paris 1947, Jul), pp 8 sq. – O. E. Heuser, "Entwicklungsmöglichkeiten der landwirtschaftlichen Betriebsorganisation", Berichte über Landwirtschaft (Hamburg & Berlin 1952), pp 77-90, especially pp 86 sqq. Cf also, for instance, Welsh Land Settlement Society, Co-operative farms and small holdings with centralized services in Wales (London 1952); J. B. Bedell, An experiment in co-operative farming? (MacDonald, Col. 1946), pp 20 sq; and J. M. Murray, Community farming (London 1952).

191b. I. Baiev, Zemedělskoto stopanstvo i kooperativnata obrabotka na zemiata (Sofia 1940), p. 45; D. Bakardzhiev, Kooperativni zemedělski stopanstva (Pleven 1940); A. K. Řeev, Kooperativno obrabotvane na zemiata 1940 godina (Sofia 1941); O. v. Franges, "Agricultural labour communities in south-eastern Europe", Monthly Bulletin of Agricultural Economics and Sociology (Rome, IIA, 1941), pp 25 sqq.

CHAPTER 6

194a. See A. Wauters, La réforme agraire en Europe (Bruxelles 1928), pp 20 sqq.

202a. The *Land Law (Ireland) Act*, 1881, 44 and 45 Vic. C 49: *Purchase of Land (Ireland) Act*, 1883, 48 and 49 Vic. C 73; *Land Law (Ireland) Acts* 1887, 1888, 1896; *Irish Land Acts*, 1903, 1909; *Sáorstat Land Acts*, 1923, 1927, 1929, 1931. Cf. J. D. Cophlan, *The Land of Ireland* (Wexford 1931), especially p. 261: J. E. Pomfret, *The struggle for land in Ireland, 1800-1923* (Princeton 1930): E. Bé-chaux, *La question agraire en Irlande au commencement du xxe siècle* (Paris 1906): E. Hooker, *Readjustments of agricultural land in Ireland* (Chapel Hill 1938). See also *Land Commission, Annual Reports*, year 1948, with an Appendix on the history and development of the Land Acts 1870 to 1946, and year 1951, on the Land Act of 1950.

202b. C. S. Smith, "A new deal for the Irish tenant", *The Farmer's Weekly* (London 1952, Feb 1), pp 55-57.

202c. E. Hooker, *Readjustments of agricultural land in Ireland* (Chapel Hill 1938), p. 117.

202d. C. S. Smith, "A new deal for the Irish tenant", *The Farmer's Weekly* (London 1952, Feb 1), pp 55-57.

203a. A. W. Ashby & I. L. Evans, *The agriculture of Wales and Monmouthshire* (Cardiff 1944), p. 128.

203b. *Smallholdings, First Report of the Smallholdings Advisory Council* (London 1949), pp 43 sqq.

203c. J. A. Venn, *The foundation of agricultural economics* (Cambridge 1933).

203d. See A. H. H. Matthews, *Fifty years of agricultural politics* (London 1915); N. Russel Smith, *Land for the small man, English and Welsh experience 1860-1937* (New York 1946); A. Richmond, *Land settlement policy* (London 1945; C. R. Fay & H. C. Fay, "The allotment movement in England and Wales", *Yearbook of International Co-operation* (London 1942), pp 82-130.

203e. A. W. Ashby & I. L. Evans, *The agriculture of Wales and Monmouth-shire* (Cardiff 1944), p. 130.

203f. *Land settlement in Scotland, Report by the Scottish Land Settlement Committee* (Edinburgh 1945), with synopsis of legislation in Appendix II.

203g. *Scotland's marginal farms, General report* (Edinburgh 1947).

204a. G. Prawitz, *Jordfrågan* (Stockholm 1951).

205a. *Die Bodenreform in Finnland 1922, Offizieller Bericht* (Helsingfors 1923).

205b. K. Haataja, "Die Ansiedlungstätigkeit in Finnland", *Siedlung und Siedlungspolitik in den Ländern Europas*, bearb. v. R. Stegemann & Fr. Schmidt (Wien & Leipzig 1939), p. 130, and idem, "Finland", *Jordpolitiken i Norden* (Stockholm 1955).

205c. M. Laisaari, "The post-war land reform in Finland", *Bank of Finland, Monthly Bulletin* (Helsinki 1948, Mar-Apr), pp 23-26.

205d. K. U. Pihkala, "The land settlement programme and its execution", *Bank of Finland, Monthly Bulletin* (Helsinki 1952, Mar-Apr), pp 24-31. See also idem, "Kolonisationsverksamheten i Finland efter kriget", *Nordisk jord-bruksforskning* (Stockholm 1949/50), pp 146-155.

206a. Th. Arnskov, "Small holdings in Denmark, 25 years' legislation", *Danish Foreign Office Journal* (Copenhagen 1924), pp 3 sqq.

206b. *Ibid*, pp 16 sqq.

207a. E. Vandervelde, *Essais sur la question agraire en Belgique* (Paris 1902); Lefuret, (pseud.), *Cinquante années de politique agraire* (Bruxelles 1936).

207b. *Monographies sur le bien-être rural en Belgique, Élaborées en vue d'une Conférence européenne pour l'étude du bien-être rural* (Bruxelles 1951), pp 64-76.

207c. W. Neukomm, "Zur Frage der Lebensfähigkeit und Existenzberechti-gung landwirtschaftlicher Kleinbetriebe", *Agrarpolitische Revue* (Zürich 1951), pp 193-200; E. Geyer, "Das neue Landwirtschaftsgesetz", *Schweizerische Monatshefte* (Zürich 1952), pp 705-714; H. Gnägi, "Das neue Landwirtschafts-gesetz und die Beiträge der öffentlichen Hand", *Agrarpolitische Revue* (Zürich 1950), pp 309-327; O. Kaufmann, *Die Neuordnung des Landwirtschaftsrechtes* (Zürich & St Gallen 1952).

208a. M. Augé-Laribé, *La politique agricole de la France de 1880 à 1940* (Paris 1950), pp 89 sq.

208b. *Loi du 12/6 1909 sur la consommation d'un bien de famille insaississable.*

208c. M. Augé-Laribé, *La politique agricole de la France de 1880 à 1940* (Paris 1950), p. 90.

208d. French C.c. 832; cf above in Chapter 4, § 141 with note (b.).

208e. For instance, R. Dumont, *Voyages en France d'un agronome* (Paris 1951).

209a. E. David, *Sozialismus und Landwirtschaft*, 2 ed. (Leipzig 1922), pp 626 sqq.

209b. *Ibid*, p. 631.

209c. *Ibid.*, pp 631 sqq, 26 sqq.

209d. Cf M. Sering, "Die Verordnung der Reichsregierung vom 29. Januar 1919 zur Beschaffung von landwirtschaftlichem Siedlungsland", *Jahrbuch für Gesetzgebung, Verwaltung und Volkswirtschaft* (Leipzig 1919), pp 83 sqq.

209e. K. Maxion, *Die bisherigen Wirkungen des Reichssiedlungsgesetzes* (Berlin 1930), pp 9 sqq.

209f. *Ibid.*, pp 14 sqq.

209g. "Gesetz betr. Ergänzung des RSG (Flüchtlingssiedlungsgesetz) vom 7 Juni 1923", *Reichsgesetzblatt* (Berlin 1923), p. 364, Cf K. Maxion, *Die bisherigen Wirkungen des Reichssiedlungsgesetzes* (Berlin 1930), p. 19.

209h. *Ibid.*, pp 22 sq.

209i. *Ibid.*, pp 39, 53, See also K. Meyer, *Ordnung und Gefüge der deutschen Landwirtschaft* (Berlin 1939), p. 290.

210a. See below, note 238(b).

211a. Cf W. Medinger, *Grossgrundbesitz, Fideikommiss und Agrarreform* (Wien & Leipzig 1919).

211b. G. Perroy, *Neuordnung ländlicher Besitztumsverhältnisse* (Salzburg 1950).

211c. "79. Bundesgesetz über das Verfahren der Agrarbehörden in den Angelegenheiten der Bodenreform (4/3 1927)", *Bundesgesetzblatt für die Republik Österreich* (Wien 1927, 11/3, Stück 22).

211d. The policy of "Besitzfestigung", i.e. an attempt to counteract the abandoning of holdings in mountain areas, was described to the author by officials in Vienna and Innsbruck; it was estimated that some 300 holdings a year could be helped by these measures. To this estimate should be compared the total number of holdings, 437,607, out of which 188,363 were described as mountain holdings. Cf also H. Kallbrunner, "The absorption of peasant hold-. ings and legislative efforts to counteract it", *Monthly Bulletin of Economic and Social Intelligence* (Rome, IIA, 1920), pp 270–276.

212a. On the results of the land reform in Hungary, see the *Statisztikai zsebkönyv* (Budapest 1948), p. 107.

213a. C. Worliczek, *Grundlagen, Grundgedanken und Kritik der tschechoslowakischen Bodenreform* (Reichenberg 1925). For figures, see, *e.g.*, *Statistical Yearbook of Czechoslovakia* (Prague 1938), pp 55 sqq.

214a. M. Constantinescu, *L'évolution de la propriété rurale et la réforme agraire en Roumanie* (Bucureşti 1925). H. L. Roberts, *Rumania* (New Haven 1951), pp 366 sqq.

215a. L. Fritscher, "Agrarverfassung und agrarische Umwälzung in Jugoslawien", *Die agrarischen Umwälzungen im ausserrussischen Osteuropa, Ein Sammelwerk* hrsg. v. M. Sering (Berlin & Leipzig 1930), pp 276–340, especially pp 336–339 on the land reform legislation in 1920 and 1925, and pp 319 sq with bibliography on the subject. Cf also R. Trouton, *Peasant renaissance in Yugoslavia 1900–1950* (London 1952), and O. v. Frangeš, "La réforme agraire en Yougoslavie", *Bulletin mensuel de renseignements économiques et sociaux* (Rome, IIA, 1934).

216a. M. Grigoroff, "La réforme agraire en Bulgarie, De la petite exploitation à la coopérative de production", *Revue du Ministère de l'agriculture* (Paris 1952), pp 135–140; K. T. Georgiev, *Agrarnata reforma v Bulgariia* (Plovdiv 1929).

217a. G. Lorenzoni, *La questione agraria albanese. Studi, inchieste e proposte per una riforma agraria in Albania*, ed. 2, including the text of the Land Reform Bill of April 13, 1930 (Bari 1930). Cf also V. Thallóczy, *Albanisch-illyrische Forschungen* (Wien 1916).

218a. P. A. Decasos, *Die Landwirtschaft im heutigen Griechenland* (Berlin 1904), pp 49–55.

218b. Chr. Evelpides, *La réforme agraire en Grèce* (Athens 1926); B. Alivisatos, *La réforme agraire en Grèce au point de vue social* (Paris 1932); Chr. Evelpidès, *E geōrgia tēs Ellados* (Athens 1944), pp 23 sq.

219a. *Inchiesta sulla piccola proprietà coltivatrice formatasi nel dopoguerra* (Rome 1933–38, 15 volumes).

219b. *La colonizzazione del latifondo siciliano* (Rome 1940): cf also J. P. M. Sánchez, *La reforma agraria italiana y la futura reforma española*, 2 ed. (Madrid 1931).

220a. See, e.g., G. M. De Jovellanos, *Informe de la sociedad economica de esta corte al real y supremo consejo de Castilla en el expediente de ley agraria* (Madrid 1795), repr. in idem, *Obras*, Vol. I (Madrid 1845), pp 25–250.

220b. C. Viñas y Mey, *La reforma agraria en España en el siglo XIX* (Santiago de Compostela 1933).

220c. For instance, F. Kriessmann, *Das spanische Agrarproblem und die Versuche zu seiner Lösung* (Stuttgart 1934); however, this author builds his opinion on the Spanish land structure on cadastre data without observing the double entries following from this.

220d. *Constitución familiar y organización de la propiedad rural en Cataluña* (Barcelona 1912); *Proyecto de ley sobre aumento de valor de la propiedad inmueble y régimen fiscal* (Barcelona 1916); *Información sobre el problema agrario en la Provincia de Cordoba* (Madrid 1919); S. Aznar, *La acción social agraria en Navarra* (Pamplona 1916). Cf also F. de los Rios, "Le problème agraire en Espagne", *Revue internationale du travail* (Genève 1925). – There was a law on inner coloni-zation as early as in 1907, but it did not produce any important results; see J. E. de Molins, *El abandono de la tierra en España* (Barcelona 1927), p. 17.

220e. S. Aznar, *Despoblación y colonización* (Barcelona 1930); M. Granados, *La reforma agraria en Europa y el proyecto español* (Madrid 1932); O. Gorni, "Le problème de la colonisation intérieure en Espagne", *Revue internationale du travail* (Genève 1929); P. Carrión, *La reforma agraria* (Madrid 1931); idem, *Los latifundios en España* (Madrid 1932); R. de Belausteguigoitia, *Reparto de tierras y producción nacional* (Madrid & Barcelona 1932); R. Juguin, *La question agraire en Andalousie* (Paris 1932).

Boletin del Instituto de reforma agraria (Madrid 1932 sqq); *Boletin de la Agrupación de propietarios de fincas rústicas de España* (Madrid 1932 sqq); A. Rodríguez-Jurado y de la Hera, *El proyecto de reforma agraria* (Madrid 1931); *Exposición y enmiendas al proyecto de reforma agraria del Exc. mo S.r Ministro de agricultura* (Madrid 1932, Mar.); *Ley de reforma agraria* (Madrid 1932); *Manual de reforma agraria . . . I–2 . . . Legislación vigente sobre comunidades campesinos* (Madrid 1932–33); P. S. Requena, *Comentarios a la Ley de reforma agraria* (Madrid 1934); J. A. Alvarez, *Acceso a la propiedad rústica y patrimonio familiar agricola* (Madrid 1935); E. H. G. Dobby, "Agrarian problems in Spain", *Geographical Review* (New York 1936).

222a. P. N. Perchin, *Zemel'noe ustroĭstvo dorevoliutsionnoĭ derevni* (Moscow & Voronezh 1928), p. 214.

222b. On the property statistics of 1905, see Appendix 5 under U.S.S.R.

222c. S. Dubrovskiĭ, *Stolypinskaia reforma* ((Moscow & Leningrad 1925–30), especially pp 359 sqq. Cf also P. I. Liashchenko, *Istoriia narodnogo khoziaĭstva SSSR*, 2 ed. (Leningrad 1950) Vol. 2, pp 264 sqq; L. E. Hubbard, *The economics of Soviet agriculture* (London 1939); N. Jasny, *The socialized agriculture of the USSR* (Stanford 1949); W. D. Preyer, *Die russische Agrarreform* (Jena 1914); C. v. Dietze, *Stolypinsche Agrarreform und Feldgemeinschaft* (Berlin 1920);

G. T. Robinson, *Rural Russia under the old regime* (New York 1949).

223a. Thus Lenin in some of his statements on the land question. Cf hereto the land statistics of 1905, as commented upon in Appendix 5, under the U.S.S.R.

223b. P. Pershin, *Uchastkovoe zemlepol'zovanie v Rossii* (Moscow 1922); cf also article on the subject in the *Bol'shaia Sovetskaia entsiklopediia*.

223c. *Code agraire 1922-25*, also reproduced in the *Annuaire International de législation agricole* (Rome, IIA. 1926).

224a. A. Thaler, *Reforma rolna* (Krakow 1937); W. Staniewics, *O programm agrarnyu w Polsce i jego wykonanie* (Warsaw 1928).

224b. T. Sinberg, "Das Siedlungswesen in Estland", *Siedlung und Siedlungspolitik in den Ländern Europas*, bearb. v. R. Stegemann & Fr. Schmidt (Wien & Leipzig 1939); H. Krause, *Die Agrarreformen in Lettland und Estland* (Berlin 1927); St. Elsbergas, *Die litauische Landreform* (Kaunas 1935).

225a. J. W. Stalin, *Complete Works* (Moscow 1949), Vol. 2, p. 158, here quoted in the translation by D. Pronin in *Land Economics* (Madison, Wis. 1950), p. 99. The italics in the quotation are those of Stalin himself.

225b. N. Jasny, *The socialized agriculture of the USSR* (Stanford 1949); S. N. Prokopovich, *Russlands Volkswirtschaft unter den Sowjets* (Zürich 1944).

225c. *Spravochnik predsedatel'ia kolkhoza*, 3 ed. (Moscow 1948), p. 4. Cf *Kolkhozy u 1929 godu, Itogi sploshnogo obsledovaniia kolkhozov* (Moscow 1931), p. xvii.

225d. See *Trud u SSSR* (Moscow 1934), p. 208, showing the sovkhozy to be organized under five different central offices. Further, *Sovkhozy, VII Vsesoiuznomu s'ezdu Sovetov, Narodnyi kommissariat zernovykh i zhivotnovodcheskikh sovkhozov SSSR* (Moscow 1935), covering about $1/5$ of the then existing sovkhozy; nonrigiving was the principle that they should include no more than 15,000–25,000 hectares of arable land each and be divided into sections of some 2,000–2,500 hectares. See also *Sovkhozy k xv godovshchine oktiabria, Sbornik* red A. P. Teriaevoi (Moscow 1932); *Sovkhozy*, red. M. A. Abraimov (Moscow 1931); S. V. Shol'ts, *Sel'skohoziaistvennaia statistika* (Moscow 1951); N. V. Vasil'ev, *Sotsialisticheskoe sel'shoe khoziaistvo na putiakh k izobiliu produktov* (Moscow 1951); I. E. Kantyshev, *Voprosy ekonomiki sovkhozov* (Moscow 1950).

226a. F. P. Koshelev, *Puti likvidatsii protivopolozhnosti mezhdu gorodom i devernet u SSSR* (Moscow 1950); S. S. Sergeev, *Organizatsionno-khoziaistvennoe ukrepleinie kolkhozov i ukrupnenie melkikh sel'skohoziaistvennykh artelei* (Moscow 1950); I. Kuvshinov, "Ukrupnenie melkikh kolkhozov – put' k novomu podionu sotsialistsicheskogo khoziaistva", *Sotsialisticheskoe sel'shoe khoziaistvo* (Moscow 1950, Aug).

226b. N. I. Anisimov, *Khoziaistvo v pervoi poslevoennoi piatiletke* (Moscow 1952), p. 97: amalgamation of the kolkhozy reduced their number from 252,000 to 123,000: no regional figures are given, but examples show that not seldom were four old kolkhozy merged into one new. – N. Khrushchov, in *Pravda* 15/9 1953, states that the kolkhozy were by then reduced in number to 94,000 (which appears to include the Baltic countries, the western parts of Belorussia and Ukraina, and the whole of Moldova – thus a larger territory than the old 242,000 kolkhozy of the late thirties); the MTS were by then 8,950 and the sovkhozy 4,700. Cf also idem, *O nekotoryikh voprosakh dal'neishego organizatsionno-khoziaistvennogo ukreplenia kolkhozov* (Moscow 1950); L. Florent'ev & I. Bochkarev, "Organizatsionno-khoziaistvennoe ustroistvo ukrepennykh kolkhozov", *Sotstalisticheskoe sel'shoe khoziaistvo* (Moscow 1950); *Kolkhoznaia Proizvodstvennaia entsiklopediia* (Kiev 1951), 2 vols; S. Fraer, "Razmery kolkhozov i ispol'zovanie sredstv proizvodstva v MTS nechernoziomnoi zony", *Sotsialisticheskoe sel'shoe khoziaistvo* (Moscow 1950, May), pp 14 sqq; F. P. Koshelev, *Osnovnoe itogi uspbteniia pervoi poslevoennoi stalinskoi piatiletki* (Moscow 1951), pp 81 sq: in the Moscow district, 26 per cent of the old kolkhozy had less than 100 hectares of sown area, 40 per cent 100-200 ha, 18 per cent 200-300 ha. Cf also L. Volin, "Soviet collective farm mergers", *Foreign Agriculture* (1951, May), pp 95 sqq.

226c. I. Glotov, "Obshchestvennoe i lichnoe v kolkhozakh", *Bol'shevik* (Moscow 1951), fasc. 24, pp 36 sqq. D. N. Kazantsev & A. A. Ruskol (ed.) *Kolkhoznoe pravo* (Moscow 1950): *Sbornik rukovodiashchikh materialov po kolkhoznomu stroitel'stvu* (Moscow 1948), pp 18 sqq, especially pp 66 sqq: pp 68 sq., it is recommended that, in case part of the land were situated more than 8 kilometers from the village center, permanent buildings should be constructed there for workmen, livestock, and implements. Cf also N.S. Grishin, article in *Sad i ogorod* (Moscow 1950), pp 7 sqq. Features of primitive labor technique, such as weeding of wheat-fields manually, are mentioned incidentally in modern Russian novels, as for instance S. P. Babaevskii, *Kavaler Zolotoi Zvezdy* (Moscow 1947–48) from the region of extensive grain growing in Northern Caucasus.

226d. M. Gendel'man & N. Murashchenko, "Zemleustroistvo ukrupennnykh kolkhozov v stepi U.S.S.R."/i.e. Ukraina/, *Sotsialisticheskoe sel'skoe khoziaistvo* (Moscow 1950, Sep); V. Smirnov & S. Akishchev, "Rost obshchestvennogo khoziaistva ukrupennykh kolkhozov", *ibid* (1950, Sep); M. Tsyrkov, "Organizatsiia khoziaistva ukrupnennego kolkhoza", *ibid* (1950, Sep).

227a. S. Udachin, "Itogi zemel'noi reformy v Sovetskoi Latvii", *Sotsialisticheskoe sel'skoe khoziaistvo* (Moscow 1947, May), pp 47 sqq, comparing the farm structure created by the latest land reform with that existing in 1939, and showing private farms to include a little more than 3/4 of the farm land of 1939; idem, *Zemel'naia reforma v Sovetskoi Latvii* (Riga 1948), with more figures, i.a. also quoting the Latvian census of 1929 (which was taken before the moderate land reform was finished, thus not showing its final result), p. 71, and material from 1905 (p. 392, farm structure percentages for all three Baltic countries). Cf also E. Jaska, *The Estonian agriculture under the Soviets* (Augsburg 1948), and E. Kareda, *Estonia in the Soviet grip* (London 1949).

227b. *Collectivization of agriculture in the Baltic countries* (New York 1952): E. Jaska, "The results of collectivisation of Estonian agriculture", *Land Economics* (Madison, Wis, 1952, Aug.), pp 212 sqq, showing, among other things, how the first collective farms were sometimes constituted of only a few of the small private farms; by 1951/52, the average Estonian kolkhoz had expanded to 440 hecares of sown area.

227c. See also articles on Latvia and Lithuania (Estonia is not yet published) in the *Bol'shaia Sove shaia Entsiklopedia*, 2 ed.

227d. P. Adamenko, "Sel'skoe khoziaistvo zadarnykh oblastei Ukrainy na putiakh kollektivizatsii", *Sotsialisticheskoe sel'shoe khoziaistvo* (Moscow 1950, Jan), pp 57–61; p. 59, it is stated that a year earlier, there were only 3,526 kolkhozy in these Western districts, with 407,000 member households, but now there were already 6,131 kolkhozy in existence, including 63 per cent of the peasantry. Examples are given of districts where the degree of collectivization was higher than the average for the area (which implicitly indicates some of the not mentioned districts to be below average). In the Zakarpatskii oblast' (i.e., formerly Czechoslovakian Carpatho-Ukraina), the two first kolkhozy had been organized in 1946, and when this article was written, there were 530, including 70 per cent of the peasant households. — The same impression is even more confirmed by articles in the *Bol'shaia Sovetskaia Entsiklopedia*, 2 ed., on Belorussia and on various Ukrainian districts.

228a. D. Warriner, *Revolution in Eastern Europe* (London 1950), chapters 7 and 8.

228b. Data on these post-war reforms can be found, e.g., in the following sources:

E. Germany: H. W. Dölling, *Wende der deutschen Agrarpolitik* (Berlin 1950);

Poland: *Rocznik statystyczny* (Warsaw 1949), p. 54;

Czechoslovakia: *Kwestia agrarna* (Warsaw 1951), pp 148 sq, and J. Kotátko, *Land reform in Czechoslovakia* (Prague 1948).

Hungary: *Kwestia agrarna* (Warsaw 1951), pp 160 sq, and A. Sándor, *Land reform in Hungary* (Budapest 1947);

Rumania: *Kwestia agrarna* (Warsaw 1951), pp 155 sq, and I. Roberts.

Rumania, Political problems of an agrarian State (New Haven 1951), p. 374;
Bulgaria: *Kwestia agrarna* (Warsaw 1951), p. 145;
Yugoslavia: M. Mirković, *Ekonomika agrarna FNRJ* (Zagreb 1950), pp 43 sqq, and B. Kidrič, *O izgradnji socijalističke ekonomike FNRJ* (Beograd 1948).
Albania: "Economic rehabilitation in Albania", *Operational analysis papers* (London 1947, Division of operational analysis, UNRRA), pp 100 sq; S. F. Burenko, "Novoe administrativno-territorial'noe delenie Albanskoĭ Narodnoĭ Respubliki", *Izvestiia vsesoiuznogo geograficheskogo obshchestva* (Moscow 1952, Jan), pp 53 sqq, and articles in *Probleme economice* (Bucharest 1950, Feb), pp 144 sq, and *Interagra* (Prague 1952, Jan-Feb), pp 103 sqq & 264 sq.

231a. Sources to the table: In general. *European agriculture, A Statement of problems*, E/ECE/175 (Geneva 1954), Chapter 4.

E. Germany: *Die Wirtschaft* (Berlin 1952, 12/12); *Neues Deutschland* (Berlin 1953), 31/7, 11/7;
Poland 1949: R. P. Rechlin, *Die Wirtschaft Polens von 1945 bis 1952* (Berlin 1953, p. 41);
Poland 1950: Interagra (Prague 1952, Jan), pp 52 sqq;
Poland 1953: *Pour une paix durable* (1953 12/6);
Czechoslovakia: *Rudé Pravo* (Prague 1953, 15/2); D. Warriner, *Revolution in Eastern Europe* (London 1950), pp 161 sq.
Hungary 1940: Z. Vas, *The fulfilment of the three-year plan* (Budapest 1950);
Hungary 1952: *Statisztikai tájékoztató* (Budapest 1953, Jan), p. 18;
Rumania 1948: *Probleme economice* (Bucharest 1951, Aug), pp 58 sq;
Rumania 1949: *Rumanian News* (Bucharest 1951, 18/11);
Rumania 1953: *Rumanian News* (Bucharest 1953 10/6);
Bulgaria; V. N. Starodubskaia, *Stroitel'stvo ekomicheshogo fundamenta sotsializma v Narodnoĭ Respubliki Bolgarii* (Moscow 1953), p. 195.

232a. *Interagra* (Prague 1952), p. 279 (after *Rolnik Polski*, Warsaw 1952 18/3) says that in 1951, the number of co-operative farms had increased by 28 per cent in comparison with 1950; the number was now 3,055, on Jan 1, 1952. The number of co-operators were to have increased by 29 per cent and the land cultivated by co-operative farms by 51 per cent.

232b. H. Minc, "Le plan sexennal d'essor économique et de construction des bases du socialisme en Pologne", *France, Direction de la Documentation Notes et études* (Paris 1950, Sep, Document No 1,377); H. Chelkowski, "Problémes de politique agricole en Pologne", *Problèmes économiques* (Paris 1951, Nov, from *Nowe Drogi*, Warsaw 1951, May-Jun); cf also the speech of H. Minc, as printed in *Polish facts and figures* (London 1951, Fall), pp 3 sqq.

232c. *Interagra* (Prague 1952), pp 330 sqq, and *ibid* (1952), p. 13.

232d. Cf I. Nagy, in a statement of July 4, 1952, *Szabad nép* (Budapest 1952, July 5): "There is a break in the development of agriculture – agriculture practically stagnated in the past years as a consequence of low investments... of negligence in giving support to the individual farmer and also as a consequence of the exceedingly speedy expansion in the cooperative sector..."

232e. *Munca* (Bucharest, 1953, Sep).

232f. V. Chervenkov stated, at the part congress in 1954 that "there is a lag in the development of agriculture compared to that of the industry", then listing the deficiencies, though without attacking the principle of speedy collectivization.

232g. W. Ulbricht in a speech of 31/10 1951, *Tägliche Rundschau* (Berlin 1951, 11/11): "Der landwirtschaftliche Produktionsplan ist darauf gerichtet, den Wohlstand der Klein- und Mittelbauern zu fördern..."

232h. *idem, Neues Deutschland* (Berlin 1953 21/9).

232i. D. Bajalica, "Reorganizacija pasivnih zadruga Bosne: Hercegovine", *Socijalistička Poljoprivreda* (Beograd 1952, Mar.).

232j. An article in *Ekonomska politika* (Beograd 1953 15/10), says that in the rural district of Kulski, in the Vojvodina, where at the beginning there were of the year 18 co-operative holdings including 60 per cent of the peasant households and $5/6$ of the land. Six of these co-operative farms were dissolved while the others became considerably diminished. Since then, however, two of the dissolved ones have been created anew, voluntarily.

234a. *Il XL anniversario della Enciclica "Rerum Novarum", Scritti commemorativi pubblicati a cura della Università cattolica del Sacro Cuore...* (Milano 1931); see also O. Kippes, *Die Bestrebungen der Bodenreform in ihrem Verhältnis zur christlichen Eigentumslehre* (Kallmünz 1933).

234b. In a neo-conservative sense H. Priebe, *Wer wird die Scheunen füllen? Sozialprobleme der deutschen Landwirtschaft* (Düsseldorf 1954).

235a. G. Medici, *L'agricoltura e la riforma agraria* (Roma 1947).

235b. G. de Rossi, *Per la riforma agraria; testo e tabelle statistiche* (Rome 1950); "Leggi di riforma fondiaria e provvedimenti connessi". *L'agricoltura italiana* (Rome 1951, special issue); cf also C. A. Resch, "Riforma fondiaria", *Genio rurale* (Rome 1951), pp 465 sqq; it is suggested that co-operation between small farmers should include also some of the heaviest field operations, such as ploughing by tractors owned by co-operatives, and that the land reform offices should provide for a layout of the small holdings in favor of such arrangements.

235c. L. Gui, "Le prime sei aziende modello", *Agricoltura* (Rome 1952, May 1), pp 5 sqq.

236a. "Ley de colonización de grandes zonas, 26/12 1939", *Boletín oficial del Estado* (Madrid 1940, 25/1).

236b. *Real decreto Ley autorizando la compra de fincas particulares para su parcelación*, 1/1 1927.

236c. The expropriation Statute is published in the *Boletín oficial* (Madrid 1946, 28/4).

236d. Cf J. A. Ubierna, *De la acción social agraria* (Madrid 1947), p. 182, where reference is made only to public utility without any comments on the wider implications of "social utility".

236e. L. Almarcha, *La cooperación como sistema económico-social*, 2 ed. (Madrid 1945); idem, *El capitalismo y el comunismo, y la cooperación* (Madrid 1947); *La obra cooperativa agraria en España, Lecciones pronunciados en el Cursillo de formación social agraria para sacerdotes, celebrado en Pamplona del 4 al 13 de agosto 1948* (Madrid 1949), especially pp 284 sqq; M. Brugarola, "La reforma de las condiciones jurídicas de la tierra".

236f. *Las organizaciones cooperativas en la teoría y en la práctica*, (Madrid 1951); *Temas de cooperación agrícola* (Madrid 1951); S. Aznar, *Estudios económico-sociales* (Madrid 1946), pp 139 sqq; "Hacia la difusión de la propie-dad" (1937); E. Sala Roca, "Ante una reforma de la propiedad agrícola", *Instituto agrícolo catalán de San Isidro, Revista* (Barcelona 1951), pp 1-3.

236f. *Obras y mejoras en el campo español, La ley de colonizaciones de interes local, Cinco anos de aplicación* (Madrid 1951); *Agricultura* (Madrid 1951, Jul), "Suplemento de colonización".

237a. L. Quartín Graça, *Subsidios para uma política agrária* (Lisboa 1949), pp 25 sqq, reproducing a speech held at a ceremony when 33 colonists (out of a planned total of 39) received their titles as owners, after five years of super-vision. Each received 81¼ hectares, plus a complete set of buildings and live stock, for 50,000 escudos, to be amortized in 30 years. The land had been cleared from a baldio (common land). Cf also *Imagens de Portugal agrícola* (Lisboa 1942), p. 17, where the work of the Junta de colonização interna is described briefly: coloni-zation was under way in six localities, among them Pegões (which was not yet finished in Jan, 1952).

238a. M. Augé-Laribé, *La politique agricole de la France de 1880 à 1940* (Paris 1950); P. Caziot, *La terre à la famille paysanne* (Paris 1921), already then claiming the preemption right realized in 1946; G. Roussel, "Terres abandon-nées ou insuffisament occupées, *Rustica* (Paris 1951, Jun 10); "L'évolution du droit en 1950 et l'agriculture, l'équipement rural", *France, Ministère de l'agricul-ture, Revue d'information juridique et social* (Paris 1951, Apr), pp 68 sqq; J. C.

Garnaud, "La modernisation gagne la campagne française", *Bulletin des agriculteurs* (Paris 1951, Jun), pp 12 sq, 51 sq.

238b. J. Baumgartner, "Die deutsche Agrarpolitik im Rahmen der Weltwirtschaft", *Landwirtschaftliches Jahrbuch für Bayern* (München 1951, Apr), pp 8 sqq; W. Ehrenforth, *Das Recht der Siedlung und Bodenreform* (München 1950); W. Neuling, *Neue deutsche Agrarpolitik* (Tübingen 1949); H. W. Dölling, *Wende der deutschen Agrarpolitik* (Berlin 1950); O. Schiller, "Um die Existenz der Kleinstbetriebe". *Agrarwirtschaft* (Hannover 1952), pp 305 sqq.

239a. *Smallholdings. First Report of the Smallholdings Advisory Council* … (London 1949), p. 1. Cf also *British Agriculture, The principles of future policy, A report of an enquiry organized by Viscount Astor and B. Seebohm Rowntree* (London 1938).

239b. *Land settlement in Scotland. Report by the Scottish Land Settlement Committee* (Edinburgh 1945); cf also *Report of the Committee on Land Settlement in Scotland* (Edinburgh 1928), and *Scotland's marginal farms, General Report* (Edinburgh 1947). On recent Irish development, see J. Johnston, *Irish agriculture in transition* (Oxford 1951).

240a. E. Nordlander, *Jordbruksreformerna 1947* (Stockholm 1947); C. E. Odhner, *Jordbruket vid full sysselsättning* (Stockholm 1952), pp 82–87; O. Söderström, "Jordbruksregleringen och dess samhällsekonomiska verkningar", *Jordbruksekonomiska meddelanden* (Stockholm 1951), pp 239–249.

CHAPTER 7

242a. H. D. Lasswell & A. Kaplan, *Power and Society* (New Haven 1950). The material treated in this chapter illustrates some of the general principles evolved by these authors.

243a. J. Gloag, *Word warfare, Some aspects of German propaganda and English liberty* (London 1939); Cf also L. W. Doob, *Public opinion and propaganda* (New York 1948); C. Hovland, "Social communication", *Reader in public opinion and communication* (Glencoe 1953); J. O. Hertzler, "Toward a sociology of language" *Social forces* (1953), pp 109 sqq, indicating that sociology has not yet paid the necessary attention to the function of language in a society, and giving a useful bibliography of recent studies of language as a community phenomenon.

243b. "The issues in the world to-day are such that readers should be on their guard against any attempt to warp their intellects or to narrow or enfeeble their judgment by tendentious literature with facts increasingly coloured and statistics even more carefully selected", statement by Winston Churchill at the opening of the Sunday Times book fair, 1937. See also H. D. Lasswell & D. Blumenstock, *World revolutionary propaganda* (New York & London 1939), and H. D. Lasswell, "The structure and function of communication in society", *Mass communications: A book of readings selected and edited for the Institute of Communications Research in the University of Illinois* by W. Schramm (Urbana 1949), pp 102–115.

243c. The definition of propaganda as the manipulation of symbols and themes to influence attitudes and decisions on controversial matters is borrowed from the writings of H. D. Lasswell. As a brief introduction, see articles by the same writer in the *Encyclopaedia of Social Sciences* (New York 1930), Vol. 1, pp 487 sq, Vol. 12 (1934), pp 521–528, and *idem*, "The theory of political propaganda". *Reader in public opinion and communication* (Glencoe 1953), pp 627–630, and *idem*, "The function of the propagandist", *International journal of ethics* (Chicago 1927–28), pp 258–268. On the use of symbols in communication, see also W. Lippmann, *Public opinion* (New York 1930).

243d. Technological propaganda, or the propaganda of facts, is described in R. K. Merton, *Social theory and social structure, Toward the codification of theory and research* (Glencoe, Ill., 1949), pp 282 sq.

244a. H. D. Lasswell, "Analyzing the content of mass communication:

A brief introduction", *Library of Congress, Experimental Division for the Study of War Time Communication, Documents*, No 11 (Washington, D.C. 1942); *idem* "Describing the contents of communications", in B. L. Smith, H. D. Lasswell & R. D. Casey, *Propaganda, Communication, and Public Opinion, A Comprehensive Reference Guide* (Princeton 1946), pp 74–117, and *idem,* "World loyalty", *The World Community*, ed. by P. Q. Wright (Chicago 1948), especially pp 207 sqq.

244b. An example of this is Heinz Paechter, B. Hellman, Hedwig Paechter & K. O. Paetel, *Nazi-Deutsch: A glossary of contemporary German usage* (New York 1944).

244c. B. L. Smith, "The political communication specialist of our times", in B. L. Smith, H. D. Lasswell & R. D. Casey, *Propaganda, Communication, and Public Opinion* (Princeton 1946); *A world of tension* (Paris, UNESCO, 1949); "The comparative study of elites: An introduction and bibliography", *Hoover Institute Studies*, Ser. B, Elites, and Ser. C, Symbols (Stanford 1951).

247a. H. D. Lasswell, *The world revolution of our time, A framework for basic policy research* (Stanford 1951).

247b. *Il contratto con i contadini* (Grosseto 1953).

247c. "I provvedimenti di riforma a favore delle zone economicamente depresse e di maggiore concentrazione fondiaria nel quadro della legislazione connessa", *L'agricoltura italiana* (Rome 1951, special issue).

247d. "Quadragesimo Anno ..." (1931, see next note), pp 19, 39.

247e. *Rerum Novarum, Encyclical letter of Our Holy Father, By Divine Providence Pope Leo XIII, on the condition of labour. Official translation* (London 1891). — *Quadragesimo Anno, After Forty Years, Encyclical letter of His Holiness Pius XI by divine providence Pope ... In commemoration of the fortieth anniversary of the encyclical "Rerum Novarum" ... Official English translation* (New York 1931). — "Discourse of His Holiness Pius XII to commemorate the 50th anniversary of the encyclical "Rerum Novarum" of Pope Leo XIII on the social question, Feast of Pentecost, June 1st, 1941 ", *Acta Apostolicae Sedis* (Città del Vaticano 1941), Cf Sister M. Claudia Carlen, I. H. M., A Guide to the encyclicals of the Roman pontiffs from Leo XIII to the present day (1878–1937) (New York 1939).

248a. V. Chervenkov: *Tasks of the co-operative farms, Report delivered on April 5, 1950, at the Second National Conference of co-operative representatives* (Sofia 1950).

248b. V. I. Lenin, "Small production in agriculture", "The peasantry and the working class", "Child labour in peasant farming", "Messrs Bourgeois on 'toiler' farming", "Speech delivered to the delegates from the committees of poor peasants of the Moscow region, November 8, 1918", "Policy towards the middle peasantry, Resolution adopted by the eighth Congress of the R. C. P. (Bolsheviks), March 23, 1919", "The Middle Peasants, Speech for a gramophone record", in V. I. Lenin, *Selected Works* (Moscow 1938), Vol. 8, pp 136–143, 184–189, Vol. 12, 283–297.

249a. *Auf dem Wege zur Kolchose, Die Sowjetisierung der Landwirtschaft in der Sowjetzone*, hrsg. vom Bundesministerium für gesamtdeutsche Fragen, (Berlin, s.a.).

249b. A. Sándor, *Land reform in Hungary* (Budapest 1947). – This pamphlet was published by the "Hungarian Bulletin", a weekly information service published by Uj Magyarország, a Hungarian non-party weekly of world politics and Hungarian intellectual life.

249c. Tanguy-Prigent, *Démocratie à la terre* (Paris 1945).

251a. C. I. Hovland & M. Weiss, "The influence of source credibility on communication effectiveness", *Public Opinion Quarterly* (Princeton 1951–52 Winter), p. 645.

251b. K. Dovring, *Striden kring Sions Sånger och närstående sångsamlingar* (Lund 1951), Vol. 1–2. Cf review by L. Fendt in the *Deutsche Literatur-Zeitung* Berlin 1954, Jul.-Aug. See also K. Dovring, "Quantitative semantics in 18th century Sweden", *Public Opinion Quarterly* (Princeton 1954–55, Winter).

251c. "Content Analysis, a new evidential technique", *The University of Chicago Law Review* (Chicago 1948), pp 910-925. — H. D. Lasswell, "Detection: Propaganda detection and the courts", chapter 9 in *Language of Politics*, ed. by H. D. Lasswell & N. Leites (New York 1949).

251d. The ideological international languages are a problem meeting all those working for international understanding. See, for instance, D. Cartwright, "The strategy of research on international conferences", in "The technique of international conferences", *International social science bulletin* (Paris, UNESCO, 1953, No 2); J. M. Goldsen, "Analysing the contents of mass communication. A step toward intergroup harmony", *International Journal of Opinion and Attitude Research* (Mexico City 1947), pp 81-92; D. Lerner, "Comparative analysis of political ideologies", *Public Opinion Quarterly* (Princeton 1951-52, Winter), pp 785 sqq.; M. Jahoda, ibid., on psychologically meaningful categories and use of words with ambivalent meanings in international political communications and on studies of the proper cultural background of these categories and words. See also E. W. Barrett, *Truth is our weapon* (New York 1953), with studies on word-concepts used in international propaganda, and H. J. Kaufmann, "Implications of domestic research for international communications research", *Public Opinion Quarterly* (Princeton 1952-53, Winter), pp 552 sqq.

252a. *Language of politics, Studies in quantitative semantics*, by H. D. Lasswell, N. Leites, and associates (New York 1949).

252b. *Quadragesimo Anno* (1931), p. 47: "Like all errors Socialism contains a certain element of truth."

254a. Aspects on these technical functions of language in ideological action are studied in the works quoted above in notes 244(a) and 252(a). See also N. Leites & I. Pool, "On content analysis", *Library of Congress, Experimental Division for the Study of War-time Communications, Documents*, No 26 (Washington, D.C. 1942) and A. Kaplan, "Content analysis and the theory of signs", *Philosophy of Science* (Baltimore 1943), pp 230-247.

253a. The configurative analysis of the world value pyramid is developed by H. D. Lasswell, *World politics and personal insecurity* (Glencoe 1950). See also *World Politics* (Princeton 1954, Apr), with "A plan of research in international communication", reported by I. de Sola Pool, pp 359 sqq. — On value analysis, see R. K. White, "Value analysis; a quantitative method for describing qualitative data", *Journal of abnormal and social psychology* (Provincetown, Mass. 1944), and idem, "Hitler, Roosevelt and the nature of war propaganda", ibid. (1949), pp 157-174.

256a. For discussion on content analysis "a priori" and "a posteriori", see D. V. McGranahan, "Content analysis of the mass media of communication", chapter 16 in *Research methods in social relations*, ed. by M. Jahoda, M. Deutsch & S. W. Cook, Vol. 2 (New York 1951), pp 539-560. For our comment, see the note to Appendix 7, last paragraph.

255a. V. McNabb, "The Pope's social encyclical", *Blackfriars* (London 1931, Jul), pp 395-402. *Blackfriars* is a monthly review published by the English Dominicans. The article here referred to gives parallel tabulations of passages from the encyclicals of Leo XIII and Pius XI, showing agreement between the two in looking on the social world as divided into two classes.

266a. The statistics quoted by Lenin to support his themes have been recorded as symbols in accordance with their function in the text. How far these particular statistics are reliable and enlightening is a question for the subject-matter experts to solve. The communication analyst can only lay bare how figures are used in the ideological battle for a certain purpose. This case also bears upon other documents where statistics appear, used as proofs in an ideological controversy, as for instance in the German document.

267a. Functional description of a slogan is made by H. D. Lasswell, *Language of politics* (George W. Stewart, Publisher, Inc. New York 1949), p. 13: "Akin to the key-symbol is the slogan, which mediates between the single word and the full-length propositions of law or philosophy. Characteristically, the slogan or maxim is a terse string of words that gain meaning by repetition and context... (quoted by courtesy of the publisher). Other definitions, so far, only variate this theme. See for instance the contributions by R. K. Merton in Chapter 10 of R.K. Merton, *Social theory and social structure* (Glencoe 1949), pp 265–285, and E. Kris, "The 'danger' of propaganda", *The American Imago* (Boston 1941).

270a. See above, note 266(a).

270b. Among works of socio-psychologists may be noted, as an introduction to the field, O. Klineberg, *Etats de tension et compréhension internationale* (Paris, UNESCO, 1951): *Tensions et conflits, Etudes de psychologie sociale* (Paris, UNESCO, 1951); N. Buchanan & H. Cantril, *How nations see each others* (Urbana 1953); L. W. Doob, *Social Psychology, An analysis of human behavior* (New York 1952); M. Jahoda, M. Deutsch & S. W. Cook, *Research methods in social relations (with special reference to prejudice)* Vol. 1–2 (New York 1951); G. W. Allport, *The nature of prejudice* (Cambridge, Mass. 1954); cf also J. Stoetzel, *Esquisse d'une théorie des opinions* (Paris 1943) and S. de Grazia, *Errors of psychotherapy* (New York 1952).

274a. H. D. Lasswell, "Why be quantitative", in H. D. Lasswell & N. Leites, *Language of politics* (New York 1949), pp 40 sqq; *idem*, "Propaganda detection and the courts", *ibid*, pp 173 sqq, showing themes and statements expressing moral weakness to be significant features in describing enemies and moral strength to be put as identical with the own self; and A. Kaplan & J. M. Goldsen, "The reliability of content analyses categories" *ibid*, pp 83 sqq.

274b. See B. Berelson, *Content analysis in communication research* (Glencoe, Ill., 1952), pp 147 sqq. (quoted by courtesy of the author).
For further systematical evaluation of the methods used in this chapter, see K. Doving, *Propaganda Analysis, The Quantitative Semantics of Biassed Communication* (forthcoming).

SYMBOLS USED IN THE TABLES

— Nil or negligible   .. Not available

. Not applicable   * Estimated by the author